# Environmental and Natural Resource Economics
## A Contemporary Approach

*Second Edition*

# Environmental and Natural Resource Economics
## A Contemporary Approach

Jonathan M. Harris

*Global Development and Environment Institute*

*Tufts University*

**HOUGHTON MIFFLIN COMPANY**     Boston   New York

Vice President, Publisher: Charles Hartford
Vice President, Editor-in-Chief: George Hoffman
Senior Sponsoring Editor: Ann West
Editorial Associate: Jim Dimock
Senior Project Editor: Nancy Blodget
Editorial Assistants: Sean McGann, Sarah Driver
Composition Buyer: Chuck Dutton
Art and Design Manager: Gary Crespo
Manufacturing Manager: Karen Banks
Marketing Manager: Mike Schenk
Marketing Associate: Kathleen Mellon

Cover image: Factory By River, © Images.com/CORBIS

Printed in the U.S.A.

Library of Congress Control Number: 2005929293
ISBN: 0-618-49633-5

123456789-QUF-09 08 07 06 05

# Contents

## 17  Industrial Ecology  *382*

### Economic and Ecological Views of Production  *382*

### Closing the Loops: The Potential of Industrial Ecology  *384*

### BOX 17-1  Beverage Bottle Recycling  *386*

### BOX 17-2  Toxic Reduction: The Problem of PVC  *388*

### BOX 17-3  Integrated Farming Systems in Asia  *392*

### Industrial Ecology on a Global Scale  *393*

### Policies to Promote Industrial Ecology  *398*

### BOX 17-4  The Kalundborg Industrial Ecosystem  *399*

## 18  Global Climate Change  *404*

### Causes and Consequences of Climate Change  *404*

### BOX 18-1  What Is the Greenhouse Effect?  *405*

### BOX 18-2  Pacific Islands Disappear as Oceans Rise  *409*

### Economic Analysis of Climate Change  *410*

### Analyzing Long-Term Environmental Effects  *415*

### Policy Responses to Climate Change  *417*

### BOX 18-3  Economists' Statement on Climate Change  *418*

### BOX 18-4  The Kyoto Protocol  *424*

# PREFACE

The second edition of *Environmental and Natural Resource Economics: A Contemporary Approach* maintains its essential focus on making environmental issues accessible to students. Its origins are in fifteen years of teaching environmental and natural resource economics at the undergraduate and graduate levels. It reflects the conviction that environmental issues are of fundamental importance, and that a broad approach to understanding the relationship of the human economy and the natural world is essential.

Typically, students come to an environmental economics course with an awareness that environmental problems are serious, and that local, national, and global policy solutions are needed. Some students may be interested in careers in environmental policy, others in gaining an understanding of issues that are likely to be relevant in their careers, personal lives, and communities. In either case, the current importance of the topics gives the course that special spark of enthusiasm that is a heaven-sent boon to any instructor trying to breathe life into marginal cost and benefit curves.

There is a distinct danger, however, that this initial enthusiasm can rather quickly be dampened by the use of a strictly conventional approach to environmental economics. A major limitation of this approach is its almost exclusive use of microeconomic techniques. The microeconomic perspective strongly implies that anything of importance can be expressed in terms of price — but many important environmental functions cannot be fully captured in dollar terms. Also, a purely microeconomic perspective makes it very difficult to focus on the inherently "macro" environmental issues such as global climate change, ocean pollution, ozone depletion, population growth, and global carbon, nitrogen, and water cycles.

For these reasons, I have tried to develop an alternative approach that presents the broader perspective that has come to be known as ecological economics as a complement to standard economic theory. Many elements of standard microeconomic analysis are essential for analyzing resource and environmental issues. At the same time, it is important to recognize the limitations of a strictly economic approach, and to introduce ecological and biophysical perspectives on the interactions of human and natural systems.

## New to the Second Edition

The second edition has been updated in response both to developments in the world of environmental policy and to comments and suggestions based on classroom use. New material in the second edition includes:

- An expanded treatment of economic valuation techniques, with more practical examples
- More in-depth discussion of "green" national income accounting, including the adoption of green accounting in China

- New sections on the impact of AIDS and declining fertility rates on population growth
- Topic boxes on controlling agricultural pollution and the development of organic agriculture
- New data on mineral price trends and energy subsidies
- Updated discussion of fisheries policies, Bush administration "Clear Skies" air pollution policy, and toxic waste management
- New data and discussion on global climate change, including new scientific evidence and policy developments

All data series have been updated to reflect recent trends. Two new appendices have been added to Chapters 3 and 8, reviewing basic supply and demand theory and national income accounting. The new appendices, and an expanded discussion of basic trade theory in Chapter 19, should enable students to review the essential economic techniques that they need for environmental and resource analysis.

## Organization of the Text

The text is structured so as to be appropriate for a variety of courses, including undergraduate courses in environmental or natural resource economics and graduate-level courses with a policy orientation. Part One provides a broad overview of different approaches to economic analysis of resources and environment, and discusses fundamental issues of economy/environment interactions. Part Two covers the basics of standard environmental and resource economics including the theory of externalities, resource allocation over time, common-property resources, public goods, and valuation. Part Three offers an introduction to the ecological economics approach, including "greening" national accounts and economic/ecological modeling.

Parts Four and Five apply these analytical approaches to fundamental environmental and resource issues. Part Four focuses on population, agriculture, and the environment. Part Five deals with the economics of renewable and nonrenewable resources at both the microeconomic and macroeconomic levels.

Part Six provides both a standard analysis of the economics of pollution control and a broader view of industrial ecology and global climate change. Part Seven brings together some of the themes from the specific topics of the earlier parts in a consideration of trade and development issues.

Each chapter has discussion questions, and the more quantitative chapters have numerical problems. A list of key terms and concepts from each chapter corresponds to an extensive glossary. Useful websites are also listed. Instructors and students are urged to make full use of the text's supporting website. The instructor website includes teaching tips and objectives, answers to text problems, and test questions. The student site includes chapter review questions and web-based exercises, and will be updated periodically with bulletins on topical environmental issues.

## Acknowledgments

The preparation of a text covering such an extensive area, in addition to the supporting materials, is a vast enterprise, and my indebtedness to all those who have contributed to the effort is accordingly great. Credit for the preparation of the web materials and glossary goes to Brian Roach, Research Associate at the Tufts University Global Development and Environment Institute, who has also provided valuable comments on the text. Other colleagues at the Institute have supplied essential help and inspiration. Research Associate Anne-Marie Codur co-authored the original version of Chapter 18 on global climate change and contributed material to the chapters on renewable resources. Especially significant has been the unwavering support of the Institute's co-Director, Neva Goodwin, who has long championed the importance of educational materials bringing broader perspectives to economics teaching.

Colleagues Frank Ackerman, Rachel Massey, Julie Nelson, Timothy Wise, and Kevin Gallagher provided insights and materials from their own work that enrich many of the text chapters. Essential research assistance for the second edition was provided by Dina Dubson and Alicia Harvie, and administrative support by Minona Heaviland.

The book has greatly benefited from the comments of reviewers, including George K. Criner, University of Maine; Ronald L. Friesen, Bluffton College; Reza Ramazani, Saint Michael's College; Barbara Street, Chaminade University; James Tober, Marlboro College; John J. Nader, Grand Valley State University; Gregory L. Poe, Cornell University; Elena Alvarez, University at Albany; and David Wishart, Wittenburg University. It also reflects much that I have learned from the work of colleagues at Tufts University and elsewhere, especially William Moomaw, Sheldon Krimsky, Julian Agyeman, Molly Anderson, Paul Kirshen, and Richard Wetzler. Others whose work has provided special inspiration for this text include Herman Daly, Richard Norgaard, Robert Costanza, Faye Duchin, Glenn-Marie Lange, John Proops, and many other members of the International Society for Ecological Economics. Colleagues who used the first edition of the text and provided crucial feedback based on course experience, as well as on their own expertise, include Fred Curtis, Drew University; John Sorrentino, Temple University; Rafael Reuveny, Indiana University; Ernest Diedrich, St. John's University; and Richard Culas, Charles Sturt University, Australia.

I hope that the book will be of use to many faculty and students from a wide variety of backgrounds. Throughout my teaching career I have felt that the best insights come from students who approach topics with an open mind and can judge the relevance and usefulness of different perspectives and techniques. As many instructors are aware, "you really learn it when you teach it," being forced to confront easy assumptions and unwarranted conclusions when challenged by intelligent students. My intention is to continue this process through the use of this text and its supporting website, which will provide an opportunity for feedback and comments on the text. Updates to the website will reflect input from instructors and students, as well as the ever-changing, ever-fascinating world of environmental and resource issues.

Jonathan M. Harris
Global Development and Environment Institute
Tufts University

# ONE

# Introduction: The Economy and the Environment

**CHAPTER FOCUS QUESTIONS**

- What major environmental issues do we face in the twenty-first century?
- How can economics help us understand these issues?
- How do economic and ecological perspectives differ, and how can we combine them to address environmental issues?

*CHAPTER*

# Changing Perspectives on the Environment

## Economics and the Environment

Over the past three decades, we have become increasingly aware of environmental problems facing communities, nations, and the world. During this period, natural resource and environmental issues have grown in scope and urgency. In 1970, the Environmental Protection Agency was created in the United States to respond to what was at that time a relatively new public concern with air and water pollution. In 1972, the first international conference on the environment, the United Nations Conference on the Human Environment, met in Stockholm. Since then, growing worldwide attention has been devoted to environmental issues.

In 1992 the United Nations Conference on Environment and Development (UNCED) focused on major global issues including depletion of the earth's protective ozone layer, destruction of tropical and old-growth forests and wetlands, species extinction, and the steady buildup of carbon dioxide and other "greenhouse" gases causing global warming and climate change. Eight years later, the United Nations Environmental Programme (UNEP) report *Global Environmental Outlook 2000* found that "environmental gains from new technology and policies are being overtaken by the pace and scale of population growth and economic development." And in 2002 the follow-up report *Global Environmental Outlook 3* stated that, while in the years following the 1972 Stockholm conference "the world has made great strides in placing the environment on the agenda at various levels from international to local . . . the level of awareness and action has not been commensurate with the state of the global environment today; it continues to deteriorate."[1]

With the exception of ozone depletion, an area in which major reduction in emissions has been achieved by international agreement, the UNEP reports offer evidence that the global environmental problems identified at UNCED in 1992 have continued or worsened. In addition, UNEP points to nitrogen pollution in freshwater and oceans, exposure to toxic chemicals and hazardous wastes, forest and freshwater ecosystem damage, water contamination and declining groundwater supplies, urban air pollution and wastes, and overexploitation of major ocean fisheries. Underlying all these problems is global population growth, adding more than 70 million people a year. The world population, which had passed 6 billion by the year 2000, is expected to grow to around 8 billion by 2030.

Scientists, policymakers, and the general public have begun to grapple with questions such as What will the future look like? and Can we respond to these multiple threats adequately and in time to prevent irreversible damage to the planetary systems that support life? One of the most important components of the problem that rarely receives sufficient attention is the economic analysis of environmental issues.

Some may argue that environmental issues transcend economics and should be judged in different terms from the money values used in economic analysis. Indeed, this assertion holds some truth. We find, however, that policies for environmental protection are often measured—and sometimes rejected—in terms of their economic costs. For example, it is extremely difficult to preserve open land that has high commercial development value. Either large sums must be raised to purchase the land, or strong political opposition to "locking up" land must be overcome. Environmental protection organizations face a continued battle with ever-increasing economic development pressures.

Often public policy issues are framed in terms of a conflict between development and the environment. The battle over logging of old-growth forest in the U.S. Northwest was typified as "jobs versus owls." Opponents of international agreements to reduce carbon dioxide emissions argue that the economic costs of such measures are too high. Supporters of increased oil production clash with advocates of protecting the Arctic National Wildlife Refuge. In developing nations, the tension between the urgency of human needs and environmental protection is even greater.

Does economic development necessarily require a high environmental price? Although all economic development must affect the environment to some degree, is "environment-friendly" development possible? If we must make a tradeoff between development and environment, how shall we decide the proper balance? Questions such as these highlight the importance of environmental economics.

## Two Approaches

In this book we describe two approaches in addressing natural resource and environmental economics. The first, or traditional, approach uses a set of models and techniques

---

[1]UNEP, 1999, 2002.

rooted within the standard *neoclassical mainstream* of economic thought[2] to apply economic concepts to the environment. The second approach, known as **ecological economics,**[3] takes a different perspective. Rather than applying economic concepts *to the* environment, ecological economics seeks to place economic activity *in the context of* the biological and physical systems that support life, including all human activities.

## The Traditional Economic Approach

Several models in economic theory specifically address environmental issues. One important application of neoclassical economic theory deals with the allocation of **nonrenewable resources** over time. This analysis is important in understanding such issues as depletion of oil and mineral resources, and also has applications to **renewable resources** such as agricultural soils. Economic analyses also address **common property resources** such as the atmosphere and oceans and **public goods** such as national parks and wildlife preserves. Because these resources are not privately owned, the economic principles governing their use differ from those affecting goods traded in the market.

Another central concept in neoclassical economic analysis of the environment is that of **externalities,** or **external costs and benefits.** The theory of externalities provides an economic framework for analyzing the costs of environmental damage caused by economic activities or the social benefits created by economic activity that improves the environment. Externalities are also sometimes referred to as **third-party effects,** because a market transaction that involves two parties—for example, someone buying gasoline from a filling station—also affects other people, such as those exposed to pollution from producing and burning the gas.

Modern environmental economic theory, built on this foundation, addresses many issues ranging from overfishing to fossil fuel depletion to parkland conservation.[4] In this text we will investigate how these economic concepts can help frame environmental questions and provide guidance for environmental policymaking.

## The Ecological Economics Approach

Ecological economics takes a broader perspective in framing environmental questions by incorporating laws derived from the natural sciences. For example, to understand the collapse of many important ocean fisheries, ecological economics refers to population biology and ecology as well as to the economic view of fish as a resource for production.

---

[2]Neoclassical price theory, based on the concepts of marginal utility and marginal productivity, emphasizes the essential function of market price in achieving an equilibrium between supply and demand.

[3]For an overview of many key articles in ecological economics, see Costanza, 1991, and Krishnan et al., 1995.

[4]See Bromley, 1995; Grafton et al., 2001; Markandya, 2001; Markandya and Richardson, 1993; Stavins, 2000; and van den Bergh, 1999, for collections of articles on environmental economics.

PART ONE   Introduction: The Economy and the Environment

Ecological economics theorists emphasize the importance of energy resources, especially fossil fuels, in current economic systems. All ecological systems depend on energy inputs, but natural systems rely almost entirely on **solar energy.** The rapid growth of economic production during the twentieth century required enormous energy inputs, and global economic systems will make even greater energy demands in the twenty-first century. Energy availability and environmental implications of energy use are central issues for ecological economics.

A fundamental principle of ecological economics is that human economic activity must be limited by the environment's **carrying capacity.** Carrying capacity is defined as the population level and consumption activities, whether of humans or animals, that the available natural resource base can sustain without depletion. For example, when a herd of grazing animals exceeds a certain size, rangeland overgrazing will diminish the potential food supply, leading inevitably to a population decline.

For the human population, the issue is more complex. The issue of food supplies is certainly relevant as the world population, more than 6 billion by 2000, grows toward a projected 8 to 10 billion. But ecological economists also point to energy supplies, scarce natural resources, and cumulative environmental damage as constraints on economic growth. They argue that the standard theory gives these factors insufficient weight, and that major structural changes in the nature of economic activity are required to adapt to environmental limits.

In this text we will consider insights from both the standard and the ecological versions of environmental economics. Sometimes the theories show significant agreement or overlap, and sometimes they produce widely differing implications. The best way to judge which approaches are most fruitful is to apply them to specific environmental issues, as we do throughout this book. First, however, we must understand the relationship between the economic system, natural resources, and the environment.

## A Framework for Understanding the Ecological Perspective

How can we best conceptualize the relationship between economic activities and the environment? One way is to start with the traditional **circular flow** diagram, used in most economics courses to depict the economic process.

### The Circular Flow Model

Figure 1-1 shows a simplified model of relationships between households and business firms in two markets: the market for goods and services and the market for factors of production. Production factors are generally defined under the headings of land, labor, and capital. The services these factors provide are "inputs" to the production of goods and services, which in turn provide the basis for households' consumption needs. Goods, services, and factors flow clockwise; their economic values are reflected in the flows of money used to pay for them, moving counterclockwise. In both markets the

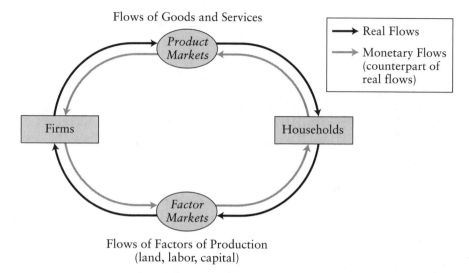

**FIGURE 1-1** *The Standard Circular Flow Model*

interaction of supply and demand determines a market-clearing price and establishes an equilibrium level of output.

Where do natural resources and the environment fit in this diagram? **Natural resources,** including minerals, water, fossil fuels, forests, fisheries, and farmland, generally fall under the inclusive category of "land." The two other major production factors, labor and capital, continually regenerate through the economic circular flow process, but by what processes do natural resources regenerate for future economic use? To answer this question, we can construct a larger "circular flow" that takes in ecosystem processes as well as economic activity (Figure 1-2).

Taking this broader view, we notice that the standard circular flow diagram also omits effects of wastes and pollution generated in the production process. These wastes from both firms and households must somewhere flow back into the ecosystem, either through land disposal or as air and water pollution.

In addition to the simple processes of extracting resources from the ecosystem and returning wastes to it, economic activities also affect broader natural systems in more subtle and pervasive ways. For example, modern intensive agriculture changes the composition and ecology of soil and water systems, as well as affecting nitrogen and carbon cycles in the environment.

Figure 1-2, although still quite simple, provides a broader framework for placing the economic system in its ecological context. As you can see, the ecological system has its own circular flow, determined by physical and biological rather than economic laws. This broader flow has only one net "input"—solar energy—and only one net "output"—waste heat. Everything else must somehow be recycled or contained within the planetary ecosystem.

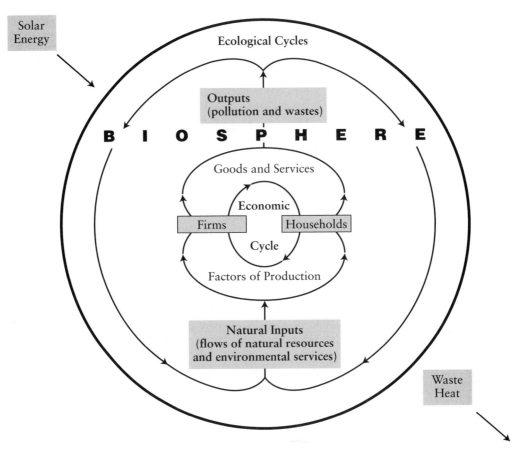

**FIGURE 1-2** *A Broader Circular Flow Model*

## *Points of Contact Between Economic and Ecological Flows*

Understanding the relationships between economic systems, natural resources, and the environment begins with defining the different functions natural systems serve.

- The environment's **source function** is its ability to make services and raw materials available for human use. Degradation of the source function can occur for two reasons: (1) **Resource depletion:** the resource declines in quantity because humans have drawn on it more rapidly than it could be regenerated; and (2) **Pollution:** contamination of the resource reduces its quality and usefulness.
- The environment's **sink function** is its ability to absorb and render harmless the waste by-products of human activity. The sink function is overtaxed when waste volume is too great in a given time period or when wastes are too toxic. When that happens, aspects of the environment on which we depend (most often soil, water, and atmosphere) become damaged, polluted, or poisoned.

These relationships between human activity and the environment define the points of contact between the inner circle of economic flows and the outer circle of ecological flows. Natural resource and environmental economics analyzes the relationships between the two circular flows: the economic system and the ecosystem.

## The Economic Valuation Approach

The traditional economic approach to analysis of natural resource and waste flows uses the same kind of **economic valuation** applied to factors of production, goods, and services. This analysis seeks to put a price on each natural resource and environmental input to the economy, including an estimated price for inputs not usually included in market transactions, such as clean air and water. Economic techniques can also be used to assess the money value of damages done by pollution and waste disposal.

By placing a money value on natural resources and environmental functions, we can include them in the inner, or economic, circular flow. This is the goal of much standard resource and environmental analysis. As we will see, a variety of methods can serve this end, including redefining or reassigning property rights, creating new institutions such as markets for pollution permits, or implicit valuation through surveys and other techniques. If we can be satisfied that these pricing mechanisms accurately reflect the "true value" of resources and of environmental damages, we can relatively easily include these factors in a market-oriented economic analysis.

## The Ecological Economics Approach

The ecological economics approach views the economic system as a subset of the broader ecosystem. In this perspective, an economic valuation expressed in prices can only imperfectly capture the complexity of ecological processes, and indeed will sometimes result in serious conflict with ecosystem requirements.

Ecological economists have often argued that standard economic pricing and valuation techniques must either be altered to reflect ecosystem realities, or must be supplemented by other forms of analysis focusing on energy flows, the carrying capacity of the environment, and the requirements of ecological balance. As we will see in our discussion of analytical techniques and of specific issues in population, energy, resources, and pollution, the standard and ecological economics perspectives will sometimes have similar practical implications, but in other cases the two approaches may lead to significantly different conclusions about appropriate resource and environmental policies.

For example, in dealing with the problem of global climate change (discussed at length in Chapter 18), a standard economic approach involves balancing the costs and benefits of avoiding future climate change. Damages caused by rising sea levels or stronger heat waves are estimated in economic terms and then compared to the costs involved in lessening climate change through reducing fossil fuel use and other measures. Policy recommendations are then formulated to maximize net economic benefits. An ecological economics approach, by contrast, looks first at the physical requirements for a stable climate, in particular the limitation of carbon dioxide and other heat-trapping gases in the atmosphere. Once the physical requirements for a stable climate are determined, the economic measures necessary to achieve this are analyzed.

Application of a standard economic approach to the problem of global climate change often results in a recommendation for more limited policy action, to avoid excessive economic costs. The ecological approach usually suggests more drastic action to preserve atmospheric balance. Cost minimization is also a concern for ecological economists, but only after the basic biophysical requirements for ecosystem stability have been met.

# Environmental Microeconomics and Macroeconomics

Another way of viewing the difference between standard and ecological approaches is in terms of a tension between microeconomic and macroeconomic perspectives on the environment.

Standard environmental economic analysis relies largely on microeconomic theory. **Environmental macroeconomics,** however, can help place the economic system in its broader ecological context.

A microeconomic perspective focuses on individual resource and environmental issues. The macroeconomic view is concerned with the interrelationship of economic growth and ecosystems.

## *Microeconomic and Valuation Techniques*

To the extent that we can succeed in putting a price on natural resources and the environment, extensions of standard microeconomic theory can help explain the process of achieving equilibrium in markets for natural resources and for **environmental services**—the capacity of the environment to absorb wastes and pollutants, capture solar energy, and in other ways provide the basis for economic activity. Analytical techniques that play an important role in **environmental microeconomics** include

- *Measuring external costs and benefits.* This means, for example, estimating a money value for damage caused by acid rain pollution. This value can then be compared to the costs of correcting the problem through pollution control technology or reduced output of polluting activities. We can **internalize externalities** through, for example, a tax on the polluting activity.
- *Valuing resources and the environment as **assets**, whether privately owned or public.* This involves considering **intertemporal resource allocation,** the choice between using a resource now or conserving it for future use. The standard economic technique to balance present and future benefits and costs is to use a **discount rate.** In this technique, a present benefit or cost receives a somewhat higher value than a future benefit or cost—how much higher depends on the discount rate employed and on how far into the future the comparison extends.

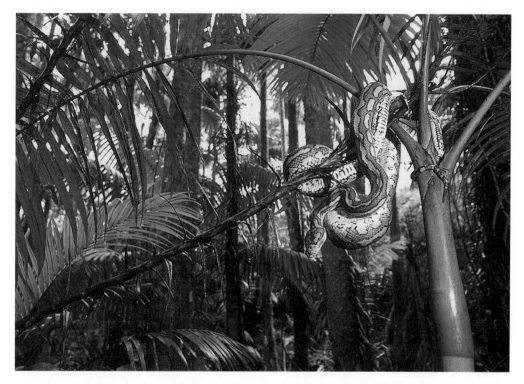

*In complex ecosystems such as rainforests, solar energy drives the cycles of life. Many such ecosystems are threatened by expansion of human activities.*

- *Devising appropriate **property rights** rules for environmental resources and establishing rules for use of common property resources and for provision of public goods.*[5] For example, a fishery may be privately owned, or it may be public with access limited by government sale of fishing licenses. Similarly, a wildlife preserve may be privately owned and managed or may be maintained as a public park.
- *Balancing economic costs and benefits through some form of **cost-benefit analysis.*** This often involves a combination of values observable in the market, such as values of land or goods, and estimates of nonmarket values, such as natural beauty and maintenance of species diversity. For example, deciding whether or not to permit construction of a ski resort on a previously undeveloped hillside would require some estimate of the recreational value of skiing, the value of alternative land uses, as well as less easily quantifiable concerns such as impact on water supplies, wildlife, and on the rural character of the area.

---

[5]*Public goods* are resources and goods available to the public without restriction. For a more precise definition, see Chapter 4.

In the context of the double circular flow shown in Figure 1-2, the above analytical techniques are derived from the smaller "economic" circle: in effect, they apply pricing concepts drawn from the economic system to the intermediate flows of natural resources and wastes that connect the two circles. These approaches seem most appropriate when we focus on a specific, quantifiable problem, such as figuring the appropriate fee to charge for a license to cut timber on government land or appropriate limits on factory air pollutant emissions.

## Environmental Macroeconomics

Valuation techniques are less effective in handling important unquantifiable values such as aesthetics, ethical issues, and **biodiversity** (the maintenance of many different interrelated species in an ecological community). They may also fail to capture the scope of **global environmental problems** that have become increasingly important in recent years. Issues such as global climate change, ozone depletion, loss of species, widespread degradation of agricultural lands, regional water shortages, forest and ocean ecosystem damage, and other large-scale environmental issues require a broader perspective. For this reason, ecological economist Herman Daly has called for development of an environmental macroeconomics,[6] which requires a different approach from the standard economic techniques discussed earlier.

Developing such a macroeconomic perspective on environmental issues requires placing the economic system in its broader ecological context. As Figure 1-2 shows, the economic circular flow is really part of a larger ecological circular flow. This ecological flow is actually made up of many cycles. **Ecological cycles** include

- The *carbon cycle,* in which green plants break down atmospheric carbon dioxide ($CO_2$) into carbon and oxygen. The carbon is stored in the plants, some of which are eaten by animals. Carbon is recombined with oxygen by animal respiration and by decay or burning of organic matter and is thus returned to the atmosphere.
- The *nitrogen cycle,* in which soil bacteria "fix," or chemically combine nitrogen from the atmosphere with oxygen and make this essential nutrient available for plant growth.
- The *water cycle,* including precipitation, runoff, and evaporation, which continually make fresh water available for plant and animal life.
- Other *organic cycles* of growth, death, decay, and new growth whereby essential nutrients are recycled through the soils to provide a continuing basis for plant and animal life.

All of these cycles rely on solar energy and operate in a complex balance that has evolved through millennia.

Seen in this context, economic activity is a process of speeding up the **throughput** of materials from the ecological cycles. The term "throughput" denotes the total use of energy and materials as both inputs and outputs of a process.

---

[6]See Daly, 1991.

Modern agriculture, for example, applies vast quantities of artificially derived nitrogen fertilizer to obtain higher crop yields. Runoff of excess nitrogen creates environmental problems and water contamination. Both agriculture and industry make heavy demands on water supplies. Together with household use, this demand can exceed the capacity of the natural water cycle, depleting reservoirs and underground aquifers.

The most important way of speeding up resource throughput is using more energy to drive the economic system. More than 80 percent of the energy used in the global economic system is derived from fossil fuels. Carbon emissions from burning these fuels unbalances the global carbon cycle. Excessive amounts of $CO_2$ accumulate in the atmosphere, alter the processes that determine the planet's climate, and thereby affect many global ecosystems.

As economic growth proceeds, the demands of the economic system on the ecological cycles grow. Energy use, resource and water use, and waste generation increase. Thus the environmental macroeconomic issue is how to balance the size of the economic system, or **macroeconomic scale,** with the supporting ecosystem. Viewing the problem in this way represents a significant paradigm shift for economic analysis, which until recently has not usually considered overall ecosystem limitations.

### *Implications of Ecologically Oriented Economics*

An ecologically oriented macroeconomics involves new concepts of national income measurement that explicitly reckon environmental pollution and natural resource depletion in calculating national income. In addition, ecological economists have introduced new forms of analysis at both microeconomic and macroeconomic levels. These new analytical techniques are based on the physical laws that govern energy and materials flows in ecosystems. Applying these laws to the economic process offers a contrasting perspective to the standard microeconomic analysis of environmental issues.

Seeking a balance between economic growth and ecosystem health has given rise to the concept of **sustainable development** (discussed in detail in Chapter 2). Forms of economic development that preserve rather than degrade the environment include renewable energy use, organic and low-input agriculture, and resource-conserving technologies. On a global scale, the promotion of sustainable development responds to the many resource and environmental issues outlined at the beginning of the chapter, viewing these issues in terms of ecosystem impacts rather than as individual problems.[7]

## A Look Ahead

How can we best use these two approaches to economic analysis of environmental issues? In the following chapters we will find out by applying the tools and methods of each to specific issues. In preparation, Chapter 2 provides an overview of the

---

[7]For surveys of the relationship between environmental economics and sustainable development, see Opschoor et al., 1999, and Harris et al., 2001. For a discussion of global ecosystem impacts of human activity, see World Resources Institute, 2000.

relationship between economic development and the environment. The microeconomic elements of resource and environmental economics are explored in detail in Chapters 3–6. Chapters 7–9 cover the concepts of ecological economics, environmental accounting, and ecosystem modeling.

In Chapters 10–18, we apply techniques of standard economic analysis and of ecological analysis to the major issues of population, food supply, energy use, natural resource management, and pollution control. Chapters 19 and 20 bring together many of these topics to focus on questions of trade, economic growth, and development as they relate to the environment.

## SUMMARY

National and global environmental issues are major challenges in the twenty-first century. Response to these challenges requires understanding the economics of the environment. Policies aimed at environmental protection have economic costs and benefits, and this economic dimension is often crucial in determining which policies we adopt. Some cases may require tradeoffs between economic and environmental goals; in other cases these goals may prove compatible and mutually reinforcing.

Two different approaches address economic analysis of environmental issues. The standard approach applies economic theory to the environment using concepts of money valuation and economic equilibrium. This approach aims for efficient management of natural resources and proper valuation of waste and pollution impact on the environment. The ecological economic approach views the economic system as a whole as a subset of a broader biophysical system. This approach emphasizes the need for economic activity that conforms to physical and biological limits.

Much of the analysis drawn from the standard approach is microeconomic, based on the workings of markets. Variations of standard market analysis can be applied to cases where economic activity has damaging environmental effects or uses up scarce resources. Other economic analyses provide insight into the use of common property resources and public goods.

Environmental macroeconomics, a relatively new field, emphasizes the relationship between economic production and the major natural cycles of the planet. In many cases, significant conflicts arise between the operations of the economic system and these natural systems, creating regional and global problems such as global climate change from excess carbon dioxide accumulation. This broader approach requires new ways to measure economic activity, as well as analysis of how the scale of economic activity affects environmental systems.

This text outlines both analytical perspectives and draws on both to help understand the major issues of population, food supply, energy use, natural resource management, and pollution. The combination of these analyses can help to formulate policies that address specific environmental problems as well as promote a broader vision of environmentally sustainable development.

## KEY TERMS AND CONCEPTS

assets
biodiversity
carrying capacity
circular flow
common property resources
cost-benefit analysis
discount rate
ecological cycles
ecological economics
economic valuation
environmental macroeconomics
environmental microeconomics
environmental services
external costs and benefits
externalities
global environmental problems

internalizing externalities
intertemporal resource allocation
macroeconomic scale
natural resources
nonrenewable resources
pollution
property rights
public goods
renewable resources
resource depletion
solar energy
source and sink functions
sustainable development
third-party effects
throughput

## DISCUSSION QUESTIONS

1. Do economic growth and sound environmental policy necessarily conflict? Identify some areas where a choice must be made between economic growth and environmental preservation and others where the two are compatible.

2. Can we put a money price on environmental resources? How? Is this impossible in any cases? Identify specific situations of valuing the environment with which you are familiar or have read about.

3. In what ways do the principles of ecological circular flow resemble those of the economic circular flow? How do they differ? Consider specific examples in the areas of agriculture, water, and energy systems.

## REFERENCES

Bromley, Daniel W., ed. *The Handbook of Environmental Economics*. Blackwell Handbooks in Economics series. Oxford, U.K., and Cambridge, U.S.: Basil Blackwell, 1995.

Costanza, Robert, ed. *Ecological Economics: The Science and Management of Sustainability*. New York: Columbia University Press, 1991.

Daly, Herman. "Elements of Environmental Macroeconomics," in Costanza, ed., 1991.

Grafton, R. Quentin, Linwood H. Pendleton, and Harry W. Nelson. *A Dictionary of Environmental Economics, Science, and Policy*. Cheltenham, U.K.: Elgar, 2001.

Harris, Jonathan M., Timothy A. Wise, Kevin P. Gallagher, and Neva R. Goodwin. *A Survey of Sustainable Development: Social and Economic Dimensions.* Washington, D.C.: Island Press, 2001.

Krishnan, Rajaram, Jonathan M. Harris, and Neva R. Goodwin, eds. *A Survey of Ecological Economics.* Washington, D.C.: Island Press, 1995.

Markandya, Anil. *Dictionary of Environmental Economics.* London, U.K.: Earthscan, 2001.

Markandya, Anil, and Julie Richardson. *Environmental Economics: A Reader.* New York: St. Martin's Press, 1993.

Opschoor, J. B., Kenneth Button, and Peter Nijkamp, eds. *Environmental Economics and Development.* Cheltenham, U.K.: Elgar, 1999.

Stavins, Robert N., ed. *Economics of the Environment: Selected Readings,* 4th ed. New York: Norton, 2000.

United Nations Environment Programme. *Global Environmental Outlook 2000: UNEP's Millennium Report on the Environment.* London, U.K.: Earthscan, 1999.

United Nations Environment Programme. *Global Environmental Outlook 3: Past, Present, and Future Perspectives.* London, U.K.: Earthscan, 2002.

van den Bergh, Jeroen C. J. M. *Handbook of Environmental and Resource Economics.* Cheltenham, U.K.: Elgar, 1999.

World Commission on Environment and Development. *Our Common Future.* New York: Oxford University Press, 1987.

World Resources Institute, United Nations Development Programme, United Nations Environment Programme, and World Bank. *World Resources 2000–2001: People and Ecosystems: The Fraying Web of Life.* Washington, D.C.: World Resources Institute, 2000.

## WEBSITES

1. **http://www.worldwatch.org/** The homepage for the Worldwatch Institute, an organization that conducts a broad range of research on environmental issues. The Worldwatch annual "State of the World" report presents detailed analyses of current environmental issues.

2. **http://www.ncseonline.org/** Website for the National Council for Science and the Environment, with links to various sites with state, national, and international data on environmental quality.

3. **http://www.emagazine.com/** Website for E/The Environmental Magazine. The site includes many archived articles on all environmental topics.

4. **http://www.unep.org/geo/geo3/** Website for the Global Environment Outlook-3, a United Nations publication. The report is an extensive analysis of the global environmental situation.

**CHAPTER FOCUS QUESTIONS**

- What is the relationship between economic growth and the environment?
- Will economic growth encounter planetary limits?
- How can economic development become environmentally sustainable?

**CHAPTER 2**

# Resources, Environment, and Economic Development

## A Brief History of Economic Growth and the Environment

Human population and economic activity have remained fairly stable during much of recorded history. Prior to the Industrial Revolution of the nineteenth century, Europe's population grew slowly and standards of living changed little. The advent of the market economy and rapid technological progress altered this pattern dramatically. Populations in Europe entered a period of rapid growth that led British classical economist Thomas Malthus to theorize that populations would outgrow food supplies, keeping the mass of people perpetually at a subsistence standard of living.

Malthus's *Essay on the Principle of Population as It Affects the Future Improvement of Society,* published in 1798, initiated a long and continuing debate on the impact of population growth. History has proved the simple Malthusian hypothesis wrong: both population and living standards in Europe rose rapidly throughout the two centuries following Malthus's *Essay.* But if we consider a more sophisticated argument, that a growing human population and economic system will eventually outrun its biophysical support systems, the debate turns out to have strong current relevance.

The controversy over population growth is intimately intertwined with resource and environmental issues. In the twenty-first century these issues, rather than the simple race between population and food supply, will strongly affect the course of economic development. It is unlikely that we will see major shortfalls in food supply on a global scale. But it is highly likely that the environmental stresses associated with a growing population and rising resource demands will require sweeping changes in the nature of economic systems.

## Measuring Growth Rates

In approaching complex growth issues, we can start with a simple economic analysis of the relationship between population and economic activity. Measuring economic output in conventional terms as **gross domestic product (GDP)**,[1] we have the simple identity

$$GDP = (Population) \times (Per\ Capita\ GDP)$$

which can then be expressed in terms of rates of growth as a relationship among **GDP growth rate, population growth rate,** and **per capita GDP growth rate:**

$$GDP\ Growth\ Rate = (Population\ Growth\ Rate)$$
$$+ (Per\ Capita\ GDP\ Growth\ Rate).[2]$$

To correct for the effects of inflation, we should use **real GDP** rather than **nominal GDP** in this equation.[3] Real per capita GDP will rise steadily, as long as real GDP growth remains consistently higher than population growth. For this to occur, productivity must also rise steadily. This increasing productivity is, of course, the key to escaping the Malthusian trap.

Increased agricultural productivity means that the portion of the population working in farming decreases, freeing labor for industrial development. Increased industrial productivity brings higher living standards. Broadly speaking, economic development has unfolded along these lines in Europe, the United States, and other industrialized nations.

## Factors Essential to Economic Growth

What determinants of increased productivity make this steady growth possible? One is accumulation of capital. Investment allows growth of **capital stock** over time: as capital stock per worker increases, the productivity of each worker increases. In addition **technological innovation** raises the productivity of both capital and labor. Standard economic growth models place no limits on this process. Provided investment continues at adequate rates, productivity and per capita consumption can continue rising far into the future.

The ecological economics perspective focuses on three additional factors as essential to economic growth. One is energy supply. Europe's economic growth in the

---

[1]Gross domestic product (GDP) is defined as the total flow of goods and services produced by an economy over a specified time period, usually a year.

[2]This relationship is derived from the mathematical rule of natural logarithms stating that if $A = BC$, then $\ln A = \ln B + \ln C$. The rates of growth of $B$ and $C$ can be expressed in terms of natural logarithms, and when added together they give the rate of growth of $A$.

[3]Nominal GDP is measured using current prices. Real GDP corrects for inflation by using a price index to calculate the constant dollar value of production.

nineteenth century depended heavily on coal as an energy source, and some writers at the time expressed concern that coal supplies might run out. In the twentieth century, oil displaced coal as the prime energy source for industry.

Currently oil, natural gas, and coal provide more than 85 percent of energy supplies for the United States, Europe, Japan, and other industrial economies, and about the same proportion of industrial energy for the world as a whole.[4] To a great extent, economic growth both in agriculture and industry has been a process of substituting fossil fuel energy for human labor. This substitution has important resource and environmental implications, which in turn affect projections of future growth.

A second fundamental factor is supplies of land and natural resources, sometimes referred to as **natural capital.** Almost all economic activities require some land use. As these activities grow, pressures increase to convert land from a natural state to agricultural, industrial, and residential uses. Some uses conflict: housing may compete with farming for rural land, and industry or road building may make land less suitable for either residential or agricultural use.

Land, of course, is fixed in supply. Except in limited cases such as the diked areas of the Netherlands, human technology cannot create more land. Natural resources vary in abundance, but mineral resources and the regenerative capacity of forests and other living resources have physical limits.

The third important factor is the **absorptive capacity of the environment** for the waste products of industrial development. This issue is not so critical when the scale of economic activity is small relative to the environment. But as national and global economic activity accelerates, the flow of waste products increases and may threaten to overwhelm environmental systems. Flows of solid wastes, sewage and liquid wastes, toxic and radioactive wastes, and atmospheric emissions all pose specific environmental problems that require local, regional, and global solutions.

## Growth Optimists and Pessimists

Debate is ongoing concerning resource and environmental factors that contribute to, and could eventually limit, economic growth. In 1972 a Massachusetts Institute of Technology research team published *The Limits to Growth,* a study that used computer modeling to project drastic resource and environmental problems looming as a result of continued economic growth (see Box 2-1).[5] This report touched off a vigorous debate between growth "optimists" and "pessimists."

For the most part, the optimists placed faith in future technological progress to tap new sources of energy, overcome any resource limitations, and control pollution problems. The pessimists pointed to the rapid growth of population and GDP, together with the already formidable array of existing environmental problems, to warn that humanity was in danger of overshooting the earth's capacity to sustain economic activity. In effect, the question was whether the successful experience of economic growth over the past two centuries can be sustained in the next century.

---

[4]U.S. Department of Energy, 2004.

[5]Meadows et al., 1972.

## 2-1    The Limits to Growth Model

The *Limits to Growth* model, presented by an MIT research team in 1972, addressed the issue of physical limits to economic growth. The study employed a model called World 3, which attempted to capture interrelationships between population, agricultural output, economic growth, resource use, and pollution. At the time, public attention was just beginning to focus on environmental issues, and the MIT study's message had a powerful impact. The team concluded that we would reach the environmental limits to global growth within a century, and that without drastic changes there was a strong likelihood of an "overshoot/collapse" outcome: "a sudden and uncontrollable decline in both population and industrial capacity."[1]

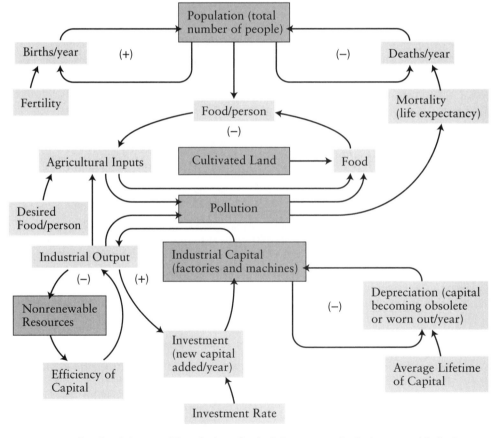

**FIGURE 2-1** *Feedback Loops of Population, Capital, Resources, Agriculture, and Pollution*

[1]Meadows et al., 1972.

*(continued on following page)*

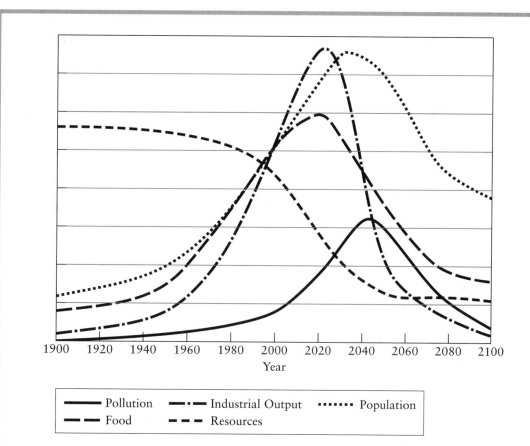

**FIGURE 2-2** *The Basic Limits to Growth Model*

Source for figures: *Beyond the Limits: Confronting Global Collapse, Envisioning a Sustainable Future.* Donella Meadows et al., copyright 1992, Chelsea Green Publishing, White River Junction, Vt., 1-800-639-4099, www.chelseagreen.com. Reprinted by permission of Chelsea Green Publishing.

The model relied heavily on exponential growth patterns and feedback effects. Exponential growth occurs when population, economic production, resource use, or pollution increases by a certain percentage each year. Feedback effects occur when two variables interact, for example, when capital accumulation increases economic output, which in turn leads to a more rapid accumulation of capital. Positive feedback effects strengthen growth trends, whereas negative feedback effects moderate them. Negative feedback effects, however, may be undesirable, for example, when limits on food supply cause population decline through malnutrition and disease.

Figure 2-1 shows a portion of the complex pattern of feedback effects in the World 3 model. The results of the model's "standard run" are shown in Figure 2-2.

*(continued on following page)*

Exponential growth in population, industrial output, and food demand generate declines in resources and increasing pollution, which force a catastrophic reversal of growth by the mid-twenty-first century.

The report also emphasized that aggressive policies to moderate population growth, resource consumption, and pollution could avoid this disastrous result, leading instead to a smooth transition to global economic and ecological stability. This conclusion received far less attention than the catastrophic predictions. The report was widely criticized for failing to recognize the flexibility and adaptability of the economic system and for overstating the danger of resource exhaustion.

In 1992, the authors of the 1972 report published another book reasserting their conclusions but with more emphasis on environmental problems such as ozone layer destruction and global climate change. Once again they stated that

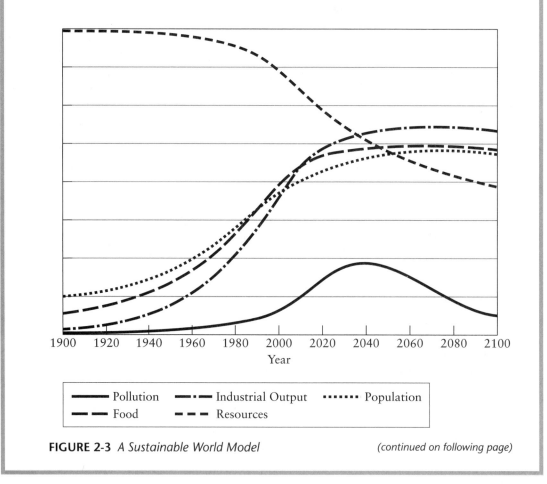

**FIGURE 2-3** *A Sustainable World Model*          *(continued on following page)*

catastrophe was not inevitable, but warned of an even more urgent need for major policy changes to achieve sustainability, with some ecological systems already being forced beyond their limits.[2] With such policy changes, the results look significantly different. In a model run showing a "transition to sustainability," policies are implemented to stabilize population, limit growth of industrial output, conserve resources and agricultural land, and control pollution. This leads to a stable, wealthier world population by the year 2050, with declining pollution levels (Figure 2-3).

---

[2]Meadows et al., 1992.

## A Summary of Recent Growth

It is worth noting that the economic growth following World War II has been extraordinary in its scope and character. In historical terms, world population and economic growth between 1800 and 1950 represented a significant increase over previous slow growth rates. Even so, the rates since 1950 have been truly remarkable.

Between 1950 and 2000, world population more than doubled; world agricultural production tripled; and world GDP and energy use quadrupled (Figure 2-4 shows trends since 1961). This, of course, has raised demands on resources and the environment to unprecedented levels. The growth process, however, is far from completed. Global population, at more than six billion by 2000, continues to increase by 1.2 percent per year, a net addition of more than 70 million people (more than the entire population of France) every year.

Together with population growth, the demand for improved living standards continues to drive overall production steadily upwards. GDP growth continues at between 2 and 3 percent per year in both developing and developed countries, with much higher rates in many developing nations such as China. At this rate, the World Bank projects that by 2030 world GDP will be 3.5 times 1990 levels—or approximately 15 times the 1950 level of GDP.[6]

Will we have enough energy, resources, and environmental capacity to sustain this level of output? We will examine many specific aspects of this question in future chapters. As an introduction, we review the main dimensions of the problem and suggest approaches to their analysis.

---

[6]World Bank, 1992 and 1999.

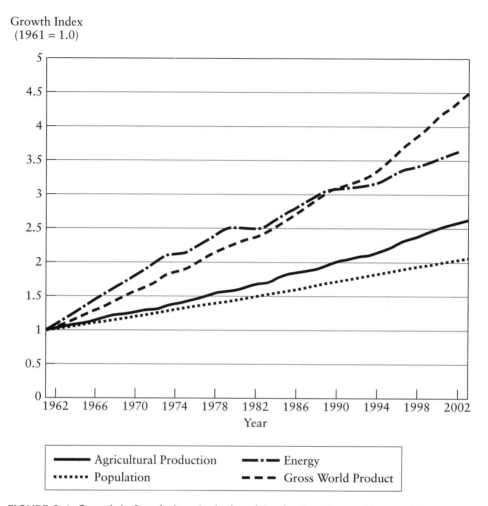

**FIGURE 2-4** *Growth in Population, Agricultural Production, Energy Use, and Gross World Product, 1961–2003*

Sources: Food and Agriculture Organization of the United Nations, FAOSTAT database 2004; United States Department of Energy, 2004; Worldwatch Institute database *Signposts 2004*. Indices based on 1961 = 1.0.

## The Future of Economic Growth and the Environment

In the economic history of the twentieth century, environmental issues gradually became more prominent. During the Great Depression of the 1930s soil erosion drew attention, and in the 1950s and 1960s concerns about pesticide use and air pollution emerged. Only in the last decades of the twentieth century, however, did environmental degradation gain recognition as a fundamental challenge to the whole economic growth process.

*Growing populations require more space for urban and residential development. Here, a housing tract covers farmland in the United States. In densely populated developing countries such as China and India, prime cropland is also being converted to urban, industrial, transportation, and residential uses.*

In the global economy of the twenty-first century, by contrast, environmental considerations will be a determining factor in shaping economic development.

## Population Growth

The first essential fact of this new global economy is our dramatically increased population. The phenomenon of **population momentum,** discussed in Chapter 10, guarantees growing populations in most countries over the next half-century. Unlike many predictions that may be quickly disproved by events, this one is virtually certain; the largest generation of children in global history has already been born. We know that these children will grow to be adults and have children of their own. Even if they have small families (and large families are now the norm in much of the world), their children will significantly outnumber the present older generations they will replace.

Thus only a huge increase in the death rate could alter the prediction of significantly higher population. Even the global AIDS crisis, despite its horrifying global spread, is unlikely to affect population projections except in a few regions. The lowest projections for the year 2030 show a 50 percent increase in global population over 1990 levels; higher-range projections show a doubling over 1990 levels to about 10 billion. More than 95 percent of this increase will occur in currently developing nations.

Although global population growth rates have been falling since the 1970s, a decline projected to continue, the total number of people added to world population (a smaller percentage of a larger total) will remain over 60 million per year over the next several decades.[7]

Such population growth raises the question of whether or not we can feed the world. Will agricultural capacity supply the needs of an extra 2, 3, or 4 billion people? We can examine this problem in several ways. The simplest question is if it is physically possible to produce sufficient grain and other foodstuffs to provide adequate nutrition for 8 to 10 billion people, given the limited global land area suitable for agriculture. The more difficult problem is whether or not it is possible to satisfy ever-growing per capita demand, including demand for "luxury" foods and meat-centered diets.

Global inequality means that widespread hunger and malnutrition persist even when the *average* food production on a national or global basis is adequate. Economic growth may improve the standard of living of the poorest (though this is not always true by any means), but it also encourages increased per capita consumption by the relatively affluent. Taking this into account, food consumption is likely to grow significantly faster than population.

Increasing global food production will require **intensification of production.** This means that each acre of land must produce significantly higher food output. The stresses imposed on land and water supplies, the increased fertilizer requirements, as well as the problems of erosion, chemical runoff, and pesticide pollution represent the real limits to agricultural expansion.

In Chapter 11 we will examine in more detail this interplay between population, social inequality, food consumption, food production, and environmental impacts. Certainly a focus on productive capacity alone is insufficient. Resource and environmental factors, as well as issues of equity, will be central in responding to the challenge of feeding much larger populations with limited resources.

In addition to agricultural land requirements, expanding populations require more space for urban, residential, and industrial development. These needs will tend to encroach on farmland, forests, and natural ecosystems. This population pressure on land is acute in countries such as India (794 people per square mile) or Bangladesh (2,320 people per square mile). In less densely populated areas such as the United States (74 people per square mile), land use remains a central environmental issue, with ever-increasing pressure from suburban developments on farmland and natural areas, and continual conflict between large scale agriculture or forestry and wilderness preservation.

## Rising Resource Use

Resource use issues also surround the question of future population and economic growth. The original argument of the 1972 *Limits to Growth* report stressed limited supplies of key **nonrenewable resources** such as metal ores and other minerals. Since then, the focus of debate has shifted. Critics of the pessimistic position on growth

---

[7]Population Reference Bureau, 2004.

limits have pointed out that new resource discoveries, new technologies for extraction and the development of substitute resources as well as expanded recycling all extend the horizon of resource use. As with food supply, the real issue may not be absolute limits on availability but rather the environmental impacts of increased **resource recovery** (mining or extraction of resources for economic use).

Mining operations, for example, are notoriously damaging to the environment. If the "average" global consumer's demand for steel rises toward the current U.S. consumption level at the same time as world population rises, requirements for iron ore will rise drastically. Plenty of iron ore remains to be extracted from the earth's crust—but at what environmental cost?

Common sense and economic theory both tell us that the highest-quality ores will be exploited first.[8] As we fall back on lower-quality ores, the energy requirements to obtain processed metal, as well as the volume of related industrial waste, rise steadily. Our present mining operations have left a legacy of scarred earth and polluted water—how will we deal with future higher-impact requirements?

### Increasing Energy Use

Expansion of resource use, like expansion of agricultural output, depends on energy supply. Energy is fundamental to economic activity and to life itself, making possible the use of all other resources. Energy resource issues are therefore of special importance. Nineteenth-century economic development relied largely on coal, and twentieth-century development on oil. Our current heavy dependence on fossil fuel resources (more than 85 percent of energy use for developed economies) poses major problems for the twenty-first-century economy.

In part these issues arise from limited supplies of fossil fuels. Currently known reserves of oil and gas will be largely depleted within 50 years. Coal reserves will last much longer—but coal is the "dirtiest" of all fossil fuels. Coal, oil, and gas burning all contribute to ground-level air pollution as well as to global carbon emissions, an important cause of **global climate change.**

Increased population and rising living standards are projected to require significantly increased energy use over the next 40 years.[9] New less-polluting sources of energy, as well as reduction in present per capita energy use in developed nations, appear essential. The economics of this transition to alternative energy sources will be discussed in Chapter 13.

### Dwindling Resources

Worldwide pressure on **renewable resources** such as forests and fisheries has become increasingly evident. **Over-harvesting of renewable resources** has caused serious

[8]The economic theory of nonrenewable resources is explained in detail in Chapter 12.

[9]As we have noted, world energy use has quadrupled during the period since World War II. A 2 percent annual rate of growth in energy use, barely sufficient to keep ahead of growing population, would double it again in 35 years. Energy use, especially in developing nations, will more likely increase at least 4 percent per annum to supply industrial growth.

environmental losses. World forest cover has declined, with particularly rapid loss of tropical forest during the past several decades.[10] After many years of steady increase, global fish catch appears close to a maximum, with major fisheries now in decline.

Exploitation of natural resources is also causing an increasing rate of species loss, posing unknown ecological hazards and diminishing the natural "inheritance" of future generations. Clearly, these pressures will only increase with rising demands for food, fuel, wood products, and fiber.

Economic theory offers an explanation for the over-harvesting phenomenon, as we will see in Chapter 4. Prescribing solutions is more difficult. Such prescriptions will certainly require a conceptual shift from regarding forests and fisheries as unrestricted **open-access resources** to perceiving them as part of a **global commons.** ("Commons" refers to resources not privately owned but managed for the social good.) Future economic development cannot simply take advantage of "free" resources such as undeveloped land and open oceans, but must be adjusted to ecological limits. In some cases, private property rights can create incentives for individual owners to conserve resources. Other situations require the development of effective regional or global common-property management policies.

## Pollution

Economic growth also brings the problem of growing volumes of **cumulative pollutants** (pollutants that neither dissipate nor degrade significantly over time) and of toxic and nuclear wastes. Controls on emissions, the traditional focus of pollution policy, are of limited use in dealing with these more insidious problems. When we deal with cumulative pollutants such as chlorofluorocarbons (CFCs), organochlorides such as DDT, or radioactive wastes, we must grapple with the legacy of all previous pollution and waste production as well as consider how our present activities will affect the future environment. This greatly complicates any economic evaluation of costs and benefits.

Air and water pollutants that are not cumulative can be controlled through specific regulatory policies. But economic growth often leads to an increased volume of such pollutants. In the area of emissions control, improved technology continually races against increased consumption (automobile use is a prime example). The economic analysis of pollution control offers policy solutions for specific emissions problems, whereas the newer theory of **industrial ecology,** explored in Chapter 17, offers an overview of the relationship of pollution-generating activities to the natural environment.

## An Ecological Approach to Economic Growth and the Environment

In reviewing these major environmental and resource challenges of the twenty-first century, we should not necessarily lean toward either an "optimistic" or "pessimistic" perspective. Indeed, these very terms may be misleading. While analysts differ greatly

---

[10]World Resources Institute, 2003, Data Table 10: Forests, Grasslands, and Drylands.

regarding appropriate responses, few dispute the importance of global environment and resource issues. As we will see, both the market-oriented approaches stressing economic system adaptability and the ecological assessment of biophysical problems have important roles to play in devising policy responses.

Chapters 10–18 will provide more detailed attention to these issues. Although in each case specific policies may address individual problems, the issues together suggest a common need for a different kind of economic analysis, one that addresses a global economy in which resource and environmental considerations are much more prominent than in the past.

Rather than approaching environmental questions as an afterthought once we have dealt with the basic economic issues of production, employment, and output growth, our concept of economics must consider the environment as fundamental to the productive process. Of course, economic production has always depended on the environment, but the scale of economic activity makes a difference. So long as human activity remained on a small scale relative to the ecosystem, we could make do with an economic theory that analyzed production and consumption without regard to their environmental impacts. Now that economic production produces such widespread environmental effects, it is essential to integrate our views of economics and environment.

If we adopt a broader perspective, we must adapt the goals of economic activity themselves to ecological realities. Traditionally, the main goals of economic activity have been seen as increased production and rising per capita consumption. But in the many ways presented above, these goals pose a threat to the **environmental sustainability** of our economic system. Either the goals or the methods we choose to achieve them must be modified as population and environmental pressures increase.

The effort to balance economic and environmental goals is addressed in the theory of **sustainable development**—economic development that provides for human needs without undermining global ecosystems and depleting essential resources. Some have complained that sustainable development is just a buzzword devoid of specific content. Others have quickly moved to appropriate the term "sustainable" to characterize only slightly modified forms of traditional economic growth. Nevertheless, the outlines of a new concept that would indeed redefine economic goals have begun to emerge.[11]

## Sustainable Development

Recall that the standard view of economic growth is defined in terms of per capita GDP, meaning that total GDP must rise faster than population. Sustainable development requires different measures. Increased output of goods and services can certainly be part of the desired outcome, but equally important is the maintenance of the ecological base of the economy—fertile soils, natural ecosystems, forests, fisheries, and water systems.

---

[11]For a review of recent theory and practice in the area of sustainable development, see Harris et al., 2001.

As we will see in Chapter 8, techniques for modifying the measurement of national income can take such factors into account. Even so, sustainable development means more than simply a different yardstick. It also implies a different analysis of the process of production and consumption.

## Sustainable Development Versus Standard Views of Economic Growth

On the production side, it is important to differentiate between renewable and non-renewable resources. Every economy must use some nonrenewable resources, but sustainable development implies conservation or recycling of these resources and greater reliance on renewables. On the consumption side, an important distinction must be drawn between wants and needs. In contrast to the standard economic paradigm, in which "dollar votes" command the marketplace and determine which goods are to be produced, sustainable development implies putting a priority on supplying basic needs before luxury goods.[12]

Also in contrast to standard economic growth theory, sustainability implies limits to **macroeconomic scale.** Rather than projecting rates of growth indefinitely into the future, some maximum level is postulated based on the **carrying capacity** of the area (and ultimately of the planet). This in turn implies a maximum level of population above which carrying capacity—the level of population and consumption that can be sustained by the available natural resource base—will be exceeded and living standards must fall.[13]

## Population and Sustainable Development

This introduction of population as a key variable in determining the limits of economic growth has implications for both developing and currently industrialized economies. For developing economies with rapid population growth rates, it means that limiting population growth is a critical element in successful development.

For industrialized economies, the role of population is different. In much of Europe and in Japan, population has stabilized, and for countries such as Germany and Russia concern has shifted to an emerging pattern of population decline. In the United States, however, population increase continues to put pressure on both national and global ecosystems. Although the U.S. population growth rate is less dramatic than that in many developing nations (0.6 percent per annum as opposed to 2–3 percent in much of Latin America, Africa, and Asia), the much larger U.S. per capita consumption means that each additional U.S. resident creates several times the additional resource demand of, for example, an additional resident of India.

---

[12]The "basic needs" approach to development, first set forth by Streeten et al. (1981), has been further developed by Stewart (1985), Sen (2000), and UNDP (1990–2004).

[13]See Daly, 1991 and 1996, on limits to macroeconomic scale.

This means that population policy must be an essential element of sustainable development. Population policy must include elements of education, social policy, economic policy, and health care, including contraceptive availability, and often runs into conflict with established religious and social mores. Still, this difficult area, generally little considered in standard economic development models, is crucial for sustainability.

## Agriculture and Sustainable Development

When we consider agricultural production systems, the general principle of relying as much as possible on renewable resources runs counter to much of standard agricultural "modernization." Modern food production is based on **input-intensive agriculture,** meaning that it depends heavily on additional fertilizer, pesticides, water for irrigation, and mechanization. All of these in turn depend on fossil fuel energy. Traditional agriculture, based on solar energy, animal power, and human labor, has generally produced lower yields than modern agriculture.

The concept of **sustainable agriculture** combines elements of traditional and modern techniques. It emphasizes maximum use of renewable resources such as crop wastes and animal manure, as well as crop rotation, intercropping of different plant types, agroforestry, efficient irrigation, minimum-till techniques, and integrated pest management (discussed in Chapter 11). It is still an open question whether this form of agriculture can equal the yields achieved with input-intensive techniques, but its environmental impacts are less damaging, or even beneficial to the environment.

## Energy and Sustainable Development

A similar issue arises as to whether **renewable energy sources** (including **solar energy**) have the capacity to replace fossil fuel dependence. The challenge is a daunting one, because renewables now supply less than 10 percent of energy in the industrialized nations. The picture is different in developing nations, where a large portion of current energy supply comes from **biomass** (wood, plant, and animal wastes). Efficient use of biomass and maintenance of forest resources can thus play an important role in energy policy. Technological advances in solar, wind, and biomass energy systems have lowered the prices of these renewable sources, and their potential for future expansion is significant both in developed and developing nations.

A huge, often unrecognized, potential lies in conservation and improved efficiency—by some estimates the developed world could reduce its energy use by about 30 percent through these techniques with little or no effect on living standards.[14] The traditional emphasis on **energy supply augmentation** (such as building new power plants) could thus give way to a focus on **demand-side management** (increasing efficiency and reducing energy consumption).

---

[14]See, for example, Intergovernmental Panel on Climate Change (IPCC), 2001, Chapter 3, "Technological and Economic Potential of Greenhouse Gas Emissions Reduction"; and the website of the American Council for an Energy-Efficient Economy, http://www.aceee.org.

Because the industrialized nations now account for three-quarters of global energy use (though only one-quarter of global population), increased energy consumption in developing nations could possibly be offset by reductions in rich nation energy use. Negotiations over global climate policy (discussed in Chapter 18) suggest that such a tradeoff may be essential to reduce overall human impacts on the world's climate.

## Sustainable Management for Natural Resources

**Sustainable natural resource management** implies a combination of economic and ecological perspectives. The economic theory of natural resource management, set forth in Chapters 14 and 15, shows how many management systems for resources such as forests and fisheries can lead to depletion or even extinction of the resource. Proper incentives and institutions can promote sustainable management. Current management systems for many of the world's fisheries and forests, however, are far from sustainable.

In the area of industrial pollution management the standard economic approach is to analyze the costs and benefits of various forms of pollution control to determine an economically optimal policy. This approach has its merits, fully considered in Chapter 16, but it is insufficient for sustainability. The best pollution control policy can be overwhelmed by growth in pollution-generating activities, especially those that produce cumulative pollutants.

Attention has therefore begun to focus on the new concept of industrial ecology as a more comprehensive approach to pollution control. Using the analogy of a natural ecosystem's capacity to recycle its own wastes, this approach attempts to analyze industrial systems as a whole to identify ways in which to minimize or avoid generating pollutants and maximize resource recycling. The application of industrial ecology techniques, discussed in Chapter 17, has potential both for restructuring existing industrial systems and for economic development in Latin America, Asia, and Africa.

In all these areas, sustainable development offers a new **theoretical paradigm** different from the standard economic approach. Considering a new paradigm of thought is justified because the global reality has changed radically from an earlier period when economic policy could be formulated with little regard to environmental impacts.

Following this logic, we might roughly distinguish three periods of economic history. In the preindustrial period, human population and economic activity remained at fairly stable levels, placing only limited demands on the planetary ecosystem. During the past two hundred years of rapid industrial and population growth, economic growth has had increasingly heavy environmental impact. The process has not been uniform; in some cases improved technology or changing industrial patterns have lessened pollution and resource demand. Still, the increasing pressures already discussed suggest that we are entering a third period during which population growth and economic activity must align with ecological carrying capacity.

The tools of economic analysis we study in Part 2 are drawn from standard economic theory, and the perspectives presented in Part 3 respond to the issues of ecological limits on economic growth. The two in combination provide a powerful toolbox of analytical techniques with which to address the multifaceted questions of the interrelationship between environment and economy.

## SUMMARY

Economic growth over time reflects both population and per capita GDP growth. This growth depends on increases in capital stock and technological progress, as well as increased supplies of energy, natural resources, and the capacity of the environment to absorb wastes.

A simple model of the relationship between population, industrial output, resources, and pollution indicates that unlimited economic growth will lead to exhaustion of resources, rising pollution, and eventual collapse of economic systems and ecosystems. However, such a model depends on assumptions about technological progress and feedback patterns among the variables in the model. A more optimistic view considers increased efficiency, pollution control, and a transition to alternative, more sustainable technologies.

During the second half of the twentieth century, unprecedented rates of growth roughly doubled population, tripled world agricultural production, and quadrupled world GDP and energy use. Continuing population and economic growth will exert even greater demands on resources and the environment during the first half of the twenty-first century. Food production, nonrenewable resource recovery, energy supply, atmospheric pollution, toxic wastes, and renewable resource management are all major issues requiring detailed analysis and policy solutions. In addition, the nature of economic growth itself must adapt to environmental and resource constraints.

The concept of sustainable development attempts to combine economic and environmental goals. Sustainable techniques for agricultural production, energy use, natural resource management, and industrial production have significant potential, but have yet to be widely adopted. A sustainable global economy also implies limits on population and material consumption. The question of the sustainability of economic activity has already become a major issue, and will be even more important in coming decades.

## KEY TERMS AND CONCEPTS

absorptive capacity of the environment
biomass
capital stock
carrying capacity
cumulative pollutants
demand-side management
energy supply augmentation
environmental sustainability
global climate change
global commons
GDP growth rate
gross domestic product (GDP)

industrial ecology
input-intensive agriculture
intensification of production
macroeconomic scale
natural capital
nominal GDP
nonrenewable resources
open-access resources
over-harvesting of renewable resources
per capita GDP growth rate
population growth rate
population momentum

productivity per capita
real GDP
renewable energy sources
renewable resources
resource recovery
solar energy

sustainable agriculture
sustainable development
sustainable natural resource
   management
technological innovation
theoretical paradigm

## DISCUSSION QUESTIONS

1. Can we safely say that history has refuted the Malthusian hypothesis? What main factors have worked against Malthus's perspective? How might that perspective still be relevant today?

2. Over the past several decades, people have worried about the world running out of oil or natural resources. Sufficient oil remains for current needs, however, and no important resources have run short. Have these fears been exaggerated? How would you evaluate them, considering both past experience and future prospects?

3. Does an improved standard of living necessarily mean more consumption? Is it possible to envision a future in which consumption of many goods and natural resources would decline? If this happened, would it mean an end to economic growth? How might perception of these questions differ between, for example, a citizen of the United States and a citizen of India?

## REFERENCES

Daly, Herman E. *Beyond Growth: The Economics of Sustainable Development.* Boston: Beacon Press, 1996.

Daly, Herman E. "Elements of Environmental Macroeconomics," in Robert Costanza, ed., *Ecological Economics: The Science and Management of Sustainability.* New York: Columbia University Press, 1991.

Food and Agriculture Organization of the United Nations, FAOSTAT database, 2004.

Harris, Jonathan M., Timothy A. Wise, Kevin Gallagher, and Neva R. Goodwin, eds. *A Survey of Sustainable Development.* Washington, D.C.: Island Press, 2001.

Intergovernmental Panel on Climate Change (IPCC). *Climate Change 2001: Mitigation.* Cambridge, U.K.: Cambridge University Press, 2001.

Malthus, Thomas Robert. *Essay on the Principle of Population as It Affects the Future Improvement of Society.* Original publication 1798.

Meadows, Donella H., et al., *The Limits to Growth.* New York: Universe Books, 1972.

Meadows, Donella H., et al., *Beyond The Limits: Confronting Global Collapse, Envisioning a Sustainable Future.* White River Junction, Vt.: Chelsea Green, 1992.

Population Reference Bureau, *2004 World Population Data Sheet*. Washington, D.C.: Population Reference Bureau, 2004.

Sen, Amartya. *Development as Freedom*. New York: Knopf, 2000.

Stewart, Frances. *Basic Needs in Developing Countries*. Baltimore: Johns Hopkins University Press, 1985.

Streeten, Paul, et al., *First Things First: Meeting Basic Needs in Developing Countries*. New York: Oxford University Press, 1981.

United Nations Development Programme (UNDP). *Human Development Report 1990–2000*. New York: Oxford University Press, 1990–2004.

United States Department of Energy. *International Energy Outlook*. Washington, D.C.: Energy Information Administration, 2004.

World Bank. *World Development Report 1992: Development and the Environment*. New York, Oxford University Press, 1992.

World Bank. *World Development Report 1998/1999: Knowledge for Development*. New York: Oxford University Press, 1999.

World Resources Institute, United Nations Development Programme, United Nations Environment Programme, and the World Bank. *World Resources 2002–2004: Decisions for the Earth: Balance, Voice, and Power*. Washington, D.C.: World Resources Institute, 2003.

## WEBSITES

1. **http://www.iisd.org/** The homepage for the International Institute for Sustainable Development, an organization that conducts policy research towards the goal of integrating environmental stewardship and economic development.

2. **http://yosemite.epa.gov/ee/epa/eed.nsf/webpages/homepage/** The website for the National Center for Environmental Economics, a division of the U.S. Environmental Protection Agency that conducts and supervises research on environmental economics. Their website includes links to many research reports.

3. **http://www.ase.tufts.edu/gdae/** The homepage for the Global Development and Environment Institute at Tufts University, "dedicated to promoting a new understanding of how societies can pursue their economic goals in an environmentally and socially sustainable manner." The site includes links to many research publications.

4. **http://www.wri.org/** The World Resources Institute website offers the biennial publication *World Resources* as well as extensive reports and data on global resource and environmental issues.

# TWO

# Economic Analysis of Environmental Issues

CHAPTER FOCUS QUESTIONS

- How can pollution and environmental damage be represented in economics?
- What economic policies effectively respond to environmental problems?
- How do property rights and market processes relate to environmental issues?

CHAPTER

# The Theory of Environmental Externalities

## External Costs and Benefits

Economic theory deals with costs and benefits. For most goods and services, economic theory represents benefits by a demand curve and costs by a supply curve. The demand and supply curves show us the **marginal benefits** and **marginal costs**—that is, the benefits and costs of producing or consuming one more unit. (See the Appendix to this chapter for a review of basic supply and demand theory.)

Consider, for example, the automobile industry. The **market demand schedule** for automobiles shows how many automobiles consumers are willing to purchase, generally indicating that more will be purchased at lower prices. The **market supply schedule** shows how many automobiles the producers will be willing to put on the market at various prices, reflecting their costs of production. Combining the two schedules gives a **market equilibrium,** which shows the price and quantity traded. So far, so good. But, as we know, automobile production and operation have significant environmental effects. Where do these appear in economic analysis?

The answer is that they do not appear in basic supply and demand analysis, nor are they reflected in the real-world market equilibrium of automobile price and quantity produced, unless specific laws and institutions are created to address them. They are what economists call **environmental externalities.**

Automobiles are a major contributor to air pollution, including both urban smog and regional problems such as acid rain. In addition, their carbon dioxide emissions contribute to global warming, and coolants escaping from older-model automobile air conditioners contribute to depletion of the ozone layer. Automobile oil is a significant cause of groundwater pollution. Automobile production involves toxic materials that may be released to the environment or may remain as toxic wastes. Road systems pave over many acres of rural and open land, and salt runoff from roads damages watersheds.

## Accounting for Environmental Costs

Clearly, automobile production and use incur many real costs not included in the manufacturer's cost schedule.[1] Neglecting these costs produces a distorted picture of reality. To improve our supply and demand analysis so as to include them, we must look for ways of **internalizing externalities**—bringing these environmental costs into our market analysis.

Our first problem in doing this is assigning a money value to environmental damages. How can we reduce the complex environmental effects we have identified to a single dollar value? There is no clear-cut answer to this question. In some cases, economic damages may be identifiable: for example, if road runoff pollutes a town's water supply, the cost of water treatment gives at least one estimate of environmental damage—but this excludes less tangible factors such as damage to lake and river ecosystems.

Identifying health problems related to air pollution and their resulting medical expenses furnishes another monetary damage estimate—but this ignores the aesthetic damage done by air pollution. Smoggy air is unpleasant, regardless of any measurable effect it has on your health. Such issues are difficult to compress into a monetary indicator. Yet if we fail to assign some value to environmental damage, the market will automatically assign a value of zero, because none of these issues are directly reflected in consumer and producer decisions about automobiles.

Various techniques exist for estimation of environmental externalities (see Box 3-1). We will examine some of these in more detail in Chapter 6. But suppose we agree for now that some significant costs exist, even if we can't measure them precisely. It is clearly important to account for these costs in economic analysis.

Figure 3-1 shows a simple way of introducing these costs into supply and demand analysis. The supply curve for automobiles ($S$) already embodies all the production costs of automobiles, including labor, capital, and raw materials. Together with the demand curve ($D$), it determines a market equilibrium $e$, with price $P_1$ and quantity $Q_1$. We simply add to these costs an estimate of the **external costs** associated with environmental damage. This gives us a new, higher curve showing the combination of market costs and external costs. This curve $S'$ depicts a **social cost** schedule—it shows the real costs to society of operating automobiles, taking into account both production costs and environmental externalities.

We could also include in social costs other externalities not strictly environmental— for example, the costs of congestion as more automobiles fill the roads. We could use the value of time wasted in traffic jams in forming a money estimate of this externality. Congestion will also raise the air pollution costs as cars idle in traffic. $S'$ reflects the

---

[1]See, for example, Cobb, 1998.

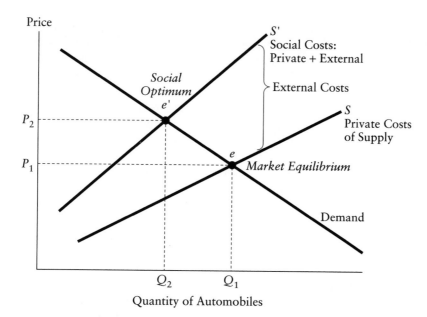

FIGURE 3-1 *Automobile Market with External Costs*

impact of all these unintended but significant effects associated with the production and use of automobiles.

Now let's consider how the introduction of externalities into supply and demand analysis affects economic equilibrium. Of course, drawing a new curve on a graph has no effect on real-world decisions to produce and purchase automobiles, but it affects our understanding of market equilibrium. In neoclassical price theory, market equilibrium, shown here at *e*, is generally considered to achieve **economic efficiency** in the automobile market. Once we introduce external costs into our analysis, this concept of efficient equilibrium changes.

Because the market process automatically balances benefits to consumers (reflected in the demand curve) and costs of production (reflected in the supply curve), it ensures that the "right amount" of cars will be produced at a price that accurately reflects production costs. But if we believe the market process misses significant extra costs—environmental externalities—we can no longer consider the equilibrium reached through the market efficient. From this point of view, the *wrong* quantity of cars is being produced at a price that *fails* to reflect true costs.

## *Internalizing Environmental Costs*

If significant externalities exist, what can correct this inefficient market equilibrium? Internalizing externalities can occur in several ways. One example would be a tax on automobiles. We could call this a **pollution tax,** whose object is not

## 3-1    The External Costs of Motor Vehicle Use

**D**riving a motor vehicle in the United States incurs not only direct costs but also external, or social, costs. Gasoline taxes cover only some external costs; others we pay in higher health-care costs, decreased environmental quality, and higher personal taxes.

Annually in the United States, motor vehicles emit about 50 million tons of carbon monoxide, 7 million tons of nitrogen oxides, as well as other toxins including formaldehyde and benzene. Annually, U.S. motor vehicle accidents kill more than 40 thousand people and injure more than 3 million. Additional external costs include natural habitat destruction from building roads and parking lots, vehicle and parts disposal, costs associated with national security in securing petroleum supplies, and noise pollution.

Delucchi's 1997 20-volume study is perhaps the most ambitious attempt to monetize the external costs of motor vehicle use. The report estimates costs associated with air pollution, crop losses, reduced visibility, national security, noise pollution, and so forth. The public sector pays some of these costs; others become external social losses.

The study used low-estimate assumptions to figure total annual monetary and nonmonetary externality costs at $99 billion and high-estimate assumptions for a figure of $879 billion. Annual public sector costs for motor vehicle infrastructure and services were estimated as $132 billion and $241 billion. Total public sector and social costs were $231 billion or $1,120 billion per year depending on the set of assumptions. (A higher estimate of global warming costs, which we discuss in Chapter 18, could raise these substantial figures even further.)

A comparable analysis (Cobb, 1998) figured at least $184 billion per year in U.S. public sector and social costs for motor vehicle use. Free-parking subsidies and cross-subsidies caused by congestion amounted to another $50–$100 billion per year.[1]

Cobb suggests an additional gasoline tax of $1.60 per gallon to internalize more social costs, although some costs would still remain. Delucchi notes that fully internalizing all costs associated with motor vehicle use would require a range of policy approaches. For example, air pollution externalities should be internalized based on a vehicle's emissions level rather than on gasoline consumption.

Although scientific and economic uncertainty render even the best attempt to internalize motor vehicle use externalities imperfect, failure to try sends a signal to consumers that the external costs are effectively zero. Delucchi and Cobb's results

---

[1]A cross-subsidy occurs when some firms or consumers pay more for a service so that others can pay less. In this case, congestion raises costs to many businesses and consumers in urban areas, while those who cause it (drivers) are not charged.

*(continued on following page)*

suggest that although fully internalizing costs may be impractical, implementing cost-internalizing policies could increase economic efficiency.

*Selected Public Sector and Social Costs of Motor Vehicle Use, 1991*
*(Billions of 1991 dollars)*

| Cost Category | Low Estimate | High Estimate |
|---|---|---|
| *Public Sector Costs* | | |
| Highways and parking | $109.7 | $196.7 |
| Pollution regulation and control | $3.2 | $8.1 |
| Highway patrol and safety | $7.4 | $8.4 |
| National security costs associated with Persian Gulf oil | $0.6 | $7.0 |
| Other public sector costs | $11.2 | $27.7 |
| *Externality Costs* | | |
| Imposed travel delays | $33.9 | $135.5 |
| Accident costs—pain, death, lost productivity, damages | $23.3 | $169.0 |
| Air pollution—human mortality and morbidity | $24.3 | $450.0 |
| Air pollution—loss of visibility | $5.1 | $36.9 |
| Air pollution—damage to crops, materials, and forests | $2.7 | $13.9 |
| Global warming | $0.5 | $9.2 |
| Noise pollution | $0.5 | $15.0 |
| Water pollution | $2.8 | $7.2 |
| Other externality costs | $6.4 | $42.6 |
| *Total public sector and externality costs* | $231.0 | $1,120.2 |

Source: Delucchi, 1997.

## SOURCES

Cobb, Clifford W. *The Roads Aren't Free: Estimating the Full Social Costs of Driving and the Effects of Accurate Pricing.* Resource Incentives Program Working Paper No. 3. San Francisco: Redefining Progress, 1998.

Delucchi, Mark A. *The Annualized Social Cost of Motor Vehicle Use in the U.S., 1990–1991: Summary of Theory, Data, Methods, and Results.* Report #1 in series: The Annualized Social Cost of Motor Vehicle Use in the United States, based on 1990–1991 data. Report number UCD-ITS-RR-96-3(1). Davis, Calif.: Institute of Transportation Studies, University of California, 1997.

ICF Incorporated. *Opportunities to Improve Air Quality through Transportation Pricing Programs.* Report prepared for the Office of Mobile Sources, U.S. Environmental Protection Agency, 1997.

U.S. Department of Transportation. *Transportation Statistics Annual Report 1999.* Report number BTS99-03, 1999.

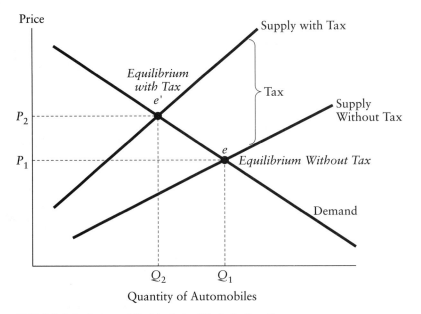

**FIGURE 3-2** *Automobile Market with Pollution Tax*

primarily to raise revenue for the government (though that will be one result), but to bring home to the purchaser of automobiles the real environmental costs of his or her actions.

Figure 3-2 shows the impact of such a tax on the market for automobiles. At the new equilibrium $e'$, the price rises to $P_2$, and the quantity consumed decreases to $Q_2$. From the point of view of economic efficiency, these are good effects. Consumers may complain about higher prices, but these prices reflect the real costs of automobile use to society. Fewer cars will be sold, which reduces pollution. We are now closer to a truly efficient equilibrium, or **social optimum,** than we were at the unmodified market equilibrium $e$.

Other issues, however, remain to be considered. What if the tax is too high? or too low? Will the same tax apply to compact cars and gas guzzlers? Might it not be better to measure and tax automobile emissions directly, rather than place a tax on automobile sales? How about taxing gasoline instead? Automobiles and gasoline are **complementary goods,** meaning that they tend to be used together. Thus we could internalize the effects of automobile pollution either by taxing cars themselves, or by taxing gas, or by taxing emissions.

Regardless of the exact mechanism we use, the idea of internalizing environmental costs through some kind of tax is well supported by economic theory. We determine the size of the tax by some process of **environmental valuation,** the topic of Chapter 6. If we are satisfied with this valuation process, a tax may be the best tool to accomplish the goal of environmental protection.

Other policies, however, may sometimes prove preferable to a pollution tax. **Government regulation,** such as tailpipe emission standards or the CAFE standards[2] requiring certain levels of average fuel efficiency, have a similar effect. They reduce total fuel consumption and total pollution. Such requirements for more efficient and less polluting engines also tend to drive up the purchase price of automobiles (although greater fuel efficiency will reduce operating costs).

## Positive Externalities

Just as it is in society's interest to internalize the social costs of pollution, it is also socially beneficial to internalize the **social benefits** of activities that generate positive externalities. For example, many suburban and rural towns have instituted open land preservation programs. Using tax incentives or public purchases, they seek to maintain or increase the amount of open and rural land. Why do they do this?

Regardless of a private landowner's particular reasons for keeping land open or using it as farmland, significant **external benefits** accrue from such uses: Others who live in town may enjoy the sight of natural areas and farmland close to their homes. A beautiful setting may significantly increase surrounding property values, whereas an industrial or residential development nearby would lower them. External benefits are not limited to town residents. Passers-by, hikers, bicyclists, and out-of-state tourists may all gain satisfaction, or **utility,** from the pleasant scenery.

Figure 3-3 shows an economic analysis of the situation. Marginal social benefits exceed marginal private benefits because they include gains to neighbors and passers-by as well as to private landowners. The market demand curve for rural uses of land will reflect private, but not social benefits, leading to an equilibrium at the **private optimum.** At the social optimum $Q_S$, including the benefits to nonowners, a larger quantity of land remains as open and rural land than at the private market equilibrium $Q_p$.

### Internalizing Environmental Benefits

From an economic point of view, policies such as tax incentives are **subsidies** for the protection of open land. It is in the social interest to encourage landowners, by lowering their costs through tax rebates or purchase of development rights,[3] to keep land in an undisturbed state. The subsidy is shown in Figure 3-4 as a downward shift in marginal private costs, increasing the quantity of open land to $Q_s$. The principle parallels the use of a tax to discourage economic activities that create negative externalities—except that in this case we want to encourage economic uses of land that have socially beneficial side effects.

---

[2]Corporate Average Fuel Economy (CAFE) refers to average standards that major automobile manufacturers must meet. For discussion of the use of standards versus taxes, see Baumol and Oates, 1993, and Tietenberg, 2000.

[3]In development-rights purchase programs, a town or state buys the rights to development on private land. The landowner retains ownership of the land but cannot use it for industrial or residential development. For further discussion of this issue see Hodge, 1995

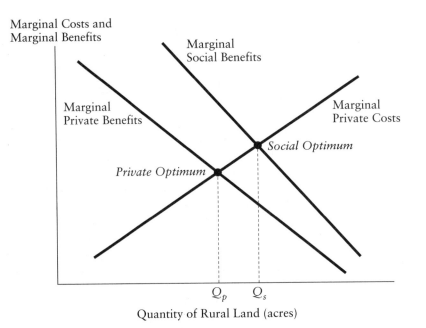

**FIGURE 3-3** *A Positive Externality*

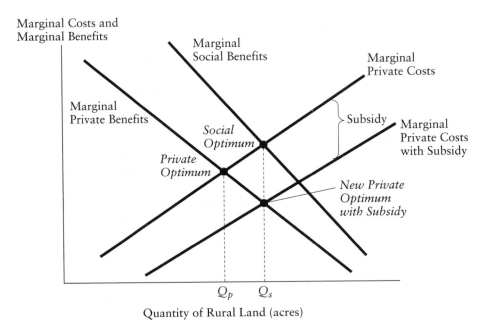

**FIGURE 3-4** *A Subsidy for Open and Rural Land Use*

# Welfare Analysis of Externalities

We can use a form of economic theory called **welfare analysis** to show why it is socially preferable to internalize externalities. The idea, as shown in Figure 3-5, is that *areas* on a supply and demand graph can be used to measure total benefits and costs.[4] The area under the demand curve shows total benefit; the area under the supply curve shows total cost. For each unit purchased, the demand curve measures the value of that unit to consumers, while the supply curve reflects the cost to suppliers.

## *Welfare Analysis Without Externalities*

The total value of $Q_0$ units purchased is shown in Figure 3-5 by areas $A + B + C$. The total cost of producing these units is area $C$. $A + B$ is the **net social benefit** from the production and consumption of $Q_0$ units—in other words, the amount by which total

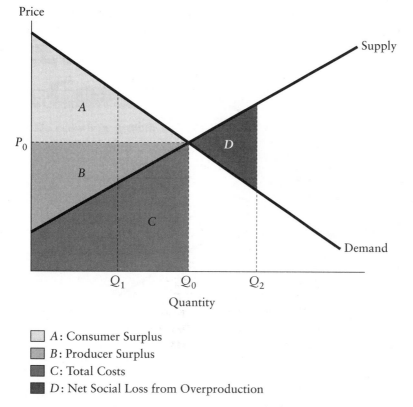

A: Consumer Surplus
B: Producer Surplus
C: Total Costs
D: Net Social Loss from Overproduction

**FIGURE 3-5** *Welfare Analysis of the Automobile Market*

---

[4]The supply and demand schedules show the *marginal* benefits and costs for each individual unit produced. Therefore, the areas under these curves in effect sum up the *total* benefits and costs for all units produced. (See Appendix for a more detailed explanation.)

benefit exceeds total cost. Part A of this net social benefit goes to consumers as **consumer surplus**—it represents the difference between their benefits from consumption of automobiles, as shown by the demand curve, and the price they pay, as shown by the horizontal line at $P_0$. Part B goes to producers as **producer surplus**—the difference between their production costs, shown by the supply curve, and the price $P_0$ that they receive.

Economists call market equilibrium efficient because it maximizes net social benefit. If we were to produce less than $Q_0$ units, or more, net benefit would be less than at $Q_0$. At $Q_1$, for example, the net benefit is only part of the area $A + B$. At $Q_2$, we realize the full net benefit $A + B$, but we also experience some **net social loss,** shown here by area $D$. The overall social benefit, then, is $A + B - D$, a lower amount than at $Q_0$. Thus $Q_0$, as we have argued, is in some sense the "right" amount to produce.

## Welfare Analysis with Externalities

If we introduce external costs (Figure 3-6), the combination of private and external costs gives a social cost curve $S'$, which lies above the ordinary supply curve. The market

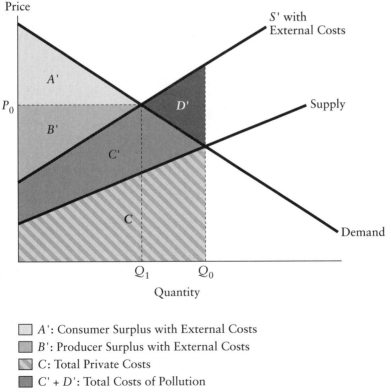

$A'$: Consumer Surplus with External Costs
$B'$: Producer Surplus with External Costs
$C$: Total Private Costs
$C' + D'$: Total Costs of Pollution
$D'$: Net Social Loss

**FIGURE 3-6** *Welfare Analysis of the Automobile Market with Pollution Costs*

equilibrium $Q_0$ no longer maximizes net social benefit. With the new higher total social cost curve, social benefit is only $A' + B'$. The area $D'$ is social loss, so that the overall net social benefit is $A' + B' - D'$. We would do better to lower production to $Q_1$, avoiding the net social loss $D'$. And of course this is exactly what we seek to accomplish with a pollution tax.

Notice that in this example the area $C' + D'$ indicates the **total cost of pollution** at point $Q_0$. But of this total cost, only $D'$ is considered net social loss. According to this analysis, some pollution costs are justifiable—provided they are outweighed by social benefits from production. Only when the combined costs of production and of pollution $(C + C' + D')$ rise above the benefits shown by the demand curve do we produce "too much" pollution.

## Optimal Pollution

This analysis leads to a concept that to some seems paradoxical: the doctrine of **optimal pollution.** At our socially optimal equilibrium $Q_1$, we still have some pollution costs (the part of $C'$ to the left of $Q_1$). According to our analysis, this is the "optimal" amount of pollution, given current production costs and technologies. But, you might object, isn't the optimal amount of pollution *zero*? How can we call any amount of pollution "optimal"?

The economist's answer would be that the only way to achieve zero pollution is to have zero production. If we want to produce virtually any manufactured good, some pollution will result. We as a society must decide what level of pollution we are willing to accept. Of course, we can strive to reduce this level over time, especially through better pollution-reducing technology, but as long as we have production, we will have an "optimal" pollution level.

Some people remain uneasy with the concept of optimal pollution. Note, for example, that if demand for automobiles increases, the demand curve will shift to the right, and the "optimal" pollution level will increase. This suggests that as global demand for automobiles rises steadily, ever-rising levels of pollution will in some sense be acceptable. Does society have a right to increase pollution just because we want more goods? This analysis would seem to imply that the answer is yes.

The issue is by no means a purely academic one. During the past thirty years, improvements in automotive technology have reduced pollution per car as well as total automotive pollution in the United States. But over the same period, the number of cars on the road and the total vehicle miles traveled have steadily increased. Also, larger cars such as sport utility vehicles have greatly increased as a percentage of the total vehicle fleet. These trends counteract the pollution reduction per car; as a result, some automobile pollutant levels such as nitrogen oxides have remained stubbornly high. Carbon dioxide emissions from the U.S. transportation sector have been on the rise since the early 1980s. In many urban areas, congestion has worsened and travel times have increased. On a global scale, the potential is enormous for increased automobile pollution as demand rises. Certainly few could call this trend "optimal."

# Property Rights and the Coase Theorem

The theory of externalities also raises another fundamental issue, that of rights. Do I have a right to drive my automobile even though it pollutes? Do others have a right to be protected from the effects of my vehicle's waste products? When we talk about prices, values, and costs, our discussion is actually about underlying rights. Patterns of resource allocation are determined by the underlying assignment of rights.

## Pigovian Tax

Let's consider a simple case of **property rights.** A factory operating in a rural area emits pollutants from its stacks. The pollutants damage the crops of the neighboring farm. The externality might be remedied by imposing a tax on the factory based on the value of the damage caused to the farmer's crops. Like the automobile tax shown earlier in Figure 3-2, this tax should reflect the farmer's marginal cost of crop damages caused by factory emissions. This method of responding to externalities is known as a **Pigovian tax,** after Arthur Pigou, a well-known British economist who published his *Economics of Welfare* in 1920. It has come to be known as the **polluter pays principle,** which sounds like a reasonable solution to many people.

However, the Pigovian approach has been criticized by economic theorists who have pointed out that assigning the responsibility for an externality is not always so simple. Suppose we take a different, less clear-cut case. A farmer drains a swamp on his property to create a field suitable for growing crops. His downstream neighbor complains that without the swamp to absorb heavy rainfalls, her land now floods—damaging her crops. Should the first farmer have the right to do what he wants on his own land, or should he be obliged to pay the second farmer the value of crop damages?

This issue involves not just externalities but also the nature of property rights. Does the ownership of land include a right to drain swamps on that land? Or is this right separate, subject to control by the community or other property owners?

## The Coase Theorem

We could resolve the problem in two ways. Suppose we say that the first farmer (we'll call him Albert) *does* have the right to drain the swamp. But let's also suppose that the net value of crops grown on the former swampland would be only $2,000, and the net value of crops damaged on the second farmer's land would be $6,000. The two farmers might reach an agreement. The second farmer (call her Betty) can offer an amount between $2,000 and $6,000—say, $4,000—to Albert in return for an agreement *not* to drain the swamp. Betty will not be happy about this, but she's better off giving up $4,000 than losing her $6,000 crop. Albert will also be better off taking the $4,000 than making a mere $2,000 growing crops on drained land. In effect, Betty purchases the right to say how the swampland will be used (without having to purchase the land itself).

We can also assign the relevant right to Betty, by passing a law stating that no one can drain swampland without the agreement of any affected parties downstream. In that case, Albert must reach an agreement with Betty before draining the swamp. With the crop values we have assumed, the same result would occur—the swamp would not be drained, because the value of doing so to Albert ($2,000) would not compensate Betty for her loss. Betty would demand at least $6,000 to grant her permission, a price too high for Albert.

Now suppose a new gourmet crop item becomes popular, a crop that grows well on former swampland and would bring Albert $10,000 in revenues. A deal is now possible—Albert would pay Betty $8,000 for the right to drain the swamp and earn $10,000 for the new crop, netting $2,000 profit for himself and leaving Betty $2,000 better off as well.

The principle at issue in this simple example has come to be known as the **Coase theorem,** after Ronald Coase, a Nobel Prize–winning economist who discussed similar examples of property rights and externalities in his famous article "The Problem of Social Cost."[5] The Coase theorem states that if property rights are well defined, and no significant **transactions costs** exist, an efficient allocation of resources will result even with externalities. Transactions costs are costs involved in reaching and implementing an agreement. These can include costs of obtaining information (such as surveying the land), time and effort spent in negotiations, and costs of enforcing the agreement. In the case of Albert and Betty, these costs should be low because they need only reach an understanding about the amount of compensation, although legal costs may be involved in formalizing an agreement.

Through negotiations, the two parties will balance the external costs against the economic benefits of a given action (in this case, draining the swamp). In the example above, the external costs were $6,000. An economic benefit of $2,000 would not justify incurring these costs, but an economic benefit of $10,000 would. Regardless of which farmer holds the property right, this "efficient" result will occur through negotiation.

The principle of the Coase theorem can also be expressed in terms of a **right to pollute.** This sounds strange, but it is similar to the principle embodied in, for example, the U.S. Clean Air Act Amendments of 1990. This act creates a system of **transferable pollution permits** to emit such pollutants as sulfur oxides and nitrogen oxides; these permits can be traded among polluting industries. Individual firms can acquire rights to increase their own pollution—provided they purchase them from other firms that reduce pollution by an equal amount. By controlling the total number of permits issued, the government can gradually reduce overall pollution.

It is also possible for public interest groups to buy up pollution permits and retire them, permanently reducing pollution totals. In effect, this system turns pollution, and pollution reduction, into marketable goods. From the economist's point of view, it has the advantage of efficiency and can be a practical application of the "right to pollute" principle.

---

[5]Coase, 1960, reprinted in Stavins, 2000.

## Applying the Coase Theorem

We can illustrate the Coase theorem by showing the marginal benefits and marginal costs of an economic activity that generates an externality. Suppose, for example, a factory emits effluent into a river, polluting the water supply of a downstream community. The factory is currently emitting 100 units of effluent. If forced to reduce effluent to zero, the company operating the factory would have to abandon a valuable production line. Thus we can say that the company gains marginal benefits from emitting pollution, and the community incurs marginal costs through damage to the water supply. We might form a reasonable quantitative estimate of these external costs by estimating the costs of water treatment. Figure 3-7 shows both marginal costs and marginal benefits.[6]

What is the optimal solution? The emission of 100 units of pollution clearly imposes high marginal costs on the community and brings the company lower marginal benefits. This is "too much" pollution. But suppose emissions were limited to 60 units. Marginal benefits to the company would then equal marginal costs to the community. A further limitation to, say, 20 units, would result in high additional loss to the company and bring only low additional benefit to the community. The efficient or "optimal" solution,

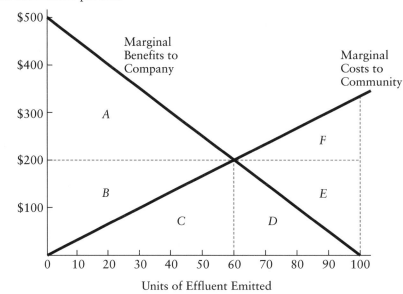

**FIGURE 3-7** *Application of the Coase Theorem*

---

[6]We will discuss a more precise analysis of the derivation of a marginal benefits schedule, based on the difference between output price and production costs, in Chapter 5.

therefore, is at 60 units of pollution. At this level the extra benefit to the company from production just balances the extra cost imposed on the community through pollution.

This solution can be achieved by assigning the pollution rights either to the company *or* to the community. Suppose the community has the right to say how much pollution can be emitted. The company can offer them up to $200 per unit for pollution permits to allow 60 units of pollution. The company can afford to pay this much; their marginal benefits from producing 60 units exceed $200 up to the sixtieth unit. It will also be to the community's advantage to accept this offer, granting permits for 60 units of pollution at $200 each. The first 60 units of pollution impose less than $200 per unit of costs on the community.

We can measure the total cost of pollution at this level as the area $C$ on the graph, or $6,000. But the amount the company pays to the community will be $B + C$ or $60 \times$ $200 = $12,000. The community can then pay $6,000 to treat the water and still come out $6,000 ahead. The company gains $A + B + C = $21,000 in benefits, pays $12,000, and has a net profit of $9,000 (area $A$).

We can also assign the right to pollute to the company. Would they then emit the full 100 units of pollution? If they did so their gain would be areas $A + B + C + D =$ $25,000. They can do better by negotiating with the community. The community will pay them up to $200 per unit, or areas $D + E = $8,000, to cut back their pollution to only 60 units. This saves the community $D + E + F = $10,667 in environmental damage or water treatment costs. They still suffer environmental costs equal to $C$, or $6,000. The company's net gain will now be $A + B + C + D + E = $29,000, better for them than the maximum pollution option. This approach may seem unfair to the community, but it leads to the same equilibrium solution—60 units of pollution emitted—as when the community held the right to control pollution levels.

This more formal demonstration of the Coase theorem shows that the participants reach the efficient solution regardless of who holds the property right governing pollution. Provided that right is clearly defined, the party who values it most highly will acquire it, with the result that the external costs of pollution and the economic benefits of production are balanced through the marketplace.

Note, however, that the assignment of the right makes a big difference in distribution of gains and losses between the two parties (see Table 3-1). The net social benefit from production is the same in both cases: area $A + B = $15,000. In one case, however,

**TABLE 3-1** *Different Assignments of Pollution Rights*

|  | *If Community Holds Rights* | *If Company Holds Rights* |
|---|---|---|
| Net Gain/Loss to Community | $12,000 payment<br>−$6,000 environ. cost<br>$6,000 | −$8,000 payment<br>−$6,000 environ. cost<br>−$14,000 |
| Net Gain/Loss to Company | $21,000 benefits<br>−$12,000 payment<br>$9,000 | $21,000 benefits<br>$8,000 payment<br>$29,000 |
| **Net Social Gain** | $15,000 | $15,000 |

this benefit is divided between the community and the company. In the other case, the community has a net loss of \$14,000 and the company a net gain of \$29,000 (for an overall social net benefit of \$29,000 − \$14,000 = \$15,000).

The value of the right to pollute, or to control pollution, is \$20,000 in this case. By redistributing that right, we make one party \$20,000 better off and the other \$20,000 worse off. The different assignments of rights are equivalent in terms of efficiency because the final result balances marginal benefits and marginal costs, but they clearly differ in terms of **equity,** or social justice.

## Limitations of the Coase Theorem

According to the Coase theorem, the clear assignment of property rights appears to promise fully efficient solutions to problems involving externalities. In theory, if we could clearly assign property rights to *all* environmental externalities, no further government intervention would be required. Individuals and business firms would negotiate all pollution control and other environmental issues among themselves once it was clear who had the "right to pollute," or the "right to be free from pollution."

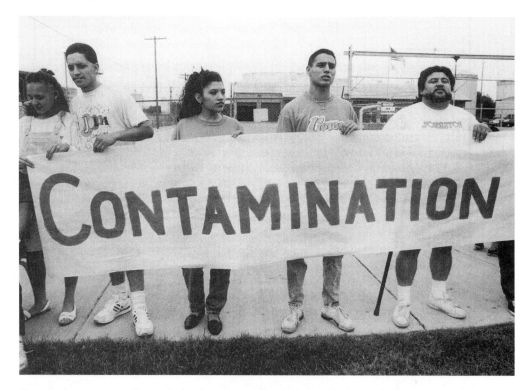

*Community protest against pollution from a gasoline tank farm in Texas. Both economic and political power affect the ability of communities to defend their environment.*

This is the basis for the approach known as **free market environmentalism.** In effect, this approach seeks to bring the environment into the marketplace by setting up a system of property rights in the environment and allowing the free market to handle issues of resource use and pollution regulation.

As we will see in dealing with specific examples in future chapters, this approach has significant potential, especially in areas such as water rights. New markets may evolve, such as a market in tradable permits for airborne pollutants. But this approach also poses significant problems, in terms of both efficiency and equity. The use of market mechanisms to solve environmental problems turns out to have crucial limitations.

## The Free Rider Effect

One important limitation derives from the assumption of no transactions costs, stated in the Coase theorem. Our previous examples have had only two parties in the negotiation. In more typical cases, environmental issues affect many parties. If, for example, fifty downstream communities are affected by pollution from a factory's effluent, negotiating effluent limits becomes cumbersome and perhaps impossible.

Suppose we assign the factory the right to pollute. The communities can then offer compensation for reducing pollution. But which community will pay what share? Unless all fifty can agree, making a specific offer to the company will be impossible. No single community, or group of communities, is likely to step forward to pay the whole bill. In fact, many may hang back, waiting for other communities to "buy off" the factory—and supply the rest with free pollution control benefits. This barrier to successful negotiations is known as the **free rider effect.**

## The Holdout Effect

A similar problem arises if the communities have the right to be free from pollution, and the factory must compensate them for any pollution emitted. Who will determine how much compensation each community receives? With all the communities situated on the same river, any single community can exercise a kind of veto power—a problem known as the **holdout effect.** Suppose forty-nine communities have hammered out an agreement with the company on permissible pollution levels and compensation. The fiftieth community can demand a much higher rate of compensation, for if they withhold their consent the whole agreement will fail and the company will be restricted to zero pollution (that is, forced to shut down).

## Public Choice Versus Private Choice

In general, the Coase theorem is inapplicable where many parties are affected. Such cases require regulation, a Pigovian tax, or other form of government intervention. The state or federal government might set a standard for waterborne effluent or a tax per unit of effluent. Although taxation has its impact through market processes, this would not be a pure market solution because government officials determine the degree of regulation or taxation. Economists call this a process of **public choice** rather than the process of **private choice** characteristic of the market solutions.[7]

## A Practical Application

An example of environmental protection using Coase theorem principles is New York City's Watershed Land Acquisition Program. The city must provide clean water to its 8 million residents. This can be done through building filtration plants, but the cost of building these plants can be avoided through watershed protection. By preserving land around the main water supplies for the city, the quality of the water can be maintained at a level that does not require filtration. The watersheds are located upstate, on lands not currently owned by the city. According to the U.S. Environmental Protection Agency:

> The Watershed Land Acquisition Program is a key element in the City's long-term strategy to preserve environmentally sensitive lands in its upstate watersheds. Land acquisition is a critical element of the City's ability to obtain filtration avoidance. Through this program, New York City has committed to soliciting a minimum of 355,050 acres of land over a ten-year period. The goal of the program is for the city to acquire, from willing sellers, fee title to or conservation easements on real property determined to be water-quality sensitive, undeveloped land. The land will be bought at fair market value prices and property taxes will be paid by the city. No property will be acquired by eminent domain. (http://www.epa.gov/ region02/water/nycshed/protprs.htm#land)

As in our Coase theorem example, all transactions here are voluntary, based on private property rights. The power of eminent domain, by which a government can compel a property owner to give up land in return for compensation (see Box 3-2), is not used. New York City has determined that it is less expensive to pay private property owners for conservation easements, which restrict land use, or to purchase the land outright, than to construct filtration plants. This market-based solution appears both environmentally effective and economically efficient.

## The Problem of Equity

Environmental policies based on private property rights and market solutions can be economically efficient, but may also raise questions of equity. Suppose that in our original example the community suffering from pollution is a low-income community. Even if the water pollution is causing serious health problems with medical costs of millions of dollars, the community may simply be unable to "buy off" the polluter. In this case, the market solution clearly is not independent of the assignment of property rights. Pollution levels will be significantly higher if the right to pollute is assigned to the company.

---

[7]For further discussion of private property rights and the environment, see Schmid, 1995.

It is also possible that, even if the right is assigned to the community, poor communities will accept location of toxic waste dumps and other polluting facilities out of a desperate need for compensatory funds.[8] Although this appears consistent with the Coase theorem—it is a voluntary transaction—many people would say that no community should be forced to trade the health of its residents for needed funds. An important criticism of free market environmentalism is that under a pure market system poorer communities and individuals will generally bear the heaviest burden of environmental costs.

A similar example would be preservation of open space. Wealthy communities can afford to buy up open space for preservation, and poor communities cannot. If communities can use zoning to preserve wetlands and natural areas, poor communities too will be able to protect their environment. Zoning, a form of government regulation, allows communities to achieve significant environmental protection while incurring relatively low enforcement costs.

Another point to note in considering Coase theorem limitations is the issue of environmental effects on nonhuman life forms and ecological systems. Our examples so far have assumed that environmental damage affects specific individuals or businesses. Certain environmental damages, however, may affect no individual directly but threaten plant or animal species with extinction. A pesticide may be harmless to humans but lethal to birds. Who will step into the marketplace to defend the preservation of nonhuman species? No individual or business firm is likely to do so, except on a relatively small scale.

Consider, for example, the activities of a group such as The Nature Conservancy, which buys up ecologically valuable tracts of land in order to preserve them. Here is an organization that *is* prepared to pay to save the environment. Their purchases, however, reach only a tiny proportion of the natural areas threatened with destruction through development, intensive farming, and other economic activities. In the "dollar vote" marketplace, purely ecological interests will almost always lose out to economic interests.

We should also note that property rights and regulating capabilities are limited to the current generation. What about the rights of the next generation? Many environmental issues have long-term implications. Rights to nonrenewable resources can be assigned today, but those resources may also be needed in the future. This important issue of resource allocation over time is the subject of Chapter 5.

As we have seen, the principle of property rights can be a powerful one, and is often explicitly or implicitly involved in environmental policymaking. But in some cases property rights may be inappropriate tools to deal with environmental problems. It may be impossible, for example, to establish property rights to the atmosphere, or to the open ocean. When we confront problems such as global warming, ocean pollution, the decline of fish stocks, or endangered species, we find that the system of private property

---

[8]Bullard, 1994, provides practical examples of the differential impact of environmental pollution on rich and poor communities. For more on "environmental justice" issues, see Massey, 2004, available at http://ase. tufts.edu/gdae/.

## 3-2    Property Rights and Environmental Regulation

Governments can apply the principle of eminent domain to appropriate private property for public purposes. However, the Fifth Amendment of the U.S. Constitution requires that the property owner be fairly compensated. Specifically, the Fifth Amendment concludes with the statement—"nor shall private property be taken for public use, without just compensation."

A government action that deprives someone of their property rights is referred to as a "takings." When the takings removes all property rights, the U.S. Constitution clearly orders full compensation. For example, if a state government decides to build a highway through a parcel of private property, the landowner must receive the property's fair market value.

A more ambiguous situation arises when a government action limits property use and, consequently, reduces property value. Instances of government regulations reducing the value of private property are often called "regulatory takings." Suppose, for example, a new law regulates timber harvesting and reduces the value of private forests. Are the landowners entitled to compensation under the Fifth Amendment?

The most notable case concerning a regulatory takings is *Lucas* v. *South Carolina Coastal Council.* David Lucas, a real estate developer, purchased two ocean-front lots in 1986 and planned to construct vacation homes. However, in 1988 the South Carolina state legislature enacted the Beachfront Management Act, which prohibited Lucas from building any permanent structures on the property. Lucas filed suit claiming that the legislation had deprived him of all "economically viable use" of his property.

A trial court ruled in Lucas's favor, concluding that the legislation had rendered his property "valueless," and awarded him $1.2 million in damages. When the South Carolina Supreme Court reversed this decision, the court ruled that further construction in the area posed a significant threat to a public resource and in cases where a regulation is intended to prevent "harmful or noxious uses" of private property no compensation is required.

The case was appealed to the U.S. Supreme Court. Although the Supreme Court overturned the state court ruling, it delineated a distinction between total and partial takings. Compensation is necessary only in cases of total takings—when a regulation deprives a property owner of "all economically beneficial uses." A regulation that merely reduces a property's value requires no compensation.

In essence, this ruling represented a victory for environmentalists because cases of total takings are rare. Partial takings as a result of government regulations, on the other hand, are common. A requirement of compensation for partial takings would

*(continued on following page)*

have created a legal and technical morass that would effectively render many environmental laws ineffective. Still, partial takings can involve significant costs to individuals and businesses, and the debate continues over equity when private costs are necessary to achieve the public good.

**SOURCES**

Ausness, Richard C. "Regulatory Takings and Wetland Protection in the Post-Lucas Era." *Land and Water Law Review* 30, no. 2 (1995): 349–414.

Johnson, Stephen M. "Defining the Property Interest: A Vital Issue in Wetlands Takings Analysis After Lucas." *Journal of Energy, Natural Resources & Environmental Law* 14, no. 1 (1994): 41–82.

Hollingsworth, Lorraine. "*Lucas* v. *South Carolina Coastal Commission*: A New Approach to the Takings Issue." *Natural Resources Journal* 34, no. 2 (1994): 479–496.

rights, which has evolved as a basis for economic systems, cannot be fully extended to ecosystems. It may be possible to use market transactions such as tradable permits for air emissions or fishing rights, but these apply to only a limited subset of ecosystem functions. In such cases, other techniques of economic analysis will be helpful in considering the interaction between human economic activity and aspects of the broader ecosystem. We will consider some of these analyses in Chapter 4.

## SUMMARY

Many economic activities have significant external effects—impacts on people not directly involved in the activity. Pollution from automobile use is an example. Market price usually fails to reflect the costs of these external impacts, leading to excessive production of goods with negative externalities.

One approach to pollution control is to internalize external costs by a tax or other instrument that requires producers and consumers of the polluting good to take these costs into account. In general, such a tax will raise the product price and reduce the quantity produced, thereby also reducing pollution. Market equilibrium then shifts toward a socially more desirable result. In theory, a tax that exactly reflects external costs could achieve a social optimum—but it is often difficult to establish a proper valuation for externalities.

Not all externalities are negative. Positive externalities result when economic activities bring benefits to others not directly involved in the transaction. Preservation of open land directly benefits those who live nearby, often raising their property values. In addition, it brings greater satisfaction to hikers, tourists, and passers-by. A positive externality can create an economic case for a subsidy to increase the market provision of the good.

The analysis of externalities implies that seeking to reduce pollution to zero is usually not appropriate. Rather, the social costs of pollution-creating goods should be balanced against their social benefits. This usually means reducing, not eliminating, pollution. In other words, an optimal level of pollution usually exists. This formulation arouses the criticism that "optimal" pollution levels may become unacceptable with increased demand and greater production of pollution-creating goods.

An alternative to taxation is the assignment of property rights to externalities. A clear legal right either to emit a certain amount of pollution or to prevent others from emitting pollution can create a market in "rights to pollute." However, this solution depends on the ability of firms and individuals to trade these pollution rights with relatively low transactions costs. Where large numbers of people are affected, or where the environmental damages are difficult to define in monetary terms, this approach is not effective. It also raises significant questions of equity, because under a market system the poor will generally bear a heavier burden of pollution.

## KEY TERMS AND CONCEPTS*

Coase theorem
complementary goods
consumer surplus
economic efficiency
environmental externalities
environmental valuation
equity
external benefit
external cost
free market environmentalism
free rider effect
government regulation
holdout effect
internalizing externalities
law of demand
law of supply
marginal benefit
marginal cost
market demand schedule
market equilibrium
market supply schedule
net social benefit
net social loss

optimal pollution
Pigovian tax
polluter pays principle
pollution tax
price elasticity of demand
price elasticity of supply
private choice
private optimum
producer surplus
property rights
public choice
right to pollute
shortage
social benefits
social cost
social optimum
subsidies
surplus
total cost of pollution
transactions costs
transferable pollution permits
utility
welfare analysis

*Including terms from Appendix.

## DISCUSSION QUESTIONS

1. Discuss your reaction to the following statement: "Solving the problems of environmental economics is simple. It is just a matter of internalizing the externalities." Does the theory of externalities apply to most or all environmental issues? What are some practical problems involved in internalizing externalities? Describe examples where the principle works well, and some where it is more problematic.

2. A pollution tax is one policy instrument for internalizing externalities. Discuss the economic policy implications of a tax on automobiles, a tax on gasoline, or a tax on tailpipe emission levels as measured at an auto inspection. How about taxing gas guzzling vehicles and subsidizing efficient hybrid vehicles? Which policy would be the most efficient? Which do you think would be most effective in reducing pollution levels?

3. According to the principle expressed in the Coase theorem, private property rights and voluntary market transactions can be effective tools for environmental policy. Discuss some cases where private property and market-based solutions can be effective, and others in which they are less appropriate. How can policymakers best combine market-oriented and public-choice mechanisms to craft effective environmental policy?

## PROBLEMS

1. Consider the following supply and demand schedule for steel:

| Price per ton ($) | 20 | 40 | 60 | 80 | 100 | 120 | 140 | 160 | 180 |
|---|---|---|---|---|---|---|---|---|---|
| $Q_D$ (million tons) | 200 | 180 | 160 | 140 | 120 | 100 | 80 | 60 | 40 |
| $Q_S$ (million tons) | 20 | 60 | 100 | 140 | 180 | 220 | 260 | 300 | 340 |

Pollution from steel production is estimated to create an external cost of sixty dollars per ton.

Show the external cost, market equilibrium, and social optimum on a graph.

What kinds of policies might help to achieve the social optimum? What effects would these policies have on the behavior of consumers and producers? What effect would they have on market equilibrium price and quantity?

2. A chemical factory is situated next to a farm. Airborne emissions from the chemical factory damage crops on the farm. The marginal benefits of emissions to the factory and the marginal costs of damage to the farmer are as follows:

| Quantity of Emissions | 100 | 200 | 300 | 400 | 500 | 600 | 700 | 800 | 900 |
|---|---|---|---|---|---|---|---|---|---|
| Marginal Benefit to factory ($000) | 320 | 280 | 240 | 200 | 160 | 120 | 80 | 40 | 0 |
| Marginal Cost to farmer ($000) | 110 | 130 | 150 | 170 | 190 | 210 | 230 | 250 | 270 |

From an economic point of view, what is the best solution to this environmental conflict of interest? How might this solution be achieved? How should considerations of efficiency and equity be balanced in this case?

## REFERENCES

Baumol, William J., and Wallace E. Oates. "The Use of Standards and Prices for Protection of the Environment." Chapter 18 in *Environmental Economics: A Reader,* edited by Anil Markandya and Julie Richardson. New York: St. Martin's Press, 1993.

Bromley, Daniel W., ed. *Handbook of Environmental Economics.* Cambridge, Mass. and Oxford, U.K.: Basil Blackwell, 1995.

Bullard, Robert D. *Dumping in Dixie: Race, Class, and Environmental Quality.* Boulder, Colo.: Westview Press, 1994.

Coase, Ronald. "The Problem of Social Cost." *Journal of Law and Economics,* vol. 3, 1960. Reprinted in Stavins, ed., 2000.

Cobb, Clifford W. *The Roads Aren't Free: Estimating the Full Social Costs of Driving and the Effects of Accurate Pricing.* San Francisco: Redefining Progress. Resource Incentives Program Working Paper No. 3, 1998.

Hodge, Ian. "Public Policies for Land Conservation." Chapter 5 in Bromley, ed., 1995.

Massey, Rachel. *Environmental Justice: Income, Race, and Health.* Tufts University Global Development and Environment Institute, 2004, available at http://ase. tufts.edu/gdae/education_materials/course_materials.html.

Stavins, Robert N., ed. *Economics of the Environment: Selected Readings.* 4th ed. New York: Norton, 2000.

Schmid, A. Allan. "The Environment and Property Rights Issues." Chapter 3 in Bromley, ed., 1995.

Tietenberg, Tom H. "Economic Instruments for Environmental Regulation." Chapter 16 in Stavins, ed., 2000.

## WEBSITES

1. **http://www.rprogress.org/** Homepage for Redefining Progress, "a nonprofit organization that develops policies and tools that reorient the economy to value people and nature first." Their site includes many publications on integrating environmental externalities into market prices.

2. **http://www.eia.doe.gov/cneaf/electricity/external/external_sum.html** A report published by the U.S. Department of Energy that estimates the magnitude of the externalities associated with electricity generation.

3. http://www.aere.org/ Website for the Association of Environmental and Resource Economists, an organization "established as a means of exchanging ideas, stimulating research, and promoting graduate training in resource and environmental economics." The AERE newsletter includes a few short articles on resource issues.

4. http://www.iisd.org/susprod/browse.asp A compendium of case studies of economic regulation, information, and planning instruments designed to promote sustainable production and consumption.

## APPENDIX: BASIC SUPPLY AND DEMAND THEORY

This text presupposes that you've had an introductory economics course. But if you haven't, or if your basic economic theory is a little rusty, then this appendix provides you with the background economic knowledge you'll need for this book.

Economists use models to help them explain complex phenomena. A model is a tool that helps us understand something by focusing on certain aspects of reality while ignoring others. No model can consider every possible factor that might be relevant, so economists make simplifying assumptions. An economic model can take the form of a simplified story, a graph, a figure, or a set of equations. One of the most powerful and widely used models in economics concerns the interaction of supply and demand. Based on several simplifying assumptions, this model provides us with insights about the changes we can expect when certain things happen as well as what types of economic policies are the most appropriate in different circumstances.

### The Theory of Demand

The theory of demand considers how consumer demand for goods and services changes as a result of changes in prices and other relevant variables. In this appendix, we'll use the market for gasoline as an example. Obviously, a lot of factors could affect consumer demand for gasoline, so we'll start off by making a simplifying assumption. For now, let's only consider how consumers' demand for gas changes when the price of gas changes—all other relevant factors are assumed constant. Economists use the Latin term *ceteris paribus,* meaning "all other things equal" or "all else being equal," to isolate the influence of only one or a few variables.

How will the quantity of gas demanded by consumers change as the price of gas changes? The **law of demand** states that as the price of a good or service increases, consumers will demand less of it, *ceteris paribus.* We could conversely state the law of demand thus: consumers demand more of a good or service when its price falls. This inverse relationship between the price of something and the quantity demanded can be expressed a couple of ways. One is a demand schedule—a table showing the quantity of a specific good or service demanded at different prices. The other way is a graph that illustrates a demand curve—the graphical representation of a demand schedule. The convention among economists is to put the quantity demanded on the horizontal axis (the *x*-axis) and price on the vertical axis (the *y*-axis).

Suppose we have collected data about how much gasoline consumers in a particular metropolitan area demand at different prices. This hypothetical demand schedule is presented in Table 1. We can see that as the price of gas goes up, people demand less of it. The data in Table 1 are expressed graphically, as a demand curve, in Figure 1. Notice that the demand curve slopes down as we move to the right, as we would expect according to the law of demand.[1]

Looking at Figure 1, we can see that at a price of $1.70 per gallon, consumers in the area will purchase 74,000 gallons of gas per week. Suppose the price goes up to $1.90 per gallon. At the higher price, we see that consumers decide to purchase less gas, 70,000 gallons per week. We call this movement along a demand curve at different prices a *change in the quantity demanded*. This is different from what economists call a *change in demand*. A change in demand occurs when the entire demand curve shifts.

What would cause the entire demand curve to shift? First, we need to realize that a change in the price of gasoline will *not* cause the demand curve to shift; it will only cause consumers to move along the demand curve in Figure 1 (that is, a change in the quantity demanded). Our demand curve in Figure 1 is stable as long as we assume that no other relevant factors are changing—the *ceteris paribus* assumption. To expand our models, let's consider several factors that would cause the entire demand curve to shift. One factor is income. If the consumers' incomes were to go up, many would decide to purchase more gas at the same price. Higher incomes would result in a change in demand. This is shown in Figure 2 where the entire demand curve shifts to the right.[2]

Another factor that would cause a change in demand is a change in the price of related goods. In our example of the demand for gas, suppose the price of public trans-

**TABLE 1** *Demand Schedule for Gasoline*

| Price ($/gal.) | $1.40 | $1.50 | $1.60 | $1.70 | $1.80 | $1.90 | $2.00 | $2.10 | $2.20 | $2.30 |
|---|---|---|---|---|---|---|---|---|---|---|
| Quantity demanded (thousand gal./week) | 80 | 78 | 76 | 74 | 72 | 70 | 68 | 66 | 64 | 62 |

---

[1]For simplicity, we have drawn this demand curve as a straight line. Real-world demand curves may have different shapes, but will generally have a downward slope.

[2]Economists generally describe demand curves as shifting to "the right" or "the left," not up or down. This is because it makes more intuitive sense to say that at a given price consumers will demand more or less than to say that consumers will purchase a given quantity at a higher or lower price.

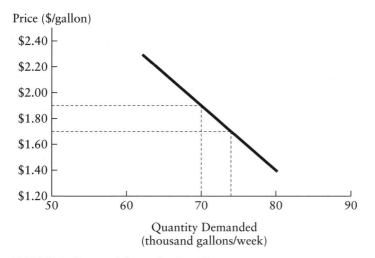

**FIGURE 1** *Demand Curve for Gasoline*

portation rose significantly. This would cause the demand for gas to increase (shift to the right) as some people decide to drive their own vehicles because public transportation is now too expensive for them. A change in consumers' preferences could also cause the demand curve for gas to shift. For example, American consumers' preferences toward larger, fuel-inefficient vehicles in recent years has caused an increase in the demand for gas. A significant change in the number of people driving would also cause a change in the demand for gas. What other factors would also cause a demand curve to shift?

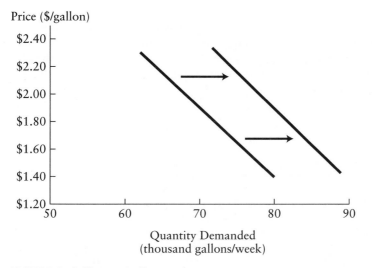

**FIGURE 2** *A Change in Demand*

## The Theory of Supply

The next step in our analysis is to consider the other side of the market. The theory of supply considers how suppliers respond to changes in the price of a good or service they supply, or other relevant factors. While low prices appeal to consumers looking for a bargain, high prices appeal to suppliers looking to make profits. As you might expect, the **law of supply** is the opposite of the law of demand. The law of supply states that as the price of a good or service increases, suppliers will choose to supply more of it, *ceteris paribus*. According to the law of supply, price and the quantity supplied change in the same direction.

Once again, we can express the relationship between price and the quantity supplied using both tables and graphs. Table 2 illustrates a supply schedule for gas, with the quantity supplied increasing as the price of gas increases. Figure 3 simply converts the data in Table 2 into a graph. Notice that the supply curve slopes upward as we move to the right.

There is also a distinction between a *change in the quantity supplied* and a *change in supply*. A change in the quantity supplied occurs when we move along a supply curve as the price of the good or service changes. This is shown in Figure 3. We see that at a price of $1.70, suppliers are willing to supply 69,000 gallons of gas. But if the price were to increase to $1.90, the quantity supplied would increase to 75,000 gallons per week.

A change in supply occurs when the entire supply curve shifts. Again, several factors might cause a supply curve to shift. One is a change in the price of input goods and services. For example, an increase in the wages paid to gasoline company employees would cause suppliers to raise the price they charge for gas, meaning a shift in the supply curve to the left as illustrated in Figure 4. Another factor that would cause a change in supply is a change in production technology. Suppose a new innovation reduces the costs of gasoline refining. In which direction would the supply curve shift in this case? What other factors would cause a change in supply?

We can now bring together both sides of the gasoline market. The price of gasoline is determined by the interaction of consumers and suppliers. We can illustrate this interaction by putting our demand and supply curves on the same graph, as shown in Figure 5. We can use this figure to determine what the price of gas will be and how much will be sold. First, suppose the price of gas was initially $2.00 per gallon. We see in Figure 5 that at this price the quantity supplied exceeds the quantity demanded. We

**TABLE 2** *Supply Schedule for Gasoline*

| Price ($/gal.) | $1.40 | $1.50 | $1.60 | $1.70 | $1.80 | $1.90 | $2.00 | $2.10 | $2.20 | $2.30 |
|---|---|---|---|---|---|---|---|---|---|---|
| Quantity supplied (thousand gal./week) | 60 | 63 | 66 | 69 | 72 | 75 | 78 | 81 | 84 | 87 |

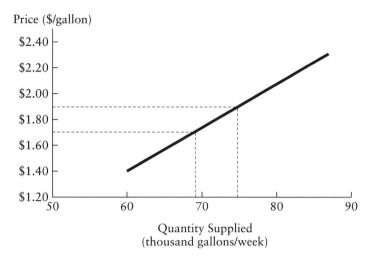

**FIGURE 3** *Supply Curve for Gasoline*

call this situation a **surplus** because suppliers have more gas than consumers are willing to buy. Rather than dumping the excess gas, suppliers will lower their price in order to attract more customers. So, in the case of a surplus we expect a downward pressure on prices.

What if the initial price were $1.50/gallon? We see in Figure 5 that at this price the quantity demanded exceeds the quantity suppliers are willing to supply. Suppliers will notice this excess demand and realize they can raise their prices, so a **shortage** will create upward pressure on prices.

**FIGURE 4** *A Change in Supply*

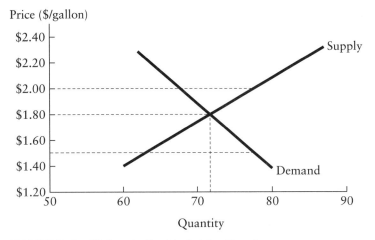

**FIGURE 5** *Equilibrium in the Market for Gasoline*

When a surplus or a shortage exists, the market will adjust attempting to eliminate the excess supply or demand. This adjustment will continue until we reach a price where the quantity demanded equals the quantity supplied. Only at this price is there no pressure for further market adjustment, *ceteris paribus*. In Figure 5, this occurs at a price of $1.80/gallon.[3] At this price, both the quantity demanded and the quantity supplied are 72,000 gallons per week. Economists use the term **market equilibrium** to describe a market that has reached this stable situation.

A market in equilibrium is stable as long as all other relevant factors stay the same, including consumers' incomes, the prices of related goods, production technology, etc. Changes in these variables will cause one (or both) curve(s) to shift and result in a new equilibrium. This is illustrated in Figure 6. Assume that an increase in consumers' incomes causes the demand curve for gas to shift from $D_0$ to $D_1$. This results in a new market equilibrium with a higher price and an increase in the quantity of gas sold. You can test yourself by figuring out what happens to the equilibrium price and quantity when the demand curve shifts in the opposite direction or when the supply curve shifts.

## *Elasticity of Demand and Supply*

Demand and supply curves indicate consumers' and suppliers' responsiveness to changes in price. While we expect all demand curves to slope downward and all supply curves to slope upward (with rare exceptions), their shapes will vary, and responses to changes in price can be minor or large. Consider again how consumers would respond to an increase in the price of gasoline. Consumers would buy less gas,

---

[3]This was the approximate market price of gasoline at the time this text was written. If by the time you read this the price of gas is higher or lower, try to explain why the price of gas has changed.

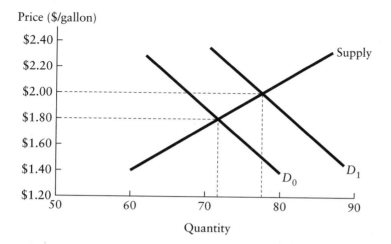

**FIGURE 6** *A New Equilibrium with a Change in Demand for Gasoline*

but, at least in the short term, probably not much less because they generally have fixed commutes to work, can't buy a new vehicle, and so on. The degree of consumer responsiveness to a change in the price of a good or service is determined by the **price elasticity of demand**.

The demand for a good is relatively *price inelastic* if the quantity demanded changes little as the price changes. This would be illustrated graphically by a relatively steep demand curve. Gasoline is an example of a good with a demand that is price inelastic. On the other hand, the demand for a good is relatively *price elastic* if the quantity demanded changes a lot as the price changes (the demand curve would be relatively flat). Can you think of goods that have relatively elastic demand curves?

We can also talk about the **price elasticity of supply**. The supply of a good is considered price inelastic if the quantity supplied changes little as price changes. A price elastic supply curve would indicate a relatively large change in the quantity supplied with a change in price.

Notice that the price elasticity of demand and supply can change as we consider a longer time period. In the short term, the demand and supply curves for gasoline are relatively inelastic. But when we consider a longer time frame, consumers can respond to an increase in gas prices by moving closer to work or buying a more fuel-efficient vehicle, and suppliers can build new refineries or drill more oil wells. So the price elasticity of demand and supply for gasoline will be higher over a longer time period.

## Welfare Analysis

The final topic we want to consider in this appendix is **welfare analysis**. Welfare analysis looks at the benefits consumers and suppliers obtain from economic transactions. Using welfare analysis, our supply and demand model becomes a powerful tool for

Price ($/gallon)

**FIGURE 7** *Consumer and Producer Surplus*

policy analysis. Our understanding of welfare analysis begins with a more detailed look at demand and supply curves.

Why do people buy things? Economists assume that people won't purchase a good or service unless the benefits they obtain from the purchase exceed what they have to pay for it. While the cost of something is expressed in dollars, quantifying benefits in dollar terms is not obvious. Economists define the net benefits a consumer obtains from a purchase as their maximum willingness to pay, less the price they actually have to pay. For example, if someone is willing to spend a maximum of $30 for a particular shirt, yet the actual price is $24, then he or she obtains a net benefit of $6 by buying it. This net benefit is called **consumer surplus**.

Notice that if the price of the shirt were $32, the consumer wouldn't purchase the shirt because the costs are greater than the benefits. When we observe people purchasing goods or services, we conclude that they are doing so because the benefits they obtain exceed their costs. If the price of a particular item rises, some people will decide not to purchase it—buying other things instead or saving their money. If the price rises further, more people will drop out of the market because the cost exceeds their maximum willingness to pay. In other words, a demand curve can also be viewed as a maximum-willingness-to-pay curve.

We can now look at Figure 7, showing the demand and supply for gasoline. The equilibrium values are the same as before ($1.80/gal. and 72,000 gallons sold) but the demand and supply curves have been extended back to the *y*-axis. Given that the demand curve shows consumers' maximum willingness to pay, the vertical difference between the demand curve (what consumers are willing to pay) and the equilibrium price (what they actually pay) is consumer surplus. Total consumer surplus in the gasoline market can be measured on our graph as an area, representing this price difference multiplied by the quantity purchased, as shown by the upper triangle in Figure 7.

We can also look at the supply curve in more detail. Economists assume that suppliers will supply an item only if the price exceeds their costs of production—in other words, if they can obtain a profit. The supply curve shows how much is needed to cover production costs. This explains the upward slope: as production increases, costs tend to rise. (At low levels of production, costs might fall as production increases, a phenomenon known as **economies of scale**, but eventually costs are likely to rise as raw materials run short, workers are paid overtime, and so forth.) In effect, the supply curve tells us how much it costs to supply each additional unit of an item. The cost to supply *one more* unit of a good is called the **marginal cost**. In other words, a supply curve is a marginal-cost curve.

Economists define the benefits producers obtain from selling an item **producer surplus.** Producer surplus is calculated as the selling price minus the cost of production. Once again, we can look at our supply and demand graph to visualize producer surplus. We see in Figure 7 that producer surplus is the lower triangle between the supply curve and the equilibrium price. The total net benefits from a market are simply the sum of consumer and producer surplus.

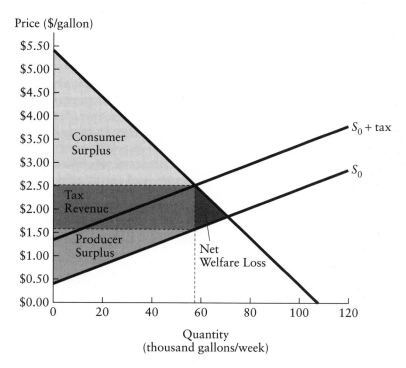

**FIGURE 8** *The Welfare Impacts of a Tax*

Using welfare analysis, we can determine how the benefits to consumers and producers change as a result of various policies. One such policy would be institution of a tax on a product. A tax on gasoline would effectively be an additional cost to producers supplying a good or service. Since the tax adds to production costs, it raises the supply curve by the amount of the tax. Figure 8 shows this new supply curve, reflecting a $1.00/gal. tax on gasoline. Notice that the equilibrium price rises, from $1.80 to about $2.55, but by an amount less than the tax.

The welfare effects of the fall on both consumers and producers. Consumer surplus has decreased but so has producer surplus. The rectangle between consumer and producer surplus indicates the tax revenues received by the government. These revenues, which used to be part of consumer and producer surplus, reflect a transfer from consumers and producers to the government. Of course, the government can then use these revenues to provide services—gasoline taxes, for example, often fund highway construction and maintenance.

Finally, note that the triangular area in Figure 8 that used to be part of consumer and producer surplus is no longer a benefit to anyone. This is the net welfare loss, or "deadweight loss," resulting from the tax. Does this imply that we should never tax anything? Of course not—as much of the text will detail. The welfare analysis we've looked at here considers only the benefits and costs to consumers and producers. There are many social justifications for the use of taxes, including environmental issues. What about those who are harmed by air pollution generated when people use gasoline in their vehicles? Clearly other impacts must be considered if we want to conduct a complete welfare analysis.

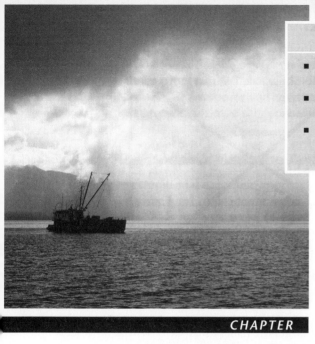

CHAPTER FOCUS QUESTIONS

- Why are resources such as fisheries often damaged through excessive use?
- What policies are effective for managing public-access resources?
- How should we preserve national parks, forests, oceans, and the atmosphere?

CHAPTER **4**

# Common-Property Resources and Public Goods

## Common Property, Open Access, and Property Rights

Property rights lie at the heart of economic analysis. In market economies, private property rights are central. This has not always been the case. In traditional or tribal societies, private property rights over resources are rare. Resources important to the life of the tribe are either held in common (as with a common grazing ground), or are not owned at all (as with animals hunted for food). Economically developed societies—we like to think of ourselves as "advanced" societies—have generally evolved elaborate systems of property rights covering most resources as well as most goods and services. But even modern industrialized nations have resources, goods, and services difficult to categorize as property.

A free-flowing river is an example. If we think of the river simply as a quantity of water flowing past people's land, we can devise rules for "ownership" of the water that allow a certain amount of water withdrawal per landowner. But what about the aquatic life of the river? What about the use of the river for recreation: canoeing, swimming, and fishing? What about the scenic beauty of the riverside?

Some of these aspects of the river might also become specific types of property. For example, in Scotland trout-fishing rights on certain rivers are jealously guarded property.

Still, it is difficult to parcel up every function of the river and define it as somebody's property. To some degree the river is a **common-property resource.** What rules apply to the use of common property?

## The Economics of a Fishery

A classic example of a common-property resource is a fishery. Inland and coastal fisheries often are governed by private, traditional, or government management systems. Fisheries in the open ocean are typically **open-access resources.** (An open-access resource can be defined as a common-property resource that lacks any system of rules governing its use.) Anyone can fish in nonterritorial waters, which means that no one owns the basic resource, the wild stock of fish. We will use this example to apply some of the basic concepts of production theory to an open-access resource.

How can we apply economic theory to a fishery? Let's start with common sense. If just a few fishing boats start operations in a rich fishing ground, their catch will certainly be good. This is likely to attract other fishers, and as more boats join the fishing fleet the total catch will increase.

As the number of fishing boats becomes large, the fishery's capacity will be strained and the catch of individual boats will diminish. We know from experience that if this process is taken too far, the output of the whole fishery can be badly damaged. At what point does it become counterproductive to put in more effort, in the shape of more boat trips? What forces may drive us past that point? Economic theory can give us insights into these critical questions of common-property resource management.

We can envision the fishery's **total product** as shown in Figure 4-1. The horizontal axis shows fishing effort, measured in numbers of boat trips. The vertical axis shows the total catch of all the boats. As the number of boat trips increases, the total product curve shown in Figure 4-1 goes through three distinct phases.

The first is a period of **constant returns to scale** (here shown from 0 to 400 boats). In this range, each extra boat finds an ample supply of fish and returns to port with a catch of 10 tons. The second is a period of **diminishing returns** to effort, shown from 400 to 850 boats. It is now becoming more difficult to catch a limited number of fish. When an extra boat puts out to sea, it increases the total catch, but it also reduces by a small amount the catch of all the other boats. The natural resource is no longer ample for all; intense competition for fish stocks makes the job tougher for all fishers.

Finally there is a period of **absolutely diminishing returns,** above 850 boats, where more boats actually *decrease* the total catch. **Overfishing** is taking place, and stocks of fish are being depleted. The fish population's ability to replenish itself is damaged, and we have the makings of both an economic and an ecological collapse.[1]

To understand the economic forces motivating the fishers, we must convert the quantitative measure of tons of fish landed into a money figure showing total revenue earned. We simply multiply the quantity of fish by the price per ton ($TR = PQ$). Let us assume a stable price of $1,000 per ton. (We are implicitly assuming that this fishery is

---

[1]Note that in this example we use a long-term production function that represents the fishery product over a period of time. Decline or collapse of fisheries, as shown in the absolutely diminishing returns section of the graph, would not take place in a single period, but over years.

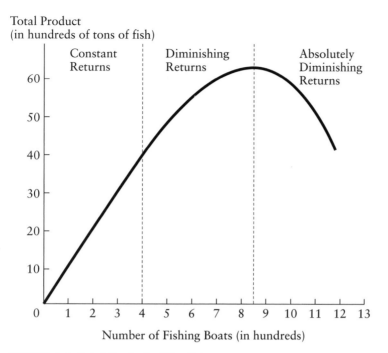

Total Product
(in hundreds of tons of fish)

Constant Returns | Diminishing Returns | Absolutely Diminishing Returns

**FIGURE 4-1** *Total Product of the Fishery*

small enough relative to the total market that its output does not significantly affect the market price. If this fishery were the market's only source of fish we would have to consider price changes also.)

We can now calculate the **total revenue** from the fishery, the **average revenue** (revenue per boat), and the **marginal revenue** (revenue added to the total by an extra boat), as shown in Table 4-1. To complete our financial data, we will also need to know the costs of operating a fishing boat. Here we will assume that the **marginal cost** of operating a boat is constant at $4,000 per boat trip. This gives us a simplified, but complete, picture of the economic forces confronting the individual fishers in this industry (Figure 4-2).

Suppose that only 400 boats are operating. What is the position of the individual boat operator? We can see from Figure 4-2 that revenues per boat are $10,000 per trip. Costs per boat are $4,000 per trip. That leaves $6,000 as net revenue, or profit.

This obviously profitable business will attract new entrants. So long as fishers have free entry into the industry, the number of boats operating will increase. Either existing fishers will acquire more boats, or new operators will enter the fishery.

## Incentives for Overfishing

Figure 4-2 also shows, however, that as more boats join the fishing fleet, the extra or marginal revenue will rapidly decline. By the time we have reached 800 boats, the marginal revenue brought in by the last 100 entrants is less than the marginal cost of

**TABLE 4-1** *Revenues and Costs for the Fishery*

| | 1 | 2 | 3 | 4 | 5 | 6 | 7 | 8 | 9 | 10 | 11 | 12 | 13 |
|---|---|---|---|---|---|---|---|---|---|---|---|---|---|
| Number of boats ($Q$ in hundreds) | 1 | 2 | 3 | 4 | 5 | 6 | 7 | 8 | 9 | 10 | 11 | 12 | 13 |
| Total fish catch (hundred tons) | 10 | 20 | 30 | 40 | 48 | 54 | 58 | 60 | 60 | 58 | 54 | 48 | 40 |
| Total value of catch ($TR$ in million $) | 1.0 | 2.0 | 3.0 | 4.0 | 4.8 | 5.4 | 5.8 | 6.0 | 6.0 | 5.8 | 5.4 | 4.8 | 4.0 |
| Total costs ($TC$ in million $) | 0.4 | 0.8 | 1.2 | 1.6 | 2.0 | 2.4 | 2.8 | 3.2 | 3.6 | 4.0 | 4.4 | 4.8 | 5.2 |
| Total net revenue ($TR$–$TC$ in million $) | 0.6 | 1.2 | 1.8 | 2.4 | 2.8 | 3.0 | 3.0 | 2.8 | 2.4 | 1.8 | 1.0 | 0 | −0.8 |
| Marginal revenue ($MR$ in thousand $) | 10 | 10 | 10 | 8 | 6 | 4 | 2 | 0 | −2 | −4 | −6 | −8 | |
| Revenue per boat ($AR$ in thousand $) | 10 | 10 | 10 | 10 | 9.6 | 9 | 8.2 | 7.5 | 6.6 | 5.8 | 4.9 | 4 | 3.1 |
| Cost per boat ($MC$, $AC$ in thousand $) | 4 | 4 | 4 | 4 | 4 | 4 | 4 | 4 | 4 | 4 | 4 | 4 | 4 |
| Net revenue per boat ($AR$–$MC$) | 6 | 6 | 6 | 6 | 5.6 | 5 | 4.2 | 3.5 | 2.6 | 1.8 | 0.9 | 0 | −0.9 |

> Marginal revenue is defined as $MR = \Delta TR/\Delta Q$
> Average revenue is defined as $AR = TR/Q$
> Marginal cost is defined as $MC = \Delta TC/\Delta Q$
> Marginal revenue is plotted *between* production levels because it represents the difference in revenues between the two levels.

operating the boats. Does this mean that operations will become unprofitable, inducing some owners to leave the industry? No, because the lower average revenues are spread throughout the fishing fleet. The average revenue, or revenue per boat, is now about $7,500, which still covers costs of $4,000, with $3,500 profit. Rather than fishers leaving the industry, considerable incentive remains for more to enter.

This process of entry will continue until average revenue falls below the marginal cost of operating a boat—in our example, when 1,200 boats are operating. Only then do individual operators find the business unprofitable, causing some to leave the industry. The market sends a "signal"—through unprofitability—that the industry is overcrowded.

But this economic signal comes far too late—too late for economic efficiency, and too late for ecological sustainability. The economically efficient number of boats would have been 650. At this point the extra benefits of adding one more boat are just balanced by the extra costs of operating that boat. The problem is that individual operators fail to "notice" that the industry as a whole is becoming less profitable above 650 boats.

So long as each boat is profitable, fishers have an incentive to continue fishing, and others see incentive to enter the fishing business. The forces of free entry and competition, which usually work to promote economic efficiency, have exactly the opposite effect in

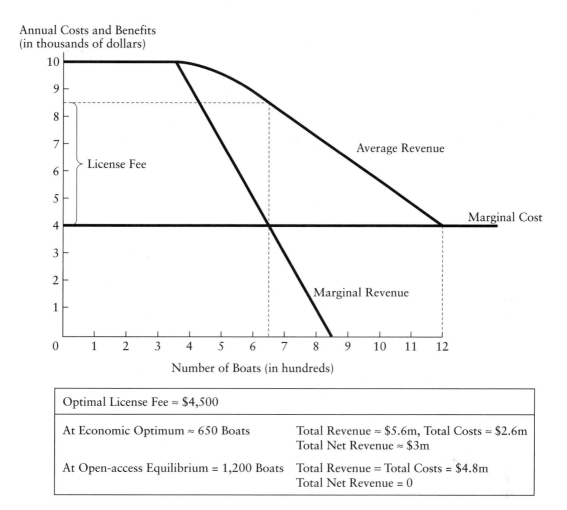

**FIGURE 4-2** *Economic Conditions in the Fishery*

this case. They encourage overfishing that ultimately destroys both the fish stocks and the profitability of all operators. The economic explanation is that fishers have free access to a crucial resource—fish stocks. Economic logic tells us that an underpriced resource will be overused, and a resource priced at zero will be squandered.

This phenomenon is sometimes referred to as the **tragedy of the commons.**[2] Because common-property resources belong to no one in particular, no one has an incentive to conserve them. On the contrary, the incentive is toward using as much as you can before someone else gets it. When resources are ample, problems are few, as in

---

[2]This concept was first introduced by Hardin, 1968. Feeny et al., 1999, give a recent assessment of the issue.

precolonial America when fish stocks were far beyond the needs or fishing abilities of the small population. When population, demand, and fishing technologies expand enough, the economic logic that we have sketched out leads to critical danger of over-fishing and even complete collapse of the fishery.

Is there a better solution? From the point of view of formal economic analysis, the **economic optimum** for this fishing industry would be at 650 boats, where marginal revenue = marginal cost. At this point the **net social benefit** from the fishing industry is maximized. Net social benefit, as we saw in Chapter 3, can be defined as total bene-fits (in this case equal to the total value of the catch) minus total costs. In this example, net social benefit equals total net revenue. Table 4-1 shows that this is indeed maxi-mized between 600 and 700 boats. The straight-line pattern of marginal revenue de-cline means that the economic optimum will be 650 boats.[3]

From an ecological point of view, this equilibrium is probably also sustainable. The **maximum sustainable yield** from this fishery occurs when 850 boats are operating and the total catch is just over 6,000 tons.[4] The economic optimum output of 650 boats is somewhat below maximum sustainable yield, which implies that the fishery can maintain ecological health at this level of output. When fishing efforts push beyond the point of maximum sustainable yield, long-term damage to the fishery—even species extinction—can occur. The **open-access equilibrium** at 1,200 boats clearly threatens such an ecological collapse, in addition to being economically inefficient.

## Policies for Fishery Management

What policies might achieve a more efficient equilibrium, protect the fishery ecosys-tem, and improve social net benefit? A simple answer suggests itself: impose a fee. If fishers must pay a **license fee,** this will reduce the economic incentive for excessive entry into the industry. Figure 4-2 illustrates the optimal level for such a fee. At the op-timal equilibrium of 650 boats, the difference between marginal cost and average rev-enue is approximately $4,500. If fishers must pay a per-boat license fee of $4,500, entry into the industry will be profitable up to 650 boats. After this, profits fall below zero, and there is no further incentive for entry.

Each fisher will now be in the position of a perfect competitor, making minimal or "normal" profit. In this case, however, the logic of competition will work to protect the ecosystem, not to destroy it. In effect, fishers must pay a fee to use a previously free resource—access to fish stocks. This policy might be politically unpopular in fishing communities, but it will prevent the industry from destroying the means of its own livelihood.

---

[3]The best placement of marginal values on a graph is halfway between the total values from which they are derived. Between 600 and 700 boats, the total revenue changes from $5.4 million to $5.8 million, and the marginal revenue value (equal to $0.4 million/100 = $4,000) is best placed at 650 boats.

[4]Assuming the total product curve is smooth, its maximum will occur at 6,025 tons when 850 boats are operating.

Another policy to achieve the same goal would be the use of a **quota,** or catch limit. Government officials may determine a quota for the entire fishery, but deciding who receives the rights to a limited fish catch can become controversial. If the right is allocated to current fishers, new entrants will be barred from the industry. Alternatively, fishers might receive **individual transferable quotas (ITQs),** which could be sold to someone entering the business. In some cases, limited rights to hunt or fish certain species are allocated to indigenous peoples. Aleut people, for example, have the right to hunt a limited number of endangered bowhead whales.

Yet another possibility is to sell fishing quotas at auction, which will lead to an economic result similar to the license fee. Any such method requires a consciously planned government intervention. Although economists often argue that markets operate more efficiently without government intervention, here is a case that *requires* government intervention to achieve an economically efficient (and ecologically sustainable) solution.

The need for social regulation of common-property resources has been well recognized throughout history. The longest place name in America is that of Lake Chargoggagoggmanchauggagoggchaubunagungamaugg, located near the town of Webster, Massachusetts. The name, a Native American phrase loosely translated as "I fish on my side, you fish on your side, and nobody fishes in the middle," reflects a long-standing principle of limited catch and conservation of resources.[5]

Population growth, high demand, and advanced technology have complicated the implementation of such sound principles. Even so, both economic theory and ecological principles tell us that we must find ways to do so or risk having our common-property resources destroyed through overuse.[6] As we will see in future chapters, the principles of common-property resource management seen in this example of a fishery will apply to many other resources such as forests, open land, and even the atmosphere.

## The Environment as a Public Good

Economists have long recognized the concept of **public goods.** Ordinary goods, such as automobiles, are generally purchased by one household, and only the purchaser enjoys their benefits. Public goods, in contrast, benefit many people, often the whole society. Public goods are said to be **nonexclusive**—that is, they are available to all for consumption—and **nonrival,** because their use by one person does not reduce their availability to others.[7]

---

[5]See Feeny et al., 1999, for a discussion of institutions for common-property management.

[6]For an extensive treatment of the economic analysis of fisheries and other natural resources, see Clark, 1990.

[7]The formal definition of a public good is "a commodity or service which if supplied to one person can be made available to others at no extra cost" (Pearce, 1992). A "pure" public good is one that the producer cannot exclude anyone from consuming. Thus a pure public good demonstrates both nonrival consumption and nonexcludability.

*North American birds such as this warbler winter in South American rainforests. Preserving rainforests protects species diversity on both continents.*

An example is the national park system of the United States. National parks are open to all, and (except where overcrowding becomes a significant problem) their use by some people does not reduce others' ability to enjoy them. Public goods are not necessarily environmental in character: the highway system and the national defense are often cited as examples of public goods. Many aspects of environmental preservation do, however, fit easily into the public goods category, because virtually everyone has an interest in a sound and healthy environment.[8]

How can we best understand the logic of demand and supply for public goods? These goods cannot be bought and sold in the same way as ordinary goods, yet their adequate supply is of crucial interest to the whole society. We begin by noting that the provision of such goods must be decided in the political arena. This is generally true of, for example, national defense. We cannot resolve the issue of national defense by having everyone buy his or her own tank. The resolution requires a political decision that takes into account some citizens' wish for more defense spending, others' for less. Once the decision is made, we all pay a share of the cost through taxes.

---

[8]Technically, national parks are not a "pure" public good because they may charge entry fees, thereby excluding nonpayers. Even so, the parks remain a public good so long as national policy allows free or low-fee entry.

Similarly, decisions regarding environmental public goods must be made through the political system. Legislatures, for example, must decide on funding for national parks. Will more land be acquired for parks? Might some existing park areas be sold or leased for development? Such decisions require an understanding of public demand for environmental amenities.

The problem, however, cannot be solved through the ordinary market process of supply and demand. In the fishery example discussed above, the problem lay on the production side—the ordinary market logic led to overexpansion of production and excessive pressure on resources. With public goods, the problem is on the demand side. The ordinary market process will lead to a low **effective demand**[9] for public goods (possibly a zero demand), despite the fact that the public needs these goods. Thus without specific government policies in this area, **undersupply of public goods** will occur.

## The Economics of Rainforest Conservation

An example may help illustrate the point. Rainforest conservation in Central and South America can be considered a public good. Such conservation certainly benefits people who tour the area and see unspoiled rainforest, whether they are local residents or foreign tourists. Many more people also gain from spin-off benefits such as preservation of species diversity and the pharmaceutical products derived from rainforest species. Bird-watchers in North America see warblers and thrushes that depend on winter habitat in rainforests. Cutting and burning of rainforest adds to atmospheric carbon dioxide, which contributes to the problem of global climate change.

Many people derive what economists call a **psychic benefit** simply from knowing that forests and species have been preserved, even if they never see the forests personally. For all these reasons, we can state with confidence that rainforest preservation yields considerable benefit. But how can we reflect this benefit in actual demand for preserved rainforest acres? The question is critical; market demands for timber, minerals, and agricultural land all create pressure to cut down rainforest for development. Can the preservation interest compete with this market demand?

Let's examine whether we can represent the benefits of preservation in market demand. Some private conservation groups have exactly that goal—to create demand for rainforest preservation. One particularly effective campaign mounted by these groups offers people the opportunity to "buy" a rainforest acre for $50. If a conservation-minded citizen chooses to respond to such an appeal, the organization promises to use her $50 contribution to purchase 1 acre of rainforest for preservation. This kind of appeal is popular because it offers direct results. In effect it sets up a new kind of market for a public good. Just as I can purchase a refrigerator, I can now "purchase" rainforest preservation.

Unfortunately, this fails to solve the problem of undersupply of public goods. To see why, we can graph the supply and demand for rainforest preservation in standard

---

[9]Effective demand is defined as demand backed up by purchasing power.

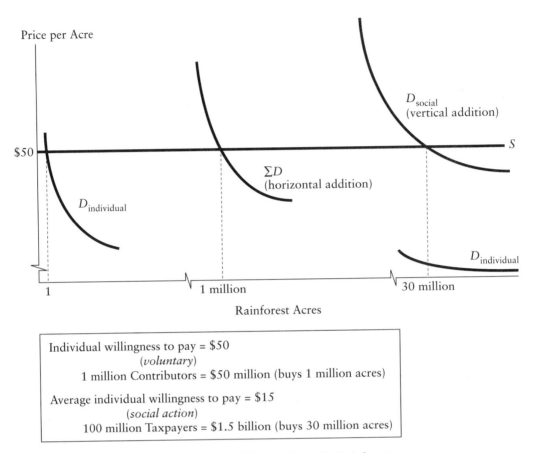

**FIGURE 4-3** *Public Good Example: How (Not) to Save the Rainforest*

economic terms, as shown in Figure 4-3. Interpreting this graph is a little tricky, but it is fully consistent both with economic theory and, as we will see, with real-world experience.

The supply function for rainforest acres preserved is simple. We assume that the going price is $50 per acre, giving us a horizontal or **perfectly elastic supply.** On the demand side, let's look first at the **individual demand schedule** of Ms. Mary Ecosmith, who sends in $50 to the appeal. We don't know the exact shape of her individual demand curve, but we do know that at the price of $50 she has demanded exactly 1 acre, and an approximate demand curve reflects this in Figure 4-3.

Now let's consider the **market demand schedule** for rainforest preservation. Just as individual demands for automobiles or refrigerators can be *added horizontally*[10] to

---

[10]Horizontal addition of demand curves means that at any given price, we add all the individual quantities demanded to obtain market demand.

obtain market demand, we can add the quantities of rainforest preservation demanded by different individuals to obtain the market demand. Let's suppose this appeal enjoys great success, and 1 million people respond, each buying 1 acre. The market demand is then shown by the curve Σ*D*, representing the *horizontal addition* of 1 million individual demand curves like Ms. Ecosmith's. One million acres of rainforest are successfully preserved, at a total cost of $50 million. (In real life, this result would be an extraordinary success, and it is unlikely that conservation organizations would do this well.)

Such a result would certainly represent some progress in promoting supply of a public good, but does it represent adequate supply? No. Estimates of the global loss rate of tropical forest indicate as much as *30 million acres* destroyed per year. Even such an extraordinarily successful conservation effort would fall far short of what is needed. Despite the creative work of conservation groups in creating a new market for this public good, it remains woefully undersupplied. In the meantime, the market demands for timber, minerals, and agricultural land continue to increase the pressure on remaining forests.

## Social Demand for Rainforest Preservation

The problem is that response to the conservation group's appeal fails to adequately reflect the true public demand for rainforest preservation. Concern about rainforest destruction is widespread; most people would probably like to see it stopped. But only a limited number of people will actually send $50. Such behavior typifies the **free-rider effect,** which we discussed in Chapter 3.

Many people will wait for someone else to contribute to a cause, even though they themselves will benefit. They are happy to see some rainforest preservation; they either neglect to write a check or they can't afford $50. Even if offered the opportunity to contribute a smaller amount, they may fear that the appeal will fail and they will have contributed money for nothing. Some people, of course, may be unconcerned about the problem—their willingness to contribute is zero. Most likely, however, many more people do care at least a little and might contribute something, but they miss the appeal or for any of the above reasons fail to respond.

In terms of economic theory, what we need is not a horizontal addition, but a *vertical addition of demand curves.* We need to add the actual benefit to each individual from rainforest preservation to find the **social benefit.** Look at the right side of Figure 4-3. Here a vertical addition shows the **social demand** for actually stopping rainforest destruction by purchasing not 1 million but 30 million acres for preservation.

The benefit to each individual is small—a tiny fraction of a cent per acre. But when we consider that practically everyone derives some benefit, it adds up to a considerable social benefit. For $1.5 billion, we could purchase the entire 30 million acres at risk. If government policy mandated such a purchase, how much would it cost taxpayers? If we consider only U.S. taxpayers, it would come to about $15 per family. This is, for comparison, less than 1 percent of the U.S. defense budget, to which each family contributes about $4,000 in taxes. Might the provision of this public good be worth the cost?

Opinions might differ on the appropriate amount, especially in a climate of budgetary cutbacks. Our point is this: effective provision of a public good requires a public decision. The efforts of private conservation groups, while commendable, are only a drop in the bucket.

Of course, our example is oversimplified. The supply cost of rainforest land is undoubtedly not perfectly elastic, and such large-scale preservation could probably not be purchased. But $1.5 billion could go a long way—much further than $50 million. Offered as debt relief, it could be a massive inducement for governments such as Brazil's to institute effective rainforest preservation plans. If Europe and Japan joined the United States in a worldwide rainforest conservation program, we could make much progress, offering developing nations significant incentive for rainforest conservation at relatively low cost. The lack of such a public effort leaves only the much smaller efforts of private conservation groups standing against the widespread market demand forces promoting rainforest conversion. Clearly, the result will be continued rapid loss of forests.[11]

Many environmental issues, such as clean air and clean water, have a similar public good nature. All land preservation policies, including wetlands, forests, wilderness, and rural area protection require government action to succeed. As we have seen, markets can help provide some of these environmental public goods, but their essential public good character places practical limits on our ability to "marketize" them. As our rainforest example shows, attempts at private provision of public goods fail to reflect many of the true public benefits of environmental preservation. Only a social decision to act together—and pay the necessary costs—will gain these public benefits for all.

## The Global Commons

Examining these examples of common-property resources and public goods extends the scope of our resource and environmental analysis. In addition, these cases relate closely to the theory of externalities, which we discussed in Chapter 3. Here, we are in a sense dealing with special cases of externalities. The fisher who adds an extra boat to the fishing grounds imposes an external cost on all the other fishers by slightly lowering the average catch. The conservation group that preserves rainforest confers an external benefit on the rest of us who, whether or not we contributed to the effort, gain a slightly improved global environment.

Extending the analysis to these examples, however, seems to raise another question. Can we really continue to define all these environmental issues as "externalities"? The use of the term seems to imply a secondary role in economic theory—external costs are added to economic analysis after the rest of the theory is essentially complete. But are these so-called externalities actually symptoms of something more fundamental?

As we consider the multitude of environmental problems that have gained increased attention in recent years, we see the rising importance of cases involving

---

[11]The initiation of some public funding for forest preservation through the Global Environment Facility (GEF) is discussed in Chapter 20.

common-property resources and public goods. Global warming, ozone layer depletion, ocean pollution, freshwater pollution, groundwater overdraft, species loss—all have clear similarities to the cases we have discussed above. The increasing prevalence of such examples has led to a new focus on the concept of the **global commons.** If so many of the earth's resources and environmental systems show the characteristics of common-property resources or public goods, perhaps we should revise our thinking about the global economy.[12]

Rather than focusing on the goals of economic growth, and dealing with the "externalities" as an afterthought, we need to recognize that the global economic system is strongly dependent on the health of global ecosystems. Evaluation of the state of these systems, and an assessment of how economic development can best be adapted to planetary limits, is essential.[13] This implies the need for new approaches to economic policy, and new or reformed institutions at the national and international level. Clearly this raises issues which go beyond the management of individual fisheries or national parks.

Proper management of the global commons poses special challenges in securing agreement among many different nations. Despite the many possibilities for conflicting views and free-rider temptations, important international agreements such as the Montreal Protocol on ozone layer depletion have been put into place to deal with threats to the global atmosphere, oceans, and ecosystems. Effective agreement on implementation has been harder to achieve in other cases, such as the Kyoto Protocol on global climate change.

We will examine some of the implications of this broader perspective on common-property issues in Chapter 7 and consider issues of managing the global commons in later chapters.

## SUMMARY

Common-property resources are those owned by a community, without specific assignment of private property rights to individuals or firms. Various possible systems for managing such resources include traditional use customs and government management. No rules limit use of open-access resources, which leads to overuse and sometimes to the collapse of the resource's ecological functions.

A classic case of resource overuse is overfishing of the oceans. Because no restrictions limit access to fisheries in the open ocean, economic incentives result in an excessive number of boats operating. Depletion of the fish stocks results, with declining revenues for all fishers. Until net revenue (revenue minus costs) reaches zero, however, incentive continues for new participants to enter the fishery. This open-access equilibrium is both economically inefficient and ecologically damaging.

Possible policy responses to overuse of open-access resources include imposing licenses or quotas. Quotas can be assigned to individual fishing boats and can be

[12]See Heal, 1999, and Johnson and Duchin, 2000.

[13]For a recent assessment of the state of planetary ecosystems, see World Resources Institute, 2000, and Millennium Ecosystem Assessment, 2005 (http://www.millenniumassessment.org).

transferable (salable). Smaller traditional societies often follow social principles of resource management, but large industrialized societies, with advanced technology for fishing and other resource extraction, require government management of open-access resources.

A similar need for active government policy arises in public goods provision. Public goods, once provided, benefit the general public rather than selected individuals. They include goods and services such as parks, highways, public health facilities, and national defense. No individual or group of individuals is likely to have sufficient incentive or funds to provide public goods, yet their benefits are great and often essential to social well-being. Many environmental public goods, such as forest and wetlands preservation, cannot be adequately supplied through the market. Government intervention and public funds are needed to achieve the social benefits that flow from providing these public goods.

The global scope of many common-property resources and public goods, including the atmosphere and oceans, raises issues regarding proper management of the global commons. New and reformed institutions are needed to manage common-property resources at the global level. The difficulty often has been to establish effective international authority to regulate activities that threaten global ecosystems.

## KEY TERMS AND CONCEPTS

| | |
|---|---|
| absolutely diminishing returns | net social benefit |
| average revenue | nonexclusive good |
| common-property resource | nonrival good |
| constant returns to scale | open-access equilibrium |
| diminishing returns | open-access resource |
| economic optimum | overfishing |
| effective demand | perfectly elastic supply |
| free-rider effect | psychic benefit |
| global commons | public goods |
| individual transferable quotas (ITQs) | quota |
| individual demand schedule | social benefit |
| license fee | social demand |
| marginal cost | total product |
| marginal revenue | total revenue |
| market demand schedule | tragedy of the commons |
| maximum sustainable yield | undersupply of public goods |

## DISCUSSION QUESTIONS

1. Would a good policy for fishery management aim at obtaining the maximum sustainable yield? Why or why not? When we speak of an optimal equilibrium from an

economic point of view, will this equilibrium also be generally ecologically sound? What might cause economic and ecological principles to conflict in fisheries management?

2. Suppose that the fishery example discussed in the chapter was *not* a common-property resource, but was a lake fishery owned by an individual or a single firm. The owner could choose to allow fishing and charge a fee for access to the lake. How would the economic logic differ from the common-property resource case? Would a greater net social benefit accrue? Who would receive this net social benefit?

3. Discuss the effects of technological improvement in an industry that uses a common-property resource. For example, consider a technological improvement in fishing equipment that cuts the costs of a fishing boat trip in half. Technological progress usually increases net social benefit. Does it do so in this case? How would government policies relating to this industry affect your answer?

4. Do you think it is possible to draw a clear distinction between private and public goods? Which of the following might be considered public goods: farmland, forest land, beachfront property, highways, a city park, a parking lot, a sports arena? What market or public policy rules should apply to providing these goods?

## PROBLEMS

1. Farmers in an arid region of Mexico draw their irrigation water from an underground aquifer. The aquifer has a natural maximum recharge rate of 340,000 gallons per day (that is, 340,000 gal/day filter into the underground reservoir from natural sources). The total product schedule for well operations looks like this:

| Wells Operating | 10 | 20 | 30 | 40 | 50 | 60 | 70 | 80 | 90 |
|---|---|---|---|---|---|---|---|---|---|
| Total Water Output (Thousand Gal/Day) | 100 | 200 | 280 | 340 | 380 | 400 | 400 | 380 | 340 |

a. The cost of operating a well is 600 pesos per day; the value of water to the farmer is 0.1 peso per gallon. Calculate total revenue (output times price) for each level of output.

b. If each well is privately owned by a different farmer, how many wells will operate? (To calculate this, first calculate average revenue, which is $TR/Q$. Note that the quantity of wells is given in units of 10.) Analyze this result in terms of economic efficiency and long-term sustainability.

c. What would be the economically efficient number of wells? (To calculate this, you will need marginal revenue, which is $MR = \Delta TR/\Delta Q$, best shown *between* two levels of output.) Show that net social benefit is maximized at this level of output.

    d. How could the socially efficient equilibrium be achieved? In this case, is the socially efficient equilibrium also ecologically sustainable?

    e. How would the answers change if the cost of well operation fell to 400 pesos per day?

2. Four towns share a common water source. By buying open land along the watershed (area from which the water flows) the towns can preserve its purity from sewage, road runoff, and such. The land demand schedule for each town based on water treatment costs saved can be expressed as

$$P = \$34,000 - 10Q_d$$

where $Q_d$ is acres purchased and $P$ is the price the town would be willing to pay.

    a. If the cost of land is $30,000 per acre, how much land will be purchased if each town operates independently? How much if they form a joint commission for land purchases? Graph the different possibilities. (If the economic theory is not clear, imagine representatives of the four towns sitting around a table, discussing the costs and benefits of purchasing different amounts of land.)

    b. Which is the socially efficient solution and why? How would the answers change if the price of land was $36,000 per acre?

    c. Discuss this in terms of the demand for clean water. Is clean water a public good in this case? Can water generally be considered a public good?

## REFERENCES

Clark, Colin W. *Mathematical Bioeconomics: The Optimal Management of Renewable Resources.* New York: Wiley, 1990.

Feeny, David, Fikret Berkes, Bonnie J. McCay, and James M. Acheson. "The Tragedy of the Commons: Twenty-Two Years Later." Chapter 8 in *Environmental Economics and Development,* edited by J. B. (Hans) Opschoor, Kenneth Button, and Peter Nijkamp. Cheltenham, U.K.: Elgar, 1999.

Hardin, Garrett. "The Tragedy of the Commons." *Science* 162 (1968).

Heal, Geoffrey. "New Strategies for the Provision of Public Goods: Learning for International Environmental Challenges." In *Global Public Goods: International Cooperation in the 21st Century,* edited by Inge Kaul et al. New York: Oxford University Press, 1999.

Johnson, Baylor, and Faye Duchin. "The Case for the Global Commons," in *Rethinking Sustainability,* edited by Jonathan M. Harris. Ann Arbor, Mich.: University of Michigan Press, 2000.

Millennium Ecosystem Assessment. *Ecosystems and Human Well-Being: Synthesis.* Washington, D.C.: Island Press, 2005.

Pearce, David W., ed. *The MIT Dictionary of Modern Economics,* 4th ed. Cambridge, Mass.: MIT Press, 1992.

World Resources Institute, United Nations Development Programme, United Nations Environment Programme, and World Bank. *World Resources 2000–2001: People and Ecosystems: The Fraying Web of Life.* Washington, D.C.: World Resources Institute, 2000.

## WEBSITES

1. **http://www.indiana.edu/~iascp/articles.html** Links to articles related to management of common-pool resources. The site is managed by the International Association for the Study of Common Property, "a nonprofit Association devoted to understanding and improving institutions for the management of environmental resources that are (or could be) held or used collectively by communities in developing or developed countries."

2. **http://www.gci.org.uk/** Homepage for the Global Commons Institute, a British organization comprised of "an independent group of people whose aim is the protection of the Global Commons." The institute mainly focuses on global climate-change issues.

## CHAPTER 5

CHAPTER FOCUS QUESTIONS

- How should we decide whether to use or conserve nonrenewable resources?
- How can we value future resource consumption?
- What will happen to prices and consumption if resources start to run out?

# Resource Allocation over Time

## Allocation of Nonrenewable Resources

Resources can be **renewable** or **nonrenewable.** Renewable resources, if properly managed, can last indefinitely. We might reasonably expect that a well-managed farm, forest, or fishery could remain productive for centuries. Nonrenewable resources, on the other hand, cannot last forever. Some may be in relatively short supply. Examples would be high-grade deposits of copper ore or crude oil supplies. This raises questions of how much of these nonrenewable resources we use today and how much we save for future use, or for future generations.

A common concern is that we are using up earth's resources too fast. Another point of view is that technological progress and adaptation will avoid resource shortages. What does economic theory have to say about this issue?

A simple version of nonrenewable resource analysis begins by assuming that we have a known, limited quantity of a resource that we can use during two different time periods. The supply of high-grade copper, for example, is relatively fixed in amount. How should we allocate this limited resource between current and future time periods?

If we consider all possible future periods, the problem becomes more complex (though not theoretically insoluble, as we will see). A simple initial model of nonrenewable resource allocation deals with only two time periods. Our economic analysis will weigh the economic value of copper in the present as compared with copper in the future. Owners of copper deposits will decide whether to exploit them immediately,

*Offshore oil drilling has increased as domestic supplies of oil become more difficult to obtain. The allocation of oil resources between present and future consumption depends on prices and on government policy.*

or to hold them for a future period, based on an estimate of probable future prices. We can formulate the problem as a simple extension of standard supply and demand theory.[1]

## Equilibrium in the Current Time Period

First, let us consider only the current time period. Figure 5-1a shows a hypothetical supply and demand for copper. From this we can derive the **marginal net benefit** curve for copper, which shows the difference between value to the consumer and cost of supply for each unit of copper. (For example, if we can extract a unit of copper for $50 and its value to the purchaser is $150, its marginal net benefit is $100.)

Graphically, marginal net benefit is the vertical difference between the supply curve and the demand curve. Marginal net benefit is generally largest for the first units extracted, then declines to zero at equilibrium (where the supply and demand curves meet). If we were to produce more than the equilibrium quantity, marginal net benefit would become negative as supply costs rise above the value to the purchaser.

---

[1]This analysis assumes no copper recycling; we'll consider the economics of recycling in Chapter 12.

**(a) Supply and Demand for Copper**

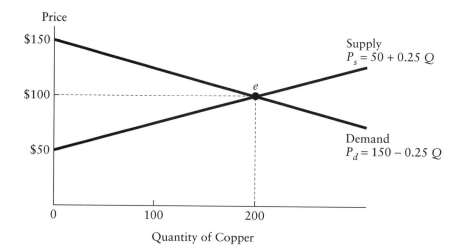

**(b) Marginal Net Benefit for Copper**

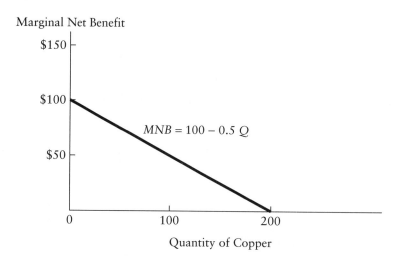

**FIGURE 5-1** *Supply, Demand, and Marginal Net Benefit for Copper*

The marginal net benefit concept is a handy way of compressing into one curve information about both supply and demand in one period. The marginal net benefit of copper in the present period is shown by curve *MNB* in Figure 5-1b.

Algebraically, if the demand and supply schedules are given by

$$P_d = 150 - 0.25Q_1$$

and

$$P_s = 50 + 0.25Q_1$$

marginal net benefit is given by

$$MNB = P_d - P_s = 100 - 0.5Q_1$$

At the supply and demand equilibrium of $Q_1 = 200$, marginal net benefit is zero, indicating that producing and consuming more than 200 units of copper will provide no additional net benefit. The area under the marginal net benefit curve shows **total net benefit** (just as the area under a demand curve shows total benefit and the area under a supply curve shows total cost).

When marginal net benefit is just equal to zero, total net benefit is maximized (as shown by the area under the marginal net benefit curve in Figure 5-1b). This corresponds to the ordinary supply and demand equilibrium for the first period, at a quantity of 200 and a price of 100. We will call this the **static equilibrium**—the market equilibrium that will prevail if only present costs and benefits are considered.[2]

### Balancing Present and Future Periods

Now let's consider the marginal net benefit of copper in the second time period. We cannot know this value for sure, of course, because no one can foretell the future, but we *do* know that a fixed quantity of copper must be divided between the two periods. Let's make a simplifying assumption that the marginal net benefit of copper in Period 2 will be *exactly the same* as in Period 1. (This assumption is not necessary for the analysis, but it will make our first example simpler.)

A graphical trick will allow us to compare the two periods. We use the horizontal axis to measure the total available quantity of copper—say, 250 units—and put the marginal net benefit curve for the first period, $MNB_1$ on this graph in the usual way. Then we put the marginal net benefit curve for the second period, $MNB_2$, as on the graph in mirror-image fashion, going from right to left. Thus we have two horizontal scales, with the quantity used in Period 1 shown left to right, and the quantity used in Period 2 shown right to left (Figure 5-2).

One more step will complete our analysis. Because we want to compare two time periods, we must translate future values into their equivalent in present values. The

---

[2]In this chapter we assume that copper production has no associated externalities. The impact of externalities on nonrenewable resource extraction will be discussed in Chapter 12.

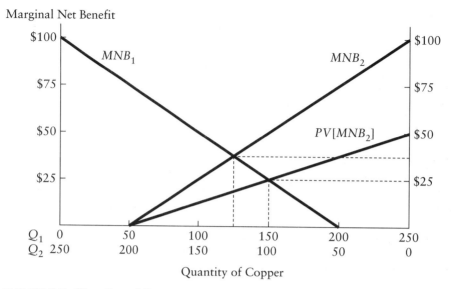

Marginal Net Benefit

**FIGURE 5-2** *Allocation of Copper over Two Time Periods*

economic concept of **present value** relies on use of a **discount rate** to convert future to present monetary values. Suppose, for example, I promise to give you $1,000—ten years from now. What is the value of this promise today?

Assuming I am trustworthy and you will definitely receive the money, the answer depends on the discount rate, reflected in financial terms as a rate of interest on deposits. Let us assume a 7.25 percent interest rate.[3] Five hundred dollars put in the bank today at compound interest would be worth almost exactly $1,000 in ten years. We can say that the present value of $1,000 to be received ten years from now is equal to $500 in cash today. In other words, you would be equally well off with $500 today or $1,000 ten years from now.[4]

Applying this principle to our copper example, let's assume that the two periods in our copper extraction example are ten years apart. (This assumption of only two extraction periods separated by ten years is of course unrealistic—but the principle that emerges from this mathematically simple example can be generalized to an *n*-period model.) Using the present value method we can convert the marginal net benefit of copper in Period 2 into Period 1 values. We do this using the formula

$$PV[MNB_2] = MNB_2/(1+r)^n$$

---

[3]For this example, we will assume this is a real interest rate, corrected for expected inflation.

[4]You might prefer to have an actual $500 to spend today. You can do so by borrowing $500 at 7.25 percent interest and paying off the loan plus accumulated interest, totaling $1,000, in ten years' time.

where $r$ is the annual discount rate and $n$ is the number of years between periods. If $r = 0.0725$ or 7.25%, and $n = 10$, we can closely approximate $PV[MNB_2]$ as

$$MNB_2/(1.0725)^{10} = MNB_2/2.$$

This present value of marginal net benefit schedule for Period 2 is shown in Figure 5-2 as a line exactly half the height of the undiscounted $MNB_2$.

## Dynamic Equilibrium for Two Periods

The reason for the special graphical format now becomes apparent. Consider the point where the two curves $MNB_1$ and $PV[MNB_2]$ cross. At this point the present value of the marginal net benefit of 1 unit of copper is *the same* in both time periods. This is the optimum economic allocation between periods since at this point no additional net benefit can be obtained by shifting consumption from one period to another. As you can see from the graph, this optimal allocation is 150 units in Period 1 and 100 units in Period 2. Algebraically, we obtain this solution by solving two equations:

$$MNB_1 = PV[MNB_2]$$

and

$$Q_1 + Q_2 = 250$$

The second equation is the **supply constraint,** which tells us that the quantities used in the two periods must sum to exactly 250, the total quantity available.

We can solve the equations as follows:

$$MNB_1 = 100 - 0.5Q_1 = MNB_2 = (100 - 0.5Q_2)/2$$

$$100 - 0.5Q_1 = 50 - 0.25Q_2$$

Because $Q_1 + Q_2 = 250$, $Q_1 = 250 - Q_2$. Substituting this in we have:

$$100 - 0.5(250 - Q_2) = 50 - 0.25Q_2$$

$$0.75Q_2 = 75$$

$$Q_1 = 150; Q_2 = 100$$

We can check the assertion that this solution is economically optimal by using the kind of welfare analysis introduced in Chapter 3 (see Figure 5-3). By choosing the equilibrium point where $Q_1 = 150$ and $Q_2 = 100$, we have achieved maximum total net benefit, shown by the shaded area $A + B$ in Figure 5-3a. (Area $A$ is the net benefit in the first period, area $B$ the net benefit in the second period.)

**FIGURE 5-3** *Different Intertemporal Resource Allocations*

Compare this result with the welfare effects of any other allocation, for example, the allocation $Q_1 = 200$, $Q_2 = 50$. As shown in Figure 5-3b, total welfare for the two periods is less with this new allocation (by the area $B_2$). By shifting 50 units from Period 2 use to Period 1 use, we have gained a first-period benefit equal to $A_2$, but lost a second-period benefit equal to $A_2 + B_2$, for a net loss of $B_2$. Total welfare is now $A_1 + A_2 + B_1$, less than the area $A + B$ in Figure 5-3a. Similarly, any other allocation we try will prove inferior to the optimal solution of $Q_1 = 150$, $Q_2 = 100$. (Try, for example, $Q_1 = 100$, $Q_2 = 150$. Show the effect of this allocation on total net benefit.)

## User Costs and Resource Depletion

Let's translate what we have learned from this algebraic and graphical analysis into more commonsense terms. We know that we can increase our benefit today by using more copper (in this example up to 200 units, which is the most we would use today if we took no account of future needs). If we chose to use only 50 units today, 200 would be left for the next period—enough to fulfill the maximum demand in that period. At any use level greater than 50 units, we start to cut into the amount of copper available for future use.

Another way of putting this would be to say that we start *imposing costs on future consumers of copper* by using up copper today. On our graph, those **user costs** show up as the steadily rising curve $PV[MNB_2]$. The more we use today, the higher these costs become. User costs are in fact a different kind of third-party cost or externality—*externalities in time*.

We can justify using up copper today so long as the benefits from doing so outweigh user costs imposed on future citizens. But once the user costs become higher than the benefits from consumption today—in our example, at any level of present consumption above 150 units—we reduce total economic welfare by our excessive present consumption.

Going back to our algebraic and graphical analysis, we define an exact value for the user cost at the Period 1 consumption level we have defined as optimal. The vertical distance to the intersection point of $MNB_1$ and $PV[MNB_2]$ shows the user cost at equilibrium. We can calculate this easily by evaluating either $MNB_1$ or $PV[MNB_2]$ at the intersection point where $Q_1 = 150$ and $Q_2 = 100$:

$$\text{user cost} = MNB_1 = 100 - 0.5(150) = 25$$

or

$$= PV[MNB_2] = 50 - 0.25(100) = 25$$

The user cost at equilibrium is thus $25.

What does this mean? Suppose we go back to the original supply and demand schedules for Period 1 (redrawn in Figure 5-4a). If we don't consider Period 2 at all, the market equilibrium in Period 1 will be 200 units of copper at a price of $100. Now suppose we add to the ordinary supply costs the user cost derived from Figure 5-2— just as we added an environmental external cost to the ordinary supply costs in the previous section. The result is shown in Figure 5-4a as the **social cost** schedule $S'$.

**(a) Market for Copper with User Costs (First Period)**

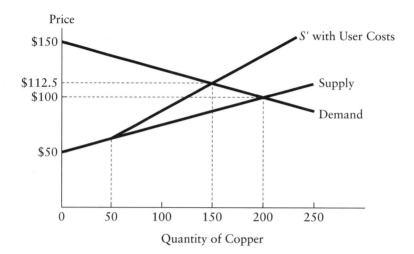

**(b) Market for Copper (Second Period)**

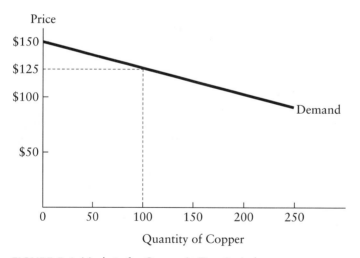

**FIGURE 5-4** *Markets for Copper in Two Periods*

A new equilibrium appears at 150 units of copper consumption, with a price of $112.50. The user cost at this new equilibrium is $25—the vertical distance between the old supply curve $S$ and the new social cost curve $S'$. With a first-period consumption of 150 units, 100 units will remain for consumption in the second period, at a second-period price of $125 (assuming demand conditions are unchanged).[5] This is shown in Figure 5-4b.

If user costs are internalized in this fashion, the new market equilibrium, known as **dynamic equilibrium,** reflects *both* the needs of the present and of the future. The higher price will send a signal to producers and consumers of the resource to produce and use less today, thereby conserving more for the future. But how will user costs be reflected in the market?

One possibility is a **resource depletion tax** imposed on copper ore production and sales. Like a pollution tax, this tax will raise the effective supply schedule to the real social cost $S'$. Other policy mechanisms could include direct government control of resource exploitation, setting aside resource deposits or maintaining stockpiles.

In certain cases, however, the market may not need government intervention to internalize user costs. This would be true especially if the time period until expected resource exhaustion is relatively short. In this case, private owners of the resource will anticipate the second-period situation and act accordingly.

If resource shortages are foreseen, profit-seeking resource owners will hold some copper stocks off the market or leave copper ores in the ground and wait for the higher prices likely to prevail in a shortage. This supply limitation will have exactly the same effect (a leftward and upward shift of the supply curve to $S'$) as the imposition of a resource depletion tax. In this case no tax is necessary—the market process will automatically adjust for anticipated future limits on copper resources.

## Hotelling's Rule and Time Discounting

What if we want to consider the real world, which presents not two periods but an infinite number of future periods? How much copper should we be prepared to set aside for 50 years from now? One hundred years? Extending our two-period analysis to a more general theory offers perspective on these issues. Such questions test the limits of our economic model and also address the interrelationship between social values and the more specific market values we deal with in economic theory.

---

[5]We can calculate the new first- and second-period prices using the original equations for the supply and demand schedules, with $25 added to the first-period supply schedule to reflect the user cost. For the first period this gives us

$$P_d = 150 - 0.25Q_1 \quad \text{and} \quad P_s = 75 + 0.25Q_1$$

Setting these equal and solving, the first-period equilibrium is

$$Q_1 = 150, \quad P_1 = 112.5$$

Because we know only 100 units remain for the second period, we can use the demand curve for the second period (which we assumed to be the same) to solve for the second-period price:

$$P_2 = 150 - 0.25(100) = 150 - 25 = 125$$

Our simple two-period example makes clear that the discount rate is a critical variable. At different discount rates, the optimal allocation of copper between the two periods will vary significantly. Let's start at one extreme—a discount rate of zero. In the example, the equilibrium allocation of copper would be 125 units consumed in each period. At a discount rate of zero, future net benefits receive *exactly the same value* as if they were current net benefits. The available copper is therefore divided evenly between the periods.

At any discount rate above zero, we favor present consumption over future consumption to some degree. At a high discount rate—say 50 percent per annum—the first-period allocation of copper is 198 units, close to the 200 units consumed in the static equilibrium case, and user costs fall nearly to zero. In general, at high discount rates we weight present benefits much more heavily than future benefits (see Figure 5-5 and Table 5-1).

We can extend this logic from one period to many periods, and even to an infinite future. The principle involved is known as **Hotelling's rule.** This rule states that in equilibrium the resource **net price** (defined as the price minus extraction costs) must rise at a rate equal to the rate of interest.

Consider an example from the perspective of a copper ore deposit owner. The owner's profit per unit extracted is equal to the net price. In deciding whether or not to produce and sell the copper, the owner will weigh the net price available today against a possible higher future net price. If the present net price, plus interest, exceeds the probable future net price, the owner will profit more by extracting the resource today and investing the proceeds, rather than waiting. If the expected future net price is higher than the net price today plus interest, it will be more profitable to sell at the future date.

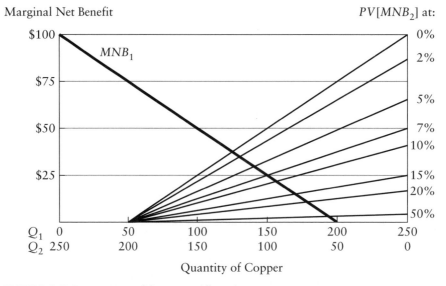

**FIGURE 5-5** *Intertemporal Resource Allocation*

**TABLE 5-1** *Different Discount Rates for Intertemporal Resource Allocation*

| Discount Rate (%) | $(1 + r)^{10}$ | $Q_1$ | $Q_2$ |
|---|---|---|---|
| 0 | 1.0 | 125 | 125 |
| 2 | 1.2 | 132 | 118 |
| 5 | 1.6 | 143 | 107 |
| 7.5 | 2.0 | 150 | 100 |
| 10 | 2.6 | 158 | 92 |
| 15 | 4.0 | 170 | 80 |
| 20 | 6.2 | 179 | 71 |
| 50 | 57.7 | 198 | 52 |

If all resource owners follow this logic, the quantity of copper supplied today will increase until today's copper price falls low enough to encourage resource owners to conserve, hoping for a better future price. At this point Hotelling's rule will hold: The expectations of future price increases will exactly follow an exponential curve $P_1(1+r)^n$, where $P_1$ is today's net price, $r$ is the discount rate, and $n$ is the number of years from the present (see Figure 5-6).

If this sounds confusing, consider this simpler, commonsense formulation: High discount rates create an incentive to use resources quickly; low discount rates create

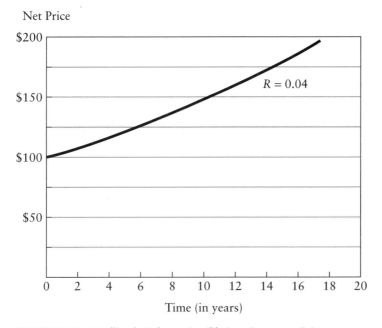

**FIGURE 5-6** *Hotelling's Rule on Equilibrium Resource Price*

greater incentive to conserve. More generally, we can say that economic theory implies the existence of an **optimal depletion rate.** Under market conditions, a nonrenewable resource will be used up at a certain "optimal" rate, and this rate will be faster at higher discount rates.[6]

Interestingly, according to this theory it is optimal to deplete certain resources to complete exhaustion over a period of time—the higher the discount rate, the shorter the time. Like the theory of optimal pollution, this sounds wrong to many people. What about the ethical imperative to leave something for future generations?

The answer in economic terms is that a discount rate based on standard commercial rates of interest will give a low weight to the well-being of future generations.[7] This leads some people to question whether we can justifiably apply present-value analysis, based on a discount rate, over long periods of time. This issue will be important in our discussion of valuation and cost/benefit analysis in Chapter 6 and of long-term sustainability in Chapter 7.

Another issue that affects the theory of exhaustible resources concerns the presence of environmental externalities in resource extraction. In this chapter we simply assumed no externalities in the production of copper, so the supply and demand curves for copper accurately reflected its social costs and benefits. In the real world, copper mining is likely to create significant environmental impacts. As higher-quality copper ores are used up, the environmental costs of recovering copper from lower-grade ores will probably rise; internalizing these costs would affect the market price and intertemporal allocation of copper. In addition, a market for recycled copper is likely to develop, providing a new source of market supply not considered in our basic analysis. Issues such as these will be dealt with more fully in Chapter 12.

## SUMMARY

Nonrenewable resources can be used in the present or conserved for future use. Economic theory offers some guidance concerning the principles of nonrenewable resource allocation over time. In essence, the net value gained from using a resource today must be balanced against the net value of its potential future use. To compare values across time periods, we use a discount rate to measure the present value of future consumption.

The concept of user costs captures the idea that, by using resources today, we impose some cost on future potential consumers. User cost is a kind of externality in time, and like other externalities should be reflected in market price to internalize all social costs. Including user costs in market price will reduce consumption today, leaving more for future use.

---

[6]We will examine the relationship of resource prices and resource extraction patterns in more detail in Chapter 12.

[7]See, for example, Howarth and Norgaard, 1995.

If resource owners foresee future resource shortages, current prices will reflect user costs. The expectation that prices will rise creates an incentive to hold resources off the market today in order to sell them at a higher price in the future. According to Hotelling's rule, in equilibrium the net price of a resource (market price minus extraction costs) must rise at a rate equal to the rate of interest. The higher the interest rate, the more likely the owner is to profit from extracting and selling a nonrenewable resource today rather than waiting for future higher prices.

Especially in figuring for long time periods, discounting reduces the significance of user costs almost to zero and creates little market incentive for conserving nonrenewable resources. If governments wish to ensure a long-term supply of certain resources, they can internalize user costs through a resource depletion tax—much as a pollution tax can internalize current externalities.

The alternative may be to exploit nonrenewable resources to exhaustion, leaving no reserves for future use. A major question is whether it is appropriate to use current discount rates to determine the allocation of resources over the long term, or whether we have a social obligation to conserve resources for future generations.

## KEY TERMS AND CONCEPTS

discount rate
dynamic equilibrium
Hotelling's rule
marginal net benefit
net price
nonrenewable resources
optimal depletion rate
present value

renewable resources
resource depletion tax
social cost
static equilibrium
supply constraint
total net benefit
user costs

## DISCUSSION QUESTIONS

1. It has been argued that any government policy aimed at nonrenewable resource conservation is an unwarranted interference with the free market. According to this point of view, the people most likely to realize that a resource is likely to become scarce are the private investors and traders who deal in the resource. If they anticipate scarcity, they will hold stocks of the resource for future profit, driving up its price and leading to conservation. Any action by government bureaucrats is likely to be less well informed than that of profit-motivated private firms. Evaluate this argument. Do you think that in some cases government should step in to conserve specific resources? If so, what policy tools should government use?

2. How could the principle of resource allocation over time be applied to environmental resources such as groundwater supplies or species diversity? Would the same kind of conclusions about optimal depletion apply or not?

## PROBLEMS

We can modify the interperiod allocation model to deal with the issue of intergenerational allocation of resources. Suppose a generation is thirty-five years and we are concerned with two generations only. Demand and supply functions for oil in the present generation are given by

$$\text{Demand: } Q_d = 200 - 5P \text{ or } P = 40 - 0.2Q_d$$

$$\text{Supply: } Q_s = 5P \text{ or } P = 0.2Q_s$$

1. Draw a demand and supply graph showing the equilibrium price and quantity consumed in this generation in the absence of any consideration of the future. Now draw a graph showing the marginal net benefits from consumption in this period at all levels of consumption up to the equilibrium level. Express the net benefit (benefit minus cost) algebraically.

2. Suppose the net benefit function is expected to be the same for the next generation, but a discount rate (interest rate) of 4 percent per annum for 35 years works out to $(1.04)^{35}$, approximately equal to 4. Total oil supply for both generations is limited to 100 units. Calculate the efficient allocation of resources between the two generations and show this graphically. (Set marginal benefits equal for the two periods, remembering to include the discount rate.)

3. What is marginal user cost for this efficient allocation? If you include this user cost in your original supply and demand graph, what is the new equilibrium? If the demand curve is the same in the second generation, what will be the price and quantity consumed in that period?

4. How would the answers differ if we used a zero discount rate? What can you conclude from this example about the general problem of allocation of resources over long time periods?

## REFERENCES

Hartwick, J. M. "Intergenerational Equity and the Investing of Rents from Exhaustible Resources." *American Economic Review* 66 (1977): 972–974.

Hotelling, Harold. "The Economics of Exhaustible Resources." *Journal of Political Economy* 39 (April 1931): 137–175.

Howarth, Richard B., and Richard B. Norgaard. "Intergenerational Choices under Global Environmental Change," in *Handbook of Environmental Economics*, edited by Daniel W. Bromley. Cambridge, Mass. and Oxford, U.K.: Basil Blackwell, 1995.

Solow, R. M. "On the Intertemporal Allocation of Natural Resources." *Scandinavian Journal of Economics* 88 (1986): 141–149.

## WEBSITES

1. **http://ideas.repec.org/a/fip/fedfer/y1988ifallp41-54.html** A paper examining the application of Hotelling's rule to exhaustible resource pricing and depletion.

2. **http://hadm.sph.sc.edu/courses/econ/dis/dis.html** A website with an interactive tutorial about discounting and present values.

3. **http://dieoff.org/page87.htm** A paper by Robert Costanza titled "Three General Policies to Achieve Sustainability." The paper includes a discussion of a natural capital depletion tax.

CHAPTER **6**

# Valuing the Environment

## Cost-Benefit Analysis

Environmental policy tools that work through market mechanisms—for example, taxes, subsidies, and transferable permits—leave the final decisions on resource use and goods production up to firms and individuals. The government acts to modify market outcomes, but not to determine the exact result. In some cases, however, governments must make specific decisions that have both economic and environmental implications. In such cases, decision-makers often use **cost-benefit analysis (CBA)**[1] to balance the positive and negative consequences of a proposed action.

Take the example of a proposed government project: the construction of a large dam. The project will have major economic benefits: hydroelectric power, a stable water supply for irrigation, and flood control. It will also have negative effects: Farmland and wildlife habitat will be flooded, communities will have to relocate, and certain fish species may become extinct. The project may create new recreational

---

[1]The terms "cost-benefit analysis" and "benefit-cost analysis" have the same meaning. We will use "cost-benefit analysis," the more common term, here.

opportunities for lake boating and fishing, but it will reduce scenic whitewater rafting and hiking.

How can we evaluate whether or not to build the dam? Some costs and benefits are relatively easy to assess. We can probably obtain good estimates of the construction costs of the dam, and of the value of hydroelectric power and irrigation water, for example. But how can we put a dollar value on the social and ecological losses that will result?

## Estimating Value

Economists use various techniques to estimate different kinds of values. The most obvious kind of value is **use value.** In this example, the value of farmland used for raising crops is a **direct use value,** which can be measured by its market price. Certainly farmers whose land is submerged by the dam waters will suffer losses at least equal to the value of their farms. These should be included in our estimates of costs associated with dam construction. Rafting on a river or hiking through the woods are also direct uses that benefit those who enjoy these activities, although the benefits may be more difficult to measure in monetary terms.

**Indirect use values** include ways in which forested lands and wetlands benefit nearby communities by filtering rainfall, preventing flooding, and absorbing potential pollution. These **environmental services** provide real economic benefits, but they may be less evident than something like crop value.

In addition to direct and indirect use values, we must also consider important kinds of **non-use values.** How can something be valuable if it is not used? Consider the fish species that might be made extinct by building the dam. Even if these species have no commercial value, many people might believe that they should be preserved. Some might argue that other species have their own rights to exist, independent of human valuation, or that the existence of many different species means that we ourselves live in a richer world—richer in an esthetic and spiritual rather than a monetary sense. In addition, we may not have a full understanding of ways in which maintaining biological diversity improves the health of ecosystems, so we may be wise to maintain diversity even without obvious benefit. We can therefore say that the endangered fish species have **existence value.** Though difficult to measure, existence value has a good theoretical justification: In economics, value is considered to flow from our desires and preferences. If we as a society prefer that endangered species not be driven to extinction, we are placing value on them, and this value may be quite high even if it is not evident in the market.

Another non-use value is **option value.** If we decide to build the dam, the flooded farms and forests will be lost forever—the decision is characterized by **irreversibility.** On the other hand, if we decide not to build the dam today, the farms and forests will be preserved, but we could still build the dam ten or twenty years from now. Thus we can preserve the option of building or preserving by simply doing nothing.

Option values are important because economies change over time, and so do the direct and indirect values of different goods, services, and environmental assets. Farmland or undeveloped natural areas might become more valuable in the future; on the other hand, the

**TABLE 6-1** *Categories of Value*

| Use Values | Non-use Values |
| --- | --- |
| Direct use value | Existence value |
| Indirect use value | Option value |
| | Bequest value |

need for hydroelectric power or irrigation water might become much greater. In either case, the decision on the dam might be made with better information at a later date.[2]

Major decisions on resource use should also take into account the value of leaving an undamaged or improved world for future generations, which economists identify as **bequest value.** Bequest value is important to individuals; it is why we make wills leaving instructions for handling our estates after our deaths. Clearly existence and bequest values are essential to environmental decision making, even though they may be difficult to put in monetary terms. The various different categories of value are summarized in Table 6-1.

## Techniques of Valuation

How can we obtain an economic measure of these different kinds of value? Economists use a variety of techniques to put **nonmarket values** such as whitewater rafting or the pollution-absorption services of a wetland into dollar terms.

### Contingent Valuation

One such approach is called **contingent valuation.** This is essentially a survey method, in which people are asked how much they would be willing to pay to preserve rafting or hiking opportunities or other environmental functions. The resulting estimate of **willingness to pay (WTP)** can be included in a cost-benefit analysis—although its reliability may be subject to challenge.

Questions arise concerning the accuracy of such survey answers. Their hypothetical nature—with no actual money involved—might lead some respondents to give unrealistically high valuations. Also, respondents might have limited knowledge of functions such as wetland pollution-absorption, leading them to underestimate the real benefits of wetland preservation.

Sometimes economists estimate **willingness to accept (WTA)** rather than willingness to pay. In the dam example, people might be asked how large a payment would adequately compensate them for the loss of hiking and rafting opportunities. WTA estimates are often much higher in dollar value than WTP estimates for the same items. This has led critics to question the usefulness of the contingent valuation approach.

---

[2]If we take this logic to its extreme, of course, we would never make any decisions on resource use—which is why we weigh option values against other values.

Consider an example. Suppose you were asked, as part of a contingent valuation survey, how much you would be prepared to pay to prevent the extinction of the blue whale, the largest animal on earth (and one of the most endangered). Depending on your level of concern, you might be willing to contribute, say, $100 to a preservation effort that you thought might be effective. Unless you were very wealthy, a significantly larger amount such as $1,000 would almost certainly be too high.[3]

But now suppose the question was phrased in WTA terms. Would you accept $1,000 to give the go-ahead for the extinction of the blue whale? Most likely you would regard such a proposal as ethically unacceptable. People who are concerned about the growing problem of species extinction might well refuse *any* amount offered. Using a WTP estimate in cost-benefit analysis may thus understate the real value of environmental assets and services, in effect tilting the playing field against environmental preservation.

This disparity between WTP and WTA is a recognized problem in economic theory, often applying to marketed as well as nonmarketed goods, but it acquires particular importance in the economic valuation of environmental issues.[4] Unlike a more ordinary economic transaction such as the purchase of a house, placing a price tag on the environment involves serious ethical and philosophical considerations. Economic values are clearly important in decision making, but can the true value of environmental preservation really be expressed in dollar terms?

Although one response would be that some things are indeed priceless, many actual decisions on environmental issues do depend on dollar values. Land preservation organizations such as The Nature Conservancy are familiar with this dilemma. Often, the reality is that if the money can be raised to preserve a natural area, it will be saved; otherwise, it will be lost to other, economically profitable uses. So even those who resent economists' efforts to put a money value on everything cannot avoid dealing with the issue of economic valuation.[5] In some cases, economic valuation studies can quantify significant public support for environmental conservation (see Box 6-1).

## Demand-Side Methods

Other techniques of valuation more closely relate to people's actual market decisions. **Hedonic pricing** attempts to value environmental services as they relate to the value of marketed goods. For example, the value of a house situated next to a conservation area is likely to be higher than that of a comparable house situated next to the town

---

[3]In a survey, not an actual contribution, you might of course claim that you were willing to pay $1,000 or more. Unless you would be prepared to back that up with real money, your inflated estimate is an example of **strategic bias**—you are attempting to bias the survey upward by stating an amount that exceeds your actual willingness to pay.

[4]A study by Horowitz and McConnell (2002) finds that the disparity between WTP and WTA is largest for nonmarketed goods such as land preservation, for which WTA exceeds WTP by a factor of 7.

[5]See the Symposium on Contingent Valuation in *Journal of Economic Perspectives* 8, no. 4 (1994) for a debate between proponents (Portney, 1994; Hanneman, 1994) and critics (Diamond and Hausman, 1994) of the use of survey techniques for valuation. Ackerman and Heinzerling, 2004, offer a strong critique of valuation in cost-benefit analysis.

## 6-1    How Much Is a Wolf Worth?

The gray wolf was one of the first animals listed under the United States Endangered Species Act of 1973. Since then, the wolf population in the northern Midwest has increased. This has often led to opposition from ranchers and others who suffer stock damage from wolves. Conservationists, and many members of the public, support wolf protection and reintroduction plans. Wolves symbolize the values of wilderness, and the presence of wolves has significant ecological benefits. By controlling deer and elk populations, wolves prevent overgrazing and promote diverse ecosystems. But they clearly cause economic losses to ranchers, farmers, hunters (whose valuable trained dogs are sometimes killed by wolves), and game farm managers. Do the benefits of wolves outweigh the costs?

Economists have attempted to answer this question through contingent valuation surveys. In a Minnesota survey, respondents were asked about their willingness to pay (WTP), a one-time tax increase to support the costs of a wolf management plan and a fund to reimburse those who suffer damage from wolves. The results indicated that respondents who live in areas near wolves have a median WTP of $5, while residents who live in central Minnesota, at a distance from wolf habitat, have a median WTP of $21. While some people were not willing to pay anything, others indicated motives for favoring wolf conservation including ethical, existence, and bequest values.

For the whole state, the aggregate WTP for wolf management is $27 million, and another $25 million for wolf damage. These amounts, if placed in a trust fund, would yield an annual income of $1.5 million for the management fund and $1.4 million for the damage fund—well above the estimated annual costs of $342,000 and $158,000, respectively. Based on these figures, the authors of the study conclude that "annual benefits exceed annual costs, indicating that the wolf population management and damage plans are efficient government policies."

### SOURCES

Chambers, Catherine M., and John C. Whitehead. "A Contingent Valuation Estimate of the Benefits of Wolves in Minnesota." *Environmental and Resource Economics* 26 (2003): 249–267.

Gorman, James. "Wolves Come Back (On Their Terms)." *New York Times,* March 16, 2004.

dump. By an econometric analysis of the various attributes that determine housing values (size, location, access to schools, and so forth), we may isolate the effect of specific environmental factors.[6] This gives a basis for estimation of a demand curve for environmental quality, which in turn allows us to estimate the benefits and costs associated with various environmental and land-use policies.[7]

Hedonic pricing has the advantage of being based on actual market decisions rather than hypothetical questions. It also has drawbacks. Separating environmental variables from other factors such as neighborhood racial makeup may be difficult. Also, hedonic analysis assumes that house buyers have perfect information about environmental quality. While hedonic price studies can often detect the influence of environmental quality, studies vary considerably in their dollar value estimates (for example, estimates of the effect of distance from a hazardous waste site on house prices vary from about $200 per mile to about $11,000 per mile).[8]

Another market-related technique is the **travel cost method.** This can be used to value the recreational attributes of environmental resources such as parks and scenic areas. A survey of visitors to a national park can indicate how far they have traveled to reach the park and estimate the amount they have spent (gas, tolls, fares, entry fees, and the value of time spent traveling) to enjoy the park's amenities. Such data can be used to simulate a demand curve, indicating how many people are willing to visit the park at different total costs for the trip. The area under the demand curve indicates the total value of the park to its visitors (using the welfare analysis outlined in Chapter 3). Note that this approach cannot represent the full ecological value of the park, nor does it capture option, existence, or bequest values.

Travel cost does, however, reflect actual choices by consumers, and often suggests greater valuations than those obtained by contingent valuation (CV) surveys. In studies of the economic value of national parks in Australia, for example, the travel-cost method consistently led to higher estimates than the CV method. Travel-cost studies of the Mount Buffalo National Park in Victoria, Australia, yielded an average estimated value of Aus $11 million (U.S. $8.25 million) for annual tourism benefits provided by the park, or about Aus $45 (U.S. $33) per visit. CV estimates were only about one-third of this amount. Both estimates were well above the current park entry fees, leading the study authors to conclude that "the economic value of the park is high and there are opportunities to introduce innovative fee schemes to enhance its revenue."[9]

## Supply-Side Methods

Whereas hedonic and travel cost methods derive value estimates from the demand side of the market, **production function** and **engineering cost** methods are based on the supply side. Here the goal is to evaluate the cost to duplicate or replace environmental

[6]Econometric analysis uses statistical techniques to estimate economic relationships.
[7]For a detailed description of the hedonic valuation method, see Hanley and Spash, 1998.
[8]Boyle and Kiel, 2001; this article provides an overview of hedonic valuation studies.
[9]Herath and Kennedy, 2004.

services. For example, a pollution treatment plant might replace wetland pollution-absorption capabilities. We can obtain engineering estimates of the size and nature of the facility required, then calculate the cost of building and operating such a plant. If the wetland is preserved, building and operating the treatment plant is unnecessary, and this **avoided cost** can provide an estimate of the value of wetland pollution control services.

In cases where individuals or corporations are liable for environmental damages, **replacement cost** or, in the case of damaged ecosystems, **habitat equivalency analysis** can estimate the monetary value of the required restitution. For example, suppose an oil spill destroys a wetland. The company responsible can be required to pay an amount sufficient either to restore the wetland to its prior ecological function, or—if that is not possible—to create a comparable wetland nearby. The cost estimates generated by these methods are typically significantly higher than those based on demand-side studies.[10]

A combination of demand and supply side methods can be used to derive an estimated dollar value for environmental services.[11] How valid are these estimates? The answer may depend on how broad a view we wish to take of the concept of value. We may often obtain a fairly good approximation of the purely **economic value** involved. However, the broader concept of **ecological value** is less easy to define.

Note that all the measures we have discussed refer to value to humans, and are defined in terms of people's ability or willingness to pay, or the capacity to provide substitutes through human productive activity. Some environmental issues, such as the preservation of endangered species, are difficult to define in such terms. We cannot recreate a species once it is extinct; we do not usually think of whole species as commodities with a market value (though individual members of a species can be bought and sold); and we may not even understand the relationships between species and their complex interactions in ecosystems. Thus although economic estimates may capture part of the value of a species (as food or as a source of medicinal products, for example), the total value may transcend economic analysis.[12]

Debate continues concerning the potential and the limits of economic valuation of environmental costs and benefits. Some issues, such as the valuation of human life, are especially controversial (see Box 6-2). We will consider this and other valuation problems in more depth later in this chapter. First, however, we need to address a specific issue of considerable importance to economic valuation: the question of time. How do we value the future? How can we balance costs and benefits today with costs and benefits at another time? Will our evaluation change depending on whether we are considering a

[10]See Woodward and Wui, 2001, and Dunford et al., 2004.

[11]For an extensive overview of valuation methods, see Smith, 1996; Hanley and Spash, 1998; and Markandya and Richardson, 1993. The application of valuation techniques to specific projects is discussed, with case studies, in Dixon et al., 1997.

[12]For differing approaches to this issue, see Pearce and Moran, 1997; Daily, 1997. For practical case studies in environmental valuation, see Garrod and Willis, 1999; Rietbergen-McCracken and Abaza, 2000.

## 6-2  Valuing Human Health and Life

**H**ow do economists value human lives? Shouldn't life be beyond monetary value? Such questions are sometimes unavoidable in performing environmental cost-benefit analyses. For example, policies for tighter control of pesticide residues may reduce the amount of cancer-causing chemicals to which children and adults are exposed (children's exposure can be a more serious concern since growing bodies may be more vulnerable to damaging effects). Such tighter regulation might cause increased production costs in the agricultural sector—say, increased labor costs to implement integrated pest management, which limits chemical use. But to measure the benefits we must place money value on reduced incidence of cancer.

One obvious measure would be the avoided cost of health care for cancer patients. To evaluate this, we need a reliable scientific estimate of the probable reduction in cancer cases, which we would multiply by the average cost of hospital care to obtain a measure of total medical costs. But what about avoided cancer deaths? Suppose our evidence indicates that several deaths per year will be avoided. How can we balance that with the increased production costs involved? Can we find an appropriate value for a life?

We might propose a simple economic estimate of what an individual contributes in terms of production of goods and services to society. This, however, would assign the life of a CEO a dollar value many times that of a manual worker, a valuation many would consider unjustified. Alternatively, if we consider what people spend on life insurance and safety precautions, we can derive an estimated value, usually in the range of several million dollars, for a human life. If, for example, someone is willing to accept a hazardous job with a one-in-one-hundred chance of death in return for an extra $20,000 in income, this implies a life valuation of $(100)(\$20,000) = \$2$ million. Or if someone is willing to spend an extra $500 for car safety features that reduce the chances of a fatal accident by 1 in 10,000, he or she is setting an implicit value of $(\$500)(10,000) = \$5$ million on his or her life.

Clearly, this kind of estimate cannot capture the full value of life. Few of us would be prepared to die for $5 million. Rather, it indicates the value of what economists call a "statistical life," based on demonstrated willingness to pay to avoid risks to life.

Many of us might object to having the value of our lives expressed in economic terms. Yet if we reject monetary valuation, we must either set the value of life at zero, which is clearly wrong, or make it infinite—meaning that *no* risks of any sort could be tolerated, which is impossible. This dilemma cannot be resolved by economists alone—it involves political and ethical judgments as well.[1]

-----

[1]For more on this debate, see Ackerman and Heinzerling, 2004, Chapter 4, and Viscusi, 1998.

period a few years from now, or several generations in the future? Many environmental issues have long-term consequences, so the question of time is a critical aspect of valuation.

## Balancing Present and Future: The Discount Rate

Economists evaluate future costs and benefits with a technique called discounting. In Chapter 5, we discussed the use of discounting for resource allocation over time. More generally, discounting, applied to *any* cost or benefit expected in the future, provides an estimate of its **present value.**

The theory behind discounting is that a dollar today is worth more than a dollar tomorrow—even correcting for inflation. The **discount rate** is the annual rate at which dollar values are considered to increase over time. Thus at an 8 percent discount rate, $1.00 today becomes $1.08 next year and $(\$1.00)(1.08^{10}) = \$2.16$ 10 years from now. Similarly, $1.00 to be received 10 years from now is worth $(\$1.00)/(1.08^{10}) = \$0.46$ today. Use of a discount rate makes sense for most financial calculations. However, its application to environmental costs and benefits is more complicated.

For longer time periods, the discount factor becomes much more dramatic. The present value of $1,000 to be received 50 years from now is only $87.20 at a 5 percent discount rate. And the present value of $1,000 to be received in 100 years is only $7.60 today (see Figure 6-1). This would mean that, according to present value theory, it is not worth spending more than $7.60 today to avoid $1,000 worth of damages 100 years from now. This has led to another serious criticism of the economic perspective. How can we justify a technique that may evaluate serious damages to future generations as less important than moderate costs today?

Discounting is essential if we consider the economics of, for example, taking a mortgage to buy a house or a loan to finance a business investment. The benefits of being able to own and live in the house starting today may well outweigh the future costs of paying interest on the mortgage over the next 20 years. Similarly, the income generated by the business investment can be compared to the annual payments on the loan.

In this case it makes sense to use the commercial discount rate, determined in current markets, to compare present benefits and future costs. Even so, can we say that a GNP gain today, or in the near future, outweighs major damage in the next generation? How should we evaluate broader environmental impacts that will continue over long periods of time?

### Applying the Discount Rate

In the case of cost-benefit evaluation of a dam project, the choice of discount rate may play a crucial role in the relative weighting of costs and benefits. Three time periods must be considered: the dam construction period (say, 3 years); the period of active dam operation (say, 50 years); and, in the case of dams prone to silting up over time, the period after the dam ceases to provide benefits (see Figure 6-2).

**(a) Present Value of $1,000 at 1% and 2% Discount Rates**

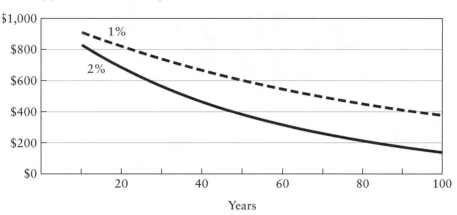

**(b) Present Value of $1,000 at 5% and 10% Discount Rates**

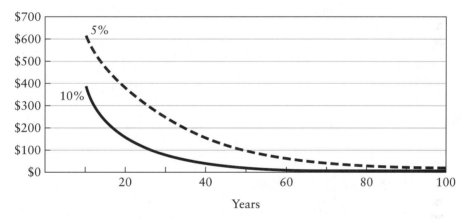

**FIGURE 6-1**  *Present Value of $1,000 at Different Discount Rates*

During the construction period we experience only costs, no benefits. Once the dam starts to operate in the fourth year, we receive benefits such as hydroelectric power, irrigation water, and flood control. But we also pay two types of costs: operating costs and external environmental and social costs (some external costs might begin before dam operation starts, but for simplicity we have assumed here that they start simultaneously with dam operation). During the 50-year expected lifetime of the dam, both benefits and costs must be reckoned. After the dam ceases to operate, the environmental and social costs may continue indefinitely. Thus the evaluation of net present value includes four components: a benefit sum from years 4–53, a construction cost sum from years 1–3, an operating cost sum from years 4–53, and an external cost sum from year 4 to infinity. All of these must be discounted back to year 0, using the formula shown in Figure 6-2. The formula for calculating costs and benefits over time

Costs and Benefits

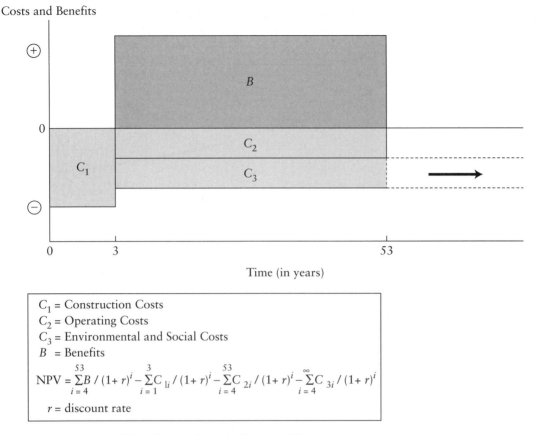

FIGURE 6-2 *Costs and Benefits of a Dam Project over Time*

looks complex, but it merely applies basic discounting theory. The present value of a future benefit in any particular year is given by

$$PV[B_i] = B_i/(1 + r)^i$$

where $i$ is the year in question, and $r$ is the discount rate. To take all future years into account, we compute

$$PV[B] = \sum_{i=1}^{n} B_i/(1 + r)^i$$

Using a similar method to compute the present value of future costs, we can then calculate the **net present value**—total benefits minus total costs—of the dam project as

$$NPV = PV[B] - PV[C]$$

<br>

| 6-3 | The Discount Rate |

If $r$ is the discount rate, the present value $PV[B]$ of a future benefit $B$ expected $n$ years from now is given by: $PV[B] = B/(1+r)^n$

Consider two extreme cases:

**Case 1: $r = 0$**

In this case the future is not discounted at all. Future costs and benefits are weighted as if they took place in the present. This is almost never the case for individuals. We are all mortals and therefore tend to favor the present more than the future. But families or whole societies may put a higher value on the future. Parents may weigh future gains or losses to their children at least as much as consumption today. Societies that set aside land for preservation as national parks and wildlife refuges willingly give up the possibilities of commercial exploitation today in order to guarantee recreational and wilderness areas to future generations.

**Case 2: $r$ is Extremely High**

In this case the future is totally neglected in favor of the short term. This situation can occur in poor societies where the struggle for survival today makes it impossible to devote any resources to future needs. But something like it can also occur in more affluent democratic societies where the vision of decision-makers extends no further than the next election, so that costs that will occur in 10, 20, or 50 years are neglected in favor of present benefits.

Let's look at implications of different discount rates for this evaluation. A *high* discount rate will mean that the benefits of the dam, which start after three years, will have a lower present value (see Box 6-3). This may make it less likely that the dam can be justified on economic grounds. On the other hand, environmental damages resulting from the dam, which may extend far into the future, will also be discounted to a relatively low present value. This might make it more likely that an environmentally destructive project will be approved.

A *low* discount rate will raise the present value of the dam's economic benefits relative to construction costs. At the same time, it will weight long-term environmental damages more heavily. Especially if these damages extend well beyond the useful life of the dam, environmental costs could factor strongly in a decision to cancel the project.

This means that neither a high nor a low discount rate is inherently better for environmental valuation. However, a low rate has been advocated in certain cases on the grounds that it better reflects future interests, including those of future generations. In the case of global climate change, for example, potential damages rise significantly over decades, or even centuries (assuming that emission levels remain high). Some analysts believe that a low discount rate is justified in evaluating these long-term effects. The same argument can be applied to other cumulative environmental problems such as soil erosion, caused by current farming practices but whose most damaging impacts may occur decades later.

### Choosing a Discount Rate

The choice of a discount rate is clearly important in cost-benefit analysis. Government agencies often specify a discount rate to be used in evaluating projects. The U.S. Office of Management and Budget (OMB) recommends the use of the real (inflation-adjusted) rate of return on government bonds. In 2004, these rates ranged from 1.6 percent for 3-year bonds to 3.5 percent for 30-year bonds. At other times, however, rates have been significantly higher. In 1996, OMB suggested a 7 percent rate. International agencies such as the World Bank often use 10 percent for project evaluation. As we have seen, a rate of 7 percent to 10 percent will have a substantial effect in discounting long-term costs or benefits. Also, it seems inconsistent to alter our assessment of long-term environmental problems based on current interest rate fluctuations arising from financial markets that have little to do with the environment.

We can try to resolve the problem by defining a **social discount rate** or **social rate of time preference (SRTP)**—a rate that attempts to reflect the appropriate social valuation of the future. We can define

$$\text{SRTP} = p + \epsilon c$$

where SRTP is the social rate of time preference;

$p$ is the "pure" rate of time preference, representing the human tendency to prefer the present over the future;

$c$ is the growth rate of consumption per capita;

$\epsilon$ is a measure of the rate at which our extra satisfaction from increased consumption declines as consumption increases (in economic terms, the elasticity of the marginal utility of consumption).

From a social point of view, setting $p$ at zero makes sense. Our well-being today is not inherently any more important than that of our children or grandchildren. This means that a positive discount rate must be based on the $\epsilon c$ term in the equation.

The principle behind the $\epsilon c$ term is that extra consumption will be of greater relative value to a poor person than to a rich one. The implication for discounting is that if we expect to be richer in the future, it is reasonable to place a higher value on consumption today (when our unfilled needs are greater) relative to the future. If our children and grandchildren will be richer than we are, favoring consumption today over consumption tomorrow may be somewhat justified.

Long-term rates of growth in per capita consumption over the past several decades have been about 2 percent. Economic studies based on consumption patterns indicate that plausible values for $\epsilon$ are near 1.5. If we set $p$ at zero, this implies a long-term discount rate of no more than 3 percent, perhaps less if we are cautious about the prospects for future growth.[13]

A different method of estimating SRTP is based on the **opportunity cost of capital.** This refers to the rate of return available on alternative investment projects. If society can obtain a 6 percent rate of return on investment, it makes no sense to settle for a project that returns only 3 percent. Estimates based on the opportunity costs of capital tend to be higher than those based on long-term consumption.

From an environmental point of view, however, this method has serious drawbacks. Human-made capital typically lasts 10 to 20 years, or 20 to 50 years for infrastructure investment such as roads and bridges. Current rates of return on investment may overestimate the long-term benefits of such investments compared to even longer-term costs.

Consider, for example, a nuclear power plant. After its productive lifetime of about 40 years, nothing is left for future generations except long-lived radioactive wastes. Even if the plant is profitable in current financial terms, its long-term social impact may be negative. The discount rate used in cost-benefit analysis should give adequate weight to these long-term costs.

The choice of a discount rate remains a controversial issue, and it is not possible to select a single rate that satisfies all the criteria of commercial viability, environmental sustainability, and social responsibility. One way of dealing with this is to use several different discount rates for cost-benefit analysis, which permits a **sensitivity analysis,** showing the relationship of the results to the choice of discount rate.

The dam project, for example, may look good at a moderate discount rate, but at a low rate the long-term environmental costs may outweigh the benefits. Therefore, decision-makers could reach different conclusions regarding net benefits of a project, depending on the relative weighting of present and future values.

Any discount rate selected may be subject to challenge. Some argue that the issue of resource and environmental considerations for the future are a matter of **intergenerational equity** and that our obligation to leave a healthy environment for future generations cannot be measured in economic terms. If we take this approach, we must distinguish between issues that can reasonably be dealt with through the economic system, and issues where moral imperatives for environmental protection must take precedence.[14]

## Dealing with Risk and Uncertainty

The evaluation of future costs and benefits may also involve issues of risk or uncertainty. For example, operating a nuclear power plant involves risk of a serious accident and major release of radiation. How great is this risk? The nuclear industry calls it small, but critics call it substantial. Any cost-benefit analysis of a nuclear power plant would have to take this issue into account.

---

[13]In a study of global climate change, Cline (1992) suggests the use of a 1.5 percent SRTP to evaluate long-term impacts of climate change. Newell and Pizer (2003) show that uncertainty about future discount rates implies that "the distant future should be discounted at significantly lower rates than suggested by the current rate."

[14]See Toman, 1994, and Page, 1997; these articles are summarized and the issue is discussed further in Harris et al., 2001, Part 1. For a discussion of conflicts between discounting and moral values, see Ackerman and Heinzerling, 2004, Chapter 8.

## *Defining Risk and Uncertainty*

Risk and uncertainty are not the same. In some cases, *risk* can be estimated with a high degree of confidence. For example, statistical studies can define the risks associated with smoking. While no one can tell whether a particular smoker will suffer an early onset of serious disease or live to a ripe old age, it is clear that smoking increases the chances of disease and death, and for a large population these risks can be calculated fairly precisely. Similarly, emissions of certain toxic atmospheric pollutants are likely to increase cancer risks, and epidemiological studies can link pollution levels to increases in cancer incidence and death rates (see Box 6-4).

*Uncertainty,* in contrast, implies a much less clearly defined understanding of the possible outcomes. The issue of global climate change, discussed in depth in Chapter 18, demonstrates this. We cannot predict the full effects of global climate change resulting from emissions of greenhouse gases. Although scientists have generally agreed on a range of possible temperature increases likely to result over the next century, the global weather system is so complex that dramatic and unpredictable events are possible.

For example, it is possible that positive **feedback effects** such as the release of $CO_2$ from melting of the Arctic tundra could add huge additional volumes of greenhouse

*Earthquake damage in Watsonville, California. Added insurance costs are required to cover earthquake risks.*

gases to the atmosphere, greatly accelerating warming. Climate change could also lead to changes in ocean currents such as the Gulf Stream, changing the climate of northern Europe to something like that of Alaska, and alterations in tropical weather patterns leading to much more violent hurricanes. But no one can determine the likelihood of these events.

## Calculating Expected Value

Well-defined risks are easier to incorporate into economic analysis than uncertain future possibilities. If we can estimate both the risk and the cost of a potential outcome, we can express its **expected value** as

$$EV[X] = p[X] \ C[X]$$

where $EV$ is expected value, $p$ is the probability of event $X$, and $C$ is its cost.

This expected value can then be used for economic analysis just like any other estimate. Suppose, for example, that building a house in an earthquake-prone area involves an annual risk of about 1 in 100 of significant earthquake damage. (This reflects the likelihood that an earthquake will occur about once every 100 years.) An insurance company will insist on a higher premium to insure such a house.

The homeowner will pay an extra amount (above the cost of ordinary insurance) equal to the expected value of annual damages. The costs of a catastrophic event—which may or may not occur—can thus be internalized, allowing a normal housing market to operate, with somewhat higher costs reflecting earthquake risks. Expected value estimates can be used in cost-benefit analysis in a similar way, assuming that the probability of the event can be predicted with reasonable confidence.

The formula for expected value does not take into account **risk aversion**—the common tendency to prefer a certain outcome to a risky one. For example, suppose you were offered the choice of gaining $100,000 versus a 50-50 chance of gaining either $200,000 or nothing. You might well prefer to take the certain $100,000, even though the expected value of the two options is the same. If risk aversion is significant, the expected value method will overestimate the value of options where some risk is involved.

How about when we do not know the probability of the event? In the dam project case, suppose that chance exists of a major earthquake that could break the dam, causing massive flooding and the loss of many lives. The chance of a major quake is considered small—say, less than 1 in 1,000—but is not known with any degree of certainty.

In this case the **precautionary principle** may apply. People in the area may be unwilling to take even a remote chance of such a huge catastrophe. A similar logic applies to the unpredictable possibilities of extreme global warming effects. We can't tell whether they will occur, but the unknown risk of such major planetary disruptions makes us properly nervous and lends urgency to efforts to reduce greenhouse gas emissions.

## 6-4   Cost-Benefit Analysis of Arsenic in Drinking Water

The case of arsenic standards for drinking water illustrates the practical diffi-culties and ambiguities of applying cost-benefit analysis (CBA). The maximum ar-senic concentration allowed in U.S. public drinking water was established at 50 parts per billion (ppb) in 1942. A 1999 report by the National Academy of Sciences concluded that the 50 ppb standard "does not achieve EPA's goal for public-health protection and, therefore, requires downward revision as promptly as possible" (National Research Council, 1999).

In 2001, the U.S. Environmental Protection Agency published the results of a CBA that estimated the costs and benefits of four new standards: 20, 10, 5, and 3 ppb (U.S. EPA, 2001). The costs of complying with each standard are relatively cer-tain. However, the benefits of each standard are much more difficult to estimate for several reasons. First, incomplete toxicological data prevents accurately determin-ing the health benefits of lowering the arsenic standard, measured in terms of re-duced illnesses and deaths. Second, the economic methods used to value these benefits are imprecise and controversial. Third, some benefits associated with lower arsenic standards can not be estimated at all.

The arsenic CBA estimates the number of lung and bladder cancer cases that would be avoided at each standard. About half of these cases would result in death. Considerable uncertainty exists over how many cancer cases would be avoided, particularly when the standard drops below 10 ppb. The CBA estimates the benefit of an avoided cancer death by placing a $6.1 million value on a statistical life. The benefit of an avoided nonfatal cancer case is valued at $607,000 based on a study of willingness to pay to avoid a case of chronic bronchitis.

The exact values chosen for these benefits fail to reflect the considerable uncer-tainty associated with such estimates. For example, the CBA's $6.1 million value of a statistical life is the average of 26 estimates ranging from $0.9 million to $20.8 million in 1999 dollars (Abt Associates, 2000).

The quantified costs and benefits indicated that the arsenic standards of 10 and 20 ppb may provide positive net benefits. The arsenic standards of 3 and 5 ppb apparently fail to provide positive net benefits. However, the CBA notes that several categories of benefits could not be quantified. Arsenic exposure has been associated with other health effects including skin cancer, kidney cancer, pul-monary effects, cardiovascular effects, and neurological effects. Treatment of water supplies to reduce arsenic levels may also reduce the levels of other con-taminants. A reduction in arsenic levels may also provide psychic benefits to users because of reduced anxiety over health effects. In light of these unquantified po-tential benefits, the CBA cannot conclude that the lower arsenic standards do not provide positive net benefits. More stringent standards, however, would impose

*(continued on following page)*

higher compliance costs that would be especially burdensome for smaller communities.

Based on this CBA, the U.S. EPA recommended a new arsenic standard of 10 ppb. However, in March 2001 the Bush administration announced it was withdrawing plans to proceed with the new standard. The administration ordered a review of the proposed standard, stating that the "scientific indicators are unclear." EPA administrator Christie Whitman said that the "standard should be less than 50 ppb" but not necessarily as low as 10 ppb. She also vowed, "When we make a decision on arsenic, it will be based on sound science and solid analysis." This set the stage for vigorous public criticism of the administration's environmental policies. In July 2001 the U.S. House of Representatives voted to direct the EPA to implement the 10 ppb standard. The 10 ppb rule became effective February 22, 2002, and systems must comply by 2006. Clearly, the issue of arsenic standards involves political and social debate as well as economic analysis.

*Estimated Costs and Benefits of Different Arsenic Standards*

| Arsenic Standard (ppb) | Compliance Costs ($ millions 1999) | Health Benefits ($ millions 1999) | Bladder and Lung Cancer Cases Avoided |
|---|---|---|---|
| 3 | $698–$792 | $214–$491 | 57–138 |
| 5 | $415–$472 | $191–$356 | 51–100 |
| 10 | $180–$206 | $140–$198 | 37–56 |
| 20 | $67–$77 | $66–$75 | 19–20 |

Source: Table III.E-7 of U.S. EPA (2001).

**SOURCES**

Abt Associates, Inc. *Arsenic in Drinking Water Rule Economic Analysis.* U.S. EPA report number EPA-815-R-00-026, 2000.

National Research Council. *Arsenic in Drinking Water.* Washington, D.C.: National Academy Press, 1999.

United States Environmental Protection Agency. "National Primary Drinking Water Regulations; Arsenic and Clarifications to Compliance and New Source Contaminants Monitoring; Final Rule." *Federal Register* 40 CFR Parts 9, 141, and 142, vol. 66 (January 22, 2001): 6975–7066.

The precautionary principle is especially appropriate when irreversibility is involved. Some types of pollution and environmental damage can be remedied by reducing emissions or allowing time for natural systems to regenerate. Others, like species loss, are irreversible. In cases where we can adjust for mistakes or change our policies to adapt to new circumstances, an economic balancing of costs and benefits may be appropriate. But when essential natural systems could suffer irreversible damage, it is better to apply a **safe minimum standard** of environmental protection.

Damage to the atmospheric ozone layer, for example, could threaten all life on earth by removing an essential barrier to destructive radiation. As a result, international treaties have sought to impose a complete ban on ozone-depleting substances, regardless of any economic benefits they offer.[15]

Dealing with issues involving risk and uncertainty requires good judgment regarding which risks can reasonably be estimated and given an expected monetary value. Inability to know outcomes with certainty does not render economic analysis of environmental impacts inappropriate. Still, we must exercise caution in order to recognize cases where economic valuation of possible outcomes may fail to capture the full impact of potential outcomes on human health or ecosystems.[16]

## Comparing Costs and Benefits

We have seen that cost-benefit analysis necessarily involves controversy as well as difficult questions of valuation and discounting. Suppose that, having grappled with these issues, we are satisfied that we have done the best job possible of measuring all the costs and benefits associated with the dam project discussed above. If the benefits outweigh the costs, should we proceed with dam construction? Not necessarily—even if we are fully confident of our valuation techniques, important issues remain regarding how we evaluate the results.

On the benefit side, we can sum up the present value of total benefits over time as

$$PV[B] = B_0 + B_1/(1 + r) + B_2/(1 + r)^2 + B_3/(1 + r)^3 \ldots B_n/(1 + r)^n$$

while the total present value of costs is

$$PV[C] = C_0 + C_1/(1 + r) + C_2/(1 + r)^2 + C_3/(1 + r)^3 \ldots C_n/(1 + r)^n$$

where period 0 is the current year, $r$ is the discount rate, and our analysis extends $n$ years into the future. To calculate the value of an infinite stream of benefits or costs with a constant annual value,[17] we can use the formula

$$PV[B] = \sum_{i=1}^{n} B_i/(1 + r)^i = B_i/r$$

[15]Loopholes in these treaties, allowing limited production in developing nations for economic reasons, constitute one major threat to their effectiveness. Another major threat is illegal production and trade.

[16]See Toman, 1994, and O'Brien, 2000, for discussion of the limitations of economic valuation.

[17]This simplified formula for the sum of an infinite discounted series can be derived mathematically; we omit the proof here.

The net present value of the project is then

$$NPV = PV[B] - PV[C]$$

while the **benefit/cost ratio** for the project is

$$PV[B]/PV[C]$$

If we are prepared to give the green light to a project whose benefits exceed its costs, we are using the **positive net present value criterion**

$$NPV = PV[B] - PV[C] > 0$$

This criterion, however, only ensures that the project has positive value, not that it is the best choice available. Suppose that the power and irrigation benefits we seek could be obtained by dams of various sizes, as shown in Figure 6-3.

If we conduct a cost-benefit analysis for the largest dam, Project III, we will find that the positive net present value criterion is satisfied: total benefits exceed total costs. Yet to go ahead with this dam would clearly be a mistake. The two smaller projects have better benefit/cost ratios. The smaller dams may offer less total hydroelectric power and irrigation benefits, but their costs, including environmental costs, are significantly lower.

This might suggest that we should use benefit/cost ratios to evaluate projects. A benefit/cost ratio may indeed give a good sense of the desirability of a single project. However, benefit/cost ratios do not provide a consistent ranking of projects. In our example, Project I has a higher benefit/cost ratio than Project II, but this does not mean that it is a better choice. Although Project II has a lower benefit/cost ratio than Project I, it returns higher total net benefits. This suggests that the best rule is to use a **maximum net present value criterion.**

We can see the logic behind this by looking at the marginal benefit and marginal cost curves, shown in the lower part of Figure 6-3, corresponding to the total benefit and total cost curves shown in the upper part. From an economic point of view, as we saw in Chapter 3, the best principle is to equate marginal benefit and marginal cost. The intersection point of the MB and MC curves satisfies maximum net present value criterion. Of the three projects in this example, Project II offers the maximum net present value. Although both Project I and Project III bring some net benefits, neither have net benefits as high as Project II.

Unfortunately, in applying this criterion in real-world situations we generally cannot "see" the marginal benefit and cost curves. Nor can we see the whole total benefit and total cost curves. We can only evaluate the costs and benefits of particular projects using the techniques we have discussed. Unless we consider a range of possible projects, we may be misled into approving a project that is not economically optimal. In this example, the fact that the benefit/cost ratio for the large dam is only slightly greater than one (total benefits only slightly exceed total costs) should serve as a warning sign that we need to investigate other possibilities.

**(a) Total Costs and Benefits of Various Dam Projects**

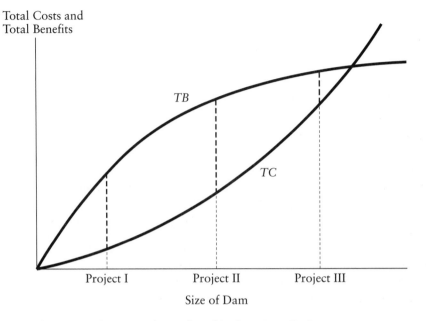

**(b) Marginal Costs and Benefits of Various Dam Projects**

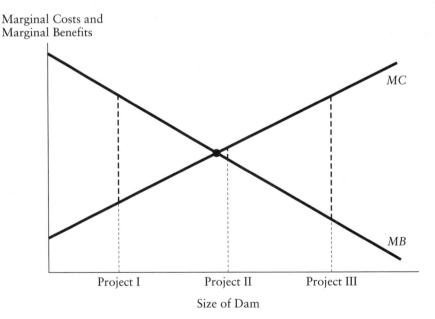

**FIGURE 6-3** *Costs and Benefits of Various Dam Projects*

# Conclusion: How Useful Is Cost-Benefit Analysis?

Valuing the environment is necessarily a troublesome endeavor. Some argue that what nature gives us is priceless and reject reducing these "services" to mere monetary values; others maintain that putting a value on ecological functions is essential because the alternative is to allow the economic system to value them at zero (see Box 6-5).

Critics of cost-benefit analysis point to the many difficulties involved in obtaining reliable estimates, and the fact that certain elements, such as spiritual value or the value of community, are essentially impossible to estimate in dollar terms. Economists generally maintain that cost-benefit analysis is a useful tool, provided it is used with proper caution. It would be unreasonable to assume that we can place a precise dollar value on everything—but in many cases economic valuations can assist decision-makers by providing specific estimates of policy impacts.

The most significant difficulty with the use of cost-benefit analysis is the requirement that we evaluate *all* costs and benefits in monetary terms to arrive at a single "bottom-line" result. One way of bypassing this problem is to use **cost-effectiveness analysis.** In this approach, economists do not attempt to decide which policy is best, but rather to analyze different means of achieving a given end.

Suppose, for example, that we have established a goal of cutting sulfur dioxide pollution, a major cause of acid rain, by 50 percent.[18] This might be done by requiring high-polluting plants to install scrubbers; by imposing taxes or fines based on emission levels; or by issuing tradable permits for certain levels of emissions, with the total number of permits not to exceed 50 percent of current levels. As we will see in more detail in Chapter 16, economic analysis can give a good estimate of the costs arising from each of these policies.

Clearly, there is a good case for adopting the least-cost method of reaching a given goal. In this approach, we do not rely on economic analysis to tell us *how much* we ought to reduce pollution—that decision is made based on other factors, including scientific evidence, political discussion, and common sense. Instead, we use economic analysis to choose the most efficient policies to achieve a desired result.

## *The Positional Analysis Alternative*

Another alternative to cost-benefit analysis, sometimes called **positional analysis,** involves consideration of broader social and political factors. Here the estimation of economic costs of a particular policy is combined with an evaluation of the effects on different groups of people, possible alternative policies, goals and objectives other than economic gain, social priorities, and individual rights. No single "bottom line" emerges, and particular outcomes may favor some groups over others.[19]

---

[18]This was in fact the goal set by the U.S. Environmental Protection Agency under the Clean Air Act Amendments of 1990.

[19]Söderbaum, 1999, discusses the basis of positional analysis.

| 6-5 | **Valuing the Global Ecosystem** |

Economists have devised various techniques to estimate nonmarket values for ecological services. These values allow us to incorporate ecosystem services into cost-benefit analyses. Most nonmarket applications estimate the value of a particular ecosystem or service, such as the value of a wetland or the value of clean air. A much more ambitious approach is to consider the value of the entire global ecosystem.

Although many would argue that the global ecosystem's value is priceless, large-scale application of nonmarket techniques is feasible. In fact, a group of researchers estimated the global value of ecosystem services in a 1997 article in the journal *Nature* (Costanza et al., 1997). The researchers considered the value of 17 ecosystem services including climate regulation, erosion control, waste treatment, food production, and recreation. They extensively reviewed nonmarket valuation studies to obtain estimates for the value of these services for each of 16 ecosystems, or biomes.

*The Global Value of Ecosystem Services*

| Biome (ecosystem) | Area (millions of hectares) | Annual Value (billions of 1994 dollars) |
|---|---|---|
| Open ocean | 33,220 | 8,381 |
| Estuaries | 180 | 4,110 |
| Seagrass/algae beds | 200 | 3,801 |
| Coral reefs | 62 | 375 |
| Shelf | 2,660 | 4,283 |
| Tropical forest | 1,900 | 3,813 |
| Temperate/boreal forest | 2,955 | 894 |
| Grass/rangelands | 3,898 | 906 |
| Tidal marsh/mangroves | 165 | 1,648 |
| Swamps/floodplains | 165 | 3,231 |
| Lakes/rivers | 200 | 1,700 |
| Desert | 1,925 | NA[1] |
| Tundra | 743 | NA[1] |
| Ice/rock | 1,640 | NA[1] |
| Cropland | 1,400 | 128 |
| Urban | 332 | NA[1] |
| TOTAL | 51,645 | 33,268 |

[1]No estimate provided.

*(continued on following page)*

The researchers estimated total annual value of the global ecosystem at $33 trillion, with a range of $16 to $54 trillion (for comparison, global GDP in 1997 was about $27 trillion). Slightly more than half of the total is for nutrient cycling services. The biomes with the highest total values are open oceans, continental shelves, and estuaries. The highest per-hectare ecosystem values are for estuaries, swamps/floodplains, and seagrass/algae beds.

The Costanza et al. research has been criticized for its attempt to use fairly simple economic methods to reduce all ecological functions to money values (Turner et al, 1998; El Serafy, 1998). Still, even the critics acknowledge "the article's potential to influence environmental discourse" and generate "rich methodological discussions" (Norgaard et al., 1998). Although any specific dollar value estimate is necessarily controversial, attempts to value the global ecosystem certainly demonstrate the significant value of ecological services and their importance in policy decisions.

**SOURCES**

Costanza, Robert Ralph d'Arge, Rudolf de Groot, Stephen Farber, Monica Grasso, Bruce Hannon, Karin Limburg, Shahid Naeem, Robert V. O'Neill, Jose Paruelo, Robert G. Raskin, Paul Sutton, and Marjan van den Belt. "The Value of the World's Ecosystem Services and Natural Capital." *Nature* 387 (May 15, 1997): 253–260.
El Serafy, Salah. "Pricing the Invaluable: The Value of the World's Ecosystem Services and Natural Capital." *Ecological Economics* 25, no. 1 (1998): 25–27.
Norgaard, Richard B., Collin Bode, and Values Reading Group. "Next, the Value of God, and Other Reactions." *Ecological Economics* 25, no. 1 (1998): 37–39.
Turner, R. K., W. N. Adger, and R. Brouwer. "Ecosystem Services Value, Research Needs, and Policy Relevance: A Commentary." *Ecological Economics* 25, no. 1 (1998): 61–65.

For example, construction of a major dam may require relocation of large numbers of people. Even if the dam's economics appear favorable, these people's rights to remain in their homes may be given a greater social priority. Such judgments cannot be made on a purely economic basis. However, valuation techniques we have discussed may be useful in defining economic aspects of what must ultimately be a social and political decision.[20]

If we do decide to use cost-benefit analysis, we will often encounter factors difficult to measure in economic terms. These unknown or immeasurable factors can be

---

[20]For a discussion of the interaction between estimation techniques and underlying values, see Gouldner and Kennedy, 1997.

represented in our summation of costs and benefits by Xs and Ys—indicating an acknowledgment of the limits of valuation techniques. (See, for example, the cost-benefit analysis of global climate change discussed in Chapter 18.)

In the chapters that follow, we will be discussing some of the broader perspectives on environmental issues that we have referred to as ecological economics. Here we will see examples of both the use and the limitations of economic valuation of the environment. Then, when we return to specific resource and environmental topics in Parts 4–6, we will see examples of how the economic analysis techniques presented in Chapters 3–6 can be applied to environmental policy issues.

## SUMMARY

Cost-benefit (also known as benefit-cost) analysis helps evaluate proposed projects and government actions. The kinds of value relevant to cost-benefit analysis include direct and indirect use values as well as non-use values such as option, existence, and bequest value. Environmental factors are often involved in cost-benefit analysis, and can be some of the most controversial to value.

Valuation techniques include contingent valuation, based on a survey that asks respondents to value environmental or other amenities in terms of their willingness to pay for them, or to accept compensation for their loss. Contingent valuation is controversial, partly because "willingness to pay" and "willingness to accept" values tend to differ substantially and partly because the survey technique is vulnerable to bias and inaccurate or inflated responses.

Other techniques more closely related to market pricing include hedonic valuation and travel cost methods. Production function and engineering values are based on the costs of replacing environmental functions such as pollution absorption by wetlands with treatment plants or other humanmade facilities.

Although these techniques can approximate some environmental values, they cannot capture the full ecological value of, for example, the preservation of endangered species. Critics have argued that pricing the environment is inherently wrong; dollar values are an inadequate metric for ecological systems. Others maintain that some valuation is essential for comparing policy options, and if done with caution will not misrepresent environmental values.

Economists use the technique of discounting to balance present and future costs and benefits. Selecting an appropriate discount rate is important and can significantly affect the results of cost-benefit studies. The socially appropriate discount rate may be different from the commercial discount rate used to evaluate investment returns.

Special issues arise when attempting to value human life and health, risk and uncertainty, and impacts on the future. While economic techniques exist that can be used in all these areas, they have often aroused further controversy. An alternative to economic valuation of risk is the precautionary principle, which states that we should avoid even a small possibility of a damaging outcome, especially when such an outcome may be irreversible. In such cases, a safe minimum standard of environmental protection may replace economic calculation.

---

## KEY TERMS AND CONCEPTS

avoided cost
benefit/cost ratio
bequest value
contingent valuation
cost-benefit analysis (CBA)
cost-effectiveness analysis
direct use value
discount rate
ecological value
economic value
engineering cost method
environmental services
existence value
expected value
feedback effects
habitat equivalency
    analysis
hedonic pricing

indirect use values
intergenerational equity
irreversibility
maximum net present
    value criterion
net present value
nonmarket values
non-use values
opportunity cost of
    capital
option value
positional analysis
positive net present
    value criterion
precautionary principle
present value
production function
    method

replacement cost
risk aversion
safe minimum standard
sensitivity analysis
social discount rate
social rate of time
    preference (SRTP)
strategic bias
travel cost method
use value
willingness to
    accept (WTA)
willingness to pay (WTP)

---

## DISCUSSION QUESTIONS

1. Suppose you are asked to conduct a cost-benefit study of a proposed coal-fired power plant. The plant will be built on the outskirts of a residential area and will emit a certain volume of pollutants. It will require a substantial amount of water for its cooling system. Industries in the region argue that the additional power is urgently needed, but local residents oppose construction. How would you evaluate social and environmental costs and weigh them against economic benefits?

2. It has been proposed that a cost-benefit analysis should be required before formulating government pollution control regulations. This would involve weighing the costs to industry of conforming to the regulations versus health and environmental benefits accrued from regulation. Do you believe this proposal makes sense? Discuss how economic, health, and environmental criteria should be balanced in formulating regulations.

3. Suppose the government of a developing nation is considering establishing a national park in a scenic forested area. Local opposition arises from those who wish

to use the forestland for timbering and agriculture. On the other hand, the national park would draw both local and foreign visitors as tourists. Could cost-benefit analysis aid the decision on whether or not to establish the park? What factors would you consider and how would you measure their economic value?

## PROBLEM

1. The World Bank is considering an application from the country of Equatoria for a large dam project. Selected project costs and benefits (dollar values) are as follows:

   Construction costs: $500 million/year for 3 years
   Operating Costs: $50 million/year
   Hydropower to be generated: 3 billion kilowatt hours/year
   Price of electricity: $0.05/kilowatt hour
   Irrigation water available from dam: 5 billion gallons/year
   Price of water: $0.015/gallon
   Agricultural product lost from flooded lands: $45 million/year
   Forest products lost from flooded lands: $20 million/year

   Additional losses are less easily quantifiable: human costs to villagers who will be forced to move, watershed damage, and ecological costs of habitat destruction. It is also possible that the new lake area may contribute to the spread of waterborne diseases.

   a. Do a formal cost-benefit analysis using the quantifiable factors listed above. Remember to distinguish between one-time costs and annual costs extending into the future. Discount all future costs and benefits to find present value. The simplest technique is to calculate costs and benefits as of dam start-up in year 4. Compound construction costs forward using the formula $C_t(1 + r)^{(4-t)}$ for years 1–3, which gives the value of the total construction costs, plus interest, as of start-up.

   For costs $C_i$ or benefits $B_i$ extending into the indefinite future, use the formulae $PV[C] = C_i/r$ or $PV[B] = B_i/r$ to obtain the value of the (infinite) stream of benefits. You may assume that the dam will operate for the foreseeable future.

   Do a complete cost-benefit analysis for *two* possible interest rates: 10 percent and 5 percent. In each case, do your figures indicate a definite "yes," definite "no," or uncertain result?

   b. Now consider an alternative project: several smaller dams constructed to avoid flooding significant agricultural areas or forestlands. For this project, total construction and operating costs are exactly half the costs of the big dam project, and power/irrigation benefits are also half as much. No damages affect farmland or forest, and the project incurs no ecological or resettlement costs. Evaluate this project and compare to the larger project at the two interest rates.

## REFERENCES

Ackerman, Frank, and Lisa Heinzerling. *Priceless: On Knowing the Price of Everything and the Value of Nothing.* New York: New Press, 2004.

Boyle, Melissa A., and Katherine A. Kiel. "A Survey of House Price Hedonic Studies of the Impact of Environmental Externalities." *Journal of Real Estate Literature* 9, no. 2 (2001): 117–144.

Cline, William R. *The Economics of Global Warming.* Washington, D.C.: Institute for International Economics, 1992.

Daily, Gretchen C., ed. *Nature's Services: Societal Dependence on Natural Ecosystems.* Washington, D.C.: Island Press, 1997.

Diamond, Peter A., and Jerry A. Hausman. "Contingent Valuation: Is Some Number Better Than No Number?" *Journal of Economic Perspectives* 8, no. 4 (fall 1994): 45–64.

Dixon, John A., et al., eds. *Economic Analysis of Environmental Impacts.* London: Earthscan, 1997.

Dunford, Richard W., Thomas C. Ginn, and William H. Desvousges. "The Use of Habitat Equivalency Analysis in Natural Resource Damage Assessments." *Ecological Economics* 48 (January 2004): 49–70.

Garrod, Guy, and Kenneth G. Willis. *Economic Valuation of the Environment: Methods and Case Studies.* Cheltenham, U.K.: Elgar, 1999.

Gouldner, Lawrence H., and Donald Kennedy. "Valuing Ecosystem Services: Philosophical Bases and Empirical Methods." In Gretchen C. Daily, ed., op. cit.

Hanley, Nick, and Clive L. Spash, eds. *Cost-Benefit Analysis and the Environment.* Cheltenham, U.K.: Elgar, 1998.

Hanneman, W. Michael. "Valuing the Environment through Contingent Valuation." *Journal of Economic Perspectives* 8, no. 4 (fall 1994): 19–43.

Harris, Jonathan M., Timothy A. Wise, Kevin P. Gallagher, and Neva R. Goodwin, eds. *A Survey of Sustainability: Social and Economic Dimensions.* Washington, D.C.: Island Press, 2001.

Herath, Gamini, and John Kennedy. "Estimating the Value of Mount Buffalo National Park with the Travel Cost and Contingent Valuation Models." *Tourism Economics* 10 (2004): 63–78.

Horowitz, John K., and Kenneth E. McConnell. "A Review of WTA/WTP Studies." *Journal of Environmental Economics and Management* 44 (November 2002): 426–447.

Markandya, Anil, and Julie Richardson. *Environmental Economics: A Reader.* Part II: Valuation Methods and Applications. New York: St. Martin's Press, 1993.

Newell, Richard G., and William A. Pizer. "Discounting the Distant Future: How Much Do Uncertain Rates Increase Valuations?" *Journal of Environmental Economics and Management* 46 (July 2003): 52–71.

O'Brien, Mary. *Making Better Environmental Decisions: An Alternative to Risk Assessment*. Cambridge, Mass.: MIT Press, 2000.

Page, Talbot. "On the Problem of Achieving Efficiency and Equity, Intergenerationally." *Land Economics* 73 (November 1997): 580–596. Also summarized in Harris et al., op. cit.

Pearce, David, and Dominic Moran. *The Economic Value of Biodiversity*. London: Earthscan, 1997.

Portney, Paul. "The Contingent Valuation Debate: Why Economists Should Care." *Journal of Economic Perspectives* 8 (fall 1994): 3–17.

Rietbergen-McCracken, Jennifer, and Hussein Abaza. *Environmental Valuation: A Worldwide Compendium of Case Studies*. London: Earthscan, 2000.

Smith, V. Kerry, ed. *Estimating Economic Values for Nature: Methods for Non-Market Valuation*. Cheltenham, U.K.: Elgar, 1996.

Söderbaum, Peter. "Valuation as Part of a Microeconomics for Ecological Sustainability." In *Valuation and the Environment: Theory, Method, and Practice*, edited by Martin O'Connor and Clive Spash. Cheltenham, U.K.: Elgar, 1999.

Toman, Michael A. "Economics and 'Sustainability': Balancing Trade-offs and Imperatives." *Land Economics* 70 (November 1994): 399–413. Also summarized in Harris et al., op. cit.

Viscusi, W. Kip. *Rational Risk Policy*. New York: Oxford University Press, 1998.

Woodward, Richard T., and Yong-Suhk Wui. "The Economic Value of Wetland Services: A Meta-Analysis." *Ecological Economics* 37 (May 2001): 257–270.

## WEBSITES

1. **http://www.rff.org/** Homepage for Resources for the Future, a nonprofit organization that conducts policy and economic research on natural resource issues. Many RFF publications available on their website use nonmarket techniques to value environmental services.

2. **http://cnie.org/NLE/CRSreports/Risk/rsk-4.cfm** A paper by the Congressional Research Service discussing the use of cost-benefit analysis as a basis for government regulations.

3. **http://www.epa.gov/safewater/arsenic.html** The EPA's 2001 cost-benefit analysis of the arsenic drinking water standard for public water supplies in the United States.

# THREE

# Ecological Economics and Environmental Accounting

**CHAPTER FOCUS QUESTIONS**

- Are natural resources a form of capital?
- How can we account for and conserve resources and environmental systems?
- What limits the scale of economic systems?
- How can we sustain economic well-being and ecosystem health in the long term?

CHAPTER **7**

# Ecological Economics: Basic Concepts

## Natural Capital

The relationships between economic and environmental issues can be viewed from a variety of perspectives. In Chapters 3–6 we applied concepts derived from standard economic analysis to environmental issues. The school of thought known as ecological economics, however, takes a different approach. Ecological economics redefines basic economic concepts to make them better applicable to environmental problems. One such fundamental concept is **natural capital.**

Most economic models of the production process focus on two factors of production: capital and labor. A third factor, usually referred to as "land," is acknowledged but usually has no prominent function in economic models. Classical economists of the nineteenth century, especially David Ricardo, author of *The Principles of Political Economy and Taxation* (1817), were concerned with land and its productivity as a fundamental determinant of economic production. Modern economics, however, generally assumes that technological progress will overcome any limits on the productive capacity of land.

Ecological economists have reintroduced and broadened the classical concept of land, renaming it *natural capital*. Natural capital is defined as the whole endowment of land and resources available to us, including air, water, fertile soil, forests, fisheries, mineral resources, and the ecological life-support systems that make economic activity, and indeed life itself, possible.[1]

In an ecological economics perspective, natural capital should be considered at least as important as humanmade capital as a basis for production. Further, a careful accounting should be made of the state of natural capital and of its improvement or deterioration, and this should be reflected in national income accounting.

## Accounting for Changes in Natural Capital

Defining natural resources as capital raises an important economic implication. A central principle of prudent economic management is to preserve the value of capital. It is generally desirable to add to productive capital over time, a process economists call **net investment.** A nation whose productive capital decreases over time (net disinvestment) is a nation in economic decline.

Sir John Hicks, Nobel laureate in economics and author of *Value and Capital* (1939), defined income as the amount of goods and services an individual or nation can consume over a period of time and remain at least as well off at the end of the period as at the beginning. In other words, you cannot increase your income by reducing your capital.

To see what this means in practice, imagine that you receive an inheritance of $1 million (few of us will ever be so lucky, but we can dream). Suppose that the million dollars is invested in bonds yielding a real return[2] of 5 percent. This will give an annual income of $50,000. However, if you decide to spend $100,000 per year from the inheritance, you will be spending $50,000 of capital in addition to the $50,000 income. This means that in future years the income will be reduced, and eventually the capital will be gone entirely. Clearly, this is different from a prudent policy of living only on income, which would allow you (and your heirs) to receive $50,000 per year indefinitely.

This principle is generally accepted insofar as humanmade capital is concerned. National income accounting includes a calculation of the wearing-out of humanmade capital over time. This **capital depreciation** is estimated annually and subtracted from gross national product to obtain net national product. To maintain national wealth requires at least enough investment to replace the capital that wears out each year. We recognize this also by distinguishing between gross and net investment. Net investment is gross investment minus depreciation, and can be zero or below zero if insufficient replacement investment occurs. A negative net investment implies a decline in national wealth.

But no similar provision is made for **natural capital depreciation.** If a nation cuts down its forests and converts them to timber for domestic consumption or export, this enters the national income accounts only as a positive contribution to income, equal to

---

[1]For a more detailed account of the development of ecological economics and its relation to economic theory, see Costanza et al., eds., 1997; and Krishnan et al., eds., 1995.

[2]Real return is return in excess of inflation.

the value of the timber. No accounting is made of the loss of standing forest, either as an economic resource or in terms of its ecological value. From the standpoint of ecological economics, this is a serious omission that must be corrected. Ecological economists have proposed revisions to national income accounting systems so as to include natural capital depreciation (we will consider these proposals in detail in Chapter 8.)

## *The Dynamics of Natural Capital*

The natural capital concept further implies that a purely economic analysis cannot fully capture the stock and flow dynamics of natural resources. As we saw in Chapter 6, economists have been at pains to devise ways of expressing natural resource and environmental factors in money terms suitable for standard economic analysis. But this only captures one dimension of natural capital.

The basic laws that govern behaviors of natural capital elements such as energy resources, water, chemical elements, and life forms are physical laws described in the sciences of chemistry, physics, biology, and ecology. Without specific consideration of these laws, we cannot gain a full understanding of natural capital.

For example, in agricultural systems, soil fertility is determined by complex interactions among chemical nutrients, microorganisms, water flows, and plant and animal waste recycling. Measuring soil fertility in terms of, say, grain output, will be valid for short-term economic calculations, but may be misleading over the long term as subtler ecological processes come into play. A purely economic analysis could result in insufficient attention to long-term maintenance of soil fertility.

Thus it is necessary to combine insights from economic analysis with ecological principles when dealing with issues of the maintenance of natural capital. This does not render the economic techniques of Chapters 3–6 irrelevant; rather they must be complemented with ecological perspectives on natural systems to avoid misleading results. Techniques advocated by ecological economists for natural capital accounting and conservation include the following:

- **Physical accounting** for natural capital. In addition to the familiar national income accounts, **satellite accounts** can be constructed to show the abundance or scarcity of natural resources and to estimate their variations from year to year. These accounts can also show pollutant build-up, water quality, soil fertility variations, and other important physical indicators of environmental conditions. Accounts that indicate significant resource depletion or environmental degradation, call for measures to conserve or restore natural capital.
- Determination of **sustainable yield** levels. As we saw in Chapter 4, economic exploitation of natural resources often exceeds ecologically sustainable levels. An ecological analysis of a natural system harvested for human use can help to determine the sustainable yield level at which the system can continue to operate indefinitely. If the economic equilibrium yield exceeds the sustainable yield, the resource is threatened, and specific protective policies are necessary. This has happened with many fisheries and forests, a topic dealt with in Chapters 14 and 15.

- Determination of the **absorptive capacity of the environment** for human-generated wastes, including household, agricultural, and industrial wastes. Natural processes can break down many waste products over time and reabsorb them into the environment without damage. Other wastes and pollutants, such as chlorinated pesticides, chlorofluorocarbons (CFCs), and radioactive wastes are difficult or impossible for the environment to absorb. Scientific analysis can offer a baseline estimate of acceptable levels of waste emissions. This will not necessarily coincide with the economic concept of "optimal pollution levels" introduced in Chapter 3.

All these measures point toward a general principle of **natural capital sustainability.** According to this principle, nations should aim to conserve their natural capital by limiting its depletion or degradation and investing in its renewal (for example, through soil conservation or reforestation programs). The difficult and controversial process of translating this general principle into specific policy rules brings into focus the differences between economic and ecological analyses. We will deal with some of these questions in more detail in Chapters 8 and 9.

## Issues of Macroeconomic Scale

Standard macroeconomic theory recognizes no limitation on an economy's scale. Keynesian, classical, and other economic theories deal with the conditions for equilibrium among the macroeconomic aggregates of consumption, savings, investment, government spending, taxes, and money supply. But with economic growth, the equilibrium level can rise indefinitely, so that a country's Gross Domestic Product (GDP) can multiply tenfold or a hundredfold over time.

With a 5 percent growth rate, for example, GDP would double every 14 years, becoming more than 100 times as large within a century. Even at a 2 percent growth rate, GDP doubles in 35 years, growing by 7 times in a century. From the point of view of mathematical computation of economic equilibrium, such growth poses no problem. But ecological economists, in particular Robert Goodland and Herman Daly, have argued that resource and environmental factors impose practical limits on feasible levels of economic activity, and that economic theory must include some concept of optimal **macroeconomic scale.**[3]

This concept is relevant both for individual economies dependent on limited resource bases, and for the global economy. Its implications for the global economy are especially important, because national economies can overcome resource limitations through international trade. The situation is illustrated in Figure 7-1. Although reminiscent of our original schematic showing the relationship between economic and ecological systems (see Figure 1-2, p. 8), Figure 7-1 also shows the economy growing within the supporting ecosystem to the point where it applies significant physical and life cycle stress.

---

[3]See Daly, 1994, and Goodland et al., 1992.

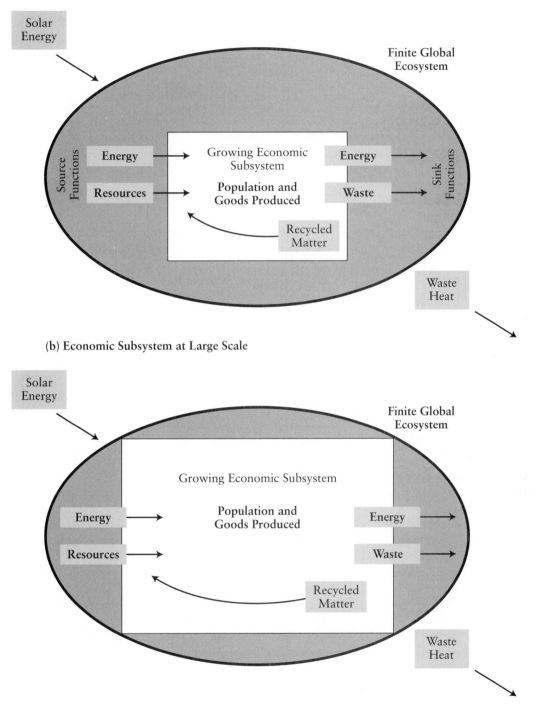

(a) Economic Subsystem at Small Scale

Solar Energy

Finite Global Ecosystem

Source Functions

Energy → Growing Economic Subsystem

Energy →

Resources → Population and Goods Produced

Waste →

Sink Functions

Recycled Matter

Waste Heat

(b) Economic Subsystem at Large Scale

Solar Energy

Finite Global Ecosystem

Growing Economic Subsystem

Population and Goods Produced

Energy →

Energy →

Resources →

Waste →

Recycled Matter

Waste Heat

**FIGURE 7-1** *The Finite Global Ecosystem Relative to the Growing Economic Subsystem*

Source: Adapted from Robert Goodland, Herman Daly, and Salah El Serafy, eds., *Population, Technology, and Lifestyle: The Transition to Sustainability.* UNESCO, 1992. Courtesy of UNESCO.

In Figure 7-1, we see that the economic system (shown as a rectangle) uses both energy and resources as inputs, and releases waste energy and other wastes into the ecosystem (shown as a circle). The combined input and waste flows can be called **throughput.**[4] The economic system shown here is an **open system,** exchanging energy and resources with the global ecosystem within which it is located. The global ecosystem has an inflow of solar energy and an outflow of waste heat, but is otherwise a **closed system.**

As the open economic subsystem grows within the closed planetary ecosystem, (shown by the enlarged rectangle in Figure 7-1b), its resource needs and waste flows are more difficult to accommodate. The fixed size of the planetary ecosystem places a scale limit on economic system growth.

We should note that this diagram refers to the *physical* growth of the economic system, measured in terms of its resource and energy demands and waste flows. It is possible for GDP to grow without higher resource requirements, especially if growth is concentrated in the service sector. Expanded automobile production, for example, requires more steel, glass, rubber, and other material inputs, as well as gasoline to operate the vehicles. But more opera productions or child-care services require few physical resources. Energy and physical resource use may also become more efficient, thus requiring less throughput of resources per unit of output. In general, though, growing GDP is associated with higher throughput of energy and resources.

Economic activity undoubtedly faces *some* scale limits. How can we determine whether the economic subsystem is in fact straining the limits of the ecosystem? One way is simply by noting the increased prevalence of large-scale or global environmental problems such as global climate change, ozone layer destruction, ocean pollution, soil degradation, and species loss. In commonsense terms as well as in ecological analysis, these pervasive problems suggest that important environmental thresholds had been reached by the late twentieth century.[5]

## *Measuring the Relationship Between Economic and Ecological Systems*

Ecological economists have also suggested a specific measure by which to link ecological and economic systems theoretically. Both systems have the function of *using energy* to support and expand the functions of life. We can thus identify energy as in some sense fundamental to all economic activity: Human labor, capital investment, and natural resource exploitation all require energy.

Living systems obtain solar energy through plant photosynthesis. As the human economic system grows, we directly or indirectly use a larger proportion of this **net primary product of photosynthesis (NPP)** to support economic activity. This appropriation of photosynthetic energy takes place through agriculture, forestry, fisheries, and

---

[4]See Daly, 1993.

[5]See, for example, Goodland et al., 1992, Chapters 1 and 2; Meadows, 1992. For a recent assessment of global ecosystem stresses, see UNEP, 2002, and World Resources Institute, 2000.

*Urban and residential sprawl requires increasing amounts of land for highways.*

fuel use. In addition, human activities convert land from natural or agricultural functions for urban and industrial uses, transportation systems, and housing construction. Humans currently appropriate about 40 percent of terrestrial (land) photosynthetic capacity and about 25 percent of the global total, including ocean ecosystems.[6]

This NPP figure implies that a doubling of economic activity will bring us close to absolute limits. As we saw in Chapter 2, such a doubling is virtually certain unless population growth or economic growth rates alter dramatically. We must, therefore, take the question of scale limits seriously. We will look at specific implications of this issue for agriculture, energy use, and other resources in Chapters 10–17, but general implications for economic theory also emerge.

Herman Daly has argued that the rapid economic growth of the twentieth century has brought us from **empty-world economics** to **full-world economics.**[7] In the "empty-world" phase, when the economic system is small relative to the ecosystem, resource and environmental limits are unimportant and the main economic activity is the exploitation of natural resources to build up humanmade capital stocks and to expand consumption. In this stage economic activity faces only the main constraint of limited quantities of humanmade capital.

---

[6]Vitousek et al., 1986.

[7]Daly, 1992.

In the "full-world" phase, however, when the dramatically expanded human economic system presses against ecosystem limits, the conservation of natural capital becomes far more important. If we do not implement adequate measures to conserve resources and protect the "full-world" environment, environmental degradation will undermine economic activity no matter how large stocks of humanmade capital may become.

This perspective differs in significant respects from standard economic theory, which generally assumes **substitutability** between resources. For example, industrially produced fertilizer might compensate for loss of fertile soil. The ecological perspective tells us that substitution is not so easy—the natural resource base for economic activity is in a sense irreplaceable, unlike humanmade factories or machinery. If this is true, we need to modify standard theories of economic growth to take into account issues of long-term sustainability.[8]

## Long-Term Sustainability

We have already mentioned sustainability in terms of natural capital, but how can we define this term more precisely? We want to limit the loss or degradation of natural capital, and to invest in its conservation and renewal. Taken in its strictest sense, this would mean that we could neither use any depletable resource, nor conduct any economic activity that would substantially alter natural systems. In a world of more than 6 billion people, largely industrialized or rapidly industrializing, this is clearly impossible. On the other hand, unrestrained resource use and ever-increasing waste generation is also unacceptable. How can we strike the balance?

We have already examined elements of the standard economic answer to this question. The theories of external economies, resource allocation over time, and common-property resource management, which we outlined in Chapters 3–5, offer economic principles on when to use and when to conserve resources, and on "optimal" pollution levels. In the long-term global context, however, these theories may be insufficient. Oriented toward individual markets, they may fail to guarantee environmental sustainability at the macroeconomic level. We need guidelines for overall conservation of the national and global resource bases. Within these guidelines, market solutions to specific resource and environmental management problems will become relevant.

We can distinguish between the concepts of **strong sustainability and weak sustainability.** ("Strong" and "weak" in this context express how demanding our assumptions are, and do not imply that one is necessarily better or worse than the other.) Strong sustainability assumes limited substitutability between natural and humanmade

---

[8]An assessment of the ecological economics of sustainability is found in Wackernagel and Long, 1999. Implications for economic growth theory are discussed in Harris and Goodwin, 2003.

capital. Weak sustainability assumes that natural and humanmade capital are generally substitutable.[9]

Taking the *strong sustainability* approach, we would keep separate accounts for humanmade and natural capital and ensure against depleting overall natural capital stocks. It would be acceptable, for example, to cut down forests in one area only if similar forests were being expanded elsewhere so that the overall forest stock remained constant. Petroleum stocks could be depleted only if alternative energy sources of equal capacity were simultaneously developed. Implementing strong sustainability would require extensive government intervention in markets and a radical change in the nature of economic activity.

*Weak sustainability* is easier to achieve. This principle allows for substitutability between natural and humanmade capital, provided that the total value of capital does not decline. This may allow us, for example, to cut down forests in order to expand agriculture or industry. It does require, however, an adequate accounting for the *value* of the cleared forest. The forest-clearing activity would be an economic loss unless the value generated in new humanmade capital equaled or exceeded the economic and ecological value of the cleared forests.

This principle is closer to standard economic theory. A private owner presumably would make such a calculation and would not willingly exchange a higher-valued resource for a lower-valued one. Government intervention would, however, be required to maintain even weak sustainability when:

- Private owners fail to consider the full ecological value of natural capital (say, a forest products company that considers timber values but is indifferent to endangered species).
- Property rights in natural resources are poorly defined, as is often true in developing nations. Short-term concession holders or illegal users can rapidly plunder a natural resource base.
- Private property owners with short-term perspectives fail to consider long-term effects such as cumulative soil erosion.
- Common-property resources or public goods are involved.
- Truly irreplaceable resources are at issue, as in the case of species extinction or limited water supplies in arid areas.

## Policy Choices and Discounting the Future

The choice between strong and weak sustainability may be difficult. In managing forest resources, for example, strong sustainability may be too restrictive, requiring a

---

[9]A discussion of the principles of strong and weak sustainability can be found in Daly, 1994. The concept of sustainability is criticized by Beckerman (1994) and defended by Daly (1995) and El Serafy (1996). Application of the weak sustainability concept is discussed by Gowdy and O'Hara (1997), while Common (1996) argues that the distinction between strong and weak sustainability is invalid. Neumayer (2003) gives a broad overview of the debate between weak and strong sustainability paradigms.

country to maintain the same area of forest cover under all circumstances. Weak sustainability, however, places no inherent limits on the amount of forest that can be cut, requiring only a sound economic accounting of its value. Although middle ground must be defined, this cannot happen simply through the market process. It must be a conscious social choice.

One crucial factor in defining this middle ground is the issue of discounting the future. Our discussions of resource allocation over time (Chapter 5) and of cost-benefit analysis (Chapter 6) have highlighted the importance of the discount rate in market choices regarding resource use. In general, the higher the discount rate, the greater the incentive to exploit resources in the present. By Hotelling's rule, private owners must expect a resource's net price to rise at a rate at least equal to the interest rate before they will conserve that resource for the future. This rarely occurs for most depletable natural resources.

Consider that at a 5 percent discount rate, owners would have to expect net resource prices to double every 14 years before they would pursue conservation rather than extract the resource immediately and invest the proceeds at 5 percent. For renewable resources such as forests, the annual yield must at least equal the market interest rate for private owners to practice sustainable management (see Chapter 15 for a full treatment of this issue). At lower yields, economic incentives favor logging the forest for immediate monetary gains. In effect, this means treating the renewable resource as a depletable resource and "mining" it out as fast as possible.

The logic of discounting imposes a stiff test on natural resource systems. Unless they can meet a certain yield level, immediate exploitation will take precedence over sustainable management. If major ecological systems and important natural resources fail this test, the resulting rush to exploit resources as fast as possible will make little provision for the future.

Here the strong sustainability principle becomes relevant: Can we trust that a world with much more humanmade capital but a severely depleted resource base will meet the needs of the future? Or should we impose a stronger principle of resource conservation to guard our own and future generations' interests?

This is not a philosophical debate about the long-term future. Critical resources such as petroleum could be largely used up within 30 to 40 years; tropical forests could be virtually eliminated in the same period; soil erosion could destroy the fertility of hundreds of millions of acres of cropland within a generation. Applying a strict commercial discounting principle, all this destruction could be seen as quite "rational" and even "optimal."

Norgaard and Howarth have argued against using market-based discount rates to guide decisions on long-term resource use.[10] They recommend using a sustainability criterion to promote **intergenerational equity.** In this view it is wrong to decide issues of long-term investment and conservation in the present simply by applying profit-maximizing criteria. This calls for social judgment on conservation of resources for the future.

[10]Norgaard and Howarth, 1991; Howarth and Norgaard, 1993. Also see Page, 1997, and Padilla, 2002.

## *Complexity, Irreversibility, and the Precautionary Principle*

Another major justification for a sustainability criterion relates to **ecological complexity** and **irreversibility**. Current ecological systems have evolved over many centuries to achieve a balance involving interactions among thousands of species of plants and animals (the total number of species is unknown, but is in the millions), as well as delicately balanced physical and chemical relationships in the atmosphere, oceans, and in freshwater and terrestrial ecosystems.

Extensive exploitation of natural resources permanently alters these ecological balances, with effects not fully predictable. In some cases, upsetting the ecological balance can lead to disaster—desertification, collapse of ocean food systems, destruction of the ozone layer, pollution of aquifers, outbreaks of super-pests resistant to insecticides, and the like. Species extinction is a clear example of irreversible damage, imposing unknown economic and ecological costs in the future.

Ecological economists therefore argue for a **precautionary principle**—we should strive for minimum interference with the operation of natural systems, especially where we cannot predict long-term effects. This principle obviously defies easy definition in economic calculations of resource value and use. Such calculations, therefore, are of value only if we can place them in the broader ecological context, whose priorities should sometimes override market equilibrium logic.[11]

As we explore resource and environment topic areas in Chapters 10–18, we will bear in mind the tension between the standard economic techniques outlined in Chapters 3–6 and the general principles of ecological economics set forth in this chapter. In addition, before addressing specific topic areas, we will examine some new analytical techniques developed by ecological economists.

One important issue is adding an environmental dimension to the measurement of economic output or GDP—or perhaps replacing GDP with a more inclusive measure of human well-being and ecosystem health. We will deal with this topic in Chapter 8. Another approach is to model the interrelationship between economic and environmental systems, focusing on flows of energy, resources, and wastes. These new approaches to economic/ecological modeling are the topic of Chapter 9.

## SUMMARY

Ecological economics gives special emphasis to the concept of natural capital. Although much of standard economics concerns the accumulation and productivity of humanmade capital, ecological economics focuses on maintaining the natural capital systems that support life and economic activity. Natural capital includes all planetary natural resources, oceans, atmosphere, and ecosystems. These must be accounted for

---

[11]Application of the precautionary principle is discussed in Raffensperger and Tickner, 1999, and Tickner and Geiser, 2004.

and should be managed according to sustainable principles so that their functions do not degrade over time.

In this perspective, economic systems cannot grow without limit, but must achieve a sustainable scale for economic activity at which the planet's ecosystems are not subjected to undue stress. Significant evidence indicates that current economic activity exceeds these limits or badly strains them. One measure of this is the proportion of photosynthetic energy appropriated for human use, now about 40 percent of terrestrial photosynthesis. Significant further growth in human demand would thus leave little room for other living systems of the earth.

The concept of sustainability, although important to managing natural capital, is difficult to define. A "weak" definition relies on the possibility of replacing natural ecosystem functions with humanmade substitutes. To the extent that this is possible, natural capital can be used up without diminishing net wealth. A "strong" definition assumes that humans have limited ability to replace natural system functions and that a sustainable society must therefore maintain most of its natural systems without significant depletion or degradation.

Long-term sustainability involves issues of discounting the future, and the question of our responsibility to provide for future generations. Economic incentives and property rights systems affect decisions regarding resource use, as does public policy on resource management. A precautionary principle is appropriate in cases where irreversible effects may result from damage to complex ecosystems. Resource conservation for future generations requires social judgment in addition to economic calculation.

The principles of ecological and of standard economics are both relevant to resource management issues. Sometimes the principles will conflict, but it is important to consider how best to apply both to specific resource and environmental issues, as well as to the measurement of economic output, human well-being, and ecosystem health.

## KEY TERMS AND CONCEPTS

absorptive capacity of the environment
capital depreciation
closed system
ecological complexity
empty-world and full-world economics
intergenerational equity
irreversibility
macroeconomic scale
natural capital
natural capital depreciation
natural capital sustainability

net investment
net primary product of photosynthesis (NPP)
open system
physical accounting
precautionary principle
satellite accounts
strong and weak sustainability
substitutability
sustainable yield
throughput

## DISCUSSION QUESTIONS

1. In what respects is natural capital similar to humanmade capital and in what respects does it differ? We often speak of a "return to capital," meaning the stream of income generated by a capital investment. Can we speak of a return to natural capital? What might be examples of investment in natural capital? Who would be motivated to make such investments? Who would suffer in the absence of such investments or if resource depletion or environmental degradation lead to "disinvestment"?

2. How can we apply the concept of optimal scale for an economy? Have the economies of the United States, Europe, and Japan reached optimal scale? Exceeded it? How about the economies of Latin America? of Africa? of other Asian economies? How would you relate the concept of optimal scale at the global level to economic growth in national economies at different levels of development?

3. Distinguish between the concepts of strong and weak sustainability and give practical examples, other than those cited in the text, for their application. Where would each concept be most appropriate? What economic policy measures would be relevant to achieving sustainability?

## REFERENCES

Beckerman, Wilfred. "Sustainable Development: Is It a Useful Concept?" *Environmental Values* 3 (1994): 191–209.

Common, Mick. "Beckerman and His Critics on Strong and Weak Sustainability: Confusing Concepts and Conditions." *Environmental Values* 5 (1996): 83–88.

Costanza, Robert, ed. *Ecological Economics*. New York: Columbia University Press, 1991.

Costanza, Robert, John Cumberland, Herman Daly, Robert Goodland, and Richard Norgaard, eds. *An Introduction to Ecological Economics*. Boca Raton, Florida: St. Lucie Press, 1997.

Daly, Herman E. *Beyond Growth: The Economics of Sustainable Development*. Boston: Beacon Press, 1994. Chapter 3 in Costanza, 1991.

Daly, Herman E. "From Empty-world Economics to Full-world Economics: Recognizing an Historical Turning Point in Economic Development." Chapter 2 in Goodland, Daly, and El Serafy, 1992.

Daly, Herman E. "On Wilfred Beckerman's Critique of Sustainable Development." *Environmental Values* 4 (1995): 49–95.

Daly, Herman E. "The Steady-State Economy: Toward a Political Economy of Biophysical Equilibrium and Moral Growth." Chapter 19 in *Valuing the Earth: Economics, Ecology, Ethics*, edited by Herman E. Daly and Kenneth N. Townsend. Cambridge, Mass.: MIT Press, 1993.

Daly, Herman E. "Operationalizing Sustainable Development by Investing in Natural Capital," in *Investing in Natural Capital: The Ecological Economics Approach to Sustainability,* edited by AnnMari Jansson et al. Washington, D.C.: Island Press, 1994.

Daly, Herman E., and John B. Cobb. *For the Common Good: Redirecting the Economy Toward Community, the Environment, and a Sustainable Future,* 2nd ed. Boston: Beacon Press, 1994.

El Serafy, Salah. "In Defense of Weak Sustainability: A Response to Beckerman." *Environmental Values* 5 (1996): 75–81.

Goodland, Robert, Herman Daly, and Salah El Serafy, eds. *Population, Technology, and Lifestyle: The Transition to Sustainability.* United Nations Educational, Scientific and Cultural Organization (UNESCO), 1992.

Gowdy, John and Sabine O'Hara. "Weak Sustainability and Viable Technologies." *Ecological Economics* 22 (1997): 239–247.

Harris, Jonathan M., and Neva R. Goodwin, "Reconciling Growth and Environment," in Jonathan M. Harris and Neva R. Goodwin, eds., *New Thinking in Macroeconomics.* Cheltenham, U.K.: Elgar, 2003.

Harris, Jonathan M., Timothy A. Wise, Kevin P. Gallagher, and Neva R. Goodwin, eds., *A Survey of Sustainable Development: Social and Economic Dimensions.* Washington, D.C.: Island Press, 2001.

Hicks, Sir John R. *Value and Capital.* Oxford, U.K.: Oxford University Press, 1939.

Howarth, Richard B., and Richard B. Norgaard. "Intergenerational Transfers and the Social Discount Rate." *Environmental and Resource Economics* 3 (August 1993): 337–358.

Krishnan, Rajaram, Jonathan M. Harris, and Neva R. Goodwin, eds. *A Survey of Ecological Economics.* Washington, D.C.: Island Press, 1995.

Meadows, Donella H., et al. *Beyond the Limits: Confronting Global Collapse, Envisioning a Sustainable Future.* White River Junction, Vt.: Chelsea Green, 1992.

Neumayer, Eric. *Weak versus Strong Sustainability: Exploring the Limits of Two Opposing Paradigms.* Cheltenham, U.K.: Elgar, 2003.

Norgaard, Richard B., and Richard B. Howarth. "Sustainability and Discounting the Future," in Costanza, 1991.

Padilla, Emilio. "Intergenerational Equity and Sustainability." *Ecological Economics* 41 (April 2002): 69–83.

Page, Talbot. "On the Problem of Achieving Efficiency and Equity, Intergenerationally." *Land Economics* 73 (November 1997): 580–596. Also summarized in Harris et al., 2001.

Raffensperger, Carolyn, and Joel Tickner. *Protecting Public Health and the Environment: Implementing the Precautionary Principle.* Washington, D.C.: Island Press, 1999.

Ricardo, David. *On the Principles of Political Economy and Taxation* in *The Works and Correspondence of David Ricardo,* edited by Piero Sraffa. Cambridge, U.K.: Cambridge University Press, 1951.

Tickner, Joel A., and Ken Geiser. "The Precautionary Principle Stimulus for Solutions- and Alternatives-based Environmental Policy." *Environmental Impact Assessment Review* 24 (2004): 801–824.

Vitousek, P. M., P. R. Ehrlich, A. H. Ehrlich, and P. A. Matson. "Human Appropriation of the Products of Photosynthesis." *BioScience* 36 (1986), no. 6: 368–373.

Wackernagel, Mathis, and Alex Long, eds. "Ecological Economics Forum." *Ecological Economics* 29 (1999): 13–60.

World Resources Institute, United Nations Development Programme, United Nations Environment Programme, and World Bank. *World Resources 2000–2001: People and Ecosystems: The Fraying Web of Life.* Washington, D.C.: World Resources Institute, 2000.

United Nations Environment Programme. *Global Environmental Outlook 3: Past, Present, and Future Perspectives.* London, U.K.: Earthscan, 2002.

## WEBSITES

1. **http://www.ecoeco.org/** The website for the International Society for Ecological Economics, a nonprofit organization "dedicated to advancing understanding of the relationships among ecological, social, and economic systems for the mutual well-being of nature and people." Their site includes links to research and educational opportunities in ecological economics.

2. **http://www.uvm.edu/giee/** Website for the Gund Institute for Ecological Economics at the University of Vermont, which "transcends traditional disciplinary boundaries in order to address the complex interrelationships between ecological and economic systems in a broad and comprehensive way." The Gund Institute sponsors the EcoValue project, which "provides an interactive decision support system for assessing and reporting the economic value of ecosystem goods and services in geographic context."

3. **http://www.biotech-info.net/precautionary.html** Information provided by the Science and Environmental Health Network (SEHN), which promotes the precautionary principle as it relates to biotechnology and food engineering. Includes articles on definitions and applications of the precautionary principle.

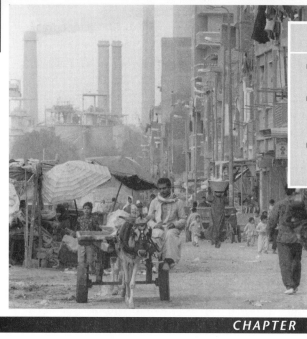

CHAPTER FOCUS QUESTIONS

- Do measures of GNP or GDP give a distorted picture of development?
- Can these measures be adjusted to better reflect environmental and resource factors?
- Do we need new, "greener" measures of national well-being?

# National Income and Environmental Accounting

## Greening the National Income Accounts

Taking the environment seriously affects how we view measures of national income and well-being. Can we say that a nation with a higher per capita national income is necessarily better off than another country with a lower per capita income? Before making this judgment, we should compare factors such as the state of the environment and natural resources in the two countries.

Standard measures of **gross national product (GNP)**, or **gross domestic product (GDP)**, are commonly used to measure a country's level of economic activity and progress in development.[1] Almost all statistics used in macroeconomic analysis are based on these measures, and most economists, as well as the general public, recognize them as standards of economic progress.

---

[1]GNP and GDP are distinguished by whether or not the foreign earnings of individuals and corporations are included in the total. See Appendix to this chapter for a discussion of this and other issues in GNP/GDP measurement.

However, critics have argued that these measures can give a highly misleading impression of economic development. Inconsistencies have long been noted in GNP/GDP measurement, such as the failure to account for unpaid work, production for domestic use, and the value of leisure time. Since GNP/GDP measures only goods traded in markets, it omits work in the household sector, including meal preparation, house cleaning, and care of the young and elderly. It does not include indicators of health, life expectancy, or educational level, nor does it reflect inequality of income. A country with extreme inequality can have a higher GDP per capita than a country where income is more equitably distributed, even though the average person in the second country is better off. We must add another major criticism of the standard GNP/GDP measure—it fails to account for environmental degradation and resource depletion.[2]

This issue can be important especially in developing nations, which depend heavily on natural resources. If a nation cuts down its forests, depletes its soil fertility, and pollutes its water supplies, this surely makes the nation poorer. Even so, national income accounts will merely record the value of the timber, agricultural produce, and industrial output as positive contributions to GNP/GDP. This may lead economic policymakers to view the nation's development in an unrealistically rosy light—at least until the effects of the environmental damage become apparent, which in some cases may be decades.

If we are measuring economic activity with, so to speak, the wrong ruler, we can hardly expect the rest of our economic analysis to be reliable. Economic growth alone does not necessarily represent true economic development, and may even lower human well-being if it is accompanied by growing inequity and environmental degradation. The attempt to define better measures of development has led to several new formulations of national income analysis that attempt to take into account resource and environmental factors.[3] (For a review of basic national income accounting, see the Appendix to this chapter.)

One approach to revising national income accounts is to estimate an economic value for **natural capital depreciation,** and subtract this estimate from the standard measure of GNP/GDP. In standard national income accounting, the **net national product (NNP)** or **net domestic product (NDP)** is calculated by subtracting the depreciation of humanmade capital such as buildings and machinery.[4] A measure of **adjusted net national product (NNP\*)** or **adjusted net domestic product (NDP\*)** extends this logic by calculating a value for natural resource depreciation and subtracting this also from GNP/GDP. Early efforts at calculating adjusted net domestic product showed significant variations from the standard measure (see Figure 8-1).

---

[2]For a survey of critiques of GNP/GDP, see England and Harris, 1997, and England, 1998.

[3]For an overview of natural resource accounting methods, see National Research Council, 1999.

[4]Depreciation is simply a measure of the loss of capital value through wear and tear. For accounting purposes, it can be calculated using a "straight-line" formula according to which, for example, a new machine is estimated to lose 10 percent of its original value each year over a 10-year period, or using more complex valuation methods.

## (a) Indonesian GDP and NDP* Adjusted for Resource Depreciation

Billion Rupiah
(in thousands)

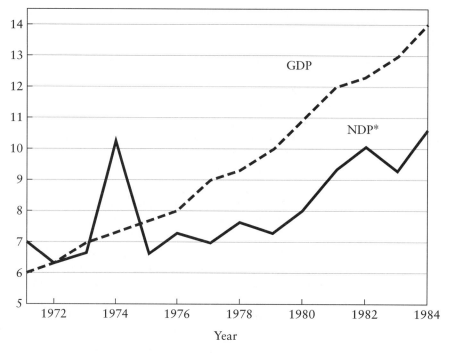

## (b) Costa Rica's Agricultural Product Before and After Resource Depreciation

Product (in billions of
1984 colonies)

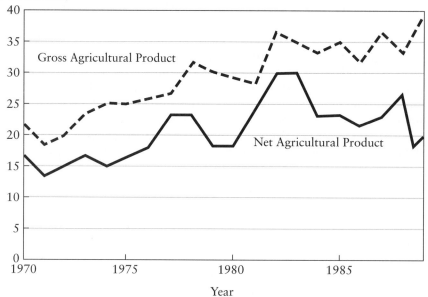

**FIGURE 8-1** *Adjusting GDP for Natural Resource Depreciation*
Sources: (a) Adapted from Robert Repetto et al., *Wasting Assets: Natural Resources in the National Income Accounts.* Washington, D.C.: World Resources Institute, 1989. Reprinted by permission of World Resources Institute. (b) Adapted from Robert Repetto et al., *Accounts Overdue: Natural Resource Depreciation in Costa Rica.* Washington, D.C.: World Resources Institute, 1991. Reprinted by permission of World Resources Institute.

In the case of Indonesia, the revised measure of NDP shows significantly slower growth than the standard measure. The Indonesian study took into account three factors: oil, forests, and soils. These were evaluated in terms of their economic value; no attempt was made to estimate non-use or ecological values. Thus this study does not provide a total estimate of natural capital depreciation but focuses on these three key sectors. Despite this admittedly limited scope, the resulting measure of depreciation lowers GDP significantly and increases over the period of the study. (The 1974 temporary spike in NDP* results from discovery of new oil reserves and high world oil prices.)

A similar study of Costa Rica found significant natural capital depreciation in agriculture, forests, and fisheries. The expanding measure of natural resource depreciation in Costa Rica, evident in the growing gap between gross and net agricultural product, arises from three factors: forest loss, unsustainable rates of soil erosion on cropland and pastures, and overfishing. The rate of nutrient loss from soil erosion is fairly constant, but the forest losses and loss of resource value due to overfishing both increase over the period 1970–1989. The gross measure of Costa Rica's overall agricultural product is generally rising over a 20-year period, but the net measure is lower for the whole period and falls during the later years.

Even more striking than the altered pattern of GDP is the impact on **net investment**. The standard measure of net investment adjusts gross investment[5] by subtracting depreciation of manufactured capital. If we include natural capital depreciation, numerous developing nations show much smaller, or even negative net investment. This has significant implications for development strategy, because investment is the most crucial economic determinant of long-term growth. These studies indicate that by failing to take into account resource and environmental depreciation we systematically overestimate the true value of investment.[6]

Figure 8-2a shows the impact of natural resource depreciation for Indonesia, as applied to investment. Note that adjusted net investment (NDI*) actually falls below zero in 1980, while gross investment is steadily rising. In Figure 8-2b, we see a similar measure for the Philippines. Here the difference between standard net investment and adjusted net investment is not so dramatic, but the use of an adjusted measure shows that a "structural adjustment" program implemented in the 1980s resulted in below-zero net investment for several years. (Structural adjustment programs, intended to

---

[5]Gross investment is total spending by businesses on capital formation.

[6]See Repetto, 1994, on the significance of natural resource accounting.

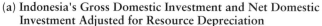
**(a)** Indonesia's Gross Domestic Investment and Net Domestic Investment Adjusted for Resource Depreciation

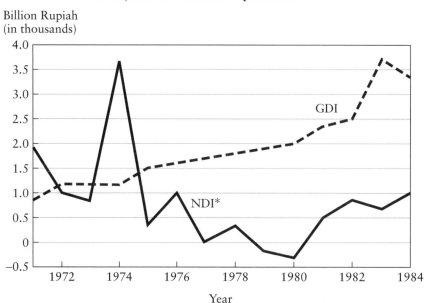

**(b)** Philippines' Investment Adjusted for Resource Depreciation

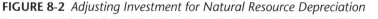

**FIGURE 8-2** *Adjusting Investment for Natural Resource Depreciation*

Sources: (a) Adapted from Robert Repetto et al., *Wasting Assets: Natural Resources in the National Income Accounts.* Washington, D.C.: World Resources Institute, 1989. Reprinted by permission of World Resources Institute. (b) Adapted from Wilfredo Cruz and Robert Repetto, *The Environmental Effects of Stabilization and Structural Adjustment Programs: The Philippines Case.* Washington, D.C.: World Resources Institute, 1992. Reprinted by permission of World Resources Institute.

impose fiscal and monetary discipline on developing nations, have often been criticized for their harsh social effects; here we see that environmental impact is another important dimension. These issues are discussed further in Chapter 20.)

As a step toward integrating economic, environmental, and social policy analysis, the World Bank's Environment Department has developed a **genuine saving** ($S^*$) measure that includes natural capital depreciation as well as foreign borrowing.[7] This measure seeks to determine how much of national income is being saved for the future, taking into account both depletion of natural resources and additions to capital stock. A genuine-saving analysis, particularly appropriate for developing countries, indicates that what may appear a development "success story" can conceal serious natural capital depletion and in some cases even a net negative genuine saving rate.

Figure 8-3 shows estimates of genuine national saving for several major regions. For Latin America, Sub-Saharan Africa, and the Middle East/North Africa the results are striking—genuine saving is low, and often significantly negative, indicating that environmental and resource degradation frequently outweigh humanmade capital accumulation. This can create a pattern of "reverse development" in which countries grow poorer over time when we account for both humanmade and natural capital. Introducing natural capital depreciation into accounting may have significant trade and macroeconomic policy implications, especially for countries that depend heavily on natural resource exports (see Box 8-2 later in this chapter).[8]

Figure 8-3a shows that East Asian developing nations have a strong positive rate of genuine saving. This does not mean that there is no significant resource depletion in these countries, but rather that such resource depletion is outweighed by a large investment in **manufactured capital**—buildings, machinery, transport networks, and other infrastructure. In Latin America, genuine saving is weaker, falling below zero in the mid-1980s. And for Sub-Saharan Africa, the picture is much worse—genuine saving becomes negative around 1979 and remains negative through the 1990s. Three factors account for this: low overall investment, high resource depletion, and extensive foreign borrowing.

In Figure 8-3b, we can see that developed nations generally have positive genuine savings. Again, this does not indicate that there is no resource depletion in these countries, but that environmental depreciation is outweighed by investment in other economic sectors. South Asia (India, Pakistan, and Bangladesh) struggles to maintain a net positive genuine savings rate, indicating that resource depletion nearly equals conventional investment. The negative figures for the Middle East and North Africa represent reduction in oil reserves. Some analysts argue that this indicates a weakness in the World Bank's method of computing genuine saving. Is it necessarily a bad thing for a country to deplete its oil reserves if the proceeds are used to raise living standards and invest in new manufactured capital? A different method of computing genuine savings

---

[7]Hamilton and Clemens, 1997; Hamilton, 2000.

[8]See El Serafy, 1997.

**(a) Genuine Saving Rates by Region, 1970–1993: East Asia/Pacific, Latin America/Caribbean, Sub-Saharan Africa**

Percentage of GNP

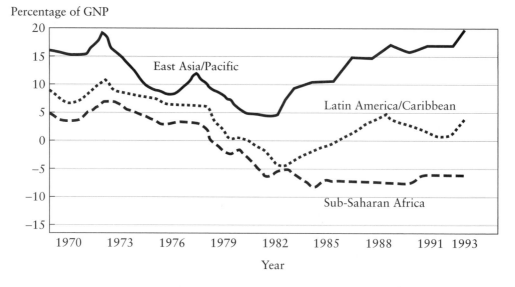

Year

**(b) Genuine Saving Rates by Region, 1970–1993: High-Income OECD South Asia, Middle East/North Africa**

Percentage of GNP

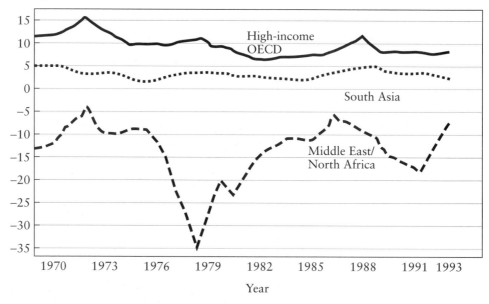

Year

**FIGURE 8-3** *Genuine National Saving*

Note: Organization for Economic Cooperation and Development (OECD) is a group of 30 more developed countries.

Source: Adapted from World Bank, *Expanding the Measure of Wealth: Indicators of Environmentally Sustainable Development.* Copyright 1997 by World Bank. Reproduced with permission of World Bank in the format textbook via the Copyright Clearance Center.

(discussed later in this chapter) would give a more positive picture, weighing new investment more heavily relative to resource depletion.[9]

## Estimating Sustainable Economic Welfare

Estimating resource depreciation is only one approach to incorporating environmental considerations into national income accounts. Another way in which standard national income accounts may overestimate a nation's economic success involves **defensive expenditures.** These are expenses associated with cleaning up pollution or attempting to repair or compensate for other environmental damage. In standard accounting, all such expenditures simply add to GDP.

For example, all U.S. government Superfund expenditures for cleaning up toxic waste sites count as contributions to GDP. The medical costs of treating diseases caused by air or water pollution similarly add to GDP. If coastal homeowners or businesses suffer property damage from an oil spill and sue for damages, the legal expenditures involved and the cleanup costs also contribute to GDP. By this logic, the more pollution damage and resulting cleanup expense a nation experiences, the better off it is—a clearly irrational position.

To take account of defensive expenditures and environmental damages, Herman Daly and John Cobb proposed an Index of Sustainable Economic Welfare (ISEW) for the United States.[10] This concept has been revised to create a U.S. **Genuine Progress Indicator (GPI).** The GPI adjusts economic output by starting with a measure of consumption adjusted for income inequality, adding the value of unpaid work, and subtracting out estimates of defensive expenditures. Rather than measuring the total amount spent on consumer durable goods (for example, refrigerators), the GPI measures *services* provided by these goods. This places a premium on more efficient and durable capital that requires less frequent expenditure but provides more services. Together with adjustments for natural resource depletion and long-term environmental damage, the GPI indicates a much slower improvement in U.S. welfare as compared to the steadily rising GDP indicator (see Table 8-1 and Figure 8-4). Per capita GPI actually declines slightly between 1975 and 2002.

Long-term resource and environmental damage such as ozone layer depletion and greenhouse gas accumulation account for much of the difference between GDP and GPI.[11] If we exclude long-term and cumulative environmental effects, the resulting measure, as shown in Figure 8-4, is closer to GDP, but still shows much less gain since 1975. Sustainable economic welfare measures similar to the GPI have been calculated for European countries and Australia, and show a similar pattern: GPI-type measures

[9]Neumayer, 2000a, criticizes the World Bank methodology and suggests a measure that assigns less weight to depletion of mineral reserves.

[10]Daly and Cobb, 1994.

[11]Some analysts have criticized the large size of these cumulative damage adjustments in GPI, while others defend them. See Neumayer, 2000b, and Lawn, 2003.

**TABLE 8-1** *Genuine Progress Indicator (United States, 2002)*

*Constant 2000 dollars (in billions)*

| | |
|---|---:|
| Personal consumption adjusted for income distribution | $5,523 |
| +services for household and volunteer labor | +2,228 |
| +services of consumer durable goods | +863 |
| +services of highways and streets | +100 |
| −consumer spending on durable goods | −1,000 |
| −cost of crime, family breakdown, loss of leisure time, and underemployment | −611 |
| −cost of commuting and automobile accidents | −660 |
| −cost of household pollution abatement | −15 |
| −cost of air, water, and noise pollution | −109 |
| −loss of wetlands, farmland, and old-growth forests | −689 |
| −depletion of nonrenewable resources | −1,578 |
| −ozone depletion, greenhouse gases, and other long-term environmental damage | −1,546 |
| +/−net capital investment | +523 |
| +/−net foreign lending or borrowing | −307 |
| **Genuine Progress Indicator** | **$2,720** |

Note: Total differs from sum of items due to rounding. + indicates a positive item, − a negative item, and +/− an item that can be positive or negative.

Source: Redefining Progress, www.rprogress.org, *The Genuine Progress Indicator 1950–2002  (2004 Update)*.

rise more or less in parallel to GDP from 1950 to 1970, but thereafter grow at a reduced rate or actually decline.[12]

## Environmental Services and Satellite Accounts

Henry Peskin and Roefie Hueting have put forward a third approach to correcting national income accounts for environmental damage.[13] They suggest defining the environment as a productive sector that contributes services to the economy, many of which remain unaccounted for because they are apparently free. Examples include provision of clean air and water, removal of carbon dioxide from the atmosphere by trees, health and recreational benefits provided by natural areas.

If these **environmental services** are impaired—say, for example, by draining a wetland—an estimate of the cost of duplicating the service must be subtracted from national output. Because wetlands perform important functions that include water purification, nutrient recycling, flood control, and provision of wildlife habitat, this estimated value could be quite high. According to current accounting methods, the wetland makes no contribution to output, but a shopping mall built on drained wetland would add to output, both through construction of the mall and through its annual sales.

All of these approaches to modifying GNP/GDP accounts have merit, but arriving at a single, uniform measure has proved difficult. Some analysts reject attempts to

---

[12]See Lawn, 2003, and http://www.foe.co.uk/campaigns/sustainable_development/progress/.

[13]See Peskin, 1991 and 1994; Hueting, 1991.

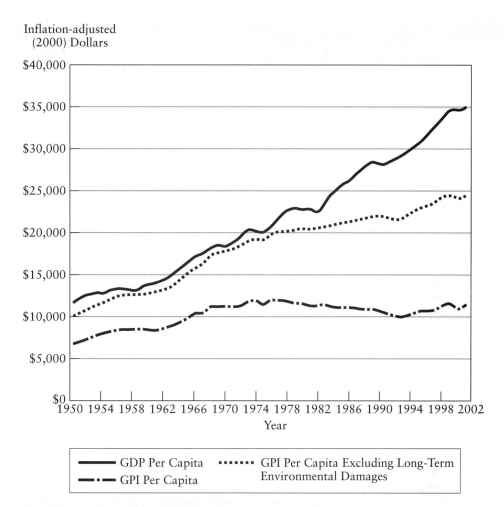

**FIGURE 8-4** *Alternative Measures of U.S. Economic Welfare*

Source: Redefining Progress, *The Genuine Progress Indicator 1950–2002 (2004 Update)*. "GPI per capita excluding long-term environmental damages" calculated from data available at www.rprogress.org.

derive a single figure for "greened" GNP/GDP. Instead, they suggest the use of **satellite accounts,** which measure environmental stocks and functions in physical terms, without necessarily attempting valuation.[14]

Satellite accounts can give a detailed picture of the natural resource base and the state of the environment by measuring such variables as forest cover, mineral resources, and water supplies and noting their changes over time (see Box 8-1). Such data are useful for different kinds of analysis. **Input-output analysis** can show the

---

[14]See Lange and Duchin, 1995.

## 8-1   Green Accounting in the Philippines

Satellite accounts do not reduce environmental accounting to a single value, as do measures such as NNP* or GPI. The satellite accounts' advantage of greater detail is offset by difficulty in interpreting and assessing data measured in different units. The system of environmental accounting adopted by the Philippines illustrates these issues well.

A 1999 article in the journal *Ecological Economics* (Bartelmus, 1999) summarizes environmental accounting data for the Philippines. One satellite account estimates the stock value of various natural resources. As seen in the table, the value of natural capital is generally on the rise in the Philippines. Still, we cannot conclude that natural capital is increasing in the Philippines. The value of natural capital may increase because of an increase in prices rather than an increase in the physical stock.

Looking further at the data, we find that between 1988 and 1994 the stock volume of forests in the Philippines decreased by 30 percent even though total forest value increased by nearly 25 percent. Thus, economic data alone may fail to identify declining natural resource stocks. This illustrates the need for "alternative or supplementary indicators linked to quantifiable standards or targets" (Bartelmus, 155).

Deducting environmental costs from net domestic product for the Philippines lowers NDP by 2 percent to 13 percent. The magnitude of the environmental deduction has been decreasing, "indicating a relative reduction in environmental costs generated by the economy" (Bartelmus, 160). A logging ban instituted in 1992 dramatically reduced the annual value of forest capital depletion. Other data indicate that the quantity of air pollutants released from electricity generators in

*The Value of Natural Capital in the Philippines (in billions of Pesos)*

| Year | Natural Capital Category | | | |
| | Forests | Minerals | Groundwater | Agricultural Land |
| --- | --- | --- | --- | --- |
| 1988 | 594 | 39 | 538 | 389 |
| 1989 | 521 | 45 | 473 | 434 |
| 1990 | 569 | 48 | 522 | 492 |
| 1991 | 557 | 54 | 542 | 580 |
| 1992 | 605 | 39 | 649 | 635 |
| 1993 | 690 | MD[1] | 719 | 688 |
| 1994 | 739 | MD[1] | 757 | MD[1] |

[1]Missing data.

*(continued on following page)*

the Philippines has remained relatively constant. The annual economic loss from groundwater depletion increased more than 40 percent between 1988 and 1994.

Although conflicting environmental data may impede an overall assessment of sustainability, a system of satellite accounts can identify problems with particular resources. Linking physical measures with economic data helps integrate environmental concerns into standard macroeconomic accounting. However, green accounting reaches "its limits when attempting to value welfare effects on human health" (Bartelmus, 169). Thus, forcing environmental accounting to accord with standard economic analysis may fail to provide the details necessary for a full environmental assessment of the country's sustainability.

**SOURCE**

Bartelmus, Peter. "Green Accounting for a Sustainable Economy, Policy Use and Analysis of Environmental Accounts in the Philippines." *Ecological Economics* 29, no. 1 (1999):155–170.

probable effects on resource stocks of various economic policies (see Chapter 9 for more on this approach). Economic valuation methods can also convert these physical measures to money measures for estimates of adjusted NNP/NDP. The United Nations has published a guide to integrated environmental and economic accounting using the satellite approach.[15]

No single system for revising national income accounts for environment and resource impacts has won general acceptance. This means that most economic analysis still relies on standard GDP or NDP measures. If the advocates of revised measures are right, we need to adjust our broader economic theories to reflect new measurements of national product and income. Even without consensus on new measurement techniques, we can explore the implications of environmental or **green accounting** approaches such as those discussed above. In the next section, we discuss their application in more analytical detail.

## Application of Environment and Resource Accounting

How can revised measures of national income guide development policy? We can identify a sustainable development path as one in which the stock of overall capital assets remains constant or rises over time. These capital stocks include manufactured capital,

---

[15]United Nations, 2000.

human capital (skills and education), and natural capital. As we discussed in Chapter 7, these different types of capital may share a degree of substitutability, but we should also take special note of critical natural capital—resources such as essential water supplies, for which no good substitutes exist.[16]

The total capital stock of an economy can thus be presented as:

$$K = K_m + K_h + K_n + K_n^*$$

where

$K_m$ is manufactured capital
$K_h$ is human capital
$K_n$ is noncritical natural capital
$K_n^*$ is critical natural capital

National income accounting must consider any changes in these categories of capital. Investment in capital is a component of standard GNP or GDP. Depreciation of manufactured capital ($D_m$) is subtracted from GDP to get NDP (net domestic product). Human capital is assumed not to depreciate (although this is only true if educational expenditures are adequate).[17] The main issue in environmental and resource accounting is to estimate and subtract depreciation of natural capital ($D_n$) to obtain adjusted net national product, NNP*.

Thus:

$$NDP = GDP - D_m$$

$$NDP^* = GDP - D_m - D_n \text{ (or } NDP^* = NDP - D_n\text{)}$$

The same adjustments are applied to total or gross investment to obtain adjusted net investment:

$$NI = I_g - D_m$$

$$NI^* = I_g - D_m - D_n \text{ (or } NI^* = NI - D_n\text{)}$$

The first question, therefore, is how to obtain an estimate of $D_n$. The pioneering study of Indonesia by Repetto et al. (1989) employed two methods: value of end-of-year stocks (for oil and timber) and productivity loss estimates (for soil). The end-of-year stocks method compares the value of standing timber or estimated oil reserves at the end

[16]Pearce and Warford (1993) discuss the concept of critical natural capital. The analytical presentation here uses the categories they propose for the definition of different kinds of capital. For an extended discussion of critical natural capital, see Ekins et al., 2003.

[17]To take this factor into account, World Bank researchers have calculated a measure of "expanded net investment" that includes educational expenditures. See World Bank, 1997, and Harris et al., 2001.

*Safety-suited workers fill bags with contaminated sand after an oil spill off Huntington Beach, California. Cleanup costs will be a positive, not a negative, in standard GDP accounts.*

of the year as compared to their value at the beginning of the year, using current prices. This method can show an increase in natural resource value if new resource discoveries are made or if prices increase during a given year (this accounts for the 1974 spike in NDP* in Figure 8-1a and NDI in Figure 8-2a). It also takes no account of forests' ecological and service values other than timber production.

Productivity loss estimates require the use of a discount rate to obtain a present value of a stream of future losses:

$$PV[\text{Loss}] = L_0 + L_1/(1 + r) + L_2/(1 + r)^2 + \ldots L_n/(1 + r)^n$$

where $L_i$ is the loss in year $i$, $r$ is the discount rate, and $n$ is the number of years. If annual losses are the same in each future year, this can be simplified to

$$PV[\text{Loss}] = L/r$$

where $L$ is the annual loss and $r$ is the interest rate.[18]

---

[18]Mathematically, the value of the sum of an infinite series $L$ is equal to $L/r$ where $r$ is the discount rate.

In Indonesia, severe highland erosion has led to soil productivity losses. If projected into the future, the present value of future losses from Indonesia's erosive agricultural production may be greater than the value of current crops.

The estimates of changes in end-of-year resource stocks and productivity loss estimates are combined to give the total value of resource depreciation for a given year. This total is subtracted from standard NDP to derive an adjusted NDP, and from net investment to obtain adjusted net investment.

In addition to natural capital depreciation, we can subtract estimates of defensive expenditures ($E_d$) and short-term pollution damage ($PD$) from $GDP$ to obtain a broader measure of **environmentally adjusted net domestic product (EDP)**:

$$\text{EDP} = GDP - D_m - D_n - E_d - PD$$

Estimates of defensive expenditures and short-term pollution damages, however, should not be subtracted from net investment, since they affect only one year's national well being. Long-term pollution damages, which lower the value of natural capital, can appropriately be subtracted from net investment.

## *Measures of True Income*

El Serafy, a critic of the end-of-year stocks method, prefers the **user cost** method.[19] This method estimates **true income** by subtracting the portion of total income that theoretically must be invested at current long-term interest rates to guarantee a continued flow of income at the same level.

The principle here is similar to an individual's investing in a retirement account. By the time the wage-earner reaches age 65, she or he hopes to have a substantial enough retirement account to provide an adequate income. In the same way, a nation with a nonrenewable resource base should invest a sufficient amount from the proceeds of selling that resource to guarantee a continued flow of income once the resource is exhausted.

The relationship of this true income ($X$) to **net receipts** ($R$) from resource sales is given by the following formula:

$$X/R = 1 - 1/(1 + r)^n$$

where $r$ is the discount rate and $n$ is the expected lifetime of the resource.

For example, if $r = .04$ and $n = 20$, $X/R = 0.55$. True income would then be 55 percent of net receipts. The user cost would be the remaining portion of net receipts, in this case 45 percent. Rather than subtracting the full value of $R$ from $GDP$ to calculate natural resource depreciation, we would then subtract only the user cost, $R - X$.

---

[19]El Serafy, 1993.

In the case of Indonesia, using this method gives a more stable estimate of NNP* than the one shown in Figure 8-1a, varying from about 5 percent to about 15 percent lower than standard GDP.[20]

The impact of proper natural resource accounting is more dramatic if we look only at the saving/investment component of GDP. Together with standard manufactured capital depreciation, the effect can be to lower adjusted net investment ($I_n^*$) close to zero or below zero. A measure of genuine saving ($S^*$) for developing nations should subtract both types of depreciation and also **net foreign borrowing (NFB)** from gross investment ($I_g$). Thus:

$$S^* = I_g - D_m - D_n - \text{NFB}$$

As shown in Figure 8-3, this adjusted saving figure gives a startling picture of low or negative saving rates in many developing nations. If we adopt the user cost method for calculating genuine savings, the adjustment is less dramatic, especially for nations that, like Saudi Arabia, depend heavily on oil revenues.

What policy implications arise from using these revised measures of national income? One obvious lesson would be the need for environmental policies to conserve natural capital. Rather than simply striving to maximize economic growth as it is conventionally defined, policymakers need an integrated plan for economic and environmental goals. El Serafy has analyzed trade and macroeconomic policy effects that arise from the failure to account adequately for resource depletion (see Box 8-2).

## Measuring Well-Being: Social and Ecological Dimensions

The field of environmental and natural resource accounting continues to develop. Policy conclusions vary, depending on the analytical approaches chosen. Many developing countries experience significant problems with obtaining adequate data.[21] Several of the following underlying issues, also reviewed in Chapters 6 and 7, have important implications for green accounting:

- **Weak versus strong sustainability.** Note that the analysis of natural capital depreciation implicitly assumes **substitutability** of different types of capital, as measured in money value. For example, the loss of $1 million in timber (natural capital) can be fully compensated for by acquiring $1 million in machinery (manufactured capital). From an accounting point of view, the value of total

---

[20]This revised estimate of Indonesian natural resource depreciation is calculated in El Serafy, 1993. Crowards, 1996, estimates natural resource depreciation for Zimbabwe at 1–3 percent, but believes that data problems and distorted prices resulting from government subsidies and price controls make this a significant underestimate.

[21]See, for example, Crowards, 1996. For a discussion of green accounting practices, see Vincent, 2000, and Lange et al., 2003.

## *8-2*  Incorrect Accounting Leads to Incorrect Policies

If economists accept conventional GDP estimates, their policy recommendations are likely to be wrong regarding natural-resource–dependent economies. Output estimates may be exaggerated by 20 percent or more, and true estimates of capital formation may prove nil or negative. Factor productivity estimates are thrown into question when neither products nor inputs are measured correctly. Capital/output ratios will be incorrect if they ignore rapid liquidation of natural capital. Sophisticated macroeconomic models based on such data will give highly questionable results for guiding long-term development.

International trade will tend to align domestic and international prices, but international prices are often distorted by agricultural subsidies, political and military interventions, and failure to internalize externalities. As a result, natural resources are likely to be sold below full environmental cost.

The impact of natural capital depletion will be especially large in estimates of national saving and investment. Estimates of "genuine saving" by the World Bank indicate that many countries' net saving and capital formation may in fact be negative, which clearly indicates lack of sustainability.

The export of natural capital also distorts exchange rates, and creates a bias against non–resource-exporting sectors, including manufacturing. Methods used to estimate exchange rate overvaluation become unreliable when proceeds from the unsustainable export of natural assets finance an import surplus. In this case, an apparently stable domestic price level is illusory, masking significant damage to non–resource-exporting sectors that must compete with artificially cheap imports. A trade deficit may be concealed or appear as a surplus in the balance of payments accounts because the proceeds of natural capital exports are recorded incorrectly in the current account.

"Greening the national accounts is more important for economic than for environmental policy . . . especially for those countries whose natural resources are rapidly eroding, and the erosion is counted misleadingly in GDP as value added. Once the accounts are greened, macroeconomic policies need to be reexamined."

**SOURCE**

El Serafy, Salah. "Green Accounting and Economic Policy." Summarized in *A Survey of Sustainable Development,* edited by Harris et al., 2001.

capital in this case is unchanged. **Weak sustainability** accepts this view of different types of capital as substitutable.

**Strong sustainability** identifies types of natural capital for which this type of substitution is considered unacceptable. This involves the concept of critical natural capital ($K_n^*$), which must be preserved and whose destruction would not be compensated for by acquisition of other forms of capital. Another interpretation of strong sustainability would suggest that if a specific resource (for example, fossil fuels) is depleted, it must be replaced by capital with a comparable function (for example, solar energy installations that produce hydrogen fuel).[22]

- **Valuation of environmental damages.** The loss-of-productivity calculation referred to above provides one measure of soil erosion damage. An alternative method might be to examine the **replacement cost** of restoring fertility to eroded lands, for example by applying fertilizer. This method was used in the World Resources Institute study of Costa Rica and has also been used in United Nations studies. This approach is weakened by the fact that applying fertilizer may not fully restore the functions of eroded soil (such as soil structure, tilth, water-retention capability, and micronutrient supplies).

- **Valuation of environmental services.** The value of environmental assets is often more than is indicated by a simple economic measure. Forests, for example, provide more than timber value. They also provide watershed stabilization, runoff control and filtration, carbon sequestration, and maintenance of biodiversity, as well as having aesthetic and recreational value. As we saw in Chapter 6, various methods can be used to estimate these nonmarket values, but they have rarely been applied to natural resource and environmental accounting. In addition, it is questionable whether any economic valuation technique can capture the full **ecological value** of these varied ecosystem services.

- **Contribution to global environmental damages.** Economic activity in one country may cause environmental damage to the atmosphere or oceans that leads to **transboundary pollution** or **global pollution.** The polluting country's national product may be unaffected, but account should be taken of environmental damage to other countries or to the world as a whole. Often this involves **cumulative pollutants.** An estimate of the effects of such cumulative damage on sustainable welfare is included in the GPI measure shown in Figure 8-4.

- **Equity and basic needs.** Increases in GDP may be unequally distributed, with most of the benefits going to the already rich. Standard measures take no account of inequity or of its practical effects on health, education, literacy, availability of clean water, and access to basic needs including food and housing. In addition to being important in themselves, these issues interrelate with environmental degradation—poverty often forces people to use resources in an unsustainable manner, and resource degradation in turn worsens poverty.

---

[22]For an extensive discussion of weak versus strong sustainability, see Neumayer, 2003.

**TABLE 8-2** *Human Development Index Scores for Selected Developing Nations*

| Nation | GDP per capita (US $ 2002) | Life Expectancy | Adult Literacy (%) | School Enrollment (%) | HDI Score |
|---|---|---|---|---|---|
| *Middle-Income Countries* | | | | | |
| Panama | $6,170 | 74.6 | 92.3 | 73 | 0.791 |
| Belize | $6,080 | 71.5 | 76.9 | 71 | 0.737 |
| Namibia | $6,210 | 45.3 | 83.3 | 71 | 0.607 |
| *Low-Income Countries* | | | | | |
| Vietnam | $2,300 | 69.0 | 69.0 | 64 | 0.691 |
| Zimbabwe | $2,400 | 33.9 | 90.0 | 58 | 0.491 |
| Angola | $2,130 | 40.1 | 42.0 | 30 | 0.381 |

Note: GDP per capita is measured in Purchasing Power Parity (PPP), indicating the value of domestic income in terms of goods-purchasing power (see Appendix to this chapter).

Source: United Nations Development Programme, 2004.

## Measures of Human Development

The United Nations Development Programme's **Human Development Index (HDI)** combines equity and basic needs measures with standard GDP. The HDI uses an adjusted measure of real per capita GDP as one component of an index that also includes life expectancy and access to education. Countries with similar conventional GDP levels often vary quite dramatically in human welfare as measured by these multivariate development indicators (Table 8-2).

For example, Panama, Belize, and Namibia have similar levels of GDP, but their HDI scores vary significantly. Panama has the highest HDI score because of high education levels and relatively long life expectancy. Meanwhile, Namibia has a low HDI score, primarily because of low life expectancy. Vietnam, Zimbabwe, and Angola also have similar GDP per capita values but widely varying HDI scores. In Vietnam, people are poor yet relatively educated and long-lived. Those in Zimbabwe are also educated but with much shorter life expectancies. In Angola, people have both low educational levels and short life expectancies.

To take account of education, the World Bank has also introduced an expanded measure of national investment, which counts all educational expenditures as an integral part of national investment.[23] Combination of this with natural capital depreciation gives a revised measure that indicates the importance of public investment in education in improving the genuine saving picture in many developing nations (Figure 8-5). For low-income nations, including a full measure of education spending approximately doubles genuine saving.

---

[23]Hamilton and Clemens, 1997.

Percentage of GNP

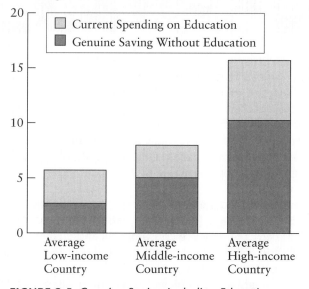

**FIGURE 8-5** *Genuine Saving Including Education*

Source: Adapted from World Bank, *Expanding the Measure of Wealth: Indicators of Environmentally Sustainable Development.* Copyright 1997 by World Bank. Reprinted with permission of World Bank in the format textbook via Copyright Clearance Center.

What can we conclude from this variety of approaches to revising or supplementing GNP/GDP measures? No single clear alternative to GNP/GDP emerges. Yet the environmental and social factors omitted in standard accounting have important implications both for policy and for our understanding of the meaning of economic development. Extensive research has been done on methods and applications of environmental accounting. The U.S. National Research Council has endorsed the concept of extending national income accounts to include the environment, and "green" national income studies have been done for many countries. Nineteen countries now maintain environmental accounting programs, and China has officially adopted the use of environmental accounts (see Box 8-3).[24] Environmental accounting efforts by international institutions such as the World Bank and the United Nations have led to more extensive reporting of social and environmental data.[25] These data will provide a basis for ongoing efforts to rethink standard measures of economic development.

---

[24]See National Research Council, 1999; Simon and Proops, 2000; Lange, 2003; and Lange et al., 2003.

[25]See World Bank, 2003; UNDP, 2004.

## 8-3    China Adopts Green GDP System

On September 1, 2004, China's State Environmental Protection Administration released a report that China had established an initial Green GDP accounting system. The new system will be launched in six pilot cities and provinces including Beijing, Jilin, Shaanxi, Guangdong, and Shanghai.

The Chinese government is paying more attention to the importance of environment and resources. For the first time, the National Bureau of Statistics included a special section on resources and the environment in its annual report on economic and social development.

According to Xu Xianchun, director-general of the department of national accounts of the National Bureau of Statistics (NBS), the Green GDP measure will deduct from traditional GDP the costs of resource consumption and environmental loss due to economic activities, and will show a different national economic growth rate. The NBS plans to adopt the calculation measures set forth by the United Nations in its comprehensive environmental economic account system. Land, forestry, mineral, and water resources will be included, as well as an energy resources account. Initial estimates are that China's growth rate will drop about 2 percentage points with environmental costs included.

China's rapid growth rate has sparked concern that the environmental base may not support resource and environmental demands. For example, China's per capita freshwater supplies are only 18.5 percent of average world levels, while consumption is more than twice that in European countries. The Ministry of Land and Resources warns that many mines must soon close due to resource depletion.

The first Chinese province to calculate Green GDP is Shaanxi, a coal-mining province south of Beijing. The province's academy of social sciences has concluded that its true economic growth has been near zero when resource depletion and environmental degradation are included. Costs attributed to pollution alone amounted to 10.9 percent of the official GDP for 2002. Depletion of coal resources, land, and water subtracted another 23 percent of GDP. According to Dong Jibing, deputy director of the Shaanxi academy, "You can see the enormous negative influence of environmental pollution and resource exploitation on Shaanxi's GDP. The (central) government should consider fiscal transfers to compensate for the contribution and sacrifice of Shaanxi."

### SOURCES

People's Daily Online (http://English.peopledaily.com.cn); *Financial Times* (London, U.K.) August 19, 2004, and Financial Times Information Global News Wire, September 3 and September 6, 2004.

## SUMMARY

Standard measures of national income such as gross national product (GNP) and gross domestic product (GDP) fail to capture important environmental and social factors. This can result in misleading measurements of national well being, potentially ignoring important environmental problems. A variety of methods can be used to correct the GNP/GDP measure or to provide alternatives.

Estimates of natural capital depreciation measure the depletion of natural resources such as oil, timber, minerals, and agricultural soils. Figures for these losses are subtracted from the standard measures of national income and investment. The results for many developing nations indicate substantial effects from natural resource depletion and environmental degradation.

For developed nations, expenditures on pollution control and cleanup, as well as the cumulative effects of long-lived pollutants, are significant factors. It is also possible to estimate the value of environmental services such as water purification, nutrient recycling, flood control, and provision of wildlife habitat. Systematic calculation of such factors can give a measure of sustainable economic welfare, which often differs significantly from GNP/GDP.

The application of modified national income accounting has wide-ranging policy implications. Nations that gain a large proportion of their export earnings from resource exports may be overestimating their economic progress. Natural resources may be sold below their true costs, leading to a net loss for the nation despite an apparent trade surplus.

Social as well as environmental conditions affect calculations of national income. Questions of human development including educational expenditures and measures of equity often interrelate with issues of environmental degradation. Despite the evident importance of these factors, there is no consensus on how to include them in national accounts. An alternative approach is to maintain satellite accounts, measuring social and environmental indicators separately from GNP/GDP. International institutions have moved toward more extensive reporting of such data, giving a basis for more accurate assessments of true national well-being.

## KEY TERMS AND CONCEPTS[†]

adjusted net domestic product (NDP*)
adjusted net national product (NNP*)
constant dollars
critical natural capital
cumulative pollutants
defensive expenditures
depreciation
ecological value
end-of-year stocks

environmental services
environmentally adjusted net
    domestic product (EDP)
equity
genuine saving ($S*$)
global pollution
green accounting
Genuine Progress Indicator (GPI)
gross domestic product (GDP)

†Including terms from Appendix.

gross domestic product (GDP) per capita
gross investment
gross national product (GNP)
human capital
Human Development Index (HDI)
input-output analysis
manufactured capital
natural capital depreciation
net domestic product (NDP)
net foreign borrowing (NFB)
net investment
net national product (NNP)
net receipts
product, spending, and income
  approaches to calculating GDP

productivity loss estimates
purchasing power parity (PPP)
real GDP
replacement cost
satellite accounts
strong sustainability
substitutability (of natural and
  manufactured capital)
transboundary pollution
true income
user cost
value-added method
weak sustainability

## DISCUSSION QUESTIONS

1. What kinds of problems arise from the focus on standard GNP/GDP measures in discussing economic policy? How do these problems differ for highly industrialized nations such as the United States and developing nations such as Indonesia?

2. What main approaches can be used to correct GNP/GDP for natural resource depletion and environmental damage? What difficulties and controversies arise in calculating these adjustments to GDP?

3. Would you consider a revised national income measure an improvement over current GNP concepts, or would you think it better to keep GNP and resource/environmental considerations separate by using satellite accounts?

4. Discuss policy implications of using a revised measure that takes into account environmental and resource depreciation. How might using revised measures affect such policy areas as macroeconomic policy, trade policy, and resource pricing policy?

## PROBLEMS

1. The following is macroeconomic information for the developing nation of Equatoria (expressed in international $ values). The Equatorian economy is composed of three sectors: agriculture, mining, and industrial.

| | |
|---|---|
| Value of Agricultural Sector Output | $800 million |
| Value of Mining Sector Output | $450 million |
| Value of Industrial Sector Output | $750 million |
| Gross Investment ($I_g$) | $550 million |

| | |
|---|---|
| Net Foreign Borrowing (NFB) | $110 million |
| Depreciation of Manufactured Capital ($D_m$) | $150 million |

Use these statistics to compute a standard measure of gross domestic product (GDP), net domestic product (NDP), and net investment ($NI = I_g - D_m$), for this three-sector economy.

Now consider the following information about natural resources and environment in Equatoria:

| | |
|---|---|
| Agricultural Area (million Ha) | 8 |
| Soil Erosion (tons/Ha/year) | 200 |
| Yield Loss Factor per 100 tons/Ha erosion | 0.75% |
| Copper Reserves (million tons) | 150 |
| Copper Extraction Per Year (million tons) | 6.0 |
| Net Price (Price—extraction costs) of Copper Per Ton | $75 |
| Industrial Pollution ($SO_2$) Per Year (thousand tons) | 750 |
| Damage Estimate Per Ton of $SO_2$ Emitted | $120 |

Use these data and the formulas on pages 164–166 to compute an environmentally adjusted measure of net domestic product (EDP) and adjusted net investment ($NI^*$). Remember that soil erosion damage will continue to affect yields in future years. Assume that industrial pollution damage is short term (affecting one year only).

To calculate the present value of future losses, use a discount rate ($r$). Experiment with discount rates of 10 percent, 5 percent, and 2 percent and compare the results (round to the nearest million).

For nonrenewable resource depletion, you will need a measure of user costs. This can be derived from the formula relating true income ($X$) from extraction of a depletable resource to net receipts ($R$):

$$X/R = 1 - 1/(1 + r)^n$$

where $n$ is the expected resource lifetime.

$$\text{User Cost} = R - X = R/(1 + r)^n$$

2. Using the same figures for Equatoria, compute a measure of genuine national savings ($S^*$), defined as gross investment minus depreciation of manufactured capital ($D_m$) minus depreciation of natural capital ($D_n$) minus net foreign borrowing (NFB):

$$S^* = I_g - D_m - D_n - \text{NFB} = NI^* - \text{NFB}$$

Suppose we have further information related to environmental policies for Equatoria:

- An effective soil conservation program can be put in place at a cost of $20/Ha.
- $SO_2$ emissions can be cut by up to 50 percent for a cost of $50 per ton of pollution reduced.

Using this information, discuss implications of your adjusted national income, investment, and savings calculations for policy in Equatoria. Be specific in your policy recommendations, remembering that Equatoria is a low-income developing nation.

## REFERENCES

Cobb, Clifford W., and John B. Cobb Jr. *The Green National Product: A Proposed Index of Sustainable Economic Welfare.* Lanham, Md.: University Press of America, 1994.

Crowards, Tom M. "Natural Resource Accounting: A Case Study of Zimbabwe." *Environmental and Resource Economics* 7 (1996): 213–241.

Cruz, Wilfredo, and Robert Repetto, *The Environmental Effects of Stabilization and Structural Adjustment Programs: The Philippines Case.* Washington, D.C.: World Resources Institute, 1992.

Daly, Herman, and John B. Cobb Jr. *For the Common Good: Redirecting the Economy Toward Community, the Environment, and a Sustainable Future.* Boston: Beacon Press, 1994.

Ekins, Paul et al. "A Framework for the Practical Application of the Concepts of Critical Natural Capital and Strong Sustainability." *Ecological Economics* 44 (2003): 165–185.

El Serafy, Salah. *Country Macroeconomic Work and Natural Resources.* World Bank Environment Department Working Paper No. 58, March 1993.

El Serafy, Salah. "Green Accounting and Economic Policy." *Ecological Economics* 21 (1997): 217–229. Summarized in *A Survey of Sustainable Development: Social and Economic Dimensions,* edited by Harris et al. Washington, D.C.: Island Press, 2001.

England, Richard W. "Measurement of Social Well-Being: Alternatives to Gross Domestic Product." *Ecological Economics* 25 (April 1998): 89–103.

England, Richard W., and Jonathan M. Harris. *Alternatives to Gross National Product: A Critical Survey.* Tufts University Global Development and Environment Institute Discussion Paper #5 (1997), available at http://www.ase.tufts.edu/gdae/publications/ archives/englandpaper.pdf.

Hamilton, Kirk. *Genuine Saving as a Sustainability Indicator.* World Bank Environment Department Papers, Environmental Economics Series #77 (October 2000), available at http://www.worldbank.org/environmentaleconomics.

Hamilton, Kirk, and Michael Clemens. "Are We Saving Enough for the Future?" Chapter 2 in *Expanding the Measure of Wealth: Indicators of Environmentally Sustainable Development,* World Bank (1997). Summarized in *A Survey of Sustainable Development: Social and Economic Dimensions,* edited by Harris et al. Washington, D.C.: Island Press, 2001.

Harris, Jonathan M., Timothy A. Wise, Kevin P. Gallagher, and Neva R. Goodwin, eds. *A Survey of Sustainable Development: Social and Economic Dimensions.* Washington, D.C.: Island Press, 2001.

Hueting, Roefie. "Correcting National Income for Environmental Losses: A Practical Solution for a Theoretical Dilemma." In *Ecological Economics,* edited by Robert Costanza. New York: Columbia University Press, 1991.

Krishnan, Rajaram et al., eds. *A Survey of Ecological Economics.* Washington, D.C.: Island Press, 1995.

Lange, Glenn-Marie. *Policy Applications of Environmental Accounting.* World Bank Environment Department Papers, Environmental Economics Series (January 2003), available at http://www.worldbank.org/environmentaleconomics.

Lange, Glenn-Marie, Rashid Hassan, Kirk Hamilton, and Moortaza Jiwanji. *Environmental Accounting in Action: Case Studies from Southern Africa.* Cheltenham, U.K.: Elgar, 2003.

Lange, Glenn-Marie, and Faye Duchin. *Integrated Environmental-Economic Accounting: Natural Resource Accounts, and Natural Resource Management in Africa.* Winrock International Institute Technical Report No. 13; also summarized in *A Survey of Ecological Economics,* edited by Krishnan et al. Washington, D.C.: Island Press, 1995.

Lawn, Philip A. "A Theoretical Foundation to Support the Index of Sustainable Economic Welfare (ISEW), Genuine Progress Indicator (GPI), and Other Related Indexes." *Ecological Economics* 44 (February 2003): 105–118.

Lutz, Ernst, ed. *Toward Improved Accounting for the Environment.* Washington, D.C.: World Bank, 1993.

National Research Council. *Nature's Number: Expanding the National Economic Accounts to Include the Environment.* (William D. Nordhaus and Edward C. Kokkelenberg, eds.) Washington, D.C.: National Academy Press, 1999.

Neumayer, Eric. "Resource Accounting in Measures of Unsustainability: Challenging the World Bank's Conclusions." *Environmental and Resource Economics* 15 (2000a): 257–278.

Neumayer, Eric. "On the Methodology of ISEW, GPI, and Related Measures: Some Constructive Suggestions and Some Doubt on the 'Threshold' Hypothesis." *Ecological Economics* 34 (September 2000b): 347–361.

Neumayer, Eric. *Weak versus Strong Sustainability: Exploring the Limits of Two Opposing Paradigms.* Cheltenham, U.K.: Elgar, 2003.

Pearce, David W., and Jeremy J. Warford. *World Without End: Economics, Environment, and Sustainable Development.* New York and Oxford, U.K.: Oxford University Press, 1993.

Peskin, Henry M. "Alternative Environmental and Resource Accounting Approaches." Chapter 13 in *Ecological Economics: The Science and Management of Sustainability,* edited by Robert Costanza. New York: Columbia University Press, 1991.

Peskin, Henry M. "Sustainable Resource Accounting." Chapter 4 in *Assigning Economic Value to Natural Resources.* National Research Council. Washington, D.C.: National Academy Press, 1994.

Repetto, Robert, et al. *Wasting Assets: Natural Resources in the National Income Accounts*. Washington, D.C.: World Resources Institute, 1989.

Repetto, Robert, et al. *Accounts Overdue: Natural Resource Depreciation in Costa Rica*. Washington, D.C.: World Resources Institute, 1991.

Repetto, Robert. "What Can Policymakers Learn from Natural Resource Accounting?" Chapter 2 in *Assigning Economic Value to Natural Resources*. National Research Council. Washington, D.C.: National Academy Press, 1994.

Simon, Sandrine, and John Proops, eds. *Greening the Accounts*. Cheltenham, U.K.: Elgar, 2000.

United Nations Department of Economic and Social Affairs, Statistics Division. *Integrated Environmental and Economic Accounting: An Operational Manual*. New York: United Nations, 2000.

United Nations Development Programme, 2004. *Human Development Report 2004: Cultural Liberty in Today's Diverse World*. New York: United Nations Development Programme.

Vincent, Jeffrey R. "Green Accounting: From Theory to Practice." *Environment and Development Economics* 5 (Feb–May 2000): 13–24.

World Bank. *Expanding the Measure of Wealth: Indicators of Environmentally Sustainable Development*. Washington, D.C.: World Bank, 1997.

World Bank. *World Development Report 2003: Sustainable Development in a Dynamic World: Transforming Institutions, Growth, and the Quality of Life*. New York: World Bank and Oxford University Press, 2003.

## WEBSITES

1. **http://www.bea.doc.gov/bea/an/0494od/maintext.htm** and **http://www.bea.doc.gov/bea/an/0494od2/maintext.htm** These 1994 articles published by the U.S. Bureau of Economic Analysis discuss the concepts and estimation of natural resource satellite accounts for the United States.

2. **http://www.rprogress.org/newprojects/gpi/index.shtml** A website from Redefining Progress on the Genuine Progress Indicator. The site includes information on how the GPI is calculated and presents trend data on the GPI.

3. **http://www.worldbank.org/environmentaleconomics** The World Bank's Environmental Economics and Indicators website. The site includes links to theoretical and empirical reports on green accounting.

4. **http://www.foe.co.uk/campaigns/sustainable_development/progress/** A discussion of sustainable economic welfare measures, including a graphical presentation of indexes for European countries, Chile, and Australia, and a step-by-step guide to constructing a sustainable development measure for the United Kingdom.

## APPENDIX: BASIC NATIONAL INCOME ACCOUNTING

In this chapter we have discussed several modifications and alternatives to traditional national income accounting. Standard accounting measures, such as gross national product (GNP) and gross domestic product (GDP), are widely accepted estimates of the health of a national economy. However, these measures have numerous technical and conceptual limitations. To understand the impetus for adjusting or replacing these measures requires background knowledge of how they are calculated and interpreted. If you have not taken an introductory macroeconomics course or need to refresh your knowledge, this appendix will help you work through the concepts presented in the chapter.

National income accounting was first developed in the United States in the 1930s to provide policymakers with information on the country's overall level of economic activity. We should realize that national income accounting was not designed to estimate the welfare of society—only the aggregate level of economic production. Also, when the accounts were designed, environmental degradation was not seen as an important issue.

For many years, the official measure of national economic activity in the United States was gross national product. GNP is defined as the final market value of all new goods and services produced by the citizens of a country over a period of time (typically one year). GNP includes goods and services produced by U.S. citizens and corporations in foreign countries but not goods and services produced within U.S. borders by foreign citizens and corporations.

In the early 1990s, the United States switched to gross domestic product as its official measure to conform with international standards developed by the United Nations. GDP measures the value of goods and services produced within the national boundaries of a country regardless of the producer's nationality. Thus GDP would exclude production by U.S. citizens and corporations in foreign countries. In practice, little quantitative difference exists between GNP and GDP. In 2003, U.S. values differed only by about 0.5 percent.

It is important to note that GNP and GDP measure only the final value of goods and services. Intermediate values are excluded to avoid double-counting. For example, consider the steps involved in producing this textbook. First, a lumber company harvested wood and sold the wood to a paper mill. The paper mill then produced paper and sold it to a printing company. The printing company then printed the text under contract with the publisher. The publisher then sold the book to a retail store for final sale to you. If we add up the prices paid by the paper mill, printing company, publisher, retail store, and you, we'll end up with a value much higher than the price you paid for the book. The more intermediate production steps taken to produce an item, the higher the sum of all the prices paid, so only the final price you paid is included in GNP.

Since it may be difficult in practice to distinguish intermediate from final goods, the accounting method generally used to compute GNP/GDP is the **value-added method,** in which the extra value added at each step of the production process is counted. In the textbook example, the value added for the paper mill is the value of its output minus the cost of inputs purchased from the lumber company. The sum of the values added at all stages of production is equal to the value of the final good.

GNP and GDP count only the production of new goods. If you purchased this book second hand from a store or another student, it would not be included in the national accounts. The sale of used products does not contribute to current economic production.

## Calculating the Value of Gross Domestic Product

As you might imagine, calculating the total value of all goods and services produced in a national economy is not a simple task. Economists use a variety of data sources to estimate aggregate production including data from tax returns, surveys of businesses and households, and government records. There are three ways to estimate GDP: the **product approach,** the **spending approach,** and the **income approach.** The product approach simply adds up the dollar value of all final goods and services produced in the economy. The spending approach adds up the expenditures of consumers, businesses, governments, and institutions for final goods and services. The income approach adds up the earnings of everyone in the economy, including wages, profits, investment income, and rental income.

In a simplified closed economy with no depreciation or inventories[1] and where all business earnings are paid out as income, all three approaches should produce the same value. In other words, if an economy produces $7 billion worth of goods and services, we can conclude that $7 billion was spent to purchase these goods and services and $7 billion in income was earned to make these purchases. Of course, the real economy is more complex and the different approaches may produce different values. For example, not everything produced in a year may be sold during that year. Economists have devised adjustment methods so that the different approach should produce the same values, but even so there remain statistical discrepancies arising from the complexity of the data or missing information.

The national accounts divide the economy into four sectors: businesses, households and institutions, governments, and the foreign sector. Using the product approach, we would add up the final goods and services produced by all businesses, households and institutions, and governments. As you might guess, using the product approach we discover that the business sector produces most of the marketed final goods and services in the economy (77 percent in 2003 for the U.S. economy). Household production, as defined in the national accounts, includes rental values and paid work within households such as maid services, child care, and gardening. However, similar household work that is not marketed, such as people cooking their own meals or cleaning their own homes, is not included in GDP. This is one common criticism of GDP. For example, essentially the same service is produced whether a household cleans their own home or hires someone to do it, but only in the latter case is the value of the service included in GDP.

---

[1]A closed economy is one without any imports or exports. Inventories are unsold goods held by businesses.

Using the spending approach, we need to consider the foreign sector in calculating GDP. We add demands by foreigners for goods produced in the United States (exports) and subtract demand by U.S. residents and institutions for foreign goods (imports). Business spending on machinery, buildings, and other goods is called **gross investment.** Governments also purchase goods and services and make investments. Using the spending approach, we find that households and institutions purchase most of the final goods and services produced in the economy (about 71 percent). The spending approach can be summarized by the equation

$$Y = C + I + G + (X - M)$$

where $Y$ represents GDP, $C$ is consumer expenditures, $I$ is business investment, $G$ is government spending on goods and services, and $(X - M)$ is net exports (exports minus imports).

Calculating GDP using the income approach, we include only income received for production that occurs within the national boundaries. The income approach includes corporate profits and rental income as well as wages and salaries. Most of the U.S. national income, about 57 percent in 2003, is paid to workers as wages and salaries.

## Adjusting for Depreciation, Population Growth, and Inflation

One reason why GDP is not the best measure of national income is that a portion of investment in capital equipment such as factories and machinery simply replaces worn-out capital. Because capital that wears out or becomes obsolete decreases national wealth, **depreciation** of this capital should be counted as a deduction from GDP. Gross investment minus depreciation is called **net investment.** If we deduct capital depreciation from GDP, we obtain a measure called **net domestic product (NDP).** The depreciation of fixed capital amounts to about 10–15 percent of GDP in the United States.

Of course, politicians and economists hope that the economy expands over time and GDP increases. But an increase in GDP does not necessarily indicate greater wealth for the citizens of a nation. GDP can increase simply because the nation has a higher population. We can account for population growth (or decline) in national accounting by calculating **GDP per capita,** equal to GDP divided by population. Data on GDP per capita also allows us to compare economic production across different nations. For example, the U.S. GDP is much greater than the GDP of Sweden, but when we adjust for population size we find that GDP per capita is higher in Sweden than in the United States.

We also must control for inflation when comparing GDP values across time. Remember that GDP is based on market prices and can grow simply because market prices have risen. So when comparing GDP data from different years we use **constant dollars.** For example, suppose we know that in general 2003 prices were twice as high as 1981 prices. If we want to compare GDP for these two years, we could compare them using 2003 dollars by doubling the GDP from 1981. Or we could compare them using 1981 dollars by dividing the GDP for 2003 by half. The first method gives us **real GDP** in 2003 dollars, while the second gives us real GDP in 1981 dollars.

**TABLE 1** *Historical Gross Domestic Product Data, United States*

| Year | Unadjusted U.S. GDP (billion $) | Unadjusted GDP per Capita (dollars) | GDP per Capita in 2003 dollars |
|---|---|---|---|
| 1950 | 294 | 1,938 | 14,796 |
| 1960 | 526 | 2,911 | 18,095 |
| 1970 | 1,039 | 5,071 | 24,048 |
| 1980 | 2,790 | 12,279 | 27,419 |
| 1990 | 5,803 | 23,262 | 32,748 |
| 2000 | 9,817 | 34,883 | 37,273 |
| 2003 | 11,004 | 37,808 | 37,808 |

The U.S. GDP has grown tremendously over recent decades. As seen in Table 1, GDP has increased by a factor of 37 between 1950 and 2003, if we don't consider any adjustments. Making an adjustment for population, we find that economic production per person has increased by about a factor of 20. Most of this increase reflects inflation. When we adjust for differences in price level by calculating real GDP per capita in 2003 dollars, we discover that economic production per person has actually increased by a factor of 2.5. This still suggests a large increase in the standard of living for the average American, but a much less significant increase than implied by the unadjusted aggregate GDP data.

## Comparing GDP for Different Countries

When comparing GDP data across nations, we can make an adjustment for **purchasing power parity (PPP)**. Even if we use currency exchange rates to put all nations' GDP per capita in U.S. dollars, we should still adjust for differences in what a dollar can purchase in different countries. For example, a U.S. dollar converted into Chinese currency will buy a lot more in China than it will in the United States. As mentioned above, Sweden has a higher GDP per capita than the United States, but when we adjust for purchasing power parity, GDP per capita is higher in the United States than in Sweden because of relatively high prices in Sweden.

Of course, GDP per capita varies widely by country. The World Bank classifies low-income countries as those that had a per capita gross national income (GNI, a measure similar to GDP) in 2003 of less than $765 annually. A total of 2.3 billion people in 2003 lived in countries classified as low-income, including India and most countries in Africa and Southeast Asia. Middle-income countries are defined as those with a per capita GNI between $765 and $9,386. These countries, including China, Russia, and most of Central and South America, had a population of 3 billion in 2003. Finally, high-income countries are those with per capita GNI above $9,386. These countries, including the United States, Japan, Australia, and the nations of western Europe, had less than a billion people in 2003.

National income accounting data illustrate the varying economic conditions of people in different nations. We can use the data to compare rates of economic development and to determine income inequality between countries, but we must be careful about interpreting national accounting data. GDP measures only the aggregate level of economic production; it does not measure social welfare. If GDP per capita goes up only because people are working longer hours, we can't conclude that they are happier. Also, GDP per capita could go up only because the wealthy members of society are becoming wealthier. GDP data tell us nothing about the level of economic inequality in a country. This and other known problems with GDP make it important to be aware of the limits of GDP as a measure of well-being—even before we consider the environmental and resource issues discussed in this chapter.

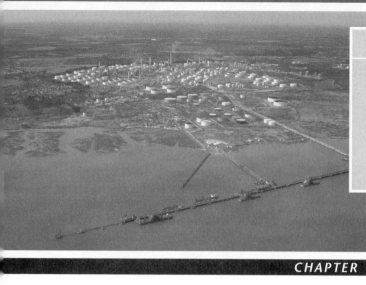

CHAPTER FOCUS QUESTIONS

- What principles explain the flow of energy and resources through the economic system?
- How do we analyze economic inputs and outputs of materials, energy, and wastes?
- What models best describe the interactions of economic and environmental systems?

CHAPTER

# Modeling Economic and Ecological Systems

## Energy and Resource Flow Analysis

Economic analysis of environmental issues focuses on markets, prices, internalization of externalities, and valuation of the environment. In Chapters 3–6, we applied concepts from economic theory to resource and environmental issues. Suppose we wish to reverse the perspective and apply the logic of physical and biological systems to the human economy, as suggested by the ecological economics perspective discussed in Chapter 7. What measure might we employ that possesses scope and explanatory power comparable to market price as a measure of value?

Ecological economics has arrived at no such single alternative measure. A prominent exponent, Richard Norgaard, has argued that the use of various analytical perspectives is essential in dealing with environmental topics, as well as other controversial issues. Norgaard maintains that "multiple insights guard against mistaken action based on one perspective."[1] He identifies this approach as **methodological pluralism:** Through a combination of perspectives we can achieve a more comprehensive picture of the problems we study.

Rather than focusing on market price, ecological analysis has tended to emphasize physical flows of resources. A particularly important flow is that of energy used by the

---

[1]Norgaard, 1989.

economic system (the analysis of energy is dealt with in detail in Chapter 13). In this chapter, we will review three approaches to modeling the economy as part of a system of physical energy flows. One is **energy flow analysis,** which evaluates the energy use by different economic processes. A second is **input-output analysis,** which provides a systematic accounting of all physical materials used by the economic system. The third is **economic/ecological modeling,** which attempts to capture a complete picture of the interactions of economic and physical systems, using concepts drawn from both economics and ecology.

## *Energy Flows and the Economic Production System*

We can apply an energy flow perspective to many different sectors of production: the energy sector itself, agriculture, mining, forestry, fishing, as well as other industrial sectors. This often gives a different picture of how these economic activities operate. A mining industry, for example, may show increasing productivity over time, measured in standard terms relative to output of labor or capital inputs. But if we concentrate on output of energy inputs per unit, we may well see declining productivity. In other words, we need increasing amounts of energy to achieve the same output, as the quality of the mined ore declines.

In this case, we are *substituting* energy for labor and capital, an economically advantageous choice so long as energy is cheap. However, it means that our economic system becomes more dependent on fossil fuels, which as we will see in Chapter 13, provide 85 percent of our commercial energy. Pollution problems associated with fossil fuels also increase.

Analysis of trends in energy use in agriculture, fisheries, metal mining, and fossil fuel extraction show varying patterns, but in many cases energy productivity, expressed as output per unit of energy input, decreases over time (Figure 9-1). This has significant implications for future industrial and energy use patterns, especially as growing populations in developing economies seek to follow the industrial growth path.

# Input-Output Analysis

Another economic technique that focuses on the physical basis of production is input-output analysis. Input-output analysis, based on a model of relationships between productive sectors in the economy, can easily be extended to apply to resource and environmental issues.

The basic input-output model describes quantitative flows between economic sectors, showing, for example, that producing an automobile might require one ton of steel, 20 square feet of glass, 100 pounds of plastic, and so on. A matrix $A$ can be constructed for the entire economy showing the inputs from each sector to every other sector (see Figure 9-2).

Each cell in the matrix shows a coefficient $a_{ij}$ indicating the amount of input from sector $i$ used in the production of one unit of output from sector $j$. This matrix can show what levels of production in each sector are required to satisfy a given total demand from consumers, investors, government, and foreign purchasers.

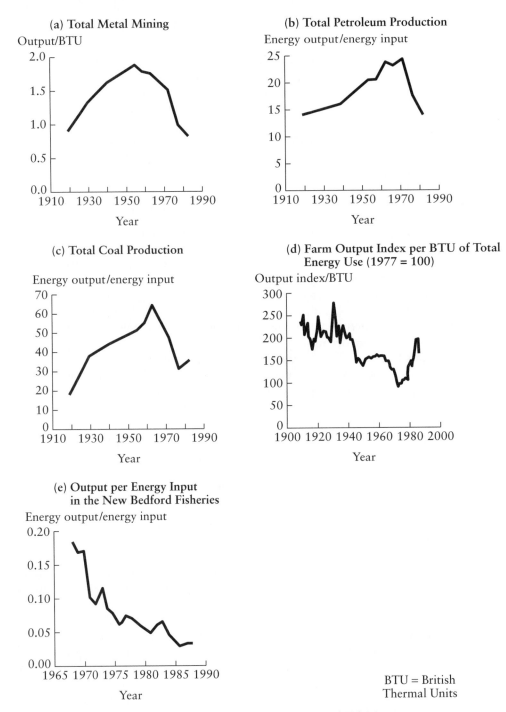

**(a) Total Metal Mining**

Output/BTU

**(b) Total Petroleum Production**

Energy output/energy input

**(c) Total Coal Production**

Energy output/energy input

**(d) Farm Output Index per BTU of Total Energy Use (1977 = 100)**

Output index/BTU

**(e) Output per Energy Input in the New Bedford Fisheries**

Energy output/energy input

BTU = British Thermal Units

**FIGURE 9-1** *Energy Productivity in Mining, Agriculture, and Fisheries*

Source: Cleveland, 1991, pp. 300–306. Adapted from *Ecological Economics: The Science and Management of Sustainability*, edited by Robert Costanza. Columbia University Press, © 1991. Reprinted with the permission of the publisher.

It is a simple task to add a matrix $B$ showing resource inputs to each sector of the economy and a matrix $C$ showing waste outputs from each sector. We can then use these matrices to calculate the resource requirements and waste outputs generated for any given level of demand. For example, if automobiles are sector 1, a projected increase of one unit in automobile production will require industrial inputs $a_{11}$ to $a_{n1}$ and resource inputs $b_{11}$ to $b_{m1}$. If steel is sector 2, an increase of one unit of steel production will generate wastes $c_{21}$ to $c_{2q}$.

The values of the parameters in the matrix cells depend on the production technologies employed. It is possible to extend this static input-output analysis to take account of changes in technology and capital stock, transforming it to a dynamic input-output analysis. Alternatively, we can compare different static analysis scenarios embodying different technologies. Thus we can consider possibilities of resource-conserving or pollution-reducing technologies, or add specific pollution-cleanup sectors to the model.

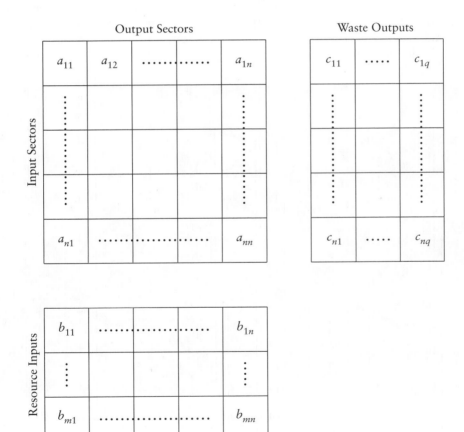

**FIGURE 9-2** *Expanded Input-Output Matrix with Resources and Wastes*

## *Analyzing National and Global Systems*

Rather than focusing on resource use and environmental impacts in only one industry, input-output analysis allows us to examine national, regional, or global effects of entire economic systems. For example, input-output models of the world economy have helped project global levels of carbon dioxide, sulfur and nitrogen oxides, and other pollutant emissions well into the twenty-first century given specific assumptions about economic growth rates in industrialized and developing nations.[2]

Input-output models are particularly useful for dealing with environmental problems, especially those that increase over time with economic growth. They allow us to combine analysis of the internal flows in the economy with measurement of the stocks and flows of resources and pollutants. However, the input-output technique also has some drawbacks.

A comprehensive input-output model requires large amounts of data input and computation, which may limit its feasibility for many specific problems. Also, some economists question the ability of such models to reflect changes in technology and production patterns. But from the ecological economist's point of view, the focus on the physical realities of production may be easier to integrate with "real world" issues of resource depletion and pollution impacts than are more abstract price-centered models.

*Daewoo Motors assembly line, South Korea. Industrial production of automobiles requires inputs of metal, plastic, and glass as well as energy.*

---

[2]Duchin and Lange, 1994.

Taking this logic a step further, the emerging theory of **industrial ecology** attempts to apply the analysis of resources, energy, and waste flows to the management of industrial activity. Industrial ecology, discussed at greater length in Chapter 17, requires the use of new analytical tools in addition to those ordinarily used by economists.[3] Input-output analysis, one way of approaching this problem, can be applied to individual industries, economic sectors, or to national or global systems.

## Economic and Ecological Modeling

More complex dynamic models of economic/ecological systems are sometimes needed to capture changes and interactions among different system components. The construction of such models must consider such factors as demographics (of human and other species), resource depletion and regeneration, stocks and flows of wastes and pollutants, as well as natural physical and biological cycles.

It boggles the imagination to think of constructing a single model that will adequately represent all these factors. We cannot safely afford to leave out any of these elements, however, in a world in which population is still growing, in which economic pressures on the environment are ubiquitous, and in which the interactions and cumulative effects of pollutants affect whole ecosystems. How can we resolve this dilemma?

Some ecological/economic modelers have chosen to approach the problem by defining areas of study in terms of systems and processes. The first step is to establish a **system boundary.** For example, we might choose to study the economy and ecology of an estuary (the wide tidal mouth of a river). Within this system boundary are numerous species of land and water plants and animals, wetlands, human settlements, factories, and a fishing industry. Numerous processes support life and economic activity within the system boundary.

Natural processes include plant photosynthesis, animals consuming plants, animal species preying on others, and the decay and regeneration of organic matter. Economic processes include household and industrial water use, pollutant and sewage discharge, factory goods production, fishing industry exploitation of marine resources, and filling wetlands for construction. We can model each of these processes, accounting for what it draws from the environment, what products it produces, and what it returns to the environment.

The model will show significant input and output flows between processes; for example, industrial discharge of pollutants may reduce yields in the fishing industry and adversely affect other plant and animal species. Filling in wetlands may increase economic output but decrease ecological activity.

We must also consider **cross-boundary flows.** The system as a whole receives solar energy, water from upstream, and goods and energy sources imported by humans. It

---

[3]For a comprehensive overview of the principles of industrial ecology, see Socolow et al., eds., 1994.

discharges water to the ocean, waste heat and carbon dioxide to the atmosphere, and outputs of goods to other communities (for example, fish caught may be shipped out and sold in cities). The first step in modeling is to note as carefully as possible all these internal processes and cross-border flows.

Of course, we can never completely describe all these flows; some will escape our attention or be impossible to measure. Even so, this view of the system is much more comprehensive than a purely economic model to which we attempt to add estimates of external costs and benefits. Our measurements of system activities will be primarily in physical terms, but we may also convert some to dollar value estimates.

## Modeling Individual Processes

We can choose to focus on a single process, noting carefully its inputs and outputs to other processes. Some of these we may ignore as insignificant to the problem under consideration. Those that we wish to analyze we must carefully measure in physical and/or value terms. For example, we could measure physical quantities of factory-emitted pollutants, or the value of damage to the fishing industry from these pollutants.

If the process we are examining is primarily economic, we may choose to express most flows in value terms, and our process model might resemble the kinds of analysis covered in Chapters 3–5 (externalities, common-property resources, and public goods). If the process is primarily ecological, we will measure the impacts of economic activity in physical terms. If a process such as the fishing industry involves both economic and ecological components, we must integrate analysis of economic incentives to fishers and demographics of fish stocks (discussed further in Chapter 14).

Figure 9-3 focuses on a single process within a system. Inputs to this process come both from other processes in the system and from outside the system. Some process outputs become inputs for other processes within the system, and others are exported out of the system. As a result, the product stock within the system changes over time.

This general framework applies both to economic and to ecological processes and can show the patterns of changes over time. For example, we might use it to track carbon storage in a forest ecosystem, taking into account inputs of carbon from the atmosphere and outputs through decay or through human exploitation of the forest.

## Modeling Complete Systems

Integrating the analysis of different processes can give a comprehensive picture of economic and ecological activity within the system boundary. Such an integrated analysis is depicted in Figure 9-4.

This example shows a schematic of economic and ecological flows in the city of Brabant, The Netherlands. Local natural resource systems provide inputs to the farms and industries of Brabant. Other inputs, including fossil fuels, are imported, and the products of industry are exported. Agricultural production in Brabant provides products both for local consumption and for export. Industry, agriculture, and households all draw on local water systems, which suffer some pollution from nitrate and

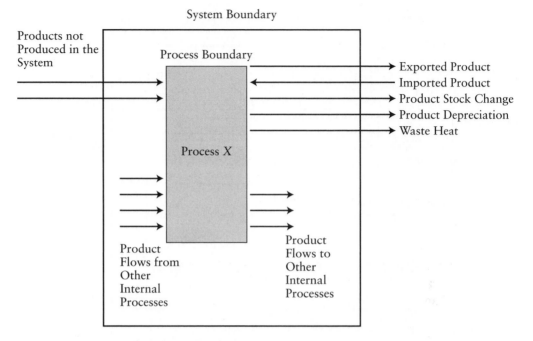

**FIGURE 9-3** *Process Flows in an Ecosystem*

Source: Hannon, 1991, p. 239. Adapted from *Ecological Economics: The Science and Management of Sustainability,* edited by Robert Costanza. Columbia University Press, © 1991. Reprinted with the permission of the publisher.

pesticides runoff. Forests provide outdoor recreation, as well as inputs for wood-processing industries. Agricultural runoff also affects forests as well as heathlands.

A model of this sort offers insight into patterns of economic production, land use, and environmental change. Although some of the system flows follow economic rules, others are biophysical in nature. Economic principles, such as conversion of land to highest-value uses, may conflict with principles of ecosystem balance such as nutrient and water recycling. The model attempts to capture the interactions between the two systems as well as their changes over time.

Computer analysis can model the changes in such a system as economic growth creates greater demands on resources and environment. The model can indicate the scale and severity of environmental pressures. In turn, we can project economic effects of environmental changes and note whether cross-border flows, such as dependence on imported energy sources, will increase.[4] (See Box 9-1.)

As we discuss issues of population, agriculture, energy, natural resources, and pollution in the following chapters we will use both standard economic and

---

[4]For an in-depth treatment of dynamic computer modeling of economic-ecological systems, see Hannon and Ruth, 1994. Discussion of practical examples of integrated economic and ecological modeling can be found in Milon and Shogren, 1995.

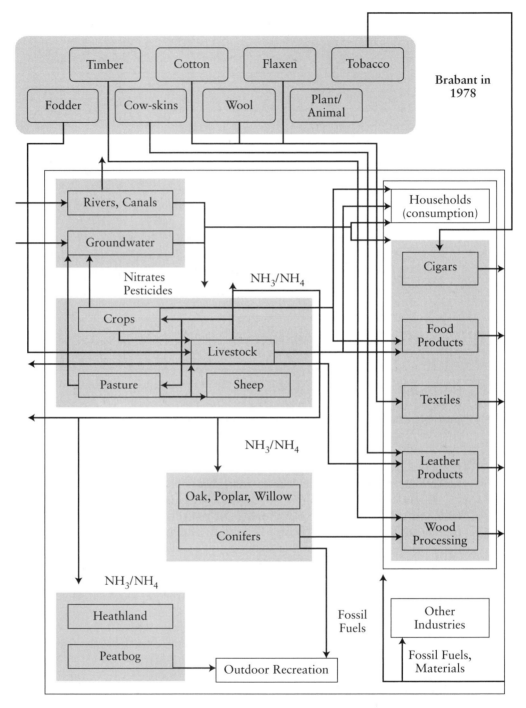

**FIGURE 9-4** *Ecological-Economic Model of Brabant, The Netherlands*

Source: Braat and Steetskamp, 1991, p. 283. Adapted from *Ecological Economics: The Science and Management of Sustainability,* edited by Robert Costanza. Columbia University Press, ©1991. Reprinted with the permission of the publisher.

ecological-economic forms of analysis. We will employ the logic of systems modeling as well as economic analysis of market prices and consumer or producer incentives. We will also draw on examples of current research in ecological economics as well as in mainstream environmental economics.

In covering both environmental and ecological perspectives, we have reviewed a formidable toolbox of analytical methods. Because different approaches give different insights, we will take an eclectic approach (meaning we'll select useful elements from varied sources). We will focus first on population, a fundamental issue in the analysis of ecological systems. We will discuss different approaches to population analysis in Chapter 10, giving a basis for the evaluation of food supply in Chapter 11, resources and energy in Chapters 12–15, and wastes and pollution in Chapters 16–18.

---

## 9-1   Modeling Sustainable Development on Greek Islands

The Northern Sporades islands in Greece face a challenge of balancing economic objectives and ecological conservation. The land environment must absorb the pressures of agricultural and urban expansion, tourism, and road development. The marine environment, rich in corals, fish, and marine mammals, attracts both tourists and fishermen, but is threatened by overuse and pollution. To study the options for economic development and conservation, researchers constructed an economic-ecological model that accounts for these varied factors.

The model has separate sections, or modules, for terrestrial and marine systems, and for population and economic activities. The economic systems of three islands, Skiathos, Skopelos, and Allonisos, and a mainland area, Pilion (Pelion), are included in the model. Over time, the model tracks growth of tourism, changes in land use, and increasing demand for fishery products. Ecological variables include stocks of fish and seals, forested area, and water supplies. Economic variables include tourism revenues, employment, and output of agriculture and fisheries (see Figure 9-5).

Various scenarios are examined for different policies regarding limiting tourism growth, managing fisheries, and agricultural incentives. Not surprisingly, high-growth scenarios offer improved economic indicators but worsened ecological outcomes. The study authors conclude that sustainable development for the region depends on a combination of economic incentives and environmental controls.

### SOURCE

Van den Bergh, Jeroen C. J. M. "Dynamic Analysis of Economic Development and Natural Environment on the Greek Sporades Islands." Chapter 7 in Milon and Shogren, eds., 1995.

*(continued on following page)*

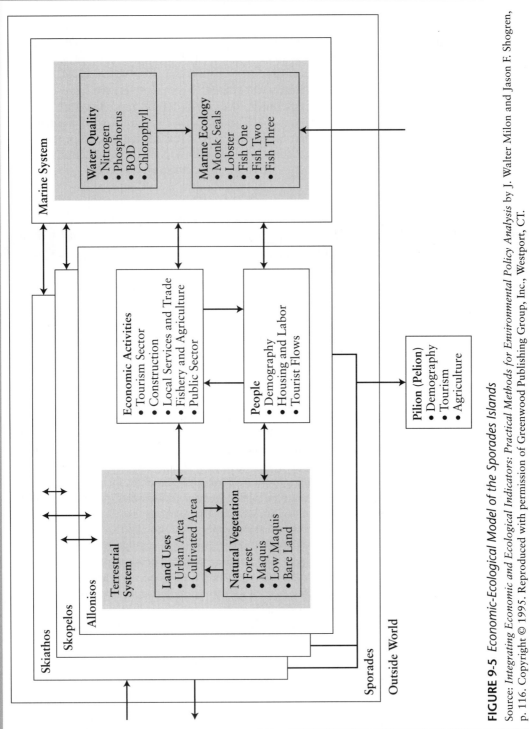

**FIGURE 9-5** *Economic-Ecological Model of the Sporades Islands*

Source: *Integrating Economic and Ecological Indicators: Practical Methods for Environmental Policy Analysis* by J. Walter Milon and Jason F. Shogren, p. 116. Copyright © 1995. Reproduced with permission of Greenwood Publishing Group, Inc., Westport, CT.

## SUMMARY

Ecological perspectives on the relationship between the economic system and the environment complement standard, market-based analysis. The differing approaches are not mutually exclusive, but offer a broader picture of economy/ecosystem interactions.

Analysis of energy and resource flows demonstrates the importance of energy supplies and high-quality resources to the economic process. Important issues concerning use of energy and resources include possible constraints on energy and resource supply, as well as the inevitable problems created by wastes and pollution. We must also consider the complex life-supporting functions of existing ecosystems. From this perspective, the potential for substituting humanmade production systems for natural functions is subject to clear ecological limits.

Input-output analysis shows resource flows through complex economic systems. It can be adapted to include resource supply and environmental impact sectors and to take account of changes in technology and capital stock. Expanded input-output models help project the resource and environmental impacts of different economic growth patterns.

Other types of modeling can also apply to economic/ecological systems. Such models attempt to capture numerous flows of materials and energy between sectors of the economy and elements of the ecosystem. These flows are measured either in physical or in value terms, and can be related to geographical data to show regional patterns. Computer analysis provides a sophisticated representation of the interaction of economic development and ecosystem modification in specific industries or for whole economies.

A combination of these techniques and of standard economic analysis offers varied insights into issues of population, agriculture, natural resources, energy, and pollution. An eclectic approach based on methodological pluralism can escape the problem of narrow theoretical models, giving a more comprehensive picture of environmental issues.

## KEY TERMS AND CONCEPTS

cross-boundary flows
economic/ecological modeling
energy flow analysis
industrial ecology

input-output analysis (static and dynamic)
methodological pluralism
solar flux
system boundary

## DISCUSSION QUESTIONS

1. What are the implications of declining output/input ratios for energy use (Figure 9-1)? Consider how the issue of energy use applies to specific areas of economic production such as agriculture, industry, and transportation.

2. Construct a simple schematic model of an economic/ecological system. Choose a relatively simple subject, such as a rural village rather than a large city. Define a system boundary and note as many process flows as you can within the system and across boundaries. How might your model be used? What kind of data would you need to complete it?

## REFERENCES

Braat, Leon C., and Ineke Steetskamp. "Ecological Economic Analysis for Regional Sustainable Development." Chapter 18 in Costanza, ed., 1991.

Cleveland, Cutler. "Natural Resource Scarcity and Economic Growth Revisited: Economic and Biophysical Perspectives." Chapter 19 in Costanza, ed., 1991.

Costanza, Robert, ed. *Ecological Economics: The Science and Management of Sustainability*. New York: Columbia University Press, 1991.

Duchin, Faye, and Glenn-Marie Lange. *The Future of the Environment: Ecological Economics and Technological Change*. New York: Oxford University Press, 1994.

Hannon, Bruce. "Accounting in Ecological Systems." Chapter 16 in Costanza, ed., 1991.

Hannon, Bruce, and Matthias Ruth. *Dynamic Modeling*. New York: Springer, 2001.

Milon, J. Walter, and Jason F. Shogren, eds. *Integrating Economic and Ecological Indicators: Practical Methods for Environmental Policy Analysis*. Westport, Conn.: Praeger, 1995.

Norgaard, Richard B. "The Case for Methodological Pluralism." *Ecological Economics* 1 (February 1989): 37–57.

Socolow, Robert, et al., eds. *Industrial Ecology and Global Change*. Cambridge, U.K.: Cambridge University Press, 1994.

## WEBSITES

1. **http://esa.org/science/publications/** Several online reports published by the Ecological Society of America that apply ecological concepts to current environmental issues.

2. **http://www.sfwmd.gov/org/wrp/elm/index.html** The Everglades Landscape Model, a regional-scale, integrated ecological model for water management in the Everglades region.

3. **http://www.uvm.edu/giee/research.htm** Ongoing research programs of the Gund Institute at the University of Vermont on dynamic spatial modeling of ecological-economic systems at multiple scales from local to global.

# Population, Agriculture, and the Environment

CHAPTER FOCUS QUESTIONS

- How fast is world population growing?
- What are the prospects for future population growth?
- What relationship exists between population and economic growth?
- How does population growth affect the global environment?

CHAPTER

# 10

# Population and the Environment

## The Dynamics of Population Growth

Human population has grown slowly throughout most of our history. Only within the past 200 years has more rapid global population growth become a reality. Figure 10-1 shows the history of global population increase during the nineteenth and twentieth centuries, with a baseline projection for the twenty-first century. As the diagram shows, in the past 100 years population growth has accelerated at a pace unprecedented in global history.

In 1800, global population had reached about 1 billion after many centuries of slow growth. In a century and a half more, the figure reached 2.5 billion. A rapid post–World War II growth acceleration doubled population to 5 billion in less than 40 years. By the year 2000, world population had passed 6 billion.

Extraordinarily rapid population growth—about 2 percent per year—took place from 1960 to 1975. At first consideration, 2 percent may not sound remarkable, but at this rate of growth population doubles in about 35 years. After 1975, the growth rate slowed, but the much larger total population meant that the absolute number of people added each year continued to increase until the 1990s (Figure 10-2).

During this period of extremely rapid growth, various authors sounded the alarm regarding the dangers of **exponential growth.** A population of 5 billion that continued

Population (in billions)

**FIGURE 10-1** *Global Population Growth and Projections, 1750–2050*
Source: United Nations Department of Economic and Social Affairs, Population Division, 2005; Repetto, 1991.

Population (in millions)

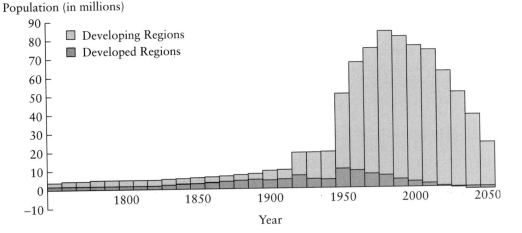

**FIGURE 10-2** *Net Annual Increase in Population Per Decade, 1750–2050*
Source: United Nations Department of Economic and Social Affairs, Population Division, 2005; Repetto, 1991.

**TABLE 10-1** *Global Population Growth Rates and Average Gross Annual Increase by Decade*

|  | 1960s | 1970s | 1980s | 1990s | 2000s (est.) |
|---|---|---|---|---|---|
| Population Growth Rate | 2.0 percent | 1.8 percent | 1.7 percent | 1.4 percent | 1.1 percent |
| Average Annual Increase (millions) | 67 | 75 | 83 | 80 | 73 |

Source: U.S. Census Bureau website, www.census.gov/ipc/www/worldpop.html, *Total Midyear Population for the World: 1950–2050*, updated 9/30/04.

to grow at 2 percent per year, for example, would reach 20 billion in 70 years and 40 billion in a little over a century. Finding food, water, and living space for such a vastly increased population would be impossible; the grim Malthusian controls of famine and disease would take over.

Authors such as Paul and Anne Ehrlich warned in *The Population Bomb* (1968) and later in *The Population Explosion* (1990) that runaway population growth could overcome all the benefits of modern science and economic growth, leaving a devastated and miserable planet. This **neo-Malthusian** perspective has gained much attention and provides the starting point for the modern debate on population growth.

Those who find the Ehrlichs' perspective overly negative often point out that **population growth rates** have been declining since the 1970s; as of the year 2000 the overall global rate was down to 1.2 percent and continuing to fall. Does this mean that population will soon stabilize, and fears of rapid growth are mere alarmism? Unfortunately not.

First, the declining growth rate is occurring at a time when total population is much higher than ever before. The global **gross annual population increase** as of 2004 was 73 million. This annual addition to the planet's human numbers is greater than the entire population of France. Each year, we now add more people than we added annually during the 1960s, when the growth *rate* was at its highest (see Table 10-1 and Figure 10-2). The equivalent of a new New York City every 6 weeks, a new France every 10 months, a new India in about 13 years—this is hardly cause for complacency. The global demographic picture is far from stabilized, and this reality will continue to underlie environmental issues for many decades.

The second reason why population is a crucial concern relates to regional patterns of population growth. It is precisely in the poorest and most hard-pressed nations that continuing population growth will be most rapid. More than 90 percent of the projected growth will come in the currently developing nations of Asia, Africa, and Latin America (Table 10-2). Many of these nations, especially in Africa, have trouble providing adequate food supplies and basic goods to their present populations.

Developed nations currently create the greatest environmental impact through their high per capita demand on resources, as well as pollution generation. If the developing nations succeed in raising living standards for their expanding populations—as China and other East Asian nations have done—their per capita demands for food and

**TABLE 10-2** *2050 Population Projections Under Three Fertility Scenarios*

| Region | 2005 Population (millions) | 2050 Population Projections (millions) | | |
|---|---|---|---|---|
| | | *Low Fertility* | *Medium Fertility* | *High Fertility* |
| Africa | 906 | 1,666 | 1,937 | 2,228 |
| Asia | 3,905 | 4,388 | 5,217 | 6,161 |
| Latin America and Caribbean | 561 | 653 | 783 | 930 |
| Europe | 728 | 557 | 653 | 764 |
| Northern America | 331 | 375 | 438 | 509 |
| Oceania | 33 | 41 | 48 | 55 |
| More developed regions | 1,211 | 1,057 | 1,236 | 1,440 |
| Less developed regions | 5,253 | 6,622 | 7,840 | 9,206 |
| **World total** | **6,465** | 7,680 | 9,076 | 10,646 |

Source: United Nations Department of Economic and Social Affairs, Population Division, 2005.

Population (in billions)

**FIGURE 10-3** *Population Projections Under Three Fertility Scenarios*

Source: Adapted from United Nations Department of Economic and Social Affairs, Population Division, *World Population Prospects: The 2004 Revision.* United Nations, 2005. The United Nations is the author of the original material. Reprinted by permission of United Nations.

resources, as well as their pollution generation, will also increase. The combined effects of population and economic growth will significantly increase environmental pressures.

## Predicting Future Population Growth

How well can we predict future population growth? The projected population shown in Figure 10-1 is a baseline prediction. Could the actual figures go much higher or much lower? As Table 10-2 and Figure 10-3 show, assumptions about changes in fertility rates significantly influence projections. The three scenarios shown cover a range of possibilities for global population in the year 2050, ranging from 7.7 to 10.6 billion people. Within this range, the major factor lending credibility to projections of continued population growth is the phenomenon of **population momentum.**

To understand population momentum, let's consider a hypothetical country, Equatoria, which has been experiencing rapid population growth for several generations. For simplicity, we'll define a generation as equal to 25 years, and divide the population of Equatoria into three age categories: under 25, 25 to 50, and over 50 years old. Suppose the population growth rate averages 3 percent per annum. (This is a high but not unprecedented rate in developing nations—the current population growth rate for Nigeria, for example, is close to 3 percent.) At this rate, each generation will be roughly twice as numerous as the preceding generation. This will give a **population age profile** shaped like a pyramid (Figure 10-4).

Now consider the future demographics of Equatoria. If this growth rate continues, the population will double every 25 years. If it is 7 million in 2000, as shown in the first part of Figure 10-4, it will be 14 million by 2025, and 28 million by 2050. No nation can long withstand the environmental and social pressures of such growth. Sooner or later, the growth rate must decline.

For this to happen, the average **fertility rate** must fall. The fertility rate is defined as the number of children borne by the average woman during her lifetime. The fertility rate in Equatoria must be over 4 children per woman to account for such rapid rates of growth. Again, this is not unusual in the developing world. The average fertility rate for Sub-Saharan Africa in 2004 was 5.6, for Nigeria 5.7, for Pakistan 4.8, for Syria 3.8, and for Nicaragua 3.8.[1]

Population policies usually seek a **replacement fertility level,** which is just over 2 children per woman (the precise number depends on the rate of infant and child mortality). At replacement fertility, each new generation will be exactly the size of the preceding one. Achieving such a lowered fertility rate usually takes many years in a country such as Equatoria. Suppose Equatoria reaches this goal. Is the population growth problem over? Absolutely not!

Imagine a fantastically effective population policy that would lower fertility to replacement level *immediately.* Equatoria's demographic future would be as shown in

---

[1]Population Reference Bureau, 2004.

**Current Population Age Structure for "Equatoria"**

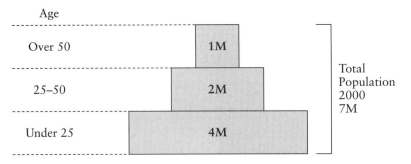

**Projected Population Age Structure for "Equatoria"**

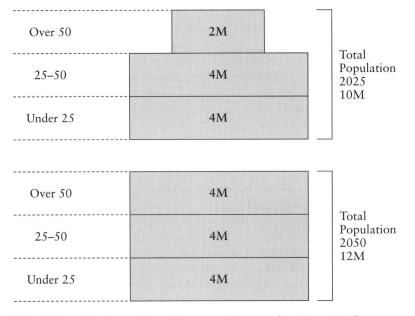

**FIGURE 10-4** *Projected Population Age Structure for "Equatoria"*

the second and third parts of Figure 10-4. Each new generation would be exactly the size of the last. The current generation of under-25s, however, is Equatoria's largest ever. Even if they only replace themselves in numbers, the population will continue to grow for two more generations.

The next generation of children will be four times as large as the current over-50 generation, meaning that the birthrate will be several times as high as the death rate for another 25 years. During the 25 years after that, the birthrate will still be about double the death rate. The population growth rate, which is the difference between birth and death rates, will remain positive. Only when the current generation of children reach the end of their lifespan will *their* grandchildren no longer outnumber them. Thus Equatoria's population will continue to grow for 50 years before it stabilizes, reaching a total of 12 million, 71 percent more than its current level.

This is the meaning of population momentum. When a nation has a history of rapid population growth, continued growth for the next several generations is virtually guaranteed, short of a massive Malthusian catastrophe that dramatically raises death rates. A more realistic projection for Equatoria might be that fertility rates, rather than falling instantaneously as in our hypothetical case, would take about a generation to reach replacement level. In this case, population would continue to grow for 75 years, finally stabilizing at well over double the 2000 level.

The case of Equatoria is not merely an abstract example. As Figure 10-5 shows, the simplified population pyramid we have described is close to reality for much of Africa. (Use Figure 10-4, frame 3, to visualize a future Africa where all **population cohorts** or age groups are at least as large as the current cohorts of young children.)

Population momentum is also considerable throughout Asia and Latin America. Projections of population growth for these regions are therefore well founded. The inexorable logic of population momentum guarantees growing human numbers well into the twenty-first century. The stable age structure of Western Europe shown in the second frame of Figure 10-5 is the exception, not the rule. This is why the lowest global population projections for 2050 are about 7.4 billion.

Population momentum makes substantial increase inevitable, but a huge difference remains between relatively low and high forecasts for the years 2030, 2050, and beyond (see Figure 10-3 and 10-6). The critical variable in these differing projections is the rate of future fertility decline. If fertility falls rapidly throughout the developing world, the global population age pyramid could approach a more stable pattern within the next 35 years. (Compare the global low fertility scenario for 2030 in Figure 10-5 with the West European population age structure in Figure 10-4.) On the other hand, a slow decline would leave the world with both a higher population and considerable remaining momentum in 2030 (as shown in the second frame of Figure 10-6).

## The Impact of AIDS

World population projections take into account the impact of diseases such as malaria, which kill millions annually. But the recent spread of HIV/AIDS has altered the picture of disease mortality. According to a 2004 United Nations report, "AIDS is the deadliest epidemic of our time. Over 22 million people have already lost their lives, and more than 42 million are currently living with AIDS. Even if a vaccine for AIDS were discovered today, over 40 million people would still die prematurely as a result of AIDS."[2] Will the spread of AIDS have a significant effect on world population growth?

The answer is yes, but the impact varies considerably by region. The United Nations' *World Population Prospects: The 2002 Revision* lowered its median 2050 population projection by 400 million from 2000; about half of this adjustment reflected an increase in projected AIDS deaths. To date, much of the heaviest impact of AIDS is in southern Africa. In seven countries in southern Africa that have an adult AIDS infection rate of 20

---

[2]United Nations, 2004a.

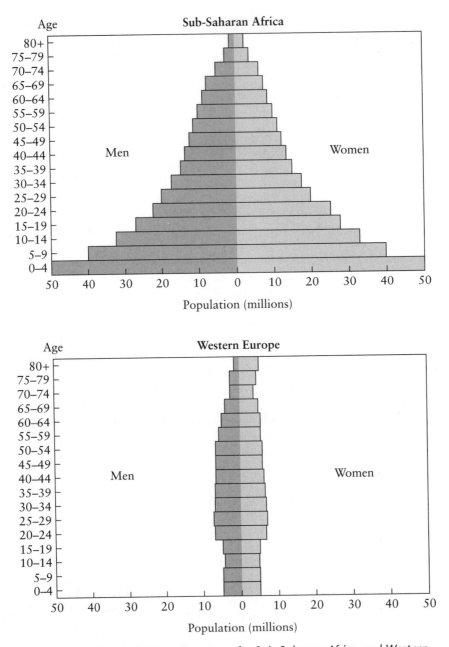

**FIGURE 10-5** *Population Age Structures for Sub-Saharan Africa and Western Europe, 1990*

Source: Adapted from Wolfgang Lutz, *The Future of World Population*. Washington, D.C.: Population Reference Bureau, 1994. Reprinted by permission of the Population Reference Bureau.

**FIGURE 10-6** *Alternative Futures for World Population*

Source: Adapted from Wolfgang Lutz, *The Future of World Population*. Washington, D.C.: Population Reference Bureau, 1994. Reprinted by permission of the Population Reference Bureau.

percent or more, AIDS-related deaths have wiped out a previously projected population growth of 75 percent by 2025. Population growth in these countries will fall to zero by about 2010. Life expectancy there has already declined by 20 to 30 years as a result of AIDS, and is projected to decline further.

For Sub-Saharan Africa as a whole, the overall picture remains one of rapid population growth. Population is projected to increase 53 percent by 2025, and will more than double by 2050. In major Asian countries such as China and India, the rate of AIDS infection is currently below 2 percent, but the danger of further spread could cause from 40 million to more than 100 million additional deaths by 2025.[3] Projected population growth for Asia is currently about 900 million by 2025. Thus AIDS, while creating a massive worldwide public health threat and humanitarian disaster, will certainly not reverse population growth except in the hardest-hit countries in southern Africa. It will, however, add enormously to the public health burden on countries already struggling with the needs of a large population of children. Many of these children will become orphans, placing enormous stress on family, social, and medical systems.

## The Theory of Demographic Transition

The third United Nations International Conference on Population and Development, meeting in Cairo in September 1994, grappled with the issue of an appropriate response to growing world population. The conference adopted the ambitious goal of stabilizing world population at about 7.27 billion by the year 2015—an increase of roughly 30 percent over 1994 levels.

If this stabilization effort fails, the conference projected population rising to 12.5 billion by 2050, more than doubling the 1994 figure. We have seen why the alternatives differ so starkly. A failure to lower fertility levels in the next two decades yields both higher population and continuing momentum. This suggests that we stand at a crucial juncture for population policy.

Current Population Reference Bureau projections indicate a world population of 7.9 billion by 2025, a net addition of 1.8 billion people over 2000 levels, with growth continuing after that toward a possible 9 billion in 2050. Thus the goal of the Cairo conference may not be achievable—but the most pessimistic projections may not occur either. Certainly the task of supplying the needs of an extra 1.5 to 3 billion people is a daunting one. The course of population growth and fertility levels over the next 20 years will profoundly affect food production, resource use, and pollution generation, issues that we consider in upcoming chapters. What, then, can an environmental or ecological economics analysis tell us about population policy?

Much thinking about the relationship between population and economic growth rests on western European experience. Western Europe's situation is considered the final stage of the **demographic transition** from high to low birth and death rates. Figure 10-7 shows the pattern of this demographic transition.

---

[3]Eberstadt, 2002.

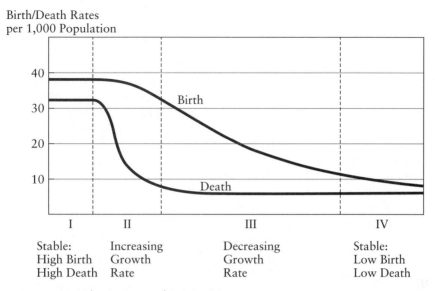

Birth/Death Rates
per 1,000 Population

**FIGURE 10-7** *The Demographic Transition*

In the first stage, corresponding to preindustrial Europe, both birth and death rates are high. Large families are common, but medical care is poor and many children die young. On average, a family produces only two surviving children. Thus the population remains about the same from generation to generation. These social conditions resemble in many ways the state of nature, where birds and animals typically produce numerous progeny to offset high rates of predation and disease. It is a harsh but ecologically stable regime.

In the second stage, industrialization takes off, as in nineteenth-century Europe. Death rates fall rapidly as standards of living, public health, and medical care improve. Birthrates remain high, however, because families still view numerous children as valuable, both to work on the farm or in the factory, and as a form of old-age insurance. If more children now survive, so much the better from the individual family's point of view. Because net population growth rate is equal to the birthrate minus the death rate (the distance between the two lines in Figure 10-7), the result is a rapidly growing population.

## Population Growth Impact

Is growing population a good or bad thing for the country as a whole? If resources are abundant, the nation's leaders may welcome it. A large labor force promotes rapid economic growth and helps in taking advantage of unexploited resources and new technology. However, this period of rapid population and economic growth probably contains some self-limiting factors.

One such factor is the improvement in social conditions likely to accompany economic growth. This development, by no means automatic, often requires hard-fought battles for social and economic reform. Eventually, however, the nation may achieve social changes characteristic of economically developed nations, including child labor laws, unemployment compensation, social security systems, private pension plans, and greater educational opportunity.

In this changed atmosphere, people's attitude toward family size changes. Smaller families now seem more desirable—a large family becomes an economic burden rather than a benefit, and greater opportunities arise, especially for women, as family size shrinks. Contraceptive techniques become more available. For all these reasons, fertility rates fall—often quite rapidly. We enter the third stage, of declining birthrates and declining net population growth rates.

Here we must remember that Figure 10-7 shows only the *rate* of population growth (the difference between birth and death rates). The total population, of course, is considerably larger at this stage, so that a lower *rate* of growth may still mean a higher net addition to population (gross annual increase) each year. Population, as we have seen, could double or triple during this period of declining birthrates. If birthrates continue to decline, however, the country will eventually reach the final stage of stabilized population with low birthrates and low death rates (stage 4).

As a retrospective view of European history, this process appears relatively benign. Despite the great hardships involved in the early stages, overall it appears that population growth, economic growth, and social progress went hand in hand, and that population growth was eventually self-limiting. The Malthusian vision failed to develop—on the contrary, larger populations typically led to better living conditions.

Does this picture fit the present global population reality? Certainly the first two stages of the demographic transition theory apply well to the developing world's experience in the second half of the twentieth century. Death rates have fallen much faster than birthrates; fertility and population growth rates rose to historic highs in the period 1950–1975. Since then, strong evidence indicates that most nations have entered the third phase, with overall growth rates falling. In many respects, however, currently developing nations' experiences differ significantly from Europe's:

- The total population numbers at issue are much larger, unprecedented in planetary history. Every decade the developing nations add population equal to the *entire* population of Europe and Russia.
- In their expansion, Europe and the United States drew on the rest of the world for natural resource supplies. The currently developed nations also have disproportionately exploited the global environment's waste absorption capacities (contributing by far the greatest proportion of greenhouse gas emissions, ozone depleting chemicals, and such). The developing world obviously will not have these options.
- There is significant uncertainty concerning the role of fertility decline. Factors that contribute to fertility decline may be present in some nations but absent in others. Projections of population stabilization depend strongly on rapid fertility decline, which may or may not occur.
- The rapid economic growth that accompanied population growth in Europe has occurred in some parts of the developing world but not in others. Africa in particular has experienced high population growth and stagnant or declining output

and food production per capita. In places where economic growth has been strong, its benefits have not filtered down to the poor, resulting in increased inequality and a greater absolute number of extremely poor people. In the "dual economies" of many Latin American countries, modern urban development coexists with extreme rural poverty and huge slums surrounding major cities. Many people have not yet achieved the improved living standards that contribute to fertility decline.

These arguments suggest that looking back to the history of population and economic growth offers insufficient insight into the population-related issues of the next 40 or 50 years. Social, economic, and environmental factors intertwine with demographics. The impacts of population growth are not limited to the developing nations; the United States faces significant continuing population growth based on a combination of natural increase and immigration (see Box 10-1). We cannot simply wait for the second, global process of demographic transition to play itself out. Rather, we must apply the best analysis and policy response possible to an issue of fundamental importance to the economic and environmental parameters of the twenty-first century.

## Population Growth and Economic Growth

What does economic theory say about population? A typical economic model, the Cobb-Douglas production function, shows economic output as a function of labor input, capital input, and technological parameters:

$$Q_t = A_t \, K_t^{\alpha} L_t^{\beta}$$

where $Q$ is total output, $K$ is the capital stock, $L$ is the labor force, $\alpha$ and $\beta$ are parameters related to the productivity of capital and of labor respectively, $A$ reflects a given state of technology, and $t$ indicates a particular time period. The values of $\alpha$ and $\beta$ are assumed to be fractions between zero and one; if $\alpha + \beta = 1$, the function shows **constant returns to scale**. This means that if labor and capital inputs were both doubled, output would also double.

Suppose that we increase only one factor, labor. Output will also increase, but by a smaller proportion than the increase in labor input.[4] If labor is roughly proportional to total population, **per capita output** will decline. As more and more labor is added, the **law of diminishing returns** comes into play, giving smaller output boosts for each additional unit of labor input. Thus in a simple economic model, population increase alone would yield falling living standards. This is a result of **capital shallowing,** which means that each worker has less capital to work with and is thus less productive.

However, few economists would view this simple logic as an accurate representation of the effects of population growth. They would point to the capital stock variable $K$, noting that if $K$ grows at a rate at least equal to $L$, output per capita will remain

---

[4]This is because the exponent $\beta$ is less than one. If, for example, $\alpha = \beta = 0.5$, doubling labor alone would increase output by a factor of 1.414. Doubling both labor and capital would increase output by a factor of 2.

## 10-1   U.S. Population Continues to Grow

**W**hen we think of population problems, we tend to focus on rapid population growth rates in developing nations. But population is far from stable in the United States as well. Although Europe has completed the demographic transition to stable population levels, both natural increase and immigration keep the U.S. population growing. U.S. fertility rates are at replacement levels, but population growth since 1950 has generated large cohorts of people still in their reproductive years, creating significant continuing population momentum.

The 1990s saw a larger increase in U.S. population than any other 10-year period in the nation's history, surpassing even the 1950s baby boom decade. Population grew from 248.7 million to 281.4 million during the 1990s, an increase of 32.7 million, or 13 percent. All 50 states increased their populations, ranging from a half percent in North Dakota to 66 percent in Nevada. Metropolitan areas sprawled out into formerly rural regions. Immigration accounted for at least one-third of the population increase, with the fastest growth in the South and West (U.S. Census Bureau, *New York Times* and *Boston Globe,* April 3, 2001).

U.S. population will likely grow for at least the next three decades. The Population Reference Bureau projects U.S. population for 2025 at 349.4 million, an increase of 68 million, or 24 percent, over 2000 levels. Projected population for 2050 is more than 400 million. The longer-term figures may be somewhat uncertain, but these numbers indicate the continuing power of population momentum combined with immigration.

Because U.S. residents have the highest resource consumption and waste generation rates on the planet, they will have much greater environmental impact than a comparable number of consumers in a low-income nation. Thus the projected U.S. population increase, although only about 3 percent of likely global population growth, has considerable significance for global environmental issues such as greenhouse gas emissions.

The increasing U.S. population will also put growing pressure on domestic land and resources. Urban and suburban sprawl, overdraft of water supplies, and air and automobile traffic congestion, will all become more difficult to manage. Population policy is clearly as relevant for the United States as it is for developing nations in considering these various environmental issues.

### SOURCES

Population Reference Bureau. *2004 World Population Data Sheet.* Washington, D.C.: Population Reference Bureau, 2004.
U.S. Census Bureau. "Largest Census-to-Census Population Increase in U.S. History As Every State Gains." http://www.census.gov/Press-Release/www/2001/cb01cn64.html.
"U.S. Population Has Biggest 10-Year Rise Ever." *New York Times,* April 3, 2001.
"Census Gain Largest Ever." *Boston Globe,* April 3, 2001.

constant or rise. In addition, **technological innovation** will tend to increase the variable *A* over time, leading to greater output for each unit of labor or capital input. Provided capital formation and technological progress are adequate, a rising standard of living can accompany population and labor force growth.

Economic theory, then, sees population growth as inherently neither good nor bad. Its effects depend on its context. If economic institutions are strong, markets work well, and environmental externalities are not great, population growth can be positive. Indeed, Ester Boserup has argued that population growth may spur technological development, especially in agriculture.[5] She finds evidence that increased population pressure forces the adoption of more efficient agricultural techniques. At least in the early stages of development, **economies of scale** may prevail; increasing population density may make possible larger-scale, more productive agriculture and industry.

## Does Population Growth Promote or Retard Economic Growth?

Some analysts generalize this argument to present a positive view of population growth both as a proof of successful advance in human technological skill and as a spur to further progress. One of the strongest proponents of this point of view, Julian Simon, suggested that we should welcome further population growth because human ingenuity will always overcome resource limitations and environmental problems.[6] Most economists and ecologists, however, reject this unqualified optimism. While acknowledging the importance of technological progress, most analyses of the overall impact of population growth present the issue as significantly more complex.

Economic theory recognizes several ways in which population growth may negatively affect economic growth:

- Increased **dependency ratios.** We have seen that a growing population typically includes a high proportion of children. Families must spend more on supporting dependent children, and thus have less to save, lowering the national savings rate. Higher spending on health and education is required, reducing funds available for capital investment. These effects tend to slow capital accumulation and economic growth. As population eventually stabilizes, dependency ratios are raised by a high proportion of elderly people, creating a different set of economic problems (see Box 10-2).
- Increased income inequality. A rapidly growing population creates excess labor supplies, which draw down wage rates. High rates of unemployment and underemployment are likely, and a large class of extremely poor people receives no benefits from economic growth. This situation prevails in many Latin American countries as well as in India, where unemployed rural laborers migrate to large cities in search of jobs, creating vast slums surrounding city centers.

---

[5]Boserup, 1981.
[6]Simon, 1996.

- Natural resource limitations. Note that natural resources do not appear as a variable in the production function used above. In theory, capital, labor, and output in this function could grow without limit. But what about resource and environmental limitations? The presence of **fixed factors,** such as a limited supply of land, will lead to diminishing returns to labor and capital. In general, economists have tended to assume that technological progress can overcome these limitations.[7] As resource and environmental problems become more pervasive and complex, however, this assumption may not hold.

- In cases of **market failure,** like the open-access fishery discussed in Chapter 4, increased population accelerates excessive depletion of the resource. Where private or social property rights are poorly defined, as in the African Sahel or the Brazilian Amazon, population pressure contributes to desertification and deforestation. Also, where externalities such as air and water pollution are uncontrolled, population growth will worsen existing pollution problems.

In an article summarizing the economic research on economic and population growth, Nancy Birdsall suggested that "the long debate over population growth and development is entering a new phase. The emphasis is now on the interaction of rapid population growth with market failures."[8] Similarly, an extensive review of the economic literature in this area concluded that

> Economic growth (as measured by per capita output) in many developing countries would have been more rapid in an environment of slower population growth, although in a number of countries the impact of population was probably negligible, and in some it may have been positive. Population's adverse impact has most likely occurred where arable land and water are particularly scarce or costly to acquire, where property rights to land and natural resources are poorly defined, and where government policies are biased against the most abundant factor of production—labor. Population's positive impact most likely occurred where natural resources are abundant, where the possibilities for scale economies are substantial, and where markets and other institutions (especially government) allocate resources in a reasonably efficient way over time and space.[9]

This statement summarizes much economic research on population growth impact. If we consider this generalization in the light of a broader ecological perspective, however, another question arises. Are the "positive" effects of population growth mainly characteristic of an earlier period in world history—what Herman Daly has referred to as the "empty world" stage in which resources and environmental absorptive capacities are abundant relative to the scale of the human economy?[10] As global population rises toward 8 billion or more, will the negative impact become dominant? To answer these questions requires a consideration of a broader, more ecologically oriented perspective on population growth.

---

[7]See, for example, Solow, 1986.

[8]Birdsall, 1989.

[9]Kelley, 1988.

[10]Daly, 1992 (as discussed in Chapter 7).

# 10-2   Fertility Decline: Is There a Birth Dearth?

Fertility, the most volatile variable in population projections, has declined worldwide, in many countries faster than expected. Has the "population problem" gone into reverse? Some analysts think so. According to Phillip Longman, "Some people think overpopulation is one of the worst dangers facing the globe. In fact, the opposite is true. As countries get richer, their populations age and their birthrates plummet. And this is not just a problem of rich countries: The developing world is getting older fast. Falling birthrates might seem beneficial, but the economic and social price is too steep to pay."[1]

Declining birthrates have different impacts in different regions. In areas such as Europe and Japan, fertility rates have largely fallen below replacement levels. These countries face the prospect of a high dependency ratio of elderly people, with a diminished work force to support them. In the developing world, a few countries are now approaching, or have reached, replacement fertility levels. As Longman acknowledges, slower population growth is likely to benefit these developing nations by lowering the child dependency ratio and providing a higher proportion of working-age people to contribute to national productivity. However, he warns that eventually these countries, many of which lack adequate social security or pension systems, will also face the problem of numerous dependent elderly.

It is important not to confuse these real issues of dependency ratios with the overall issue of population growth. Even the lowest global projections show well over a billion additional population by 2025, almost all of it in the developing world. There is a wide dispersion in fertility rates, and areas of high fertility, such as Africa, are likely to see population doubling before 2050, even taking into account the impact of AIDS. Rates of population growth are slower in Latin America and Asia, but increases of 200 million and 1 billion, respectively, are projected for these areas. Thus Longman's prescription of trying to deal with the situation by policies to promote fertility seems unwise for the developing world, even if it might be relevant for Europe, where fertility has fallen to an average of 1.4 children per woman.

Lower fertility in India, for example, has gone hand-in-hand with improvement of women's status and economic well-being.[2] Stabilizing populations also lessens pressure on scarce water supplies, arable land, and other resources. Increases in the average age of a country's population are an inevitable result of a demographic transition to lower birth rates. In this sense, the issue of "graying" populations is one that the world must confront sooner or later—unless population grows without limit.

---

[1]Longman, 2004.

[2]"Population Estimates Fall as Poor Women Assert Control." *New York Times*, March 10, 2002.

# Ecological Perspectives on Population Growth

Whereas the standard economic perspective sees no inherent limitations on population or output growth, the ecological approach is based on the concept of **carrying capacity,** which implies practical limits to the population that can occupy a certain region. This certainly applies to animal populations in nature.

If, for example, a herd of grazing animals exceeds the land's carrying capacity, food will run short, many individuals will starve, and the population will drop to more sustainable levels. Predator species are even more tightly constrained in numbers, based on the available prey populations. Because animals live by consuming either other animals or plants, all life on Earth depends on the ability of green plants to capture solar energy. The available **solar flux,** or flow of sunlight to the earth's surface, thus ultimately determines carrying capacity.

*Vietnamese family-planning posters contrast a large family in poverty with a prosperous small family.*

Can human populations escape the logic of carrying capacity? Certainly we have successfully stretched its limits. We have used artificial fertilizers to increase agricultural outputs. Fossil fuel and nuclear energy provide far more power for our industrialization than any solar flux we currently capture either directly through solar energy systems or indirectly through hydroelectric and wind power. Through these means more than 6 billion people can live on a planet that a century ago supported only about 1.5 billion.

However, this expansion of carrying capacity carries significant ecological cost. The extraction of large quantities of fossil fuels and mineral stocks causes environmental degradation both in production and through the waste products generated. Some wastes and pollutants are cumulative—their negative environmental effects build up over time.

A prime example is global warming caused by burning fossil fuels, known as the **greenhouse effect.** While increasing Earth's carrying capacity today, we build up problems for the future. Soil erosion, depletion of aquifers, and buildup of long-lived toxic and nuclear wastes are all cumulative processes. Many of these issues already pose major problems—how much worse will they become if a significantly larger population is consuming at higher per capita levels than today?

Ecologists identify three major areas in which current economic activities are systematically undermining the planet's long-term carrying capacity. One is erosion and degradation of topsoil; topsoil losses worldwide are currently estimated at 24 billion tons annually, with nearly 11 percent of the world's vegetated land suffering moderate to extreme degradation. A second is overuse and pollution of fresh water supplies—a problem in virtually every country, reaching critical levels in China, India, and parts of the former Soviet Union. The third, and perhaps most serious, is the loss of biodiversity, with more species driven to extinction every year than at any time in the preceding 65 million years of planetary history.[11]

## *The Impact of Population, Affluence, and Technology*

We can conceptualize the interrelationship of population, economic growth, and environment in an equation linking all three, known as *IPAT*:

$$I = P \times A \times T$$

where

$I$ = Environmental impact (units of pollution)
$P$ = Population
$A$ = Affluence measured as output/person
$T$ = Technology variable measuring pollution per unit of output

---

[11]Ehrlich, Ehrlich, and Daily, 2003; Postel, 2003.

This equation is an identity, a mathematical statement that is true by definition. The right side of the equation can be mathematically stated as follows:

$$(\text{Population}) \times (\text{Output/Population}) \times (\text{Pollution/Output})$$

"Population" and "Output" cancel out because they occur both in numerator and denominator, leaving only "Pollution"—which is the same as the left variable $I$ (units of pollution).

Thus we cannot argue with the equation itself. The only questions are the levels of the variables and what determines them. What do we know about these questions?

We have seen that global population is projected to increase by 40–50 percent over the next 50 years, according to the United Nations medium-variant projection (see Table 10-2 and Figure 10-5). We also know that average per capita consumption, the $A$ variable, is steadily increasing throughout the world. If per capita consumption grows at 2 percent per year, which most development economists would view as a minimally satisfactory rate, it will increase by a factor of 2.7 in 50 years. The combined impact of $A$ and $P$ will therefore multiply the right side of the equation by a factor of three to four.

What about the technology variable $T$? Improved technology could lower the pollution per unit of GDP—let us say by a factor of 2. This would still leave us with a significantly increased level of overall pollution. Given the current level of concern about environmental problems, this seems unacceptable. In order to project lower overall environmental impact, we will need technological improvements that would lower environmental impact by a factor of 4 or more.

Of course, a mathematical abstraction such as *IPAT* gives little insight into the specifics behind these broad concepts. *IPAT* has faced strong criticism on the grounds that it covers up some basic issues concerning causes of population growth, consumption distribution, and the workings of markets. One obvious concern is highly unequal consumption per capita throughout the world.

The one-quarter of the world's population living in developed countries accounts for roughly three-quarters of global consumption. Poverty, lack of basic health services, and poor education in many developing nations contribute to high population growth rates. This suggests a crucial need to focus on issues of inequality rather than only on total population or economic output.[12]

Some economists criticize *IPAT* as a highly abstracted view that ignores the capacity of markets to improve efficiency, delivering more goods while using fewer resources and creating less pollution. This perspective was summarized in the World Bank's 1992 report *Development and the Environment:*

> Under present productivity trends, and given projected population increases, developing country output would rise by 4–5 percent a year between 1990 and 2030 and by the end of the period would be about five times what it is today. Industrial country output would rise more slowly but would still triple over the period. World output by 2030 would be 3.5 times what it is today, or roughly $69 trillion (in 1990 prices).

---

[12]Hynes, 1993.

If environmental pollution and degradation were to rise in step with such a rise in output, the result would be appalling environmental pollution and damage. Tens of millions more people would become sick or die each year from environmental causes. Water shortages would be intolerable, and tropical forests and other natural habitats would decline to a fraction of their current size. Fortunately, such an outcome need not occur, nor will it if sound policies and strong institutional arrangements are put in place.[13]

This puts the focus on "sound policies and strong institutional arrangements" rather than on absolute limits on population or economic growth. Nonetheless, the World Bank's presentation makes it clear that the pressures of population and growing output increase the urgency of environmental threats.

Perhaps the economic and ecological perspectives can converge. Even if we cannot identify a fixed carrying capacity for the planet, population growth at the levels we are now experiencing clearly increases virtually all resource and environmental stresses (see Box 10-3). This makes progress on all fronts vital—reducing population growth, moderating the growth of consumption, improving social equity, and introducing environmentally friendly technologies.[14]

## Population Policies for the Twenty-First Century

In recent years, the population policy discussion has shifted. Past debate was dominated by the conflict between "optimists" who saw no problem in increasing population and "pessimists" who predicted catastrophe. Now elements of consensus are emerging. Most analysts accept that increasing population places extra stress on the environment and resources and agree that slower population growth in the future is essential. How will we accomplish this?

Nations have sometimes attempted to control population growth by government compulsion. The most prominent example of this is China's draconian "one-child family" policy. Although effective in a strongly controlled economy such as communist China's, such policies have also been discredited in most other nations both on human rights grounds and because they fail to alter basic incentives regarding fertility.

Birthrates can fall rapidly, however, when people—especially women—reach higher levels of education and literacy and enjoy better employment opportunities. Significant voluntary reduction of birthrates in many East Asian countries as well as in the state of Kerala in India has resulted from higher levels of basic education, health care, and job security.[15]

In analyzing which population policies are most effective, Nancy Birdsall focuses on the link between high fertility and poverty and the resulting vicious circle of negative social and environmental outcomes. She identifies a significant range of policies that can help both to slow population growth and to improve economic efficiency and output.

---

[13]World Bank, 1992.

[14]For an overview of different perspectives and projections on population, see Cohen, 1995; Baudot and Moomaw, 1999; and Harris et al., eds., 2001, Part 4: Population and Urbanization.

[15]The cases of China and Kerala are reviewed in Sen, 1999, pp. 219–224.

## 10-3 Humanity's Ecological Footprint

**S**ubstantial research has focused on measuring human impact on the environment. Humans affect the environment in multidimensional ways. From a policy perspective, there may be advantages to converting all these effects to a single index. Further, this index should be measured in units that we can easily understand and interpret.

One such index calculates environmental impacts using "ecological footprints." Originally developed by Wackernagel and Rees (1996), the ecological footprint (EF) concept attempts to convert human impact into equivalent units of biologically productive land area. In other words, a person's ecological footprint is the amount of land required to support his or her lifestyle.

Some effects convert easily to land-area footprints. For example, demand for meat converts to pasture area needed to raise livestock. For others, such as carbon dioxide emissions from burning fossil fuels, the EF approach estimates the area of vegetation required to absorb the carbon.

Calculation of a country's ecological footprint requires data on more than 100 factors, including demand for food products, timber, energy, industrial machinery, office supplies, and vehicles. A demonstration of the detailed calculations involved in obtaining a country's ecological footprint, using Italy as an example, is available at http://www.iclei.org/iclei/efcalcs.htm. An individual ecological footprint calculator can be found at www.earthday.net.

Comparing a region's ecological footprint to its available land helps determine whether the region creates a sustainable environmental impact. The following table presents per capita ecological footprints and available productive land for 20 selected countries and the world. The per capita ecological footprints are much higher in developed countries, such as the United States, Australia, and Canada, than in developing countries such as India, Bangladesh, and Ethiopia.

Most countries, developed or developing, currently run at an ecological deficit. The global per capita impact of 2.8 hectares per person exceeds the available biologically productive land on Earth (2.0 hectares per capita). In other words, the EF approach indicates that current global environmental impact is not sustainable, implying a depletion of natural capital.

The concept and methodology of ecological footprints remains controversial. The March 2000 *Ecological Economics* journal presented a forum of 12 articles related to the ecological footprint concept. Some of the articles are particularly critical of the approach. For example, Ayres (2000) claims that the EF concept "is too aggregated (and too limited in other respects) to be an adequate guide for policy purposes at the national level." Other researchers, while recognizing that the EF

*(continued on following page)*

approach requires further refinement, believe it is a valuable analytical tool with policy relevance. Herendeen (2000) notes that the "EF, as modified and improved, is an excellent tool to illustrate the larger picture, and the details." At the least, the debate over the EF methodology has raised awareness of the need to go beyond the rhetoric of sustainability toward quantifiable results.

*Ecological Footprints of Nations*

| Country | Ecological Footprint (ha/cap) | Available Productive Land (ha/cap) | Ecological Surplus or Deficit (ha/cap) |
|---|---|---|---|
| Australia | 9.0 | 14.0 | 5.0 |
| Bangladesh | 0.5 | 0.3 | −0.2 |
| Canada | 7.7 | 9.7 | 1.9 |
| China | 1.2 | 0.8 | −0.4 |
| Denmark | 5.9 | 5.2 | −0.7 |
| Ethiopia | 0.8 | 0.5 | −0.3 |
| France | 4.1 | 4.2 | 0.1 |
| Iceland | 7.4 | 21.7 | 14.3 |
| India | 0.8 | 0.5 | −0.3 |
| Italy | 4.2 | 1.3 | −2.9 |
| Japan | 4.3 | 0.9 | −3.4 |
| Mexico | 2.6 | 1.4 | −1.2 |
| Nigeria | 1.5 | 0.6 | −0.9 |
| Norway | 6.2 | 6.3 | 0.1 |
| Peru | 1.6 | 7.7 | 6.1 |
| Russian Federation | 6.0 | 3.7 | −2.3 |
| Singapore | 6.9 | 0.1 | −6.8 |
| Spain | 3.8 | 2.2 | −1.6 |
| United States | 10.3 | 6.7 | −3.6 |
| Venezuela | 3.8 | 2.7 | −1.1 |
| WORLD | 2.8 | 2.0 | −0.8 |

Source: Wackernagel et al., 1999.

### SOURCES

Ayres, Robert U. "Commentary on the Utility of the Ecological Footprint Concept." *Ecological Economics* 32, no. 3 (2000): 347–349.
Herendeen, Robert A. "Ecological Footprint Is a Vivid Indicator of Indirect Effects." *Ecological Economics* 32, no. 3 (2000): 357–358.
Wackernagel, Mathis, et al. "National Natural Capital Accounting with the Ecological Footprint Concept." *Ecological Economics* 29, no. 3 (1999): 375–390.
Wackernagel, Mathis, and William Rees. *Our Ecological Footprint: Reducing Human Impact on Earth.* Stony Creek, Conn.: New Society, 1996.

Prominent among these are promotion of education and other social programs, improvement in the status of women, and improved nutrition and health care, including contraceptive availability.[16]

These policies tend to lower fertility rates, and Birdsall identifies them as win-win policies that benefit both the economy and the environment through voluntary moderation of population growth. Sound macroeconomic policies, improved credit markets, and improved conditions for agriculture are also important in promoting broad-based growth and poverty reduction, which in turn is essential to population–environment balance.

Such policies are essential to avert serious environmental and social breakdowns in many developing nations. As people struggle to respond to higher demands on the land, slower population growth allows crucial breathing space—time to innovate and adapt. Higher population growth rates can lead to serious environmental degradation—not because of an absolute limit on carrying capacity, but because the means and incentives to adopt new techniques were not forthcoming in time.

Urban areas, where population growth is most rapid, often experience major social and infrastructure problems. Urban populations in Asia and Africa are projected to double over the next 30 years.[17] Inadequate housing and sanitation, congestion, air and water pollution, disruption of water cycles, solid waste problems and soil contamination are typical of large cities in the developing world. Attempts to respond to massive social and environmental problems in cities are frustrated by continuing rapid and unplanned growth. Moderation of overall population growth must be an essential component of efforts to achieve urban sustainability.[18]

Population growth has been a major factor in shaping development patterns during the second half of the twentieth century and will continue to play a central role during the first half of the twenty-first century. The differing perspectives of economists, ecologists, demographers, and other social theorists all contribute toward developing effective policies that can promote population stabilization and population–environment balance.

In later chapters, we will use this overview of population as our basis for examining specific stresses associated with growing population and higher consumption levels—in agriculture, energy use, demands on natural resources, and pollution generation. In Chapter 20 we will return to the issue of sustainable global futures for a growing human population.

## SUMMARY

Global population grew rapidly during the second half of the twentieth century. Although population growth rates are now slowing, total annual additions to global population remain high. With a global population of 6 billion in the year 2000, growth is

[16]See Birdsall, 1994.

[17]United Nations, 2004b.

[18]See Harris et al., 2001, Part 4: Population and Urbanization.

projected to continue for at least the next three decades, reaching a level of 7.6 to 10.6 billion by 2050. Over 90 percent of the projected growth will be in the developing nations of Asia, Africa, and Latin America.

Population projections offer no certainty about actual future numbers, but the population momentum phenomenon guarantees significant further growth. Currently, average fertility rates (number of children per woman) remain high throughout the developing world. Although fertility rates are generally falling, decades will pass before population growth stabilizes.

Europe has accomplished the demographic transition from rapid population growth to a relatively stable population. In the United States, growth continues both due to population momentum and annual immigration. In the developing world, the demographic transition is far from finished, and significant uncertainty remains about future birth rates. Economic growth, social equity, access to contraception, and cultural factors all play a role.

The economic analysis of population growth emphasizes the potential of other factors such as technological progress to offset the effects of population growth. Under favorable conditions for economic and technological progress, population growth may be accompanied by rising living standards. However, rapid population growth accompanied by social inequity and significant environmental externalities may lead to a decline in living standards.

An ecological perspective recognizes more stringent limits to the population carrying capacity of regional and global ecosystems. Greater population increases the demand for materials, energy, and natural resources, which in turn increases pressures on the environment. Given the extent of existing environmental damage, especially where this damage is cumulative or irreversible, the challenge of providing for significantly larger populations poses severe challenges to the earth's ecosystems.

Compulsory population control policies generally fail to alter basic incentives regarding fertility. More effective population policy measures include improved nutrition and health care, greater social equity, women's education, and contraceptive availability.

## KEY TERMS AND CONCEPTS

| | |
|---|---|
| capital shallowing | law of diminishing returns |
| carrying capacity | market failure |
| constant returns to scale | neo-Malthusianism |
| demographic transition | per capita output |
| dependency ratios | population age profile |
| economies of scale | population cohort |
| exponential growth | population growth rate |
| fertility rate | population momentum |
| fixed factors | replacement fertility level |
| greenhouse effect | solar flux |
| gross annual population increase | technological innovation |

## DISCUSSION QUESTIONS

1. What criteria would you use to evaluate the argument between the neo-Malthusians, who see population growth as the major problem facing humanity, and those who argue that population growth is a neutral, or even positive factor for economic development? How would you assess the relative urgency of population concerns in the United States (population growth rate 0.6 percent per annum), India (1.7 percent per annum), and Uganda (3.0 percent per annum)?

2. "Every extra mouth brings with it an extra pair of hands. Therefore we do not have to worry about growing population." Relate this statement to the more formal economic analysis of labor force and production. To what extent is the statement true? To what extent is it misleading?

3. The concept of carrying capacity is a useful one for ecological analysis of animal and plant populations. Is it also useful for analyzing human population growth? Why or why not?

## REFERENCES

Birdsall, Nancy. "Economic Analyses of Rapid Population Growth." *World Bank Research Observer* 4 (January 1989): 173–198.

Birdsall, Nancy. "Government, Population, and Poverty: A Win-Win Tale." In *Population, Economic Development, and the Environment,* edited by Kerstin Lindahl-Kiessling and Hans Landberg. New York and Oxford, U.K.: Oxford University Press, 1994.

Baudot, Barbara, and William Moomaw, eds. *People and Their Planet: Searching for Balance.* New York: St. Martin's Press, 1999.

Boserup, Ester. *Population Growth and Technological Change: A Study of Long-Term Trends.* Chicago: University of Chicago Press, 1981.

Cohen, Joel E. *How Many People Can the Earth Support?* New York: Norton, 1995.

Daly, Herman E. "From Empty World Economics to Full-World Economics: Recognizing an Historical Turning Point in Economic Development." In *Population, Technology and Lifestyle: The Transition to Sustainability,* edited by Goodland, Daly, and El Serafy. Washington, D.C.: Island Press, 1992.

Eberstadt, Nicholas. "The Future of AIDS." *Foreign Affairs* (November/December 2002): 22–45.

Ehrlich, Paul R. *The Population Bomb.* New York: Ballantine, 1968.

Ehrlich, Paul R. and Anne H. Ehrlich. *The Population Explosion.* New York: Simon and Schuster, 1990.

Ehrlich, Paul R., Anne H. Ehrlich, and Gretchen Daily. "Food Security, Population, and Environment." In Lorey, ed., 2003.

Harris, Jonathan M., Timothy A. Wise, Kevin Gallagher, and Neva R. Goodwin, eds. *A Survey of Sustainable Development: Social and Economic Perspectives.* Washington, D.C.: Island Press, 2001.

Hynes, H. Patricia. *Taking Population out of the Equation: Reformulating I=PAT.* North Amherst, Mass.: Institute on Women and Technology, 1993.

Kelley, Allen C. "Economic Consequences of Population Change in the Third World." *Journal of Economic Literature* 26 (December 1988): 1685–1728.

Longman, Phillip. "The Global Baby Bust." *Foreign Affairs* (May/June 2004): 64–79.

Lorey, David E., ed. *Global Environmental Challenges of the Twenty-first Century: Resources, Consumption, and Sustainable Solutions.* Wilmington, Delaware: Scholarly Resources, 2003.

Lutz, Wolfgang. *The Future of World Population.* Washington, D.C.: Population Reference Bureau, 1994.

Population Reference Bureau. *2004 World Population Data Sheet.* Washington, D.C.: Population Reference Bureau, 2004.

Postel, Sandra. "Water For Food Production: Will There Be Enough in 2025?" In Lorey, ed., 2003.

Repetto, Robert. *Population, Resources, Environment: An Uncertain Future.* Washington, D.C.: Population Reference Bureau, 1991.

Sen, Amartya. *Development as Freedom.* New York: Knopf, 1999.

Simon, Julian L. *The Ultimate Resource 2.* Princeton, N.J.: Princeton University Press, 1996. (Original publication as *The Ultimate Resource*, 1981.)

Solow, Robert. "On the Intertemporal Allocation of Natural Resources." *Scandinavian Journal of Economics* 88 (1986): 141–149.

United Nations Department of Economic and Social Affairs, Population Division. *The Impact of AIDS.* New York: United Nations, 2004a.

United Nations Department of Economic and Social Affairs, Population Division. *World Population Prospects: The 2004 Revision.* New York: United Nations, 2005.

United Nations Department of Economic and Social Affairs, Population Division. *World Urbanization Prospects: The 2003 Revision.* New York: United Nations, 2004b.

World Bank. *World Development Report 1992: Development and the Environment.* New York and Oxford, U.K.: Oxford University Press, 1992.

## WEBSITES

1. **http://www.prb.org/** Homepage for the Population Reference Bureau, which provides data and policy analysis on U.S. and international population issues. Their World Data Sheet provides demographic data for every country in the world.

2. **http://www.un.org/esa/population/unpop.htm** Website for the United Nations Population Division, which provides international information on population issues including population projections.

3. **http://www.populationconnection.org/** Homepage for Population Connection, a nonprofit organization that "advocates progressive action to stabilize world population at a level that can be sustained by Earth's resources."

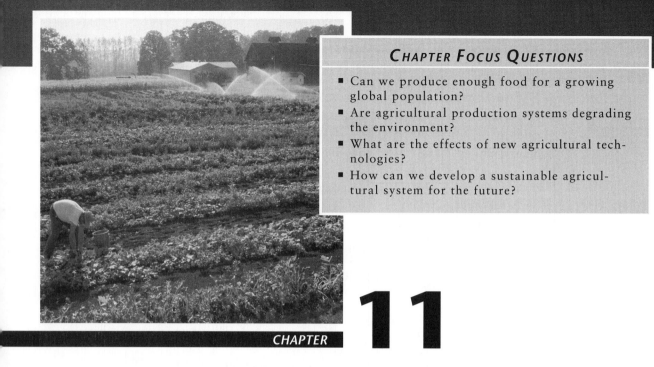

**CHAPTER FOCUS QUESTIONS**

- Can we produce enough food for a growing global population?
- Are agricultural production systems degrading the environment?
- What are the effects of new agricultural technologies?
- How can we develop a sustainable agricultural system for the future?

**CHAPTER** **11**

# Agriculture, Food, and Environment

## Feeding the World: Population and Food Supply

Food supply constitutes a fundamental relationship between any human society and its environment. In the wild, animal populations wax and wane based largely on food availability. For many centuries, human numbers were also linked closely to food abundance or scarcity. In the past two centuries, increasingly productive agricultural technology has spurred a significant increase in human population.

Despite unprecedented population growth, average world per capita food production rose during the second half of the twentieth century. Figure 11-1 shows this trend for the important category of cereal crops. Many economic theorists assert, based on this trend, that history has disproved the Malthusian argument that population would outrun food supply. Before we dismiss concerns over food limitations, however, we must consider several factors that cast a different light on the issues of population, agriculture, and the environment.

- *Land Use.* Since World War II agricultural land use has expanded considerably, but the expansion has slowed (see Figure 11-2a). The land most suitable for

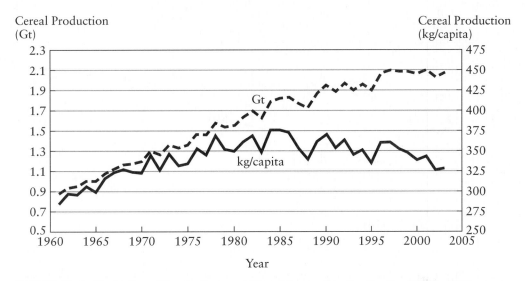

**FIGURE 11-1** *World Cereal Production and Cereal Production Per Capita, 1961–2003*
Source: FAO, 2004.

agriculture is already being farmed, and most remaining lands are marginal in quality. Also, urban and industrial encroachment is cutting into agricultural land and available farmland per person is steadily decreasing (Figure 11-2b). To feed the world better, we must continually increase productivity on this shrinking per capita acreage.

- *Consumption patterns.* Existing food supplies are distributed according to market demand, which strongly favors upper-income consumers. Per capita grain consumption in the United States, for example, is more than three times that in the developing world. This is not because U.S. citizens eat more grains, but because three-quarters of U.S. domestic grain use goes to animal feed. The meat-centered U.S. diet thus requires nearly four times as much agricultural output per person as a typical diet for, say, a citizen of Mexico.

- *Inequalities in food distribution.* On average enough food is produced to provide an adequate diet for everyone on earth. In practice, however, many low-income areas suffer from a **nutritional deficit,** meaning that between 500 million and 1 billion people receive inadequate nutrition.

- *Environmental impact of agriculture.* As agricultural land use has expanded, more marginal and fragile lands have come under the plow. The result is increased erosion, deforestation, and loss of wildlife habitat. Erosion and depletion of nutrients in the soil mean that a **renewable resource** is being turned into a **depletable resource,** and soil fertility is being "mined" over time. Increased irrigation, crucial to modern agriculture, also brings many environmental problems in its wake, including salinization, alkalinization, and waterlogging, as well as overdraft of ground water and pollution of surface water.

**(a) Total World Arable and Permanent Cropland**

Cropland
(in millions of hectares)

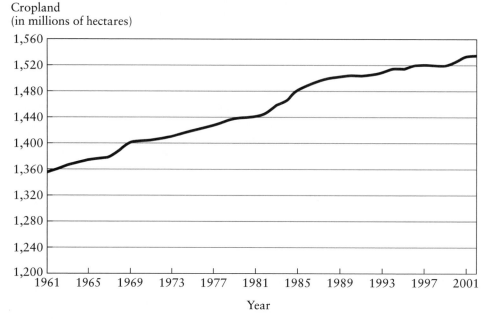

Year

**(b) World Arable and Permanent Cropland Per Capita**

Hectares
per Capita

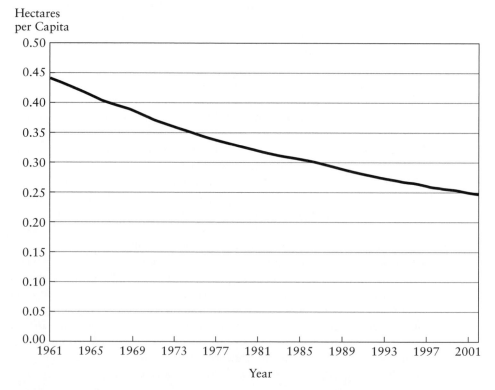

Year

**FIGURE 11-2** *World Cropland and Cropland Per Capita, 1961–2002*

Source: FAO, 2004.

Runoff from chemical fertilizer and pesticide use pollutes land and water and contributes to atmospheric problems such as global warming and ozone depletion. Depletion of **biodiversity** and the creation of "super-pests" resistant to pesticides are also results of intensive agriculture. At a minimum, management of these problems is an important issue in the economics of agriculture. More broadly, this complex of environmental issues raises questions about the global agricultural system's capacity to sustain growing populations without unacceptable environmental damage.

These factors contribute to a more sophisticated perception of the problems involved in feeding an expanded world population. Rather than focusing on the simple dichotomy of population and food, we must examine interactions between population, per capita food consumption, and the environment.

If growing population does not necessarily mean famine, it may nonetheless create irresistible pressures on available agricultural land that increase environmental degradation and leave future generations with a depleted agricultural base. This is occurring in developing nations such as Haiti and Ethiopia that have permanently lost much productive land to erosion and soil degradation. We must, therefore, examine more carefully the realities behind the macroeconomic statistics showing increasing agricultural output.

## Trends in Global Food Production

First, let us take a more careful look at the trends in global food production shown in Figure 11-1. The total output of grains appears to rise over the whole period from 1961 to 2003.[1] The per capita production figures, however, tell a different story. From 1961 to 1985, we see a slow but steady increase in output per capita. This increase—about 0.5 percent per year—is of crucial importance. It means that people throughout the world are experiencing gradually improving average nutritional levels. Of course, as we have noted, not all benefit equally, but to some extent "a rising tide lifts all ships."

During the later years, however, we notice a change. Per capita output no longer increases, and appears to decline after 1985. Does this represent some fundamental change in the dynamics of world agriculture?

Some analysts, such as Lester Brown of Worldwatch Institute, have suggested that it does. Citing many of the environmental problems mentioned above, Brown argues that ecological limits already reached will prevent further rapid expansion in agricultural output. In this view, the 1980s represent a major turning point. Agricultural yields leveled off worldwide and total grain production no longer outpaced population growth: " . . . the next four decades could be a mirror image of the last four, with grain availability levels in 2030 returning to those of 1950."[2] This, of course, would have enormous implications for economic development and for the nutritional status of the world's poorest people.

---

[1]Grain, or cereal, output is easily measured and is a fairly good proxy for total food output. Grain consumption accounts for about 50 percent of food consumption worldwide and up to 70 percent in many developing nations.

[2]Brown and Kane, 1994. See also Brown, 2004.

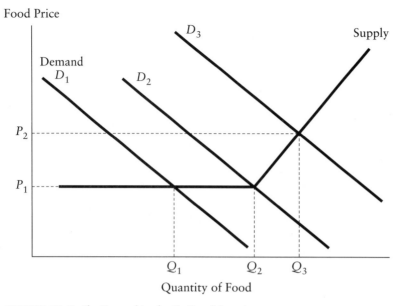

Food Price

**FIGURE 11-3** *Elastic and Inelastic Food Supply*

How can we evaluate Brown's hypothesis? From an economic perspective, the main question is one of price. If indeed agriculture experienced supply limitations, we would expect to see rising food prices as demand grows. The simple supply and demand analysis in Figure 11-3 shows this principle. Where **elasticity of supply** is high, as in the left half of the graph, demand increases from $D_1$ to $D_2$ with no significant upward pressure on price. With inelastic supply, in the right portion of the graph, rising demand ($D_2$ to $D_3$) causes a sharp upward move in price.

As Figure 11-4 shows, no sustained increase has occurred in prices for cereal crops. Taking inflation into account, real food prices have declined since the 1970s. What then explains the change in per capita production trends after 1985? Economists such as Amartya Sen have argued that it is a demand-side rather than a supply-side phenomenon. In this view, a general slowdown in economic growth during the 1980s, a result of world recession and debt problems in many developing nations, lowered people's purchasing power for food as well as for other goods. Thus "food output [was] held back by a lack of effective demand in the marketplace"[3] rather than by environmental constraints on production. In addition, much of the global slowdown in cereal production during the 1990s can be attributed to lower farm subsidies in the United States and Europe, as well as the economic breakdown in the former Soviet Union.[4] Brown also acknowledges that part of the decline in per capita grain output is

[3]Sen, 2000.
[4]Smil, 2000.

**FIGURE 11-4** *U.S. Producer Price Indices for Selected Cereal Crops, 1961–2001*
Source: FAO, 2004.

associated with an increase in the efficiency with which grain is converted into animal protein.[5]

These factors indicate that the decline in per capita grain output since 1985 does not constitute a crisis in food supply. The fact that prices are generally stable or declining, however, does not preclude significant environmental impact on food production. In many developing nations, the poor bear the greatest burden of economic recession, increasing the problem of inequality of distribution. At the same time, the marginal lands farmed by the poor suffer the greatest damage from erosion and other environmental problems.

Loss of food-buying power for the poor, combined with a decline in the productive capacity of marginal farmlands, would clearly impair nutrition with little impact on world prices. Stagnation or decline in per capita production of grain in South America and Sub-Saharan Africa (see Figure 11-5) may result primarily from weakening demand, but in these areas environmental damage to marginal lands is also widespread.

––––––––––

[5]Brown, 2004.

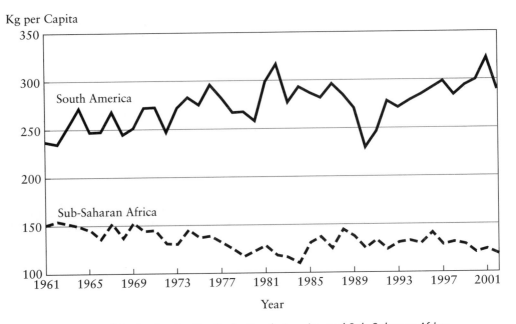

**FIGURE 11-5** *Cereal Production Per Capita for South America and Sub-Saharan Africa, 1961–2002*

Source: FAO, 2004.

## Land Use and Equity Issues

The issue of unequal distribution is linked to that of land use. We have already noted that most good agricultural land is currently in production. In a market economy, land will generally be used for the highest valued crop, as shown in Figure 11-6.

Here land is rated by quality on the horizontal axis, with the highest quality land on the left side, and quality declining as we move to the right. The vertical axis shows the value of crops grown on the land. This **crop value index** will differ depending on how the land is used. Some crops require higher-quality land and produce higher value per acre. Other crops grow on land of varying quality but produce less market value per acre. In economic terms, the crop value index represents the **marginal revenue product** of the land, which is equal to the **marginal physical product** (quantity of a particular crop) times the price of the crop.

For example, in Mexico much land is devoted to growing corn and beans for local consumption. But growing broccoli and strawberries for export produces higher revenues. The intersection of the two crop value lines $D_1$ and $E_1$ shows how the land will be divided between production for export and production for domestic use. On the high-quality land to the left of point $A$, the most valuable product is the export crop, and the land will be used for this. Corn and beans will be grown on the lower-quality land to the right of point $A$.

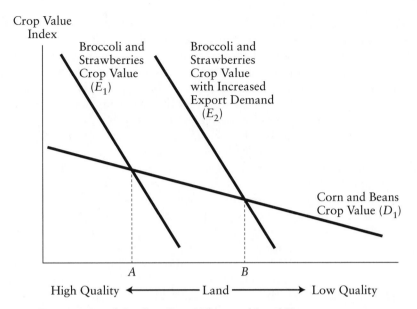

**FIGURE 11-6** *Land Quality, Crop Value, and Land Use*

Now suppose that demand for export crops increases, as shown by crop value line $E_2$, while demand for domestic foods remains the same. The crop value line for export products rises, reflecting higher prices for broccoli and strawberries. As a result, the land use pattern changes, with export production expanding up to point $B$ and domestic production squeezed onto lower-quality land to the right of point $B$. In Mexico today, this land use trend is accelerating as a result of the North American Free Trade Agreement (NAFTA).

What does this imply for the environment and for the nutritional status of the population? One likely result is that larger commercial farms will displace smaller farmers who lack good access to export markets. This will increase pressure on the marginal farmlands (to the right on the graph). Hill slopes, forest margins, and arid lands all are especially vulnerable to the kind of environmental degradation that results when displaced people move onto whatever land is available. We see the effects of this throughout much of Africa, Latin America, and Asia.

If revenues from export crops are unequally distributed, poorer peoples' diets will worsen as less corn and beans are produced for domestic consumption. Small farmers who share in export revenues can buy imported foods with the proceeds from cash crops, but more frequently they will lose out to larger producers in export markets.

## Projections for the Future

Population projections for the first half of the twenty-first century show total world population reaching a level close to 8 billion by 2025. What new stresses will the additional demand for food place on the environment? Will we exceed agricultural **carrying capacity?**

Will we experience food shortages? The grain production figures shown in Table 11-1 illustrate some implications of projected increases in global population.

As of 2003, the world produced about 2 billion metric tons of grain (column 2). If evenly distributed, this would provide each person with 337 kilograms of grain (cereals) per year—approximately one kilogram, or 2.2 pounds, per day. This grain crop required about half of the world's cropland. The other half was devoted to vegetables, fruits, oilseeds, root crops, and nonfood crops such as cotton.

This level of output, evenly distributed, would be adequate to provide each person with a mostly vegetarian diet, supplemented with a little meat, fish, or eggs—a diet characteristic of much of the developing world. The largely meat-centered diet characteristic of most of the developed world, however, requires much larger amounts of grain per person—not consumed directly, of course, but used for livestock feed. About three-quarters of the U.S. domestic consumption of cereal, for example, goes to feed cattle, pigs, and poultry.

Globally, therefore, distribution of the existing output is significantly unequal. Annual grain consumption in the United States is about 900 kg per capita, including direct consumption and livestock feed. In the developing world, it averages about 270 kg per capita. Consumption levels throughout much of the developing world are just sufficient for an adequate non-meat-centered diet, but inequality of distribution within countries leaves many of the poorest with inadequate levels of food consumption.

As economic development proceeds, per capita demand for food rises. This is partly because poorer people can afford to buy more basic foods, and partly because middle-class consumers shift toward a meat-based diet. Between 1950 and 1985, per capita grain consumption rose slowly but steadily throughout the world, at about 0.5 percent per year. Assuming that the slowdown in consumption growth after the mid-1980s was primarily due to limited purchasing power, we can expect this trend of increasing per capita consumption to continue. As we look ahead to the future, we must prepare to provide for both an increased total population, and a higher average consumption per person.

## Future Yield Requirements

The population projections in Table 11-1 for the year 2025 (column 4) are in the middle range of published estimates. Note that more than 95 percent of the population growth will take place in developing nations. When we combine this population growth with a modest projected increase in per capita consumption, it is clear that grain consumption will nearly double in the developing world (column 5).[6] On the other hand, agricultural land area will increase little (as discussed above). Output per hectare of land in developing nations must therefore rise by at least 50–75 percent (compare columns 3 and 6).[7]

---

[6]The rate of increase in per capita consumption assumed here is 0.5 percent per annum. Faster economic growth could significantly increase this if diets shift toward meat products as incomes rise.

[7]1 hectare = 2.477 acres.

**TABLE 11-1** *Population and Cereal Consumption Projections for 2025*

| Region | 1. Population 2003 (millions) | 2. Cereal Production 2002–2004 Average (MMT) | 3. Cereal Yields 2002–2004 Average (Kg/Ha) | 4. Projected Population 2025 | 5. Projected Cereal Requirements in 2025 (MMT) | 6. Projected Yield Requirements for Self-Sufficiency in 2025 (Kg/Ha) |
|---|---|---|---|---|---|---|
| World | 6,301 | 2,120 | 3,153 | 7,934 | 2,911 | 3,940 |
| Developed Nations | 1,329 | 891 | 3,783 | 1,257 | 774 | 3,381 |
| Developing Nations | 4,973 | 1,228 | 2,813 | 6,677 | 2,136 | 4,189 |
| Developing Nations (excluding China) | 3,661 | 829 | 2,325 | 5,201 | 1,534 | 3,618 |
| Africa | 851 | 125 | 1,254 | 1,323 | 291 | 2,720 |
| Latin America and Caribbean | 543 | 151 | 3,012 | 685 | 223 | 4,281 |
| Asia | 3,823 | 1005 | 3,221 | 4,778 | 1,648 | 5,119 |
| Asia (excluding China) | 2,512 | 605 | 2,610 | 3,302 | 1,026 | 4,351 |
| China | 1,312 | 400 | 4,984 | 1,476 | 603 | 7,019 |
| U.S. and Canada | 326 | 391 | 5,339 | 386 | 372 | 4,384 |
| Europe (excluding Russia) | 583 | 343 | 4,271 | 585 | 319 | 3,895 |
| Russia | 143 | 75 | 1,891 | 137 | 61 | 1,238 |
| Oceania | 32 | 32 | 1,748 | 41 | 16 | 1,258 |

MMT = million metric tons, MHa = million hectares. One metric ton = 1,000 kilograms(Kg).
Sources: Harris, 1996; FAOSTAT Agriculture Database http://apps.fao.org; Population Reference Bureau, 2004 *World Population Data Sheet.*

Column 6 of Table 11-1 shows the increases in agricultural yields required for self-sufficiency in grain production (supplying domestic demand without imports) in developed and developing nations. Average yields in the developing world must rise from the present 2.8 metric tons per hectare to more than 4 metric tons per hectare.[8] For the developing world, excluding China, yields must increase by 70 percent over present levels. Yields in Asia as a whole must rise from 3 to 5 metric tons per hectare. Yields in Africa would need to more than double for self-sufficiency in 2025.

Of course, not every region must achieve self-sufficiency; grain can be imported from countries with surplus capacity. The possibilities for meeting demand through increased trade, however, are limited. If we assume that most nations can achieve, but not exceed, yield levels similar to those now reached in the developed nations, both Asia and Africa will significantly increase their import demands.

According to recent studies, net cereal imports by developing countries will nearly double by 2020, from 104 to 201 million metrics tons.[9] Where will this extra export production come from? Current world cereal exports are predominantly from North America and Europe. Both of these areas already have very high yields, suggesting that future yield increases may be difficult to achieve. In addition, current Census Bureau projections show U.S. population rising from 293 million in 2004 to 338 million by 2025 and over 400 million by 2050. If this larger U.S. population consumes the same kind of meat-centered diet Americans now favor, there will be a significant added grain demand for animal feed. These combined demand pressures could lead to rising grain prices, confronting the world's poorest countries with the problem of purchasing a larger volume of more expensive food imports.

Analysts who offer a more optimistic view of the future rely on two factors. One is reduced population growth. As we have seen, population growth estimates show significant variation. If we accept the low-range projections, pressures on the global agricultural system are significantly less.[10] The other factor is yield increases. Some regions have achieved grain yields of 6 to 9 metric tons per hectare (6,000 to 9,000 kilograms per hectare). If this success could be extended worldwide, grain production would be more than ample.[11]

However, these population and yield variables may move in the opposite direction. Population may rise higher than medium projections. Environmental problems, including water shortages and global climate change, might endanger even present levels of yields in major regions. It seems prudent to prepare for unpleasant as well as pleasant surprises. If we take this approach, the critical question becomes the **environmental sustainability** of agricultural production. To assess the likelihood of an adequate solution to the food problem, we must consider in more detail the environmental stresses associated with pushing our agricultural systems toward their limits.

---

[8]1 metric ton = 1,000 kilograms.

[9]Pinstrup-Andersen and Pandya-Lorch, 2001.

[10]See, for example, Seckler, 1994.

[11]Waggoner, 1994, provides a good example of optimism on yields.

# Agriculture's Impact on the Environment

## Soil Erosion and Degradation

With the exception of some hydroponics and aquaculture, almost all agriculture depends on soil. Soil, as we have noted, can be either a renewable or a depletable resource. Ideally, agricultural techniques would not degrade soils and would replenish soil productivity over time through **nutrient recycling** from crop residues. If this were the case, agricultural output would be truly sustainable and could continue at present levels indefinitely.

Unfortunately, the situation in almost all the world's major agricultural areas is quite different: soil erosion and degradation is widespread. From 30 to 50 percent of the earth's surface is affected by erosion and soil degradation. Erosion damages crop productivity by reducing the availability of water, nutrients, and organic matter; water resources are also degraded by sediments and pollutants associated with erosion. Soil loss rates are typically highest in developing countries:

> Severe soil erosion is occurring in most of the world's agricultural regions, and the problem is growing as more marginal land is brought into production and less crop residues are returned to the soil. Soil loss rates in Europe range between 10 and 20 tons/hectare/year. In the United States, soil erosion on cropland averages 16 t/ha/yr. In Asia, Africa, and South America, soil erosion rates on cropland range between 20 and 40 t/ha/yr.[12]

The United Nations Environmental Programme's Global Assessment of Soil Degradation (GLASOD) estimates that erosion severely degrades an additional 5 to 6 million hectares of land each year.[13] As well as soil loss from erosion, further soil degradation occurs from over-irrigation, overgrazing, and destruction of trees and ground cover.

## The Economics of Erosion and Erosion Control

In many cases, farmers can greatly reduce erosion and soil degradation by **crop rotation and fallowing**—alternating grain and legume crops and taking the land out of production every several years. The farmer's costs include foregoing revenues in any year when the land is out of production and possibly settling for lower revenues in years when the land produces other than highest value crops. Farmers must make an economic calculation as to whether the immediate costs of erosion control are worth the long-term benefits.

Consider a simple example. Suppose a farmer can obtain $100,000 in annual revenues by continually growing the highest value crops with no provision for rebuilding soils or erosion control. Under these conditions, erosion will cause an annual decline of about 1 percent in yield. An effective erosion control program will reduce revenues by $15,000 per year. Is the program worth it to the farmer?

---

[12]Pimentel, 1993.

[13]Oldeman et al., 1990.

The answer depends on the **discount rate** used to balance present versus future costs. One percent yield loss means a monetary loss of $1,000. But this is not just a one-time loss; it will continue into the future. How do we evaluate this stream of losses resulting from one year's erosion? In economic terms, we apply a discount rate as discussed in Chapters 5 and 6. Suppose we select a 10 percent discount rate. The **present value** of the stream of losses extending indefinitely into the future is equal to

$$PV = (-\$1,000)(1/0.10) = -\$10,000$$

The benefits of erosion control are thus $10,000—not enough, in this example, to justify $15,000 lost revenue. Under these conditions, it is economically optimal to continue the erosive practices—but it is certainly not ecologically sustainable. Following this economic logic, the farmer will leave severely degraded land for the next generation.

Unfortunately, many farmers face exactly this kind of economic pressure to maximize short-term revenues. Note that if we used a lower interest rate—say 5 percent—the benefits of erosion control, calculated at $20,000, would exceed the costs and in theory make erosion control economically beneficial. Even so, the short-term losses might still be difficult to accept. An ecologically sound soil management policy thus depends on the farmer's foresight, relatively low interest rates, and the financial flexibility to invest in erosion control today for long-term benefits.

Off-farm effects of erosion are an additional problem. In many areas, major dams have silted up with eroded soil, ultimately destroying their potential for power generation and wasting billions in investments. Heavy siltation also causes extensive damage to river ecology. Because these costs are **externalities** from the farmer's point of view, social decision is required to respond to this aspect of erosion damage.

## Fertilizer Use

The steady increase in average yields characteristic of modern agriculture depends strongly on increased fertilizer use. Figure 11-7 shows this pattern for major world regions over the past 30 years. Increased fertilizer use is clearly associated with higher yields. Over time, nations tend to shift from traditional agriculture with low fertilizer input to modernized agriculture's heavy fertilizer use and high yields. Following this trend, food output has generally outpaced population growth over the long term.

## Environmental Effects of Fertilizer Use

What are the environmental applications of this "modernizing" process in agriculture? In general, modern agricultural techniques rely on a "package" of inputs including fertilizer, pesticides, irrigation, mechanization, and high-yielding crop varieties. In Figure 11-7, fertilizer per hectare serves as what economists call a **proxy variable** for this whole package: higher use of fertilizer correlates so strongly with higher use of the other inputs that measuring fertilizer use alone gives us a good idea of the degree of agricultural modernization. Each of these inputs, however, relates to specific environmental problems,

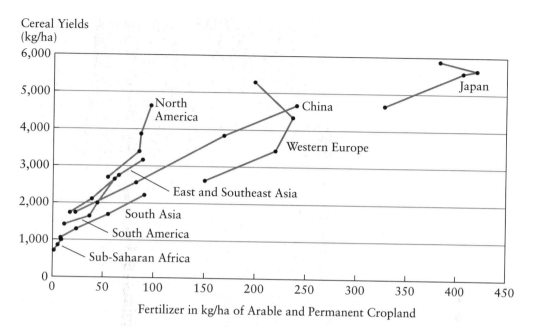

**FIGURE 11-7**  *Yield/Fertilizer Relationship for Major Regions Using Averaged Data for the Periods 1961–1970, 1971–1980, 1981–1990, 1991–2000*
Source: FAO, 2004.

and as high-yield input use has increased, so has the seriousness of these environmental problems.

Fertilizer supplies nutrients to the soil, and thence to crops. Most fertilizers supply the three major nutrients of nitrate, phosphate, and potassium. But a significant portion of the nutrients applied do not reach the crops as intended. Instead, they leach into ground and surface water, where they become serious pollutants.

Excessive nitrate in water is damaging to human health. Nitrates and phosphates also promote unwanted algae growth that chokes out other life in rivers, lakes, and even oceans. Most agricultural areas in the U.S. Midwest and West suffer from these problems. In the Gulf of Mexico, a huge "dead zone" caused by agricultural runoff covers an area of 18,000 km$^2$, and threatens commercial and recreational fisheries. In the Mediterranean, large portions of the sea have suffered severe ecological damage from agricultural runoff pollution, with giant mats of algae blanketing coastlines in the Aegean Sea and elsewhere. Inefficient and excessive fertilizer use have created especially severe agricultural problems in the formerly communist economies of Russia and East Europe. Inland seas such as the Black and Caspian Seas have experienced extinctions of numerous local species as a result.

Another damaging effect of excessive fertilizer use is more subtle. As large amounts of nitrate, phosphate, and potassium are added to the soil year after year, other nutrients present in smaller quantities—called **micronutrients**—become depleted.[14] This gradually reduces both yields and nutritional values of the crops. Like erosion, these can be long-term effects, which leaves little incentive for farmers to respond to them so long as short-term yields are high.

Fertilizer production is energy intensive. In effect, modern agriculture replaces solar energy and human labor with energy extracted primarily from fossil fuels.[15] Agricultural energy consumption thus contributes to all of the environmental problems associated with fossil fuel energy consumption discussed in Chapters 13 and 18. Agriculture accounts for about 3–5 percent of total energy use; although not the major component of energy-related issues, this percentage is significant, particularly for developing countries with growing populations who must buy imported energy.[16] Fertilizer use also contributes directly to various global atmospheric problems including global warming and ozone depletion.

Some analysts find it significant that artificial nitrogen applied to crops now exceeds the amount supplied through natural nitrogen fixation by soil microorganisms. Such a large intervention in the earth's **nitrogen cycle** must have ecological consequences. Furthermore, the use of fertilizer is projected to increase steadily to provide the yields needed for the twenty-first century.

## Pesticide Use

Like fertilizer use, pesticide use has risen rapidly with the spread of modern agriculture (see Figure 11-8). Pesticide use in the United States has leveled off after approximately doubling between the 1960s and 1980s, but worldwide pesticide use is still rising. Numerous health and environmental problems have accompanied this increase. Pesticides may affect agricultural workers directly—pesticide poisoning is a serious and widespread problem throughout much of the developing world. Residues in food affect consumers: measurable levels of chlorinated pesticides can be found in breast milk, and the cumulative impact of many pesticides on the human body is a serious concern. The carcinogenic effects of many pesticides are well known, and a more recent focus of research has been effects on reproductive systems.

Pesticides also affect ecosystems in various ways. Groundwater pollution from pesticides is a common problem in agricultural areas (see Box 11-1). Unintended extermination of beneficial species can lead to pest outbreaks far worse than the original problem. Since World War II (when the chemistry for many pesticides emerged), rapidly expanding pesticide use has paralleled an equally rapid expansion in **resistant pest species** (Figure 11-9). Similarly, excessive use of antibiotics in animal feed has encouraged the development of antibiotic-resistant microbes.

These developments are no surprise to ecologists, who understand the dangers of upsetting a natural species balance. However, such consequences are difficult to quantify

---

[14]Micronutrients include boron, copper, cobalt, and molybdenum. Although some of these substances can be damaging in large amounts, trace amounts are important for plant growth and human nutrition.

[15]For a detailed analysis of this process, see Martinez-Alier, 1987; Cleveland, 1994.

[16]See, for example, Hall, 1993.

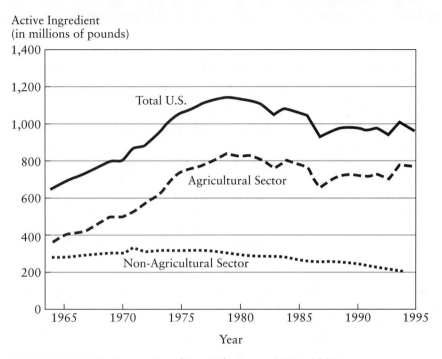

Active Ingredient
(in millions of pounds)

**FIGURE 11-8** *U.S. Conventional Pesticide Usage 1964–1995*
Source: U.S. EPA, 1994/1995.

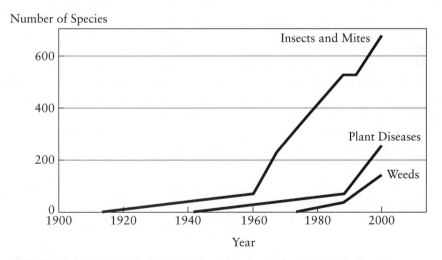

Number of Species

**FIGURE 11-9** *Increase in Resistant Pest Species in the Twentieth Century*
Source: Adapted from Gary Gardner, "Preserving Agricultural Resources," in Brown et al., *State of the World 1996*. Washington, D.C.: Worldwatch Institute, 1996. Reprinted by permission of Worldwatch Institute.

Agricultural pollution from erosion, fertilizers, and pesticides often poses a more difficult policy problem than pollution from well-defined industrial sources. Runoff from agriculture is called **nonpoint source pollution,** meaning that it originates from a wide area, affecting water supplies and downstream communities. In addition, factory farms pose a huge problem of animal wastes released into water supplies. According to the Environmental Protection Agency, hog, chicken, and cattle waste has polluted 35,000 miles of rivers in 22 states and contaminated groundwater in 17 states. Pollution from livestock is associated with many types of waterborne disease, as well as problems like bacterial outbreaks (which have plagued the Chesapeake Bay), red tides, algae blooms, and the dead zone in the Gulf of Mexico.

Reducing nonpoint source pollution requires altering production methods in agriculture. The use of fertilizers, pesticides, and intensive farming methods can bring benefits in terms of reduced prices to consumers. But while these benefits are automatically internalized into market mechanisms—farmers who can produce more cheaply will gain greater market share—external costs are not considered. Thus government policies must help ensure that agricultural input and output prices reflect true social costs and benefits.

This implies reducing subsidies for agricultural inputs, as well as subsidies directed at increasing production. On the other hand, support for research and promotion of alternative, lower-polluting techniques can be justified on the grounds of internalizing positive externalities. Strict regulation of factory farming, and incentives for nonfactory livestock production, may raise prices to consumers, but lower prices cannot be justified on economic grounds if they fail to reflect full social costs.

Particularly in the developing world, where use of pesticides is steadily rising, information and support for production methods with lower pesticide use requires government commitment and investment. In the 1980s Indonesia invested as much as $1 million per year in research and training in ecologically oriented pest control, following a destructive infestation of the brown planthopper, which had spiraled out of control when excessive pesticide use eliminated its natural predators. The Indonesian program has been a success—crop yields have increased by 12 percent with lower environmental impacts—but replication of such programs depends on initial investments, often hard to come by in developing nations.

**SOURCES**

U.S. Environmental Protection Agency, http://www.epa.gov/agriculture/anafoidx.html
Wilson, Clevo, and Clem Tisdell, "Why Farmers Continue to Use Pesticides Despite Environmental, Health, and Sustainability Costs." *Ecological Economics* 39 (December 2001): 449–462.

Karlsson, Sylvia I. "Agricultural Pesticides in Developing Countries." *Environment* 46, no. 4 (May 2004): 22–42.

in monetary terms or to introduce into farm-level decision making. In addition, vested interests—the manufacturers of agricultural chemicals—seek to expand pesticide use.

As with other issues of technological impact on the environment, **information asymmetry** is a problem.[17] Pesticide producers generally know the most about the chemical composition and potential effects of pesticides. With thousands of different compounds on the market, mastering this information—even if it is available—would be practically impossible for pesticide consumers. Government regulators have trouble keeping up with the rapid introduction of new compounds and usually must narrow their focus to, for example, carcinogenicity. In such circumstances it is unlikely that the **external costs** of pesticide use will be fully understood and internalized. Regulatory issues have become even more complex with the introduction of genetically modified crops, often by the same chemical companies that are major producers of agricultural pesticides (see Box 11-2).

## Irrigation and Water Resources

The spread of irrigation has been just as important as increased fertilizer use in expanding agricultural output. Irrigation greatly improves yields and often permits **multiple cropping** in areas dependent on seasonal rains. The most optimistic projections of further yield increases in developing-nation agriculture rely heavily on expanded irrigation.[18] But, as with fertilizer and pesticides, the short-term benefits of irrigation often link to long-term environmental damage.

Poor drainage causes irrigation water to build up underground, eventually waterlogging fields. In tropical areas, water that reaches the surface evaporates rapidly, leaving behind a buildup of dissolved salts and leading to **salinization and alkalinization of soils.** In the Indian Punjab, for example, millions of hectares of land have been damaged by salinization. Irrigation also increases fertilizer and pesticide runoff, polluting local surface and groundwater.

The farmland most dependent on irrigation often lies in precisely those arid regions where water is in short supply. This leads to overdraft of groundwater—pumping out underground reservoirs faster than the natural water cycle can refill them—a classic example of the **common property resource** problem discussed in Chapter 4. No individual farmer has an incentive to limit water use. As a result, currently productive agriculture regions face a waterless future once the aquifers are exhausted. The Ogallala aquifer that supports much of irrigated agriculture in the western United States is as much as 50 percent depleted in some areas, and its level continues to fall. Rapid declines in groundwater levels are also taking place in India, North China, central Asia.

Withdrawals from rivers in arid areas can be equally damaging. Agricultural water demand has led to serious salinization problems in the Colorado River basin in the western United States as well as an international dispute over the increased salinity of the

---

[17]Economists speak of *information asymmetry* when participants in a market economy have different levels of information access. In the case of agricultural technologies, consumers of food products, and even government regulators, may be unaware of the nature and dangers of pesticide residues.

[18]See, for example, Alexandratos, 1994.

## 11-2  Genetically Modified Foods: A Controversial Technology

An estimated 60 million acres in the United States, and more than 100 million acres worldwide, were cultivated with genetically modified (GM) crops in 2000. Although proponents list a variety of potential benefits from GM crops, opponents argue that widespread use of GM products creates health and environmental hazards. Opposition to introduction of genetically modified organisms and use of genetically modified ingredients in regular consumer products first started and is still strong in the European Union, but concern seems to be spreading worldwide as more countries restrict or consider restricting GM foods.

### GM Foods: Concerns and Proposed Benefits

Proponents claim that the marriage of biotechnology and agriculture has great potential for providing safe, pest-resistant, adaptive, high-yielding, and nutritious food for a growing world population. They argue that certain genetic modifications would produce foods with a variety of beneficial qualities such as corn that produces a toxin that kills a corn boring beetle, a frost-resistant tomato inserted with a fish gene, and salmon that grow faster and are more resistant to cold. High-yielding GM crops could replace lower-yielding crops in developing countries, and engineering vitamins into crops such as rice could provide a more nutritious diet for poor consumers. This would not only help feed the increasing population in those countries but would also decrease the conversion rate of natural forests into agricultural land.

Opponents of GM foods claim that any social benefits are outweighed by the chance of a large-scale eco-catastrophe. Crossing the species boundaries inherent in the natural structure, according to these critics, can have disastrous implications for nature as well as for human health. Genetically modified plants could cross breed with natural varieties to produce strains that could wreak havoc on the natural environment. Also, widespread use of such pesticide-producing plants could promote the emergence of resistant "super-pests." Genetically modified corn threatens native corn varieties in Mexico, and the U.S. Forest Service has warned that genetically engineered grass "has the potential to adversely impact all 175 national forests and grasslands."[1] Even a small chance of such a major disaster, critics contend, is not worth the benefits of GM crops.

---

[1]"Mexico Is Warned of Risk from Altered Corn," *New York Times,* March 13, 2004; "Genes from Engineered Grass Spread for Miles," *New York Times,* September 21, 2004.

*(continued on following page)*

### Issues of Corporate Control

Formulating GM crops requires heavy investment in research and development. To earn back their investments, companies must ensure that only those who pay for them use their products. Traditionally farmers, especially in developing countries, buy an initial consignment of seeds and subsequently save part of their crops as seeds for future cultivation. Biotechnology corporations can patent their products and ensure, through threat of legal action, that farmers buy a new consignment of seed for every season or pay royalties. Some companies have attempted to genetically modify seeds so that the subsequent crop seeds are sterile or create crops usable only with another product made by the same company. Critics claim that such developments can create monopolistic situations in which a few companies control the supply of major crop seeds. Such a market would place small-scale farmers and developing countries at a strong disadvantage.

Staunch anti–GM foods stances are causing trade conflicts between GM food producers such as the United States and importing countries. European governments, some Asian governments, and U.S. activists are calling for labeling on foods that contain GM ingredients and the right to exclude GM products from their markets. Some farmers and industry lobbyists, mainly in the United States, contend that GM and non–GM foods will have to be grown, transported, stored and processed separately, which will lead to higher prices. In addition, they claim, labeling will stigmatize products. Most countries have agreed to the need for further research on the safety of GM foods. In 2003, the U.S. Agriculture Department announced stricter rules for crops that are genetically modified to produce pharmaceuticals or industrial chemicals.[2]

The debate on genetically modified foods includes powerful arguments on both sides. Decisions will have important implications for environmental sustainability, food security, and international trade and politics.[3]

---

[2]"U.S. Imposes Stricter Rules for Genetically Modified Crops." *New York Times,* March 7, 2003.

[3]For more on both sides of this debate, see Rissler and Mellen, 1996, and Paarlberg, 2000.

---

river water crossing the border into Mexico. Perhaps the worst case of excessive irrigation demand is the Aral Sea in the former Soviet Union; this entire inland sea is drying up as a result of water withdrawals (primarily for cotton production) from the rivers that feed it.[19]

Limits on water supplies may be the most significant constraint on future agricultural expansion in large areas of the world. Irrigation accounts for 65 percent of total water withdrawal worldwide and more than 80 percent in developing countries.[20]

---

[19]For an extensive discussion of the problems of irrigated agriculture, see Postel, 1999.

[20]Harris, 1990.

Most of China and the Indian subcontinent are close to the limits of their available water supply, and urban/industrial water demand is rising steadily. Much of Africa is arid or semi-arid, as are large areas in west and central Asia, and in the western United States. Despite clear economic incentives to expand irrigation, both externality and common-property resource problems associated with irrigation mean that this expansion is likely to intensify resource and environmental problems.

## Sustainable Agriculture for the Future

Many of the resource and environmental issues we discussed in Chapters 3–5 are relevant to the analysis of agricultural production. Erosion and soil degradation, as we have noted, make soil a depletable resource and impose **user costs** on future generations. Fertilizer runoff and pesticide pollution are classic examples of externalities. Excessive pumping of water from rivers and aquifers demonstrates the problem of overuse of common-property resources. Problems such as resistant pest species and loss of biodiversity impose ecological costs that may be difficult to evaluate in monetary terms, as we saw in Chapter 6.

*A rice farmer levels his plowed field in Bali, Indonesia. Traditional techniques, such as the use of draft animals, agroforestry, and multicropping, are ecologically sustainable but have often been displaced by modernized agriculture.*

Ecological analysis offers us a somewhat different understanding of the relationship between agriculture and the environment. Rather than seeing agricultural production as a process of combining inputs (including land, water, fertilizer, and pesticides) to maximize output, the ecological economist would argue that agriculture is a process of intervention in the natural **biophysical cycles** responsible for plant growth. These include the carbon cycle, nitrogen cycle, water cycle, and similar cycles for other plant nutrients.

In a natural state, solar energy drives these cycles. Traditional agriculture departs little from these natural cycles. Modernized agriculture relies on extra inputs of energy, water, nitrogen, and synthetic chemicals. This gives higher yields, but creates imbalances in all the natural cyclical processes. From this perspective, soil degradation, fertilizer and pesticide pollution, and water overdraft are results of disrupting natural cycles. To use another ecological concept, modern agriculture expands carrying capacity but only at the cost of increasing ecological stresses.

Both the economic and the ecological perspectives can influence our definition of **sustainable agriculture.** A sustainable agricultural system should produce a stable level of output without degrading the environmental systems that support it. In economic terms, this means no significant uninternalized externalities, user costs, or excessive use of common-property resources. From an ecological point of view, a sustainable system minimizes disruption to natural cycles. This suggests supply-side and demand-side techniques that may be appropriate for sustainable agriculture.

Production techniques such as organic fertilization from recycled plant and animal wastes, crop rotation, and **intercropping** grains and legumes help maintain the soil's nutrients balance and minimize need for artificial fertilizer. The use of reduced tillage, terracing, fallowing, and **agroforestry** (planting trees in and around fields) all help to reduce erosion. **Integrated pest management (IPM)** uses natural pest controls such as predator species, crop rotation, and labor-intensive early pest removal to minimize use of chemical pesticides.

Efficient irrigation techniques and the use of drought- and salt-tolerant crop varieties can reduce water use. Species diversity is promoted by multiple cropping (planting several different crops in the same field) rather than the **monoculture** (extensive plantings of a single crop) typical of modernized agriculture.

According to the National Research Council report *Alternative Agriculture*,[21] farms using organic techniques have been fairly successful in equaling the yields and economic record of neighboring high-input farms in Iowa, Pennsylvania, Ohio, Virginia, and California. This is a positive indication that environmentally friendly techniques may be economically feasible in larger scale agriculture. However, the barriers to implementing this kind of farming in the United States and worldwide are considerable.

One major problem is access to information. Alternative techniques tend to be both **labor intensive** and **information intensive.** In developed countries, only a minority of farmers know enough about the complex techniques of organic and low-input agriculture to make them pay. It's much easier to read the instructions on a bag of fertilizer or a canister of pesticide. In developing countries, traditional low-input farming systems have often been displaced by modernized "Green Revolution" techniques.

---

[21]National Research Council, 1989.

In recent years, organic agriculture has expanded rapidly, but it still represents a small portion of total agricultural production (see Box 11-3). Government policies, such as the establishment of organic standards and reform of agricultural subsidy policies, will have an important influence on the future of organic farming.

## Policies for Sustainable Agriculture

Without strong economic incentives to alter production methods, combined with widespread information and support for alternative techniques, most farmers will stay with established methods. A shift to alternative agriculture will require a combination of government policy and market incentives.

Important market incentives include the prices of fertilizer, pesticides, irrigation water, and energy. Many governments have policies that directly or indirectly subsidize these prices. According to a well-established principle of agricultural economics, price ratios for agricultural inputs determine the course of **induced innovation** in agriculture.[22] If fertilizer is cheap relative to land and labor, the farm sector will develop and implement fertilizer-intensive methods. By providing low-cost fertilizer, farm chemicals, and water for irrigation, governments promote agricultural productivity—but at environmental cost.

Policies to subsidize energy development also promote the trend to more highly mechanized and input-dependent agriculture. Changing these policies would support development of a more labor- and information-intensive agriculture with less environmental impact. In developing nations with large pools of unemployed and underemployed labor, promotion of labor-intensive agricultural development might have considerable employment as well as environmental benefits.

Removing energy and input subsidies would send a price signal to farmers to use less input-intensive techniques. Before they can respond effectively to these price incentives, however, farmers need information on alternative techniques—otherwise higher input prices will simply make food more expensive. Developing nations can combine valuable knowledge of traditional agricultural techniques with modern innovations provided energy-intensive monoculture does not sweep away traditional knowledge.

Agricultural subsidies in developed nations were estimated at $362 billion in 1998.[23] Most of these subsidies are environmentally destructive, promoting increased input and energy use. While developed nations typically promote production, resulting in agricultural surpluses, developing nations often reduce incentives for agricultural production by policies that lower prices paid to farmers. The goal is to provide cheap food for consumers, but the effect is to discourage local production. Widespread use of these counterproductive economic policies in agriculture leaves much scope for policy reforms that could benefit both food supply and the environment. Damaging subsidies could be removed or shifted to favor environmentally sound techniques and agricultural research. Better prices and improved credit systems for farmers can encourage both increased production and investment in soil conservation.

---

[22]Ruttan and Hayami, 1998.

[23]Myers and Kent, 2001, Chapter 3: Agriculture.

# 11-3  Organic Agriculture on the Rise

Organic production, representing about $26 billion of production worldwide, is the most rapidly growing sector of agriculture. According to a report by the Organization for Economic Cooperation and Development (OECD), organic agriculture now constitutes only 2 percent of production within the OECD (essentially the world's higher-income countries) but is growing at a rate of 15–30 percent annually. The growth responds to the demand of consumers in high-income countries who are prepared to pay a premium for foods grown without pesticides or genetic modification. Advantages of organics are perceived to include health and environmental benefits, improved food quality and taste, accessibility of fresh produce, and helping small-scale local producers.

While yields tend to be lower and labor costs higher on organic farms, profitability is also higher as a result of price premiums and, in some cases, government support payments. Market-based policy approaches to promote organic agriculture include certification and labeling schemes, now adopted by almost all OECD countries. The European Union has a single, "harmonized" standard for organic agriculture, and the United States has put federal organic standards in place. Compliance with these standards helps exporters expand organic production, but the multiplicity of standards can be confusing.

Some European governments have undertaken promotional campaigns to encourage consumption of organic products. A few countries require public institutions such as schools and hospitals to purchase organic food. Many governments provide direct financial support to organic farmers, justifying this subsidy as a return for providing external benefits of environmental protection—for example, reducing nitrate, phosphate, and pesticide flows into water supplies. A small percentage of public agricultural research is also devoted to organic systems.

The OECD report concludes that conventional agriculture still retains an advantage due to government production subsidies and failure to address the problems of negative externalities associated with conventional systems. "Such policies provide incentives to adopt farming practices that increase production rather than those, like organics, which stress quality. . . . Governments need to address the externalities in conventional agriculture to provide a better use of resources and a more level playing field for organic systems."

**SOURCE**

Organisation for Economic Co-operation and Development, *Organic Agriculture: Sustainability, Markets, and Policies*. Wallingford, U.K.: CABI, 2003.

An example of an environmentally positive agricultural subsidy is the U.S. Conservation Reserve Program. Started in 1985, this program now covers 34 million acres of former cropland. Farmers receive payments to remove environmentally sensitive land from production, reducing erosion, protecting wetlands and water supplies, and providing habitat for wildlife, including endangered species. At a cost of $1.8 billion annually, this program internalizes positive externalities, helps to preserve family farms, and provides greater land use option value for the future.

On the demand side, it is clear that population size is a major determinant of food demand and indirectly of agricultural pressures on the environment. The ecological concept of carrying capacity implies some maximum population that the planet's resources can sustainably support. Our discussion of agricultural futures indicates that we are close to that capacity, and may have exceeded it if we consider long-term issues of soil erosion and water overdraft. Population policy is therefore a central element in limiting the impact of agricultural production on the environment.

The other major demand-side variable is diet. As we have seen, a meat-centered diet implies much higher land, water, and fertilizer requirements per capita than a mostly vegetarian diet. Using land resources to produce meat for export also increases environmental pressures in developing nations. Thus, reducing meat consumption in developed nations and slowing the trend toward meat-centered diets in newly industrializing nations are important components of long-term sustainability.

Abolishing input subsidies will increase the relative price of meat as compared to more input-efficient foods, and health motivations may lead to reduced demand for meat in developed nations. To the extent that consumers shift their preferences toward more vegetables, including more organically grown produce, the incentives to producers to employ less environmentally damaging techniques will grow.

The environmental problems associated with agriculture are complex and cannot be solved by simple cost internalization policies—though these will help. It will take major changes in consumer behavior, production techniques, and government price and agricultural policies to move toward a sustainable agricultural system. The urgency of these issues will grow as population increases and cumulative soil and water impacts increase. The high-input agriculture that has been central to increasing world output during recent decades will not meet the needs of the twenty-first century without significant changes to promote sustainability.

## SUMMARY

Food production has outpaced population growth during the past century, allowing for slowly rising global per capita food consumption. However, food distribution is significantly unequal, with up to 1 billion people receiving inadequate nutrition. Most suitable agricultural land is already being farmed, leaving relatively little room for further expansion. Yields have risen, and continue to rise, but greater productivity has been accompanied by rising environmental impact, including erosion, soil degradation, and fertilizer and pesticide runoff.

Rates of growth in agricultural output have slowed, but prices of basic foods are stable or declining, indicating that supply limits have not been reached. In many areas of the developing world per capita consumption has grown slowly, stagnated, or declined. Inequitable access to food means that basic food crops can be displaced by luxury or export food crops, increasing pressures on the poor and on environmentally vulnerable marginal lands.

Projections of future demand show a near doubling of food demand in the developing world over the next several decades. With little potential for land expansion, meeting this demand will require dramatic increases in yields. The challenge is to achieve this in an environmentally sustainable manner. Existing environmental effects associated with agricultural production make this a formidable task.

Erosion causes declining soil fertility as well as significant off-farm damage. Farmers facing short-term financial pressures often find investment in long-term conservation difficult. Fertilizer use has led to extensive runoff pollution and excessive nitrate release, affecting both water supplies and the atmosphere. Pesticide applications are associated with steadily increasing numbers of resistant pest species, as well as with other negative effects on ecosystems. Poorly planned irrigation systems have led to water overdraft and pollution as well as soil damage.

Future policies must promote agricultural sustainability. Practices such as crop rotation, intercropping, agroforestry, and integrated pest management can reduce input requirements and environmental impact while maintaining high yields. Efficient irrigation and land management techniques have great potential, but require appropriate economic incentives for farmers to adopt them. Removing energy and input subsidies and providing information on environmentally sound techniques must accompany more equitable and efficient distribution and consumption patterns.

## KEY TERMS AND CONCEPTS

agroforestry
biodiversity
biophysical cycles
carrying capacity
common-property resource
crop rotation and fallowing
crop value index
depletable resource
discount rate
elasticity of supply
environmental sustainability
external costs
externalities
induced innovation
information asymmetry
information-intensive techniques
integrated pest management
intercropping

labor-intensive techniques
marginal physical product
marginal revenue product
micronutrients
monoculture
multiple cropping
nitrogen cycle
nonpoint source pollution
nutrient recycling
nutritional deficit
present value
proxy variable
renewable resource
resistant pest species
salinization and alkalinization of soils
sustainable agriculture
user costs

## DISCUSSION QUESTIONS

1. What evidence would you use to evaluate the proposition that the world is reaching maximum carrying capacity in terms of food supply? Some analysts believe that the world's agricultural capacity is quite adequate for a population of 10 billion people. Do you feel comfortable with this assertion? Is it useful to attempt to evaluate maximum carrying capacity, or should we just wait and see how markets adjust to increased food demand?

2. Which of agriculture's environmental effects are most amenable to market solutions? Consider the on-farm and off-farm effects of erosion, for example. What kinds of incentives might induce greater erosion control? How much can private initiative accomplish and how much must rely on government policy?

3. How can we define the concept of sustainable agriculture? Can high-input agriculture be sustainable? Is organic agriculture sustainable? How is our current agricultural system not sustainable, and what kinds of policies are appropriate responses to problems of nonsustainability? How would you evaluate the economic costs and benefits of such policies?

## REFERENCES

Alexandratos, Nikos. *The Outlook for World Food and Agriculture to the Year 2010.* Rome, Italy: United Nations Food and Agriculture Organization, 1994.

Brown, Lester, and Hal Kane. *Full House: Reassessing the Earth's Population Carrying Capacity.* New York: Norton, 1994.

Brown, Lester R. *Outgrowing the Earth: The Food Security Challenge in an Age of Falling Water Tables and Rising Temperatures.* New York: Norton, 2004.

Cleveland, Cutler J. "Reallocating Work Between Human and Natural Capital and Agriculture: Examples from India and the United States." In *Investing in Natural Capital: The Ecological Approach to Sustainability,* edited by Jannson et al. Washington, D.C.: Island Press, 1994.

Food and Agriculture Organization of the United Nations (FAO). FAOSTAT Agriculture Database, 2004.

Gardner, Gary. "Preserving Agricultural Resources." In *State of the World 1996,* edited by Brown et al. Washington, D.C.: Worldwatch Institute, 1996.

Hall, Charles A. S. "The Efficiency of Land and Energy Use in Tropical Economies and Agriculture." *Agriculture, Ecosystems and Environment* 46. Amsterdam: Elsevier, 1993: 1–30.

Harris, Jonathan M. *World Agriculture and the Environment.* New York: Garland, 1990.

Harris, Jonathan M. "World Agricultural Futures: Regional Sustainability and Ecological Limits." *Ecological Economics* 17 (May 1996): 95–115.

Martinez-Alier, Juan. "Modern Agriculture: A Source of Energy?" Chapter 2 in *Ecological Economics: Energy, Environment, and Society.* Oxford, U.K.: Blackwell, 1987.

Myers, Norman, and Jennifer Kent. *Perverse Subsidies: How Tax Dollars Can Undercut the Environment and the Economy.* Washington, D.C.: Island Press, 2001.

National Research Council. *Alternative Agriculture.* Washington, D.C.: National Academy Press, 1989.

Oldeman, L. R., R. T. A. Hakkeling, and W. G. Sombroek. *Global Assessment of Soil Degradation.* Wageningen, Netherlands: ISRIC/UNEP, 1990.

Paarlberg, Robert. "The Global Food Fight." *Foreign Affairs* 79 (May/June 2000): 24–38.

Pimentel, David, ed. *World Soil Erosion and Conservation.* Cambridge, U.K.: Cambridge University Press, 1993.

Pinstrup-Andersen, Per, and Rajul Pandya-Lorch. *The Unfinished Agenda: Perspectives on Overcoming Hunger, Poverty, and Environmental Degradation.* Washington, D.C.: International Food Policy Research Institute, 2001.

Postel, Sandra. *Pillar of Sand: Can the Irrigation Miracle Last?* Worldwatch Institute Book. New York: Norton, 1999.

Rissler, Jane, and Margaret Mellen. *The Ecological Risks of Engineered Crops.* Cambridge, Mass.: MIT Press, 1996.

Ruttan, Vernon W., and Yujiro Hayami. "Induced Innovation Model of Agricultural Development." In *International Agricultural Development* (3rd ed.), edited by Carl K. Eicher and John M. Staatz. Baltimore: Johns Hopkins University Press, 1998.

Seckler, David. *Trends in World Food Needs: Toward Zero Growth in the 21st Century.* Winrock International Institute for Agricultural Development, Center for Economic Policy Studies Discussion Paper No. 18, 1994.

Sen, Amartya. "Population: Delusion and Reality." *New York Review of Books,* September 22, 1994.

Sen, Amartya. "Population, Food and Freedom." Chapter 9 in Sen, *Development as Freedom.* New York: Knopf, 2000.

Smil, Vaclav. *Feeding the World: A Challenge for the Twenty-First Century.* Cambridge, Mass.: MIT Press, 2000.

United States Environmental Protection Agency. *Pesticides Industry Sales and Usage Report,* 1994/1995.

Waggoner, Paul E. *How Much Land Can Ten Billion People Spare for Nature?* Council for Agricultural Science and Technology, Task Force Report No. 121, February 1994.

## WEBSITES

1. **http://www.ers.usda.gov/** Website for the Economic Research Service, a division of the U.S. Department of Agriculture with a mission "to inform and enhance public and private decision making on economic and policy issues related to agriculture, food, natural resources, and rural development." Their website provides links to a broad range of data and analysis on U.S. agricultural issues.

2. **http://www.fao.org/** Website for the Food and Agriculture Organization of the United Nations, an organization "with a mandate to raise levels of nutrition and standards of living, to improve agricultural productivity, and to better the condition of rural populations." Their website includes a huge amount of data on agriculture and food issues around the world.

3. **http://www.ota.com/** Homepage for the Organic Trade Association, "a membership-based business association representing the organic industry in Canada, the United States, and Mexico." Their website includes press releases and facts about the organic agriculture industry.

4. **http://www.cals.cornell.edu/extension/nabc/** Homepage for the National Agricultural Biotechnology Council, a nonprofit group with membership from more than 30 research and teaching institutions designed to provide a forum for the evaluation of agricultural biotechnology. Several reports available on their website concern the impact of agricultural biotechnology.

5. **http://www.oecd.org/agr/** Website for the Food, Agriculture, and Fisheries division of the Organisation for Economic Co-operation and Development. The site offers data, trade information, and discussions of environmental issues, including a web page on biotechnology.

# Energy and Resources

CHAPTER FOCUS QUESTIONS

■ Are we running out of nonrenewable resources?
■ What are the environmental costs of mining mineral resources?
■ How do economic incentives affect recycling of nonrenewable resources?

CHAPTER **12**

# Nonrenewable Resources: Scarcity and Abundance

## The Supply of Nonrenewable Resources

The planet holds a fixed quantity of **nonrenewable resources,** including metal and nonmetal minerals, coal, oil, and natural gas. We have extensive supplies of certain resources, such as iron; others, such as mercury or helium, are in relatively limited supply. The global economy is using up these resources—often at increasing rates. Is this a cause for alarm? The authors of the original *Limits to Growth* report[1] thought so in 1972, and repeated a similar warning 20 years later in *Beyond the Limits*:

> Human use of many essential resources and generation of many kinds of pollutants have already surpassed rates that are physically sustainable. Without significant reductions in material and energy flows, there will be in the coming decades an uncontrolled decline in per capita food output, energy use, and industrial production.[2]

Limited, nonrenewable resources cannot, of course, last forever, but issues regarding their use are complex, involving changes in resource supply and demand as well as the wastes and pollution generated in their consumption. In this chapter we examine the dynamics of nonrenewable resource use; in Chapter 13 we will look more specifically at the

---

[1]Meadows et al., 1972.

[2]Meadows et al., 1992, p. xv.

use of energy resources, and in Chapters 16 and 17 we will examine analyses of pollution generation and resource recycling.

In our initial analysis in Chapter 5, we considered the allocation of a mineral resource over several time periods. We assumed that both the resource quantity and quality were fixed. The economic principles derived from this simple example, including the analysis of **user costs** and **Hotelling's rule** for resource pricing, are important, but a more sophisticated analysis must deal with real-world conditions. We usually see many different resource qualities (for example, different grades of copper ore), and we rarely know with complete certainty the location and total quantity of resource deposits.

## *Physical Supply and Economic Supply*

The **economic supply** of a nonrenewable resource differs from its **physical supply.** The physical supply (in the earth's crust) is finite but generally not precisely known. The **economically recoverable reserves** provide the measure most commonly used in, for example, calculations of resource lifetime. However, this figure changes over time for three main reasons:

- The resource is extracted and used over time, diminishing reserves.
- New resource deposits are discovered over time, increasing reserves.
- Changing price and technological conditions can make more (or less) of the known reserves economically viable. These factors make predictions of resource lifetimes an inexact science.

A mineral resource such as copper is classified through a combination of geologic and economic measures (Figure 12-1).

In geological terms, resources are classified by available quantities, shown as the horizontal dimension in Figure 12-1. **Identified reserves** are those whose quantity and quality are already known. A portion of these identified reserves have been **measured** within a 20 percent margin of error; another portion are **indicated** or **inferred** based on geological principles. In addition, **hypothetical** and **speculative** amounts of the resource are as yet undiscovered, but likely to exist in certain geological situations.

Economic factors create another dimension to resource classification, shown vertically in Figure 12-1, with the most economically profitable resources toward the top. Resources of high enough quality to be profitably produced are identified as **economic reserves. Subeconomic resources** are those whose costs of extraction are too high to make production worthwhile. However, if prices rise or extraction technologies improve, these deposits may become profitable.

The fact that economic reserves can be expanded in both geological and economic dimensions renders projections using a **static reserve index** unreliable. A static reserve index simply divides economic reserves by the current rate of use for an estimate of **resource lifetime:**

$$\text{Expected Resource Lifetime} = \frac{\text{Economic Reserves}}{\text{Annual Consumption}}$$

| | | Identified | | | Undiscovered | |
|---|---|---|---|---|---|---|
| | | Demonstrated | | Inferred | Hypothetical (in known districts) | Speculative (in undiscovered districts) |
| | | Measured | Indicated | | | |
| Economic | | Reserves | | | | |
| Subeconomic | | | | | | |

← ————————— Increasing Geologic Assurance ————————— →

Increasing Economic Feasibility ↑

**FIGURE 12-1** *Classification of Nonrenewable Resources*

Source: Adapted from U.S. Bureau of Mines and U.S. Geological Survey, *Geological Survey Bulletins 1450-A* and *1450-B,* 1976. Available at http://www.usgs.gov.

Of course, current consumption is not necessarily a good indication of future use. With growing population and economic output, we can expect nonrenewable resource use to grow—although substitution and changing consumption patterns will affect rates of growth. An **exponential reserve index** assumes that consumption will grow exponentially over time, leading to more rapid resource exhaustion.

Calculations made in 1972 using both static and exponential reserve indices indicated that major mineral reserves would be exhausted within several decades—projections clearly not borne out.[3] Why not? Because reserves have grown with new discoveries and new extractive technologies. However, we cannot simply dismiss predictions of resource exhaustion. Even with reserve expansion, planetary resources are ultimately limited.

The relevant question is how resource consumption, new technology, and discovery will interact to affect prices, which in turn will affect future patterns of resource demand and supply. To better understand these factors, we need a more sophisticated economic theory of nonrenewable resource use.

## Economic Theory of Nonrenewable Resource Use

What determines the rate at which we extract and use nonrenewable resources? An individual firm operating a mine or other resource extraction operation, must be guided

---

[3]Meadows et al., 1992.

by the principle of maximization of **resource rents.**[4] Consider a firm operating a bauxite (aluminum ore) mine. If the firm is in a competitive industry, it is a **price taker** and sells its output at the market price, over which it has no control. It can, however, control the amount of the resource extracted in any period.

In general, as more of the resource is extracted the marginal cost of extraction will rise. Obviously, if the **marginal extraction cost** rises above the market price, producing the bauxite becomes unprofitable. Price must at least equal marginal cost to make production worthwhile. Unlike other competitive industries where price equals marginal cost in equilibrium, resource-extracting firms typically operate at an output level at which price exceeds marginal cost (Figure 12-2). Such firms must seek to maximize the value of rents not just in one period, but over an extended period of time.

The rent for the firm in any specific period $i$ is given by:

$$R_i = P - MC(q_i)$$

where $q_i$ is the quantity of the resource extracted in the $i^{\text{th}}$ period.

The present value of a stream of rents extending into the future is given by

$$PV[R] = R_0 + R_1/(1 + r) + R_2/(1 + r)^2 + R_3/(1 + r)^3 + \cdots + R_n/(1 + r)^n$$

$$= \sum_{i=0}^{n} R_i/(1 + r)^i$$

where $R_i$ is the rent accruing to the firm in the $i^{\text{th}}$ period.

To maximize the present value of the rent stream, the firm must adjust the extraction quantity in each period until the rent rises at a rate equal to the discount rate, so that the present value of the rent in each period is the same,[5] or:

$$R_0 = R_1/(1 + r) = R_2/(1 + r)^2 = R_3/(1 + r)^3 = \cdots = R_n/(1 + r)^n$$

When all the firms in a resource-extracting industry operate on this principle, the rent, or **net price** (price minus extraction costs) must rise over time in accordance with Hotelling's rule (which we discussed in Chapter 5). The common-sense explanation for this is that if production is very profitable today, firms will produce more. The increased production will lower today's price, while the reduced reserves available for future production will raise expected future prices. This process will continue until Hotelling's rule is satisfied—the net price rises over time at a rate equal to the discount rate, and the discounted value of rents is equalized over time.

---

[4]*Economic rent* is the income derived from ownership of a scarce resource. In a resource-extracting industry, the usual principle of profit maximization thus becomes the maximization of resource rents.

[5]The firm seeks to equalize discounted marginal profit for each period. If a greater marginal profit is expected in a given period, it will be advantageous to increase production planned for that period until all periods yield the same discounted marginal profit.

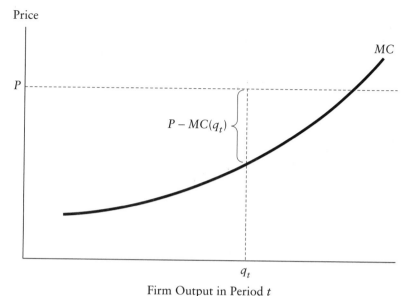

Firm Output in Period $t$

**FIGURE 12-2** *Resource Rent for the Competitive Firm*[6]

If marginal extraction costs fall over time, perhaps due to improved technology, net price may rise while the market price of the resource declines. However, if extraction costs are stable, we would expect the market price of the resource to rise over time. Since this has not yet occurred for most resources, the effects of Hotelling's rule may only become evident when specific resources move closer to exhaustion.

The principle of rent maximization has a more immediately relevant implication: Higher-quality resources will be exploited first. Suppose, for example, that a firm owns two bauxite deposits, one high grade and one low grade. Marginal costs of production for the high-grade resource will be relatively low, so a high rent can be obtained by producing today. Costs of extracting the low-grade deposit are significantly higher. Even if extracting the low-grade deposit today would be marginally profitable, waiting until market prices rise or until better technology makes extraction less costly will be a better strategy.

This explains why resources that are subeconomic today (see Figure 12-1) can become economic in the future, possibly increasing the amount of economically recoverable reserves—at the same time that extraction has diminished the physical reserves.

The basic theory of nonrenewable resource extraction also implies that limited resource stocks will be exploited to exhaustion. So long as the price continues to rise, delaying some production will remain profitable. But every resource has a maximum

---

[6]This diagram and Figure 12-3 have been adapted from Hartwick and Olewiler (1998), which provides a more advanced discussion of the economic theory of nonrenewable resource extraction.

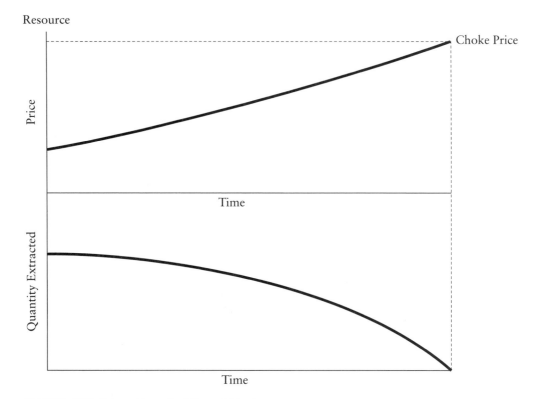

**FIGURE 12-3** *Exhaustion of a Mineral Stock*

price, called the **choke price,** at which the quantity demanded falls to zero. By the time the choke price is reached, producers will have extracted and sold all economically viable reserves. Figure 12-3 shows the **price path** and **extraction path** for a resource stock being exploited to exhaustion.

## Long-Term Trends in Nonrenewable Resource Use

How well does this theory of resource depletion fit with real-world experience? A classic study by Barnett and Morse[7] showed that most mineral resource prices fell from the Industrial Revolution through the mid-twentieth century. At the same time, global nonrenewable resource consumption steadily expanded. Three major factors were responsible:

- continual resource discovery
- improved resource extraction technology
- **resource substitution,** such as use of plastics in place of metals

---

[7]Barnett and Morse, 1963.

I:   Falling Price, Exponentially Increasing Resource Consumption
II:  Stable Price, Steadily Increasing Consumption
III: Rising Price, Slowing Rate of Increase of Consumption
IV:  Price Increasing to Choke Point, Consumption Falling to Zero

**FIGURE 12-4** *Hypothetical Nonrenewable Resource Use Profile*

Despite the unreliability of reserve estimates and indices of depletion, new discoveries and improved extraction technologies cannot extend nonrenewable resource lifetimes forever. In addition, the economic incentive to deplete high-quality reserves first means that over time the remaining reserves will be of lower quality, and more difficult and expensive to extract. Thus we can predict a long-term **resource use profile** similar to that shown in Figure 12-4.

In the early stages of resource exploitation, price falls as new discoveries and improved technology make the resource easier to obtain. In Stage II, prices are stable as increasing consumption (tending to pull prices up) balances further discovery and technological improvement (tending to pull prices down). In Stage III, demand starts to press against resource limitations, and prices begin to rise. Finally, rising price limits consumption, which eventually falls to zero as price reaches the choke point.

As we will see in Chapter 13, a profile of this kind applies to certain regional fossil fuel resources and may also apply to global use of fossil fuels. For mineral resources in general, the picture is more mixed. Considerable controversy exists as to whether a resource profile similar to Figure 12-4 applies to most minerals. Where it does apply, an interesting question is whether we are currently in Stage I, II, or III, and therefore whether we can expect falling, stable, or rising prices. We review this debate in the next section.

## Global Scarcity or Increasing Abundance?

As we have noted, predictions of nonrenewable resource exhaustion have thus far not been borne out. In fact, despite growing consumption, new discoveries and improved technology have led to increased reserves of most minerals. Figure 12-5 shows this trend over time for copper, lead, and zinc.

Table 12-1 shows current estimates of reserves and of a static reserve index for major minerals. In general, the static reserve indices show expected resource lifetimes ranging from several decades to several centuries. The predictive power of a static reserve index is limited, because it does not take into account new discoveries or improved extraction technology.

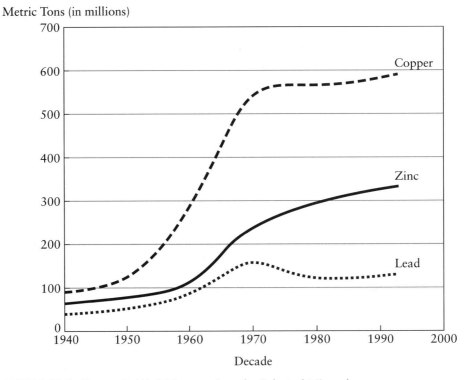

**FIGURE 12-5** *Change in World Reserve Base for Selected Minerals*
Source: Hodges, 1995, p. 1306.

**TABLE 12-1** *Reserve Estimates for Selected Minerals*

| Mineral | Annual Consumption (thousand metric tons) | Total Reserves (thousand metric tons) | Reserve Base (thousand metric tons) | Reserve Index (years) | Reserve Base Index (years) |
|---|---|---|---|---|---|
| Aluminum | 103,625* | 23,000,000 | 28,000,000 | 222 | 270 |
| Cadmium | 20 | 600 | 1,200 | 30 | 60 |
| Copper | 10,714 | 340,000 | 650,000 | 32 | 61 |
| Iron Ore | 959,609 | 71,000,000 | 160,000,000 | 74 | 167 |
| Lead | 5,342 | 64,000 | 130,000 | 12 | 24 |
| Mercury | 6.6 | 120 | 240 | 18 | 36 |
| Nickel | 882 | 49,000 | 150,000 | 56 | 170 |
| Tin | 218 | 9,600 | 12,000 | 44 | 55 |
| Zinc | 6,993 | 190,000 | 430,000 | 27 | 62 |

Source: Derived from World Resources Institute, 1994; and U.S. Geological Survey, 2001.

*Annual consumption of bauxite ore.

The **reserve base index** reflects a broader estimate of potential reserves and therefore a longer predicted lifetime. Even with this broader index, however, we note that several important minerals have relatively short projected lifetimes, including tin, zinc, copper, lead, and mercury. Are we then likely to see increasing prices for these minerals?

Current data does not indicate an increasing price trend for most minerals. Figure 12-6 shows the trends for copper, lead, and zinc. While prices for all three turned upward in the 1980s, prices have been stable or declined since 1990, and future prospects remain uncertain.[8]

One important physical consideration, not generally reflected in economic models, is the distribution of different qualities of mineral ore in the earth's crust. The bulk of available reserves are of considerably lower grade than those now exploited commercially. Studies of mineral abundance have often assumed a relatively smooth distribution pattern similar to that shown in Figure 12-7a. If this is accurate, the market should indicate mineral resource depletion with gradually rising prices from higher extraction costs.

However, the relative abundance of high- and low-grade ore may also be uneven, showing a pattern similar to Figure 12-7b, with a significant quality gap between ores currently being mined and lower-grade reserves. If this is the case, when the high-grade reserves are exhausted, recovering lower-grade ores will be significantly more difficult and expensive as well as more environmentally damaging. The lower the ore grade, the greater the volume of wastes generated in producing minerals of marketable quality.

[8]Berck and Roberts, 1996.

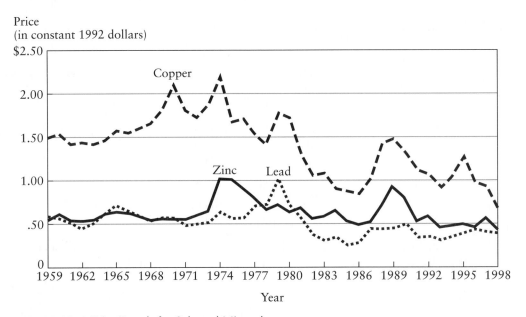

**FIGURE 12-6** *Price Trends for Selected Minerals*
Source: U.S. Geological Survey, *Metal Prices in the United States through 1998,* available at http://minerals.usgs.gov/minerals/pubs/metal_prices/.

## Internalizing Environmental Costs of Resource Recovery

While it is unlikely that we will ever completely "run out" of a resource, we may well exhaust high-grade deposits, resulting in higher private and environmental costs of resource recovery. Figure 12-8 shows the implications of this for resource price profiles. If environmental costs are internalized, a price profile reflecting the full social costs of resource extraction will show an earlier turning point than one showing extraction costs alone.

We should consider both direct and indirect environmental costs associated with resource recovery. Typically, mining produces vast quantities of wastes, some extremely toxic, as well as other damage to land and water (see Tables 12-2 and 12-3). As the resource grade declines, the quantity of mining wastes per ton of product increases.

In addition, lower-grade resources typically require more energy per unit to produce.[9] Although the basic price path will reflect the higher costs of energy, energy production will also create significant environmental externalities. These could be internalized into the price of energy, but generally are not. (More on this in Chapters 13 and 18.)

If we include these indirect environmental damages, the resource price path will turn up sooner and more sharply, reaching the "choke price" at a significantly earlier time. Figure 12-9 shows the likely effects of internalizing environmental costs on the resource consumption profile.

---

[9]Cleveland, 1991.

**(a) Smooth Distribution**

**(b) Uneven Distribution**

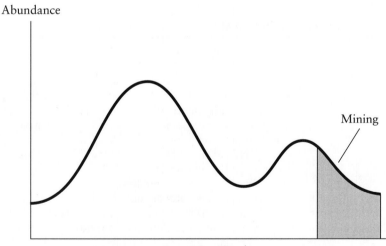

**FIGURE 12-7** *Distribution of Mineral Ores in the Earth's Crust*
Source: Adapted from Skinner, 1976.

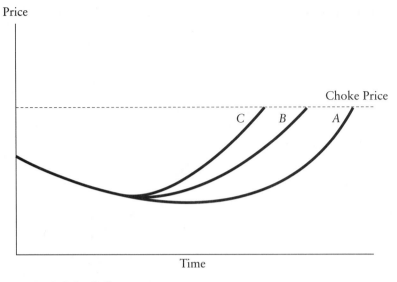

Price

Choke Price

C   B   A

Time

A: Basic Price Path
B: Price Path with Direct Environmental Costs
C: Price Path with Direct and Indirect Environmental Costs

**FIGURE 12-8** *Resource Price Profile with Environmental Costs*

**TABLE 12-2** *The Environmental Costs of Mining*

| Activity | Potential Impact |
| --- | --- |
| Excavation and Ore Removal | Destruction of plant and animal habitat, human settlements, and other features (surface mining) |
|  | Land subsidence (underground mining) |
|  | Increased erosion; silting of lakes and streams |
|  | Waste generation |
|  | Acid drainage and metal contamination of lakes, streams, and groundwater |
| Ore Concentration | Waste generation (tailings) |
|  | Organic chemical contamination |
|  | Acid drainage and metal contamination |
| Smelting/Refining | Air pollution (including sulfur dioxide, arsenic, lead, cadmium, and other toxics) |
|  | Waste generation (slag) |
|  | Impact of producing energy (most energy used for mineral production goes into smelting and refining). |

Source: Excerpted from John E. Young, *Mining the Earth*, Worldwatch Paper 109, pp. 17, 19. ©1992. Reprinted by permission of Worldwatch Institute. www.worldwatch.org.

**TABLE 12-3** *Environmental Impacts of Selected Mineral Projects*

| *Mineral/Location* | *Environmental Impacts* |
|---|---|
| Copper mining and smelting Ilo-Locombo area, Peru | 600,000 tons of sulfur compounds emitted per year; nearly 40 million cubic meters of tailings containing copper, zinc, lead, aluminum, and traces of cyanides are dumped into the sea each year, along with 800,000 tons of slag. |
| Phosphate Mining Nauru, South Pacific | When mining is complete in 5–15 years, four-fifths of the 2,100-hectare South Pacific island will be uninhabitable. |
| Carajás Iron Ore Project Pará State, Brazil | Wood requirements for smelting iron ore will deforest 50,000 hectares of tropical forest each year. |
| Nickel Smelters Russia | Two nickel smelters near the Norwegian and Finnish borders pump 300,000 tons of sulfur dioxide into the atmosphere, along with lesser amounts of heavy metals. More than 200,000 hectares of local forests are dying as a result, and local residents suffer health effects. |
| Mamut Copper Mine Sabah Province, Malaysia | Local rivers are contaminated with high levels of chromium, copper, iron, lead, manganese, and nickel. |
| Gold Mining Amazon Basin, Brazil | Rivers are clogged with sediment and 100 tons of mercury are released into the ecosystem each year. |

Source: Excerpted from John E. Young, *Mining the Earth*, Worldwatch Paper 109, pp. 17, 19. ©1992. Reprinted by permission of Worldwatch Institute. www.worldwatch.org.

**FIGURE 12-9** *Resource Consumption Profile with Backstop Resource or Recycling. Internalization of environmental costs causes virgin resource consumption to peak at $T_1$ instead of $T_2$.*

*Scrap steel to be recycled for industrial use in Youngstown, Ohio. Recycled metals provide about 50 percent of U.S. iron and steel consumption.*

Whereas the basic consumption profile rises until higher prices start to constrain demand and then falls fairly rapidly, including environmental costs in price leads to an earlier flattening out of **virgin** or **primary resource** consumption.[10] Resource consumers will have an incentive to shift to backstop resources or to **recycle** the resource where possible. A **backstop resource** can substitute for the original product, but at a higher price—it will enter the market only when the price rises to a certain level. Recycling is an option for many nonrenewable resources, especially metals, and becomes more cost-effective as the price of the virgin resource rises.

Note that with this modified consumption profile, supplies of the primary resource last longer. Consumption shows a less rapid turnaround, and technological infrastructure can adapt to the use of backstop and recycled resources. Both on these grounds and because it is generally good policy to internalize externalities, a pricing policy that encourages an earlier transition away from dependence on primary resources may be advisable.

---

[10]A *virgin resource* is one that has been newly extracted, as opposed to one being reused or recycled. These are also known as *primary resources*.

Some assessments of global resource availability present an optimistic view of the future based on the relatively long projected lifetimes of some resources, and the possibilities for substitution in the case of those with shorter reserve indices.[11] However, this approach takes little account of the growing environmental problems resulting from recovery of lower-grade resources. In addition to environmental costs today, depleting high-grade resources also imposes user costs (discussed in Chapter 5) on future generations. Future resource users will both pay higher prices and suffer greater environmental damages from their use of low-grade resources.

Recycling resources today lessens both present and future costs resulting from primary resource use. The recycling process also has its own costs, including capital costs of recycling facilities and labor, transportation, and energy costs. It makes sense, therefore, to examine the economics of recycling and its effects on resource use.

## The Economics of Recycling

In theory, effective recycling could significantly extend the lifetimes of many nonrenewable resources. However, recycling has both economic and physical limits.

The second law of thermodynamics (the principle of increasing entropy, which we will discuss further in Chapter 13) implies that perfect recycling is impossible. Some loss or degradation of material will always occur during the process of fabrication, use, and recycling. In addition, recycling requires new inputs of energy. In economic terms, we must compare recycling costs to the costs of using primary materials to determine when recycling will be both physically possible and economically advantageous.

Figure 12-10 shows the economics of recycling from the manufacturer's point of view. The obvious advantage to the manufacturer is that using recycled materials saves the cost of purchasing new inputs. Reading from left to right in Figure 12-10, the total cost of virgin materials declines as the proportion of recycled inputs rises. On the other hand, the cost of recycled materials rises in a nonlinear manner, indicating that as we approach a theoretical 100-percent recycling, increasing the proportion of recycled materials becomes difficult and expensive.

In this hypothetical example, the optimum mix of virgin and recycled materials, shown by the minimum point on the total private cost curve, is 40 percent recycled. This, however, neglects environmental and disposal costs. These costs are typically external—not borne by the manufacturer. Environmental costs include air and water pollution from mining and fabrication of primary materials. Disposal costs are paid by consumers or municipalities, who have no control over the proportion of virgin materials the manufacturer uses (although community decisions on recycling may eventually affect industry incentives, as discussed in Chapter 17).

If we include environmental and disposal costs associated with virgin material use, the optimum proportion of recycled materials rises to 70 percent in this example (the minimum point on the total private plus environmental cost curve). If a tax is imposed on primary resources to internalize environmental impact and disposal costs, manufacturers

---

[11]See, for example, Goeller and Zucker, 1984.

Total Costs

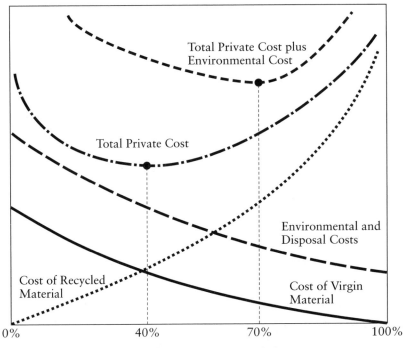

**FIGURE 12-10** *Total Costs of Recycling*

Source: This graph is adapted from a simplified version of a cost analysis by Walter O. Spofford, Jr., "Solid Residual Management: Some Economic Considerations," *Natural Resources Journal.* Vol. 11, July 1971: 561–589. Reprinted by permission. Spofford analyzed paper recycling, but the economic principle illustrated here applies to recycling of any material.

will find that they can minimize overall input costs, including the tax, by using 70 percent recycled material.

We can also examine recycling's private and social equilibrium levels in terms of the corresponding marginal cost curves, as shown in Figure 12-11. Profit-maximizing producers will balance the marginal cost of recycling with the marginal cost of virgin materials. If we internalize **external costs** through a tax that reflects the true social costs, their decisions will shift in favor of using more recycled materials.

## Policies to Promote Recycling

Even without significant policies to internalize environmental costs, metals recycling has generally been on the increase. In the United States, nearly 50 percent of metals consumption now comes from recycled scrap (Figure 12-12). Among the metals with the highest annual consumption, aluminum has a 40 percent recycled content, copper about

Marginal Costs

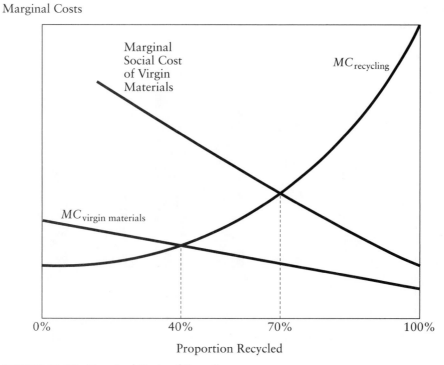

**FIGURE 12-11** *Marginal Costs of Recycling*

Percent by Weight

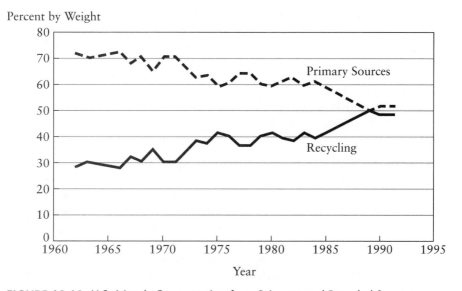

**FIGURE 12-12** *U.S. Metals Consumption from Primary and Recycled Sources*
Source: Adapted from Carol Hodges, "Mineral Resources, Environmental Issues, and Land Uses." Reprinted from *Science* 268 (June 2, 1995), p. 1307.

Scrap Metal (percent)

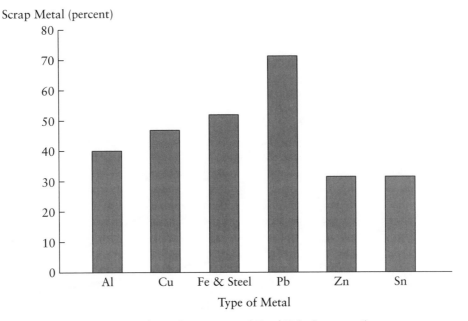

FIGURE 12-13 *Scrap Metal as a Percentage of Total U.S. Consumption*
Source: Adapted from Carol Hodges, "Mineral Resources, Environmental Issues, and Land Uses."
Reprinted from *Science* 268 (June 2, 1995), p. 1307.

45 percent, and iron and steel about 55 percent. Lead recycling, at about 70 percent, significantly reduces highly toxic lead residues in the environment (Figure 12-13).

These recycling rates are significant in terms of extending resource lifetimes as well as reducing economic and environmental costs. If global metal recycling rates could be increased to over 50 percent, resource lifetimes would be more than double those based on using only virgin materials. In addition, pollution from metal mining and fabrication, as well as problems of waste disposal, would drop significantly.

What kinds of policies would best promote increased recycling of nonrenewables? Policy options for increasing recycling include the following:

- *Altering public policies that encourage rapid resource extraction.* Governments often make mineral resources available for exploitation at extremely low cost. For instance, the U.S. General Mining Act of 1872 offers mineral exploitation rights on government land at a few dollars an acre—a price unchanged in more than a century. Despite efforts to change the law to recapture a portion of resource rents through more adequate royalty payments,[12] mining interests have been successful in preventing amendments or new rules. In addition to lost revenues, low prices for valuable resources promote resource overuse and excessive external and user costs.

---

[12]A *royalty* is a payment to the owner of a scarce resource for the use of that resource.

- *Imposing taxes on the use of primary resources.* As Figure 12-11 shows, internalizing environmental costs through a tax promotes increased use of recycled materials. However, because the cost of virgin materials usually represents only a small portion of the final product cost, a tax alone may have little effect on consumption patterns.[13]

- *Combining market incentives for recycling with measures to promote the technology and infrastructure needed for recycling systems.* A phenomenon known as **technological lock-in** leads an industry that has once acquired a certain kind of plant and machinery—in this case production technology using primary resources—to continue investing in the same kind of plant. Changing over a whole industry from one production system to another involves heavy costs and requires a significant amount of initial capital. Tax incentives, support for research and development of recycling technologies, and **government procurement**—programs that guarantee a certain government demand for recycled materials—can help jump-start this process.

- *Municipal programs and institutions to promote recycling.* Curbside recycling pickup makes recycling waste materials much easier for consumers and businesses. Communities can often recoup the costs of curbside recycling through sale of recyclable materials, as well as through reduced disposal costs. Even if these programs require a subsidy, they can be justified on environmental grounds. Municipal recycling institutions create the basis for mining the waste stream—obtaining metals and other materials from waste rather than from mineral deposits or other primary resources. Increased supplies of recycled materials will lower their prices, making them more attractive to manufacturers as inputs.

- *Consumer incentives such as **deposit/return systems** or **pay-by-the-bag** rules for collecting nonrecyclable garbage.* These give consumers a financial incentive to recycle and impose a cost for failing to recycle. In general, these consumer incentives prove much more effective if combined with other institutional mechanisms for recycling such as curbside pickup or rules requiring manufacturers to identify different kinds of material to facilitate recycling.

Promoting recycling can be environmentally beneficial both for nonrenewable and renewable resources. Metal recycling reduces the need for ore mining, plastics recycling reduces demand for primary petroleum products, and paper recycling (as we will discuss in Chapter 15) lessens demand pressures on forests.

Energy resources, however, cannot be recycled, and energy is a requirement for both primary resource extraction and recycling. According to the second law of thermodynamics, usable energy is inevitably degraded into waste heat after use.[14]

For this reason, energy deserves special attention in our analysis of resource use. In the following chapters, we will consider the full cycle of resource use, including pollution and waste generation from resource consumption. We will focus our examination on energy resources in Chapter 13, consider the economics of renewable

---

[13]See Ackerman, 1996, Chapter 2.

[14]We can use captured waste energy from electricity production to heat buildings, a process called **cogeneration,** but after a single use this energy, too, escapes to the atmosphere as waste heat.

resources in Chapters 14 and 15, and analyze pollution control policies in Chapter 16. In Chapter 17, we will return to the overall cycle of resource use and waste management and the emerging field of **industrial ecology.**

## SUMMARY

Nonrenewable resources are limited in supply, but available reserves can be expanded either by new discovery or by increasing recovery of lower-grade deposits. Concerns over exhaustion of major nonrenewable resources have so far not been borne out. Despite growing demand, new discoveries and improved technology have increased available reserves of key minerals.

The economic theory of nonrenewable resource use implies that the net price (price minus extraction costs) of a resource of given quality will rise over time. Profit-maximizing firms will exploit high-grade resources first. As lower-grade resources enter the market, the energy and environmental costs of recovery will tend to rise. Because technological progress and expanded resource availability can offset these price effects, resource price projections remain uncertain.

Global reserves of major minerals vary from great abundance to relatively limited stocks. A broader measure of the reserve base indicates projected lifetimes of several hundred years for certain minerals, but only several decades for others.

The mining process generates many toxic wastes and has extensive negative environmental effects on land and water. Internalizing the full environmental cost of resource recovery would encourage a shift to renewable resource use or recycling, rather than increased consumption of virgin resources.

In the United States, more than 40 percent of metal production currently uses recycled scrap. Although complete recycling is impossible, recycling rates for most major metals can increase considerably. In addition to extending nonrenewable resource lifetimes, recycling significantly reduces environmental damage associated with the production of virgin materials.

Public policies to promote recycling include raising royalty payments for access to minerals on public lands, internalizing environmental costs through taxes on primary resource use, developing technology and infrastructure, and government procurement of recycled products.

Although metals, plastics, and paper can be recycled, energy resources cannot be recycled. Energy is an essential input both for primary resource extraction and for recycling, giving energy resources a special importance in the analysis of nonrenewable resource use.

## KEY TERMS AND CONCEPTS

backstop resource
choke price
cogeneration
deposit/return systems

economic reserves (economically
   recoverable reserves)
economic supply (of a resource)
exponential reserve index

external costs
extraction path
government procurement
Hotelling's rule
hypothetical and speculative
  resources
identified reserves
indicated or inferred reserves
industrial ecology
marginal extraction cost
measured reserves
net price (of a resource)
nonrenewable resources
pay-by-the-bag systems
physical supply (of a resource)

price path
price taker
primary resource
recycling
reserve base index
resource lifetime
resource rents
resource substitution
resource use profile
static reserve index
subeconomic resources
technological lock-in
throughput
user costs
virgin resource

## DISCUSSION QUESTIONS

1. Is scarcity of nonrenewable resources a major problem? What kinds of physical and economic measures are relevant to understanding this issue, and in what ways can some measures be misleading? What do you think will be the main issues relating to nonrenewable use in the twenty-first century?

2. What is the significance of the distribution pattern of mineral ores in the earth's crust (Figure 12-7)? How would mineral extraction economics be affected if minerals show a nonuniform distribution pattern (Figure 12-7b) rather than a uniform pattern (Figure 12-7a)? What would this imply for government policy?

3. Some critics of municipal recycling programs have argued that they are uneconomic because they cost more than ordinary waste disposal. What economic factors would you use to evaluate this argument? What relationship exists between recycling incentives for end-users and incentives for manufacturers to use recycled materials? How can environmental costs be internalized at various stages of the production cycle?

## REFERENCES

Ackerman, Frank. *Why Do We Recycle? Markets, Values, and Public Policy.* Washington, D.C.: Island Press, 1996.

Barnett, Harold J., and Chandler Morse. *Scarcity and Growth: The Economics of Natural Resource Availability.* Baltimore: Johns Hopkins University Press, 1963.

Berck, Peter, and Michael Roberts. "Natural Resource Prices: Will They Ever Turn Up?" *Journal of Environmental Economics and Management* 31 (1996): 65–78.

Cleveland, Cutler J. "Natural Resource Scarcity and Economic Growth Revisited: Economic and Biophysical Perspectives." Chapter 19 in *Ecological Economics: The Science and Management of Sustainability*, edited by Robert Costanza. New York: Columbia University Press, 1991.

Goeller, H. E., and A. Zucker. "Infinite Resources: The Ultimate Strategy." *Science* 27 (1984): 456–462.

Hartwick, John M., and Nancy D. Olewiler. *The Economics of Natural Resource Use.* 2nd ed. Reading, Mass.: Addison Wesley Longman, 1998.

Hodges, Carol A. "Mineral Resources, Environmental Issues, and Land Use." *Science* 268 (June 2, 1995): 1305–1312.

Meadows, Donella H., et al. *The Limits to Growth*. New York: Universe Books, 1972.

Meadows, Donella H., et al. *Beyond the Limits: Confronting Global Collapse, Envisioning a Sustainable Future*. Post Mills, Vt.: Chelsea Green, 1992.

Skinner, B. J. "A Second Iron Age Ahead?" *American Scientist* 64 (1976): 263.

Spofford, Walter O., Jr. "Solid Residual Management: Some Economic Considerations." *Natural Resources Journal* 11 (July 1971): 561–589.

U.S. Geological Survey. *Mineral Commodity Summaries*. USGS, January 2001.

World Resources Institute. *World Resources 1994-95*. New York and Oxford, U.K.: Oxford University Press, 1994.

Young, John E. *Mining the Earth*. Worldwatch Paper 109. Washington, D.C.: Worldwatch Institute, 1992.

## WEBSITES

1. http://imcg.wr.usgs.gov/usbmak/c831.html  A report detailing the U.S. government classification scheme to measure mineral reserves.
2. http://minerals.usgs.gov/  The website for the Minerals Resources Program of the U.S. Geological Survey. The site includes links to extensive technical data as well as information about the environmental implications of mining.
3. http://minerals.usgs.gov/minerals/pubs/commodity/recycle/  Information on metals recycling in the United States.
4. http://www.epa.gov/msw/index.htm  The EPA's website on municipal waste management. It includes information about recycling, pay-as-you-throw programs, and waste management nationally and in each state.

## CHAPTER FOCUS QUESTIONS

- What special role does energy play in economic systems?
- What are our current energy uses and future energy needs?
- Are we in danger of energy shortages?
- Can we shift from fossil-based energy systems to alternative systems?

CHAPTER

# 13

# Energy: The Great Transition

## Energy and Economic Systems

Energy is fundamental to economic systems and indeed to all life. On deep ocean floors, far below the reach of sunlight, giant tube-worms and other strange life forms cluster around heat vents. Energy from the earth's interior drives their metabolic processes. On the earth's surface, and at shallower ocean levels, all plant life depends on sunlight, and all animal life depends directly or indirectly on plants.[1] Our own equally critical need for energy is partly camouflaged in a modern economy. Measured in terms of gross domestic product, energy resources represent only about 5 percent of economic output. Yet the other 95 percent depends absolutely on energy inputs.

In less developed, agrarian economies the dependence is more evident. People's basic need for food calories is, of course, a need for energy input. Traditional agriculture is essentially a method of capturing **solar energy** for human use. Solar energy captured in firewood meets other basic needs for home heating and cooking.

---

[1]The few plants that can live without direct sunlight make use of soil nutrients deposited by the decay of other plants.

As economies develop and become more complex, energy needs increase greatly. Historically, as supplies of firewood and other **biomass** proved insufficient to support growing economies, people turned to **hydropower** (also a form of stored solar energy), then to coal, and then to oil and natural gas as major energy sources. In the past half-century, nuclear power has entered the energy mix.

Each stage of economic development has been accompanied by a characteristic energy transition from one major fuel source to another. Today, fossil fuels—coal, oil, and natural gas—are by far the dominant energy source in industrial economies. The twenty-first century will see a further great transition in energy sources. The nature and speed of this transition is a fundamental issue in the relationship of the economy to the environment.

From the point of view of economic analysis, the most important factor affecting energy use is its market price. Distortion of this price, for example by government subsidies, leads to inefficient energy use. A major goal of energy policy, in this view, should be to avoid or to correct such distortions. But we must also consider the need to internalize externalities such as the impacts of pollution and the user costs of resource depletion, as well as the environmental advantages of conservation and renewable energy sources. The existence of positive or negative externalities may justify government subsidy or tax policies directed at particular energy sectors.

We can also take a broader, more ecologically oriented, perspective on energy. Theorists of the ecological economics school see energy as fundamental to economic development, and focus on a crucial distinction between the **stock** of nonrenewable fossil fuel reserves and the renewable **flow** of solar energy.[2] In this perspective, the period of intensive fossil fuel use that began in the nineteenth century amounts to a one-time, unrepeatable bonanza—the rapid exploitation of a limited stock of high-quality resources.

Because so much of the **capital stock** and **energy infrastructure** of modern economic systems rely on fossil fuel use, any transition away from fossil-fuel dependence will involve massive restructuring and new investment. The considerable economic implications of this justify a special focus on energy use as a central economic and environmental issue.

## Economic and Ecological Analyses of Energy

What makes energy special? To answer this question we turn to the physical laws of thermodynamics. The **first law of thermodynamics** states that energy can be neither created nor destroyed (although energy can be transmuted into matter, or matter into energy, through nuclear processes). This means that all physical processes, including all life processes and all economic systems, merely move or transform matter and energy. But these processes are also subject to the **second law of thermodynamics**.

---

[2]For the classic assertion of energy's critical role in the economy, see Georgescu-Roegen, 1971. An overview of differing analytical perspectives on energy can be found in Krishnan et al., 1995, pp. 169–224.

The second law relates to the concept of **entropy.** Entropy is defined as a measure of *unavailable* energy—energy in a form that is not available to do work. The second law states that entropy increases in all physical processes. The best way to grasp the significance of this rather slippery concept is through an example.

Consider the process of burning a lump of coal. The coal in its original state contains available or free energy. In this form it is said to have low entropy. Once it is burned, the energy is dissipated. According to the first law, the energy is not destroyed, but it is now in an unavailable or bound form. In ordinary terms, the coal has been transformed into ashes and waste heat. In this form, it has high entropy—and is no longer a potential energy source.

All economic processes, as well as all life processes, transform low-entropy inputs into high-entropy waste products in accordance with the second law. Therefore all economic processes are limited by the availability of low-entropy resources. These come in two forms: stocks of nonrenewable terrestrial resources such as fossil fuels, and a flow of renewable energy from the sun. Our current economic activities depend heavily on the use of limited stocks. Ultimately we must adapt our economic system to use the flow of solar energy, or **solar flux.**

Another way of looking at the concept of entropy offers further insights into energy use. We can consider entropy as a measure of *disorder* in a system. The coal in our previous example represents a highly ordered form of matter and energy, whereas the ashes and waste heat from its burning are a more disorderly form. Thus we see a correspondence between orderliness and available energy. As entropy and disorder increase in any environment, that environment becomes less useful to support life. Wastes and pollution represent a high-entropy state of matter and energy. According to the second law, all life processes and all economic systems must necessarily generate increasing amounts of high-entropy wastes while consuming low-entropy resources.

We can see, then, two kinds of problems associated with energy use. One is the depletion of limited stocks of energy resources. Another is the inevitable generation of wastes and pollution through energy use. Recall from Chapter 1 the expanded circular flow diagram (Figure 1-2), which showed cycles of resources and environmental services, but a one-way flow, or **throughput** of energy. Whereas labor, capital, renewable resources, and some recyclable resources can be regenerated through the expanded circular flow, energy cannot. In this sense energy throughput, constrained both by resource availability and by the pollution arising from its use, represents a fundamental factor determining levels of economic activity.[3]

## Economic Perspectives on Energy Supply

We can also analyze energy's role in resource supply using more conventional economic theory. In Chapter 12 we noted that the **economic supply** of nonrenewable resources differs from the **physical supply.** The reserves of any given nonrenewable

---

[3]The concept of throughput, introduced by Georgescu-Roegen (1971), is discussed extensively in Daly, 1991.

resource are fixed in physical terms, but the economically recoverable proportion of these reserves varies with changing prices and technology.

Energy reserves have a specific importance in this process because energy is essential to the recovery of other resources. For example, if we use up high-grade copper ores, recovering copper from lower-grade ore will generally require more energy per unit of copper recovered. Recalling our discussion of the economics of nonrenewable resource extraction in Chapter 12, we can see that so long as the marginal cost of extra energy does not drive the price of copper above what the market will bear, firms will keep bringing lower-grade ores into production.

The economic logic of extraction of energy reserves, however, has a crucial difference from other mineral reserves. Energy must of course be expended to recover these reserves, giving rise to the concept of **net energy ratio.** If we expend a quantity of energy $Y$ to obtain a quantity of energy $Z$ from reserves, the net energy ratio = $Z/Y$. If this ratio falls below 1, then we expend more energy than we receive, which is clearly uneconomic. A net energy ratio of 1 thus represents an absolute limit on energy production.

Most current energy production is far from this margin, but the net energy ratio is close to 1 for certain forms of energy, such as ethanol produced in high-energy-input agriculture. Political forces such as effective farm lobbies, or the desire for energy self-sufficiency, have led countries including the United States and Brazil to mandate ethanol use. But unless ethanol is produced from agricultural wastes, it is difficult to justify this policy on the grounds of saving energy, because producing it uses almost as much energy as it provides.

Abundant available energy reserves are essential for recovering nonrenewable resources and for economic production in general. Limitations on other resource supplies can be overcome—provided we have enough energy. Also, as we saw in Chapter 11, the output of renewable resources such as productive soils can be boosted by extra energy inputs. Agricultural and industrial system productivity depends on the continued supply of high-quality energy. Although we can seek out alternative energy sources, we cannot evade the laws of thermodynamics, which tell us that the scale of economic activity is limited by available energy supplies.

## Economic and Thermodynamic Efficiency

This unique relationship between energy and economic activity can lead to significant tension between the concepts of **economic efficiency** and **thermodynamic efficiency.** As we know, economic efficiency is a central goal of economic theory and policy. But paradoxically, increased economic efficiency can lead to lower thermodynamic efficiency—more energy use to obtain a given output. The availability of cheap energy creates an economic incentive to shift toward energy-intensive production methods. Rather than conserving energy, which would be thermodynamically efficient, low prices encourage individuals and firms to substitute energy for labor and capital.

For example, it is much more energy efficient to walk or ride a bicycle for short trips. But if gas is cheap, many people will choose to drive instead, burning gallons of gas to move tons of steel in order to save a small amount of labor time. From a strictly economic point of view, nothing is wrong with this—the consumer has made the rational decision that he or she prefers paying a small price for gas to making the effort to walk or bicycle. But this kind of decision, multiplied millions of times, can significantly affect a society's energy consumption.

The same kind of logic affects the economic behavior of business. Commercial farms won't employ relatively costly labor if they can do the same job at lower cost with energy-using machinery. Over time, more firms will shift to more energy-intensive methods if these are more profitable. And as high-grade ores are used up, one strategy for keeping productivity high in resource-extracting industries is to use more energy. Some studies suggest that increased energy use per unit output is a common trend in many resource-based industries and agriculture.[4]

The dependence of modern economic systems on cheap energy was dramatically demonstrated during the 1970s, when sudden increases in oil prices caused economic crisis, inflation, and recession throughout the world economy. Prices rose in this case not because of natural shortages but through successful action by a powerful **cartel** of oil-producing nations.

By acting together to restrict supply, the OPEC[5] cartel quadrupled world oil prices. For a time, this focused much attention on the importance of energy and the need for conservation and alternative energy sources. However, as the cartel's power waned over time, oil prices fell and efforts to promote energy-saving investment were abandoned.

Could the energy crises of the 1970s recur? Low oil prices and abundant supplies during the 1990s encouraged complacency, but prices rose again after 2000, reaching $50 per barrel in 2004. This price, while not as high in real (inflation-adjusted) terms as the price spike of 1979–1981, suggested that world energy demand might be outrunning supply. With China and India entering the market as major consumers of imported oil, pressure on existing oil reserves has been significantly increased.

As we look ahead to the longer term, we must consider the changing picture of both energy supply and demand. On the supply side, fossil fuel energy reserves have global limits, as well as much more stringent regional limits. On the demand side, global energy demand is steadily increasing. Although total demand in the currently developed economies is fairly stable, almost all developing economies show rapid rates of growth in energy demand. We can assess future economic and environmental implications of global energy use with a more specific look at current trends and future resource availability.

## Energy Trends and Projections

Global energy use has grown rapidly (Figure 13-1). All fossil fuel use has expanded steadily, particularly oil consumption. Currently more than 80 percent of the world's energy comes from fossil fuel sources. If we consider commercial energy sources only, about 85 percent comes from fossil fuels.

---

[4]See Cleveland, 1991, and Figure 9-1 in this text.

[5]Organization of Petroleum Exporting Countries.

Quadrillion
BTUs per Year

**FIGURE 13-1** *World Marketed Energy Consumption*

Note: "Other" category is primarily hydroelectric power and excludes non-marketed traditional biomass fuels.
Source: Meadows et al., 1992; U.S. Department of Energy, 2004.

Hydroelectric power and nuclear power are the major nonfossil fuel sources of industrial energy. Alternative sources such as wind, biomass, and solar power currently supply only a small fraction of total energy needs in industrialized countries (Figure 13-2). In many developing nations, biomass remains a significant portion of total energy supply, but in most of these countries commercial energy demand is swiftly increasing.

Crude oil is the largest single world energy source, followed by coal and natural gas. Hydroelectric power contributes about 8 percent, and nuclear power about 7 percent of world energy. In the United States, energy uses are divided between transportation (26 percent), industry (38 percent), and residential and commercial (36 percent) as shown in Figure 13-2, and the worldwide breakdown of energy use is similar.

We can expect the continued steep upward slope of total world energy demand since 1950 to continue. World energy consumption in 2000 was close to double that of 1970, and World Bank projections show future world energy demand approaching another doubling by about 2030, with almost all the increase in presently developing nations. This would still leave per capita consumption in presently developing nations at less than one-third of what presently developed nations consume (Figure 13-3).

How will we meet this massive increase in world energy demand? Standard projections see fossil fuels mostly supplying the increase. "High-growth" energy use projections for 2050 by the World Energy Council and the International Institute for Applied

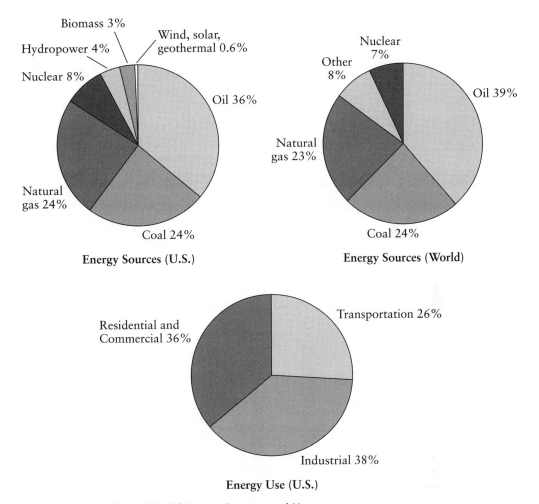

**FIGURE 13-2** *U.S. and World Energy Sources and Use*

Note: World energy-use patterns resemble U.S. patterns in the division between residential/commercial, transportation, and industrial uses. Percentages may not sum to 100% due to rounding.

Source: Data from U.S. Department of Energy, 2003, 2004 (http://www.eia.doe.gov).

Systems Analysis show huge increases in fossil fuel use, as well as in nuclear power (Figure 13-4a).

This may be technically possible based on available fossil fuel reserves. In 1994, the World Resources Institute estimated that about 40 years' proved reserves of oil remained, 50 years' supply of natural gas, and more than 200 years of coal reserves.[6] In addition, new discoveries and improved technology for resource recovery can increase

---

[6]World Resources Institute, 1994, p. 169.

**(a) Total Consumption**

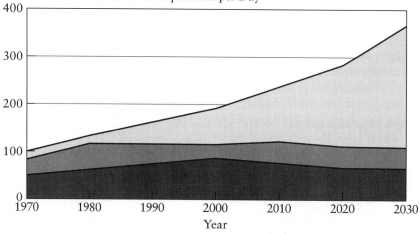

Millions of Barrels of Oil Equivalent per Day

**(b) Per Capita Consumption for OECD and Developing Countries**

Barrels of Oil Equivalent per Year

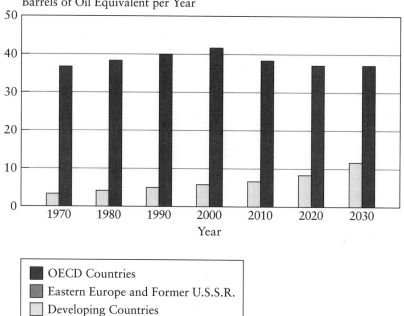

■ OECD Countries
■ Eastern Europe and Former U.S.S.R.
□ Developing Countries

**FIGURE 13-3** *Past and Projected Energy Consumption, 1970–2030*

Note: The Organisation for Economic Co-operation and Development (OECD) consists of 30 of the world's more developed countries. Mexico and several East European nations joined OECD after these projections were made.

Source: Adapted from *World Development Report 1992* by World Bank. Reprinted by permission of The World Bank via Copyright Clearance Center.

(a) World Total Primary Energy Consumption — High Growth;
Ample Oil and Gas

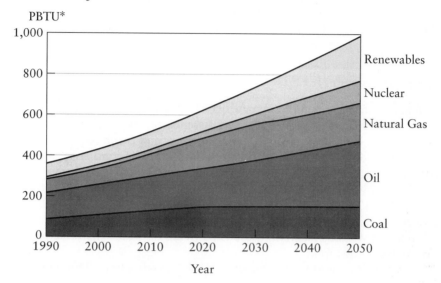

(b) World Total Primary Energy Consumption — Ecologically
Driven; New Renewables with Nuclear Phaseout

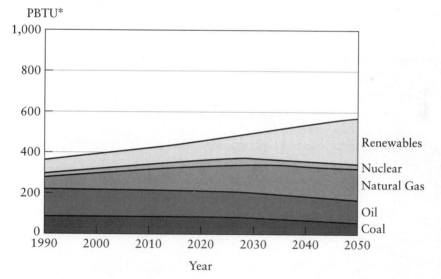

*PBTU = Quadrillion British Thermal Units

**FIGURE 13-4** *Projections of World Energy Use to 2050 by Fuel Source*
Source: International Institute for Applied Systems (IIASA) and the World Energy Council
(WEC), 1998.

the level of proved reserves, as discussed in Chapter 12. But is this energy future either economically feasible or environmentally desirable? An alternative projection, relying on conservation and greater use of renewable sources, shows little or no increase in fossil fuel use by 2050 (Figure 13-4b). A central issue is the future of world oil production, since oil is now the predominant fossil fuel.

## Patterns of Energy Use

According to a theory advanced by petroleum geologist M. King Hubbert in 1956, the typical pattern of energy resource use over time resembles a bell curve. In the early period of resource exploitation, prices fall, discovery and production expand, and consumption grows exponentially. Eventually limited supplies and rising resource recovery costs force a turnaround, and consumption starts to fall.

As Figure 13-5 shows, the **Hubbert curve** projection has worked out well for U.S. oil production. Oil output in the continental United States peaked by 1980, and has been declining since then. If U.S. oil production continues to follow the Hubbert model, reserves will be essentially exhausted by 2040. Much the same pattern applies to natural gas production.

The picture for world oil production is a little different. Through about 1980, world oil production followed the steadily increasing pattern that represents the upslope of a Hubbert curve (Figure 13-6). After the sharp oil price increases of the 1970s, global production and consumption of oil leveled off for about 20 years. According to the original Hubbert curve pattern, world oil production would have peaked by about

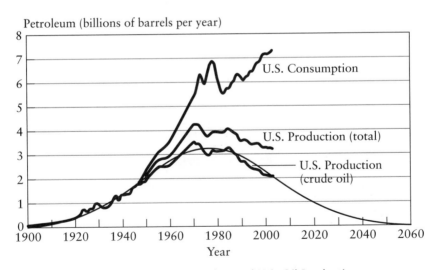

**FIGURE 13-5** *The Hubbert Curve and Actual U.S. Oil Production*

Note: U.S. Production (total) includes natural gas plant liquids and other domestic supply in addition to crude oil.

Source: Gever, 1991; U.S. Department of Energy, 2003, 2004.

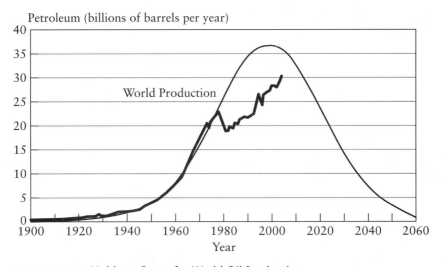

Petroleum (billions of barrels per year)

**FIGURE 13-6** *Hubbert Curve for World Oil Production*
Sources: Gever, 1991; U.S. Department of Energy, 2002, 2005.

2000, but this prolonged slowdown in consumption has extended the projected lifetime of world oil reserves.

The picture for natural gas is similar to oil; U.S. natural gas production peaked in 1971, while world production is still increasing. Proven natural gas reserves are slightly larger relative to current consumption than are oil reserves.

World coal reserves are plentiful, and at present consumption rates would last for at least 200 years. Supply constraints are thus not an issue for coal use. Far more important are the environmental implications of expanded coal use. Coal mining, especially strip-mining, often generates significant environmental damage, and coal-burning is a major contributor both to regional acid rain and smog problems and to global carbon dioxide accumulation.

## The Future of World Oil Production

Because oil currently supplies 39 percent of global commercial energy needs (see Figure 13-2), oil supply and demand represent a crucial element of the future energy picture. Recent analyses indicate a renewed concern with future oil limits. The International Energy Agency projects a resumption of the Hubbert curve pattern of rising oil demand.[7] If such demand increases occur, the production curve peak, at which supply constraints start to choke off consumption, will occur within the next few decades. James MacKenzie uses a range of figures for **estimated ultimately recoverable (EUR) supplies** of oil to project peaking sometime between 2007 and 2020 (Figure 13-7).

---

[7]International Energy Agency, 2004.

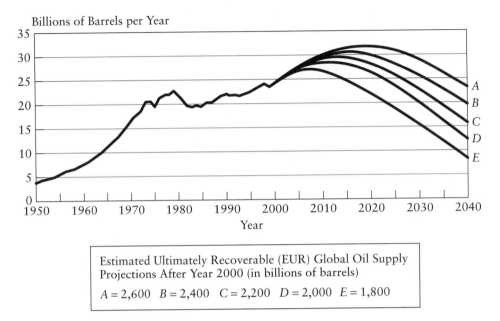

**FIGURE 13-7** *Actual and Projected World Oil Production, 1950–2040*

Source: Adapted from MacKenzie, *Oil as a Finite Resource: When Is Global Production Likely to Peak?*, Washington, D.C.: World Resources Institute, 1996. Reprinted by permission of World Resources Institute.

Petroleum geologists Colin Campbell and Jean Laherrère argue that, unlike the 1970s energy crisis,

> The next oil crunch will not be so temporary. Our analysis of the discovery and production of oil fields around the world suggests that within the next decade, the supply of conventional oil will be unable to keep up with the demand.
>
> This conclusion contradicts the picture one gets from industry reports, which boasted of 1,020 billion barrels of oil (Gbo) in "proved" reserves at the start of 1998. Dividing that figure by the current production rate of about 23.6 Gbo a year might suggest that crude oil could remain plentiful and cheap for 43 more years—probably longer, because official charts show reserves growing.[8]

According to Campbell and Laherrère, optimistic official estimates suffer from three major errors. One is accepting inflated estimates of "proved" reserves provided by governments of former Soviet countries and others who may have political reasons to exaggerate their holdings. A second error is ignoring probable growth in demand. The third is omitting the well-established economic principle of **diminishing returns,** which tells us that as oil fields are exploited, the per-unit costs of obtaining

---

[8]Campbell and Laherrère, 1998.

the remaining oil will rise. Campbell and Laherrère update Hubbert's analysis to project a peak in world oil production by 2010.

What would a peak in conventional oil production in the not-too-distant future imply? As we know from Chapter 12, an environment of rising prices would accompany this change in supply/demand balance. This in turn would encourage substitution of other fuels for oil.

A rise in use of natural gas would be likely (natural gas can be liquefied for use as a transport fuel in addition to its use in domestic heating and industrial power generation). The expected lifetime of natural gas reserves, however, is not much longer than that of oil reserves. It would also be possible to obtain oil from tar sands and oil shale deposits, although recovery from these sources, like coal strip-mining, has potentially high environmental costs.

A further issue with future oil production concerns the regional distribution rather than the total quantity of reserves. Oil reserves are disproportionately concentrated in the Middle East, and natural gas reserves are predominantly located in the Middle East and former Soviet countries. This gives rise to both economic and security concerns for countries lacking oil supplies or for countries like the United States with declining oil production and increasing import dependence (as shown by the gap between U.S. consumption and production in Figure 13-5).

As production in oil fields outside the Middle East starts to decline, the concentration of a larger proportion of the remaining oil production in a limited number of countries increases the likelihood of a successful cartel. This suggests that an economic infrastructure that relies heavily on oil could be vulnerable:

> . . . The growing dependence on imported oil in general and Persian Gulf oil in particular has several potentially serious implications for the nation's economic and national security. First, the United States is expected to be importing nearly 60 percent of its oil by [2006], with roughly a third of that oil coming from the Persian Gulf. Our trade deficit in oil is expected to double, to $100 billion a year, by that time—a large and continual drag on our economic health. To the extent that the Gulf's recapture of the dominant share of the global oil market will make price increases more likely, the U.S. economy is at risk.[9]

## The Economics of Alternative Energy Futures

Two factors could dramatically alter the projections discussed above. On the demand side, significant energy conservation and increased end-use efficiency could considerably lower projections of demand growth. On the supply side, the renewable resources that currently provide only a small proportion of the world's energy needs (Figure 13-2) could become much more significant. However, these changes would require a combination of market price signals and government energy policies promoting energy efficiency and renewables.

---

[9]Romm and Curtis, 1996.

*Windmills in San Gorgonio Pass, Palm Springs, California. California's energy policies encourage development of renewable energy sources.*

Technologies for highly efficient energy use could achieve dramatic reductions in energy consumption with little or no effect on living standards. In most developed nations, energy use per dollar of GDP has declined steadily with technological progress and a shift to a more service-based economy. Developing nations have the opportunity to take advantage of existing technologies for more efficient and less environmentally damaging energy systems. Energy demand will certainly grow in the developing world, but this does not necessarily mean reliance on inefficient or highly polluting sources.[10]

Simply by using the most efficient known technologies, energy use in developed nations could be cut by up to 50 percent with no loss in living standard.[11] If this were to occur, global energy demand would be almost flat through 2020. The percentage of global energy use attributable to (presently) developed nations would decline from 70 to 35 percent, while (presently) developing nations could increase energy use from 30 to 65 percent of the global total. This would provide for the inevitable growth in population and allow a modest rise in per capita energy consumption (and a much bigger rise in living standards) among presently developing nations.

---

[10]See Reddy and Goldemberg, 1990.

[11]Intergovernmental Panel on Climate Change, 1996.

This scenario has many obvious advantages from an environmental point of view. All forms of pollution associated with energy use would drop, including atmospheric carbon dioxide accumulation. Countries with limited domestic energy sources would benefit from greater self-sufficiency and less import dependence. And lifetimes of limited oil and other fossil fuels reserves would be extended significantly.

## The Central Role of Energy Prices

Given these advantages, what stands in the way of a high-energy-efficiency future? The central economic issue is low current prices for energy. Even though increasing energy efficiency by a factor of 2 or more may be technically feasible, it is not necessarily economically profitable. This may seem strange, but recall our earlier distinction between economic and thermodynamic efficiency. So long as energy prices remain low, energy-intensive methods may remain the optimal economic strategy.

Significant costs accompany developing and installing energy efficient technologies. Why should a business firm bother to take on these costs if their current energy bills are already low? Why should a homeowner or car driver worry much about furnace and appliance efficiency or gas mileage if oil and gas costs are only a small percentage of domestic expenses? We choose to spend our time, effort, and money in areas that bring us the greatest return. If energy costs are low, other areas of our lives and businesses are more likely to receive attention and attract economic investment.

Energy pricing is equally central to developing nonfossil fuel energy sources. Costs of solar and renewable energy sources have declined rapidly since 1980 (Figure 13-8).

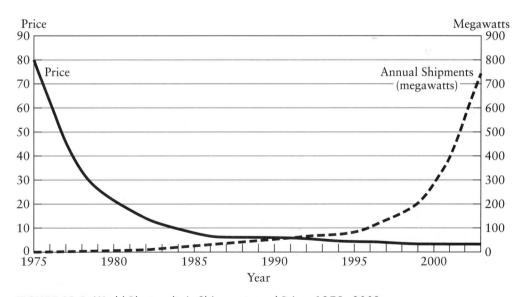

**FIGURE 13-8** *World Photovoltaic Shipments and Prices 1975–2003*
Sources: Worldwatch Institute: Database 2001, and *Signposts 2004*; U.S. Department of Energy, 2004.

## 13-1    Energy Subsidies: Tilting the Playing Field

**E**nergy is the third most heavily subsidized economic sector, after road transportation and agriculture. Governments often see cheap energy as an essential for economic development. In most cases, fossil fuel industries are the favored recipients for government largesse. In the United States, annual energy subsidies during the 1990s were $25 billion, of which fossil fuel and nuclear energy subsidies accounted for $21 billion. Energy subsidies in Western Europe were $16 billion, of which more than $10 billion went to fossil fuels and $4.6 billion to nuclear power.

Developing nations also subsidize fossil fuels, although nations such as China and India have recently reduced their levels of price supports, encouraging greater efficiency. A recent (2001) estimate of total developing-nation fossil fuel subsidies is $60 billion, down from $100 billion in 1991.

Economic theory suggests that taxes can internalize the many negative externalities associated with fossil fuels, but subsidies have the opposite effect, encouraging both greater consumption and a bias towards dirtier fuels such as coal and oil. To a limited degree, governments have started to redirect subsidies toward alternative energy sources. Benefits of removing or redirecting subsidies include economic efficiency gains, reduced overall energy consumption, reduced $CO_2$ emissions, and reduced local and regional pollution including acid rain and smog. Damage to agricultural production, health costs, and lives lost to pollution-related illnesses could all be reduced, as well as easing pressure on government budgets.

**SOURCE**

Myers, Norman, and Jennifer Kent. *Perverse Subsidies: How Tax Dollars Can Undercut the Environment and the Economy,* Chapter 4: Fossil Fuels and Nuclear Energy. Washington, D.C.: Island Press, 2001.

Some alternative power sources, such as wind and biomass energy, have reached the margin of competitiveness in the mass market, but in only a few instances have they crossed that margin into large-scale commercial feasibility. Solar power is competitive for hot water heating, but not yet for power supply. In addition to price, other institutional issues have been important in preventing alternative energy sources from gaining a significant market share.

The extensive infrastructure investment in fossil fuels—existing power stations, machinery, and transportation systems—creates considerable momentum for continued fossil fuel use. In addition, extensive direct and indirect government subsidies support fossil fuel industries. Worldwide, many governments artificially lower energy prices in order to promote industrial growth (see Box 13-1). Also, in many cases centralized power authorities are heavily committed to investment in standard coal or oil-powered plants, and state regulatory policy makes it difficult for competitors to enter the market.

From an economic point of view, subsidizing fossil fuels is bad policy. As we saw in Chapter 3, the economic case for a subsidy must rest on external benefits associated with product use. But fossil fuels provide few external benefits and incur many external costs.

Low fossil fuel prices can properly be viewed as a **market failure,** omitting the external costs of health and environmental damages as well as military expenditures associated with maintaining access to oil. A rationale exists for internalizing user costs imposed by exhausting prime fossil fuel deposits, and for carbon taxes to reflect the long-term external costs of atmospheric carbon dioxide accumulation. Internalizing all these costs would shift the competitive balance between fossil fuels and renewables strongly in favor of renewables.

## Policies for Future Energy Development

What kinds of government policies are most important to energy development? The answers differ somewhat for industrialized and developing nations. Industrialized nations already have an extensive energy infrastructure and strong momentum for continued fossil fuel use. Major infrastructure investments often have lifetimes of 50 years or more.

Large coal- or oil-fired power plants, electric grids reaching even remote areas, extensive highway systems, as well as cities designed for road traffic and energy-inefficient buildings dependent on fossil-fueled heating systems—all these encourage the continued use of presently cheap fossil fuels. Nuclear energy, sometimes promoted as an alternative to fossil fuels, has significant economic and environmental problems (see Box 13-2). Nonetheless, significant opportunities exist for modified or new infrastructure oriented toward conservation and alternative energy.

Historically, electric power generation has been treated as a regulated monopoly. This often leads to a perverse system of incentives whereby utilities are rewarded (with rate increases) for adding central power-station generating capacity and at the same time discouraged from conservation or efficiency initiatives that would lower power use. The barriers to entry in this system also make it difficult for more efficient producers and small-scale power generators to enter the market.

Regulators could create a rate structure that rewards utilities for conservation and requires them to purchase power from small producers. Recent emphasis, however, has been on **deregulation** of electric power.

Proponents of deregulation cite several favorable environmental effects. Market competition forces large, centralized power stations that use coal, oil, or nuclear fuel to compete with smaller power producers. Market incentives also favor the installation of highly efficient natural gas turbine **cogeneration** technology.

Gas turbine plants have significantly higher conversion efficiencies than conventional coal- or oil-fired plants—that is, they convert a higher proportion of the chemical

## 13-2   Nuclear Power: Coming or Going?

In the 1950s nuclear power was promoted as a safe, clean, and cheap source of energy. Proponents of nuclear power stated that it would be "too cheap to meter," and predicted that nuclear power would provide about one-quarter of the world's commercial energy and most of the world's electricity by 2000 (Miller, 1998).

Currently, nuclear power provides only about 7 percent of the world's energy and 17 percent of the world's electricity. Most forecasts predict a decline in nuclear energy production in the coming decades. No new nuclear power plants have been ordered in the United States since 1978. Among developed countries, only Japan, Korea, and possibly Finland are currently planning new nuclear plants.

Despite this projected decline, some have proposed a renewed expansion of nuclear power. Surprisingly, one of the touted benefits of nuclear power is environmental. Unlike fossil fuels, generating electricity using nuclear power does not emit carbon dioxide, the primary greenhouse gas. Is nuclear power an industry headed for extinction or is it entering a renaissance?

Accidents such as those at Three Mile Island and Chernobyl created significant public concern over the safety of nuclear power. These concerns remain—the results of a May 2001 Gallup survey indicate that 46 percent of Americans consider nuclear power too dangerous even if it would solve the country's energy problems. Recent nuclear technologies such as pebble-bed reactors and passive safety features reduce the chance of a major nuclear accident, but the problem of storage of long-lived nuclear wastes remains unsolved.

The main weakness of nuclear power is economic. Existing nuclear power plants have lower operating costs than coal or natural gas plants, and new nuclear technologies promise even lower production costs. However, building new nuclear power plants requires considerable capital costs. Recent analysis by the International Energy Agency (IEA, 2001) estimates the capital costs of a modern nuclear power plant at $2,000 per kw, compared to $1,200 per kw for coal and $500 per kw for a combined-cycle gas plant. The IEA notes that "high capital cost is the single most important economic factor weakening the prospects for new nuclear power plants."

Nuclear power has benefited from substantial government subsidies. Between 1974 and 1998, the U.S. government spent more than $40 billion (in 1999 dollars) for research and development of nuclear technology. Another important subsidy is provided by the Price-Anderson Act, which limits the liability of nuclear power operators in the event of an accident. About half of all government-financed energy research and development in developed countries is currently directed toward nuclear power.

*(continued on following page)*

Electricity markets worldwide are in the process of deregulation. Subject to market forces and declining subsidies, nuclear power's revival may never materialize. The IEA states that "nuclear power must increasingly face the future on its economic merits and drawbacks as judged by electricity markets." New nuclear power plants may simply be too expensive to compete in the market.

**SOURCES**

International Energy Agency. IEA, 2001. Nuclear Power in OECD Countries.
Miller, G. Tyler, Jr. *Living in the Environment,* 10th edition. Belmont, Calif.: Wadsworth, 1998.
*The Economist.* "Special Report, Nuclear Power: A Renaissance That May Not Come." May 19, 2001, pp. 24–26.

energy of natural gas into electricity. Cogeneration means that the heat produced in the process is captured and used, rather than released as waste heat. Thus these plants combine thermodynamic and economic efficiency. Nitrogen oxide emissions drop by 90 percent, and carbon dioxide by 60 percent. Under deregulation, these new highly efficient plants will tend to replace older, less-efficient plants.

The outlook for renewable energy under deregulation is less clear. As Figure 13-8 shows, prices for solar and renewable sources have fallen toward the margin of competitiveness but in most cases have not crossed this margin. To gain a significant market share, these sources need an extra boost in the form of subsidies, tax rebates, or content standards. U.S. deregulation laws have mainly been introduced at the state level, and they vary in structure, but many include provisions to encourage use of renewables.

On the demand side, a possible conflict exists between deregulation and conservation. One goal of deregulation is to provide lower prices to consumers; but lower prices encourage higher usage and more energy-intensive technology. Energy suppliers may offer customers a "package" of power supply and energy-saving technology. For instance, a supplier could offer a long-term contract including installation of efficient lighting and heating systems as well as power supply. The consumer's net cost would be less than the energy costs of a less-efficient system. However, such comprehensive power-and-conservation service may or may not thrive in a deregulated marketplace. So long as competition focuses primarily on lowering the price of delivered energy, incentives to conserve will be weak.

Other important policies that will affect the course of energy development include the following:

- *Subsidy shifts.* Governments can remove direct and hidden subsidies for fossil fuels and provide subsidies or tax incentives for alternative energy development.

Such a shift is economically justifiable based on the external costs of fossil fuels and the relative environmental and security benefits of renewables. Temporary subsidies may help new technologies achieve sufficient market share and **economies of scale** to become commercially viable. Many renewable technologies can achieve significant cost reductions with increases in production volume. In the United States, California's energy policy has given renewables sufficient initial support to make them a significant part of that state's energy mix and to lower overall costs closer to commercially competitive levels.

- *Infrastructure investment.* Transportation—primarily automobile transport—has long been a major government spending area. Improving public transit and urban design to allow light rail and bicycle transportation, as well as "clean" fleets of buses running on alternative fuels, can contribute to significant reductions in energy use and pollution in this sector. High-speed intercity rail can be nearly as fast as air transport, and is much more energy efficient.
- *Research and development (R&D).* This includes government-sponsored research and tax policies that encourage corporate R&D in energy efficiency and renewables. Cutting-edge technologies that have high efficiencies and low to zero pollution such as fuel cells, wind turbines, and photovoltaics, have begun to penetrate commercial markets, despite a relatively slim share of government R&D support, which has concentrated on fossil fuels and nuclear technology.
- *Efficiency standards.* High implicit consumer discount rates (Box 13-3) often mean that buildings, appliances, and vehicles remain energy inefficient even when efficient technologies are available and economical. Mandatory regulations such as building codes and fuel efficiency standards can help correct this market failure. Industries have historically resisted imposition of such regulations—for example, the automobile industry has always fought fuel efficiency standards. A compromise approach is mandatory **efficiency labeling,** common for appliances such as dishwashers and refrigerators. This provides better information to consumers—however, so long as energy prices remain low it may be ineffective in promoting a shift to use of higher-efficiency products.

## *Energy Policy Options for Developing Nations*

The policies outlined above have particular importance for developing nations because of their rapidly expanding energy sectors. Developing nations are still creating energy infrastructure and have the opportunity to choose a different energy path from that of industrialized nations. As cities grow, for example, they can favor designs and plans for public transit and bicycle use over automobile-dependent transport systems.

Many developing nations are particularly well situated to take advantage of solar energy potential, both because of abundant sunshine and because the solar installation can substitute for the expansion of the electric grid to remote areas. Solar electric systems may be economically advantageous for villages not currently connected to a national grid. When the avoided costs of extending the grid are taken into account, solar electric systems are cost-effective.

## 13-3    Implicit Discount Rates and Energy Efficiency

**A** major problem in increasing appliance energy efficiency arises from *high implicit discount rates.* Suppose that a consumer can purchase a standard refrigerator for $400 or an energy-efficient model for $500. The energy-efficient model will save the consumer $5 per month in energy costs. From an economic point of view, we can say that the return on the extra $100 invested in the efficient model is $5 × 12 = $60/year or 60 percent.

Anyone who was offered a stock market investment that would bring a guaranteed 60 percent annual return would consider this a tremendous opportunity, but the refrigerator buyer may well turn down the chance to make this fantastic return. She or he will likely place more weight on the immediate decision to spend $400 versus $500 and therefore choose the cheaper model. We could say that the consumer is implicitly using a discount rate of greater than 60 percent to make this judgment—a consumer behavior difficult to justify economically, yet very common.

Policies especially relevant to the energy sectors of developing nations include the following:

- Eliminate widespread energy subsidies that primarily benefit fossil fuels development. These subsidies, often justified as a way of promoting industrialization, waste scarce government funds and increase import dependence for non–oil-producing countries.
- Eliminate tariff systems that raise the cost of efficient equipment and technologies; facilitate technology transfer and development of technical expertise in energy efficiency and renewable technologies.
- Institute regulatory reform to break up powerful electricity-generation boards whose policies strongly favor construction of centralized coal- and oil-fired or nuclear facilities.[12]

In the long term, **solar hydrogen** systems might allow tropical countries in effect to export sunlight. Hydrogen can be produced with photovoltaic or wind power by water electrolysis. It can be used in fuel cells to generate power without the pollutants and carbon dioxide associated with fossil fuel use.[13]

---

[12]Policies summarized from Kats, "Achieving Sustainability in Energy Use in Developing Countries." Chapter 9 in *Making Development Sustainable,* edited by Holmberg, 1992.

[13]See Dunn, 2001, for an extensive discussion of hydrogen energy systems.

Rather than becoming dependent on imported fossil fuels, countries with abundant sunlight could both supply their own energy needs and become net exporters. Technically feasible, this nonpolluting energy system would require a shift in the relative costs of fossil and renewable energy to become commercially viable.

The vast projected growth in energy demand in developing nations increases the need for a transition to renewable energy sources in the twenty-first century. Current government policies as well as temporary abundance and low oil and coal prices, however, keep us on a fossil-fuel–dependent path.

Local and regional pollution from fossil fuel use, along with security considerations, may impel countries toward stronger policies promoting alternative paths. A decisive issue may well be global climate change implications of continued and expanded fossil fuel use. We address this topic, the subject of extensive research efforts and much controversy, in Chapter 18.

## SUMMARY

Energy is an input fundamental to economic systems. Current economic activity depends overwhelmingly on nonrenewable fossil fuels including oil, coal, and natural gas. Renewable sources such as hydroelectric, wind, and solar power currently provide less than 10 percent of the energy supply in industrialized economies.

The laws of thermodynamics provide a basis for understanding the special role of energy. Energy can be used to expand the production of other nonrenewable resources, or to recycle them, but energy itself cannot be recycled. High-quality energy sources are essential to economic growth. Efficient energy use is desirable, but cheap energy often encourages thermodynamically inefficient uses.

World energy demand has expanded rapidly and is projected to double by 2030. Oil supplies are sufficient for several decades, but production could peak within a decade or two. World oil reserves are disproportionately located in the Middle East, and growing demand for limited supplies may strengthen producer cartels. Coal, which is more abundant, is often associated with significant environmental damage.

Alternative energy sources could grow in importance in the future. Prices for alternative sources such as wind and solar power have declined. Increased efficiency and energy conservation have great potential, but existing infrastructure and government subsidies continue to favor fossil fuel use. Policies that could promote a shift to alternative sources include eliminating fossil fuel subsidies, promoting research and development, and imposing efficiency standards.

Developing nations can reduce fossil fuel dependence by using renewable sources, acquiring energy-efficient capital, and promoting localized rather than centralized electricity generating systems. Ultimately, a shift to a solar-based economy could benefit developing nations in tropical and subtropical areas, which could take advantage of abundant sunshine to develop self-sufficient energy systems and perhaps export hydrogen fuel produced by solar energy.

## KEY TERMS AND CONCEPTS

biomass

capital stock

cartel

cogeneration

deregulation

diminishing returns

economic efficiency

economic supply

economies of scale

efficiency labeling

efficiency standards

energy infrastructure

entropy

estimated ultimately recoverable (EUR) supplies

first law of thermodynamics

flow

Hubbert curve

hydropower

market failure

net energy ratio

physical supply

research and development (R&D)

second law of thermodynamics

solar energy

solar flux

solar hydrogen

stock

thermodynamic efficiency

throughput

## DISCUSSION QUESTIONS

1. Given that energy production represents only about 5 percent of economic output, why should we place special importance on this sector? Is there any significant difference between an economic system that relies on nonrenewable energy supplies and one that uses primarily renewable sources? Should governments implement policy decisions about energy use, or should market allocation and pricing alone determine energy use patterns?

2. Discuss the concept of entropy as it relates to energy use. What do the thermodynamic laws imply for economic analysis of energy supplies, consumption, and environmental impact? How does this relate to the rapid expansion of energy use in the twentieth century and to projections for further expansion in the future?

3. In the 1970s, energy shortages had significant worldwide economic impact. Was this a one-time phenomenon or could it recur? Did it relate primarily to demand-side or supply-side factors? How have energy demand and supply changed since the 1970s, and how have these changes affected energy prices and consumption patterns? Are further significant changes likely?

4. Many people argue that a transition to renewable energy sources would be good policy from both economic and environmental points of view. Yet such a transition has not occurred and does not seem imminent. Do you think a shift away from fossil fuel dependence would be beneficial? What economic factors and policy decisions are likely to significantly affect whether or not and how rapidly such a shift occurs?

## REFERENCES

Campbell, Colin, and Jean Laherrère. "The End of Cheap Oil." *Scientific American,* March 1998, 78–83.

Cleveland, Cutler. "Natural Resource Scarcity and Economic Growth Revisited: Economic and Biophysical Perspectives." Chapter 19 in *Ecological Economics,* edited by Robert Costanza. New York: Columbia University Press, 1991.

Daly, Herman E. *Steady-State Economics.* 2nd ed. Washington, D.C.: Island Press, 1991.

Dunn, Seth. *Hydrogen Futures: Toward a Sustainable Energy System.* Worldwatch Paper No. 157. Washington, D.C.: Worldwatch Institute, 2001.

Georgescu-Roegen, Nicholas. *The Entropy Law and the Economic Process.* Cambridge, Mass.: Harvard University Press, 1971.

Intergovernmental Panel on Climate Change (IPCC). *Climate Change 1995, Volume 3: Economic and Social Dimensions of Climate Change.* New York: Cambridge University Press, 1996.

International Energy Agency. *World Energy Outlook 2004.* Available at http://www.iea.org.

International Institute for Applied Systems (IIASA) and the World Energy Council (WEC). *Global Energy Perspectives.* Laxenburg, Austria, 1998. Available at http://www.worldenergy.org.

Kats, Gregory. "Achieving Sustainability in Energy Use in Developing Countries." Chapter 9 in *Making Development Sustainable,* edited by Johan Holmberg. Washington, D.C.: Island Press, 1992.

Krishnan, Rajaram, Jonathan M. Harris, and Neva Goodwin, eds. *A Survey of Ecological Economics.* Washington, D.C.: Island Press, 1995.

MacKenzie, James J. *Oil as a Finite Resource: When Is Global Production Likely to Peak?* Washington, D.C.: World Resources Institute, 1996.

Meadows, Donella H., Dennis L. Meadows, and Jørgen Randers. *Beyond the Limits.* Post Mills, Vt.: Chelsea Green, 1992.

Reddy, Amulya, and José Goldemberg. "Energy for the Developing World." *Scientific American,* September 1990, 110–118.

Romm, Joseph, and Charles Curtis. "Mideast Oil Forever?" *Atlantic Monthly,* April 1996, 54–74.

U.S. Department of Energy, Energy Information Administration. *Annual Energy Review 2003.* Washington, D.C.: U.S. Government, 2003. http://www.eia.doe.gov.

U.S. Department of Energy, Energy Information Administration. *International Energy Annual 2002.* Washington, D.C.: U.S. Government, 2002. http://www.eia.doe.gov.

U.S. Department of Energy, Energy Information Administration. *International Energy Outlook, 2004.* Washington, D.C.: U.S. Government, 2004. http://www.eia.doe.gov.

U.S. Department of Energy, Energy Information Administration. *International Petroleum Monthly,* February 2005. Washington, D.C.: U.S. Government, 2005. http://www.eia.doe.gov.

World Bank. *World Development Report 1992,* Chapter 6: "Energy and Industry." New York: Oxford University Press, 1992.

World Resources Institute. *World Resources 1994–95.* New York: Oxford University Press, 1994.

*Worldwatch Institute Database Disk.* Washington, D.C.: Worldwatch Institute, 2001.

Worldwatch Institute. *Signposts 2004: Essential Data, Timelines and Analyses of Global Trends* (CD-ROM). Washington, D.C.: Worldwatch Institute, 2004.

## WEBSITES

1. **http://www.eia.doe.gov/** Website for the Energy Information Administration in the U.S. Department of Energy. Provides a wealth of information about energy demand, supply, trends, and prices.

2. **http://www.cnie.org/NLE/CRSreports/Energy/** Access to energy reports and issue briefs published by the Congressional Research Service.

3. **http://www.nrel.gov/** The website for the National Renewable Energy Laboratory in Colorado. NRE conducts research on renewable energy technologies including solar, wind, biomass, and fuel cell energy.

4. **http://www.rmi.org/** Homepage for the Rocky Mountain Institute, a nonprofit organization that "fosters the efficient and restorative use of resources to create a more secure, prosperous, and life-sustaining world." RMI focuses mostly on promoting increased energy efficiency in industry and households.

5. **http://www.eere.energy.gov/** Website for the Energy Efficiency and Renewable Energy Network within the U.S. Department of Energy. The site includes extensive information on energy efficiency and renewable energy sources as well as links to thousands of other sites.

6. **http://www.eesi.org/** The Environmental and Energy Study Institute (EESI), a nonprofit organization dedicated to promoting "transitions to social and economic patterns that sustain people, the environment, and the natural resources upon which present and future generations depend." EESI develops public policy initiatives on energy, agriculture, climate, and transportation.

**CHAPTER FOCUS QUESTIONS**

- What ecological and economic principles govern fisheries?
- Why are so many of the world's fisheries suffering from overexploitation?
- What policies can be effective in conserving and rebuilding fisheries?

CHAPTER **14**

# Renewable Resource Use: Fisheries

## Principles of Renewable Resource Management

The expansion of human economic activity, as we noted in Chapter 2, has had major impact on the planet's renewable natural resources. In the early twenty-first century most of the world's major fisheries are depleted or in decline, tropical forest area continues to shrink at about 30 million acres per year, and groundwater withdrawals continue to deplete aquifers in all major water-scarce regions of the globe.[1] Clearly, management of renewable resources remains a major continuing issue. What economic and ecological principles underlie sustainable—or unsustainable—management of renewable resources?

We can view resources simply as inputs into the economic production process, or, in a broader view, analyze **renewable resources** in terms of their own internal logic of equilibrium and regeneration. In some resource management approaches, these two perspectives are compatible, but in others they clash. For example, should the governing principle in managing natural systems be ecological diversity or maximum yield? The problem of integrating economic and ecological goals is essential to the management of natural resource systems.

---

[1]World Resources Institute, 2000; UNEP, 2002.

In Chapter 1, we identified the relationships between the human economy and natural systems in terms of **source function** and **sink function**. The source function is the provision of materials for human use, and the sink function is the absorption of waste products from human activity. We have already considered aspects of these functions in dealing with agriculture, nonrenewable resources and atmospheric carbon absorption. **Sustainable management** of renewable resources involves maintaining the resource's source and sink functions in such a way that its quality and availability remain stable over time. Although this certainly seems like a desirable goal, some forms of management tend to encourage unsustainable use.

We have already seen an example of how managing a fishery as an **open-access resource** can lead to overfishing and depletion of stocks (Chapter 4). However, management by a private owner or by a government authority also can lead to unsustainable practices. The reason lies in the difference between economic principles and ecological principles.

Economic principles of resource management include profit maximization, efficient production, and efficient intertemporal resource allocation. We saw in Chapters 4 and 5 how these principles apply in general to resource use. When we examine fisheries, forests, and water systems in more detail we see that these economic principles are sometimes, but not always, consistent with sustainable management.

The ecological principles underlying renewable resource systems are a little more difficult to express in simple terms. One basic rule derived from ecological principles is that of **maximum sustainable yield (MSY)**—no more of the resource should be harvested or withdrawn annually than can be regenerated or replenished by the natural processes of resource cycling and the capture of solar energy. Maximum sustainable yield, as we have already seen in Chapter 4, can be included in an economic analysis and may be consistent with economic goals under some circumstances.

But we must also consider that most natural systems are characterized by **ecological complexity.** Fisheries typically include many species of fish as well as other forms of animal and vegetable marine life. Natural forests usually have a variety of tree species, provide habitat for many animal species, as well as symbiotic or parasitic insects, fungi, and microbial life. Water systems generally include different kinds of aquatic habitat, some of which, like wetlands, play a crucial role in balancing the water cycle and maintaining water quality.

Human management of natural ecosystems must of necessity be a compromise between economic and ecological goals. In almost every case, human use of natural ecosystems will alter their state to some degree. Even so, we can usually manage ecosystems without destroying their **resilience**—defined as the capacity to recover from adverse impacts—or exceeding their maximum sustainable yield. To do so, however, requires a degree of restraint that may or may not be consistent with economic principles of profit maximization and economic institutions of resource ownership. In this chapter and Chapter 15 we will investigate this tension between economic and ecological principles as it applies to the management of fisheries, forests, and water systems.

## Ecological and Economic Analyses of Fisheries

In our initial analysis of fisheries in Chapter 4, we viewed the fishery as a productive system whose output—fish—was an economic good. But fisheries are fundamentally biological systems, so a more complete view should start with a biological analysis and examine its economic implications.

The field of **population biology** identifies a general theory of population change for an organism, such as a species of fish, in the natural environment. Figure 14-1 shows a basic pattern of population change over time characteristic of many species in a natural state. This graph shows two paths for population change over time. Above a minimum critical population necessary for survival ($X_{min}$), population will grow from point $A$ to a natural equilibrium, in balance with food supply, following a **logistic curve** of growth over time.[2]

With a small population and abundant food supply, the population initially grows at a steady rate, in a near-exponential pattern. Limits on food supply and living space slow the rate of population growth. Beyond point $B$, known as an **inflection point**,[3]

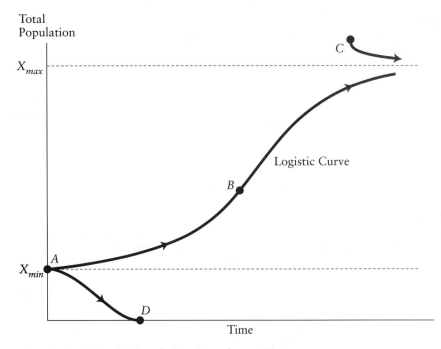

**FIGURE 14-1** *Species Population Growth over Time*

---

[2]A logistic curve is an S-shaped growth curve tending toward an upper limit. For an exposition of the mathematical analysis of logistic growth, see Hartwick and Olewiler, 1998, Chapter 4: The Economics of the Fishery.

[3]At an inflection point, the curvature of the line changes from positive (upward) to negative (downward). In the terminology of calculus, the second derivative goes from positive to negative and is equal to zero at the inflection point.

annual growth declines and population eventually approaches an upper limit $X_{max}$. Should the population ever exceed this limit—for example, reaching point $C$ due to a temporary increase in available food—it will rapidly decline from point $C$ back to $X_{max}$ once normal food supply conditions return.

If the population falls below the critical $X_{min}$ level, it will decline to extinction (point $D$). This can happen if disease, predation, or excessive harvesting by humans reduces the population to an unsustainably low level. The passenger pigeon in North America provides a classic case in which excessive harvesting led to extinction of a wild species. At one time, abundant food supply in the forests of North America made the passenger pigeon perhaps the most numerous species on the continent. Unrestrained hunting reduced it to a few scattered remnants, which died out by the late nineteenth century.

In general, species populations in a natural state are determined by the environment's **carrying capacity**—the supply of food and other life support naturally available. Human exploitation of renewable resources must be consistent with this carrying capacity to avoid ecological disruption and possible population collapse.

The population growth pattern shown in Figure 14-1 can be viewed in a different graphical format by relating the stock (population size) to its growth per year (Figure 14-2). Stock size now appears on the horizontal axis and annual growth on the vertical axis. The arrows indicate the direction of population change. When growth rates are positive (above $X_{min}$) the population is expanding toward $X_{max}$, while below $X_{min}$ it is declining toward zero.

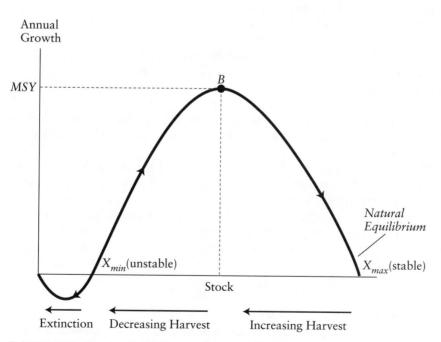

**FIGURE 14-2** *Species Population and Annual Growth*

We can now see that $X_{min}$ is an **unstable equilibrium.** At this population, a slight increase will set the species on the road to recovery; a slight decrease will head it to extinction. Many endangered species are in this position. For example, barely enough North American whooping cranes survive to maintain a nesting population, and scientists hope to nudge the number upward to recovery. But a single major incidence of natural disaster or disease could eliminate the species.

By contrast, $X_{max}$ is a **stable equilibrium.** In a natural state, the population will tend to this equilibrium. A smaller population will grow, while a larger population will shrink. Thus while some oscillation might occur around the equilibrium, the population will not tend to explode or to crash.[4]

In this form, the population growth graph clearly shows the maximum sustainable yield (*MSY*) at the top of the curve. The potential sustainable harvest of fish equals the total annual growth. If this amount is taken for human use, the population will remain constant. It will therefore be possible to exploit the fish stock at any population level between $X_{max}$ and $X_{min}$, with the maximum possible harvest at point *B*.

## Deriving an Economic Analysis from Biological Principles

Note that so far we have followed a strictly biological analysis, without considering economic implications. But we have derived a graph close to the economic graph of **total product** used for the fishery in Chapter 4. If we view Figure 14-2 from right to left, starting at the natural population equilibrium $X_{max}$, we can see how the economic graph of total product is derived.

Suppose Figure 14-2 describes a fish population in its natural state—say, the codfish population off New England when the first European colonists arrived.[5] As fishing effort increases, the stock will decline. However, this leads to a *higher* annual increment of fish. This is because a somewhat smaller stock of fish, with an unchanged food supply, can reproduce more rapidly. This pattern continues until point *B*, the maximum sustainable yield or *MSY*.

If fishing continues beyond *MSY*, however, the pattern changes. Both the fish stock and the annual increment decline. Larger harvests progressively reduce both stock and yield until eventually the fish population may face danger of extinction as $X_{min}$ is approached.

The economic view of this biologically derived pattern is shown in Figures 14-3 and 14-4. Figure 14-3 relates fishing effort (measured in number of boat-days) to total returns. The total product, measured in tons of fish, can be converted to money terms by multiplying by the price of fish.[6] The resulting total revenue (*TR*) curve has the same general shape as the yield curve in Figure 14-2, and in fact corresponds closely to that curve. Increased fishing effort moves right to left in Figure 14-2, but left to right in Figure 14-3. We measure the horizontal axes on the two graphs in different units,

---

[4]For an advanced treatment of fisheries dynamics, see Clark, 1990.

[5]The levels of fishing engaged in by Native American tribes before European colonization would have had little impact on the natural equilibrium.

[6]For this example, we assume a stable market price for fish.

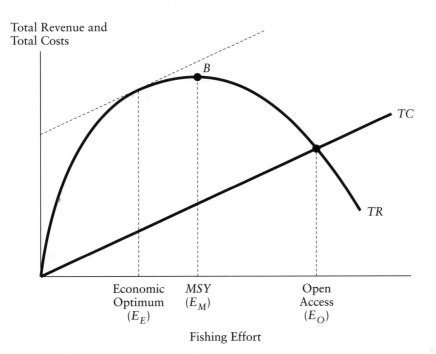

FIGURE 14-3 *Total Revenues and Costs in the Fishery*

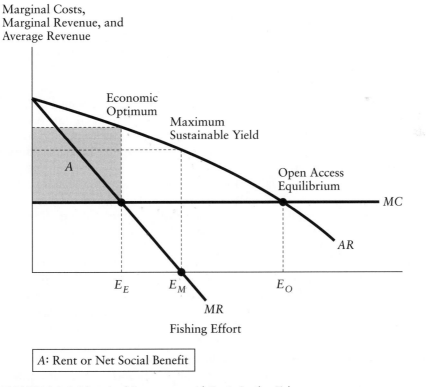

*A*: Rent or Net Social Benefit

FIGURE 14-4 *Marginal Revenues and Costs in the Fishery*

because one measures fish population and the other fishing effort, but in general as fishing effort increases fish population decreases.

Fishing, of course, also involves costs. The total cost ($TC$) curve shown in Figure 14-3 is linear, implying a constant cost per unit of fishing effort. Other patterns for total cost curves are possible, but in general total costs will increase as fishing effort increases. The combination of costs and revenues shown here allows us to identify two possible equilibrium positions:

1. the **economic optimum**, $E_E$, where the slopes of the total revenue and total cost curves are equal, or Marginal Revenue = Marginal Cost;
2. the **open-access equilibrium**, $E_O$, where $TR = TC$, or Average Revenue = Marginal Cost.

These equilibria can be more easily identified using the marginal and average cost and revenue curves shown in Figure 14-4. The maximum sustainable yield appears on the economic graphs as $E_M$, where $TR$ is maximized and $MR = 0$.

The open-access equilibrium $E_O$, as discussed in Chapter 4, occurs only when average revenue equals marginal cost, which means that profits throughout the fishing industry have fallen to zero. So long as the industry is profitable, new entrants will continue to increase the pressure on the fish population, driving total revenues down until $TR = TC$. This position is both economically and ecologically undesirable, but is the likely outcome unless policies to limit entry are in place.

From the economist's point of view, open-access equilibrium leads to **rent dissipation**—the loss of much of the potential social benefit from the fishery. A single owner of the fishery could capture the potential rent by limiting operations to $E_E$. This potential rent is the shaded area $A$ in Figure 14-4. The difference between average revenue and marginal cost shows the rent per unit of effort, and area $A$ shows the total rent. With open access, this economic benefit is lost.

Note the relationship of the economic optimum ($E_E$), maximum sustainable yield ($E_M$), and open-access equilibrium ($E_O$) in Figure 14-4. The economic optimum lies to the left of maximum sustainable yield, and the open-access equilibrium lies to the right. As we saw in Chapter 4, the economic optimum might be achieved through use of a **license fee** or **quota system**.

In cases where the fishery is localized, such as on a small lake, the economic optimum could be achieved through **private ownership**. A profit-seeking owner, or group of owners acting together, would have an incentive to limit fishing effort to $E_E$. This would maximize profits, and would also have the effect of avoiding overexploitation of the fishery.

Referring back to the biological graph (Figure 14-2), we see that the economic optimum will lie to the right of *MSY* (point *B*), in a sustainable range. Although total fish stocks will drop as a result of the fishing effort, a high annual growth rate will allow the system to maintain resilience, or bounce-back capacity. The open-access equilibrium, in contrast, lies to the left of *MSY*.

As we move further to the left of *MSY*, both harvest and annual growth decline, and eventually the fish stock may be in danger of extinction. As fish harvests decline, fish prices are likely to rise, increasing the marginal and average revenue curves in

Figure 14-4, thus pushing the open-access equilibrium further to the right and hastening the spiral toward collapse of the fishery.[7]

Unfortunately, the open-access equilibrium is common in fisheries throughout the world. Figure 14-5 shows data from Philippine fisheries, in which open-access has led to effort levels exceeding first the maximum economic yield *MEY* (corresponding to $E_M$ in the above analysis), then the maximum sustainable yield *MSY*. It is interesting to note how this actual historical data corresponds closely to our theoretical patterns for the economics of a fishery. We can clearly see how, by the 1980s, fishing had exceeded the maximum sustainable yield and catches of both demersal (sea-bottom) and pelagic (ocean) fisheries had begun to decline.

## The Economics of Fisheries in Practice

Fishing in open seas is a typical illustration of a situation where the **tragedy of the commons,** as discussed in Chapter 4, is likely to occur. Individual fishers tend to have little incentive to practice conservation, for they know that if they do not catch the available fish, someone else probably will. Without limits in place, fishers try to catch as many fish as they possibly can. Technological improvements that make it easier to find and catch fish only make matters worse.

Many traditional societies have evolved rules limiting the seasons or days when particular seafood species could be harvested (for example, prohibiting fishing at spawning season), or the amount to be taken. In recent years these rules have in many cases been swept aside, in part due to population pressures. Other reasons why the balance might break down include **institutional failure,** such as when an outside interest acquires the power to override the community's traditional patterns of property rights.[8]

In industrial societies, **overfishing** rapidly affects whole fisheries. Management institutions often are overwhelmed by rising demands. Today the problem is global in scope:

> In 1871, the U.S. government created its first federal conservation agency, the Commission of Fish and Fisheries, in response to the decline of fisheries off the coast of New England and in inland lakes. Fishery declines were nothing new even in 1871—in the mid-1800s drastic declines of whales had captured people's attention.
>
> [Today] as a result of excessive exploitation and other abuses, most of the highly prized marine fisheries around the world are on the verge of collapse. The warning signs are clear: 11 of the world's 15 most important fishing areas and 60 percent of major fish species are in decline, according to the U.N. Food and Agriculture Organization (FAO).[9]

The scale of fishing operations has increased dramatically with the introduction of modern vessels such as commercial trawlers. Between 1970 and 1990, global fleet

---

[7]The process of fishery collapse cannot be fully shown in a static-equilibrium model such as Figure 14-4. More complex dynamic models are required to show the effects of disequilibrium leading to collapse (see, for example, Clark, 1990).

[8]See Schlager and Ostrom, 1993; McGinnis and Ostrom, 1996.

[9]McGinn, 1998, p. 11. See also McGoodwin, 1990; Fairlie et al., 1995.

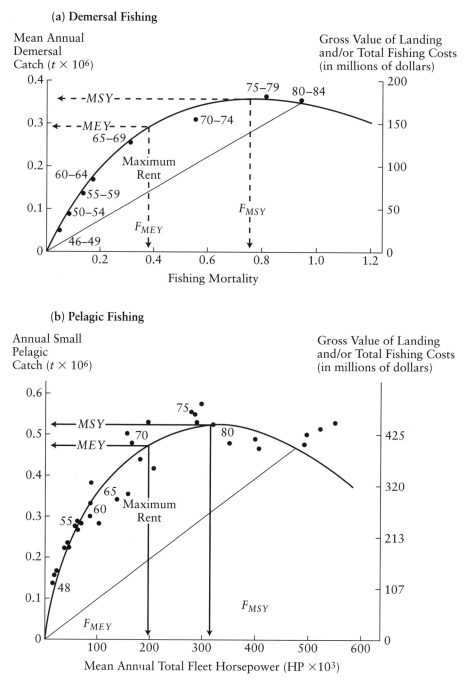

**(a) Demersal Fishing**

**(b) Pelagic Fishing**

**FIGURE 14-5** *Open Access in Philippine Fisheries*

Source: Adapted from "The Overfishing of Marine Resources: Socioeconomic Background in Southeast Asia," by Pauly, D., and Thia-Eng, C., in *Ambio*, Vol. 17, no. 3, p. 203. Reprinted by permission of *Ambio*.

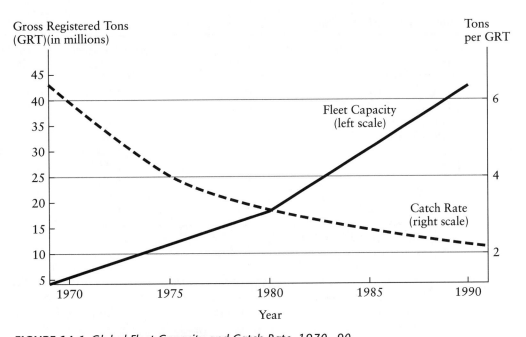

**FIGURE 14-6** *Global Fleet Capacity and Catch Rate, 1970–90*
Source: Adapted from Anne Platt McGinn, *Rocking the Boat: Conserving Fisheries and Protecting Jobs.*
Worldwatch Paper no. 142. Washington, D.C.: Worldwatch Institute, 1998. Reprinted by permission of
Worldwatch Institute, http://www.worldwatch.org

capacity more than quadrupled, whereas the average catch per boat (catch rate)
dropped by a factor of three (see Figure 14-6).

Clearly, an open-access situation is economically irrational. It also poses further
ecological problems because modern fishing methods often cause a high death rate
among nontarget species. One-fourth of all catches are discarded, because they are
either undersized or nonmarketable. This wasted portion of the global harvest is called
**bycatch.** "Global bycatch was estimated at more than 28 million tons in 1994 . . . bycatch is associated with industrialized fishers who use indiscriminate gear to catch as
much as they can, but generally keep only the fish they are legally permitted to catch
or those that make money."[10]

Although identifying the maximum sustainable yield for a fishery can help maintain an individual species, the issues of ecological sustainability are more complex. Depleting one species may lead to an irreversible change in ocean ecology as other species
fill the ecological niche formerly occupied by the harvested species.[11] For example,
dogfish and skates have replaced overfished cod and haddock in major areas of the

[10]McGinn, 1998.

[11]See Hagler, 1995; Ogden, 2001.

**TABLE 14-1** *Declining Major Fisheries in the World*

| Ocean Area | Estimated Annual Potential (million tons) | Year Potential Reached | Decline from Peak Yield |
|---|---|---|---|
| East Central Atlantic | 4 | 1984 | −22% |
| Northwest Atlantic | 4 | 1971 | −38% |
| Southeast Atlantic | 3 | 1978 | −53% |
| West Central Atlantic | 2 | 1987 | −28% |
| East Central Pacific | 3 | 1988 | −13% |
| Northeast Pacific | 4 | 1990 | −12% |
| Southwest Pacific | 1 | 1991 | −13% |
| Antarctic | 0.2 | 1980 | unavailable |
| World | 82 | 1999 | unavailable |

Sources: FAO, 1997; McGinn, 1999.

North Atlantic fishery, and are now themselves threatened with overfishing. Fishing techniques such as trawling, in which nets are dragged along the bottom of the ocean, are highly destructive to all kinds of benthic (bottom-dwelling) life. In large areas of the Atlantic, formerly productive ocean floor ecological communities have been severely damaged by repeated trawling.

While some fisheries remain in a healthy state, and others have recovered after fishing limitations have been imposed, many major ocean fisheries appear to have been exploited beyond the point of maximum sustainable yield (Table 14-1). The issue of open-access and proper fishery management is thus both a national and a global problem. Existing institutions for fishery management are often not sufficient to control the economic pressures leading to depletion of ocean resources.[12]

## Policies for Sustainable Fisheries Management

From an economic point of view, **market failure** occurs in open-access fisheries because important productive resources—lakes and oceans—are treated as free resources, and are therefore overused. A simple solution is to place a price on the resource.

Certainly no private owner of a small lake, for example, would allow unlimited numbers of people to fish for free, depleting the stock of fish until the resource was worthless. The owner would charge a fee to fish, yielding income for the owner (part of which might go to restocking the lake) and limiting the number of people who would fish. Although the owner's motivation would be to collect **economic rent,**[13] the people fishing would also benefit—despite having to pay a fee—because they would have access to continued good fishing instead of suffering depletion of the fish stock.

---

[12]See Hanna, 1999.

[13]Economic rent is the return that flows to the owner of a scarce resource.

*Effective regulatory policies such as Individual Transferable Quota (ITQ) systems can restore profitability and ecological stability to depleted fisheries.*

An ocean fishery does not allow the private ownership solution. The oceans have been called a common heritage resource—they belong to everyone and no one. But under the 1982 **Law of the Sea** treaty, agreed to under United Nations auspices, nations can claim territorial rights to many important offshore fisheries. They can then limit access to these fisheries by requiring a fishing license within their Exclusive Economic Zones (EEZs), which extend 200 miles from their coastlines.

Fishing licenses can be sold for a set fee, or a limited number can be sold at auction. In effect, this establishes a price for access to the resource. Notice that we can also view this as *internalizing a negative externality*. Each fisher now must pay a price for the external costs imposed on one fishery by adding one extra boat. The economic signal such a price sends will result in fewer people entering the fishery.

This approach, however, will not necessarily solve the problem of overinvestment. A boat owner who buys a license will have added incentive to obtain the maximum catch by investing in new equipment such as sonar devices to track fish, bigger nets, and more powerful engines to travel further. He or she will be more likely to spend as much time as possible at sea, to earn the maximum return on the investment in the license and equipment. If all fishers do this, the depletion problem may remain serious. Governments can respond by imposing quotas on total catch, but area-wide quotas are often difficult to enforce and meet fierce resistance from fishers.[14]

---

[14]See Townsend, 1990, for a survey of the effects of entry restrictions in fisheries.

One possible policy response that combines regulation with the use of market mechanisms is a system of **individual transferable quotas** (ITQs). Like transferable emissions permits, ITQs impose a maximum limit on the quantity of fish that can be taken. Anyone purchasing such a permit can catch and sell a certain number of fish—or can sell the permit and fishing rights to someone else. Assuming the quota limits can be enforced, the total catch from the fishery will not exceed a certain predetermined level.

To determine the maximum sustainable yield level, policymakers must consult marine biologists, who can estimate the sustainable level of fish population. Once ecological sustainability has been assured, the permit market will promote **economic efficiency.** Those who can fish most effectively will be able to outbid others to acquire the ITQs. Although ITQ systems have been successful in certain areas, they have also led to complaints that they promote concentration in the fishing industry and squeeze out small fishers.[15]

A more difficult problem concerns species that are highly migratory. Tuna and swordfish, for example, continually travel between national fishing areas and the open ocean. Even with good policies for resource management in national waters, these species can be harvested as an open-access global resource, which almost inevitably leads to stock declines. Only an international agreement can solve an issue concerning global commons.

In 1995, the first such agreement was signed: the Convention on Highly Migratory and Straddling Stocks. This convention embodies a principle of ecological economics introduced in Chapter 6: the **precautionary principle.** This principle suggests that, rather than waiting until depletion is obvious, fishery access should be controlled before problems appear, with measures to limit the total catch rate, establish data collection and reporting systems, and minimize bycatch through the use of more selective gear.[16]

## Demand-Side Issues: Changing Consumption Patterns

People in developed countries currently consume 40 percent of the global fish catch; the other 60 percent is consumed in the developing world, where fish is an important protein source.[17] Increasing population and income in developing countries will likely produce steady growth in global demand for fish and fish products, but supply expansion, at least from wild fisheries, may be close to its limits.

After increasing rapidly between 1950 and 1990, the world fish catch now appears to have leveled off; per capita catch has increased little over the past 30 years, and may have started to decline (Figure 14-7). Most ocean and inland fisheries are at or near their capacity limits, with many already in decline (see Table 14-1). Atlantic fisheries have been especially pressured as many fishing nations compete for access, and fishery management within the 200-mile EEZs has been inadequate.[18]

---

[15]See Duncan, 1995; Arnason, 1993; Young, 1999.

[16]McGinn, 1998.

[17]Ibid.

[18]A recent article in *Nature* magazine suggests that China has systematically overestimated fishery production and that world fish catch may actually have peaked in the early 1990s (Watson and Pauly, 2001). On Atlantic fisheries, see Harris, 1998.

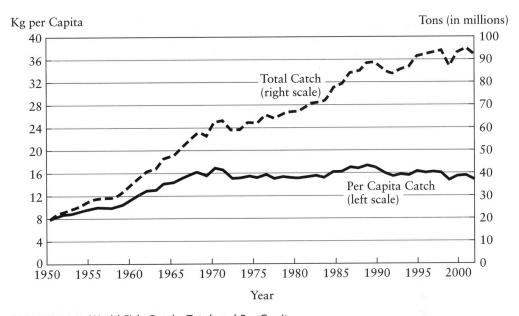

**FIGURE 14-7** *World Fish Catch, Total and Per Capita*

Note: Recent data may need to be revised downward due to overestimation of China's fish catch.

Source: Worldwatch Institute, *Signposts 2004,* based on FAO FISHSTAT Statistical Database, http://www. fao.org/fi/statist/fisoft/FISHPLUS.asp, updated 2003.

About one-third of world fish production—30 million tons—goes to nonfood uses such as fishmeal and oils.[19] Alternative use of soymeal and other sources of protein in animal and fish feed would relieve pressure on fisheries and potentially make more fish available for direct human consumption. This would depend, of course, on increased output of land-grown protein products such as soybeans, which as we saw in Chapter 11 may pose other environmental issues.

Changes in human consumption patterns are also important. Public education campaigns that identify fish and seafood produced with environmentally damaging techniques may lead consumers to avoid these species. For example, a boycott of swordfish aimed at stopping the decline of this species has gained the support of numerous restaurant chefs and consumers.

**Ecolabeling,** which identifies products produced in a sustainable manner, has the potential to encourage sustainable fishing techniques. Products of certifiably sustainable fishing practices can often command a slightly higher market price. By accepting this price premium, consumers implicitly agree to pay for something more than the fish they eat. They pay a little extra for the health of the ocean ecosystem and the hope of a

[19]McGinn, 1998.

## 14-1    Fishery Policies in Practice: Successes and Failures

Environmental economics shows that fisheries often require some form of community or government management to avoid overuse of a common-property resource. But many government fishery management policies have been counter-productive, worsening overfishing and hastening depletion of stocks. This is especially true of fishery subsidies, which include grants, loans, tax incentives, discounted insurance, and fuel tax credits, as well as support for research and development on more effective fishing methods. Globally, fishery subsidies amount to about $20 billion per year, and almost all these subsidies contribute to excess capacity and overfishing.

Policies imposing catch limits have been more successful in preventing depletion of stocks and in some cases helping stocks to recover. But these policies are often bitterly contested, since limits on fishing days or permitted catch reduce fishing incomes. In New England fisheries, for example, a recent decision by a federal judge found that catch restrictions have not succeeded in rebuilding cod and other groundfish stocks; the court imposed even more stringent rules, which the fishing industry contends will destroy their livelihood. Canada recently closed its historic Atlantic cod fishery entirely, citing catastrophic decline of stocks.

Is there a better way? Countries such as New Zealand and Australia have pioneered the use of transferable fishing quotas. In effect, this establishes property rights in ocean fisheries. New entrants into the industry must purchase licenses from current owners. With overall catch strictly limited, fish stocks have flourished and the value of the fishing permits has steadily risen. This gives fishers an incentive to conserve. "Why hurt the fishery?" says an Australian lobsterman. "It's my retirement fund. No one's going to pay me $35,000 a pot if there are no lobsters left. If I rape and pillage the fishery now, in ten years my licenses won't be worth anything."

Unlike New England lobstermen, who must tend up to 800 lobster traps to squeeze out a living from scarcer, smaller, and short-lived lobsters, their Australian counterparts can make an excellent living from 60 traps, in which they catch larger lobsters. "Fishing may be the only economic activity in which you can make more money by doing less work," says a biologist who monitors the Australian lobster fishery. "By fishing less, the fishermen leave more lobsters out there to produce more eggs, which will make it easier for them to catch lobsters in the future. The lobsters are thriving and the fishermen are spending more time at home with their families."

Transferable quota systems face opposition from critics who fear that corporations will take over public waters by buying up licenses. But it would be possible to protect small operators by limiting the number of permits any individual or

*(continued on following page)*

corporation can own. According to Richard Allen, a Rhode Island lobsterman who is lobbying for an Australian-type system, "Many people complain that it's unfair to lock anyone out of the fishery . . . but with the current system we have fisheries that we're all locked out of. I can't go out and fish for halibut and swordfish—there aren't any left. I would rather have a healthy fish stock and the option to buy access to it."

**SOURCES**

Fishermen and biologist quotes from John Tierney, "A Tale of Two Fisheries," *New York Times,* August 27, 2000; Beth Daley, "Drastic Cuts Ordered in New England Fishing: Judge's Decision Seen as Heavy Blow to Industry," *Boston Globe,* April 27, 2002; Colin Nickerson, "Canada Declares an End to Cod Fishing," *Boston Globe,* April 25, 2003; subsidy estimate from Myers and Kent, 2001.

supply of fish to feed people in the future as well as in the present. These consumer choices give the fishing industry a financial incentive to use sustainable methods.

In economic terminology, we can say that consumers are *internalizing the positive externalities* associated with sustainable fishing techniques through their willingness to buy ecolabeled products. Governments or well-respected private agencies can oversee **certification** of sustainable fish products. A prominent example is "dolphin-safe" ecolabeling, which has been instrumental in reducing the numbers of dolphin killed as bycatch during tuna fishing.

Another area where governments policies can assist in internalizing positive externalities is the judicious use of **subsidies**—for example, to assist in developing or acquiring equipment designed especially to release bycatch, or to avoid major disturbances of the seabed. This may moderate political opposition from fishing communities to government intervention aimed at eliminating destructive fishing practices. Unfortunately, most current fishery subsidies are counterproductive, increasing economic incentives for overfishing (see Box 14-1).

## Aquaculture: New Solutions, New Problems

The most rapidly growing area of fish production is **aquaculture**—fish farming, often in large offshore pens. Aquaculture is largely responsible for recent increases in world fish production (see Figure 14-8). However, from an environmental point of view aquaculture may pose as many questions as it solves.

While traditional aquaculture systems often raised several species of fish in ecologically healthy combination with crops and animals, modern systems rely on **monoculture** of economically profitable species such as salmon and shrimp. Such systems have

*A salmon farm in Washington. Aquaculture offers significant potential for expanding fish supplies, but it can also lead to ecological damage and degradation of wild stocks through interbreeding with escaped fish or the spread of disease.*

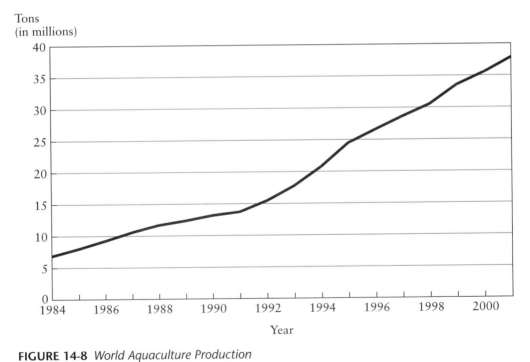

**FIGURE 14-8** *World Aquaculture Production*

Source: Worldwatch Institute, *Signposts 2004*, based on FAO FISHSTAT Statistical Database, http://www.fao.org/fi/statist/fisoft/FISHPLUS.asp, updated 2003.

## 14-2 Scientists Criticize Salmon Aquaculture

**D**espite their image as potential saviors of the world's beleaguered fisheries, some of the most successful forms of fish farming may do more harm than good by depleting marine resources and polluting the water, according to a paper in the journal *Science*.

Researchers from Stanford University and the Environmental Defense Fund argue that salmon and shrimp aquaculture are especially damaging to the environment because the animals are carnivorous, consuming smaller fish that could have been eaten by humans or other marine life.

The world's salmon farmers fed their fish 1.8 million tons of wild fish to harvest just 644,000 tons of salmon. At the same time, water pollution from shrimp and salmon farms has grown. Salmon farms in Norway alone discharge nutrients in their feces equivalent to a city of at least 1.7 million people. In addition, farmed fish can spread diseases and parasites to wild stocks, and escaped fish can degrade the wild genetic pool.

Shrimp farming, which has grown 700 percent since the 1980s, also leaves a trail of ecologically crippled ponds in China, Thailand, and Indonesia where low-income people formerly harvested shellfish.

"Rapid growth in shrimp and salmon farming has clearly caused environmental degradation, while contributing little to world food security" the paper concludes.

### SOURCES

"Fish Farming Pollutes, Harms Marine Life," by Scott Allen. *Boston Globe*, October 30, 1998, p. A13. Reprinted by permission of *Boston Globe* via Copyright Clearance Center.

"Salmon Aquaculture in the Pacific Northwest: A Global Industry with Local Impacts," *Environment* 45, 8 (October 2003).

significant negative externalities (see Box 14-2). Excess food and fish wastes contaminate the aquatic environment, and captive fish can spread disease to wild stocks or, if they escape, degrade the wild gene pool. Shrimp farms, which often replace mangrove forests, are especially ecologically destructive:

In the short term, intensive shrimp farming is highly profitable: in a year, an individual shrimp farmer can make up to $10,000 per hectare for intensive production rates of 4 to 5 tons per hectare. This compares to the roughly $1,000 per hectare that a species such as milkfish or carp generates. But these economic returns do not account for ecological—and economic—losses such as habitat degradation. By converting diverse ecosystems to simple ones, fish farmers and the public lose a host of ecological goods such as fish, shellfish, timber, charcoal, and other products. They also lose services that coastal ecosystems provide, such as filtering and purifying water, cycling nutrients, removing contaminants and buffering the land from coastal storms and severe weather. A study of the Matang mangrove in Malaysia revealed that its value for coastal protection alone exceeded the value of farmed shrimp by 170 percent.[20]

On a modest local scale, inland aquaculture can be environmentally beneficial, encouraging multiple use of water systems for crops such as rice as well as fish ponds. Asia has a long tradition of ecologically sound aquaculture, and Africa and other developing areas show considerable potential for its further development.[21] Whether ocean aquaculture can be practiced on a large scale without irreversible damage to ecosystems remains to be seen.

Given the rapid growth in aquaculture, regulatory policy should encourage less resource-intensive forms of production. Reviving and encouraging traditional pond systems, which integrate well with local environments and available resources, would help minimize aquaculture's impact on the environment.

Aquaculture will undoubtedly be a component of a strategy for sustainable fisheries management, but it cannot compensate for the damage done by unrestricted access to wild fisheries. A comprehensive approach including supply management, demand modification, and sustainable forms of aquaculture will be required to meet the needs of a still-growing world population.

## SUMMARY

A renewable natural resource system such as a fishery involves both economic and ecological principles. In a natural state, fish populations reach an equilibrium level based on the carrying capacity of the environment. Human exploitation of the resource can be sustainable provided it is consistent with this natural carrying capacity.

Economic analysis of the fishery suggests that economically efficient resource use should be compatible with ecological sustainability. However, open-access conditions in many fisheries create a strong tendency toward overexploitation.

On a global scale, fishing fleet capacity has exceeded maximum sustainable yield, leading to declining catch rates in most ocean fisheries. The total world fish catch increased steadily from 1950 to 1990, but has leveled off since then. Per capita catch rates have not increased over the past 30 years. Destructive fishing techniques have damaged marine habitat and altered ocean ecology, diminishing productivity.

Policies for maintaining sustainable yield and rebuilding depleted fisheries can involve a combination of regulation and market mechanisms. International conventions have set guidelines for territorial rights and management practices. Nations can require fishing licenses or impose quotas to limit access to the fishery. Area-wide quotas can be

---

[20]McGinn 1998, pp. 48–49.

[21]See Brummett and Williams, 2000.

difficult to enforce, but systems of individual transferable quotas have been successfully implemented.

Fish is an important protein source, especially in the developing world, where demand can be expected to grow as population and income rise. More efficient consumption patterns and increased aquaculture will be important as wild fish catches reach or exceed sustainable limits.

Consumption patterns can be modified to promote more sustainable fisheries management through consumer awareness and certification or ecolabeling programs. Aquaculture has great potential but can also involve significant environmental costs. Small-scale and traditional inland aquacultural systems often tend to be more environmentally beneficial than large-scale commercial operations.

## KEY TERMS AND CONCEPTS

aquaculture
bycatch
carrying capacity
certification
ecolabeling
ecological complexity
economic efficiency
economic optimum
economic rent
individual transferable
 quotas (ITQs)
inflection point
institutional failure
Law of the Sea
license fee
logistic curve
market failure
maximum sustainable yield
 (*MSY*)

monoculture
open-access equilibrium
open-access resource
overfishing
population biology
precautionary principle
private ownership
quota system
renewable resources
rent dissipation
resilience
sink function
source function
stable equilibrium
subsidies
sustainable management
total product
tragedy of the commons
unstable equilibrium

## DISCUSSION QUESTIONS

1. What is the basic reason for fishery depletion? What factors have made this problem especially severe in the modern period? Relate this issue to the difference between economic and ecological analyses of a fishery.

2. Discuss the advantages and disadvantages of the following policies for fisheries management: private ownership, government regulation through licensing, the use of individual transferable quotas (ITQs). In what circumstances might each one be appropriate?

3. Explain the interrelationship between the following concepts as they relate to fisheries: economic rent, maximum sustainable yield (*MSY*), economic efficiency, ecological sustainability. How should these concepts help guide fisheries management policies?

## PROBLEMS

1. Suppose that a fishery is characterized by the following relationship between total fish stock and annual growth:

| STOCK (thousand tons biomass) | 10 | 20 | 30 | 40 | 50 | 60 | 70 | 80 | 90 | 100 | 120 |
|---|---|---|---|---|---|---|---|---|---|---|---|
| GROWTH (tons) | 0 | 800 | 1600 | 2400 | 2800 | 3000 | 2800 | 2200 | 1200 | 0 | −1200 |

Construct a graph showing the relationship between stock and growth, and another graph showing the growth *rate* at each stock level (for example, at stock = 60,000 tons, yield = 3,000 tons, growth rate = 5%). What stock level corresponds to the maximum growth rate? What stock level gives the maximum sustainable yield? What will be the stable and unstable equilibrium stock levels for this fish population in a natural state?

2. Now assume that we can translate this population/yield relationship into an economic relationship between fishing boats operating and total product:

| BOATS | 0 | 100 | 200 | 300 | 400 | 500 | 600 | 700 | 800 | 900 |
|---|---|---|---|---|---|---|---|---|---|---|
| TOTAL PRODUCT (tons) | 0 | 1200 | 2200 | 2800 | 3000 | 2800 | 2400 | 1600 | 800 | 0 |

Fish prices average $1,000/ton, and the cost to operate a fishing boat for a year is $4,000.

Construct a graph showing total revenues and total costs in the fishery as a function of the number of boats operating. Now derive graphs showing marginal and average revenue and marginal cost. Use your graphs to analyze equilibrium in the fishery under the following conditions:

(a) A natural state with no fishing industry
(b) A fishing industry obtaining the maximum sustainable yield from the fishery

(c) A fishing industry operating under an efficient management plan, with economically optimal returns

(d) A fishing industry characterized by open access

What does this economic analysis suggest concerning government policy on fisheries management? Should such policies be based on the concept of maximum sustainable yield? Are other significant considerations not reflected in this analysis?

## REFERENCES

Arnason, R. "The Icelandic Individual Transferable Quota System: A Descriptive Account." *Marine Resource Economics* 8 (1993): 201–218.

Brummett, Randall E., and Meryl J. Williams. "The Evolution of Aquaculture in African Rural and Economic Development." *Ecological Economics* 33 (May 2000): 193–203.

Clark, Colin. *The Optimal Management of Renewable Resources.* 2nd ed. New York: Wiley, 1990.

Duncan, Leith. "Closed Competition: Fish Quotas in New Zealand." *The Ecologist* 25 (March/April, May/June 1995): 97–104.

Fairlie, Simon, Mike Hagler, and Brian O'Riordan. "The Politics of Overfishing." *The Ecologist* 25 (March/April, May/June 1995): 46–73.

Food and Agriculture Organization of the United Nations (FAO). *The State of World Fisheries and Aquaculture, 1996.* Rome: FAO, 1997.

Hagler, Mike. "Deforestation of the Deep: Fishing and the State of the Oceans." *The Ecologist* 25 (March/April, May/June 1995): 74–79.

Hanna, Susan S. "Strengthening Governance of Ocean Fishery Resources." *Ecological Economics* 31 (November 1999): 275–286.

Harris, Michael. *Lament for an Ocean: The Collapse of the Atlantic Cod Fishery.* Toronto, Ontario: M&S, 1998.

Hartwick, John M., and Nancy D. Olewiler. *The Economics of Natural Resource Use.* Reading, Massachusetts: Addison Wesley Longman, 1998.

McGinn, Anne Platt. *Rocking the Boat: Conserving Fisheries and Protecting Jobs.* Worldwatch Paper No. 142. Washington, D.C.: Worldwatch Institute, 1998.

McGinn, Anne Platt. *Safeguarding the Health of Oceans.* Worldwatch Paper No. 145. Washington, D.C.: Worldwatch Institute, 1999.

McGinnis, Michael, and Elinor Ostrom. "Design Principles for Local and Global Commons." In *The International Political Economy and International Institutions,* Vol. 2. Edited by Oran P. Young. Cheltenham, U.K.: Edward Elgar, 1996.

McGoodwin, James R. *Crisis in the World's Fisheries: People, Problems, and Politics.* California: Stanford University Press, 1990.

Myers, Norman, and Jennifer Kent. *Perverse Subsidies: How Tax Dollars Can Undercut the Environment and the Economy.* Washington, D.C.: Island Press, 2001.

Ogden, John C. "Maintaining Diversity in the Oceans." *Environment* 43 (April 2001): 28–37.

Schlager, Edella, and Elinor Ostrom. "Property Rights and Coastal Fisheries: An Empirical Analysis." In *The Political Economy of Customs and Culture: Informal Solutions to the Commons Problem*, edited by Terry L. Anderson and Randy T. Simmons. Lanham, Md.: Rowman and Littlefield, 1993.

Townsend, Ralph E. "Entry Restrictions in the Fishery: A Survey of the Evidence." *Land Economics* 66 (1990): 361–378.

United Nations Environmental Programme. *Global Environmental Outlook 3: Past, Present, and Future Perspectives.* London, U.K.: Earthscan, 2002.

United Nations Food and Agriculture Organization (FAO). *Review of the State of World Fishery Resources: Marine Fisheries.* Rome: FAO, 1997.

Watson, Reg, and Daniel Pauly. "Systematic Distortions in World Fisheries Catch Trends." *Nature* 414 (November 2001): 534–536.

World Resources Institute, United Nations Development Programme, United Nations Environment Programme, and the World Bank. *World Resources 2000–2001: People and Ecosystems.* Washington, D.C.: World Resources Institute, 2000.

Worldwatch Institute. *Signposts 2004: Essential Data, Timelines, and Analyses of Global Trends* (CD-ROM). Washington, D.C.: Worldwatch Institute, 2004.

Young, Michael D. "The Design of Fishing Rights Systems: The New South Wales Experience." *Ecological Economics* 31 (November 1999): 305–316.

## WEBSITES

1. **http://www.nmfs.noaa.gov/** Website for the National Marine Fisheries Service, a division of the National Oceanic and Atmospheric Administration that provides information on marine harvest, prices, and ecosystem health in the United States. The NMFS is also responsible for management of endangered marine species.

2. **http://osu.orst.edu/Dept/IIFET/** Homepage for the International Institute of Fisheries Economics and Trade, an organization of researchers devoted to an exchange of information on issues of fishery economics and management.

3. **http://fisheries.fws.gov/** Website of the U.S. Fish and Wildlife Service devoted to freshwater fisheries and habitat conservation. Includes links to information on the relationship between environmental quality and fishery health.

CHAPTER FOCUS QUESTIONS

- What economic and ecological principles relate to forest management?
- How can we best implement sustainable-forestry policies?
- What is the extent of global water scarcity, and what economic incentives encourage water management?

CHAPTER

# 15

# Ecosystem Management: Forest and Water Systems

## The Economics of Forest Management

Forests, like fisheries, are primarily biological systems. When we exploit them for human use, both ecological and economic analyses can help us understand principles of effective management. Just as with fisheries, natural growth rate is fundamental in forest ecology and provides a link between ecological and economic analyses. An important factor in forest management policy is the cumulative nature of forest growth: biomass accumulated years, decades, or even centuries ago will still remain available for use if left undisturbed. Thus choices about time of harvesting are important in forest management.

If we measure the volume of standing timber in a forest over time, we obtain a **logistic curve** similar to that for the growth of a fishery (Figure 15-1). However, the logic of harvesting is somewhat different. From an economic point of view, we can see a standing forest as an **asset,** or **stock,** that can also yield a **flow** of **use value** to humans. If a forest is privately owned, the owner will balance the asset value against the stream of income available from use. A simplified example will demonstrate the economic principle involved.

Consider a forest with 100,000 tons of standing timber, and a growth rate of 5,000 tons additional biomass per year. At a price of $100 per ton, the value of the forest if it is **clear-cut** (logged all at one time) is $10 million. A policy of sustainable management, in which the annual harvest is no more than the annual growth, would yield $500,000 per year.

Volume of Wood

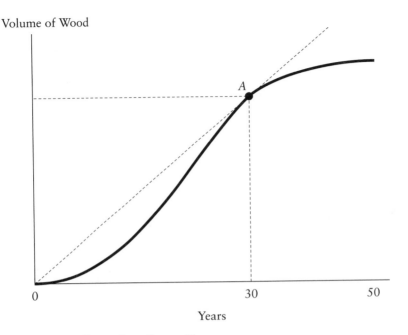

0                                30              50

Years

**FIGURE 15-1** *Forest Growth over Time*

Which is economically preferable? It depends on the **discount rate.** At 4 percent, the present value ($PV$) of the sustainable yield alternative is

$$PV = \$500,000/.04 = \$12.5 \text{ million.}$$

At 6 percent it is

$$PV = \$500,000/.06 = \$8.33 \text{ million.}$$

Comparing these figures with the $10 million present value of an immediate clear-cut, we find that at the lower discount rate, sustainable management is economically preferable, but at the higher rate the owner will do better with a clear-cut.

From the owner's point of view, the clear-cut revenue of $10 million can be invested at 6 percent to give $600,000 per year, a more lucrative option than the $500,000 from sustainable management. Thus a financial variable, the commercial rate of interest, will dominate private forest management policy. Forests with a growth rate below the going rate of interest are destined to be harvested as fast as possible. U.S. corporate forest management frequently applies this logic, especially when forest owners have high-interest debt to pay off.

This simple example fails to consider forest replanting and regrowth. We can apply a more sophisticated version to determine economically optimum harvesting periods (years from planting to cutting in plantation forestry).

Consider a forest's biological growth pattern. Figure 15-1 shows that a young forest grows more rapidly than a mature forest. The **mean annual increment (MAI),** or average growth rate, is obtained by dividing the total **biomass,** or weight of timber, by the age of the forest. Graphically, the MAI at any point on the growth curve is defined by the slope of a straight line from the origin to that point. The maximum MAI occurs where a line from the origin is exactly tangent to the curve (point *A* in Figure 15-1).

One possible rule for harvesting would be to cut at a period that maximized the MAI (30 years in Figure 15-1). This would result in the highest total volume of timber and highest average annual revenues over time, assuming a constant price for timber.

To find an economic optimum, however, we must consider two other factors. One is the cost of harvesting—the labor, machinery, and energy required to cut the timber and transport it to market. The other important factor, as our earlier example showed, is the discount rate. Both revenues and costs must be discounted to calculate the present value of various harvesting policies.

The economic optimum can be determined by comparing total revenue to total cost for different possible harvesting periods (Figure 15-2), then discounting this figure to obtain the present value of expected future profits (Figure 15-3). Total revenue (*TR*) is equal to the volume of timber harvested multiplied by its price. The shape of the *TR* curve therefore resembles that of the logistic curve in Figure 15-1. Total costs (*TC*) include planting and harvesting costs, with harvesting costs rising proportionately to the volume of timber. Total revenue minus total cost indicates the profit from harvesting at some future point. Profits expected at a future time must be discounted to calculate their present value. The point at which the discounted value of (*TR*–*TC*) is maximized gives

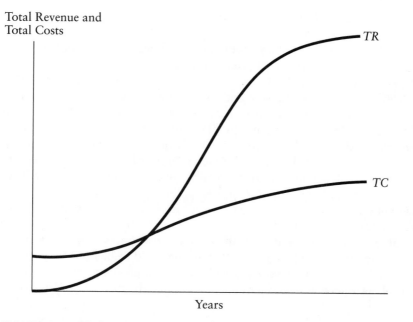

**FIGURE 15-2** *Timber Revenues and Costs over Time*

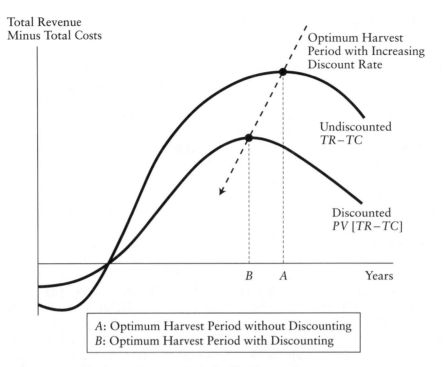

Total Revenue Minus Total Costs

Optimum Harvest Period with Increasing Discount Rate

Undiscounted *TR–TC*

Discounted *PV [TR–TC]*

B   A   Years

A: Optimum Harvest Period without Discounting
B: Optimum Harvest Period with Discounting

**FIGURE 15-3** *Optimum Harvest Period with Discounting*

the **optimum rotation period** for harvesting, from the point of view of economic profitability.[1]

At higher discount rates, the present value of expected future income shrinks. Thus the higher the discount rate, the shorter will be the optimum harvesting period. Figure 15-3 shows undiscounted *TR–TC* and the present value of discounted *TR–TC*. The discounted *PV[TR–TC]* curve is lower, and its maximum occurs at an earlier year. As discount rates rise, the optimum rotation period shortens, as indicated by the arrow.

This principle helps to explain why plantation forestry is generally based on fast-growing softwood trees. Slower-growing hardwoods or mixed forest might be profitable over the long term, but at a commercial rate of discount the present value of slower-growing trees will be too low to be attractive to timber companies. The determination of commercial interest rates depends on financial factors unrelated to ecological systems—but interest rates can have significant impact on ecosystem management.

This economic logic also helps explain pressure on old-growth forests. Standing forests that may have taken hundreds of years to grow represent an economic asset that can be harvested for immediate profit. Replantings tend to be in faster-growing species. Although replanting an entire forest with a single fast-growing species represents a significant ecological loss, commercially speaking it may be the most profitable option.

---

[1]For a more detailed treatment of the economics of timber harvesting and optimal rotation periods, see Hartwick and Olewiler, 1998, Chapter 10.

The principles of commercial forest management can often conflict with ecological goals. Although it may be possible to internalize some of the social costs and benefits related to forest management, for vast areas of privately owned or open-access forest, market profitability is the only management principle. This has led to serious problems of forest and biodiversity loss throughout the world.

## Forest Loss and Biodiversity

Human activity has reduced forest area in some cases and increased it in others, as well as changing forest biodiversity. Worldwide, about two-thirds of tropical deforestation results from slash-and-burn agricultural techniques rather than directly from timbering. However, opening up forest areas with logging roads often allows access and encourages destructive agricultural techniques. In Asia and parts of Latin America, logging is directly responsible for half or more of the forest area lost.[2]

As human populations have increased, a typical pattern has been to cut down old-growth forests and replace them with planted and second-growth forests. This gives rise to a U-shaped curve showing the change in total forested area as population densities increase (Figure 15-4). Most tropical areas of the world remain on the downward-sloping portion of this curve, suffering net forest loss. Many temperate zones have a stable or increasing forest area, having eliminated much of their natural forest and replaced it with planted forest.[3]

Losses of tropical forest have been severe over the past several decades. Estimates of forest loss range from 50,000 $km^2$ to 170,000 $km^2$ per year. From 1980 to 1995, Africa and Latin America lost about 10 percent of their forests, while Asia and Oceania lost more than 6 percent.[4]

Even in areas where forest area is stable or increasing, the threat to biodiversity from economic uses of forests may still be great. Cultivated forests tend to be **monocultures**— huge stands planted with a single species selected for maximum economic return. Such artificial forests displace natural forests, which provide habitat for many more species. Over a long period of time it is possible to regenerate diverse forests, but economic incentives to manage forests for diversity are often lacking.

The maximum sustainable yield principle may not be enough to achieve ecosystem sustainability. Forest managers can maintain sustainable yield merely by replanting all logged areas with a single species of fast-growing tree. This offers sustainable flows of timber and income for the forest owner but destroys the original complexity of the forest ecosystem to the detriment of many animals and plants that thrive in a multispecies forest.

Ecologist C. S. Holling has identified the principle of **resilience** as central to ecosystem sustainability.[5] Resilience is a "bounce-back" capacity—the ability of an ecosystem to recover from disruption (for example, a forest fire or pest infestation). In general, complex ecosystems display more resilience than simple systems. If a plantation forest

---

[2]United Nations Environmental Programme (UNEP) 1999, p. 38.

[3]Myers, 1996, surveys the state of world forests.

[4]World Resources Institute 2000, pp. 90–91.

[5]See Holling, 1986; Common and Perrings, 1992.

Proportion of
Land under Trees

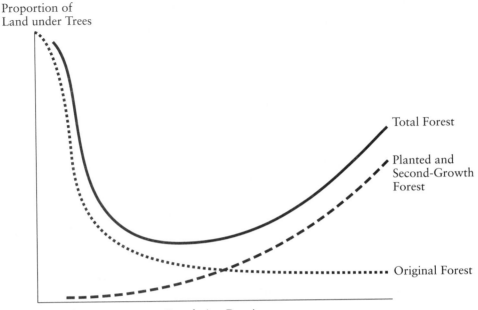

Population Density

**FIGURE 15-4** *Deforestation and Tree Cover*

contains only one species of tree, an attack by a single pest may destroy the entire forest. A forest with many species is much more likely to withstand pest attacks. The proportion of species within the forest may change, but its ecological integrity and health will survive.

Species extinction has accelerated in the past decades, and loss of **biodiversity** is likely to be one of the most critical environmental problems of the coming century (see Box 15-1).[6] Biological diversity can be viewed economically as a significant positive externality associated with preservation of existing forests and ecosystems—or as a negative externality associated with their loss. These externalities are not reflected in the commercial exploitation of forests for timber. We must account for them, however, in any policy for sustainable forest management.

## Economic and Demographic Pressures on Forests

Economic forces that promote forest destruction include a steadily increasing global market for wood products, leading to declining forest area or conversion to ecologically less-desirable plantation forestry. Rising demand alone, however, does not fully explain forest destruction. Overexploitation is often the result of **institutional failure.** Many governments either allow open access to forests, or encourage **under-pricing** of forest resources by selling logging rights well below their market value.[7]

---

[6]See Wilson, 1988 and 1992; Ehrlich and Daily, 1993.

[7]See Panayotou, 1993, Chapter 3, for a discussion of policy failures in forest management.

## 15-1   Loss of Biodiversity

**W**hy does biodiversity matter? Loss of a single species of beetle may never be noticed and seems to have no economic impact. But any species may have vital pharmaceutical or medical value, and cumulatively the existence of many species promotes crucial ecosystem resilience. In 1990, a compound derived from twigs and leaves from a tree in the Malaysian rainforest was found to stop the spread of one of the two strains of HIV that causes AIDS. But when researchers returned for more

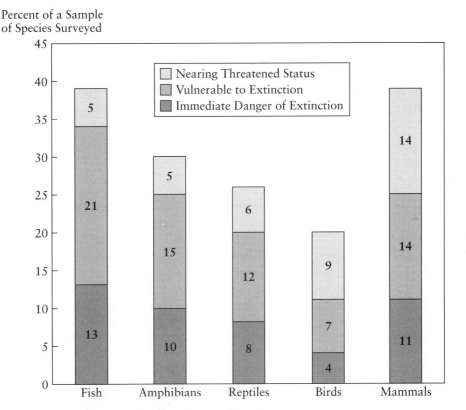

**FIGURE 15-5** *Threatened and Endangered Species*

Source: World Conservation Union, *IUCN Red List of Threatened Animals*, 1996. Adapted from Tuxill, 1998.

*(continued on following page)*

samples, they found that the stand of trees had been felled, and no other trees in the vicinity yielded the crucial ingredient.[1]

In addition to possible medical and commercial losses, the loss of even a single species can alter the balance of an ecosystem, causing ripple effects on other species and on ecosystem resilience. Our knowledge of the world's biodiversity, and of scale of biodiversity losses, is limited.

> Perhaps the biggest unknown in the debate over mass extinctions is how many species exist. Scientists know that the 1.4 million named species represent a small portion of existing wildlife, though estimates of the total vary from 10 million to 100 million. Because species density is highest in tropical forests, every large swath that falls or burns is likely to contain beetles, plants, fungi, insects or animals that could vanish before ever coming to human notice.[2]

An extensive review of worldwide animal species conservation by the International Union for the Conservation of Nature (IUCN) led to the publication of the *1996 Red List* of threatened and endangered species. This study concluded that about 10 percent of birds and 25 percent of mammals face threat of extinction. While the survey covers only a fifth of reptile species, an eighth of amphibians, and a tenth of fish, 20 percent of the reptiles and amphibians surveyed and more than 33 percent of the fishes surveyed were considered threatened (Figure 15-5).[3]

---

[1]Scott Allen, "Loss of a tree means loss of an HIV blocker," *Boston Globe,* November 10, 1992.
[2]*New York Times,* June 2, 1998, E7.
[3]Tuxill, 1998.

---

In some cases, local communities have traditionally managed forests in a sustainable manner—until they lose control over the resource to governments and logging companies. Governments often grant logging concessions and sometimes monopolies to timber companies. They have also encouraged large agricultural firms to encroach on the forest for extensive cattle ranching, as in Brazil and Central America, or for cash-crop cultivation of coffee, tobacco, and other export crops, as in Indonesia, other Asian countries, and Latin America.

Demographic pressure also contributes to forest loss. Governments have encouraged settlements in formerly undisturbed forest areas as a means of accommodating population growth. These new settlers often lack knowledge of forest management, and their practices of exploitation and agricultural encroachment may have deep and lasting ecological impact.[8] Although poor policies are usually more to blame for forest loss than simple population pressure (Box 15-2), rising global population has been accompanied by a general trend of decline in forested area over a long period (Figure 15-6).

---

[8]See Abramovitz, 1998, for many specific examples of destructive government forest policies.

## 15-2    Institutional Failures in Forest Management

"Much forest exploitation and conversion is encouraged and subsidized by governments. In both developed and developing countries, these policies result in forests being sold at prices far below what the timber alone is worth. In Belize, a Malaysian logging firm paid about $1 a hectare for timber rights. Indonesia's give-away timber concessions cost the government $2.5 billion in lost revenues in 1990 alone. In the United States, timber sales from national forests lost over $1 billion from 1992 to 1994. . . . Subsidies for below-cost logging, processing, roads, and infrastructure are so large that governments are essentially paying private interests to take the timber and convert the land to other uses.

"Globalization and the lowering of barriers to international trade and invest-ment allow corporations to roam the world seeking more profitable forest opportu-nities. Legal international trade in forest products has almost tripled since 1970. Meanwhile, illegal and unrecorded trade has likely expanded far faster, encouraged by lax enforcement of domestic forest laws and gaps in international ones. The Brazilian government, for example, estimates that 80 percent of the timber harvest in the Amazon violates the law.

"As some Asian nations have depleted their forest resources, they have turned elsewhere to satisfy their domestic consumption needs and the demands of their forest industries. Companies that have grown wealthy from domestic timber ex-ploitation are using their capital to expand elsewhere. . . . One Malaysian company controls 60–85 percent of the logging concessions in Papua, New Guinea. In 1996, the area of Amazon forest under concession to Asian timber companies quadrupled to more than 12 million hectares.

"Few forest communities have been successful in gaining recognition for their customary rights. Their right of occupancy has been banned in some cases, and disregarded in others. . . . In Brazil and Venezuela, hard-won indigenous reserves have been invaded by miners, loggers, and settlers. In Indonesia, the government created a real-life **tragedy of the commons** when it declared in 1967 that it had sole jurisdiction over the nation's forests. Customary rights to common areas, which had evolved as a complex and sustainable management system over many generations, were not legally recognized. The government . . . was unable to police the nation's vast forests, and the communities who are in the forest no longer had the power to stop exploitation by outsiders. One analysis concluded that "the tra-ditional rights of millions of people have been handed over to a relatively small number of commercial firms and state enterprises."

### SOURCE

Adapted from Janet N. Abramovitz, *Taking a Stand: Cultivating a New Relationship with the World's Forests,* Worldwatch Paper no. 140, ©1998. Reprinted with permission of Worldwatch Institute. www.worldwatch.org.

Billion Acres                                                                      Billion Persons

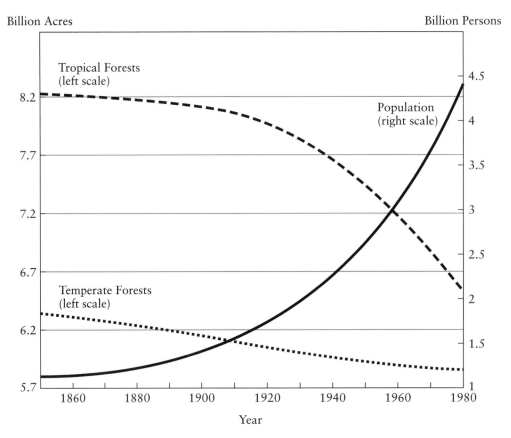

Year

**FIGURE 15-6** *Long-Term Deforestation and Population Growth*
Sources: World Resources Institute, 1987, p. 272; United Nations, 2001.

## Policies for Sustainable Forest Management

Both economic and ecological theory can offer guidance in devising better approaches to forest management. Better policy approaches can be implemented both on the supply side, by promoting sustainable forestry, and on the demand side, by changing consumption patterns, reducing wastes and expanding recycling.

### Supply Side: Property Rights and Pricing Policies

A major issue in forest management throughout the developing world is the need for secure **property rights.** Individuals and communities whose land tenure is insecure, including many migrants, have little incentive to conserve forests. Economic necessity forces them to exploit the forest for maximum short-term gain and then move on. If granted secure tenure, they will have an interest in a continuing flow of income from the forest, including forest products other than timber, such as fruits, latex (from rubber-tapping), or shade-grown coffee.[9]

Stable communities also have incentives to maintain forests in order to enjoy their accompanying positive externalities. A village or community situated in the mountains, for example, may undertake a program of reforestation both to sustain the supply of wood and also because trees retain soils on the slopes, preventing erosion. Forested ecosystems also help to provide a stable supply of fresh water and prevent flooding.

Some positive externalities associated with forest maintenance or reforestation are global in nature. Forests remove and store atmospheric carbon, reducing the concentration of carbon dioxide in the atmosphere and lowering the risks of global climate change. This may bring no immediate benefit to the local community, but future global climate change agreements may well provide compensation to nations that preserve or expand their forest cover.[10] In the future, a country might be able to earn income from its forests by keeping them in place rather than by cutting them down for timber export. The carbon storage function of tropical forests has been estimated at $3.7 trillion, assuming a carbon storage value of $20 per ton (see Box 15-3).[11]

Another critical issue is **full pricing** of forest concessions. Government policies of low-cost sales of timber constitute **subsidies** to major logging corporations, as well as an inducement to corrupt practices such as payoffs to government officials for valuable concessions. The many negative externalities of overexploiting forests make this a particularly inappropriate use of a subsidy, which should be used only where clear positive externalities exist.[12]

Economic theory supports secure property rights and full pricing of resources. The ecological perspective adds another important dimension to forest management issues: Forests must be recognized as complex ecosystems to be managed as such, both to preserve healthy ecosystems and to supply a wide array of goods and services for current and future generations. These ecological goals often differ from the priorities of private landowners, who seek to manage the forest for profitability, often selecting fast-growing species and cutting timber on a short cycle rather the longer, natural cycle that allows a mature forest to develop.

Government policy can encourage sound forest management by such measures as tax breaks for sustainable forestry or limitations on clear-cutting. From an economic-theory perspective, the positive externalities associated with good forest management justify such policies. Programs have also begun for **certification** of sustainably produced wood so that consumers and public agencies can encourage sound practices by their

---

[9]Shade-grown coffee leaves forest trees standing, with coffee bushes beneath, whereas sun-grown coffee requires complete removal of forest cover.

[10]Under the Kyoto Protocol, which was negotiated in December 1997 and which entered into force in February 2004, nations committed to reducing their greenhouse gas emissions must include in their calculations the changes to their carbon stock resulting from "afforestation, deforestation, and reforestation." See discussion in Chapter 18.

[11]See Myers, 1996.

[12]See Panayotou, 1998, pp. 78–79, on policies for fully pricing forest concessions.

## 15-3   Forest Carbon Storage Valuation in Zimbabwe

One of the many benefits of forests is that trees and other plants store carbon dioxide in their tissue, called carbon sequestration. Net increases in plant biomass generally increase carbon storage, essentially removing $CO_2$ from the earth's atmosphere. As discussed in Chapter 18, $CO_2$ is an important greenhouse gas that influences the global climate. Thus, efforts to increase forest cover or prevent forest loss provide a positive externality by tempering climate change.

One of the reasons for overexploitation of forests is that positive externality values are not reflected in market transactions. Estimates of these values can be used to support efforts to preserve forests. A 2000 article in the journal *Ecological Economics* (Kundhlande et al., 2000) provides estimates of the carbon sequestration benefits for the savanna region of Zimbabwe.

The authors use a value of $25 per ton for the benefits of carbon sequestration. Future benefits are discounted at a rate of 5 percent annually. The present value of carbon sequestration is estimated to be around $300 per hectare. This value is significant, but less than the potential agricultural value of land, which is about $600 per hectare. Thus, based on carbon storage benefits alone, policies to prevent the conversion of forests to agricultural land are not economically justified. In combination with other forest values, however, carbon storage values might alter the economic logic of forest conversion.

A study of forest management in Australia (Creedy and Wurzbacher, 2001) indicates that inclusion of carbon storage values increases the optimal rotation period for harvesting, and including other ecological values of the forest may increase it to infinity (meaning it would be economically optimal to conserve the forest indefinitely).

A complete accounting of forest benefits may indicate that forest preservation is justified but, as we saw in Chapter 6, obtaining valid estimates of all values may be difficult. Forest policies based solely on market behavior "fail to fully account for the numerous functions and values that are not captured through market transactions. Forest use decisions that ignore those benefits that are not normally exchanged in markets introduce distortions in resource allocation, often with detrimental environmental consequences" (Kundhlande et al., 2000).

### SOURCES

Creedy, J., and A. D. Wurzbacher. "The Economic Value of a Forested Catchment with Timber, Water, and Carbon Sequestration Benefits." *Ecological Economics* 38 (2001): 71–83.

Kundhlande, G., W. L. Adamowicz, and I. Mapaure. "Valuing Ecological Services in a Savanna Ecosystem: A Case Study from Zimbabwe." *Ecological Economics* 33 (2000): 401–412.

purchasing choices. Experience shows that many consumers are willing to pay a premium above market price for sustainably produced wood. In 2002, the Forest Stewardship Council (FSC) identified 27 million acres of certified forest worldwide—although only 3.6 million acres were in developing nations.[13]

In cases where complex and old-growth forest ecosystems can only be effectively protected through preservation as parkland, government or private conservation agencies can acquire them as **public goods.** In many developing nations buffer zones around parkland allow local communities to pursue sustainable exploitation of forest products. This can overcome local hostility to parks on the part of villagers who resent the loss of access to forest resources.

Often a key factor is the availability of credit on reasonable terms to villagers who invest in replanting and **agroforestry** (mixing tree crops with food crops). As we have seen, a high interest rate encourages a short planning horizon, and low-cost credit can encourage profitable investment in long-term resource conservation.

## Demand Side: Changing Consumption Patterns

As we have noted, overall demand for wood products has risen steadily. The increase in paper consumption has been especially rapid (Figure 15-7). Like other forms of consumption, paper consumption is unequally distributed: U.S. paper use is 341 kilograms per person per year, while in Germany per capita consumption is 200 kilograms, in Brazil 35 kilograms, and in India only 4 kilograms.

> If everyone in the world consumed as much as the average American, the world would be using nearly seven times as much paper. And by 2050 it would be 11 times as much. If, on the other hand, paper use stabilized at today's global average—50 kilograms a year per person—paper consumption in 2050 could be held to 1.7 times today's level.[14]

Expanded recycling of paper and other wood products has significant potential to reduce pressure on forests. Worldwide, 43 percent of wastepaper is now recycled. Developing countries such as India typically recover and reuse many paper products and often import and recycle scrap paper from industrialized nations.

Low prices for paper and other wood products serve both as an incentive for greater consumption and a disincentive to expanded recycling. In some cases, direct and indirect subsidies for forest exploitation encourage use of virgin rather than recycled paper. Internalizing environmental externalities into prices would encourage greater efficiency at all stages of the production cycle. Properly pricing wood products would increase prices for nonrecycled paper and all one-time-use wood products relative to recycled-materials prices, thereby encouraging a higher recycling rate.[15]

---

[13]World Resources Institute, 2003.

[14]Abramovitz, 1998.

[15]Data on paper consumption and recycling from Abramovitz, 1998; Abramovitz and Mattoon, 1999. For more on paper recycling, see Chapter 17.

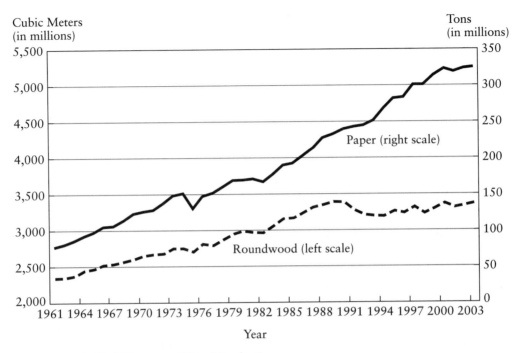

**FIGURE 15-7** *World Paper and Wood Production*

Source: Worldwatch Institute, *Signposts 2004*; FAO, FAOSTAT database 2004.

## Water: Depletion and Renewal

Water, because it can be reused indefinitely if not severely polluted, can be characterized as a renewable resource. Water is continually transferred between the atmosphere, rivers, lakes, and the oceans in a process known as the **water cycle** (Figure 15-8). But stocks of water such as underground aquifers are also depletable resources. Some aquifers have such long replenishment times as to be essentially nonrenewable on a human time-scale.[16] Thus analysis of water systems combines elements of renewable- and nonrenewable-resource theory. Water also has a unique and essential ecological function.

Many of the principles of renewable-resource management apply to water systems, but water availability is subject to absolute limits. Although water is reusable, the amount available in a given region is limited to the total **freshwater runoff,** of which only about a third is **stable supply.**

Each year, evaporation fueled by the sun's energy lifts 500,000 cubic kilometers of moisture into the atmosphere each year—86 percent from the oceans and 14 percent from the land. An

---

[16]Aquifers under the Sahara, for example, are thousands of years old and are sometimes referred to as "fossil water."

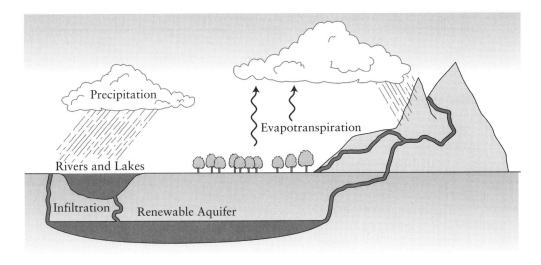

**FIGURE 15-8** *The Water Cycle*

equal amount falls back to earth as rain, sleet, or snow, but it is distributed in different proportions: whereas the continents lose about 70,000 cubic kilometers through evaporation, they gain 110,000 through precipitation. As a result, roughly 40,000 cubic kilometers are transferred from the sea to the land each year. . . . Two-thirds runs off in floods, leaving about 14,000 cubic kilometers as a relatively stable source of supply.[17]

This stable supply is about 7,000 cubic meters per person, but it is unevenly distributed. Some areas are **water-abundant,** and others are **water-scarce.** Hydrologists[18] have established that, considering the water needs of modern societies, a threshold of 2,000 cubic meters per person per year represents the level above which a population can be sustained comfortably by the water available. Between 1,000 and 2,000 cubic meters per person, the situation is "water-stressed," below 1,000, "water-scarce," where "lack of water becomes a severe constraint on food production, economic development and protection of natural systems."[19]

Table 15-1 lists countries already experiencing water stress or scarcity. Considering that the developing countries on this list will continue to experience rapid population growth over the next half-century (with some projected to double in population) the water problem is likely to worsen in the coming decades.[20]

---

[17]Postel, 1992, p. 27.

[18]Hydrology is the scientific study of water's distribution and movement on the earth's surface, underground, and in the atmosphere.

[19]Postel, 1992, p. 29. See also Falkenmark and Widstrand, 1992.

[20]For an extensive recent analysis of the world's water resources, see Gleick, 2000.

**TABLE 15-1** *Water-Scarce and Water-Stressed Countries*

| | Water-scarce countries (renewable water supply per capita < 1,000 cubic meters) | | Water-stressed countries (renewable water supply per capita < 2,000 cubic meters) | |
|---|---|---|---|---|
| Sub-Saharan Africa | Kenya | 947 | Burkina Faso | 1024 |
| | Rwanda | 638 | Eritrea | 1577 |
| | | | Ethiopia | 1666 |
| | | | Lesotho | 1456 |
| | | | Malawi | 1461 |
| | | | Somalia | 1413 |
| | | | South Africa | 1131 |
| | | | Sudan | 1981 |
| | | | Zimbabwe | 1530 |
| Middle East & North Africa | Algeria | 460 | Iran | 1900 |
| | Egypt | 830 | Morocco | 936 |
| | Israel | 265 | Syria | 1541 |
| | Jordan | 169 | | |
| | Kuwait | 10 | | |
| | Libya | 108 | | |
| | Saudi Arabia | 111 | | |
| | Tunisia | 577 | | |
| Europe | | | Belgium | 1781 |
| | | | Czech Republic | 1283 |
| | | | Germany | 1878 |
| | | | Poland | 1598 |
| Asia | | | China | 2186* |
| | | | India | 1822 |
| | | | S. Korea | 1471 |
| | | | Uzbekistan | 1968 |

*China, at 2,186 cubic meters per capita, falls just above the water-stress benchmark, but distribution of water resources within China is uneven, and areas in North China suffer severe water stress.

Source: World Resources Institute, 2003.

## Increasing Supply: Aquifers and Dams

The two sides to the water-population equation are supply and demand. We can respond to scarcity by either increasing supply or decreasing demand. Past water management policies generally oriented toward increasing supply; systematic conservation policies have only recently begun to attract attention.

Many countries and regions that face water scarcity problems rely on water from underground aquifers. Aquifers are replenished or **recharged** by rainfall, but in most

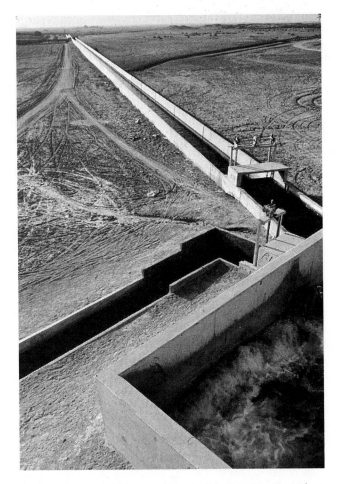

*An irrigation and drainage system in Saudi Arabia. Agriculture in water-scarce countries is heavily dependent on irrigation.*

cases use rates greatly exceed recharge rates. Countries such as Saudi Arabia and Libya are relying on "fossil" groundwater from ancient aquifers in desert areas that have practically no recharge and are likely to be exhausted in the next 40 to 60 years.

Almost all major water-scarce areas of the world suffer from **groundwater overdraft**—withdrawal of water exceeding aquifer recharge capacity, resulting in declining water tables. In the western United States, the Ogallala aquifer is severely depleted, and irrigated area has started to shrink. Similar problems affect aquifers in North China, India, Pakistan, Mexico, and many other countries.

Another way of increasing water supply is damming surface flows. Dams can capture floodwater that would otherwise be unavailable for human use, as well as providing

## 15-4    Water Scarcity, Pollution , and Politics in Mexico

In Mexico, a growing population struggles to cope with problems of scarce and polluted water supplies. About 15 million Mexicans, or 16 percent of the population, have no access to drinking water services. In rural areas of Mexico only 52 percent of the people have access to drinking water services.

While local water shortages do exist in some arid regions of Mexico, the more prominent problems concern water quality and politics. Nearly every river and stream in Mexico is polluted, and 73 percent of the nation's water supply, including both surface and ground water, is contaminated. The health costs of drinking water contamination in Mexico have been estimated at $3.6 billion annually. While Mexico needs to build more water treatment plants, it does not even have the money to maintain existing plants. None of the 13 treatment plants in Chiapas State are operating because of a lack of money to perform necessary repairs.

The aquifer that supplies Mexico City is nearly depleted, and water is pumped nearly a mile uphill, from as much as 125 miles away. Enough water leaks annually from cracks in supply pipes to provide for the water needs of Los Angeles. Ground water pumping in Mexico City is lowering its underground aquifer by as much as 11 feet per year, causing streets and buildings to bend and sink.

Water is a powerful political issue in Mexico. Allocation of water has been based on political alliances, and water supply can be cut off to punish political opponents. The 2000 presidential election of Vincente Fox, ending over 70 years of rule by the Institutional Revolutionary Party (PRI), was partly a result of his promise to increase water supplies. One possibility for funding improvements in drinking water supplies is to reduce implicit and explicit government subsidies—water subsidies comprise over 1 percent of the federal budget. Large mining, ranching, and farming businesses, who consume at least 70 percent of the nation's water, currently obtain water for free; a proposed law would start charging these companies for water.

A solution to Mexico's water problems will require institutional and market reforms. For many years in Mexico, water, like power, has flowed toward the wealthy. Proposed reforms include increased private sector involvement in providing water. A movement is also underway to decentralize water management and increase public participation in decisions regarding water issues.

### SOURCES

Hazin, Lilian Saade. "Toward More Efficient Urban Water Management in Mexico" (2001). Available at http://www.gdrc.org/uem/water/mexsaade.htm.
Weiner, Tim. "Mexico Grows Parched, with Pollution and Politics," *New York Times*, April 14, 2001.

hydroelectric power. Worldwide, 40,000 large dams and about 800,000 small dams are now in operation.[21] More dams are being built, but the best sites are already in use. Existing dams often suffer problems of siltation, and new large dam proposals have been criticized for the environmental and social damage resulting from the flooding of large areas.[22]

Given the vast amounts of seawater on the planet, **desalination** has appeal as a potential source of virtually unlimited supply. Here, however, cost is a significant barrier. Desalination is expensive: one to two dollars per cubic meter, four to eight times average urban water costs and ten to twenty times the current cost of water for agricultural use. Although desalination is an important source of supply in some arid regions, it is likely to provide only a small proportion of global freshwater supply.[23]

## Demand: Always More Water?

The three major sectors of water use are agricultural, industrial, and domestic use. Agriculture is by far the biggest consumer of water, accounting for two-thirds of freshwater demand worldwide. Although 83 percent of the world's cropland is rain-fed, the 17 percent that requires irrigation produces more than 40 percent of the world's food supply.[24] Arid and semi-arid countries, most of which are in the developing world, rely heavily on irrigation for food production.

Irrigation is thus a cornerstone of global food security. However, current irrigation demands are pressing against or exceeding water supply limits in many areas, and the rate of expansion of irrigated land—a key factor in agricultural output growth—has slowed significantly.

Industrial demand has also grown rapidly in the developing world. Many industries in the early phases of economic development are water-intensive. Urbanization and improvement of standards of living have promoted increased domestic water demand. Between 1900 and 2000, freshwater consumption rose over sixfold, more than double the rate of population growth (see Figure 15-9).[25] In future, the combined growth of urban, industrial, and agricultural demand will clearly increase water demand significantly, especially in the developing world. In countries such as China and Mexico, widespread water pollution from agricultural and industrial uses greatly increases the problem of providing adequate water supplies for growing populations (see Box 15-4).

---

[21]Postel, 1999, p. 81.

[22]See World Commission on Dams, 2000.

[23]Postel, 1992, pp. 45–46; Gleick, 2000, Chapter 5.

[24]Postel, 1999, p. 42.

[25]UNEP, 1999, p. 4.

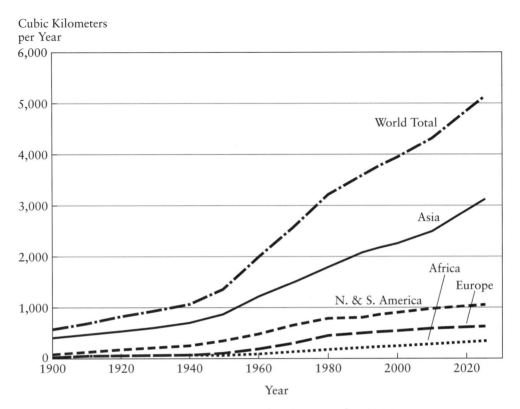

Cubic Kilometers per Year

**FIGURE 15-9** *Global Water Demand, Historical and Projected to 2025*
Source: Gleick, 2000, pp. 50–53.

## Policies for Sustainable Water Management

We can alter the current trend of ever-increasing water demand through policies to increase water use efficiency. Whereas traditional irrigation by flooding or channeling water by gravity is inefficient (60 percent of the water is lost by evaporation or infiltration), new techniques of **microirrigation** by drip systems allow an efficiency of 95 percent.[26] Recycling and reuse of wastewater can reduce water demand in many industries. Leak detection and repair, as well as efficient appliances, can help improve urban and domestic water efficiency.

The most important way to induce more efficient water use is through appropriate water pricing. Prices should serve as indicators of economic scarcity, reflecting physical limits and environmental externalities. For various social and political reasons however, governments have maintained low water prices, particularly for agricultural supply.

---

[26]Postel, 1992, p. 104.

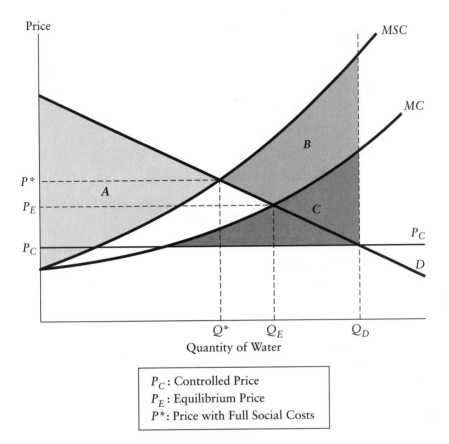

**FIGURE 15-10** *Effects of Subsidized Water Pricing*

Governments often build, maintain, and operate irrigation systems with public funds and then charge prices well below actual cost. These policies of subsidizing water have created an artificial climate of water abundance—even in arid areas like the western part of the United States—that has favored wasteful and inefficient water use. Setting prices closer to the real cost of supplying water would encourage farmers to shift to more efficient methods of irrigation, as well as giving city dwellers and manufacturers an incentive to conserve, recycle, and reuse their supplies.

Figure 15-10 shows how pricing policies affect water supply and demand. The figure shows total water demand (*D*) together with the marginal cost of supplying water (*MC*). In addition, the full marginal social cost (*MSC*) is shown, taking into account such factors as damage to ecosystems or depletion of aquifers. It is reasonable to assume that these costs increase with larger water withdrawals.

Setting a water price ($P_C$) below true marginal cost leads to an excessive demand of $Q_D$. This can create problems. Because quantity demanded exceeds quantity supplied, some form of government allocation or rationing will be required. But the government will also feel pressure to subsidize the supply of water. In this example, an increase in supply to $Q_D$ would require a government subsidy equal to area $C$. Significant net social loss due to external or user costs may also be associated with excessive water consumption, as shown by area $B$.

Full marginal-cost pricing would lead to an equilibrium at the lower supply level of $Q_E$, with a price of $P_E$. If we include full social costs, the price would be $P^*$, with quantity consumed of $Q^*$. This would be the best solution, leading to a net social benefit equal to area $A$, and avoiding the external costs $B$ and subsidy payment $C$. This pricing policy would promote economic efficiency as well as internalization of environmental costs. Political pressures for a lower water price, however, are likely to make this full-pricing policy difficult to implement.[27]

Government policy can also promote the development of water markets. Establishing clear rules regarding water rights will facilitate a water trading system through which a market price for water can be established. This can promote both conservation and further development of water resources. Possible drawbacks to such a system include encouraging excessive withdrawals from rivers and groundwater, and placing insufficient value on in-stream uses of water, including recreational and ecological functions. In addition, water rights systems raise significant issues of equity, because more affluent users can bid water away from lower-income farmers or domestic consumers.

## Conclusion: Reconciling Economic and Ecological Principles

A general conclusion from the basic economic theory of renewable resource management is that *economically* efficient use of natural resources, although generally more sustainable than open-access exploitation, is not necessarily sustainable from an *ecological* perspective. An important goal of natural resource management, therefore, must be to reconcile the differing principles of economics and ecology.

As we have noted, ecological sustainability has dimensions not reflected in the economic analyses of resource use. Whereas economic sustainability is concerned primarily with sustaining a flow of income over time, ecological sustainability depends on resilience—the "bounce-back" capacity of ecosystems affected by economic exploitation or by natural phenomena such as disease or weather extremes. Resilience depends on **ecological complexity,** an essential element of sustainable natural systems. Economic harvesting with maximum profit in mind often destroys complexity.

A key determinant of natural resource management is technology. We saw in Chapter 14 that as fishing technologies become more "productive" in an economic sense, fisheries are more likely to be overexploited. Technological progress accelerates economic growth, but relatively slow-growing natural resource systems come under greater pressure from the demands of economic "efficiency."

Similarly, old-growth forests are doomed to clear-cutting in a forestry regime that places a premium on rapid growth and shorter harvesting periods, and that can bring to bear powerful equipment for timber removal. Total forested area may not decline,

---

[27]Panayotou, 1998, pp. 165–168, provides examples of the role of pricing in water resource management. Seidenstat et al., 2002, offer a selection of global case studies in efficient water management policies.

but natural forest will be replaced with ecologically less diverse second-growth forest, or with fast-growing plantation monocultures. In rapidly growing developing economies, many natural resource systems, traditionally harvested in a relatively sustainable manner, come under much heavier pressure as a market logic prevails and modern technology penetrates remote areas.

On the other hand, technologies such as paper recycling and efficient irrigation have great potential for conservation of scarce resources. Given the proper incentives, ecologically friendly technology can promote less wasteful resource use, recycling, and more efficient consumption.

A related issue is **social sustainability.** Indigenous communities dependent on forest products are threatened by more intensive, "modernized" methods of forest exploitation. Local fishing communities have often been devastated by economically more productive trawlers that push fish stocks to collapse. Social sustainability and resource sustainability are mutually dependent.

Policies for natural resource management must also consider continuing growth in overall demand. We have seen how growing demand has increased the impact of market failures in fisheries, forests, and water systems. Although policies aimed at increasing economic efficiency can improve resource management at the *micro*economic level, they can also increase overall stress on natural systems at the *macro*economic level. More efficient resource use requires less resource input per unit of consumption, but may also encourage expanded consumption by lowering prices.

An **ecosystems management** model stressing the ecological integrity of fisheries, forests, and water systems may provide more appropriate policy guidance. In such a model, economic efficiency principles can be extremely important, as reflected in the need for secure land tenure institutions, suitable price incentives, and credit extension to rural communities. But the principles of economic efficiency alone can also conflict with long-term natural resource sustainability. Effective natural resource systems management must therefore consider both economic and ecological principles.

## SUMMARY

Forest management policies can be derived from the ecological principles of forest growth. Forest growth patterns imply an optimum rotation period for commercial timber. However, this commercial optimum neglects other ecological functions of forests.

Deforestation and conversion of natural forest to plantation cause significant biodiversity loss. Values associated with biodiversity represent significant externalities rarely reflected in market prices.

Growing demand for wood and wood products increases pressure on forests. Open access to many forests creates incentives for short-term exploitation without investment in replanting or sustainable forestry. In addition, many governments subsidize excessive forest clearance by making public lands available to timber companies at low prices.

Policies that encourage secure tenure and support for small-scale forestry enterprises and agroforestry can create incentives to maintain environmentally stable forests. In addition to timber, forests can provide income from other products such as fruit and latex. Certification programs for sustainably produced forest products can benefit from some consumers' willingness to pay a premium for certified wood. Public good and carbon storage functions also represent positive economic values of standing forest.

Like forests, water systems are under pressure from steadily growing agricultural, industrial, and urban demand. Many countries experience permanent water stress, defined as less than 2,000 cubic meters per capita available supply. Shortages will become more serious as population grows.

Increasing supply by pumping from aquifers has led to groundwater overdraft in major water-scarce areas throughout the world. Construction of dams also increases available supply, but most major dam sites are already being exploited, and new dam construction often involves major environmental and social costs.

Proper water pricing can promote conservation and encourage technologies for efficient water use. Government policies, however, often subsidize water, thereby encouraging over-use. A better approach for both forests and water systems is ecosystems management, aimed at balancing economic and ecological functions.

## KEY TERMS AND CONCEPTS

agroforestry
asset
biodiversity
biomass
certification
clear-cut
desalination
discount rate
ecological complexity
ecosystems management
flow
freshwater runoff
full pricing
groundwater overdraft
institutional failure
logistic curve
mean annual increment (MAI)

microirrigation
monoculture
optimum rotation period
property rights
public goods
recharge of aquifers
resilience
social sustainability
stable water supply
stock
subsidies
tragedy of the commons
under-pricing
use value
water-abundant and water-scarce areas
water cycle

## DISCUSSION QUESTIONS

1. Unlike ocean fisheries, forests can be privately owned, and in fact many millions of acres of forests are owned and managed by private corporations. In economic theory, private ownership should create incentives for efficient management. To what extent is this true of privately owned forests? Is efficient management also beneficial to the environment?

2. How can the timber values of forests be balanced with their value in supporting biodiversity? What changes in property regimes and forest management policies could help achieve the dual goals of economic profitability and environmental preservation?

3. In what ways do economic and ecological analyses of water systems resemble those of forests and fisheries? How do they differ? Which water management problems can be addressed through market mechanisms, and which require some form of government or social management?

## PROBLEMS

1. XYZ Forest Products owns a 2,000-acre tract of forest land. 1,000 acres are currently planted in hardwood trees (oak, beech, etc.) and 1,000 in softwoods (pine). An acre of either kind of forest contains a biomass (standing timber) of 200 tons/acre. Hardwoods, however, grow more slowly: an acre of hardwoods will add 10 tons/acre/year of new growth, whereas an acre of softwoods will add 20 tons/acre/year. The current age of the hardwoods is 40 years, and of the softwoods 20 years; both are currently at their maximum levels of mean annual increment.

   The going prices are $500 per ton for hardwood and $300 per ton for softwood. These prices are expected to remain stable for the indefinite future (in real terms). Two management practices are possible: clear-cutting or sustainable timbering, in which the amount of biomass removed annually just equals annual growth. Costs of clear-cutting are $40 per ton (for either kind of tree), and costs of sustainable timbering are $70 per ton.

   Analyze the profit-maximizing forest management policy XYZ corporation will pursue if

   (a) Real interest rates are 3 percent per annum;
   (b) Real interest rates are 5 percent per annum.

2. Now assume that XYZ is taken over by the Gargantua conglomerate, which has $100 million in debt at an 8 percent real interest rate. Analyze their probable forest management practice.

   Comment on the role of the interest rate here and suggest a government policy on forest management. What other considerations not apparent in the data given here would affect policy formulation? What would you recommend if the forest were publicly rather than privately owned? How might your recommendations differ for forest management in developed versus developing nations?

## REFERENCES

Abramovitz, Janet N. *Taking a Stand: Cultivating a New Relationship with the World's Forests.* Worldwatch Paper No. 140. Washington, D.C.: Worldwatch Institute, 1998.

Abramovitz, Janet N., and Ashley T. Mattoon. *Paper Cuts: Recovering the Paper Landscape*. Worldwatch Paper No. 149. Washington, D.C.: Worldwatch Institute, 1999.

Common, Mick, and Charles Perrings. "Towards an Ecological Economics of Sustainability." *Ecological Economics* 6 (July 1992): 7–34.

Ehrlich, Paul R., and Gretchen C. Daily. "Population Extinction and Saving Biodiversity." *Ambio* 22 (May 1993): 64–68. Summarized in *A Survey of Sustainable Development,* edited by Harris et al., 176–178. Washington, D.C.: Island Press, 2000.

Falkenmark, Malin, and Carl Widstrand. *Population and Water Resources: A Delicate Balance*. Washington, D.C.: Population Reference Bureau, 1992.

Gleick, Peter H. *The World's Water 2000–2001: The Biennial Report on Freshwater Resources*. Washington, D.C.: Island Press, 2000.

Hartwick, John M., and Nancy D. Olewiler. *The Economics of Natural Resource Use*. 2nd ed. New York: Addison Wesley, 1998.

Holling, C. S. "The Resilience of Terrestrial Ecosystems: Local Surprise and Global Change." In *Sustainable Development of the Biosphere,* edited by W. C. Clark and R. E. Munn. Cambridge, U.K.: Cambridge University Press, 1986.

Myers, Norman. "The World's Forests: Problems and Potentials." *Environmental Conservation* 23 no. 2 (1996): 156–168. Summarized in *A Survey of Sustainable Development,* edited by Harris et al., 183–188. Washington, D.C.: Island Press, 2000.

Panayotou, Theodore. *Green Markets: The Economics of Sustainable Development*. San Francisco: Institute for Contemporary Studies Press, 1993.

Panayotou, Theodore. *Instruments of Change: Motivating and Financing Sustainable Development*. London, U.K.: Earthscan, 1998.

Postel, Sandra. *Last Oasis: Facing Water Scarcity*. Worldwatch Environmental Alert Series, edited by Linda Starke. New York: Norton, 1992.

Postel, Sandra. *Pillar of Sand: Can the Irrigation Miracle Last?* New York: Norton, 1999.

Seidenstat, Paul, David Haarmeyer, and Simon Hakim, eds. *Reinventing Water and Wastewater Systems: Global Lessons for Improving Water Management*. New York: Wiley, 2002.

Tuxill, John. *Losing Strands in the Web of Life: Vertebrate Declines and the Conservation of Biological Diversity*. Worldwatch Paper No. 141. Washington, D.C.: Worldwatch Institute, 1998.

United Nations Department of Economic and Social Affairs, Population Division. *World Population Prospects: The 2000 Revision*. United Nations, 2001.

United Nations Economic and Social Council. *World Population Prospects: The 1998 Revision*. United Nations, 1998.

United Nations Environmental Programme. *Global Environmental Outlook 2000*. London, U.K.: Earthscan, 1999.

Wilson, E. O., ed. *Biodiversity*. Washington, D.C.: National Academy Press, 1988.

Wilson, E. O. *The Diversity of Life*. New York: Norton, 1992.

World Commission on Dams. *Dams and Development: A New Framework for Decision-Making*. London, U.K.: Earthscan Publications, 2000. Also at www.dams.org.

World Resources Institute and International Institute for Environment and Development, *World Resources 1987*. New York: Basic Books, 1987.

World Resources Institute, United Nations Development Programme, United Nations Environment Programme, and the World Bank. *World Resources 2000–2001: A Guide to the Global Environment*. Washington, D.C.: World Resources Institute, 2000.

World Resources Institute, United Nations Development Programme, United Nations Environment Programme, and the World Bank. *World Resources 2002–2004: Decisions for the Earth: Balance, Voice, and Power*. Washington, D.C.: World Resources Institute, 2003.

Worldwatch Institute. *Signposts 2004: Essential Data, Timelines, and Analyses of Global Trends* (CD-ROM). Washington, D.C.: Worldwatch Institute, 2004.

## WEBSITES

1. **http://www.fs.fed.us/sustained/siteindex.html** The U.S. Forest Service's website, with links to information on sustainable forest management.

2. **http://www.fsc.org/fsc/** Homepage for the Forest Stewardship Council, a leader in the development of an international forest products labeling plan that certifies products grown in a sustainable manner.

3. **http://www.ran.org/info_center/index.html** Links to information about rainforests from the Rainforest Action Network, an environmental group that campaigns to protect rainforests around the world.

4. **http://www.wri.org/water/** The World Resources Institute's website about freshwater issues. The site includes discussion papers on freshwater issues as well as extensive data.

5. **http://www.iwrn.net/** Website of the Inter-American Water Resources Network, with links to other water-related organizations and publications.

# PART SIX

# Pollution: Impacts and Policy Responses

CHAPTER

# 16

# Pollution: Analysis and Policy

## The Economics of Pollution Control

One of the services provided by natural systems is a **sink function**—the capacity to absorb wastes and **pollution**. Although essential to human life and economic systems, this function has often been abused by excessive pollution. This raises two questions for environmental policy. First, how much pollution is acceptable—given that any society must emit some waste products? Second, how can we best control or reduce pollution to this acceptable level?

### How Much Pollution Is Too Much?

If we take an economic approach to answering this question, we need to compare marginal costs and benefits associated with a pollution-generating activity. We saw in Chapter 3 that this leads to the concept of an **optimal pollution level**—the amount of pollution that exactly balances marginal social benefits and marginal social costs. Another way of looking at this is to consider the marginal cost of pollution control versus the marginal cost of pollution damage (Figure 16-1). In this approach, pollution reduction is worthwhile so long as control costs are less than the benefits gained in terms of reduced damage.

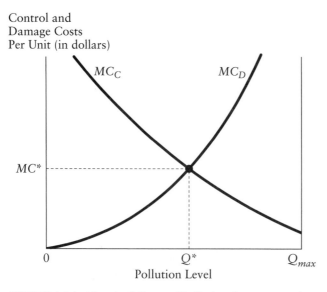

Control and
Damage Costs
Per Unit (in dollars)

**FIGURE 16-1** *Marginal Costs of Pollution Damage and
Control*

## Picking a Pollution Control Policy

In Chapter 3 we discussed **pollution taxes** or charges levied per unit emitted. Other options include regulation, in which the government sets specific limits on emissions, or
**transferable pollution permits,** which allow firms to emit only the level of pollution for
which they have permits. Transferability implies that firms can buy and sell these permits, with low-emitting firms able to sell extra permits, and high-emitting firms able to
purchase additional permits.

In this chapter, we will approach the questions of the level and method of pollution control primarily in terms of economic analysis. At the same time, we will bear in
mind the limitations of a purely economic perspective. In dealing with the impacts of
pollution, we may not be able to measure all relevant costs and benefits in economic
terms. This is especially true when multiple pollutants affect the environment, when
cumulative ecosystem damage and degradation is at issue, or when subtle effects of
persistent pollutants are poorly understood.

In such cases, economic analysis may not capture the full scope of ecosystem effects.
Economic analysis, however, is essential to understand how pollution control policies affect firms and individuals, and the role that economic incentives play in altering behavior
with regard to the production and consumption of pollution-generating products.

## Marginal Costs and Benefits of Pollution Control

Let us look first at the question of pollution levels. Figure 16-1 shows a general analysis applicable to many pollution control issues. The horizontal axis shows the quantity
of pollution emitted in a particular industry, with pollution levels increasing from left

to right. The maximum level, $Q_{max}$, shows the expected amount of pollution with no pollution control. As pollution control policies are implemented, the amount of pollution will drop below $Q_{max}$, moving from right to left on the horizontal axis.

$MC_D$, the marginal cost of damage, shows the marginal costs associated with pollution emissions. These tend to rise in a nonlinear, upward-curving pattern, indicating that incremental emissions are proportionally more damaging once the environment is already polluted. This is consistent with both common sense and scientific evidence—a small amount of automobile exhaust on a clear day may be a mere annoyance, but the same amount added to a smog-choked intersection at rush hour could trigger significant breathing and health problems. We can also think of $MC_D$ as showing the marginal *benefits* of pollution reduction.

$MC_C$, the marginal cost of control, rises as pollution levels fall (moving from right to left on the graph). This also makes sense in terms of practical experience. It is generally easier to clean up the first few units of pollution than to reduce pollution to low levels. As we approach zero emissions, the control costs are likely to soar, and for many pollutants a zero level would require shutting down production entirely.

Economic theory indicates that the optimum level of control is $Q^*$—where the marginal damage cost exactly equals the marginal control cost ($MC^*$). At $Q^*$, the cost of cleaning up one more unit of pollution is greater than the benefit it brings in reduced damages. On the other hand, cleaning up one less unit will increase damages by more than it reduces control costs. Therefore $Q^*$ is the most efficient level of cleanup. This balancing of marginal control cost with marginal damage cost is known as the **equimarginal principle.**[1]

It is easy enough to find $Q^*$ on our graph, but how can we identify it in real life? This is not so easy, because we are unlikely to know the shape and location of the $MC$ curves with any precision. As we saw in Chapter 6, valuation of environmental damages is an imprecise science and involves many judgment calls. Control costs may be easier to estimate based on industry experience, but these too are often uncertain.

Industries often estimate control costs at higher levels than actually occur when control policies go into effect. For example, the automobile industry has often argued that controlling tailpipe emissions would boost vehicle costs by a large margin. In practice, the implementation of significantly tighter vehicle emission standards has had little impact on costs.

Similarly, the electric power industry predicted high costs for sulfur oxide ($SO_X$) reduction, but the real costs (as shown by the price of $SO_X$ emissions permits, discussed below) were considerably lower. On the other hand, control costs can run much higher than estimated, as has often proved the case for cleaning up toxic waste facilities.

Despite these uncertainties, the equimarginal principle is central to the economic analysis of pollution control policies. Even if we cannot define the precise goal, we know that it will be better to use efficient policies—those that give the greatest result for

---

[1]The equimarginal principle can also apply to marginal control costs for different firms or different techniques, as we will see in our discussion of pollution control policies. Tietenberg distinguishes between the "first equimarginal principle" of equating marginal costs and benefits and the "second equimarginal principle" of equalizing marginal control costs among firms. See Tietenberg, 2003, Chapters 2 and 3.

the lowest cost—rather than inefficient policies that bring relatively higher costs and reduced benefits. Economic analysis can help us formulate efficient policies and analyze the advantages and disadvantages of different approaches. In the following sections, we will consider possible options for pollution control from this point of view.

## Pollution Control Policies: Standards, Taxes, Permits

One option for pollution control is direct regulation of pollution-creating activities. Government departments such as the U.S. Environmental Protection Agency can set **emissions standards** for particular industries or products, subject to legislative guidelines. Many people experience such standards at an annual automobile inspection. Cars must meet certain standards for tailpipe emissions; a car that fails must correct the problem before receiving an inspection sticker.

What are the advantages and disadvantages of standards from the economic perspective? The clear advantage is that standards can specify a definite result. This is particularly important in the case of substances that pose a clear hazard to public health. By imposing a uniform rule on all producers, we can be sure that no factory or product will produce hazardous levels of pollutants.

Systems that require all economic actors to meet the same standard, however, may have the problem of inflexibility.[2] Fixed standards work well when pollution-generating activities are similar. For example, different models of automobiles are sufficiently alike to impose the same emissions rules on all.[3] But consider an industry with many plants of different sizes and ages. Will it make sense to have the same rule for every plant? A particular standard might be too difficult for the older plants to meet, forcing owners to shut them down. On the other hand, the same standard might be too lax for more modern plants, allowing them to emit pollution that could have been eliminated at low cost.

In the case of an industry with many different plants, a **market-based pollution control** system may make sense. One such system is a tax, or per unit charge, for emissions. As we saw in Chapter 3, a pollution tax reflects the principle of **internalizing externalities.** If producers must bear the costs associated with pollution by paying a per unit charge, they will find it in their interests to reduce pollution so long as the marginal control costs are less than the tax.

Once again, $Q_{max}$ is the level of pollution emitted with no controls. If, as shown in Figure 16-2, a uniform charge or pollution tax equal to $T_1$ is imposed, pollution will

[2]Some economists refer to government-set standards as **command-and-control** systems, comparing them unfavorably to market-based mechanisms. We avoid this terminology here, because it conveys unnecessary bias. "Command and control" summons up images of failed communist economic systems. Rather, we will seek to evaluate different policies on their merits, without preconceptions as to which is better. Goodstein (2005, Chapter 14) shares this reservation about the use of the term.

[3]A problem has arisen, though, with sport utility vehicles, which are defined as light trucks and thus avoid strict emissions control standards. For this reason, the Environmental Protection Agency has moved to tighten standards for SUVs.

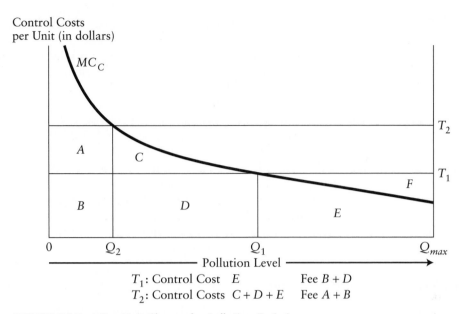

Control Costs per Unit (in dollars)

$T_1$: Control Cost   $E$           Fee $B + D$
$T_2$: Control Costs   $C + D + E$     Fee $A + B$

**FIGURE 16-2** *A Per-Unit Charge for Pollution Emissions*

fall to $Q_1$. Producers will find it preferable to reduce pollution to this level, at a total cost of $E$ (the area under the marginal control cost curve between $Q_1$ and $Q_{max}$), rather than paying a fee equal to $E + F$ on these units. They will also have to pay a total charge equal to $B + D$ on the quantity $Q_1$ of pollution they continue to emit. Thus their total cost arising from pollution control plus charges will be $B + D + E$. This is less than $B + D + E + F$, which they would have to pay if they undertook no pollution reduction.

If the per-unit charge is set higher, at $T_2$, producers will reduce pollution to $Q_2$. This will involve control costs of $C + D + E$, and pollution charges of $A + B$. The extra units of pollution reduction involve higher marginal costs, but so long as these costs are less than $T_2$ producers will find it worthwhile to undertake the extra expense and thus avoid paying the fee on the units of pollution between $Q_1$ and $Q_2$.

Which of these pollution tax levels is correct? To find out, we must measure the real costs of pollution damage. Notice that the marginal cost of damage curve shown in Figure 16-1 has been omitted in Figure 16-2. This is consistent with real-life policymaking, in which we rarely have a precise measure of damages in economic terms. This raises the possibility that the pollution charge will be set too high, or too low.

Notice, however, that for any given tax level producers' response will be **economically efficient.** In the case where different producers have different control costs, they can decide independently as to which level of pollution control makes sense for them. Those who have high control costs will reduce less, but pay a higher total charge for pollution emitted. Those who can cut pollution at low cost will reduce more, thereby reducing the charges they must pay.

This cost-minimizing logic ensures that cleanup expenses are directed to wherever they can achieve the most. Here we have a different application of the equimarginal principle—marginal control costs are being equalized among all producers.[4] If the tax level reflects the true damage costs, it will also be true that marginal control costs for all producers are equal to marginal benefits from damage reduction.

We can note that the same goal of efficient pollution reduction may be achieved by the use of a subsidy rather than a tax. If producers are paid per unit of pollution reduced, they will make a similar judgment about the level of pollution reduction that is most profitable. For example, if a subsidy equal to $T_1$ is offered for each unit of pollution control, producers will find it worthwhile to cut pollution to $Q_1$, paying area $E$ in control costs but collecting $E + F$ in subsidy for a net profit of $F$. This has the same policy effect as a tax of $T_1$, but a different distributional implication: Rather than collecting revenues $B + D$, the government pays $E + F$, leaving the producers better off by $B + D + E + F$. Politically, this approach may be more acceptable to industry, but it may also make pollution control unacceptably costly in terms of government budgets.

## Transferable Pollution Permits

Economic efficiency in pollution control is clearly an advantage. One disadvantage of pollution charges, however, is that it is generally impossible to predict the total amount of pollution reduction a given charge will produce. It depends on the shape of the $MC_C$ curve shown in Figure 16-2, which as we have noted is usually not known to policymakers.

Suppose that the policy goal is a more precise and definite reduction in pollution levels within a region. For example, in 1990 the U.S. Environmental Protection Agency set a goal of 50 percent reduction in sulfur and nitrogen oxide ($SO_X$ and $NO_X$) emissions that cause acid rain. What is the best way to achieve such a specific target, while also achieving economic efficiency?

One approach, used in the U.S. Clean Air Act Amendments of 1990, is to set up a system of transferable pollution permits. The total number of permits issued equals the desired target level of pollution. These permits can then be allocated to existing firms or sold at auction. Once allocated, they are fully transferable, or tradable, among firms or other interested parties. Firms can choose for themselves whether to reduce pollution or to purchase permits for the pollution they emit—but the total volume of pollution emitted by all firms cannot exceed a maximum amount set by the total number of permits.[5]

Within this system, however, private groups interested in reducing pollution could purchase permits and permanently retire them, thus reducing total emissions below the original target level. The permits also may be issued for a specific time period, after which fewer permits will be issued, resulting in lower overall pollution levels. Figure 16-3 illustrates a simplified version of a transferable permit system.

---

[4]Tietenberg, 2003, refers to this as the "second equimarginal principle."

[5]For an in-depth account of the background and implementation of the 1990 Clean Air Act Amendments, see Goodstein, 2005, Chapters 13 and 15.

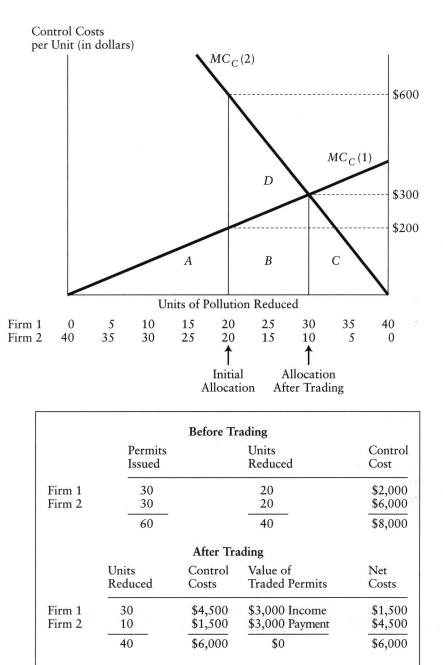

FIGURE 16-3  *A Transferable Pollution Permit System*

In this simplified example we assume only two firms, each emitting 50 units of pollution. The policy goal is a total reduction of 40 units of pollution. The sum of reductions by the two firms must therefore equal 40. However, the marginal control costs for the two firms differ. Figure 16-3 shows the different ways in which a total reduction of 40 units can be distributed between the two firms.

The marginal cost of control ($MC_C$) curves for the two firms are plotted in different directions on the same axis, with pollution reduction by Firm 1 going from left to right, and for Firm 2 from right to left. This is merely a graphical trick to make it easy to identify the point at which the equimarginal principle is satisfied (that is, the point at which the marginal control costs for the two firms are equal).

The two firms together are emitting 100 units of pollution. To achieve the 40-unit reduction goal, a total of 60 permits must be issued. Suppose that the initial allocation of permits is 30 to each firm. If permits cannot be traded, each firm must cut back its emission from 50 to 30—a net reduction of 20. This is shown in the middle of the graph. At this point, the marginal control cost is $200 for Firm 1 and $600 for Firm 2. This is the same result that would occur if a uniform regulation limited each firm to a maximum of 30 emissions units.

This result achieves the policy goal in terms of emissions reductions, but it is economically inefficient. Each firm's total control cost can be seen on the graph as the area under the $MC_C$ curve.[6] Firm 1's total cost for pollution control is area $A$ (= $2,000), and the total cost for Firm 2 is areas $B + C + D$ (= $6,000). The combined cost to achieve 40 units of pollution reduction is $A + B + C + D$ (= $8,000). However, the firms can improve their own positions, and overall economic efficiency, by trading permits.

It will be advantageous for Firm 1, which has lower control costs, to reduce pollution by 10 additional units (for a total of 30 reduced), thus using only 10 permits and selling the extra 10 permits to Firm 2. Firm 2 will find it worthwhile to purchase 10 permits, allowing it to reduce pollution by only 10 units. The equilibrium price for the permits will be $300, which represents the value of marginal control costs for both firms at the point where Firm 1 is reducing by 30 units and Firm 2 by 10 units.

At this new equilibrium, total control cost for Firm 1 is areas $A + B$ (= $4,500), and total cost for Firm 2 is area $C$ (= $1,500). The combined cost is $6,000. The same pollution reduction goal has been achieved at a lower cost. Area $D$ (= $2,000) represents the net savings from this more efficient solution. Figure 16-3 shows the costs with and without trading. Notice that trading reduces the total costs for each firm, as well as the combined costs.

In a sense, a transferable permit system combines the advantages of direct regulation and an emissions charge system. It allows policymakers to set a definite limit on total pollution levels, while using the market process to seek an efficient method of achieving the goal. It is economically advantageous for the firms involved, as our example shows, allowing a given amount of pollution reduction for the minimum economic cost. In addition, other interested parties can strengthen pollution control by purchasing

---

[6] In mathematical terms, total cost $= TC = \int_0^q MC \, dq$ where $q$ is units of pollution reduced.

and retiring permits, and pollution controls can be tightened over time by reducing the overall number of permits issued.

The trading equilibrium shown in Figure 16-3 is consistent with the equimarginal principle, because at the trading equilibrium the marginal control costs for all firms are equal. (Our example used only two firms for simplicity, but the principle can easily apply to an industry with many firms.) This uniform marginal control cost will also be the equilibrium price of a pollution permit. Firms will benefit by purchasing permits whenever the permit price is below marginal control costs or selling permits whenever the permit price exceeds these costs.

It does not necessarily follow, however, that a transferable permit system is always the ideal pollution control policy. Transferable permits have been used successfully for sulfur dioxide reduction under the Clean Air Act Amendments of 1990, and have been widely discussed as a tool for reduction of global carbon dioxide emissions (more on this in Chapter 18). But numerous factors must be considered in deciding whether pollution taxes, permits, or direct regulation are the best policy tools for a particular goal. In the next section, we review some of these issues and look at some examples of pollution control in practice.

## Pollution Control Policies in Practice

One major factor in formulating effective pollution control policies is the nature of the pollution involved. Are its effects primarily **local, regional,** or **global?** Do the effects increase linearly with the amount of pollutant, or are there **nonlinear or threshold effects?** (See Figure 16-4.)

Consider, for example, a heavy metal pollutant such as lead. If a productive facility is emitting lead as a pollutant, this poses a grave health threat to those living in the vicinity of the plant. A small amount of lead in the blood can lead to serious neurological and mental damage, especially in children. We can say that the threshold for

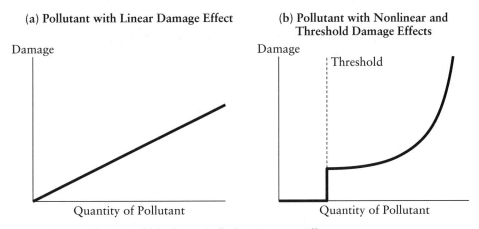

**(a) Pollutant with Linear Damage Effect**

Damage

Quantity of Pollutant

**(b) Pollutant with Nonlinear and Threshold Damage Effects**

Damage

Threshold

Quantity of Pollutant

**FIGURE 16-4** *Linear and Nonlinear Pollution Damage Effects*

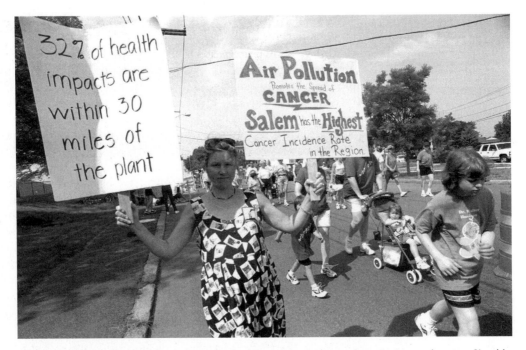

*Environmental activists rally for tighter emissions controls at power plants in Massachusetts. Six older plants are responsible for 90 percent of the state's power plant pollution. In 2001, Massachusetts imposed tougher regulations that require cuts of as much as 75 percent in nitrous oxide and sulfur dioxide pollutants.*

acceptable levels of lead in the environment is low, and above this threshold damage can be severe (Figure 16-4b).

Another important factor in this case is the distribution of the pollutant's impact. The worst effects are likely to be local—although lead pollution can spread throughout the environment, the highest concentrations are likely to be near to the producing plant.[7]

Market mechanisms such as pollution taxes or permits are generally ineffective in preventing damage from lead pollution. Under a permit system a high-polluting but profitable plant could simply purchase permits and continue polluting, with serious consequences for local residents. Similarly, the managers of such a plant might choose to pay a pollution tax rather than cut back emissions. These market-based systems might achieve regional or national control of overall lead emissions, but they would fail to protect local residents. In a case like this, regulations must specify strong emissions standards for every plant in order to protect the public. For leaded gasoline or lead paint, complete prohibition is the only effective policy.

---

[7]In the case of leaded gasoline, the pollution is spread widely through automobile exhaust, making lead a regional pollutant.

Market-based policies work better in the case of **uniformly mixed pollutants.** Sulfur oxides ($SO_X$) are an example. These gases, which contribute to acid rain, are emitted by many productive facilities, especially coal- and oil-fired power plants. They are carried by the wind over wide areas, creating regional pollution. In devising policies to limit these regional damages, it makes little difference which sources reduce pollution output, provided that the desired reduction targets are met. This is therefore a good case for the application of a tax or permit scheme.

As we have noted, the Clean Air Act Amendments of 1990 utilized transferable permits with successful results. Considerable overall reduction in $SO_X$ emissions has been achieved, and the price of an emissions permit has fallen as emissions reduction technology has improved (see Box 16-1).[8]

Policy issues become more complex regarding **nonuniformly mixed pollutants.** These pollutants are emitted in varying concentrations and remain at different levels in different locations. Trading programs are less appropriate when the impact of a given amount of pollutant may be more or less severe depending on local conditions. This is commonly the case when dealing with water pollution, which involves differing conditions in streams, rivers, lakes, oceans, and groundwater.

## *Policies for Controlling Water Pollution*

Consider the case of water pollution in a large river that runs past many urban, industrial, and agricultural areas. The river will carry different types of pollution from many different sources. Some of these are likely to be **point source pollution** emitters, like waste pipes from factories or sewage treatment plants. A large portion may also be **nonpoint source pollution.** This could include agricultural fertilizer and pesticide runoff, as well as runoff of oil, salt, and other pollutants from roads and urban areas.

In this case the important factor may be the **ambient pollution level** in the river, meaning the concentration of pollutants per cubic meter of water. Some acceptable threshold level may exist for ambient pollution (as shown in Figure 16-4b). If pollution exceeds this level, regulations for point source pollution reduction must be calculated based on the contribution of particular sources to the ambient level. This may vary depending on the location and nature of the source. Because of the difficulty in devising a pollution charge or tradable permit system in this case, point source water pollution control has generally depended on specific regulations for different kinds of emitters, including sewage facilities and industrial plants.

Under the U.S. Clean Water Act of 1977, the 1987 Water Quality Act, and the Safe Drinking Water Act of 1974, together with its 1986 and 1996 amendments, standards are set for achieving fishable and swimmable waters, with higher standards for community drinking water. The Environmental Protection Agency is charged with

---

[8]Sanchez, 1998, discusses how the Clean Air Act Amendments promoted technological progress in emissions reduction; Joskow et al., 1998, and Stavins, 1998, examine the operation of the market for emissions rights. Burtraw et al., 1998, finds that Clean Air Act Amendments benefits considerably outweigh costs, and Jorgenson and Wilcoxen, 1998, evaluate the act's overall economic impact.

## 16-1   Sulfur Dioxide Emissions Trading

The 1990 Clean Air Act Amendments created a national program to allow trading and banking of sulfur dioxide ($SO_2$) emissions. Electricity firms that emit $SO_2$ may trade permits, or allowances, to other firms. Unused allowances may be "banked" for use in future years. By reducing the total number of allowances allocated, national $SO_2$ emissions can be gradually reduced.

Economic theory suggests that a system of transferable pollution permits can produce the same level of pollution reduction as a universal standard but at lower cost. Dallas Burtraw, an economist with Resources for the Future, notes that the "$SO_2$ allowance market presents the first real test of economists' advice and therefore merits careful evaluation" (Burtraw, 2000, p. 2). After more than 10 years of practice, has the $SO_2$ trading system produced significant cost savings?

To evaluate the policy, the effects of emissions trading must be isolated from other factors. Declining prices for low-sulfur coal in the 1990s and technological advances would have reduced the costs of lowering emissions even without a trading system. Further complicating the analysis, Burtraw notes that the trading scheme is responsible for spurring innovation in pollution reduction technologies and organizational behavior. Separating the savings induced by the emissions trading program from other factors is difficult.

Using statistical techniques, a group of researchers estimated the annual cost savings directly associated with trading as $250 billion, in 1995 dollars, for the period 1995–2000 (Carlson, 2000). The cost savings increase to $784 billion annually after 2000, as all electricity plants are covered by the program (from 1995 to 2000 only the dirtiest plants were covered). The number of trades in the first few years of the program was lower than expected because of price uncertainty, regulatory factors, state mandates of coal use, and other factors (U.S. GAO, 1994). Cost savings could be increased as policies are changed to encourage more trading.

Overall, the $SO_2$ trading plan has been effective in reducing national emissions. Actual $SO_2$ emissions are about 35 percent below the allowable cap (U.S. GAO, 1997) but banked allowances could be utilized in the future to increase emissions. Although the cost savings are not as large as originally expected, they "are substantial and contribute to the tremendous success of the program" (Burtraw, 2000, p. 24).

Lessons learned from the $SO_2$ trading policy can be applied to other environmental issues, particularly $CO_2$ trading to reduce global warming. Agreements for other pollutants should reduce "administrative complexities," "set more objectively based reduction goals, and encourage a more rapid phase-in of the reduction process" (Ackerman and Moomaw, 1997, p. 66).

*(continued on following page)*

**SOURCES**

Ackerman, Frank, and William Moomaw. "SO$_2$ Emissions Trading: Does it Work?" *Electricity Journal,* vol. 10 (1997): 61–66.

Burtraw, Dallas. "Innovation Under the Tradable Sulfur Dioxide Emission Permits Program in the U.S. Electricity Sector." Resources for the Future Discussion Paper 00–38, 2000.

Carlson, Curtis, Dallas Burtraw, Maureen Cropper, and Karen L. Palmer. "Sulfur Dioxide Control by Electric Utilities: What Are the Gains from Trade?" *Journal of Political Economy,* vol. 108 (2000): 1292–1326.

U.S. General Accounting Office. Overview and Issures on Emissions Allowance Trading Programs, GAO/T-RCED-97-183, 1997.

U.S. General Accounting Office. Allowance Trading Offers an Opportunity to Reduce Emissions at Less Cost, GAO/RGED-95-30, 1994.

determining the best practical technology for this goal and, in the longer term, the "best achievable technology"—a more demanding requirement. Mandates for improved technology at sewage and industrial plants have been accompanied by federal grants to municipalities, a form of subsidy for pollution control.

Nonpoint source pollution has proved more difficult to control. The widespread origins of this kind of pollution require **watershed management,** which involves modified industrial and agricultural practices as well as protection of land surrounding public water supplies. Watershed management can involve various policy instruments, including market-based instruments such as taxes on fertilizer and pesticides, or subsidies for erosion control or pollution-reduction technology. In addition, zoning regulations to prevent the location of new polluting facilities and federal or state purchase of conservation land are likely to be important elements of a watershed management policy.[9]

## Policy Choice: Pollution Taxes Versus Tradable Permits

Clearly, market-based policies can play a significant role in pollution control. Both pollution taxes and tradable permits can promote efficiency, although as we have seen they are not always the most appropriate policies.[10] When market-based policies are indicated, a further question arises: Which market-based policy is best? Also, if we choose taxes, at what level should they be set? And if we choose permits, how many should be issued and to whom?

The choice of taxes versus permits relates closely to the shapes of the marginal cost of control and marginal cost of damage curves shown in Figure 16-1. In analyzing the

---

[9]For an extensive analysis of nonpoint source pollution, see Rigano, 1994; and Miltz et al., 1998.

[10]An overview of the applicability of market-based environmental policies is provided by Stavins and Whitehead, 1997. The analysis presented in this section is based on Weitzman, 1974.

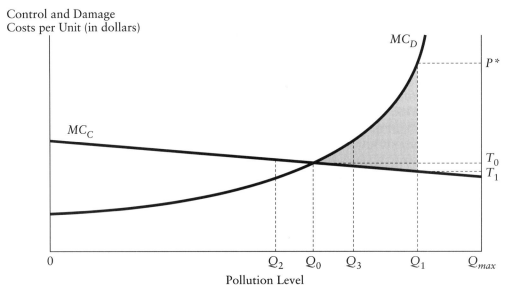

Control and Damage
Costs per Unit (in dollars)

**FIGURE 16-5** *Pollution Control with Steep Marginal Damage Costs*

way in which these policies work, we focused on issues related to the marginal cost of control curve. But in the choice of policies, we must also consider the marginal cost of damage and the interrelationships between the two curves. A couple of examples will show why this is important.

Suppose that for a particular pollutant the marginal costs of damage are steep, or inelastic: That is to say, they rise quickly as the level of pollution increases. On the other hand, the per unit costs of control for this pollutant tend to be fairly stable, with marginal cost rising only slowly as pollution reduction increases. This is shown in Figure 16-5.

In this case, a pollution tax is risky, because a small error in setting the tax level can lead to a large increase in pollution damage. In Figure 16-5, the appropriate tax level to balance marginal damage and control costs would be $T_0$, with resulting pollution level $Q_0$. But setting the tax slightly lower, at $T_1$, would cause firms to cut back on pollution control to $Q_1$, with marginal damage costs rising to $P^*$. The large shaded triangle shows the net social loss from this extra pollution damage.

This pattern of damage costs might be associated with a pollutant such as methyl mercury, which can cause serious nerve damage above a low tolerance threshold. In this case, a quantity-based control system would be a much more effective policy. Transferable permits or direct regulation could limit emissions to $Q_0$. A small error in either direction in setting the quantity control level ($Q_2$ or $Q_3$) would cause a much smaller net social loss (the small triangular areas between the marginal cost and damage curves from $Q_0$ to $Q_2$ or from $Q_0$ to $Q_3$).

A contrasting case occurs when the marginal cost of damage curve is relatively flat, but the marginal cost of control curve is steep, as shown in Figure 16-6. Here, control costs rise rapidly above a certain level, while damage costs are fairly stable.

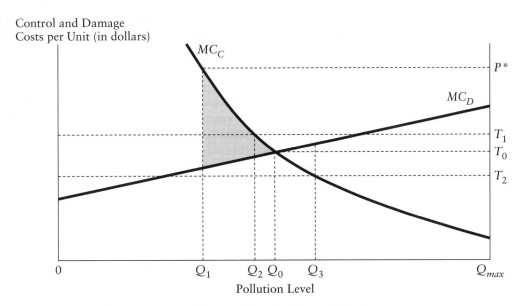

FIGURE 16-6 *Pollution Control with Steep Marginal Control Costs*

In this case quantity controls pose the more serious risk of error. The ideal quantity control would be at $Q_0$, but an excessively strict control at $Q_1$ would cause a rapid rise in marginal control costs, to $P^*$, with net social loss shown by the large shaded triangle. On the other hand, a tax policy could deviate from the appropriate level of $T_0$ without having much negative effect either in excessive cost or excessive damage. The impact of a tax policy with a tax level set too high ($T_1$) or too low ($T_2$) causes only a small deviation from the $Q_0$ control level, with net social losses equal to the small triangles between $MC_C$ and $MC_D$ between $Q_0$ and $Q_2$ or $Q_0$ and $Q_3$.

Industry spokespersons often argue that excessively rigid government regulations force high control costs for limited benefits. As we have seen, these arguments sometimes amount to crying wolf. Where industrywide control costs may genuinely be high, however, a tax or pollution charge will allow firms to make their own decisions about pollution control. They will not be forced to undertake exorbitant expenditures, but at the same time the tax will require them to account for the internalized social costs of pollution. For example, a tax on fertilizer or pesticides could encourage farmers to seek more environmentally friendly production techniques while allowing the use of chemical inputs where cost-effective.

## Structuring Pollution Control Policies

A further issue in the use of market-based pollution control concerns how we allocate permits in a tradable permit system. One approach is to issue permits to existing firms, requiring new firms entering the industry to purchase permits on the open market.

## 16-2    Grandfathering and Air Pollution Control

The Clean Air Act of 1970 "grandfathered" coal-fired power plants built before 1970, exempting them from the law's pollution standards in the expectation that they would eventually be closed. But as of 2000, many of these plants were still in business, producing far more pollution than more modern plants.

The act also specified that when older plants were modernized to make appreciably more energy, they had to comply with the same emission standards as new plants. The State of New York and the federal Environmental Protection Agency sued more than 100 plants, claiming that they had made major modifications without installing required pollution controls.

The first results of these suits came when the Virginia Electric Power Company agreed to spend $1.2 billion to cut harmful pollutants from eight coal-burning plants, and the Tampa Electric Company pledged to spend $1 billion to switch a plant from coal to cleaner natural gas.

Federal and state regulators thus acted to close the loophole created by the "grandfathering" language of the 1970 act. The results of these suits may eventually lead to significant clean-up at many more plants across the country.

### SOURCE

"Power Plants to Cut Emissions Faulted in Northeast Smog." *New York Times,* November 16, 2000; editorial, November 20, 2000.

This obviously favors existing firms, who receive something of value (the permits) at no charge. However, it may be the most politically acceptable policy, because it will minimize industry opposition.

An alternative approach is a permit auction, in which permits are sold to the highest bidder. This has the advantage of bringing in government revenues that could be used to lower taxes elsewhere in the economy (we will discuss this possibility in greater detail in Chapters 17 and 18). Tradable permits sold at auction are economically similar to pollution taxes; the market-determined permit price is equivalent in effect to a per-unit pollution charge.

A related issue is **grandfathering** of existing plants. This refers to a system in which strict pollution control regulations are applied to new plants, but existing plants are allowed to comply with less-demanding standards (or no standards at all). This is intended to avoid excessively high marginal control costs, but is clearly biased toward existing plants, and is open to abuse (see Box 16-2).

## The Impact of Technological Change

Finally, when considering the effectiveness of different policies we should evaluate their relationship to technological progress in pollution control. The marginal control cost curves we have used in our analysis are not fixed over time. With technological progress, control costs can be reduced. This raises two issues. First, how will changing control costs affect the policies we have discussed? Second, what incentives do these policies create for the development of improved pollution control technologies?

Figure 16-7 shows how the level of pollution control will vary with different policies and technological change. Suppose we start with control costs of $MC_C$ and initial pollution levels of $Q_{max}$. A pollution tax at the level $T_0$ will lead to reduction of pollution to the level $Q_0$. A permit allocation of $Q_0$ permits will have the same effect, with a market-determined permit price of $P_0$. Now suppose that technological progress lowers controls costs to $MC_C^*$. How will firms react?

In the pollution tax case, firms will have an incentive to increase pollution control, reducing pollution levels to $Q_1$. By doing so they save area $A$ (the difference between the new control costs and the pollution taxes they were formerly paying on units $Q_0$ to $Q_1$). With permits, however, the result will be different. Given the lower control costs, the permit price will fall to $P_1$. (Recall from Figure 16-3 that the equilibrium permit price is equal to marginal control costs.) The total units of pollution will remain the same at $Q_0$—equal to the total number of permits issued.

In fact, the permit system may have a seemingly perverse effect. If control costs fall drastically for some firms (those using newer technology), the permit price will fall, allowing plants with older technology to purchase more permits and actually increase

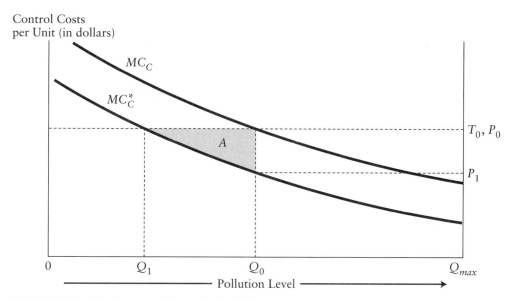

**FIGURE 16-7** *The Impact of Technological Change*

## 16-3 Clean Air and Clear Skies: Economics and Politics

**U.S.** regulatory policy on air pollution has focused on "criteria" air pollutants including particulates, sulfur dioxide, carbon monoxide, nitrogen oxide, and ground-level ozone. In addition, the 1990 Clean Air Act Amendments introduced controls on other toxic air pollutants such as airborne mercury. Enforcement has been based on establishing air quality standards for these pollutants, and mandating technological standards for new and existing plants (with more rigorous standards for new plants).

In 2003, the Bush administration introduced a new proposal for air pollution policy called Clear Skies. This plan proposed to extend the principle of pollution trading from sulfur dioxide (see Box 16-1) to other air pollutants including nitrogen oxide and mercury. Advocates of this proposal cited the greater economic efficiency of trading programs as compared with the current, state-by-state program based on technology mandates. Opponents argued that it actually weakens environmental protection, as compared with the existing Clean Air Act rules.

The Clear Skies initiative proposes a 70 percent cut in power plant pollution by 2018. Most of this reduction would come in the later years, with more pollution allowed during the first half of the period than would occur under existing law. Also, Clear Skies provides for no regulation of carbon dioxide emissions, linked to global warming (see Chapter 18).

A particular focus of criticism has been the inclusion of airborne mercury in a trading program. Unlike sulfur and nitrogen oxides, mercury (a heavy metal) is not a uniformly mixed pollutant. Produced primarily by coal-fired power plants, mercury can concentrate in "hot spots" and is a powerful nerve toxin, posing an especially serious threat to pregnant women and young children. Nearly every state has issued fish consumption warnings due to mercury-poisoned waters. Even if overall mercury emissions are reduced, dangerous local concentrations could remain as high-polluting plants purchase permits to continue operating.

As of early 2005, Congress was divided on the Clear Skies proposal and charges flew over the release of a report by the Environmental Protection Agency's inspector general charging that agency managers had deliberately downplayed the risks of mercury emissions to favor industry. Even without the Clear Skies legislation, the EPA plans to implement many of the bill's provisions through regulatory rules. Basic issues of balancing economic efficiency and environmental protection have thus become the focus of fierce political controversy.

emissions. This surprising effect of better pollution control technology leading to *more* pollution by some firms could, however, be avoided by reducing the total number of permits issued.

Following the same logic, we can conclude that pollution taxes provide a better incentive for the development of improved technology. With a fixed pollution charge, any firm can save money by installing improved control technology. With permits, some firms can "free-ride" on the technological progress of others, while actually increasing their emissions. For this reason, the authorities responsible for a permit scheme must be alert to changes in technology, tightening the allocation of permits over time to provide an incentive for the development of better pollution-control methods. Some recent proposals to expand pollution trading programs have drawn criticism for providing insufficient incentives for improvements in pollution control (see Box 16-3).

## Cumulative and Global Pollutants

Pollution problems are often long-lived. Organochloride pesticides such as DDT, polychlorinated biphenyls (PCBs), and chlorofluorocarbons (CFCs) remain in the environment for many decades. As emissions of such **cumulative pollutants** continue, their total accumulations in land, air, water, and living things steadily increase.

The kinds of analyses that we have discussed regarding marginal costs of pollution damage are appropriate for **flow pollutants**—those that have a short-term impact and then dissipate or are absorbed harmlessly into the environment. For cumulative or **stock pollutants,** however, we need a different kind of analysis and different control policies.

The issues of cumulative pollution are especially important for **global pollutants.** Carbon, methane, and chlorofluorocarbons emitted into the atmosphere last for decades and have worldwide effects. Pollutants such as DDT and other persistent pesticides also spread worldwide and are found in high concentrations in the bodies of people and animals in the Arctic, where these substances have never been used.

Polychlorinated biphenyls (PCBs) formerly used as insulators in electrical systems have caused severe river pollution that remains a major problem decades after their use was banned. Methyl mercury absorbed by fish in rivers and oceans can prevail for many years, becoming more concentrated as it moves up the food chain. As the importance of such issues increases, we must consider appropriate responses. Often these may be quite different from the policies used to respond to shorter-term air and water pollution.

Consider the case of ozone-depleting substances, which include chlorofluorocarbons (CFCs) as well as other chemicals such as the pesticide methyl bromide. The damaging effects of CFCs were first identified in the 1970s, but many years passed before the scale of the problem was sufficiently well understood to motivate significant action on a global scale. These gases, used for cooling equipment such as automobile air conditioners as well as in other industrial applications, eventually migrate to the upper levels of the atmosphere, where they attack the earth's protective ozone layer.

As the ozone layer thins, damaging solar radiation penetrates, causing problems such as increased incidence of skin cancer as well as complex ecological damage.

## 16-4   Has Ozone Depletion Peaked?

In October 2000, NASA data showed that the ozone hole over Antarctica had reached a size of nearly 11 million square miles, an area more than three times the size of the United States. This was the largest measurement ever reported. Record-low temperatures in the stratosphere are believed to have promoted the expansion of the ozone hole during the Southern Hemisphere's spring season.

For two days, a small part of the hole extended north from Antarctica to Punta Arenas, a southern Chilean city of about 120,000 people, exposing residents to high levels of ultraviolet (UV) radiation. This was the first time the ozone hole had extended over a major population center. Too much UV radiation can cause skin cancer and destroy tiny plants at the beginning of the food chain.

Somewhat better news was reported in October 2001. The hole did not grow any larger and may have peaked in 2000. "This is consistent with human-produced chlorine compounds that destroy ozone reaching their peak concentrations in the atmosphere, leveling off, and beginning a very slow decline," according to NASA scientist Samuel Oltmans. However, recovery of the ozone layer to levels observed before 1980 is expected to take at least 50 years.

In 2003, the ozone hole once again reached a record size of 11 million square miles, but in 2004 it peaked at just over 9 million square miles, apparently indicating no clear increasing or decreasing trend.

**SOURCES**

Lilley, Ray. Associated Press, "Ozone Hole Opens over Chile City." *Boston Globe,* October 6, 2000.

Schmid, Randolph. "New Data Show Ozone Hole Is No Longer Getting Worse." *Boston Globe,* October 17, 2001.

The Ozone Hole Inc. (compiling data from The British Antarctic Study, NASA, UNEP, EPA, and other sources). http://www.theozonehole.com

Complete destruction of the ozone layer would end most life on Earth, as few organisms could withstand the intense radiation that would result. Thus the problem is extremely grave, and alarm has increased as holes in the ozone layer have widened over the polar regions (Box 16-4).

To analyze the issue of ozone depletion, we must consider both emissions and accumulation of CFCs. Figure 16-8 shows the relationship between the two in simplified form. Unlike our previous graphs, this one includes time, shown on the horizontal axis. The graph shows an emission pattern over three time periods of 20 years each. In the first period, emissions increase steadily. In the second, a freeze is imposed on

(a) Emissions

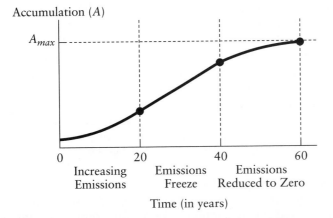

(b) Accumulation

**FIGURE 16-8** *Emissions and Accumulation of a Stock Pollutant*

emissions levels, with no further increase permitted—but emissions continue at the level they had already reached. In the third period, emissions drop steadily to an eventual zero level.[11]

Note the relationship between emissions and accumulations. As emissions rise at a steady rate, shown by the straight line in the first part of the upper graph, accumulations rise at an increasing rate.[12] Accumulations continue to rise steadily even when a

---

[11]This is rather over-optimistic for CFCs and other ozone-depleters. Loopholes in international agreements, as well as illegal production and trade, have made the goal of zero emissions an elusive one.

[12]In mathematical terms, this relationship can be expressed as $A = \int_0^t e\, dt$, meaning that accumulation can be measured as the integral of emissions over time.

freeze is imposed on emissions during the second period. Only when emissions are cut to zero in the third period does the rate of increase in accumulations start to slow, finally reaching a maximum accumulation that occurs 40 years after the maximum emission level was reached.

This simplified diagram conveys the essence of the problem. Since damages are related to accumulations, not emissions, environmental impact becomes steadily more severe, continuing for many years after control measures are taken. Dealing with cumulative pollutants requires urgent action and stringent policy measures. Even with such measures irreversible damage may occur. The environmental accumulations on our graph will take many decades after year 60 before they decline to a safe level.

The extreme urgency of the ozone depletion problem prompted an international agreement known as the Montreal Protocol, reached in 1987, to phase out the use of ozone-depleting substances. Subsequent amendments to the protocol strengthened and accelerated its implementation. Despite this unprecedented and generally effective international agreement, serious problems with loopholes have allowed continued production by some developing nations, and illegal trade in CFCs and other ozone depleters has been difficult to control. While emissions have declined as a result of the protocol, accumulations have continued to rise.[13]

The history of the ozone depletion problem shows the difficulty of responding adequately to cumulative pollutants. This is especially true when impacts are global, because effective action requires agreement among many governments. Unfortunately, ozone depletion is by no means the only problem with cumulative and global implications. Global climate change, as we will see in Chapter 18, shows a similar pattern of steadily accumulating **greenhouse gases** that cause atmospheric warming. Many industrial chemicals also are long-lived and persistent in the environment, making it impossible to limit policy analysis to short-term marginal damage effects.

The kinds of analysis and policy we have reviewed in this chapter have limited value in dealing with cumulative pollution problems. Market-based systems such as tradable permits have been used for transitional periods; for example, during the U.S. phase out of CFCs. A tradable permit system has been proposed for carbon emissions related to global warming. An effective response to the long-lived environmental impact of many human industrial and agricultural activities, however, requires fundamental changes in industrial systems.

In Chapters 17 and 18 we view pollution problems in a broader perspective. Chapter 17 deals with **industrial ecology,** which aims at an overall reduction of human environmental impact, and Chapter 18 focuses in greater depth on the problem of **global climate change** resulting from emissions of carbon dioxide and other gases.

---

[13]For an overview of the implementation of the Montreal Protocol, see Brack, 1996; Benedick, 1998; and LePrestre et al., 1998.

## SUMMARY

The principle of economic efficiency in environmental policy implies a balance between the marginal costs and benefits of pollution control. This has implications both for the level of control and the policies used to achieve it. Although the principle of balancing marginal costs and benefits is simple in theory, its application to real-world issues is often complex and involves judgment about both goals and policies.

One possible market-based policy is a per-unit tax on pollution emissions. The tax level should reflect the damage caused by the pollution. A pollution tax allows individual firms to decide how much pollution reduction to undertake. Least-cost pollution control options will be selected first. However, choosing the tax level requires an accurate estimate of damage costs, which may be difficult to reduce to monetary terms.

Transferable pollution permits, another market-based policy, allow setting a target for total pollution reduction. The permit price is then set through the market mechanism, as firms trade permits amongst themselves. This, in theory, combines the advantages of a definite amount of pollution reduction with an economically efficient process. However, it is only suitable for specific pollution control efforts under particular conditions.

Market-based policies often fail to control pollutants that exhibit nonlinear and threshold damage effects, as well as pollutants with local rather than regional impact. Specific emissions standards may be needed for these pollutants, especially those that produce potentially severe health or ecological damage. For nonuniformly mixed water pollutants, ambient pollution level rather than emission levels must be the focus of policy. This may require different kinds of policies for different emitters.

Important considerations in the choice of pollution policy include the patterns of costs and damages as well as options for improved pollution-control technology. Policies should be selected with a view to minimizing unnecessary costs or damages, and promoting technological progress in pollution control.

An especially difficult problem arises in the case of long-lived, cumulative pollutants such as DDT, PCBs, and ozone-depleting substances. In these cases, controlling emissions levels is insufficient, and it will often be necessary to reduce emissions to zero to avoid unacceptable levels of damage.

## KEY TERMS AND CONCEPTS

ambient pollution level
command-and-control policies
cumulative pollutant
economic efficiency
emissions standards
equimarginal principle
flow pollutant
global climate change

global pollutant
grandfathering
greenhouse gases
industrial ecology
internalizing externalities
local and regional pollutants
market-based pollution control
nonlinear or threshold effects

nonpoint source pollution
nonuniformly mixed pollutants
optimal pollution level
point source pollution
pollution
pollution tax

sink function
stock pollutant
transferable pollution permits
uniformly mixed pollutants
watershed management

## DISCUSSION QUESTIONS

1. How practical is the idea of an optimum pollution control level? How is it possible to establish such a level in practice? Can this be done solely based on economic analysis, or must we take into account other factors?

2. Suppose that your state has a problem with pollution in rivers and lakes, from both residential and industrial sources. You are asked to advise on appropriate pollution control policies. Which kinds of policies would be appropriate? How would you decide whether to recommend standards, pollution taxes, or permits, or some other policy? What factors (for example, different kinds of pollution) would go into your decision?

3. Why is an emissions freeze not an adequate policy response to a cumulative pollutant such as chlorofluorocarbons (CFCs)? What kinds of policies are more appropriate, and why are these policies often especially difficult to implement?

## PROBLEM

Two power plants are currently emitting 8,000 tons of pollution each (for a total of 16,000 tons). Control costs for Plant 1 are given by $MC_c(1)=.02Q$ and for Plant 2 by $MC_c(2)=.03Q$, where $Q$ represents the number of tons of pollution reduction. Analyze the effects of the following policies in terms of control costs for each firm, total control costs, government revenues, and total pollution reduction:

(a) A regulation requiring each plant to reduce its pollution by 5,000 tons.
(b) A pollution tax of $120 per ton of pollution emitted.
(c) A transferable permit system in which permits for emission of 6,000 tons of pollution are issued, 3,000 to each plant (use a diagram similar to Figure 16-3, showing 10,000 tons of total pollution reduction).

## REFERENCES

Benedick, Richard Elliott. *Ozone Diplomacy; New Directions in Safeguarding the Planet.* Cambridge, Mass.: Harvard University Press, 1998.

Brack, Duncan. *International Trade and the Montreal Protocol.* Royal Institute of International Affairs, Energy and Environment Programme. London, U.K.: Earthscan, 1996.

Burtraw, Dallas, et al. "Costs and Benefits of Reducing Air Pollutants Related to Acid Rain." *Contemporary Economic Policy* 16 (October 1998): 379–400.

Goodstein, Eban. *Economics and the Environment*. 4th ed. New York: Wiley, 2005.

Jorgenson, Dale W., and Peter J. Wilcoxen. "The Economic Impact of the Clean Air Act Amendments of 1990." In *Energy, the Environment, and Economic Growth*, edited by Dale Jorgenson. Cambridge, Mass.: MIT Press, 1998.

Joskow, Paul L., Richard Schmalensee, and Elizabeth M. Bailey. "The Market for Sulfur Dioxide Emissions." *American Economic Review* 88 (September 1998): 669–685.

LePrestre, Phillipe G., et al. *Protecting the Ozone Layer: Lessons, Models, and Prospects*. Boston: Kluwer, 1998.

Miltz, D., et al. "Standards versus Prices Revisited: The Case of Agricultural NonPoint Source Pollution." *Journal of Agricultural Economics* 39 (September 1998): 360–368.

Rigano, James P. "The Regulation of Non-Point Source Pollution." In *The Environment: Global Problems, Local Solutions*, edited by James E. Hickey and Linda A. Longmire. Westport, Conn., and London, U.K.: Greenwood Press, 1994.

Sanchez, Carol M. "The Impact of Environmental Regulations on the Adoption of Innovation: How Electric Utilities Responded to the Clean Air Act Amendments of 1990." In *Research in Corporate Social Performance and Policy*, vol. 15, edited by James E. Post. Stamford, Conn., and London, U.K.: JAI Press, 1998.

Stavins, Robert. "What Can We Learn from the Grand Policy Experiment? Lessons from SO$_2$ Allowance Trading." *Journal of Economic Perspectives* 12 (Summer 1998): 69–88.

Stavins, Robert, and Bradley Whitehead. "Market Based Environmental Policies." In *Thinking Ecologically: The Next Generation of Environmental Policy*, edited by Marian R. Chertow and Daniel C. Esty. New Haven, Conn.: Yale University Press, 1997.

Tietenberg, Tom. *Environmental and Natural Resource Economics*. 6th ed. New York: Addison-Wesley, 2003.

Weitzman, Martin. "Prices versus Quantities." *Review of Economic Studies* 41, no. 4 (October 1974): 477–491.

## WEBSITES

1. **http://www.epa.gov/airmarkets/** The EPA's website for acid rain regulation. Includes extensive information about the SO$_2$ emissions trading program.

2. **http://www.etei.org/** Homepage for the Emissions Trading Education Initiative, a project of the Environmental Defense Fund and the Emissions Marketing Association. The site includes case studies as well as extensive links and a bibliography.

3. **http://www.epa.gov/ozone/** The EPA's website about the ozone layer and ozone depletion. The site includes scientific information on ozone depletion, information about the Montreal Protocol and CFC substitutes, and a glossary of terms.

4. **http://www.rff.org/** Website of Resources for the Future, featuring many publications dealing with the benefits of pollution reduction and different approaches for regulating pollution.

**CHAPTER FOCUS QUESTIONS**

- Can the principle of recycling apply to the entire industrial system?
- Can modern agriculture become compatible with ecological systems?
- Can growing world demands for materials be met without disrupting the global environment?

CHAPTER **17**

# Industrial Ecology

## Economic and Ecological Views of Production

We started this book with the observation that economic systems inevitably use resources and produce wastes. In Chapters 4, 5, and 12–15 we discussed the economics of resources, and in Chapters 3 and 16 we looked at methods of internalizing environmental costs and controlling pollution. Although the standard environmental economics approach is to examine these issues separately, they are clearly connected.

In this chapter we survey the flows of resources and wastes through the economic system—what we call **throughput**—and develop a new perspective on policies to improve resource management and reduce wastes and pollution.

Robert and Leslie Ayres, in an exposition of the basic principles of **industrial ecology,** summarize the relationship between resource use and waste generation as follows:

> As a point of departure, we note that every substance extracted from the earth's crust, or harvested from a forest, a fishery, or from agriculture, is a potential waste. Not only is it a potential waste, it soon becomes an actual waste in almost all cases, with a delay of a few weeks to a few years at most. The only exceptions worth mentioning are long-lived construction materials.

In other words, materials consumed by the industrial economic system do not physically disappear. They are merely transformed to less useful forms. . . . It follows from this simple relationship between inputs and outputs—a consequence of the law of conservation of mass—that economic growth tends to be accompanied by equivalent growth in waste generation and pollution.[1]

The economic view of production is as a process of transforming raw materials into finished products. This "straight-line" process—from raw materials to final product—must necessarily create the unwanted by-products of pollution and wastes. In addition, once products wear out, they too become wastes.

For many years, economic theory generally paid little attention to what happens to these wastes. Environmental and resource economics may be seen as an effort to respond to the "loose ends" of the production process—the inputs of resources and outputs of wastes. More generally, we can think of the entire economic process as being embedded within a broader set of ecosystem processes, as we indicated with the expanded circular flow diagram in Figure 1-2 in Chapter 1.

Natural systems, in contrast to economic systems, typically follow a cyclical pattern, with wastes being recycled and reused. Healthy natural systems show no buildup of pollution and wastes. Inorganic elements such as water and nitrogen cycle through the system. Dead and decayed organic materials form the basis of fertile soils from which new vegetable life can grow, in turn supporting new animal life. Rather than creating a problem requiring solution or disposal, wastes become inputs at a new stage in the cycle.

Can this principle apply to the economic system? Many resource inputs are **nonrenewable,** but opportunities often exist for resource **recycling.** As we saw in Chapter 12, recycling promotes resource conservation—fewer new resources are needed—and it also reduces the volume of wastes generated by the industrial system. Taking a broader view, we can think of the entire economic production process as a circular flow in which wastes (except for waste energy) can potentially become the raw materials for future production.

## Making Wastes into Inputs

Figure 17-1 illustrates the economic view of the industrial process. Industrial ecology applies ecosystem principles of recycling to the industrial realm, replacing the straight-line process with a circular pattern, as shown in Figure 17-2. "In industrial ecology, economic systems are viewed not in isolation from their surrounding systems, but in concert with them . . . it is the study of all interactions between industrial systems and the environment."[2]

Think of individual industries as composed of an interlocking pattern of different materials cycles. Figure 17-3 shows a more complete view of a typical industrial cycle,

---

[1]Ayres and Ayres, 1996, p. 1.

[2]Graedel, 1994, p. 23.

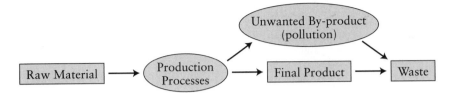

**FIGURE 17-1** *"Straight-Line" Pattern of Traditional Industrial Processes*

taking into account the various stages in the processes of production and consumption. The complexity of real-life industrial processes offers many potential **feedback loops** within the total process: opportunities to reuse waste materials from production or consumption as inputs at an earlier stage in the process.

A specific example gives some insight into the policy challenges associated with creating a system of industrial ecology. Producing plastic beverage bottles (Box 17-1) offers various opportunities for recycling materials either into new bottles or into other products. Whether or not consumers and producers will take advantage of such opportunities depends on how profitable it is to do so. Important economic issues include incentives for recycling—such as bottle deposit/return systems—and the institutions that support recycling, such as curbside collection of used bottles and other recyclables.

## Closing the Loops: The Potential of Industrial Ecology

Current economic systems have developed primarily based on incentives associated with the "straight-line" production pattern shown in Figure 17-1. Reorienting the economic system toward more environmentally benign industrial ecology goals requires major **technological innovation** aimed at

- Minimizing the output of unwanted by-products such as pollution and $CO_2$ emissions.

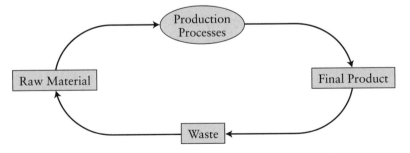

**FIGURE 17-2** *Cyclic Production Processes of Industrial Ecology*

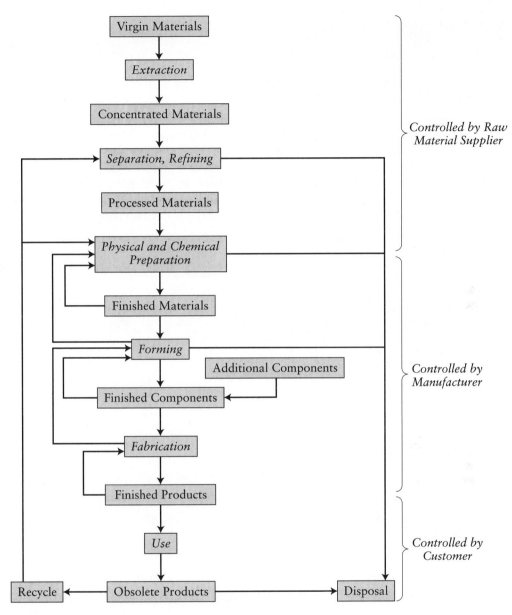

**FIGURE 17-3** *The Total Industrial Ecology Cycle*

Source: Adapted from R. Socolow et al., eds. *Industrial Ecology and Global Change.* Cambridge, U.K.: CUP, 1994. Reprinted with the permission of Cambridge University Press.

## *17-1*   Beverage Bottle Recycling

The basic ingredient in widely used plastic beverage bottles is polyethylene teraphthalate (PET). Used PET is easily recyclable into fibers for carpets or insulation for sleeping bags, pillows, and ski jackets. With chemical treatment, it can make polyurethane foam insulation or polyester resin bathtubs, and can also be repolymerized for new bottles and other PET products (Figure 17-4).

The U.S. PET bottle recycling rate is about 40 percent. About 35 percent of all synthetic carpeting sold in the United States contains material from used soft-drink bottles. With improved economic incentives, plastics recycling shows significant further expansion possibilities.

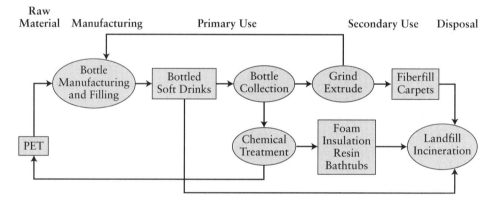

FIGURE 17-4 *Beverage Bottle Industrial Life Cycle*

**SOURCES**

Frosch and Gallopoulos, 1992.

R. Socolow et al., 1994, p. 344. Reprinted with the permission of Cambridge University Press.

- Recycling the wastes from industrial processes and worn-out goods into raw materials for further production.

Robert and Leslie Ayres identify four major strategies for increasing the ecological efficiency of resource use and reducing wastes and pollution:

- **Dematerialization:** achieving the same economic goal using less material by increasing materials use efficiency.
- **Materials substitution:** replacing a scarce, hazardous, or high-polluting material with a more environmentally benign substitute.

- Repair, reuse, **remanufacturing,** and recycling: variations on the feedback loops shown in Figure 17-3. (*Remanufacturing* refers to the installation of new parts in used appliances and machines to extend their useful life.)
- **Waste mining:** retrieving usable materials from urban, industrial, or agricultural waste streams.[3]

Each of these strategies implies specific economic incentives and institutions. *Dematerialization* has occurred in many industries simply as a consequence of technological progress and increased efficiency. Aluminum beverage cans, for example, contain 30 percent less metal than they did in the 1970s, and aluminum cans themselves replaced cans made of much heavier metal used in earlier decades. Achieving the same function (delivering the beverage to the consumer) using less material benefits the supplier, as well as the environment, cutting resource use and reducing the waste stream even if cans are not recycled.

Market incentives have led to *materials substitution.* Many uses of copper, for example, have been replaced by plastics, optical fibers, and lighter metals such as aluminum. Government regulation has contributed to the partial replacement of metal-based pigments in paint with organic pigments, reducing the dangers of lead paint poisoning and the amounts of lead and other heavy metals in the waste stream.[4]

Some market-driven substitutions, however, may be worse for the environment. For example, organo-chloride compounds such as polyvinyl chloride (PVC), associated with environmental hazards and health risks, have expanded in use due to their relatively low cost in many industrial and commercial products (see Box 17-2).

An extensive review of the evidence on dematerialization and materials substitution concludes that, while considerable evidence indicates that many economic production processes have grown "lighter," using less material per unit of output, this does not necessarily result in less overall environmental impact. Trends of declining input use per dollar of GDP must be balanced against increasing overall demand as GDP grows. To separate, or "decouple," GDP growth from materials inputs would require that output can grow while input use remains constant. However, " . . . there is no compelling macroeconomic evidence that the U.S. economy is "decoupled" from material inputs; and we know even less about the net environmental effects of many changes in materials use."[5]

Although *recycling* has increased in recent years, economic incentives to recycle materials vary considerably. Recycling certain materials, such as aluminum, is profitable because of considerable savings in energy use and other costs as compared to the use of virgin materials. As we noted in Chapter 12, a significant portion of other metal production also uses scrap or recycled inputs.

Materials such as paper and plastics can be recycled effectively, but the profitability of recycling these materials varies. Thus successful paper and plastic recycling

---

[3]Ayres and Ayres, 1996, p. 13–14.

[4]Ayres and Ayres, 1996, p. 12.

[5]Quote from Cleveland and Ruth, 1999, p. 45; see also Ayres et al., 2004.

## 17-2 Toxics Reduction: The Problem of PVC

Polyvinyl chloride (PVC) is one of the most widely used plastics. It is used in numerous products including outdoor furniture, sewer pipes, toys, credit cards, storage containers, electrical wire insulation, and medical equipment. However, health and environmental concerns arise throughout the life cycle of PVC products. PVC production can expose workers to carcinogens and other toxic chemicals. The use of PVC products, such as medical equipment and toys, poses dangers from the leaching of chemical additives. PVC's most common use is in construction materials but in the event of a building fire, PVC products release hydrochloric acid fumes. Disposal of PVC is also problematic as incineration produces toxic emissions and disposal in landfills can contaminate soil and groundwater.

With some plastics, such as PET (see Box 17-1), an industrial ecology approach emphasizes "closing the loop" through recycling and the production of new products using recycled materials. However, recycling of PVC products is limited, primarily because most PVC products contain various additives that inhibit recycling. In Europe, where PVC recycling efforts are the most aggressive, only about 3 percent of post-consumer PVC is recycled.

Addressing the environmental concerns of PVC requires a broader approach, such as that undertaken by Denmark. The country has instituted an effort to eliminate the incineration of PVC waste. Still, about half of PVC waste is incinerated because many PVC products can not be identified as containing PVC. Denmark has also placed a tax on certain PVC products, and eco-labels are not permitted on goods containing PVC. Finally, the country is actively encouraging the development of PVC alternatives.

In many instances, **life-cycle analysis**—taking into account the full economic and environmental impacts of a product from production to disposal—suggests that PVC alternatives are both cheaper and less damaging to the environment and human health. For example, vinyl flooring is inexpensive to purchase and install, but alternative flooring materials, such as cork and linoleum, are cheaper when the product lifespan and maintenance costs are taken into consideration. PVC alternatives are also available for sewer pipes, medical supplies, and many other applications.

The limited possibilities for an environmentally friendly cyclical PVC system suggest the long-term goal of reducing or eliminating PVC production. Regional or national regulations can encourage the switch to PVC-free alternatives. For example, Canada has banned the use of PVC in food packaging. A Japanese law requiring the recycling of packaging materials has encouraged manufacturers to switch to non-PVC packaging. Companies including Nike, Sony, and IKEA have also taken voluntary steps to reduce or eliminate the use of PVC in their products.

**SOURCE**

Frank Ackerman and Rachel Massey, *The Economics of Phasing out PVC,* available at http://www.ase.tufts.edu/gdae/pubs/rp/economics_of_pvc.pdf. Reprinted by permission of Frank Ackerman and Rachel Massey.

programs often depend on some degree of government support. *Repair and remanufacturing* tend to be labor-intensive. Countries with relatively high labor costs often forgo these activities in favor of replacement with new products.

*Waste mining* is "the recovery of low-value byproducts and wastes for use as industrial raw materials . . . such sources are often somewhat more difficult, or more costly to exploit than natural sources"[6] For this reason, effective waste mining requires government policy either to internalize the costs of generating wastes or to encourage their reuse. Both *technological innovation* and *institutional support* (such as curbside recycling programs or government purchase of recycled materials) are important in developing a thriving market for recyclables.[7]

The development of "green technologies" to reduce materials use and waste generation can be encouraged by economic incentives. Examples include **green taxes** (Pigovian taxes on negative externalities) and **green subsidies** (subsidies for environmentally friendly technologies that provide positive externalities), as well as **transferable permit** systems. Table 17-1 gives examples of environmentally oriented economic policies in practice.

## Making Agriculture Compatible with Natural Ecosystems

The connection between agricultural production and ecological systems is obvious; yet modernized agriculture borrows many of its operating principles from industry. Economic and ecological values may conflict in the drive to maximize agricultural output.

Modern production techniques generally focus on increasing agricultural yields per acre cultivated through the use of inputs such as chemical fertilizers, pesticides, and intensive irrigation (Figure 17-5). However, as we saw in Chapter 11, this type of agriculture can damage the environment. Chemical inputs can pollute groundwater and rivers, and pesticides can kill beneficial species and disturb the food chain of the surrounding ecosystems. Excessive irrigation can deplete water supplies and contribute to erosion, soil degradation, and groundwater pollution.

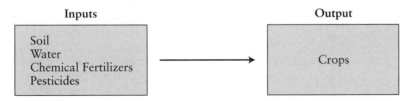

Inputs | Output

Soil
Water
Chemical Fertilizers
Pesticides

Crops

**FIGURE 17-5** *The Economic "Straight-Line" View of Agricultural Production*

---

[6]Ayres and Ayres, 1996, p. 15.

[7]See Ackerman, 1996.

**TABLE 17-1** *Selected "Green" Tax and Permit Systems*

| Environmental Problem | Policy | Country, Year | Description |
|---|---|---|---|
| Excessive water demand | Tradable water rights | Chile, 1981 | Existing users grandfathered. Rights to new suppliers auctioned. Total water use capped. |
| Solid waste | Toxic waste charge | Germany, 1991 | Toxic waste production fell more than 15 percent in three years. |
| | Solid waste charge | Denmark, 1986 | Recycling rate for demolition waste increased from 12 percent to 82 percent over 6–8 years. |
| Water pollution | Fees to cover waste-water treatment costs | Netherlands, 1970 | Main factor behind 86–97 percent drop in industrial heavy metals discharges and substantial drops in organic emissions. |
| | Fertilizer sales taxes | Sweden, 1982 and 1984 | Revenues fund agricultural subsidies and education programs on fertilizer use reduction. Use of nitrogen dropped 25 percent; potassium, 60 percent; phosphorus 64 percent. |
| Acid rain | Nitrogen oxide charge on electricity producers | Sweden, 1992 | Refunded as electricity production subsidy. Contributed to 35 percent emissions reduction in two years. |
| $SO_2$ air pollution | Sulfur permit system | U.S., 1995 | Nearly all permits allocated free to past emitters. Emissions cut to about half the 1980 level by 2000; cost of compliance far lower than predicted. |
| Ozone depletion | Ozone-depleting substance tax | U.S., 1990 | Smoothing and enforcing phase-outs. |
| | Chlorofluoro-carbon permit system | Singapore, 1989 | Half of permits auctioned, half allocated to past producers and importers. |
| Global climate change | Carbon dioxide tax | Norway, 1991 | Emissions appear 3–4 percent lower than they would have been without the tax. |
| Uncontrolled development | Tradable development rights | U.S., New Jersey pinelands, 1982 | Land use plan sets density limits on development in forested, agricultural, and designated growth zones. In growth zones, developers may build beyond density limits if they buy excess credits from landowners. |

Source: Roodman, 1997.

An ecological view of agricultural production sees crop output as one part of a diverse **agroecological system,** including water, carbon, nitrogen and other nutrient cycles (Figure 17-6). To maintain the long-term sustainability of this system, cultivation practices must minimize chemical inputs and rely more on **organic techniques,** which return nutrients to the soil, control pests by natural methods, and are not harmful to other species. Agriculture of this type may not offer such high single-crop yields in the short term, but will allow farmers to raise a variety of crops and animals without damaging ecosystems or polluting water supplies.

Just as with industrial systems, economic incentives are key in developing more ecologically balanced agricultural production. Subsidies for fertilizer, pesticides, and water encourage the "straight-line" approach of high input use accompanied by problems such as chemical runoff and water overdraft. Removing such subsidies encourages more efficient use of inputs and recycling of natural organic nutrients.

Subsidy removal, however, can cause hardship for farmers who depend on purchased inputs. For this reason, other policies such as provision of information on organic techniques, agricultural credit for soil conservation and small-scale irrigation development, and transportation and marketing assistance must accompany the removal of subsidies, particularly in developing countries where many farmers are poor and have limited access to credit and markets.

Many traditional agricultural systems operated in greater harmony with natural cycles, using a diverse pattern of multiple crops and animal husbandry (Box 17-3 and Figure 17-7). The challenge today is to preserve or regain the ecological benefits of such systems while also achieving the high yields essential to providing an adequate diet to still-growing populations.

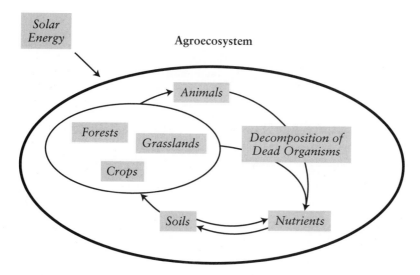

**FIGURE 17-6** *The Ecological View of Agroecological Cycles*

## 17-3  Integrated Farming Systems in Asia

Integrated Farming Systems (IFS) involving aquaculture have been used in Asia for many centuries. The IFS uses "natural processes involving natural organisms under the most favorable conditions for optimum yields. The main objective is to enhance nutrient cycling and energy flow in ecosystems in order to obtain maximum benefits in food and fiber and to recycle residues completely and economically." The system "combines livestock, aquaculture, agriculture, and agroindustry on every farm, and reinforces the microbial or biochemical process as input for subsequent ones."[1]

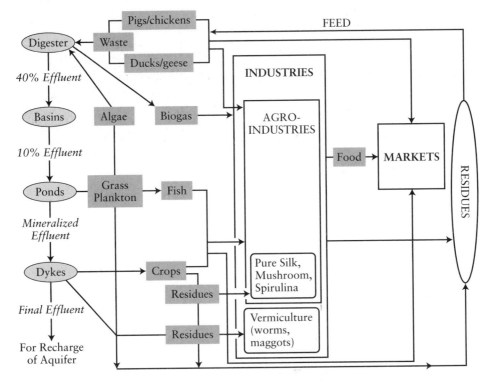

**FIGURE 17-7** *Feedback Loops in an Integrated Farming System*

Source: Adapted from George L. Chan, "Aquaculture, Ecological Engineering: Lessons from China." *Ambio*, November 1993, p. 492. Reprinted by permission of *Ambio*. Published by the Royal Swedish Academy of Sciences.

[1]McGinn, 1998.

*Fish farms and rice paddies along the border of Shenzhen and Hong Kong. Recycling of nutrients and wastes can maintain ecological balance in agricultural systems producing multiple outputs.*

## Industrial Ecology on a Global Scale

Efforts to improve materials use efficiency take place against a backdrop of steadily increasing material consumption. Figure 17-8 shows the steady growth of world materials production over a 30-year period. "In 1995, nearly 10 billion tons of industrial and construction minerals, metals, wood products, and synthetic materials were extracted or produced globally. This is more than double the level of 1963. This 10 billion tons does not include hidden flows of material—the billions of tons that never entered the economy but were left at mine sites or smelters. Factoring in these flows would at least double and possibly triple the global total materials load."[8]

As shown in Table 17-2, per capita material consumption rates differ widely between developed and developing countries. Each U.S. citizen consumes about 10 tons of materials per year (not including mining wastes), about six times the world average.

---

[8]Gardner and Sampat, 1998, p. 14.

Billions of Tons

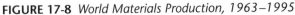

**FIGURE 17-8** *World Materials Production, 1963–1995*

Source: Adapted from Gardner and Sampat, *Mind Over Matter: Recasting the Role of Materials in Our Lives.* Worldwatch Paper no. 144. Washington, D.C.: Worldwatch Institute, 1998. Reprinted by permission of Worldwatch Institute, http://www.worldwatch.org.

Thus if everyone in the world consumed at U.S. levels, materials consumption would hypothetically increase sixfold. Material flows at this level would be impossible to sustain, but even short of this seemingly impossible level, population and GDP growth will certainly lead to significantly greater demands in the coming decades.

It is therefore important to examine the potential impact of vastly increased materials flows on planetary ecosystems. This is a broader issue than the question of nonrenewable resource supplies that we examined in Chapter 12. Even if supplies of most resources are adequate, the mining, fabrication, use, and disposal of materials has environmental impacts at each stage of the cycle.

On a planetary scale, evidence is mounting that materials consumption by humans is causing significant disruptions in the **global materials cycles** that support life on earth:

> In the grand cycles, atoms of carbon, nitrogen, sulfur, and phosphorous cycle back and forth from living plants and animals to the soil, atmosphere and oceans. The winds and water currents of earth move these atoms global distances. . . . All four grand cycles are now strongly influenced by human activity. . . .
>
> The carbon cycle has been perturbed by fossil fuel use, deforestation, and changes in agriculture and animal husbandry. . . . The nitrogen cycle has been perturbed especially by worldwide fertilizer use, which has grown rapidly and steadily for more than 40 years.

**TABLE 17-2A** *Growth in World Materials Production, 1960–1995*

| Material | Production in 1995 (million tons) | Per Capita Production (tons per capita) | Increase since Early 1960s (factor of change) |
|---|---|---|---|
| Minerals | 7,641 | 1.34 | 2.5-fold |
| Metals | 1,196 | 0.20 | 2.1-fold |
| Wood Products | 724 | 0.12 | 2.3-fold |
| Synthetics | 252 | 0.04 | 5.6-fold |
| All Materials | 9,813 | 1.72 | 2.4-fold |

**TABLE 17-2B** *Growth in U.S. Materials Consumption, 1900–1995*

| Material | Consumption in 1995 (million tons) | Per Capita Consumption (tons per capita) | Increase since 1900 (factor of change) |
|---|---|---|---|
| Minerals | 2,410 | 9.16 | 29-fold |
| Metals | 132 | 0.50 | 3-fold |
| Wood Products | 170 | 0.64 | 14-fold |
| Synthetics | 131 | 0.49 | 82-fold |
| All Materials | 2,843 | 10.81 | 18-fold |

Source: Adapted from Gardner and Sampat, *Mind Over Matter: Recasting the Role of Materials in Our Lives.* Worldwatch Paper no. 144. Washington, D.C.: Worldwatch Institute, 1998, p. 16. Reprinted by permission of Worldwatch Institute. www.worldwatch.org. Per capita production figures based on population estimates from Population Reference Bureau, *World Population DataSheet 1995.*

Secondary impacts on the nitrogen cycle have resulted from high-temperature combustion and from [other] agricultural practices.[9]

The sulfur and phosphorous cycles are also strongly affected by industrial emission of sulfur compounds and by mining of phosphate rock for fertilizer. Nitrogen and phosphorous cycles provide plant nutrients beneficial to agriculture but also capable of creating ecological havoc by promoting excessive growth of algae and other opportunistic species that choke out other plant and animal life. Sulfur compounds cause acid rain and other damaging effects on ecosystems and also affect weather patterns. In Chapter 18 we will examine effects of the disruption of the global carbon cycle on climate and ecosystems.

Clearly, the projected continuing rise in world materials consumption will pose even greater problems of ecosystem disruption on regional and global scales. The most likely strategies for counteracting this trend include increased efficiency and recycling to reduce human global impact. The record to date, however, is not encouraging. Significant

[9]Socolow et al., 1994, p. 117. See Ayres et al., 1994, on carbon and nitrogen cycles.

**TABLE 17-3** *Gains in Materials Efficiency and Offsetting Factors*

| Product | Efficiency Gains | Offsetting Factors |
|---|---|---|
| Plastics in Cars | Use of plastics in U.S. cars increased by 26 percent between 1980 and 1994, replacing steel in many uses and reducing car weight by 6 percent. | Cars contain 25 chemically incompatible plastics that, unlike steel, cannot be easily recycled. Thus most plastic in cars winds up in landfills. |
| Bottles and Cans | Aluminum cans weigh 30 percent less today than they did 20 years ago. | Cans replaced an environmentally superior product—refillable bottles. |
| Lead Batteries | A typical automobile battery used 30 pounds of lead in 1974, but only 20 pounds in 1994, with improved performance. | U.S. domestic battery shipments increased by 76 percent in the same period, more than offsetting the efficiency gains. |
| Radial Tires | Radial tires are 25 percent lighter and last twice as long as bias-ply tires. | Radials are more difficult to retread. Sales of passenger car retreads fell by 52 percent in the United States between 1977 and 1997. |
| Mobile Phones | Weight of mobile phones dropped tenfold between 1991 and 1996. | Subscribers to cellular telephone service jumped more than eightfold in the same period, nearly offsetting the gains from weight decreases. |

Source: Adapted from Gardner and Sampat, *Mind Over Matter: Recasting the Role of Materials in Our Lives.* Worldwatch Paper no. 144. Washington, D.C.: Worldwatch Institute, 1998, p. 29. Reprinted by permission of Worldwatch Institute. www.worldwatch.org.

improvements in efficiency and reduction in the **intensity of materials use (IU)**, defined as the quantity of material used per unit of economic output,[10] have tended to be offset by economic growth and additional materials-related environmental impact (see Table 17-3).

## Measuring the Impacts of Global Growth

In Chapter 10 we introduced the $I = PAT$ equation that links environmental impact, population, affluence, and technology. The global industrial ecology challenge can be viewed in terms of this equation as follows:

change in $P$ = increase in population (at least 30 percent growth predicted 2000–2025)

change in $A$ = economic growth (2.5 percent per capita per year would give 85 percent growth by 2025)

total change in $(P \times A) = (1.3)(1.85) =$ a factor of 2.40 over 2000 levels by 2025.

---

[10]Cleveland and Ruth, 1999

The technology factor *T* is defined as the environmental impact per unit of output. If the technology factor—closely related to the intensity of materials use (material use per unit of economic output or *IU*)—remained unchanged, by 2025 environmental impact would be multiplied by a factor of 2.4 over 2000 levels.

In order to hold environmental impact unchanged, *IU* would have to be reduced by about 60 percent. In other words, if total output is 2.4 times as great in 2025, but the impact per unit of output is 0.4 of the current level, the net impact would be (0.4)(2.4), which approximately equals 1, indicating no change in net impact. To reduce the environmental impacts of economic activity below today's level, the reduction in *IU* would have to be even greater.

How likely is it that this kind of gain will occur? A study of industrial economies shows that energy intensity (energy use per dollar of GDP) has declined steadily since 1970 (see Figure 17-9). In almost all cases, this has been offset by GDP growth, so that total energy use has increased. But countries can take widely divergent energy paths,

**FIGURE 17-9** *Declining Energy Intensity in Industrial Economies, 1970–2002*

Note: Data for Germany is for West Germany only prior to 1991.

Source: OECD, 1991; U.S. Department of Energy, Energy Information Administration, *International Energy Annual 2002,* posted June 2004 at http://eia.doe.gov/iea.

some with much less impact on the global carbon cycle than others.[11] With deliberate policy effort, much greater reductions in energy and materials intensity could be achieved.

A Worldwatch Institute report identifies strategies for promoting recycling and increased efficiency.[12] These include integrating recycling into all industrial stages, as the industrial ecology paradigm implies. In addition, redefining "output" in terms of services rather than goods could make firms seek to lower, rather than increase, physical product sales.

For example, if utilities were reoriented toward delivering heating, cooling, and light rather than gas or electricity, they could specialize in retrofitting homes and businesses for high efficiency, thereby profiting by selling *less* of their physical output. Substitution of new materials and nonfossil fuel energy sources in production and goods could considerably reduce environmental impacts. To be truly effective, these changes on the production side would need to be complemented by a new consumer ethic of **sufficiency**—a goal of having enough to support a comfortable life, but no more—rather than ever-growing consumption. (We will discuss this important issue of restraint in consumption in Chapter 20.)

## Policies to Promote Industrial Ecology

In Chapters 12 and 16 we discussed many microeconomic policies aimed at conserving resources, internalizing the full costs of resource extraction, and reducing pollution. All of these policies are relevant to promoting industrial ecology. We cannot, however, respond on the necessary scale to global issues surrounding expansion of materials use and waste generation without macroeconomic policies as well.

Industrial ecology advocates have called for nothing less than a reorientation of the structure and goals of the entire economic system. This would require a combination of microeconomic and macroeconomic policies including the following:

- Systematic "green" tax reform to shift the tax burden from income and capital to resource consumption and waste emissions.
- Global and national limits on carbon emissions, possibly implemented through a system of tradable permits (more on this in Chapter 18).
- Local and regional planning processes to restructure industrial and transportation systems for maximum recycling and minimum energy use and waste generation (see Box 17-4 on the Kalundborg industrial ecosystem).
- Promotion of **environmental design**—engineering products for environmental compatibility, recyclability, and minimal toxicity. Incentives for environmental design can include **certification** of "green" products by government or independent agencies.

---

[11]Moomaw and Tullis, 1994.

[12]Gardner and Sampat, 1998.

## 17-4   The Kalundborg Industrial Ecosystem

**C**reating a system of industrial ecology requires coordination among many different firms as well as government policy support. An outstanding example of such **industrial symbiosis** is the town of Kalundborg, Denmark, as described by John Ehrenfeld and Nicolas Gertler in the *Journal of Industrial Ecology:*

> Eleven physical linkages comprise much of the tangible aspect of industrial symbiosis in Kalundborg. The town's four main industries—Asnaes Power Station, a 1,500-megawatt coal-fired power plant; a large oil refinery operated by Statoil; Novo Nordisk, a manufacturer of pharmaceuticals and enzymes; and Gyproc, a plasterboard manufacturer—and several users within the municipality trade and make use of waste streams and energy resources, and turn by-products into raw materials.

> Firms outside the area also participate as recipients of by-product-to-raw material exchanges. The symbioses evolved gradually and without a grand design over the past 25 years, as the firms sought to make economic use of their by-products and to minimize the costs of compliance with new, ever-stricter environmental regulations.

(Figure 17–10 shows patterns of material flows among firms.)

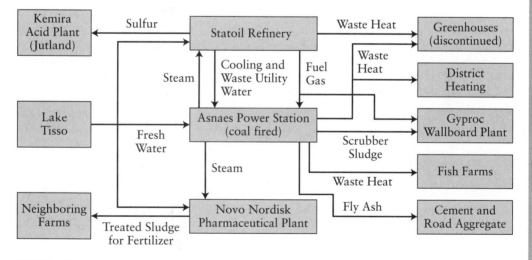

**FIGURE 17-10** *Industrial Linkages at Kalundborg*

Source: From John Ehrenfeld and Nicolas Gertler, "Industrial Ecology in Practice: The Evolution of Interdependence at Kalundborg," *Journal of Industrial Ecology*, 1:1 (Winter 1997), pp. 67–69. Copyright ©1997 by Yale University and the Massachusetts Institute of Technology. Reprinted by permission.

- Research and development of new technologies such as **solar hydrogen** and **fuel cells**[13] that capture and use solar energy to replace fossil fuels.
- Macroeconomic policies aimed at stability, sufficiency, and equity rather than continual economic growth.

Clearly, this vision is far from current reality. Present pollution control policies primarily respond to specific problems, but not the "macro" problems of economic growth and ecosystem disruption. However, industrial ecology theorists argue that we are not far from important **technological thresholds** that could introduce radically different—and much less environmentally damaging—industrial, agricultural, and energy systems.[14]

Would shifting toward an industrial ecology model impose large costs on consumers and producers? According to Harvard Business School professor Michael Porter, improving environmental performance can actually give firms a competitive advantage and help them to cut costs. The **Porter hypothesis** suggests that although shifting to environmentally sound production patterns can involve short-term costs, it can benefit firms in the long run by putting them "ahead of the curve" of government regulation and helping them establish a technological lead in processes and products that will gain international market share over time.[15] In addition, energy-efficient firms will be well placed to deal with future price increases in energy—a strong possibility, as we discussed in Chapter 13. Other research indicates that investment in new environmentally sound technology has a positive job-creation effect that prevents net job loss from stronger environmental regulation.[16]

The **Industrial Revolution** of the nineteenth century fundamentally altered both production systems and perceptions of economic goals. It may well be that in the twenty-first century the survival of planetary ecosystems will depend on a similar revolution in thought and practice, replacing standard industrial production and modernized agriculture with ecologically oriented systems. If so, we are only in the beginning stages of this transformation. Most of our policies and practices remain more suited to the earlier industrial era in which ecosystem impacts were only a minor consideration.

In the next chapter, we will examine one of the most prominent issues related to industrial impacts on global ecological cycles—greenhouse gas emissions and global climate change.

## SUMMARY

Industrial ecology adopts an overview of the entire process of resource use and waste generation in all sectors of the economy. Rather than viewing this as a series of "straight-line" processes from raw materials to final products and wastes, industrial

---

[13]Solar hydrogen systems use solar energy to split water into hydrogen and oxygen. The hydrogen and oxygen are then recombined in a fuel cell to provide energy with only water vapor emissions. Fuel cells can also use fossil fuels such as methane, but without the pollution resulting from burning fuels.

[14]See Ayres and Ayres, 1996, pp. 304–306.

[15]Porter, 1991.

[16]Goodstein, 1999.

ecology applies the cyclical logic of natural ecosystems. In a fully cyclical process, almost all wastes are recycled to become inputs to new processes.

Natural systems are based on complete cycles, with no buildup of pollution or wastes. Industrial systems may be designed to follow a similar cyclical pattern, by maximizing opportunities to recycle wastes at every point in the industrial production and consumption process.

Strategies for making the economic process more compatible with natural systems include increasing material use efficiency, finding substitutes for high-polluting or hazardous materials, reuse and recycling, and retrieving materials from urban, industrial, and agricultural waste streams. These strategies may be promoted through market processes, government policies, or economic incentives such as "green" taxes or subsidies.

Modern agriculture shares the "straight-line" focus on increased output that characterizes industrial systems. This has led to patterns of high input use and serious resource and environmental impact. A more environmentally benign agricultural system could be based on low-input techniques that conserve and recycle nutrients and water. Many traditional agricultural systems follow this approach, and traditional agriculture principles can combine with modern technological innovations to promote sustainable agroecological systems.

On a global scale, the effects of improved efficiency of materials use are outweighed by increased demand resulting from population and economic growth. Considerable further growth will occur throughout the developing world in coming decades, increasing pressures on resources and the environment. Human intervention significantly affects major planetary cycles including carbon, nitrogen, sulfur, and phosphorous.

Offsetting growth in population and per capita consumption will require dramatic reductions in intensity of materials use and environmental impact. Technological possibilities exist for achieving this goal, but local, regional, national, and global policy initiatives are needed to promote technologies that can make industry compatible with planetary ecosystems.

## KEY TERMS AND CONCEPTS

agroecological systems
certification
dematerialization
environmental design
feedback loops
fuel cells
global materials cycles
green subsidies
green taxes
industrial ecology
Industrial Revolution
industrial symbiosis
intensity of materials use (IU)
life-cycle analysis

materials substitution
nonrenewable resources
organic techniques
Porter hypothesis
recycling
remanufacturing
solar hydrogen
sufficiency
technological innovation
technological thresholds
throughput
transferable (pollution) permits
waste mining

## DISCUSSION QUESTIONS

1. What opportunities can you think of for developing industrial ecology in particular industries or regions? What kinds of economic incentives and government policies would be most effective in promoting ecosystem-friendly economic production?

2. What is the consumer's role in industrial ecology? In standard economic theory, consumers maximize their utility by consuming goods and services. How must this perspective be modified in an economic system oriented toward industrial ecology?

3. What economic barriers to developing agroecosystems use organic techniques? Note that the organic food industry, once a small "niche" market, has become a multibillion-dollar industry. Yet "industrialized agriculture" still produces most of our food with high synthetic chemical input. What economic factors will determine the future course of agricultural production?

## REFERENCES

Ackerman, Frank. *Why Do We Recycle? Markets, Values, and Public Policy.* Washington, D.C.: Island Press, 1996.

Ayres, Robert U., and Leslie W. Ayres. *Industrial Ecology: Towards Closing the Materials Cycle.* Cheltenham, U.K.: Elgar, 1996.

Ayres, Robert U., William H. Schlesinger, and Robert H. Socolow et al. "Human Impacts on the Carbon and Nitrogen Cycles." Chapter 9 in Socolow et al., eds., 1994.

Ayres, Robert U., Leslie W. Ayres, and Benjamin Warr. "Is the U.S. Economy Dematerializing? Main Indicators and Drivers." Chapter 3 in van den Bergh and Janssen, 2004.

Chan, George L. "Aquaculture, Ecological Engineering: Lessons from China." *Ambio,* November 1993.

Cleveland, Cutler, and Matthias Ruth. "Indicators of Dematerialization and the Materials Intensity of Use." *Journal of Industrial Ecology* 2, no. 3 (1999): 15–50.

Ehrenfeld, John, and Nicholas Gertler. "Industrial Ecology in Practice: The Evolution of Interdependence at Kalundborg." *Journal of Industrial Ecology* 1, no. 1 (1997): 67–79.

Frosch, R. A., and N. E. Gallopoulos. "Towards an Industrial Ecology." In *The Treatment and Handling of Wastes*, edited by A. D. Bradshaw et al. London, U.K.: Chapman and Hall for the Royal Society, 1992.

Gardner, Gary. "Preserving Agricultural Resources." In *State of the World 1996*, edited by Brown et al. Washington, D.C.: Worldwatch Institute, 1996.

Gardner, Gary, and Payal Sampat. *Mind Over Matter: Recasting the Role of Materials in Our Lives.* Worldwatch Paper 144. Washington, D.C.: Worldwatch Institute, 1998.

Goodstein, Eban. *The Trade-Off Myth: Fact and Fiction about Jobs and the Environment.* Washington, D.C.: Island Press, 1999.

Graedel, Thomas. "Industrial Ecology: Definition and Implementation." Chapter 3 in Socolow et al., eds., 1994.

McGinn, Anne Platt. *Rocking the Boat: Conserving Fisheries and Protecting Jobs.* Worldwatch Paper no. 142. Washington, D.C.: Worldwatch Institute, 1998.

Moomaw, William, and Mark Tullis. "Charting Development Paths: A Multicountry Comparison of Carbon Dioxide Emissions." Chapter 10 in Socolow et al., eds., 1994.

Organisation for Economic Co-operation and Development (OECD). *Environmental Indicators: A Preliminary Set.* Paris, France: OECD, 1991.

Porter, Michael E. "America's Green Strategy." *Scientific American* (April 1991): 168.

Roodman, David M. *Getting the Signals Right: Tax Reform to Protect the Environment and the Economy.* Worldwatch Paper No. 134, May 1997.

Socolow, R., C. Andrews, F. Berkhout, and V. Thomas, eds. *Industrial Ecology and Global Change.* Cambridge, U.K.: Cambridge University Press, 1994.

Van den Bergh, Jeroen C. J. M., and Marco Janssen, eds. *Economics of Industrial Ecology: Materials, Structural Change, and Spatial Scales.* Cambridge, Mass.: MIT Press, 2004.

## WEBSITES

1. **http://mitpress.mit.edu/** Search "industrial ecology" to find the *Journal of Industrial Ecology*, "designed to foster both understanding and practice in the emerging field of industrial ecology," and other books and reports on industrial ecology in practice.

2. **http://www.epa.gov/opptintr/dfe/** The EPA's website for the Design for the Environment Program, an initiative that "helps businesses incorporate environmental considerations into the design and redesign of products, processes, and technical and management systems." The site includes descriptions of many successful applications of industrial ecology.

3. **http://www.worldbank.org/research/greening/cover.htm** An online version of "Greening Industry," a World Bank report on ways to resolve apparent conflicts between economic development and environmental quality in developing countries.

**CHAPTER FOCUS QUESTIONS**

- How serious a problem is global warming/ global climate change?
- Can economic theory help evaluate the impact of climate change?
- What policies most effectively address climate change?

CHAPTER

# 18

# Global Climate Change

## Causes and Consequences of Climate Change

Concern has grown in recent years over the issue of global climate change.[1] In terms of economic analysis, **greenhouse gas** emissions, which cause planetary warming, represent both **environmental externalities** and overuse of a **common-property resource.**

The atmosphere is a **global commons** into which individuals and firms can release pollution in the shape of gases and particulates. Global pollution creates a "public bad" affecting everyone—a negative externality with wide impact. Many countries have environmental protection laws to limit release of **local and regional pollutants.** In economic terminology, such laws to some degree **internalize externalities** associated with local and regional pollutants.

Few controls exist for carbon dioxide ($CO_2$), the major greenhouse gas, which has no short-term damaging effects at ground level. Atmospheric accumulations of carbon dioxide and other greenhouse gases, however, will have significant effects on world weather, although there is uncertainty about the probable scale and timing of these effects (see Box 18-1).

---

[1]The problem, frequently called **global warming**, is more accurately referred to as **global climate change.** A basic warming effect will produce complex effects on climate patterns—with warming in some areas, cooling in others, and increased climatic variability.

# 18-1   What Is the Greenhouse Effect?

The sun's rays travel through a greenhouse's glass to warm the air inside, but the glass acts as a barrier to the escape of heat. Thus plants that require warm weather can be grown in cold climates. The global greenhouse effect, in which the earth's atmosphere acts like the glass in a greenhouse, was first described by French scientist Jean Baptiste Fourier in 1824.

Clouds, water vapor, and the natural greenhouse gases carbon dioxide ($CO_2$), methane, nitrous oxide, and ozone allow inbound solar radiation to pass through, but serve as a barrier to outgoing infrared heat. This creates the natural **greenhouse effect** that makes the planet suitable for life. Without it, the average surface temperature on the planet would average about −18 degrees Celsius (0 degrees Fahrenheit), instead of approximately 15 degrees Celsius (60 degrees Fahrenheit).

"The possibility of an *enhanced* or *manmade* greenhouse effect was introduced by the Swedish scientist Svante Arrhenius in 1896. Arrhenius hypothesized that the increased coal burning, which had paralleled the process of industrialization, would lead to an increased concentration of carbon dioxide in the atmosphere and warm the earth."[1] Since Arrhenius's time, greenhouse gas emissions have grown dramatically. Carbon dioxide concentrations in the atmosphere have increased by 25 percent over preindustrial levels. In addition to increased burning of fossil fuels such as coal, oil and natural gas, manmade chemical substances such as chlorofluorocarbons (CFCs) as well as methane and nitrous oxide emissions from agriculture and industry contribute to the greenhouse effect.

In 1988, the United Nations Environment Programme and the World Meteorological Organization together established the Intergovernmental Panel on Climate Change (IPCC) to provide an authoritative international statement of scientific opinion on climate change. With respect to human-caused greenhouse effect, the IPCC concluded in 2001 that "there is new and stronger evidence that most of the warming observed over the last 50 years is attributable to human activities."

Current emissions trends will lead to a doubling of greenhouse gas concentration over preindustrial levels by about 2050. Using general circulation models—large mathematical models of the atmosphere—scientists can simulate the effect of increased greenhouse gas concentrations. The IPCC projects a global average temperature increase of 1 to 6 degrees Celsius, or 2 to 10 degrees Fahrenheit, which would have significant impact on climate throughout the world.

**SOURCES**

Cline, 1992; Fankhauser, 1995; IPCC, 1996, 2001.

---

[1]Fankhauser, 1995.

If indeed the effects of climate change are likely to be severe, it is in everyone's interest to lower emissions for the common good. Thus we can also view climate change as a *public good* issue. If no agreement or rules on emissions exist, actions by individual firms, cities, or nations are likely to be inadequate, for the reasons discussed in Chapter 4 regarding the economics of public goods. In this situation, only a strong international agreement binding nations to act for the common good can prevent serious environmental consequences.

Because $CO_2$ and other greenhouse gases continuously accumulate in the atmosphere, stabilizing or "freezing" emissions will not solve the problem. This is a case of a **stock pollutant**: only major reductions in emissions levels will prevent ever-increasing atmospheric accumulations. Development of national and international policies to combat global climate change is a huge challenge, involving many scientific, economic, and social issues. In this chapter we will address these issues of analysis and policy, using techniques and concepts developed in earlier chapters.

## Trends and Projections for Temperature Change

Despite two global conferences dealing with the issue—the 1992 United Nations Conference on Environment and Development (UNCED) at Rio de Janeiro and a 1997 meeting in Kyoto, Japan—as well as numerous follow-up negotiating sessions, progress on combating global climate change has been slow. Global greenhouse gas emissions continue to rise (see Figure 18-1).

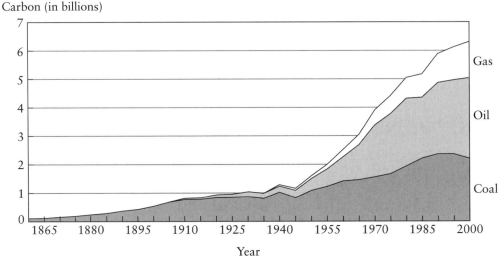

**FIGURE 18-1** *Carbon Emissions Due to Fossil Fuel Consumption, 1860–2000*
Source: Carbon Dioxide Information Analysis Center (CDIAC), http://cdiac.esd.ornl.gov/.

Temperature Variation (in °C)

**FIGURE 18-2** *Temperature Trend, Northern Hemisphere 1860–2000*

Source: Data from the Carbon Dioxide Information Analysis Center (CDIAC), http://cdiac.esd.ornl.gov/, and IPCC, 2001.

Note: Temperature variations are shown in degrees C relative to 1961–1990 mean, using a five-year average of data since 1860. Data point for 2000 is average of 1998–2000.

Increasing accumulations of greenhouse gases have caused the earth's surface temperature to rise perceptibly. Although some warming may be a natural trend, the Intergovernmental Panel on Climate Change (IPCC) has determined that human-caused impact on the atmosphere has "contributed substantially to the observed warming over the last 50 years."[2] Temperatures have risen about 1 degree Celsius (1.8 degrees Fahrenheit) over the last century (see Figure 18-2).

The IPCC scientists project that continued greenhouse gas emissions will further increase average temperatures between 1 and 6 degrees Celsius (about 2 to 10 degrees Fahrenheit) over the next century (Figure 18-3). This steady rise in the earth's average temperature will have many significant effects on climate. For example, one effect of climate change is likely to be a rise in sea level as the volume of seawater

---

[2]"A Shift in Stance on Global Warming Theory: International Panel Highlights Role of Humans in Climate Change." *New York Times*, October 26, 2000. See also Trenberth, 2001.

Temperature (in °C)

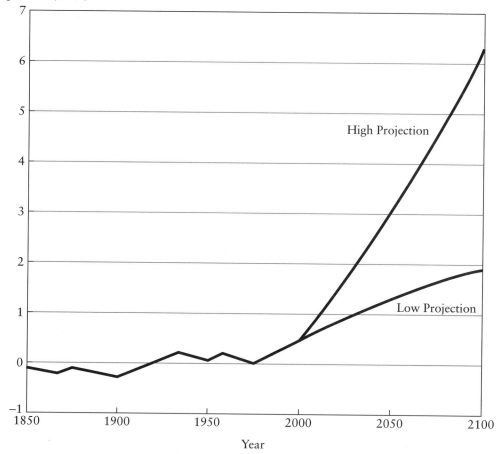

**FIGURE 18-3** *Global Temperature Trends Projected to 2100*
Source: IPCC, 2001.

expands and polar ice caps and glaciers melt. This will have serious effects on islands and low-lying coastal areas (see Box 18-2).

By early 2005, the urgency of the climate change issue increased with new reports of climate change impacts. Melting of Antarctic ice shelves and glaciers
alarmed scientists, and conclusive evidence of deep-ocean warming patterns provided further evidence of human-induced warming and led to predictions of
increased hurricane intensity.[3] The five hottest years on record occurred during

---

[3]Andrew Revkin, "Antarctic Glaciers Quicken Pace to Sea; Warming is Cited," *New York Times,*
September 24, 2004; Larry Rohter, "Antarctica, Warming, Looks Ever More Vulnerable," *New York
Times,* January 25, 2005; Beth Daley, "Greenhouse Gas Buildup Seen as Risk to Oceans," *Boston
Globe,* July 16, 2004; "Researchers Present What They Call Conclusive Evidence of Global Warming
from Greenhouse Gases," *Chronicle of Higher Education,* February 18, 2005.

## *18-2*  Pacific Islands Disappear as Oceans Rise

Two islands in the Pacific Ocean nation of Kiribati—Tebua Tarawa and Abanuea—have disappeared as a result of rising sea level. Others, both in Kiribati and in the neighboring island nation of Tuvalu, are nearly gone. So far the seas have completely engulfed only uninhabited, relatively small islands, but the crisis is growing all along the shores of the world's atolls.

Populated islands are already suffering. The main islands of Kiribati, Tuvalu, and the Marshall Islands (also in the Pacific) have suffered severe floods as high tides demolish sea walls, bridges and roads, and swamp homes and plantations. Almost the entire coastline of the 29 Marshall Islands atolls is eroding. World War II graves on its main Majuro atoll are washing away, roads and subsoils have been swept into the sea, and the airport has flooded several times despite the supposed protection of a high sea wall.

The people of Tuvalu are finding it difficult to grow their crops because the rising seas are poisoning the soil with salt. In both Kiribati and the Marshall Islands families are desperately trying to keep the waves at bay by dumping trucks, cars and other old machinery in the sea and surrounding them with rocks.

The story is much the same far away in the Maldives. The Indian Ocean is sweeping away the beaches of one-third of its 200 inhabited islands. "Sea-level rise is not a fashionable scientific hypothesis," says President Gayoom. "It is a fact."

*Low-lying islands, estuaries, and marshes are threatened by sea-level rise.*

*(continued on following page)*

The seas are rising partly because global warming is melting glaciers and nibbling away at the polar ice caps, but mainly because the oceans expand as their water warms. Scientists' best estimate is that these processes will raise sea levels by about 1.5 feet over the next century, quite enough to destroy several island nations.

The higher the seas rise, the more often storms will sweep the waves across the narrow atolls and carry away the land—and storms are expected to increase as the world warms up. Many islands will become uninhabitable long before they physically disappear, as sea contaminates the underground freshwater supplies on which they depend.

**SOURCE**

Adapted from Geoffrey Lean, "They're Going Under; Two Islands Have Disappeared Beneath the Pacific Ocean—Sunk by Global Warming." *The Independent* (June 13, 1999): 15. Extracted from an article by Geoffrey Lean first published in *The Independent on* Sunday 13 June 1999. Used with permission of *The Independent*.

1998–2004, and NASA scientists predicted that 2005 could be the warmest year since records started being kept in the late 1800s.[4]

The onset of climate change poses a choice between **preventive strategies and adaptive strategies.** Consider, for example, the damage caused by rising sea levels. The only way to stop this would be to prevent the climate change itself. It might be possible to adapt to changed conditions by building dikes and sea walls to hold back the higher waters. Those who live close to the sea—including whole island nations that could lose most of their territory to sea-level rise—are unlikely to endorse this mitigation strategy. But a successful prevention strategy would require convincing most of the world's countries to participate. Is it in their interest to do so? To answer this question, we must find a way to evaluate the effects of climate change.

## Economic Analysis of Climate Change

Scientists have modeled the results of a projected doubling of accumulated carbon dioxide in the earth's atmosphere. Predicted effects include

- Land area loss, including beaches and wetlands, to sea-level rise
- Loss of species and forest area
- Disruption of water supplies to cities and agriculture

---

[4]Timothy Gardner, "2005 Could be Warmest Year on Record—NASA," *Reuters*, February 10, 2005; Lisa Buckley, "Global Temperature Rise Accelerating," Earth Policy Institute, http://www.earth-policy.org.

- Increased air conditioning costs
- Health damage and deaths from heat waves and spread of tropical diseases
- Loss of agricultural output due to drought

Beneficial outcomes might include

- Increased agricultural production in cold climates
- Lower heating costs

In addition, other less-predictable but possibly more damaging effects include

- Disruption of weather patterns, with increased frequency of hurricanes and other extreme weather events
- Sudden major climate changes, such as a shift in the Atlantic Gulf Stream, that could leave Europe's climate similar to Alaska's.
- Positive **feedback effects**,[5] such as increased carbon dioxide release from warming arctic tundra, which would speed up global warming.

How can we evaluate such possible impacts? In attempting to respond to this question, economists have employed **cost-benefit analysis,** which we introduced in Chapter 6. Others have criticized this approach as an attempt to put a monetary valuation on issues with social, political, and ecological implications that go far beyond dollar value. We will examine economists' efforts to place the issue in a cost-benefit context, then return to the debate over whether this effort is appropriate and what policies should be implemented.

We can evaluate policy responses to climate change by first considering a **business as usual** scenario in which no action is taken to limit greenhouse gas emissions. According to World Bank projections, global energy use will have nearly doubled by about 2030, with the greatest growth coming from developing nations.[6] Figure 18-4 illustrates the resulting dramatic increase in carbon emissions.

Today, the developed nations are responsible for most carbon emissions, with much higher per capita emissions rates, especially in the United States (Figure 18-5). The largest projected increase in emissions, however, will be in the currently developing nations. By 2020, developing nations will approximately equal developed nations in total emissions. But note that even with this large increase, per capita emissions levels will remain much lower in developing nations. With expected population and economic growth, emissions increases in the developing world are unavoidable. Thus global emissions reductions will require significant policy action by developed nations, as well as eventual limits on developing-nation emissions.

## Cost-Benefit Studies of Global Climate Change

In performing a cost-benefit analysis, we must weigh the consequences of allowing this uncontrolled emissions scenario to proceed versus the costs of policy action to prevent it. We can do this by estimating the damages from uncontrolled global climate change.

---

[5]A feedback effect occurs when an original change in a system causes further changes that either reinforce the original change (positive feedback) or counteract it (negative feedback).

[6]World Bank, 1992.

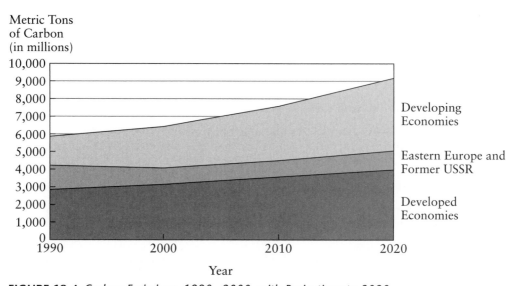

**FIGURE 18-4** *Carbon Emissions, 1990–2000, with Projections to 2020*

Source: U.S. Department of Energy, 2004, "International Energy-Related Environmental Information," available at http://www.eia.doe.gov/emeu/international/environm.html.

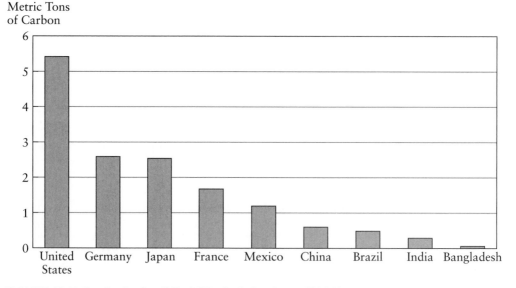

**FIGURE 18-5** *Per Capita Fossil-Fuel $CO_2$ Emission Rates (2000)*

Source: Carbon Dioxide Information Analysis Center (CDIAC), http://cdiac.esd.ornl.gov/.

Strong policy action to prevent climate change will bring benefits equal to the value of these damages.[7] Then we must compare these to benefits to the costs of taking action. Various economic studies have attempted to estimate these benefits and costs. Table 18-1 shows the results of one such study for the U.S. economy.

The study is based on an estimated doubling of $CO_2$ over preindustrial levels. When the monetized costs are added up, the total annual U.S. damages are estimated at approximately $60 billion (1990 dollars). This is about 1 percent of U.S. GDP. Although different economic studies come up with different estimates, most of them are in the range of 1 to 2 percent of GDP. Cost estimates for larger temperature change over the longer term rise to about 5 percent of GDP (Table 18-1, column 2).

Note, however, the Xs, Ys, and Δs in the totals—unknown quantities that cannot easily be measured. The value of species loss, for example, is difficult to estimate in dollar terms: The estimates used here show a cost of at least $4 billion in the short term and $16 billion in the long term, with an additional unknown cost denoted as Δ.

Other monetized estimates could also be challenged on the grounds that they fail to capture the full value of potential losses. For example, oceanfront land is more than just real estate. Beaches and coastal wetlands have great social, cultural, and ecological value. Their market value fails to reflect the full scope of damage society will suffer if they are lost.

In addition, these estimates omit the possibility of the much more catastrophic consequences that *could* result if weather disruption is much worse than anticipated. A single hurricane, for example, can cause more than $10 billion in damage, in addition to loss of life. For example, in November 1998, a severe hurricane caused massive devastation and the loss of more than 7,000 lives in Central America. In 2004, Florida was hit by four hurricanes causing more than $20 billion in damages. If climate changes cause severe hurricanes to become much more frequent, the estimate here of less than $1 billion in annual losses could be much too low. Another "X" value—human morbidity (disease)—could be large if warmer weather conditions allow tropical diseases to significantly extend their range.

Clearly, these damage estimates are imprecise and open to many criticisms, but suppose we decide to accept them—at least as a rough estimate. We must then weigh the estimated benefits of policies to prevent climate change against the costs of such policies. To estimate these costs, economists use models that show how inputs such as labor, capital, and resources produce economic output.

To lower carbon emissions, we must cut back the use of fossil fuels, substituting other energy sources that may be more expensive. Some economic models predict that this substitution would reduce GDP growth. One major study showed GDP losses ranging from 1 to 3 percent of GDP for most countries, with higher potential long-term losses for coal-dependent developing nations such as China.[8]

---

[7]These benefits of preventing damage can also be referred to as **avoided costs.**

[8]Manne and Richels, 1992.

**TABLE 18-1** *Estimates of Annual Damages to the U.S. Economy from Global Climate Change (Billions 1990 $)*

| | $2 \times CO_2 (+2.5°C)$ | *Long-term Warming (+10°C)* |
|---|---|---|
| Agriculture | 17.5 | 95.0 |
| Forest loss | 3.3 | 7.0 |
| Species loss | $4.0 + \Delta$ | $16.0 + \Delta'$ |
| Sea-level rise | | 35.0 |
|   Building dikes, levees | 1.2 | |
|   Wetlands loss | 4.1 | |
|   Drylands loss | 1.7 | |
| Electricity requirements | 11.2 | 64.1 |
| Nonelectric heating | −1.3 | −4.0 |
| Human amenity | $Xa$ | $Ya$ |
| Human life | 5.8 | 33.0 |
| Human morbidity | $Xm$ | $Ym$ |
| Migration | 0.5 | 2.8 |
| Hurricanes | 0.8 | 6.4 |
| Construction | $+/- Xc$ | $+/- Yc$ |
| Leisure activities | 1.7 | 4.0 |
| Water supply | 7.0 | 56.0 |
| Urban infrastructure | 0.1 | 0.6 |
| Air pollution | | |
|   Tropospheric ozone | 3.5 | 19.8 |
|   Other | $Xo$ | $Yo$ |
| **Total** | $61.6 + Xa + Xm + Xo + \Delta' +/- Xc$ | $335.7 + Ya + Ym + Yo + \Delta +/- Yc$ |

Source: Adapted from William R. Cline, *The Economics of Global Warming,* Washington, D.C.: Institute for International Economics, 1992. Reprinted by permission of Institute for International Economics.

If both costs and benefits of an aggressive carbon abatement policy fall in the range of 1 to 3 percent of GDP, how can we decide what to do? Much depends on our evaluation of future costs and benefits. The costs of taking action must be borne today or in the near future. The benefits of taking action (the avoided costs of damages) are further in the future. Our task, then, is to decide today how to balance these future costs and benefits.

As we saw in Chapter 9, economists evaluate future costs and benefits by the use of a **discount rate.** The problems and implicit value judgments associated with discounting add to the uncertainties that we have already noted in valuing costs and benefits. This suggests that we should consider alternative approaches—including techniques that incorporate ecological as well as economic costs and benefits.

*A family walks through the destruction left by Hurricane Mitch in Honduras in 1998. More severe hurricanes are a possible result of global climate change.*

## Analyzing Long-Term Environmental Effects

Two major economic studies dealing with cost/benefit analysis of climate change have come to significantly different conclusions about policy. According to analysis by William Nordhaus,[9] the **economic optimum** would be a small reduction in greenhouse gas emissions below the business-as-usual emissions growth shown in Figure 18-4. This would require few changes in the carbon-based energy path typical of current economic development.

In contrast, a study by William Cline recommends "a worldwide program of aggressive action to limit global warming" that includes cutting carbon emissions well below present levels and freezing them there with no future increase.[10] This would involve major changes in current patterns of energy use. What explains the dramatic difference between these two cost/benefit analyses?

The two studies used similar methods to assess benefits and costs. The main differences were that the Cline study considered long-term effects and used a low discount rate

[9]Nordhaus, 1993; Nordhaus and Boyer, 2000.

[10]Cline, 1992 and 2004.

(1.5 percent) to balance present and future costs. Thus even though costs of aggressive action appeared higher than benefits for several decades, the high potential long-term damages sway the balance in favor of aggressive action today.

As we saw in Chapter 6, the present value (*PV*) of a long-term stream of benefits or costs depends on the discount rate. A high discount rate will lead to a low present valuation for benefits that are mainly in the longer-term, and a high present valuation for short-term costs. On the other hand, a low discount rate will lead to a higher present valuation for long-term benefits. The estimated net present value of an aggressive abatement policy will thus be much higher if we choose a low discount rate.

While both the Cline and Nordhaus studies used standard economic methodology, Cline's approach gives greater weight to long-term ecological effects. These effects are significant both for their monetary and nonmonetary effects. In the long term, damage done to the environment by global climate change will have significant negative effects on the economy, too. Thus these long-term effects have a high monetary value, as shown in Figure 18-6. But a standard discount rate of 5 to 10 percent reduces the present value of significant future damages to relative insignificance.

An ecologically oriented economist would argue that the fundamental issue is the stability of the physical and ecological systems that serve as a planetary climate-

Percent of GDP

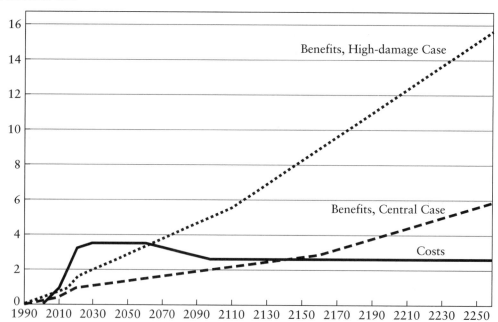

**FIGURE 18-6** *Long-Term Costs and Benefits of Abating Global Climate Change*
Source: Adapted from William R. Cline, *The Economics of Global Warming*, Washington, D.C.: Institute for International Economics, 1992. Reprinted by permission of Institute for International Economics.

control mechanism. This means that **climate stabilization** should be the goal, rather than economic optimization of costs and benefits. Stabilizing greenhouse gas emissions is insufficient; at the current rate of emissions carbon dioxide and other greenhouse gases will continue to accumulate in the atmosphere. Stabilizing the accumulations of greenhouse gases will require a significant cut below present emission levels.

Any measure taken to prevent global climate change will have economic effects on GDP, consumption, and employment, which explains the reluctance of governments to take drastic measures to reduce $CO_2$ emissions. But these effects may not necessarily be negative.

A comprehensive review of economic models of climate change policy shows that the economic outcomes predicted for carbon reduction policies depend heavily on the modeling assumptions used.[11] The predicted effects of stabilizing emissions at 1990 levels range from a 2 percent decrease to a 2 percent *increase* in GDP. The outcomes depend on a range of assumptions including

- The efficiency or inefficiency of economic responses to energy price signals.
- The availability of noncarbon "backstop" energy technologies.
- Whether or not nations can trade least-cost options for carbon reduction.
- Whether or not revenues from taxes on carbon-based fuels are used to lower other taxes.
- Whether or not **external benefits** of carbon reduction, including reduction in ground-level air pollution, are taken into account.

Thus emissions reduction policies could range from a minimalist approach of slightly reducing emissions growth to a dramatic $CO_2$ emissions reduction of 50 percent or more. Most economists who have analyzed the problem agree that action is necessary (see Box 18-3), but there is a wide range of opinion on how drastic this action should be and how soon it should occur. The world's nations have acknowledged the problem and are negotiating over plans to achieve emissions reductions. The scope of the reductions now being discussed, however, falls well short of that necessary for climate stabilization.

Whatever the outcome of these negotiations, any serious effort to reduce carbon emissions will require the kinds of economic policies to deal with negative externalities that we discussed in Chapter 3. We will now turn to an analysis of possible policies.

## Policy Responses to Climate Change

Two types of measures can be used to address climate change: Preventive measures tend to lower or mitigate the greenhouse effect, and adaptive measures deal with the consequences of the greenhouse effect and try to minimize their impact.

[11]Repetto and Austin, WRI, 1997.

| 18-3 | Economists' Statement on Climate Change |

I. The review conducted by a distinguished international panel of scientists under the auspices of the Intergovernmental Panel on Climate Change has determined that "the balance of evidence suggests a discernible human influence on global climate." As economists, we believe that global climate change carries with it significant environmental, economic, social, and geopolitical risks, and that preventive steps are justified.

II. Economic studies have found that there are many potential policies to reduce greenhouse-gas emissions for which the total benefits outweigh the total costs. For the United States in particular, sound economic analysis shows that there are policy options that would slow climate change without harming American living standards, and these measures may in fact improve U.S. productivity in the longer run.

III. The most efficient approach to slowing climate change is through market-based policies. In order for the world to achieve its climatic objectives at minimum cost, a cooperative approach among nations is required—such as an international emissions trading agreement. The United States and other nations can most efficiently implement their climate policies through market mechanisms, such as carbon taxes or the auction of emissions permits. The revenues generated from such policies can effectively be used to reduce the deficit or to lower existing taxes.

Note: The above statement has been endorsed by more than 2,500 economists, including eight Nobel Laureates.

**SOURCE**

From Redefining Progress, Oakland, California, http://www.rprogress.org.

Preventive measures include

- Reducing emissions of greenhouse gases, either by reducing the level of emissions-related economic activities or by shifting to more energy-efficient technologies that allow the same level of economic activity at a lower level of $CO_2$ emissions.
- Enhancing **carbon sinks.**[12] Forests recycle $CO_2$ into oxygen; preserving forested areas and expanding reforestation have a significant effect on net $CO_2$ emissions.

---

[12]Carbon sinks are areas where excess carbon may be stored. Natural sinks include the oceans and forests. Human intervention can either reduce or expand these sinks through forest management and agricultural practices.

Adaptive measures include

- Construction of dikes and seawalls to protect against rising sea levels and extreme weather events such as floods and hurricanes.
- Shifting cultivation patterns in agriculture to adapt to changed weather conditions in different areas.

An economic approach suggests that we should apply cost-effectiveness analysis in considering such policies. This differs from cost-benefit analysis in having a more modest goal: Rather than attempting to decide whether or not a policy should be implemented, cost-effectiveness analysis asks what is the most efficient way to reach a policy goal.

In general, economists favor approaches that work through market mechanisms to achieve their goals. Market-oriented approaches are considered cost-effective—rather than attempting to control market actors directly, they shift incentives so that individuals and firms will change their behavior to take account of external costs and benefits. In Chapter 16 we discussed the economics of **pollution taxes** and **transferable, or tradable, permits.** Both of these are potentially useful tools for greenhouse gas reduction. Other relevant economic policies include measures to create incentives for the adoption of **renewable energy sources** and **energy-efficient technology.**

## Policy Tools: Carbon Taxes

The release of greenhouse gases in the atmosphere is a clear example of a negative externality that imposes significant costs on a global scale. In the language of economic theory, the market for carbon-based fuels such as coal, oil, and natural gas takes into account only private costs and benefits, which leads to a market equilibrium that fails to correspond to the **social optimum.**

As we have seen, a standard remedy for internalizing external costs is a per-unit tax on the pollutant. For carbon dioxide emissions, this would be a **carbon tax,** levied exclusively on carbon-based fossil fuels. Such a tax will raise the price of carbon-based energy sources, and so give consumers incentive to conserve energy and to shift demand to alternative sources (Figure 18-7). Demand may also shift from carbon-based fuels with a higher proportion of carbon, such as coal, to those with relatively lower carbon content, such as natural gas.

> Carbon taxes would appear to consumers as energy price increases. But since taxes would be levied on primary energy, which represents only one part of the cost of delivered energy (such as gasoline or electricity) and more important, since one fuel can in many cases be substituted for another, overall price increases may not be jolting. Consumers can respond to new prices by reducing energy use and buying fewer carbon-intensive products (those that require great amounts of carbon-based fuels to produce). In addition, some of these savings could be used to buy other less carbon-intensive goods and services.
>
> Clearly, a carbon tax creates an incentive for producers and consumers to avoid paying the tax by reducing their use of carbon-intensive fuels. Contrary to other taxed items and activities, this avoidance has social benefits—reduced energy use and reduced $CO_2$ emissions.

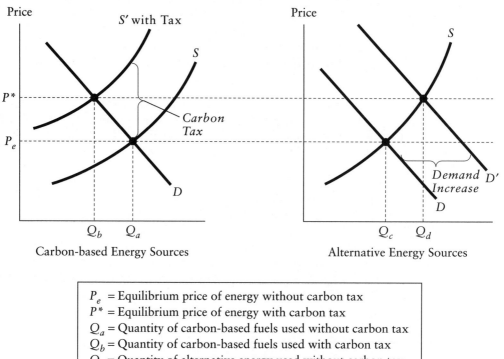

FIGURE 18-7 *The Economic Effects of a Carbon Tax*

Thus, declining tax revenues over time indicate policy success—just the opposite of what happens when tax policy seeks to maintain steady or increasing revenues.[13]

Consider Table 18-2, which shows the impact different levels of carbon tax will have on prices of coal, oil, and gas. A $10 per ton carbon tax, for example, raises the price of a barrel of oil by $1.30, which is about 3 cents a gallon. Will this affect people's driving or home heating habits much? Probably not—we would not expect a high **price elasticity of demand** for gasoline or heating oil, since these commonalities are viewed as necessities.

Figure 18-8 shows a cross-country relationship between gasoline prices and per capita use. Notice that the pattern of this relationship resembles a demand curve: Higher prices are associated with lower consumption, lower prices with higher

[13]From Robert Dower and Mary Zimmerman, *The Right Climate for Carbon Taxes.* World Resources Institute, 1992. Reprinted by permission of World Resources Institute, Washington, D.C.

**TABLE 18-2** *Alternative Carbon Taxes on Fossil Fuels*

|  | *Coal* | *Oil* | *Natural Gas* |
|---|---|---|---|
| Tons of carbon per unit of fuel | 0.605/ton | 0.130/barrel | 0.016/ccf (hundred cubic feet) |
| Average price (2003) | $17.98/ton | $27.56/barrel | $4.98/ccf |
| *Carbon tax amount per unit of fuel:* | | | |
| $10/ton of carbon | $6.05/ton | $1.30/barrel | $0.16/ccf |
| $100/ton of carbon | $60.50/ton | $13/barrel | $1.60/ccf |
| $200/ton of carbon | $121/ton | $26/barrel | $3.20/ccf |
| *Carbon tax as a percent of fuel price:* | | | |
| $10/ton of carbon | 34% | 5% | 3% |
| $100/ton of carbon | 340% | 47% | 32% |
| $200/ton of carbon | 673% | 94% | 64% |

Source: Adapted from Poterba, 1993. Price data from U.S. Department of Energy, 2003.

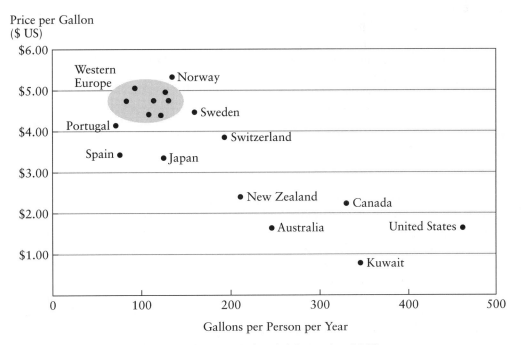

**FIGURE 18-8** *Gasoline Price Versus Use in Industrial Countries, 2003*
Source: U.S. Department of Energy, 2004. Figure adapted from Roodman, 1997, with updated data.

consumption. The relationship shown here, however, is not the same as a demand curve; because we are looking at data from different countries, the assumption of "other things equal," needed to construct a demand curve, doesn't hold.

People in the United States, for example, may drive more partly because travel distances (especially in the western states) are greater than in many European countries. But Figure 18-8 does indicate a clear price/consumption relationship. The data shown here suggest that it would take a fairly big price hike—in the range of $0.50–$1.00 per gallon or more—to affect fuel use substantially.

A much larger tax would be needed to promote a major shift away from fossil fuels. According to most studies, stabilizing global $CO_2$ emissions would require a carbon tax of at least $200 per ton.[14] This would significantly increase fuel prices (see Table 18-2), which would certainly affect consumption patterns. In addition, the long-term price elasticity of demand would be greater, as higher prices for carbon-based fuels promoted development of alternative technologies.

But would such a tax ever be politically feasible? Especially in the United States, high taxes on gasoline and other fuels would face much opposition, especially if people saw it as infringing on their freedom to drive. Note that in Figure 18-8 the United States has by far the highest fuel consumption per person, and the lowest price except for Kuwait.

But let's note two things about the proposal for substantial carbon taxes:

First, **revenue recycling** could redirect the revenue from such taxes to lower other taxes. Much political opposition to high energy taxes comes from the perception that they would be an *extra* tax—on top of the income, property, and social security taxes that people already pay. If a carbon tax was matched, for example, with a substantial cut in income and social security taxes, it might be more politically acceptable.

The idea of increasing taxes on economic "bads" such as pollution and reducing taxes on things we want to encourage, such as labor and capital investment, is fully consistent with principles of economic efficiency.[15] Rather than a net tax increase, this would be a **revenue-neutral tax shift**—the total amount of taxes paid to the government is unchanged.

Second, if such a tax shift did take place, individuals or businesses whose operations were more energy efficient would actually save money. The higher cost of energy would also create a powerful incentive for energy-saving technological innovation. Economic adaptation would be easier if the higher carbon taxes (and lower income and capital taxes) were phased in over time. The potential economic advantages of a tax shift have led some economists to argue that carbon taxes would bring a **double dividend** of economic and environmental benefits. Others suggest that significant economic costs would result, especially from a substantial carbon tax, but that these costs would be less with revenue recycling than without.[16]

---

[14]Manne and Richels, 1992; Nordhaus and Boyer, 2000; Cline, 2004.

[15]To encourage higher investment, carbon tax revenues could be used to lower capital gains or corporate taxes.

[16]See Gouldner, 2002, for a review of the literature on the double dividend debate.

## Policy Tools: Tradable Permits

As we have seen, one alternative to a pollution tax is a system of tradable pollution permits. In the international negotiations over greenhouse gas reduction, extensive discussion has focused on the implementation of a tradable permit system for carbon emissions. Such a system would work as follows:

- Each nation would be allocated a certain permissible level of carbon emissions. The total number of carbon permits issued would be equal to the desired goal. For example, if global carbon emissions are 6 billion tons and the goal is to reduce this by 1 billion, permits for 5 billion tons of emissions would be issued.
- Permit allocation would meet agreed-on targets for national or regional reductions. For example, under the 1997 Kyoto Protocol agreement, the United States agreed to set a goal of cutting its greenhouse emissions 7 percent below 1990 levels by 2008–2012. Japan agreed to a 6 percent cut, and Europe to an 8 percent cut. (The United States has since withdrawn from the Kyoto Protocol—see Box 18-4.)
- Nations could trade permits among themselves. For example, if Japan failed to meet its target, but Europe exceeded its target, Japan could purchase permits from Europe.
- The permits might also be tradable among firms, with countries setting targets for major industrial sectors, and allocating permits accordingly. Firms could then trade among themselves, or internationally.
- Nations and firms could also receive credit for reductions that they help to finance in other countries. For example, European firms could earn credit for installing efficient electric generating equipment in China, replacing highly polluting coal plants.

From an economic point of view, a tradable permit system would encourage implementing least-cost carbon reduction options. Depending on permit allocations, it might also mean that developing nations could transform permits into a new export commodity by choosing a noncarbon path for their energy development. They could then sell permits to industrialized nations that had not met their reduction requirements.

The stumbling block to an international tradable permit system is obtaining agreement on the target levels. Developing nations have resisted *any* limitations on their emissions—which are currently much lower per capita than those of industrialized nations—until the developed nations show significant progress in reducing theirs. But some developed nations, such as the United States and Australia, are reluctant to implement any reduction policy until developing nations have signed on to some commitments (see Box 18-4).

## The Economics of Tradable Carbon Permits

To demonstrate the economic impact of a tradable carbon permit system, we can use the analytical concept of **marginal net benefit** introduced in Chapter 5. Figure 18-10a

## 18-4   The Kyoto Protocol

The December 1997 Kyoto Conference, held under the auspices of the United Nations, produced an agreement on greenhouse gas reduction called the Kyoto Protocol. Unlike the entirely voluntary Framework Convention on Climate Change (FCCC), agreed to at the Rio Conference on Environment and Development in 1992, the Kyoto Protocol is binding on its signatory nations. Despite U.S. opposition, the Kyoto Protocol was ratified by enough countries to enter into force on February 16, 2005. Industrialized countries accepted goals for specific emissions reductions by 2012. Developing countries would not accept specific emissions limits, arguing that developed nations must first live up to their responsibility to cut their much greater per capita emissions.

Under the Kyoto Protocol, the **Clean Development Mechanism** allows cooperative projects, such as construction of highly efficient power plants in developing countries, through which an industrialized country can receive emissions reduction credit for aid given to a developing country. Another cooperative or **joint implementation** mechanism is sink enhancement, where common efforts between industrialized countries and developing countries promote forest conservation and reforestation.

These mechanisms do not add up to a global tradable permit system. Trading will be possible between nations that have agreed to specific emissions limits. Within the European Union, emissions trading began on January 1, 2005. For a global emission trading system to work, all nations must accept emissions caps, which would require agreed-on limits for both developed and developing nations.

The major issue following adoption of the Kyoto Protocol is how to bring in the major emitters not now covered—The United States, China, and India—and how to move beyond Kyoto's relatively modest goals of a reduction of about 5 percent below 1990 emissions levels for industrialized nations that have ratified the protocol.

The United States is the world's largest emitter of greenhouse gases, accounting for about 25 percent of global $CO_2$ emissions. U.S. emissions have risen steadily since 1990, and are projected to continue rising through 2010 (see Figure 18-9). The Bush administration has rejected the Kyoto Protocol but has not proposed alternative measures to control greenhouse gases. While China and India are far below the United States in per capita emissions (see Figure 18-5), their rapid economic growth means that their fuel use and carbon emissions will increase rapidly. Developing countries as a whole currently account for about 40 percent of global emissions but will overtake the developed countries by 2025, according to the International Energy Agency.

*(continued on following page)*

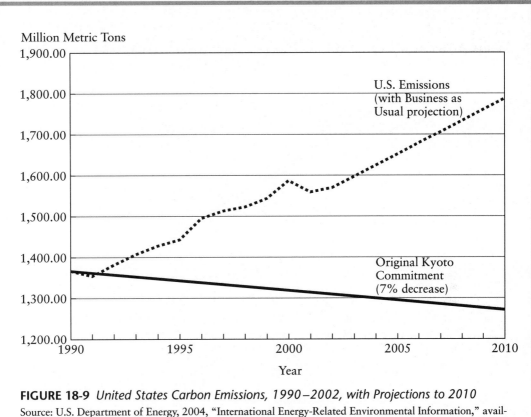

**FIGURE 18-9** *United States Carbon Emissions, 1990–2002, with Projections to 2010*

Source: U.S. Department of Energy, 2004, "International Energy-Related Environmental Information," available at http://www.eia.doe.gov/emeu/international/environm.html; IPCC, 2001.

shows the marginal net benefit of carbon emissions to producers and consumers.[17] The emissions level $Q_E$ will result with no emissions limits—this is the market equilibrium, where consumers and producers maximize total net benefits, without taking into account environmental externalities.

Under a permit system, $Q^*$ represents the total number of permits issued. The equilibrium permit price will then be $P^*$, reflecting the marginal net benefit of carbon emissions at $Q^*$. Emitters who gain benefits greater than $P^*$ from their emissions will want to purchase permits, while those whose emissions benefits are less than $P^*$ will do better to reduce emissions and sell any excess permits.

Figure 18-10b shows three possible carbon reduction strategies. Replacement of plants using existing carbon-emitting technologies is possible, but will tend to have high marginal costs. Reducing emissions through greater energy efficiency has lower

---

[17]As we saw in Chapter 5, the marginal net benefit curve is derived from the demand and supply curve (in this case for carbon-based fuels), showing the marginal benefits of the product minus the marginal costs of supply.

**(a) Determination of Carbon Permit Price**

MNB$_C$ = Marginal net benefits of carbon emissions

Q$_E$ = Quality of carbon emissions without permit system

Q$^*$= Quantity of carbon permits issued

P$^*$= Equilibrium price of carbon permit

**FIGURE 18-10A** *Least-Cost Carbon Reduction with Tradable Permits—*
*Determination of Carbon Permit Price*

marginal costs, as does carbon storage through forest area expansion. The permit price $P^*$ will govern the relative levels of implementation of each of these strategies.

Nations and corporations subject to the trading scheme can decide for themselves how much of each control strategy to implement and will naturally favor the least-cost methods. This will probably involve a combination of approaches. If, for example, one nation undertakes extensive reforestation, they are likely to have excess permits, which they can sell to a nation with few low-cost reduction options. The net effect will be the worldwide implementation of the least-cost reduction techniques.

This system combines the advantages of economic efficiency with a guaranteed result—reduction to overall emissions level $Q^*$. The problem, of course, is to achieve agreement on the initial allocation of permits. Measurement problems may also arise, as well as issues such as whether to count only commercial carbon emissions or to include emissions changes resulting from forest and land use patterns.

**(b) Carbon Reduction with a Permit System**

| | |
|---|---|
| $MC_A$ = Marginal costs of carbon reduction by plant replacement | |
| $MC_B$ = Marginal costs of carbon reduction by increased energy efficiency | |
| $MC_C$ = Marginal costs of carbon reduction by forest area expansion | |
| $P^*$ = Equilibrium price of carbon permit | |
| $Q_a$ = Units of carbon reduced by plant replacement | |
| $Q_b$ = Units of carbon reduced by increased energy efficiency | |
| $Q_c$ = Units of carbon reduced by forest area expansion | |

**FIGURE 18-10B** *Carbon Reduction with a Permit System*

## Policy Tools: Subsidies, Standards, R&D, and Technology Transfer

Although political problems may prevent the adoption of effective carbon taxes or transferable permit systems, other policy measures have potential to lower carbon emissions. These include the following:

- *Shifting **subsidies** from carbon-based to noncarbon-based fuels.* As noted in Chapter 13, many countries currently provide direct or indirect subsidies to fossil fuels. Eliminating these subsidies would alter the competitive balance in favor of alternative fuel sources. If these subsidy expenditures were redirected to renewable sources, especially in the form of tax rebates for investment, it could promote a boom in investment in solar, photovoltaics, fuel cells, biomass and wind power—all technologies currently at the margin of competitiveness in various areas.

- The use of *efficiency standards to require utilities and major manufacturers to increase efficiency and renewable content in power sources.* A coal-fired generating plant achieves about 35 percent efficiency, and a high-efficiency gas-fired cogeneration facility achieves from 75 percent to 90 percent efficiency. Current automobile fuel-efficiency standards do not exceed 27.5 miles per gallon, but efficiencies of up to 50 miles per gallon or more can be achieved with proven technologies, including hybrid vehicles already in widespread use. Tightening standards over time for plants, buildings, vehicles, and appliances would hasten the turnover of existing, energy-inefficient capital stock.

- *Research and development (R&D) expenditures directed toward commercializing alternative technologies.* Both government R&D programs and favorable tax treatment of corporate R&D for alternative energy can speed commercialization. The existence of a noncarbon "backstop" technology significantly reduces the economic cost of measures such as carbon taxes.

- *Technology transfer to developing nations.* As we have seen, the bulk of projected growth in carbon emissions will come in the developing world. Many energy development projects are now funded by agencies such as the World Bank and regional development banks. To the extent that these funds can be directed toward noncarbon energy systems, supplemented by other funds dedicated specifically to alternative energy development, it will be economically feasible for developing nations to turn away from fossil-fuel intensive paths, achieving significant local environmental benefits at the same time.

## The Future of Climate Change Policy

Will the limited policy measures now being taken to control greenhouse emissions be sufficient? Recent evidence of increased rapidity of climate change suggests that the cumulative impact of emissions may be more severe than anticipated, with a significant risk of sudden or severe climate change. Arctic ecosystems have shown clear signs of breakdown as temperatures rise, raising the possibility of feedback effects from tundra melting, which would further accelerate global warming.[18] A report prepared for the U.S. Department of Defense cited the possibility of large-scale drought in critical agricultural regions; a collapse of the North Atlantic Gulf Stream, causing an abrupt shift to much colder temperatures in Europe and the northern United States, and widespread civil unrest and mass migration caused by disruption of water and food supplies.[19] The

---

[18]See Richard B. Alley, "Abrupt Climate Change," *Scientific American,* November 2004; Clifford Kraus, "Eskimos Fret as Climate Shifts and Wildlife Changes," *New York Times,* September 6, 2004.

[19]Peter Schwartz and Doug Randall, "An Abrupt Climate Change Scenario and Its Implications for U.S. National Security," October 2003, available at http://www.ems.org/climate/pentagon_climate_change.html.

costs of such developments would clearly be high, putting us well into the higher range of estimates in Table 18-1, amounting to hundreds of billions of dollars per year.

At the same time, the Intergovernmental Panel on Climate Change estimates that stabilizing atmospheric $CO_2$ levels would require reduction of $CO_2$ emissions to a small fraction of current levels. This goal is far beyond the Kyoto Protocol targets and would require major policy intervention to redirect the world's economies toward noncarbon energy sources. However, the IPCC also finds that opportunities for reductions of 30–70 percent in greenhouse gas emissions are available at a net cost below $100 per ton of carbon equivalent; a substantial portion of these cuts would have low or even zero marginal cost. According to these figures, the IPCC's maximum estimated reduction, 5 billion tons, could be achieved at a net cost of several hundred billion dollars—a large amount but probably less than the cost of the high-scenario damages, even using standard discount rates. Certainly the low-cost cuts look like a good investment.

Economic analysis could thus justify much more aggressive climate change policy, but significant political barriers stand in the way of such policies, especially in the United States. Nonetheless, as the ratifying nations move to implement the Kyoto Protocol, and as attention focuses on future policies "beyond Kyoto," the economic policy measures discussed in this chapter will certainly become increasingly important in the future. Political leaders and the public will determine how strongly we will respond to this major issue of the twenty-first century, but economic policies will be central to accomplishing the goals we choose.

## SUMMARY

Climate change, arising from the greenhouse effect of heat-trapping gases, is a global problem. All nations are involved in both its causes and consequences. Current developed nations are the largest greenhouse gas emitters, but emissions by developing nations will grow considerably in coming decades.

The most recent scientific evidence indicates that effects during the twenty-first century may range from a global temperature increase of 1 degree Celsius (2 degrees Fahrenheit) to as much as 6 degrees Celsius (10 degrees Fahrenheit). In addition to simply warming the planet, other predicted effects include disruption of weather patterns and possible sudden major climate shifts.

An analysis of costs and benefits can serve as an economic analysis of climate change. The benefits in this case are the damages potentially averted through action to prevent climate change; the costs are the economic costs of shifting away from fossil fuel dependence, as well as other economic implications of greenhouse gas reduction.

Cost-benefit studies have estimated both costs and benefits in the range of several percent of GDP. However, relative evaluation of costs and benefits depends heavily on the discount rate selected. Because damages tend to worsen with time, the use of a high discount rate leads to a lower evaluation of the benefits of avoiding climate change. In addition, effects such as species loss and effects on life and health are difficult to measure in monetary terms. Also, depending on the assumptions used in economic models, the impact of policies to avoid climate change on GDP could range from a 2 percent decrease to a 2 percent increase in GDP.

Policies to respond to global climate change could be preventive or adaptive. One widely discussed policy is a carbon tax, which would fall most heavily on fuels causing the highest carbon emissions. Revenues from such a tax could be recycled to lower taxes elsewhere in the economy. Another policy option is tradable carbon emissions permits, which could be bought and sold by firms or nations, depending on their level of carbon emissions. Both these policies have the advantage of economic efficiency, but it has been difficult to obtain the political support necessary to implement them. Other possible policy measures include shifting subsidies away from fossil fuels, strengthening energy efficiency standards, and increasing research and development of alternative energy technologies.

The Kyoto Protocol mandating reductions of greenhouse gases by industrialized nations went into force in 2005, but the United States refused to participate. Effective climate change policy in the future will require involvement of the United States as well as China, India, and other developing nations. Much more ambitious reduction targets will be needed to avoid the costs associated with long-term climate change.

## KEY TERMS AND CONCEPTS

avoided costs
business as usual
carbon sinks
carbon tax
Clean Development Mechanism
climate stabilization
common-property resource
cost-benefit analysis
cost-effectiveness analysis
discount rate
double dividend
economic optimum
efficiency standards
energy-efficient technology
environmental externalities
externalities/external costs and benefits
feedback effect
global climate change
global commons
global warming

greenhouse effect
greenhouse gases
internalizing externalities
joint implementation
local and regional pollutants
marginal net benefit
pollution taxes
preventive and adaptive strategies
price elasticity of demand
public good
renewable energy sources
research and development (R&D)
revenue recycling
revenue-neutral tax shift
social optimum
stock pollutant
subsidies
technology transfer
transferable (tradable) pollution permits

## DISCUSSION QUESTIONS

1. Do you consider cost-benefit analysis a useful means of addressing the problem of climate change? How can we adequately value the melting of arctic ice caps, inundation of island nations, and similar climactic impacts? What is the appropriate role of economic analysis in dealing with questions that affect global ecosystems and future generations?

2. Which policies might most effectively address climate change? How can we decide which combination of policies to use? What kinds of policies would economists especially recommend? What are the main barriers to effective policy implementation?

3. The process for formulating and implementing international agreements on climate change policy has been plagued with disagreements and deadlocks. What are the main difficulties in agreeing on specific policy actions? From an economic point of view, what kinds of incentives might induce nations to enter and carry out agreements? What kinds of "win-win" policies might overcome negotiating barriers?

## PROBLEMS

1. Suppose that the terms of an international agreement require reduction of U.S. $CO_2$ emissions by 200 million tons and those of Brazil by 50 million tons. These are the emissions reduction policy options for each country:

| Policy Options | Total Emissions Reduction (million tons carbon) | Cost ($ billion) |
|---|---|---|
| *United States:* | | |
| A: Efficient machinery | 60 | 12 |
| B: Reforestation | 40 | 20 |
| C: Replace coal-fueled power plants | 120 | 30 |
| *Brazil:* | | |
| A: Efficient machinery | 50 | 20 |
| B: Protection of Amazon forest | 30 | 3 |
| C: Replace coal-fueled power plants | 40 | 8 |

a. Which policies are most efficient for each nation in meeting their reduction targets? How much will be reduced using each option, at what cost, if the two nations must operate independently? Assume that any of the policy options can be partially implemented at a constant marginal cost. For example, the United States could choose to reduce carbon emissions with efficient machinery by 10 million tons at a cost of $2 billion. (Hint: Start by calculating the average cost of carbon reduction in dollars per ton for each of the six policies.)

b. Suppose a market of transferable permits allows the United States and Brazil to trade permits to emit $CO_2$. Who has an interest in buying permits? Who has an interest in selling permits? What agreement can they reach to meet the overall emissions reduction target of 250 million tons at the least cost? Can you estimate a range for the permit price to emit one ton of carbon? (Hint: Use your average cost calculations from Question a.)

2. Suppose that the annual consumption of an average American household is 2,000 gallons of oil in heating and transportation and 300 ccf (hundred cubic feet) of gas in cooking. Use the figures in Table 18-2 on the effects of a carbon tax to calculate how much an average American household would pay per year with an added tax of $10 per ton of carbon. (One barrel of oil contains 42 gallons.) Assume that this relatively small tax initially causes no reduction in the demand for oil and gas. Figuring 100 million households in the United States, what would be the U.S. Treasury revenue from such a carbon tax?

What would be the national revenue from a tax of $200 per ton of carbon? Consider the issue of the impact of increased prices on consumption—a reasonable assumption about consumption elasticity might be that a $200 per ton tax would cause the quantity of oil and gas consumed to decline by 20 percent. How might the government use such revenues? What would the impact be on the average family? Consider the difference between the short-term and long-term impacts.

## REFERENCES

Cline, William R. *The Economics of Global Warming.* Washington, D.C.: Institute for International Economics, 1992.

Cline, William R. "Climate Change." Chapter 1 in Bjørn Lomborg, ed., *Global Crises, Global Solutions.* Cambridge, U.K.: Cambridge University Press, 2004.

Dower, Roger C., and Mary Zimmerman. *The Right Climate for Carbon Taxes, Creating Economic Incentives to Protect the Atmosphere.* Washington, D.C.: World Resources Institute, 1992.

Fankhauser, Samuel. *Valuing Climate Change: The Economics of the Greenhouse.* London, U.K.: Earthscan, 1995.

Gouldner, Lawrence H. "Environmental Taxation and the Double Dividend: A Reader's Guide," in *Environmental Policy Making in Economies with Prior Tax Distortions.* Cheltenham, U.K.: Elgar, 2002.

Intergovernmental Panel on Climate Change (IPCC). *Climate Change 1995, Volume 1: The Science of Climate Change.* Cambridge, U.K.: Cambridge University Press, 1996.

Intergovernmental Panel on Climate Change (IPCC). *Climate Change 2001, Volume 1: The Scientific Basis.* Cambridge, U.K.: Cambridge University Press, 2001.

Manne, Alan S., and Richard G. Richels. *Buying Greenhouse Insurance: The Economic Costs of CO_2 Emissions Limits.* Cambridge, Mass.: MIT Press, 1992.

Nordhaus, William D. "Reflections on the Economics of Climate Change." *Journal of Economic Perspectives* 7 (Fall 1993): 11–25.

Nordhaus, William D., and Joseph Boyer. *Warming the World: Economic Models of Global Warming*. Cambridge, Mass.: MIT Press, 2000.

Poterba, James. "Global Warming Policy: A Public Finance Perspective." *Journal of Economic Perspectives* 7 (Fall 1993): 47–63.

Repetto, Robert, and Duncan Austin. *The Costs of Climate Protection: A Guide for the Perplexed*. Washington, D.C.: World Resources Institute, 1997.

Roodman, David M. *Getting the Signals Right: Tax Reform to Protect the Environment and the Economy*. Worldwatch Paper 134. Washington, D.C.: Worldwatch Institute, 1997.

Trenberth, Kevin E. "Stronger Evidence of Human Influence on Climate: The 2001 IPCC Assessment." *Environment* 43 (May 2001): 8–19.

U.S. Department of Energy, Energy Information Administration. *Annual Energy Review 2003*. Washington, D.C.: U.S. Government, 2003.

U.S. Department of Energy, Energy Information Administration. *International Energy Outlook 2004*. Washington, D.C.: U.S. Government, 2004.

World Bank. *World Development Report 1992: Development and the Environment*. Washington, D.C.: World Bank, 1992.

## WEBSITES

1. **http://www.epa.gov/globalwarming/** The global warming website of the U.S. Environmental Protection Agency. The site provides links to information on the causes, impact, and trends related to global climate change.

2. **http://www.ipcc.ch/** The website for the Intergovernmental Panel on Climate Change, a United Nations–sponsored agency "to assess the scientific, technical, and socioeconomic information relevant for the understanding of the risk of human-induced climate change." Their website includes assessment reports detailing the relationships between human actions and global climate change.

3. **http://climate.wri.org/** World Resource Institute's website on climate and atmosphere. The site includes several articles and case studies, including research on Clean Development Mechanisms.

4. **http://unfccc.int/** Homepage for the United Nations Framework Convention on Climate Change. The site provides data on the climate change issue and information about the ongoing process of negotiating international agreements related to climate change.

5. **http://www.weathervane.rff.org/** A website sponsored by Resources for the Future devoted to climate change issues. The site includes several research papers on the trading of greenhouse gas emissions permits.

# SEVEN

## Environment, Trade, and Development

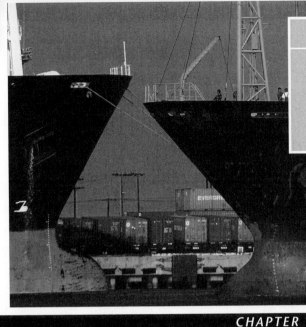

CHAPTER FOCUS QUESTIONS

- What effects does expanded trade have on the environment?
- Should regional and global trade agreements include environmental protection?
- What policies can promote sustainable trade?

# 19

# World Trade and the Environment

## Environmental Impact of Trade

World trade expansion has raised the issue of the relationship between trade and the environment. Is trade good or bad for the environment? The answer is not obvious. The production of goods for import and export, like other production, often has environmental effects. Will these effects increase or decrease with expanded trade? How will they affect the exporting nation, the importing nation, or the world as a whole? Who is responsible for responding to environmental problems associated with trade? Questions such as these have received increasing attention in recent years.

International attention first focused on these issues in 1991, when the Mexican government challenged a U.S. law banning tuna imports from Mexico. The U.S. Marine Mammal Protection Act prohibited tuna-fishing methods that killed large numbers of dolphins, and banned tuna imports from countries that used such fishing methods. The Mexican government argued that this U.S. law violated the rules of the **General Agreement on Tariffs and Trade (GATT)**.

According to the free-trade principles that provided the basis for GATT and for its successor, the **World Trade Organization (WTO)**, countries cannot restrict imports except in limited cases such as protecting the health and safety of their own citizens. A GATT dispute panel ruled that the United States could not use domestic legislation to protect dolphins outside its own territorial limits.

Although Mexico did not press for enforcement of this decision, the tuna/dolphin case opened a major controversy over issues of trade and environment. In a similar case in 1999, the World Trade Organization ruled that the United States could not prohibit shrimp imports from countries using fishing methods that killed endangered sea turtles.

The implications of this and the earlier tuna/dolphin decision could affect many other international environmental issues, including forest protection, ozone depletion, hazardous wastes, and global climate change. All these issues relate to international trade. If individual countries cannot use trade measures to protect the global environment, how will it be possible to devise effective policies to respond to these issues?

To address these questions, we need to reexamine the theory and practice of international trade. Most economists believe that expanded trade is generally beneficial, promoting increased efficiency and greater wealth among trading nations. But what if expanded trade causes environmental damage?

At the national level, the standard economic policy response to environmental impact is to implement policies that internalize externalities, as discussed in earlier chapters. At the international level, however, the picture is more confusing. The burden of environmental externalities associated with trade may be borne by importers, exporters, or by others not directly involved in producing or consuming traded goods. The authority to formulate and enforce environmental policies usually exists only at the national level. This can create significant problems when environmental impacts are transnational, because most international trade agreements make no provision for environmental protection.

## Comparative Advantage and Environmental Externalities

We can use economic theory to analyze gains and losses associated with environmental effects of trade. The theory of **comparative advantage** tells us that both trading partners gain from trade by specializing in goods they can produce most efficiently. This basic theory does not consider **environmental externalities** associated with the production or consumption of goods. Consider Figure 19-1, which uses automobiles as an example of an imported good's welfare effects.

In the absence of trade, domestic supply and demand would be in equilibrium at $Q^*$, with a domestic price of $P^*$. With trade, both production and consumption of automobiles will change. If there are no barriers to trade, automobiles can be imported at the world price $P_w$, which is lower than the domestic price.[1] Domestic production falls to $Q_1$, while domestic consumption rises to $Q_2$. The quantity of imports is shown as $(Q_2 - Q_1)$.

---

[1]This example shows trade in a relatively small country whose demand has no affect on world price—hence world price is shown as constant.

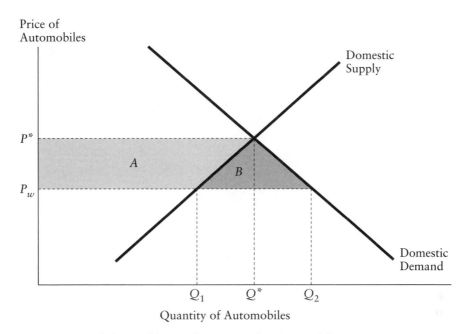

**FIGURE 19-1** *Gains and Losses from Importing Automobiles*

How does trade affect domestic economic welfare? Domestic producers of automobiles lose area *A* because they now sell fewer cars at a lower price. Domestic consumers gain areas *A + B* because they can now buy more cars at the same lower price. The net gain from trade is therefore $(A + B) - A = B$.

But this leaves out any environmental externalities associated with trade. Consider Figure 19-2, which adds two curves showing two types of environmental externalities: **production externalities,** caused by automobile production, and **consumption externalities** resulting from automobile use.[2] The production externalities are shown as added costs on the supply side, and the consumption externalities as lowered benefits on the demand side. The resulting welfare impacts resulting from trade are represented by the shaded areas *C* and *F*. The reduction in domestic production means that the country gains area *C* in reduced environmental costs—costs shifted to countries producing cars for export. Increased automobile consumption and use, however, cause increased environmental damage equal to area *F*.

This has important implications for trade theory. In the basic trade case without externalities, we can unambiguously claim overall **gains from trade.** Even though one group (automobile producers) loses, consumers' gains outweigh these losses. Once we

---

[2]In Chapter 3 we combined both types of externality for simplicity. Here, because production and consumption can take place in different countries, we must treat them separately.

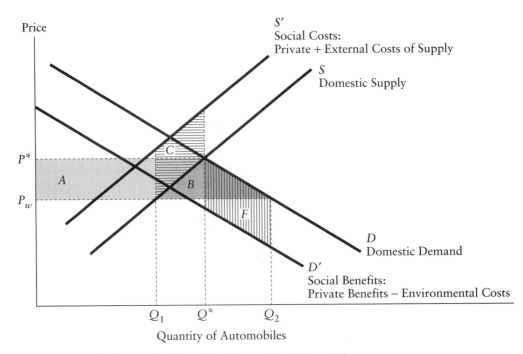

**FIGURE 19-2** *Environmental Impacts of Importing Automobiles*

introduce externalities, however, we can no longer be so sure of net gains from trade. It depends on the nature and size of the environmental damages C and F. Policy actions by the importing and exporting countries could internalize these external costs, but unless we know such policies will be implemented, we cannot be sure of a net gain from trade.

## Environmental Effects of Expanding Resource Exports

Environmental effects must also figure in the analysis of how trade affects an exporting country. In Figure 19-3 we use timber exports as our example. In the ordinary analysis of trade without externalities, production of timber increases from $Q^*$ to $Q_2$, while domestic consumption decreases to $Q_1$, leaving $(Q_2 - Q_1)$ for export. Timber producers gain areas $A' + B'$ because with trade they can produce and sell more timber at the higher world price $P_w$. Domestic timber consumers lose $A'$, being able to afford less timber at the higher price. The net gain to the country is $B'$.

The external costs associated with additional timber production—which could include land and watershed degradation as well as user costs, option values, and ecological costs—are shown by the area of $C'$. We cannot tell for sure how $B'$ and $C'$ compare in size. Thus we cannot unambiguously claim net benefits from trade to this exporting country. In more commonsense terms, it is not clear that the economic

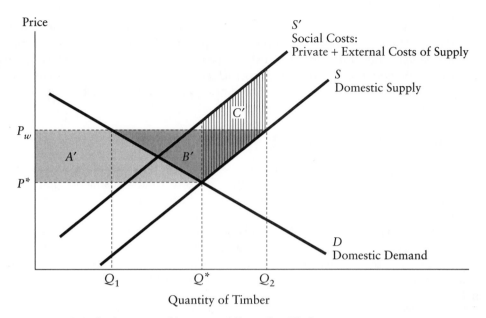

**FIGURE 19-3** *Environmental Impacts of Exporting Timber*

benefits of increased exports outweigh the environmental damage associated with expanded logging.[3]

Our examples, of course, represent a simple model of trade, but the conclusion that environmental costs may seriously affect net gains from trade is far-reaching. In the real world, hundreds of countries trade trillions of dollars' worth of products. Where significant environmental externalities occur, trade will reallocate these externalities among countries.

It may be possible to **export pollution** by importing goods whose production creates heavy environmental impact. In addition, expanded trade tends to increase the scale of production for the individual countries and world as a whole, meaning that the total volume of pollution and environmental damage is likely to increase. Trade also necessarily involves energy use for transportation, with resulting air pollution and other environmental consequences. Indirect environmental effects of trade might also occur, for example when larger-scale export agriculture displaces peasant farmers onto marginal lands such as hillsides and forest margins, leading to deforestation and soil erosion. Specific kinds of trade, such as trade in toxic wastes or endangered species, can have obvious negative environmental impact.

Trade may also have environmentally beneficial effects. Freer trade may help spread environmentally friendly technology, and the tendency of trade to promote

[3]Consumption externalities may also be associated with timber (as in our previous automobile example), but we have omitted them in Figure 19-3, as they are unlikely to be significant.

more efficient production may reduce materials and energy use per unit of output. In addition, trading nations may come under pressure to improve environmental standards when product quality or transboundary impacts are at issue.[4] How can we balance the economic gains from trade against the reality that trade shifts environmental impact, sometimes increasing and sometimes decreasing total external costs?

## Trade and Environment: Policy and Practice

Many developing countries grow agricultural crops for domestic sale as well as for export. With increased trade—often a major feature of "structural adjustment" policies required by international agencies such as the International Monetary Fund and the World Bank—the area devoted to export crops increases. What are the environmental effects of shifting to export crops? In some cases they can be significant and harmful. A study of Mali, for example, finds that development of cotton as a cash export crop "has substantially increased the cultivated area and markedly reduced the fallow period. . . . The environmental effects are evident in land degradation and soil erosion owing to overcultivation, insufficient fallow, and the use of marginal land against a backdrop of increasing aridity."[5]

On the other hand, export crops may sometimes be more environmentally friendly than the domestic crops they replace. In Latin America and Africa, tree crops such as coffee and cocoa can help prevent erosion. In Kenya, the rapidly expanding horticulture export sector has had mixed environmental effects. Some flower growers apply pesticides intensively, with both health and environmental impacts. Excessive water use for irrigation is also an issue in water-poor Kenya. Prime agricultural land used for horticulture may displace food production; on the other hand, employment on flower farms may provide an alternative to exploitation of marginal lands for subsistence farming. The flowers are flown to Europe by jet, raising the issue of transportation energy use, but the energy consumed in jet fuel approximately equals the energy needed to grow similar flowers in heated greenhouses in Europe. Some Kenyan growers produce "Fairtrade" flowers under a code that reduces water and pesticide use and guarantees higher wages to workers, giving them a steady and reliable income.[6]

Much depends not on trade alone, but on domestic political conditions. **Dualistic land ownership,** with large landowners wielding considerable political power and small farmers being displaced by export-oriented agriculture, can be doubly damaging to the environment. In Central America, for example, improved transportation and trade infrastructure led to "a technical shift to higher-profit, input-dependent farming. Maize and beans gave way to cotton, tomatoes, strawberries, and bananas. The value of farmland naturally increased, which benefited privileged landowning elites but led many poor farmers to be promptly evicted. These farmers had no choice but to move on to drier

---

[4]Examples could include pesticide residues in food or water pollution in rivers that cross national borders.

[5]Reed, ed., 1996, pp. 86 and 96.

[6]See http://www.fairtrade.org.uk/products_roses.htm, http://www.biotech-monitor.nl/2004.htm, and http://www.pan-uk.org/ for more on the Kenyan flower industry.

lands, forests, hillsides, or lands with shallow and less fertile soils." At the same time the affluent farmers "use their influence to demand environmentally damaging input subsidies, which in turn lead them to overmechanize, overirrigate, and overspray."[7]

Health and safety issues arising in trade are not always easily resolved at either the domestic or international levels. For example, domestic regulations that prohibit the sale of toxic pesticides may not apply internationally. "Goods that are restricted in domestic markets, on the grounds that they present a danger to human, animal or plant life or health, or to the environment, may often be legally exported. This may cause a problem for the importing country, where information is lacking on whether and why the product is banned: exporters may make false declarations, customs authorities (particularly in developing countries) may lack adequate product testing facilities."[8]

According to **GATT Article XX,** countries may restrict trade in order to "conserve exhaustible natural resources" or to protect "human, animal or plant life or health." However, interpretation of this special exception to free trade rules has led to fiercely contested disputes among countries.

For example, European nations have refused to allow imports of U.S. beef produced with hormone supplements. The United States has argued that since there is no proven harm to human health this is an illegal barrier to trade. The Europeans, however, cite the **precautionary principle:** because their consumers are concerned about the possible effects of hormones, shouldn't they have the prerogative to decide what they will allow for domestic consumption?

## Product and Process Issues

A similar issue has arisen over the use of genetically engineered crops. Although the United States allows unlabeled genetically engineered foods, these are widely opposed in Europe. Should European countries be able to ban the import of genetically engineered foods? The issue has enormous implications both for agribusinesses that see great profit potential in genetic engineering and for many consumers who strongly oppose it.

The issue is further complicated because much of the opposition to genetic engineering is based not on possible human health effects (which, if proved, would be a valid reason for trade restrictions under Article XX), but on the likely environmental repercussions of genetically engineered crops. Pollen from such crops can easily spread into the environment, disrupting fragile ecosystems and possibly creating "superweeds" resistant to herbicides. But under GATT and WTO rules, the production *process* is not an acceptable cause for trade restrictions. Only if the *product* itself is harmful can a country impose controls.

For example, if pesticide residues at dangerous levels are detected on fruit or vegetables, import of those products can be banned. But if pesticide overuse is causing environmental damage in the producing areas, the importing nation has no right to

---

[7]Paarlberg, 2000, p. 177.

[8]Brack, 1998, p. 7.

act. Similarly, if unrestricted logging is destroying rainforests, countries may not impose a ban on the import of unsustainably produced timber.

Globalization of trade can also create "boomerang" effects through the transboundary exchange of externalities. For example, pesticides banned in the United States are often exported to developing countries. Poor laborers who apply pesticides without safety precautions suffer harmful effects, as do adults and children who drink water from streams polluted by runoff. In addition, harmful effects return to the United States through trade in fruits containing residues of dangerous chemicals.

The **process and production methods (PPM) rule** removes an important potential weapon for international environmental protection. If a nation fails to act to protect its own environment, other countries have no trade leverage to promote better environmental practices. Only if a specific **multilateral environmental agreement (MEA)** such as the Convention on International Trade in Endangered Species (CITES) is in place are import restrictions permissible.

This principle was at issue in the tuna/dolphin and shrimp/turtle decisions, in which trade authorities ruled that nations had no jurisdiction over extraterritorial environmental issues. But such issues are more and more common in an increasingly globalized world. Simply waiting for the producing country to "clean up its act" is likely to be insufficient.

Trade can affect domestic as well as international policy, weakening the autonomy of nations to define their own environmental and social policies. Concerns have arisen of a **"race to the bottom,"** in which nations reduce environmental and social standards in order to gain competitive advantage.

> Producers located in member states enforcing strict process standards will suffer a competitive disadvantage compared with producers located in member states enforcing less strict standards. . . . [F]aced with the prospect of their industries suffering a competitive disadvantage when compared with companies located in low-standard jurisdictions, member states may choose not to elevate environmental standards or may even relax current standards.[9]

According to several economic studies, there is "relatively little evidence to support the hypothesis that environmental regulations have had a large adverse effect on competitiveness," and few cases exist of **pollution havens**—countries that attract manufacturing firms due to weak environmental regulations.[10] But competitive pressures may nonetheless exert a "chilling" effect on countries considering strict environmental laws.

The North American Free Trade Agreement (NAFTA) has produced cases in which corporations have challenged environmental regulations as barriers to trade.[11]

---

[9]Brack, 1998, p. 113.

[10]See Jaffe et al., 1995 (quoted); Cole, 2003; and Gallagher, 2004.

[11]The parties to the NAFTA are the United States, Canada, and Mexico. Discussions are underway to create a Free Trade Area of the Americas (FTAA), which would extend NAFTA-like trade rules to all of North and South America.

The Canadian asbestos industry sought to remove U.S. restrictions on the sale of cancer-causing asbestos products, and the U.S. pesticide industry challenged strong Canadian pesticide regulations. In one case, Ethyl Corporation (based in the United States) successfully overturned a Canadian ban on importation and sale of the gasoline additive MMT, a chemical suspected to cause nerve damage. Canada was required not only to eliminate the ban, but also to pay $13 million to compensate Ethyl Corporation for legal costs and lost sales.

Trade expansion may also have direct or indirect beneficial effects on the environment. According to comparative advantage theory, trade causes countries to become more efficient in their use of resources, thereby conserving resources and avoiding waste. Trade liberalization also removes distortionary subsidies and pricing policies, improving the efficiency of resource allocation. For example, widespread subsidies on chemical fertilizers and pesticides promote environmentally harmful farming methods—but trade agreements often prohibit such subsidies to domestic producers. Eliminating these subsidies would promote both economic efficiency and environmental sustainability.

Trade may also encourage the spread of environmentally friendly technology. In energy production, for example, many developing and formerly communist nations depend heavily on old, inefficient, high-polluting power plants. Trade can facilitate the replacement of these plants with modern, highly efficient facilities or (as in India) encourage a growing wind-power sector. Multinational companies, sometimes seen as offenders in the exploitation of developing country resources, can also introduce efficient technologies into industrial sectors. Multinationals may respond to domestic political pressures to develop cleaner industrial processes and then disseminate those processes throughout their worldwide operations.

> Foreign investment affects the environment in many ways. In resource-based industries, especially oil extraction and mineral mining, it can lead to significant local environmental degradation as demonstrated in, for example, Nigeria, Indonesia, and Papua New Guinea. Foreign investment in the manufacturing sector, on the other hand, can lead to the employment of later vintage and possibly less resource- and pollution-intensive technology.[12]

One way of capturing trade's differing effects on the environment is to distinguish between **scale, composition, and technique effects.** Trade promotes growth (increased scale), changes in industrial patterns (composition), and improvements in technological efficiency (technique). The combination of the three effects may increase or decrease pollution levels or balance out to leave pollution levels unchanged. One study of sulfur dioxide pollution found that, on balance, trade reduces pollution levels,[13] but this may not be true for other pollutants (see Box 19-1).

[12]Neumayer, 2001, p. x.

[13]Antweiler, Copeland, and Taylor, 2001.

| 19-1 | The Environmental Kuznets Curve Debate |

**D**efenders of expanding global trade have often relied on the **Environmental Kuznets Curve (EKC)** principle, which asserts that environmental damage increases in the early stages of growth, but diminishes once nations reach higher levels of income (see Figure 19-4). According to this theory, after passing through a "dirty" stage of development, nations will put effort into "cleaning up" and may also shift to less-polluting production methods. More open trade will therefore accelerate the process of achieving both economic growth and a cleaner environment.

Do empirical data support the EKC principle? The picture is mixed. A study by Grossman and Krueger found it effective for a limited number of air and water pollutants.[1] Other important environmental pollutants such as nitrogen oxides, carbon monoxide, carbon dioxide, methane, and tropospheric ozone, were not included,

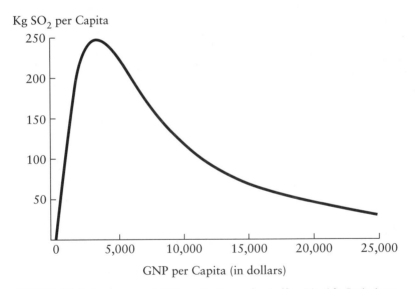

**FIGURE 19-4** *Environmental Kuznets Curve for Sulfur Dioxide Emissions*
Source: Adapted from Panayotou, T., *Empirical Tests and Policy Analysis of Environmental Degradation at Different Levels of Development*, 1993. Reprinted by permission of the author.

---

[1]Grossman and Krueger, 1995. The pollutants they tested were sulfur dioxide, smoke, and particulate matter in air; oxygen loss, fecal contamination, and heavy metal contamination in water.

*(continued on following page)*

nor were municipal wastes or measures of ecosystem degradation such as species loss, soil degradation, or groundwater depletion.

According to a World Bank study, carbon dioxide emissions and municipal wastes continued to increase with economic growth. And even those pollutants that seem to conform to an EKC have high enough "turning points," ranging from $2,000 to $12,000 in income, to imply a considerable increase in pollution for most of the world's developing nations before any improvement would be noted.

According to one EKC study, the estimated global "turning point" for sulfur dioxide would not come until 2085, by which time global emissions would be 354 percent above 1986 levels. Suspended particulate matter would peak in 2089 at 421 percent higher emissions, and nitrogen oxides in 2079 with 226 percent higher emissions.[2] Another review of EKC studies suggested that ". . . using different indicators, more explanatory variables than income alone and the estimation of different models, the EKC results are not generally reproduced. This should be a warning to those who too superficially have concluded that economic growth is, by nature, a benefit for the environment and that economic growth can be prescribed as the remedy to environmental problems."[3]

Clearly, trade-led growth can have significant environmental impacts. Although economic growth may increase the capabilities of nations to promote environmental protection, avoiding unacceptable levels of environmental damage will require specific policies to reduce pollution.

---

[2]Selden and Song, 1994.

[3]Rothman and de Bruyn, 1998, p. 145. See also Stern, 2004.

## Trade Agreements and the Environment

A variety of institutional and policy approaches have been suggested to balance the goals of trade benefits and environmental protection, some similar to the standard free-trade model, and some significantly different. Let's examine several of them.

### The World Trade Organization Approach

This approach retains the overarching policy goal of free or "liberalized" trade, pursued for five decades through "rounds" of trade agreements under the General Agreement on Tariffs and Trade, which became the World Trade Organization in 1994. The GATT and WTO, whose membership now includes more than 120 nations, have worked to lower tariffs and nontariff barriers to trade, as well as eliminate subsidies for export industries.

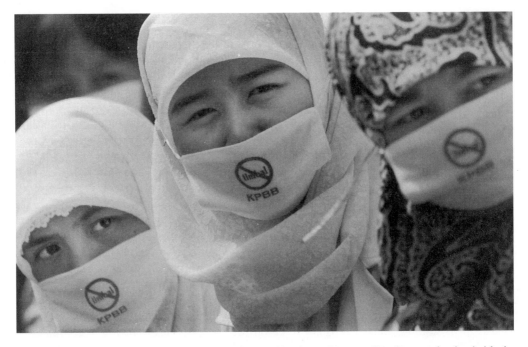

*Indonesian environmental activists protest air pollution levels in Jakarta, calling for use of unleaded fuels. Signs on the masks say "no lead." Many cities in developing nations have high levels of air pollution.*

Although the WTO recognizes a special exception to trade rules under Article XX for resource conservation and environmental protection, its panel rulings have interpreted this narrowly. WTO authorities tend to be suspicious of "green protectionism"—the use of trade barriers to protect domestic industry from competition under the guise of environmental regulation. They are also unsympathetic to nations' efforts to affect environmental policy outside their borders through trade measures.

From the WTO perspective, environmental policy responsibility should remain at the national level. As far as possible, decisions on international trade policy should not be complicated with environmental issues. This is consistent with an economic principle known as the **specificity rule**: policy solutions should directly target the source of the problem. Using trade measures to accomplish environmental policy goals is therefore a **second-best solution** likely to cause other, undesired effects such as economic losses from trade restriction.

This argument, placing the responsibility for environmental policies on national governments, has been criticized on several grounds. It fails to consider the competitive pressures that may encourage trading nations to reduce environmental protections, as well as the weak regulatory institutions in many developing countries. It is also inadequate for dealing with truly **transboundary** or **global pollution** problems.

## The North American Free Trade Agreement (NAFTA) Approach

In 1993, the United States, Canada, and Mexico signed the NAFTA agreement, lowering trade barriers across the continent. During negotiations, environmental groups argued strongly that freer trade could lead to negative environmental consequences, pointing to the severe environmental problems already affecting the *maquiladoras*—tariff-free industrial zones along the Mexican border. As a result, a side agreement, the North American Agreement on Environmental Cooperation (NAAEC), set up the tripartite Commission for Environmental Cooperation (CEC), and another side agreement, the North American Agreement on Labor Cooperation (NAALC), dealt with labor issues.

This specific attention to social and environmental aspects of trade was remarkable and almost unprecedented in trade agreements. Although this unusual aspect of NAFTA persuaded some environmental groups in the United States to support the agreement, the CEC has few enforcement powers. It may respond to a country's failure to enforce existing environmental regulations, but its role is generally limited to producing a fact-finding report and recommendations to the government involved.

The opening of agricultural sector trade under NAFTA has both social and environmental effects, as small corn farmers in Mexico are unable to compete with cheaper grain imported from the United States. The migration of displaced farmers from rural to urban areas will intensify urban environmental pressures, as well as creating greater pressure for illegal migration across the U.S./Mexico border. In addition, the genetic diversity characteristic of small-scale farming may be threatened, which could result in the loss of a "living seed bank" of great importance to world agriculture.[14]

In the area of industrial pollution, NAFTA has had both positive and negative impacts. Mexican environmental enforcement has improved, but increased industrial concentrations have led to worsened local environmental quality in some areas. A recent review of NAFTA's environmental provisions concludes that they have "fallen well short of the aspirations of the environmental community" and "should be strengthened in the next phase of NAFTA."[15] But efforts to expand NAFTA to Central and South America, in the Free Trade Area of the Americas (FTAA) and Central America Free Trade Agreement (CAFTA), have drawn opposition from critics who argue that these proposed agreements have even weaker social and environmental provisions.

One of the most controversial aspects of NAFTA is its Chapter 11, which protects foreign investors. Under this provision, investors who claim damage to their business from environmental regulations can sue governments to recover damages, and several suits have been successful. In 1999, when California ordered a phase-out of the gasoline additive and groundwater contaminant MTBE, the Canadian manufacturer Methanex sued for $1 billion in compensation. The issue of investor rights agreements has since become a major controversy in other international trade agreements.[16]

---

[14]See CEC, 1999, Issue Study 1: Maize in Mexico; and Nadal, 2000.

[15]Hufbauer et al., 2000, p. 62. See also Deere and Esty, 2002, and Gallagher, 2004.

[16]See Mann, 2001, available at http://www.iisd.org/publications/.

## *The European Union Approach*

The European Union is unusual in being a free-trade area with its own legislative and administrative institutions. Unlike the North American CEC, the European Union has the power to make environmental regulations binding on its member countries. This is known as **harmonization of environmental standards.** Note, however, that this policy solution involves more than free trade; it entails the creation of a supranational authority with the power to set environmental standards.

Regional trade area policies also raise the issue of "harmonizing up" versus "harmonizing down." Some countries may be forced to tighten their environmental policies to meet EU standards, but others may find their environmental standards weakened. The EU overturned a law requiring returnable bottles in Denmark as a barrier to trade, and Norway chose not to join the EU in part out of fear that they would be compelled to modify strict domestic environmental regulations.

It is relatively rare for trade agreements to include the kind of enforceable supranational environmental regulations that exist in the European Union. Although the Standards Code adopted after the Uruguay Round GATT negotiations in 1992 calls for international harmonization of environmental standards, no basis exists for this process to be other than voluntary. Indeed, critics have argued that harmonization undertaken in the closed, business-dominated atmosphere of the WTO standards committees would in many cases be likely to harmonize standards down rather than up.

## *Multilateral Environmental Agreements (MEAs)*

It has long been recognized that some environmental problems require international solutions. The first international treaty dealing with trade and the environment was the *Phylloxera* agreement of 1878, restricting trade in grapevines to prevent the spread of pests that damage vineyards. In 1906 an international convention was adopted banning the use of phosphorus in matches. Phosphorus was responsible for serious occupational disease among match workers, but it was the cheapest ingredient for matches. Only an international convention could prevent any exporting country from gaining competitive advantage by using phosphorus in match production.[17]

Since then, numerous international treaties have responded to specific environmental issues. These include conventions protecting fur seals, migratory birds, polar bears, whales, and endangered species. Transboundary and global environmental issues have been addressed in the Montreal Protocol on Substances that Deplete the Ozone Layer (1987), the Basel Convention on Hazardous Wastes (1989), the Antarctica Treaty (1991), and the Convention on Straddling and Highly Migratory Fish Stocks (1995). In 1997 the Kyoto Protocol on Climate Change established guidelines for reducing greenhouse gas emissions, including important trade-related measures.

These international treaties have addressed the environmental consequences of production methods in ways that individual nations cannot. "The local imposition of

---

[17]Charnovitz, 1996, pp. 176–177.

PPM (Process and Production Measures) standards on domestic manufacturing industry is obviously a national prerogative, but it should not be used to restrict imported products, whatever the process used for their production. This kind of action would be in conflict with the GATT. If PPMs are included as appropriate measures within a Multilateral Environmental Agreement (MEA), however, this would be much more acceptable, as their imposition would be multilateral rather than unilateral."[18]

Serious questions remain, however, about the compatibility of MEAs with WTO rules. Which set of international agreements should take precedence in the case of a conflict? For example, the Kyoto Protocol encourages the subsidized transfer of energy-efficient technology to developing nations—but this provision could violate the WTO's prohibition of export subsidies. Whereas national laws such as the U.S. Marine Mammal Protection Act have been found incompatible with WTO rules, so far no major test case has addressed conflict between an MEA and a trade agreement.

## Strategies for Sustainable Trade

The emerging twenty-first century global economy will be characterized both by resource and environmental limits and by a much more important role for the presently developing nations. Expanded global trade will bring benefits in terms of increased efficiency, technology transfer, and the import and export of sustainably produced products. But we must also evaluate the effects of trade in terms of social and ecological impacts.

A World Bank review of trade and environment issues finds that "many participants in the debate now agree that (a) more open trade improves growth and economic welfare, and (b) increased trade and growth without appropriate environmental policies in place may have unwanted effects on the environment."[19] This implies that future trade agreements must take environmental sustainability more explicitly into account. Introducing sustainability into trade policy will require institutional changes at global, regional, and local levels.

### "Greening" Global Environmental Organizations

At the global level, advocates of institutional reform have proposed setting up a **World Environmental Organization (WEO)**[20] that would counterbalance the World Trade Organization much as national environmental protection agencies balance departments of finance and commerce. This would create a global environmental advocacy organization but might also lead to conflict and deadlock with other transnational institutions.

Another approach would be to "green" existing institutions, broadening the environmental and social provisions of the GATT's Article XX and altering the missions of the World Bank and International Monetary Fund to emphasize sustainable trade development objectives (discussed further in Chapter 20).

---

[18]Brack, 1998, p. 65.

[19]Fredriksson, 1999, p. 1.

[20]See Runge, 1994, Chapter 6; and Esty, 1994, Chapter 4.

The idea of a World Environmental Organization may seem visionary, but it has gained significant support. According to Sir Leon Brittan, vice president of the European Commission: "Setting environmental standards within a territory may be fine, but what about damage that spills over national borders? In a rapidly globalizing world, more and more of these problems cannot be effectively solved at the national or bilateral level, or even at the level of regional trading blocs like the European Union. Global problems require global solutions."[21]

A World Environmental Organization could serve as an umbrella for the implementation of existing multinational environmental agreements, as well as promoting further agreements consistent with global sustainable development strategies. **Global public goods** such as biodiversity, ozone layer protection, climate stabilization, and protection of oceans and water systems, would be the responsibility of the WEO.

A WEO could also play a role in negotiating trade agreements on agricultural subsidies, seeking to redirect farm subsidies to soil conservation and development of low-input agricultural techniques. As global $CO_2$ emissions continue to rise, energy sector trade may need to accommodate a carbon tax or tradable permit scheme, as discussed in Chapter 18. Global agreements on forest and biodiversity preservation are also likely to involve specific trade restrictions, tariff preferences, or labeling systems. In all these areas, a powerful advocate for environmental interests would have a major impact on the shaping of trade treaties and regulations.

## *Local, Regional, and Private Sector Policies*

The trend toward globalization, which increasingly subjects communities to the logic of the global marketplace, may conflict with the goal of strengthening local and regional policies promoting sustainable development. Reserving powers of resource conservation and management to local and national institutions is important to sustainable resource management. Most environmental protection policies are implemented at the national level, and it is important to maintain national authority to enforce environmental standards.

In regional groupings such as NAFTA that involve no supranational rule-making body, trade agreements could give special status to national policies aimed at sustainable agriculture and resource management. NAFTA rules currently give precedence to international environmental treaties (such as the Basel Convention on hazardous wastes, the Montreal Protocol on ozone depleting substances, and CITES on endangered species). This principle could be expanded to all national environmental protection policies, and effective sanctions for environmental violations could be established.

Regional trade and customs unions such as the European Union, with elected supranational policymaking bodies, can be responsible for environmental and social regulation to the extent that their legitimate democratic mandate allows. Transboundary issues are a logical area for supranational bodies to carry out environmental rule-making. Where they are empowered to intervene in national policymaking, the process can be oriented toward "harmonizing up" rather than "harmonizing down" environmental

---

[21]Brack, 1998, pp. 19–20.

standards. This means that countries within a free-trade area must retain the power to impose higher social and environmental standards where they see fit.

The development of **certification** and labeling requirements for sustainably produced products can arise from public or private initiative. Germany's "green dot" system for recyclable and recycled goods is one example. Private, nongovernmental organizations have also set up certification systems for goods such as coffee and timber. "Fair trade" networks certify socially and environmentally responsible production of traded goods. While representing only a tiny proportion of trade, the fair-trade industry has experienced rapid rates of sales growth.[22]

It is evident that there are many different approaches to reconciling the goals of trade and environment policy. In an article reviewing the debate on trade and environment, Daniel Esty concludes that ". . . there is no real choice about whether to address the trade and environment linkage; this linkage is a matter of fact. . . . Building environmental sensitivity into the trade regime in a thoughtful and systematic fashion should therefore be of interest to the trade community as well as environmental advocates."[23] Achieving this goal will be a major challenge for trade negotiators at both regional and global levels for the foreseeable future.

## SUMMARY

Trade expansion can often have environmental implications. Trade may increase environmental externalities at the national, regional, or global level. Although it is usually economically advantageous for countries to pursue their comparative advantage through trade, trade may have environmental repercussions such as increased pollution or natural resource degradation.

The environmental impacts of trade affect both importers and exporters. Agricultural cropping patterns altered by the introduction of export crops may involve environmental benefit or harm. Secondary effects of trade may arise from the disruption of existing communities, increased migration, and impact on marginal lands. Industrial pollution may increase, decrease, or shift in regional impact.

International trade agreements make provisions for resource conservation and environmental protection, but these are usually limited exceptions to a general principle of free trade. In the World Trade Organization, countries may consider the environmental impact of a product, but not of its production processes. This has led to numerous trade disputes over whether specific measures are justified on the grounds of protection of life and health, or are simply disguised protectionism.

Policy responses to trade and environment issues can occur at the national, regional, or global level. The European Union is an example of a free-trade area that includes institutions for transnational environmental standards enforcement. The North American Free Trade Agreement was accompanied by a side agreement setting up an environmental monitoring authority, the Commission for Environmental Cooperation, but this body has little enforcement power.

---

[22]For more on fair trade, see http://www.fairtradefederation.org/ and http://www.equalexchange.com/.

[23]Esty, 2001, pp. 114 and 126–127. See also Harris, 2000.

Multilateral environmental agreements (MEAs) address specific transboundary or global environmental issues. Conflicts between MEAs and World Trade Organization rules are possible, but have so far been avoided. Proposals have also been made for a World Environmental Organization to oversee global environmental policy and to advocate for environmental interests in the world trade system.

Where effective environmental protection policies are lacking at the regional or global level, national policies must address trade-related environmental issues. Certification and labeling requirements, instituted by governments or by private nongovernmental organizations, can help to promote consumer awareness and "greener" corporate practices in international trade.

## KEY TERMS AND CONCEPTS

certification
comparative advantage
consumption externalities
dualistic land ownership
environmental externalities
Environmental Kuznets Curve (EKC)
exporting pollution
gains from trade
GATT Article XX
General Agreement on Tariffs and Trade (GATT)
global pollution
global public goods
harmonization of environmental standards

multilateral environmental agreements (MEAs)
pollution haven
precautionary principle
process and production methods (PPM) rules
production externalities
race to the bottom
scale, composition, and technique effects
second-best solution
specificity rule
transboundary pollution
World Environmental Organization (WEO)
World Trade Organization (WTO)

## DISCUSSION QUESTIONS

1. What are the welfare implications of trade in toxic wastes? Should such trade be banned, or can it serve a useful function? Who should regulate trade in toxic wastes, individual nations, local communities, or a global authority?

2. Can harmonizing environmental standards solve the problem of environmental externalities in trade? How would harmonization issues differ in NAFTA, the European Union, and the World Trade Organization? Would harmonization promote economic efficiency as well as environmental improvement, or might it lead to lower environmental standards?

3. What should be done if the provisions of a multilateral environmental agreement in conflict with the principles of the World Trade Organization? Which should take precedence, and who should have the authority to decide? Which economic, social, and ecological principles should influence such issues?

# REFERENCES

Antweiler, Werner, Brian R. Copeland, and M. Scott Taylor. "Is Free Trade Good for the Environment?" *American Economic Review* 91, no. 4 (September 2001): 877–908.

Brack, Duncan, ed. *Trade and Environment: Conflict or Compatibility?* London: Royal Institute of International Affairs, 1998.

Commission for Environmental Cooperation (CEC). *Assessing Environmental Effects of the North American Free Trade Agreement: An Analytic Framework and Issue Studies.* Montréal, Québec, Canada: CEC, 1999.

Charnovitz, Steve. "Trade Measures and the Design of International Regimes." *Journal of Environment and Development 5*, no. 2 (1996): 168–169.

Cole, Matthew A. "Trade, the Pollution Haven Hypothesis, and the Environmental Kuznets Curve: Examining the Linkages." *Ecological Economics* 48 (January 2004): 71–81.

Deere, Carolyn L., and Daniel C. Esty. *Greening the Americas: NAFTA's Lessons for Hemispheric Trade.* Cambridge, Mass.: MIT Press, 2002.

Esty, Daniel C. *Greening the GATT: Trade, Environment, and the Future.* Washington, D.C.: Institute for International Economics, 1994.

Esty, Daniel C. "Bridging the Trade-Environment Divide." *Journal of Economic Perspectives* 15, no. 3 (2001): 113–130.

Fredriksson, Per G., ed. *Trade, Global Policy, and the Environment.* World Bank Discussion Paper No. 402. Washington, D.C.: World Bank, 1999.

Gallagher, Kevin P. *Free Trade and the Environment: Mexico, NAFTA, and Beyond.* Stanford, Calif.: Stanford University Press, 2004.

Grossman, Gene, and Alan Krueger. "Economic Growth and the Environment." *Quarterly Journal of Economics* 110, no. 2 (1995): 353–377.

Harris, Jonathan M. "Free Trade or Sustainable Trade? An Ecological Economics Perspective." Chapter 5 in *Rethinking Sustainability: Power, Knowledge, and Institutions,* edited by Jonathan Harris. Ann Arbor, Mich.: University of Michigan Press, 2000.

Hufbauer, Gary C., Daniel C. Esty, Diana Orejas, Luis Rubio, and Jeffrey J. Scott. *NAFTA and the Environment: Seven Years Later.* Policy Analyses in International Economics 61. Washington, D.C.: Institute for International Economics, 2000.

Jaffe, Adam B., et al. "Environmental Regulation and the Competitiveness of U.S. Manufacturing." *Journal of Economic Literature* 33 (March 1995): 132–163.

Mann, Howard. *Private Rights, Public Problems: A Guide to NAFTA's Controversial Chapter on Investment Rights.* Winnipeg, Canada: International Institute for Sustainable Development, 2001, available at http://www.iisd.org/publications.

Nadal, Alejandro. *The Environmental and Social Impacts of Economic Liberalization on Corn Production in Mexico.* London, U.K.: World Wildlife Fund and Oxfam UK, 2000.

Neumayer, Eric. *Greening Trade and Investment: Environmental Protection without Protectionism.* London, U.K.: Earthscan, 2001.

Paarlberg, Robert. "Political Power and Environmental Sustainability in Agriculture," Chapter 7 in Harris, ed., 2000.

Panayotou, Theodore. "Empirical Tests and Policy Analysis of Environmental Degradation at Different Levels of Development." Geneva, Switzerland: International Labour Office Working Paper WP238, 1993.

Reed, David, ed. *Structural Adjustment, the Environment, and Sustainable Development.* London, U.K.: World Wide Fund for Nature, 1996.

Rothman, Dale, and Sander de Bruyn. "Probing into the Environmental Kuznets Curve Hypothesis" (Introduction to Special Issue on the Environmental Kuznets Curve), *Ecological Economics* 25, no. 2 (1998): 143–145.

Runge, C. Ford. *Freer Trade, Protected Environment: Balancing Trade Liberalization and Environmental Interests.* New York: Council on Foreign Relations Press, 1994.

Selden, Thomas M., and Daqing Song. "Environmental Quality and Development: Is There a Kuznets Curve for Air Pollution?" *Journal of Environmental Economics and Management* 27, no. 2 (1994): 147–162.

Stern, David I. "The Rise and Fall of the Environmental Kuznets Curve." *World Development* 32, no. 8 (August 2004): 1419–1439.

## WEBSITES

1. **http://www.wto.org/english/tratop_e/envir_e/envir_e.htm** The World Trade Organization's website devoted to the relationship between international trade issues and environmental quality. The site includes links to many research reports and other information.

2. **http://www.oecd.org/ech/** The website for the trade division of the Organisation for Economic Co-operation and Development. The site includes many publications on trade issues, including trade and the environment.

3. **www.cec.org/** Homepage for the Commission for Environmental Cooperation, created under the North American Free Trade Agreement "to address regional environmental concerns, help prevent potential trade and environmental conflicts, and to promote the effective enforcement of environmental law." The site includes numerous publications on issues of trade and the environment.

4. **http://gurukul.ucc.american.edu/ted/ted.htm** The Trade & Environment Database (TED) includes a collection of about 700 case studies on trade and the environment.

5. **http://www.iisd.org/trade/handbook/** This handbook, a joint effort of the International Institute for Sustainable Development and the United Nations Environment Programme, provides a guide to trade, environment, and development issues.

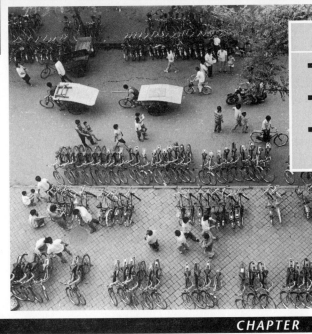

CHAPTER FOCUS QUESTIONS

- Do the goals of economic development and environmental sustainability conflict?
- How can current development institutions be "greened"?
- What will be the central environment and development issues for the twenty-first century?

CHAPTER 20

# Institutions for Sustainable Development

## The Economics of Sustainable Development

All nations seek economic development. Economic development policies, however, have taken little heed of the environment until relatively recently. Only within the past 40 years have currently developed nations recognized the need for specific policies to protect the environment. In many nations, the concept of environmental protection is even more recent.

The United States, for example, set up its Environmental Protection Agency in 1970. Prior to this, a conservation movement, active for nearly a century, had focused primarily on protection of public lands. The idea that the industrial system should be subject to some sort of environmental controls was not an integral part of economic development theory or practice for most of the twentieth century.

In the twenty-first century, it is clear that the issues of environment and development cannot be separated. This has given rise to the concept of **sustainable development**. In

457

1987, the World Commission on Environment and Development addressed the issue of conflicts between environment and development by proposing a definition:

> Sustainable development is development that meets the needs of the present without compromising the ability of future generations to meet their own needs.[1]

This view of development suggests that the standard perspective of equating economic development with economic growth may need to be altered. From an economic point of view, development improves the situation of future generations by increasing their **capital stock.** Having more capital enables a country to produce more goods and deliver a higher standard of living to its citizens. But if, in the process of producing this stock of manufactured capital, we degrade or destroy **natural capital,** we may actually leave future generations worse off. Indeed, we may leave ourselves worse off, because some environmental pollution damage may immediately affect our lives and health.

The implications of making development sustainable differ for developed and developing nations. Currently developed nations typically have large capital stocks and extensive infrastructure including power plants, highways, factories, extensive urban and suburban business and residential construction, dams, irrigation systems, and many other elements essential to modern economic production. This is both an advantage and a disadvantage in trying to achieve environmental sustainability.

On the one hand, greater economic capacity and advanced technology makes instituting environmental protection systems more possible and affordable. On the other, developed nations with large existing stocks of resource-using, waste- and pollution-generating capital and consumer demand for a continual flow of products may encounter **technological lock-in** such as a dependence on fossil fuels and the technologies associated with them. A lock-in may also be social—an example might be American reluctance to consider alternatives to automobile-based transport.

Developing nations have a different set of problems in achieving sustainability. Starting from much lower income levels, a major social and economic goal is increasing production. As we have seen, developing nations also tend to have considerable population growth momentum. The combination of increased population and economic growth creates strong pressure for rising resource use and increased generation of wastes and pollution.

At the same time, developing nations may have greater choice as to the development path they will pursue. They are not necessarily committed to following a resource-intensive, high waste-generating pattern of economic growth. As later participants in development, they may have access to improved technologies and avoid costly environmental errors made by the developed nations. They will also, however, find themselves competing with developed nations for limited resources and limited environmental absorption capacities for global pollutants such as $CO_2$ (see Box 20-1).

A critical issue is whether developed and developing nations can cooperate to promote environmentally sustainable development paths. As we saw in the Chapter 18 discussion of global climate, agreement can be difficult to reach. Developing nations

---

[1]World Commission on Environment and Development, 1987, p. 8.

| 20-1 | China and the Future of the Global Environment |

$\mathbf{A}$ major factor affecting the future of the global environment is China's ability to develop economically without causing serious and irreversible ecological damage. With a population of 1.3 billion, China already uses about 11 percent of the world's commercial energy and is responsible for emitting about 14 percent of global $CO_2$ emissions. However, China is also experiencing rapid economic growth. Between 1991 and 2000 China's GDP grew at an average annual rate of 9.0 percent (WRI, 2003). For comparison, GDP in the United States grew at an annual average rate of 2.4 percent during the same period.

Significant further economic development appears likely for China. Consider that per capita motor vehicle ownership in China is only about 0.015 of the U.S. level. Per capita energy use and $CO_2$ emissions in China are well below the comparable values for Mexico and Thailand (see table). What will happen to the environment if China's growth continues?

Even with relatively low per capita impacts, the large total population in China (about 21 percent of global population) means that China already causes significant global environmental impacts. China is soon expected to pass the United States as the world's largest energy consumer and emitter of carbon dioxide. If China used the same amount of energy per capita as Americans do, global energy use would nearly double. China's consumption of grain, meat, coal, steel, and fertilizer has already surpassed that of the United States, although per capita consumption of these commodities remains well below U.S. levels.

As a result of rapid growth in industrial and agricultural production, "China is facing an ecological and health crisis. Heavy air pollution contributes to respiratory illnesses that kill up to 300,000 people a year." Rivers are heavily polluted with factory wastes and fertilizer runoff, with few controls on emissions (*New York Times*, September 12, 2004).

China, still a relatively poor country, resists suggestions by developed countries to limit economic development for the benefit of the global environment. As noted by Mark Hertsgaard (1999, p. 210), "China has little patience with Western finger-pointing on the climate-change issue, regarding it as a cynical means of constraining China's economic development." Currently, China appears willing to sacrifice environmental quality for economic growth.

Hope may lie in China's continued integration into the international community. Financial and technical assistance could provide China with the ability to develop efficient processes that reduce energy consumption by half (Hertsgaard, 1999). All nations have a stake in the issue because the negative environmental

*(continued on following page)*

consequences of increased resource use and pollution by China will be global in scope. The credibility of Western nations in helping to find an environmentally friendly development path for China will depend on their willingness to take effective measures to reduce their own environmental impacts.

*Environmental Data for Selected Countries*

| Country | 2003 Population (millions) | Energy Consumption[1] Per Capita | Total | $CO_2$ Emissions[2] Per Capita | Total | Motor Vehicles[3] Per 1,000 People | Total |
|---|---|---|---|---|---|---|---|
| Bangladesh | 138 | 153 | 20 | 0.2 | 29 | 1 | 0.1 |
| China | 1,288 | 896 | 1,139 | 2.2 | 2,790 | 12 | 15.7 |
| France | 60 | 4,371 | 266 | 6.2 | 362 | 575 | 33.9 |
| India | 1,064 | 515 | 531 | 1.1 | 1,071 | 10 | 10.1 |
| Japan | 127 | 4,099 | 521 | 9.3 | 1,185 | 572 | 72.6 |
| Mexico | 102 | 1,532 | 152 | 4.3 | 424 | 159 | 15.6 |
| Thailand | 62 | 1,235 | 76 | 3.3 | 199 | 106 | 6.3 |
| United States | 291 | 7,996 | 2,281 | 19.8 | 5,602 | 779 | 217.2 |
| World | 6,272 | 1,686 | 10,010 | 3.8 | 22,995 | 137 | 805.4 |

Source: World Bank, World Development Indicators database, http://devdata.worldbank.org/dataonline/. Subscription available at http://www.worldbank.org/data/

[1]Commercial energy from all sources, measured in kilograms of oil equivalent per capita, 2001 data. Totals in million metric tons of oil equivalent.

[2]Emissions from industrial processes, measured in metric tons of $CO_2$ per capita, 2000 data. Totals in million metric tons.

[3]Includes automobiles, buses, and freight vehicles. Date of data varies (generally 2000). Totals in millions of vehicles.

## SOURCES

Brown, Lester R. *China Replacing the United States as World's Leading Consumer.* http://www.earth-policy.org/Updates/Update45.htm.

Hertsgaard, Mark. "Our Real China Problem," in *Annual Editions, Environment 99/00,* edited by John L. Allen. Guilford, Conn.: Dushkin/McGraw-Hill, 1999.

World Resources Institute. *World Resources 2002–2004: Decisions for the Earth: Balance, Voice, and Power.* Washington, D.C.: World Resources Institute, 2003. Available at http://www.wri.org/wr2002/index.html.

Yardley, Jim. "Rivers Run Black, and Chinese Die of Cancer," *New York Times,* September 12, 2004.

argue that the richer countries should "clean up their act" first. Developed countries worry that the vast growth of production expected in the developing world will swallow up gains from efficiency and pollution control, unless developing nations modify their economic goals. This difference in perspectives need not lead to deadlock. Many possibilities exist for mutual progress toward environmental improvement—but the scale of the problems is daunting.

## New Goals and New Production Methods

To bring the argument down to earth and develop a sense of what the principles summarized at the beginning of this section mean for development policies, we can examine specific areas of economic activity. In each, sustainability implies a major shift from existing techniques and organization of production.

- **Agriculture.** Feeding an expanding population at higher per capita levels of consumption will impose significant strain on global soil and water systems.[2] The response to this must be twofold. On the production side, current high-input techniques associated with soil degradation and water pollution and overdraft must give way to organic soil rebuilding, integrated pest management, and efficient irrigation. This in turn implies much greater reliance on local knowledge and participatory input into the development of farming systems.[3]

    On the consumption side, probable resource limitations on production will necessitate both population growth limits and greater food distribution equity and efficiency. As discussed in Chapter 10, effective policies can simultaneously promote social equity and moderate population growth, including women's education and health and family planning services. Distribution and dietary patterns will need to emphasize affordable basic foodstuffs and vegetable-based proteins and nutrients.

- **Energy.** Both supply limits and environmental impact, in particular the accumulation of greenhouse gases, will require a transition away from fossil fuels well before 2050. A restructured energy system would be significantly less centralized, adapted to local conditions and taking advantage of opportunities for wind, biomass, and off-grid solar power systems. This is unlikely to occur without a major mobilization of capital resources for development of **renewable energy sources** in countries now rapidly expanding their energy systems.

- **Industry.** As the scale of global industrial production grows well beyond current levels, which themselves represent a quadrupling over 1950 levels, the inadequacy of "end-of-pipe" pollution control will be increasingly apparent. As we saw in Chapter 17, the concept of **industrial ecology** implies the restructuring of whole industrial sectors based on a goal of reducing emissions and reusing materials at all stages of the production cycle. A broad cooperative effort between corporations and government is essential to achieve this goal.

[2]Harris and Kennedy, 1999; Pinstrup-Andersen and Pandya-Lorch, 1998.
[3]Pretty and Chambers, 2000.

## 20-2  Community Resource Management in India

The role of local communities is often central in developing sustainable agriculture and forestry policies. A case in point is the Arabari experiment in India's West Bengal. This region was suffering rapid deforestation in the 1970s, leading to a government program to offer villagers alternatives to the illegal cutting of firewood. Local residents were offered employment opportunities planting trees and grass in deforested areas. Through a revenue-sharing arrangement with the Forest Department, the villagers received 25 percent of the income from sales of sustainably produced trees. In return, they were given the responsibility of protecting the forest from illegal cutting.

After 15 years, degraded forest areas had been rehabilitated, and economic conditions for the villagers had improved significantly. The success of the initial experiment led to its expansion to more than 700 villages. By 1989 Village Protection Committees were managing the restoration of more than 70,000 hectares of degraded lands in West Bengal.

In Haryana, India, a cooperative project between government agencies, nongovernmental organizations, and villagers led to the construction of a system of small dams for irrigation and erosion protection, and to the protection of local forests. Instead of cutting the forests for grazing lands, villagers were encouraged to grow fiber and fodder grasses as well as trees. This provided the basis for the success of small rope-making businesses and milk sales, as well as dramatically increased crop yields.

Similar successes with small-scale local farming and land management programs has been reported in Nepal, Indonesia, Kenya, Niger, and Sri Lanka, among other developing countries. Effective group management structure and cooperation among all parties is essential to the success of such programs.

### SOURCES

Panayotou, Theodore. *Green Markets: The Economics of Sustainable Development.* San Francisco, Calif.: Institute for Contemporary Studies (ICS) Press, 1993.

Poffenberger, M. *Joint Management of Forest Lands: Experiences from South Asia.* New Delhi: Ford Foundation, 1990.

Pretty, Jules N., and Robert Chambers. "Toward a Learning Paradigm: New Professionalism and Institutions for Agriculture," *Rethinking Sustainability: Power, Knowledge, and Institutions,* edited by Jonathan M. Harris. Ann Arbor, Mich.: University of Michigan Press, 2000.

- **Renewable resource systems.** As we have discussed, world fisheries, forests, and water systems are severely overstressed. With even greater demands on all systems expected in the twenty-first century, reform is needed at all levels of institutional management. Multilateral agreements and global funding must conserve transboundary resources; national resource management systems must shift from exploitative goals to conservation and sustainable harvesting; and local communities must participate fully in resource conservation (see Box 20-2).

Each of these areas poses social and institutional as well as economic challenges. Environmental sustainability is thus linked to **social sustainability.** Existing institutions of all kinds, including corporations, local and national governments, and transnational organizations, must adopt policies for sustainable development if the problems that motivated development of the concept are not to grow worse. Democratic governance, participation, and the satisfaction of basic needs are an essential part of a new approach to development.[4]

## Reforming Global Institutions

Major global institutions such as the World Bank, the International Monetary Fund (IMF), and the World Trade Organization (WTO) have as their goal promoting economic development. Only relatively recently have environmental considerations acquired a prominent role in World Bank policymaking. As we saw in Chapter 19, environmental issues remain controversial at the WTO. The IMF does not include environmental factors in its mandate, but its monetary policies have significant implications both for the environment and for relations between developed and developing countries.

A major theme in both IMF and World Bank policy has been **structural adjustment.** This refers to a package of conditions linked to loans to developing countries, intended to promote market-oriented economic reform. Generally these conditions include fiscal and monetary measures aimed at balancing government budgets and restraining money supplies to avoid inflation. In addition, countries often must reduce barriers to trade, correct overvalued exchange rates, and privatize state-controlled enterprises.

A study by the Worldwide Fund for Nature (WWF) reviewed the social and environmental impact of structural adjustment policies promoted by the IMF and World Bank.[5] The WWF researchers found that environmental effects were mixed, but negative effects seemed predominant in many cases. Environmentally positive results included the following:

- Shifting terms of trade to favor the agricultural sector provides farmers with more income to finance on-farm investment.
- Increased farm income reduces poverty-induced degradation of marginal lands.

---

[4]See Harris et al., 2001.

[5]Reed, 1997.

*A Nicaraguan worker picks cotton. Structural adjustment programs can have varied effects on agricultural production and the environment. Some export crops are less erosive, but increased pesticide use on crops such as cotton can be harmful to workers and ecosystems and can pollute water supplies.*

- Reduced subsidies for agricultural inputs reduce fertilizer and pesticide overuse.
- Some export crops produce less erosion than the local crops they replace.
- Better macroeconomic management increases investment flows.
- Market-oriented microeconomic policies improve industrial efficiency.

On the other hand, negative environmental effects included the following:

- Small farmers displaced by imports or unable to take advantage of export opportunities increase rural-to-urban migration and pressures on marginal lands and forests.
- Rising prices for agricultural inputs promote unsustainable extension of agricultural production onto marginal lands.
- Faster growth in the mining and industrial sectors leads to increased environmental damage and larger waste flows.
- Extension of pasture for cattle production and beef export promotes faster deforestation.
- Imports of inefficient used vehicles greatly increase urban pollution.
- Government agricultural extension services, environmental protection expenditures, and social services all decline under conditions of budget stringency.

- Reduced educational and health spending leads to lower school attendance, increased disease, and weakened population and family planning policy implementation.

The study concludes that structural adjustment policies have led to increased consumption of renewable and nonrenewable resources, greater pressure on environmental **sink functions** of pollution absorption, a drawdown of natural capital, and a weakening of environmental institutional capacity. "The weakening of environmental institutions represents a major setback in moving countries towards sustainable development paths."[6]

The WWF study recommends integrating environmental issues into the planning of macroeconomic reforms. Specific proposals include

- Implementation of national environmental accounting systems.
- Reinvestment of incomes from nonrenewable resource extraction.
- Increased agricultural extension and credit policies.
- Stronger environmental regulation for emerging industries.
- Increased social services and health-care spending, with a special focus on women's education and health care.
- Targeted small-scale lending policies (microlending) to encourage small local enterprises.
- Targeted food assistance and distributional equity policies.

This analysis suggests that economic reform and environmental goals are compatible, but only if policies are specifically designed for sustainable outcomes. Neglecting the environment leads to long-term problems that can undermine economic goals as well. Also, environmental and social issues are clearly linked. Deteriorating conditions for the poor are likely to accentuate environmental problems, which in turn worsen poverty. Thus development policy must include the dual goals of poverty reduction and environmental improvement.

## Promoting Environmentally Sustainable Development

In the 1980s and 1990s the World Bank was frequently a target of protest for funding environmentally destructive projects such as large dams and forest clearance. Partly as a result, the bank shifted its lending policies to give much greater prominence to the environment. The World Bank's total active environment and natural resource management (ENRM) portfolio increased from less than $1 billion in 1988 to $11.2 billion in 2004.[7] On an annual basis, ENRM lending reached a high of 17.2 percent of total lending in 1994 but has since fallen to 6.5 percent (Figure 20-1).

These projects include both a "brown agenda" (pollution management) and a "green agenda" (natural resource conservation). They include projects on forest management,

---

[6]Reed, 1997, p. 351.

[7]World Bank, 2004.

**FIGURE 20-1** *World Bank Environmental Lending*

Note: Environment and Natural Resource Management (ENRM) lending is shown as annual total spending (left scale) and as a percent of total World Bank lending (right scale).

Source: World Bank, *Environment Matters: Annual Review*. Washington, D.C.: World Bank, 2004. Reprinted by permission of The World Bank via Copyright Clearance Center.

integrated pest management, watershed rehabilitation, energy efficiency and renewables, and water management and sewer systems. Some of these loans are coupled with grants from the Global Environment Facility (GEF), jointly managed by the World Bank, the United Nations Environment Programme (UNEP), and the United Nations Development Programme (UNDP) (see Box 20-3).

In addition, all World Bank projects are screened for potential environmental impact. "A growing number of sector projects include environmental components or incorporate environmental considerations into the project design."[8] Rural development projects increasingly emphasize land resource management, soil and water conservation, and training in sustainable farming techniques. Urban development projects include water and sanitation upgrading and solid waste management. Energy lending includes promotion of energy efficiency and renewable energy sources, as well as development of cleaner fossil fuels such as natural gas.

Despite significant improvement in the environmental content of World Bank policies, critics still maintain that "the World Bank and the IMF pay insufficient heed to the profound effects of [their] policies on the ecological health and the social fabric of the recipient countries."[9] Because these institutions provide loans, not grants, the

[8]World Bank, 2000, p. 10.

[9]French, 2000, p. 196.

| 20-3 | The Global Environment Facility |
|------|----------------------------------|

The Global Environment Facility (GEF), initiated in 1990, is jointly administered by the United Nations Environment Programme (UNEP), the United Nations Development Programme (UNDP) and the World Bank. In 1994 the GEF was restructured and expanded, with $2 billion in funding. Its mission is to support global environmental projects including biodiversity conservation, ocean ecosystem protection, and reduction of greenhouse gases and ozone-depleting substances.

Unlike the World Bank and the IMF, the GEF provides grants and concessional funds rather than loans. Often a GEF grant may be paired with a World Bank environmental loan to increase its impact at lower cost to the receiving nation.

The GEF operates on the economic rationale that the global community as a whole should bear the **incremental costs** of environmental protection beyond what developing nations are prepared to pay. For example, the installation of energy-efficient and renewable power systems has local benefits, but also contributes to the global effort to limit greenhouse gas emissions. It seems reasonable, therefore, that the recipient nation should pay some of the cost in the form of loan repayments, but wealthier nations should also underwrite part of the cost through GEF.

In practice, applying this incremental-cost concept has been tricky. Critics have argued that it is difficult to separate global and national benefits. Also, the pairing of regular World Bank grants with GEF loans may actually promote greater environmental damage in some cases. For example, in Ecuador, a logging company received $4 million in World Bank funds as well as a $2.5 million GEF grant. The company was required to set up a forest reserve, but also expanded logging on a much greater area. In Egypt, a $242 million World Bank loan to develop a coastal resort was paired with a $4.75 million GEF loan for conservation activity. In such cases, the GEF component may serve as a rationale for accelerated resource exploitation.

**SOURCES**

Barnes et al., 1995; World Bank, 2004; Shiva, 2000.

funds must eventually be repaid. To promote debt repayment, the lenders emphasize export promotion, but "the pressure to export can lead countries to liquidate natural assets such as forest and fisheries, thereby undermining longer-term economic prospects."[10] In addition, large bureaucratic institutions dealing in billions of dollars often are poorly prepared to connect to sustainable initiatives at the local level.

---

[10]Ibid.

## *Local Development Projects*

Some of the most encouraging stories of sustainable development projects are those funded by **nongovernmental organizations (NGOs)** and European governments. A review by Friends of the Earth and the National Wildlife Federation cites dozens of successful local development projects.[11] These include

- Organic farming cooperatives in the Philippines
- **Extractive reserves** in the Brazilian rainforest promoting multiple-product forest management and conservation
- Aquatic ecosystem management including rice and fish cultivation
- Sustainable forestry and rehabilitation of deforested lands in the Peruvian Amazon
- Forest conservation, rehabilitation, and biodiversity classification in Costa Rica
- Rural solar power installation in the Dominican Republic
- Soil restoration and conservation technologies in Honduras
- Oilseed production and processing in Tanzania and Zimbabwe
- Promoting bicycle transportation in Lima, Peru
- Family planning and health services in Colombia and Pakistan
- Women's cooperatives for farming, food processing, and light industry in Nigeria
- **Agroforestry** programs in Guatemala, Haiti, and Indonesia
- Recycled paper production in India

These examples of sustainable development in practice demonstrate that the goals of economic development, poverty reduction, and environmental improvement can be successfully combined (see Box 20-4). However, the principles embodied in these small-scale projects are rarely reflected in national and global economic priorities. This suggests the continuing need for a major reorientation of economic development policies.

# Policies for Sustainable Development

The goals of sustainable development policies can be viewed in terms of **strong and weak sustainability,** as discussed in Chapters 7 and 8. In general, advocates of *strong sustainability* argue that natural systems should be maintained intact wherever possible. They identify **critical natural capital**—such as water supplies—as resources to preserve under all circumstances. In this view, for example, maintaining soil's natural fertility is essential—even if it is possible to compensate for degraded soils with extra fertilizer. Under the more moderate approach of *weak sustainability,* some degradation or loss of natural capital is acceptable if it is compensated for by accumulation of manufactured capital.

Either concept of sustainability—but especially the strong version—implies limits to economic growth. Economic activity that relies heavily on natural resources, raw materials, and fossil fuels cannot grow indefinitely. Because the planetary ecosystem

---

[11]Barnes et al., 1995.

## 20-4    Sustainable Urban Management in Curitiba, Brazil

About half of the world's population currently lives in urban areas and urbanization rates are expected to increase in the future. Achieving environmental sustainability will require an integration of ecological principles into urban management. While most cities have grown without significant regard to environmental impacts, exceptions exist as role models for other communities.

The city of Curitiba, Brazil, has grown in population from 300,000 in 1950 to about 2 million. Faced with this growth pressure, the city has demonstrated that urban environmental problems can be addressed with creativity, strong leadership, and public participation despite limited financial resources. Rather than relying on a single master plan, city officials have taken a flexible approach with constant input from local residents.

A key component of Curitiba's success is the attention given to transportation issues. Zoning laws foster high-density development along transportation corridors served by buses. The bus system transports more than 1 million passengers per day. Gasoline use per capita and air pollution levels in Curitiba are among the lowest in Brazil.

The city has protected drainage areas to control flooding by converting these areas into public parks. Curitiba could not afford a large-scale recycling plant, but public education programs have been successful in reducing wastes and increasing recycling rates. In areas where streets are too narrow for garbage trucks to enter, incentives for community garbage collection have been created by exchanging filled garbage bags for bus tokens, parcels of surplus food, and school notebooks. In another program, older public buses are converted to mobile schools and travel to low-income neighborhoods.

The example of Curitiba shows that progress toward environmental sustainability is possible even in an urban area with increasing population and high poverty rates. "The lesson to be learned from Curitiba is that creativity can substitute for financial resources. Any city, rich or poor, can draw on the skills of its residents to tackle urban environmental problems" (World Resources Institute, 1996).

### SOURCE

World Resources Institute. *World Resources 1996–97: The Urban Environment.* New York: Oxford University Press, 1996.

Resource-using
Economic Activities

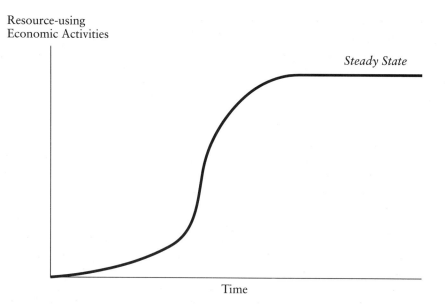

**FIGURE 20-2** *Growth Reaching a Steady State*

has certain limits, limits must also apply on a **macroeconomic scale**—the overall level of resource use and goods output. Herman Daly has argued for the long-term need to reach a plateau, a **steady state economy** in terms of the consumption of material and energy resources.[12]

This concept differs radically from the standard view of economic growth, in which GDP increases indefinitely on an **exponential growth** path—for example, 4 percent GDP growth per year. In the limits-to-growth perspective, national and global economic systems must follow what is called a **logistic curve** pattern in which economic activity approaches some maximum, at least in terms of resource consumption (Figure 20-2).

This analysis necessarily implies constraints on material consumption, but activities that involve no resource consumption or are environmentally neutral or environmentally friendly, could grow indefinitely. Such activities could include services, arts, communication, and education. Once basic needs are met and moderate levels of consumption achieved, the concept of sustainable development implies that economic development should be increasingly oriented toward these kinds of inherently "sustainable" activities.[13]

Currently much of development theory and policy promotes continuous economic growth. What kind of policies would promote sustainability? Are the goals of economic growth and sustainability compatible?

---

[12]See Daly, 1996, and Ekins et al., 2003.

[13]See Durning, 1992.

Some ecological economists view "sustainable growth" as a contradiction in terms. They point out that no system can grow without limit. However, certain kinds of economic growth are essential. The large number of people in the world who lack basic needs require more and better food, housing, and other goods.

In high-consumption societies, improved well-being might be achieved through expanded educational and cultural services that, as we have noted, have no negative environmental impact. But unregulated economic growth is unlikely to be either equitable or environmentally benign. A report by the U.S. National Research Council calls for a twenty-first century **sustainability transition** that involves stabilizing population, reducing hunger and poverty, and maintaining the planet's life support systems and living resources.[14] Such a transition would involve major investments in health, water, sanitation, and education, as well as alternative energy sources and environmental protection. Currently, no national governments or international institutions are prepared to undertake such investments on anything like the necessary scale. But if the world moves toward such a reorientation of policy at the macroeconomic level in the future, microeconomic policies of the type discussed throughout this book would become increasingly relevant.

## Specific Policy Proposals

Such policies might include approaches that we have already touched on in previous chapters:

- *Green taxes that would shift the tax burden away from income and capital taxation and onto fossil fuel use, resource extraction, and pollution generation.* This would discourage energy- and material-intensive economic activities while favoring the provision of services and labor-intensive activities.[15] A **revenue-neutral tax shift** could match every dollar collected in new energy and resource taxes with a dollar of income, payroll, corporate or capital gains tax reduction.[16]
- *Elimination of agricultural and energy subsidies that encourage overuse of energy, fertilizer, pesticides, and irrigation water.* This could be matched with promotion of sustainable agricultural systems including nutrient recycling, crop diversification, and natural pest controls, minimizing the use of artificial chemicals and fertilizer.
- *Greater* **recycling** *of materials and use of renewable energy.* The principles of industrial ecology suggest redesigning industrial systems to imitate the closed-cycle patterns of natural systems and reuse as many materials as possible with minimal waste output.

---

[14]National Research Council, 1999.

[15]Labor-intensive production systems use large amounts of labor relative to other factors of production. Similarly, energy-intensive systems use large amounts of energy. For example, automobile transport is energy-intensive; bicycle transport is labor-intensive.

[16]See Hamond et al., 1997, summarized in Harris et al., 2001.

- *Efficient transportation systems that replace energy-intensive automotive transport with high-speed trains, public transit, increased bicycle use, and redesign of cities and suburbs to minimize transportation needs.* The use of highly fuel-efficient cars would be important in countries such as the United States with extensively developed automobile-centered systems. Some developing countries might avoid large-scale automobile dependence by relying instead on bicycles and efficient public transit.
- *Accelerated development of renewable energy systems such as solar, hydroelectric, wind, and geothermal power, as well as new technologies such as fuel cells and high-efficiency industrial systems.* As we saw in Chapter 13, redirection of current fossil fuel subsidies to create market incentives for alternative energy sources is essential to this process.

Analysis of development policy must take account of long-term sustainability. Policies oriented toward economic growth alone risk damage to the broader "circular flow" of the **biosphere,** unless they include consideration of environmental impact and sustainable scale. This adds a new dimension to the debate over development policy, a dimension that will be increasingly important for both developed and developing economies.

As world population continues to grow, and economic activity expands at an even faster rate, sustainability will become both more important and more difficult to achieve. This is the major challenge of the twenty-first century, and both economic and ecological understanding will be needed to formulate global, national, and local responses.

## SUMMARY

Sustainable development has been defined as development that meets present needs without damaging the basis for meeting future needs. This implies increasing and improving manufactured capital without destroying natural capital. The needs of a growing population must be met without increasing resource demands and pollution generation beyond the supportive capacity of ecosystems.

For developed nations, this implies both moderation in consumption growth and adoption of more environmentally friendly technologies. Developing nations, for whom growth in consumption is essential, can avoid production methods that have high resource demands and environmental repercussions. Mutual cooperation between developed and developing nations toward these goals is essential but often difficult to achieve.

Major reforms must occur in agricultural, industrial, and energy systems, as well as in renewable resource management. Low-input and organic agriculture, energy-efficient and ecologically sound industrial development, as well as better fishery and forest management, are all important components of a balanced economic/environmental system. In addition, population stabilization is central to sustainability in all these areas.

An inherent tension exists between the ideas of sustainability and economic growth. Although the two are not necessarily incompatible, we cannot have unlimited economic growth with finite resources. Future economic growth must therefore turn more toward areas such as services, communication, arts, and education that contribute to human welfare but have relatively low resource requirements.

Major global finance institutions such as the World Bank have begun to recognize the necessity of specific policy initiatives to promote more sustainable development and reorient their development lending accordingly. However, resource-intensive and pollution-generating development strategies remain common. Small-scale projects financed privately or by individual countries have often been more successful in achieving the dual goals of poverty reduction and environmental conservation.

Sustainable development strategies attempt to balance the imperatives of economic growth with the limits of planetary resources and pollution absorption capacity. Modification of global goals of economic growth will be essential for sustainability in the twenty-first century.

## KEY TERMS AND CONCEPTS

agroforestry
biosphere
capital stock
critical natural capital
exponential growth
extractive reserves
green taxes
incremental costs
industrial ecology
logistic curve
macroeconomic scale
natural capital
nongovernmental
   organizations (NGOs)

recycling
renewable energy sources
revenue-neutral tax shift
sink functions
social sustainability
steady state economy
strong sustainability
structural adjustment
sustainable development
sustainability transition
technological lock-in
weak sustainability

## DISCUSSION QUESTIONS

1. Comment on the original definition of sustainable development: "development that meets the needs of the present without compromising the ability of future generations to meet their own needs." Do you consider this definition useful or so ambiguous or vague as to lack applicability? How might you make it more precise? What alternative definitions might you use?

2. How would you seek to balance the goals of economic growth and environmental sustainability? To what extent are these goals necessarily in conflict?

3. Which specific policies do you consider of greatest importance in promoting environmentally sustainable development? In which areas is the world making progress toward sustainability, and where are the most serious problems?

## REFERENCES

Barnes, James N., Brent Blackwelder, Barbara J. Bramble, Ellen Grossman, and Walter V. Reid. *Bankrolling Successes: A Portfolio of Sustainable Development Projects*. Washington, D.C.: Friends of Earth and National Wildlife Federation, 1995.

Daly, Herman E. *Beyond Growth: The Economics of Sustainable Development*. Boston: Beacon Press, 1996.

Durning, Alan. *How Much Is Enough: The Consumer Society and the Future of the Earth*. Worldwatch Environmental Alert Series, edited by Linda Starke. New York: Norton, 1992.

Ekins, Paul, et al. "A Framework for the Practical Application of the Concepts of Critical Natural Capital and Strong Sustainability." *Ecological Economics* 44 (March 2003): 165–185.

French, Hilary. "Coping with Ecological Globalization." Chapter 10 in *State of the World 2000,* edited by Brown et al. New York: Norton, 2000.

Hamond, M. Jeff, Stephen J. DeCanio, Peggy Duxbury, Alan H. Sanstad, and Christopher H. Stinson. *Tax Waste, Not Work*. Washington, D.C.: Redefining Progress, 1997.

Harris, Jonathan M., and Scott Kennedy. "Carrying Capacity in Agriculture: Global and Regional Issues." *Ecological Economics* 29, no. 3 (1999): 443–461.

Harris, Jonathan M., Timothy A. Wise, Kevin P. Gallagher, and Neva R. Goodwin, eds. *A Survey of Sustainable Development: Social and Economic Dimensions*. Washington, D.C.: Island Press, 2001.

National Research Council, Board on Sustainable Development. *Our Common Journey: A Transition Toward Sustainability*. Washington, D.C.: National Academy Press, 1999, http://www.nap.edu/catalog/9690.html.

Pinstrup-Andersen, Per, and Rajul Pandya-Lorch. "Food Security and Sustainable Use of Natural Resources: A 2020 Vision." *Ecological Economics* 26, no. 1 (1998): 1–10.

Pretty, Jules, and Robert Chambers. "Towards a Learning Paradigm: New Professionalism and Institutions for Agriculture." In *Rethinking Sustainability: Power, Knowledge, and Institutions,* edited by Jonathan M. Harris. Ann Arbor, Mich.: University of Michigan Press, 2000.

Reed, David, ed. *Structural Adjustment, the Environment, and Sustainable Development*. London, U.K.: Earthscan, 1997.

Shiva, Vandana. "Conflicts of Global Ecology: Environmental Activism in a Period of Global Reach." Original publication in *Alternatives* 19 (1994): 195–207; summarized version in Harris et al., eds., *A Survey of Sustainable Development*, 2001.

United Nations Department for Economic and Social Information and Policy Analysis, Statistical Division. *Integrated Environmental and Economic Accounting*. New York: United Nations, 1993.

World Bank. *Environment Matters: Annual Review.* Washington, D.C.: World Bank, 2004.

World Commission on Environment and Development. *Our Common Future.* New York: Oxford University Press, 1987.

## WEBSITES

1. **http://www.gefweb.org/** Homepage for the Global Environmental Facility, a funding agency "established to forge international cooperation and finance actions to address four critical threats to the global environment: biodiversity loss, climate change, degradation of international waters, and ozone depletion." The site includes publications and a summary of projects funded by the GEF.

2. **http://www.panda.org/resources/programmes/mpo** Homepage for the World Wildlife Fund's Macroeconomics for Sustainable Development Programme, designed to "analyze the impact of macroeconomic practices, and to promote alternative approaches that integrate environmental and social concerns into macroeconomic planning and application." The site includes publications and case studies.

3. **http://www.unep.org/** The United Nations Environmental Programme website, including the GEO Yearbook 2004/5, focusing on major policy developments and instruments that have a bearing on sustainable development.

4. **http://www.iisd.org/** The International Institute for Sustainable Development contributes to sustainable development by advancing policy recommendations on international trade and investment, economic policy, climate change, measurement and indicators, and natural resources management.

5. **http://millenniumassessment.org** Reports by the Millennium Ecosystem Assessment, a United Nations project "strengthening capacity to manage ecosystems sustainably for human well-being," including the 2005 report *Ecosystems and Human Well-Being.*

# Glossary

**absolutely diminishing returns** an increase in one or more inputs results in a decrease in output. (4)

**absorptive capacity of environment** the ability of the environment to absorb and render harmless waste products. (2, 7)

**adjusted net national product (NNP\*)/net domestic product (NDP\*)** the value obtained by subtracting both humanmade and natural resource depreciation from gross national product or gross domestic product. (8)

**agroecological systems** systems of agricultural production in which crop output is integrated with a diverse ecological system. (17)

**agroforestry** growing both tree and other plant crops on the same piece of land. (11, 15, 20)

**ambient pollution level** the concentration of a pollutant measured in terms of pollutant quantity per volume of air, water, or soil. (16)

**aquaculture** raising fish for harvest in controlled conditions. (14)

**asset(s)** something with market value, including financial assets, physical assets, and natural assets. (1, 15)

**average revenue** total revenue divided by quantity sold. (4)

**avoided cost(s)** costs avoidable through environmental preservation or improvement. (6, 18)

**backstop resource** a resource that can substitute for a preferred resource but at a higher price. (12)

**benefit/cost ratio** the ratio of total benefits to total costs; a ratio greater than one indicates net benefits. (6)

**bequest value** value people place on the knowledge that a resource will be available for future generations. (6)

**biodiversity** the maintenance of many different interrelated species in an ecological community. (1, 11, 15)

**biomass** energy supply from wood, plant, and animal wastes. (2, 13, 15)

**biophysical cycles** the circular flow of organic and inorganic materials in ecosystems. (11)

**biosphere** all areas on earth that contain life forms, including air, soil, land, and water. (20)

**business as usual** a policy of maintaining the status quo; for example, estimates of greenhouse gas emissions levels if no policy measures counteract global climate change. (18)

**bycatch** fishery catch discarded because it is undersized or nonmarketable. (14)

**capital depreciation** a deduction in national income accounting for the wearing-out of capital over time. (7)

**capital shallowing** a decrease in the availability of capital per worker leading to reduced productivity per worker. (10)

**capital stock** the existing quantity of capital in a given region, including manufactured, human, and natural capital. (2, 13, 20)

**carbon sinks** portions of the ecosystem with the ability to absorb certain quantities of carbon dioxide, such as forests and oceans. (18)

**carbon tax** a per-unit tax on goods and services based on the quantity of carbon dioxide emitted during the production or consumption process. (18)

**carrying capacity** the level of population and consumption sustainable by the available natural resource base. (1, 2, 10, 11, 14)

**cartel** a group of independent organizations working together to regulate production and prices; the OPEC cartel nations significantly influence oil production and price. (13)

**certification** the process of certifying products that meet certain standards, such as certifying produce grown using organic farming techniques. (14, 15, 17, 19)

**choke price** the minimum price of a good or service that would result in a zero quantity demanded. (12)

**circular flow** a diagram that indicates the ways resources, such as goods, money, wastes, and energy, move through an economy or ecosystem. (1)

**Clean Development Mechanism** a component of the Kyoto Protocol that allows industrialized countries to receive credits for helping developing countries reduce their carbon emissions. (18)

**clear-cut** the process of harvesting all trees within a given area. (15)

**climate stabilization**   the policy of reducing fossil fuel use to a level that would not increase the potential for global climate change. (18)

**closed system**   a system that exchanges no energy or resources with another system; except for solar energy and waste heat, the global ecosystem is a closed system. (7)

**Coase theorem**   the proposition that if property rights are well defined and there are no transactions costs, an efficient allocation of resources will result, even if externalities exist. (3)

**cogeneration**   the process of using waste energy to produce heat from electricity generation. (12, 13)

**command-and-control policies**   regulation policies that dictate standards or equipment, such as a policy that limits allowable automobile emissions or requires catalytic converters. (16)

**common-property resource(s)**   a resource not subject to private ownership and available to all, such as a public park or the oceans. (1, 4, 11, 18)

**comparative advantage**   the theory that trade benefits both parties by allowing each to specialize in goods they can produce with relative efficiency. (19)

**complementary goods**   goods that tend to be used together, such as gasoline and automobiles. (3)

**constant returns (to scale)**   a proportional increase (or decrease) in one or more inputs results in the same proportional increase (or decrease) in output. (4, 10)

**consumer surplus**   the benefits consumers receive from a product in excess of the amount they pay for it. (3)

**consumption externalities**   externalities associated with consumption of a good, such as pollutant emissions from automobiles. (19)

**contingent valuation**   an economic technique that surveys people regarding their willingness to pay for a good or service such as preservation of hiking opportunities or air quality. (6)

**cost-benefit analysis (CBA)**   a tool for policy analysis that attempts to monetize all the costs and benefits of a proposed action to determine the net benefit. (1, 6, 18)

**cost-effectiveness analysis**   a policy tool that determines the least-cost approach for achieving a given goal. (6, 18)

**critical natural capital**   elements of natural capital for which no good humanmade substitutes exist, such as basic water supplies and breathable air. (8, 20)

**crop rotation and fallowing**   an agricultural system involving growing different crops on the same piece of land at different times and regularly taking part of the land out of production. (11)

**crop value index**   an index indicating the relative value of production of different crops on a given quantity of land. (11)

**cross-boundary flows**   the transport of materials or information across a given physical boundary. (9)

**cumulative pollutant(s)/pollution**   pollutants that do not significantly dissipate or degrade over time. (2, 8, 16)

**defensive expenditures**   expenditures made to clean up pollution or repair or compensate for environmental damage. (8)

**demand-side management**   an approach to energy management that stresses increasing energy efficiency and reducing energy consumption. (2)

**dematerialization**   the process of achieving an economic goal through a decrease in the use of physical materials, such as making aluminum cans with less metal. (17)

**demographic transition**   the tendency for first death rates and then birth rates to fall as a society develops economically; population growth rates first increase and eventually decrease. (10)

**dependency ratios**   the ratio of the number of people in a society who depend on others for their livelihood divided by the number who do not depend on others. (10)

**depletable resource**   a renewable resource that can be exploited and depleted, such as soil or clean air. (11)

**deposit/return systems**   systems that encourage recycling by charging consumers a deposit when they purchase certain goods such as beverages in recyclable containers or batteries; the deposit is returned when the consumer returns the recyclable material to an appropriate location. (12)

**deregulation**   the process of converting a market dominated by a regulated monopoly or oligopoly to a market with competition. (13)

**desalination**   the removal of salt from ocean water to make it usable for irrigation, industrial, or municipal water supplies. (15)

**diminishing returns**   a proportional increase (or decrease) in one or more inputs results in a smaller proportional increase (or decrease) in output. (4, 13)

**direct use value**   the value one obtains by directly using a natural resource, such as visiting a national park. (6)

**discount rate**   the annual rate at which future benefits or costs are discounted relative to current benefits or costs. (1, 5, 11, 15, 18)

**double dividend**   the hypothesis that an increased reliance on environmental taxes while reducing other market-distorting taxes not only provides environmental benefits but also increases economic efficiency. (18)

**dualistic land ownership**   an ownership pattern, common in developing countries, where large landowners wield considerable power and small landowners tend to be displaced. (19)

**dynamic equilibrium**   a market equilibrium that results when present and future costs and benefits are considered. (5)

**ecolabeling**   a label on a good that provides information concerning the environmental impact of producing the good. (14)

**ecological complexity**   the presence of many different living and nonliving elements in an ecosystem interacting in complex patterns; ecosystem complexity implies that human impact on ecosystems may be unpredictable. (7, 14, 15)

**ecological cycles**   the flow of energy and natural resources through ecosystems. (1)

**ecological economics**   an economic perspective that views the economic system as a subset of the broader ecosystem and subject to biophysical laws. (1)

**ecological value**   the value of ecosystem resources and services not expressed in markets. (6, 8)

**economic/ecological modeling**   construction of models that attempt to capture interactions between economic and biophysical systems. (9)

**economic efficiency**   an allocation of resources that maximizes net social benefits; perfectly competitive markets in the absence of externalities are efficient. (3, 13, 14, 16)

**economic optimum**   a result that maximizes an economic criterion, such as efficiency or profits. (4, 14, 18)

**economic rent**   income that accrues to the owner of a scarce resource. (14)

**economic reserves (economically recoverable reserves)**   the quantity of a resource identified as economically feasible to extract given current prices and technology. (12)

**economic supply (of a resource)**   the amount of a resource that is available based on current prices and technology. (12, 13)

**economic value/valuation**   the value of a good or service, expressed in monetary terms. (1, 6)

**economies of scale**   expanded output increases returns per unit of input. (10, 13)

**ecosystems management**   a system of resource management that stresses long-term ecosystem sustainability. (15)

**effective demand**   the total demand for goods and services based on ability to pay; consumers must have sufficient income to translate needs into effective demand. (4)

**efficiency labeling**   labels on goods that indicate energy efficiency, such as a label on a refrigerator indicating annual energy use. (13)

**efficiency standards**   regulations that mandate efficiency criteria for goods, such as fuel economy standards for automobiles. (13, 18)

**elasticity of demand**   see *price elasticity of demand.*

**elasticity of supply**   see *price elasticity of supply.*

**embodied energy**   the total energy required to produce a good or service, including both direct and indirect uses of energy. (9)

**emissions standards**   regulations that set the maximum amount of pollutants that may be legally emitted by an industrial facility or product. (16)

**empty-world and full-world economics**   the view that economic approaches to environmental issues should differ depending on whether the scale of the economy relative to the ecosystem is small (an empty world) or large (a full world). (7)

**end-of-year stocks**  the stock of natural resources, such as timber and oil, at the end of a year; used as a supplement to national income accounting. (8)

**energy flow analysis**  evaluation of the energy produced and used by physical and economic processes. (9)

**energy infrastructure**  a system that supports the use of a particular energy source, such as gas stations and roads that support gasoline-powered automobiles. (13)

**energy supply augmentation**  an approach to energy management emphasizing increase in energy supplies, such as building more power plants or increasing oil drilling. (2)

**energy-efficient technology**  a technology that minimizes the amount of energy used to perform a specific task, such as the use of compact fluorescent light bulbs to supply light. (18)

**engineering cost method**  an approach to economic valuation that determines the monetary costs of duplicating or replacing environmental services. (6)

**entropy**  a measure of the unavailable energy in a system; according to the second law of thermodynamics entropy increases in all physical processes. (13)

**environmental design**  the design of products or processes to limit environmental impact, such as manufacturing a product for eventual recycling or reducing materials requirements. (17)

**environmental externalities**  environmental impacts of an economic activity that are not reflected in the market costs or prices associated with the activity. (3, 18, 19)

**Environmental Kuznets Curve (EKC)**  the theory that a nation's environmental impact increases in the early stages of economic development but eventually decreases above a certain level of income. (19)

**environmental macroeconomics**  an analysis that places the human economic system in an ecological context to balance the scale of the economic system within ecological constraints. (1)

**environmental microeconomics**  the use of microeconomic techniques such as economic valuation, property rights rules, and discounting to determine an efficient allocation of natural resources and environmental services. (1)

**environmental services**  ecosystem services such as nutrient cycling, water purification, and soil stabilization; these services benefit humans and support economic production. (1, 8)

**environmental sustainability**  the continued existence of an ecosystem in a healthy state; ecosystems may change over time but do not significantly degrade. (2, 11)

**environmental valuation**  assigning monetary values to environmental goods and services using economic techniques. (3)

**equimarginal principle**  the concept that benefits are maximized when marginal benefits equal marginal costs, or when marginal costs of achieving a given goal by different methods are equalized. (16)

**equity**  fairness in the relative distribution of goods or services across a population; can be applied to income and environmental quality. (3, 8)

**estimated ultimately recoverable (EUR) supplies**  an estimate of the total amount of a nonrenewable resource that will ultimately be extracted. (13)

**existence value**  the value people place on the continued existence of a resource, such as the benefit one obtains from knowing an area of rainforest is preserved even though one will never visit it. (6)

**expected value**  an estimate of the value of an event or outcome whose likelihood is uncertain, calculated by mutiplying its probability by its cost or benefit. (6)

**exponential growth**  a value that increases by the same percentage in each time period, such as a population increasing by the same percentage every year. (10, 20)

**exponential reserve index**  an estimate of a resource lifetime based on existing economic reserves and a projected continuing percentage increase in resource use rates. (12)

**exporting pollution**  importing goods whose production involves environmental impact, thereby avoiding domestic impacts. (19)

**external benefit(s)**   a benefit, not necessarily monetary, not reflected in a market transaction. (1, 3, 18)

**external cost(s)**   a cost, not necessarily monetary, not reflected in a market transaction. (1, 3, 11, 12, 18)

**externalities**   an effect of a market transaction on individuals or firms other than those involved in the transaction. (1, 11, 18)

**extraction path**   the extraction rate of a resource over time. (12)

**extractive reserves**   a forested area managed for sustainable harvests of nontimber products such as nuts, sap, and extracts. (20)

**feedback loops/effects**   the process of changes in a system leading to other changes that either counteract or reinforce the original change. (6, 17, 18)

**fertility rate**   the average number of live births per woman in a society. (10)

**first law of thermodynamics**   the physical law stating that matter and energy cannot be created or destroyed, only transformed. (13)

**fixed factors**   production factors whose quantity cannot be changed in the short run. (10)

**flow**   the quantity of a variable measured over a period of time, such as the flow of a river past a given point measured in cubic-feet per second. (13, 15)

**flow pollutant**   a pollutant that has a short-term impact and then dissipates or is absorbed harmlessly into the environment. (16)

**free market environmentalism**   the view that a more complete system of property rights and expanded use of market mechanisms is the best approach to solving issues of resource use and pollution control. (3)

**free rider effect**   the incentive for people to avoid paying for a resource when the benefits they obtain from the resource are unaffected by whether or not they pay; results in the undersupply of public goods. (3, 4)

**freshwater runoff**   the amount of freshwater that flows across a given area in a period of time, including water usable for human water supplies and flood waters. (15)

**fuel cells**   using a chemical reaction between a fuel and an oxidant to produce electricity directly. (17)

**full pricing**   the inclusion of both internal and external costs in the price of a product. (15)

**gains from trade**   the net social benefits that result from trade. (19)

**GATT Article XX**   the GATT provision stating that a country can restrict trade to conserve exhaustible natural resources or to protect human and animal life or health. (19)

**GDP growth rate**   the annual change in GDP, expressed as a percentage. (2)

**General Agreement on Tariffs and Trade (GATT)**   a multilateral trade agreement providing a framework for the gradual elimination of tariffs and other barriers to trade; the predecessor to the World Trade Organization. (19)

**Genuine Progress Indicator (GPI)**   a national income accounting measure that subtracts defensive expenditures from output and accounts for natural resource depletion, pollution damages, income inequality, and nonmarketed services. (8)

**genuine saving ($S^*$)**   a measure that estimates the amount of national income being saved, taking into account natural-resource depletion, net foreign borrowing, and net additions to capital stock. (8)

**global climate change**   the changes in global climate, including temperature, precipitation, and storm frequency and intensity, that result from changes in greenhouse gas concentrations in the atmosphere. (2, 16, 18)

**global commons**   global common property resources such as the atmosphere and the oceans. (2, 4, 18)

**global environmental problems**   environmental problems with global impact, such as global climate change and species extinction. (1)

**global materials cycles**   the natural cycling of atoms of certain chemicals, such as nitrogen, carbon, and sulfur, between living beings, soil, air, and water. (17)

**global pollution/pollutant(s)**   pollutants that can have global impact such as carbon dioxide and chlorofluorocarbons (CFCs). (8, 16, 19)

**global public goods**   environmental goods or services that benefit all people, such as biodiversity and climate stabilization. (19)

**global warming** the increase in average global temperature as a result of emissions from human activities. (18)

**government procurement** programs that guarantee a certain government demand for a good or service. (12)

**government regulation** direct government control through the use of a specific rule or standard, as applied for example to permissible pollution emission levels. (3)

**grandfathering** a policy of exempting existing industrial facilities from complying with new environmental standards or regulations. (16)

**green accounting** approaches to national income accounting that attempt to incorporate the depletion of natural capital and other environmental benefits and costs. (8)

**green subsidies** subsidies on a good or service based on the reduction of environmental impact. (17, 20)

**green taxes** taxes based on the environmental impact of a good or service. (17, 20)

**greenhouse effect** the effect of certain gases in the earth's atmosphere trapping solar radiation, resulting in an increase in global temperatures and other climatic changes. (10, 18)

**greenhouse gases** gases such as carbon dioxide and methane whose atmospheric concentrations influence global climate by trapping solar radiation. (16, 18)

**gross annual population increase** the total numerical increase in population for a given region over one year. (10)

**Gross Domestic Product (GDP)** the value of all new final goods and services produced within the physical borders of a country regardless of the citizenship of the producer during a period of time (typically a calendar year). (8)

**GDP per capita** the GDP of a country divided by the population of the country. (8)

**gross investment** the total investment in new capital, such as office buildings and machinery, in an economy during a given period of time. (8)

**Gross National Product (GNP)** the value of all new final goods and services produced by residents of a particular country regardless of where the production takes place during a period of time (typically a calendar year). (8)

**groundwater overdraft** the withdrawal of water from an underground aquifer at a rate greater than the recharge rate. (15)

**habitat equivalency analysis** a methodology used to determine the payment required to compensate for damages to ecological resources, set at a level sufficient to provide for restorative ecological projects that supply services equal to what was damaged. (6)

**harmonization of environmental standards** the equalization of environmental standards across countries, as in the European Union. (19)

**hedonic pricing** the use of statistical analysis to explain the price of a good or service as a function of several components, such as explaining the price of a home as a function of the number of rooms, the caliber of local schools, and the surrounding air quality. (6)

**holdout effect** the ability of a single entity to hinder a multi-party agreement by making disproportionate demands. (3)

**Hotelling's rule** a theory stating that in equilibrium the net price (price minus production costs) of a resource must rise at a rate equal to the rate of interest. (5, 12)

**Hubbert curve** a bell-shaped curve showing the production rate of a nonrenewable energy resource over time. (13)

**human capital** knowledge, skills, and abilities possessed by individuals in the labor force, reflecting investments in education and training. (8)

**Human Development Index (HDI)** a national income accounting technique, developed by the United Nations Development Programme, that combines GDP with data on life expectancy, literacy, and school enrollment to obtain an HDI score. (8)

**hydropower** the generation of electricity from the energy in flowing water. (13)

**hypothetical and speculative resources** the quantity of a resource not identified with certainty but hypothesized to exist. (12)

**identified reserves** the identified quantity of a resource; includes both economic and subeconomic reserves. (12)

**income approach to GDP** An approach to measuring GDP that adds up the total income received within an economy, including wages, profits, investment income, and rental income. (8)

**incremental costs**   costs of environmental protection in developing countries in excess of what the country is prepared to pay without foreign assistance. (20)

**indicated or inferred reserves**   resources that have been identified but whose exact quantity is not known with certainty. (12)

**indirect use values**   ecosystem benefits not valued in markets, such as flood prevention and pollution absorption. (6)

**individual demand schedule**   the relationship between price and quantity demanded for a particular individual. (4)

**individual transferable quotas (ITQs)**   tradable rights to harvest a resource, such as a permit to harvest a particular quantity of fish. (5, 14)

**induced innovation**   innovation in a particular industry resulting from changes in the relative prices of inputs. (11)

**industrial ecology**   the application of ecological principles to the management of industrial activity. (2, 9, 12, 16, 17, 20)

**Industrial Revolution**   the period during the late eighteenth and nineteenth centuries characterized by mechanization of production and a significant increase in industrial output. (17)

**industrial symbiosis**   the process of linking industrial production such that the wastes from one industry become production inputs for other industries. (17)

**inflection point**   the point on a curve where the second derivative equals zero, indicating a change from positive to negative curvature or vice versa. (14)

**information asymmetry**   a situation where different agents in a market have different knowledge or access to information. (11)

**information-intensive techniques**   production techniques that require specialized knowledge; usually these techniques substitute knowledge for energy, produced capital, or material inputs, often reducing environmental impact. (11)

**input-intensive agriculture**   agricultural production that relies heavily on machinery, artificial fertilizers, pesticides, and irrigation. (2)

**input-output analysis (static and dynamic)**   a modeling approach that determines the physical or economic relationships between sectors of an economy; a static analysis does not account for changes in technology and capital stock, but a dynamic model does account for these changes. (9)

**institutional failure**   the failure of governments or other institutions to prevent resource overexploitation, or the use of policies that promote resource overexploitation and environmental damage. (14, 15)

**integrated pest management**   the use of methods such as natural predators, crop rotations, and pest removal to reduce pesticide application rates. (11)

**intensification of production**   increasing production rates with a limited supply of resources, such as increasing agricultural yield per acre. (2)

**intensity of materials use (IU)**   the quantity of physical materials used per unit of economic output. (17)

**intercropping**   an agricultural system involving growing more than one crop on a piece of land at the same time. (11)

**intergenerational equity**   the distribution of resources, including humanmade and natural capital, across human generations. (6, 7)

**internalizing externalities**   using approaches such as taxation to incorporate external costs and benefits into market decisions. (1, 3, 16, 18)

**intertemporal resource allocation**   the way resource consumption is distributed over time. (1)

**irreversibility**   environmental damage that cannot be reversed, such as the extinction of species. (6, 7)

**joint implementation**   cooperative agreements between nations to reduce carbon emissions. (18)

**labor-intensive techniques**   production techniques that rely heavily on labor input. (11)

**law of demand**   the economic principle stating that the quantity of a good or service that consumers are willing to buy will decrease as the market price rises or, conversely, that the quantity demanded will increase as the price falls. (3)

**law of diminishing returns**   the principle that a continual increase in production inputs will eventually yield decreasing marginal output. (10)

**law of supply**   the economic principle stating that the quantity of a good or service suppliers are willing to sell will increase as the market price rises or, conversely, that the quantity supplied will decrease as the price falls. (3)

**Law of the Sea**   a 1982 international treaty regulating marine fisheries. (14)

**license fee**   the fee paid for access to a resource, such as a fishing license. (4, 14)

**life cycle analysis**   analysis of the costs and environmental impacts of a product, including all stages of its production, use, and disposal. (17)

**local and regional pollutants**   pollutants that cause damage only within the area where they are emitted. (16, 18)

**logistic curve**   an S-shaped growth curve tending toward an upper limit. (14, 15, 20)

**macroeconomic (system) scale**   the total scale of an economy; ecological economics suggests that the ecosystem imposes scale limits on the macroeconomy. (1, 2, 7, 20)

**manufactured capital**   physical assets produced by humans for use in the production of other goods and services. (8)

**marginal benefit**   the benefit of producing or consuming one more unit of something. (3)

**marginal cost**   the cost of producing or consuming one more unit of something. (3, 4)

**marginal extraction cost**   the cost of extracting an additional unit of a nonrenewable resource. (12)

**marginal net benefit**   the net benefit of the consumption or production of an additional unit of a resource; equal to marginal benefit minus marginal cost. (5, 18)

**marginal physical product**   the additional quantity of output produced by increasing an input level by one unit. (11)

**marginal revenue**   the additional revenue obtained by selling one more unit of a good or service. (4)

**marginal revenue product**   the additional revenue obtained by increasing input by one unit; equal to marginal physical product multiplied by marginal revenue. (11)

**market demand schedule**   the relationship between the price of a good or service and the quantity consumers are willing to purchase. (3, 4)

**market equilibrium**   the interaction of supply and demand resulting in a price at which no excess demand or supply exists. (3)

**market failure**   the failure of certain markets to provide a socially efficient allocation of resources. (10, 13, 14)

**market supply schedule**   the relationship between the price of a good or service and the quantity producers are willing to produce. (3)

**market-based pollution control**   the use of market incentives to control pollution levels, such as pollution taxes or tradable permits. (16)

**materials substitution**   changing the materials used to produce a product, such as using plastic pipe instead of copper in plumbing systems. (17)

**maximum net present value criterion**   a decision rule stating that policies should be designed to maximize net present values; the maximum net present value occurs when the marginal benefits of an action just equal the marginal costs. (6)

**maximum sustainable yield (MSY)**   the maximum quantity of a natural resource that can be harvested annually without depleting the resource stock or population. (4, 14)

**mean annual increment (MAI)**   the average growth rate of a forest; obtained by dividing the total weight of timber by the age of the forest. (15)

**measured reserves**   identified resources whose quantity is known with certainty. (12)

**methodological pluralism**   the view that a more comprehensive understanding of problems can be obtained by using a combination of perspectives rather than just one perspective. (9)

**microirrigation**   irrigation systems that increase water use efficiency by applying water in small quantities close to the plants. (15)

**micronutrients**   nutrients present in low concentrations in soil, required for plant growth or health. (11)

**monoculture**   an agricultural system involving the growing of the same crop exclusively on a piece of land year after year. (11, 14, 15)

**multilateral environmental agreements (MEAs)**   international treaties between nations on environmental issues, such as the Convention on International Trade in Endangered Species. (19)

**multiple cropping**   an agricultural system involving growing more than one crop on a piece of land. (11)

**natural capital**   the available endowment of land and resources including air, water, soil, forests, fisheries, minerals, and ecological life-support systems. (2, 7, 20)

**natural capital depreciation**   a deduction in national accounting for loss of natural capital, such as a reduction in the supply of timber, wildlife habitat, or mineral resources. (7, 8)

**natural capital sustainability**   conserving natural capital by limiting depletion rates and investing in resource renewal. (7)

**natural resources**   resources that occur in a natural state and are valuable for economic activity, such as minerals, timber, and soils. (1)

**neo-Malthusianism**   the modern version of T. R. Malthus's argument that human population growth can lead to catastrophic ecological consequences and an increase in the human death rate. (10)

**net energy ratio**   the quantity of energy obtained from a process such as oil recovery, divided by the energy used in the process. (13)

**net foreign borrowing (NFB)**   the amount borrowed by a country less the amount lent to other countries; gross investment is adjusted by NFB and depreciation to determine net domestic investment or savings. (8)

**net investment**   the process of adding to productive capital over time, calculated by subtracting depreciation from gross, or total, investment. (7, 8)

**net national product (NNP)/net domestic product (NDP)**   the value obtained by subtracting the depreciation of humanmade capital from gross national product or gross domestic product. (8)

**net present value**   the present value of a stream of benefits minus the present value of a stream of costs. (6)

**net price (of a resource)**   the price of a resource minus production costs. (5)

**net primary product of photosynthesis (NPP)**   the biomass energy directly produced by photosynthesis. (7)

**net receipts**   returns from the sale of a resource, equal to revenues minus production costs. (8)

**net social benefit**   the social gain that results when total benefits exceed total costs, including external benefits and costs. (3, 4)

**net social loss**   the social loss that results when total costs exceed total benefits, including external benefits and costs. (3)

**nitrogen cycle**   the conversion of nitrogen into different forms in the ecosystem, including the fixation of nitrogen by symbiotic bacteria in certain plants such as legumes. (11)

**nominal GNP**   gross national product measured using current dollars. (2)

**nonexclusive good**   a good available to all users; one of the two characteristics of public goods. (4)

**nongovernmental organizations (NGOs)**   privately funded, and commonly nonprofit, organizations involved in research, lobbying, provision of services, or development projects. (20)

**nonlinear or threshold effects**   effects such as the health damage from a pollutant that do not increase linearly with the quantity of the pollutant. (16)

**nonmarket values**   the values people place on goods or services not traded in markets. (6)

**nonpoint source pollution**   pollution difficult to identify as originating from a particular source, such as groundwater contamination from agricultural chemicals used over a wide area. (16)

**nonrenewable resources**   resources available in fixed supply, such as metal ores and oil. (1, 2, 5, 12, 17)

**nonrival good**   a good whose use by one person does not limit its use by others; one of the two characteristics of public goods. (4)

**nonuniformly mixed pollutants**   pollutants that have different effects in different areas, depending on where they are emitted. (16)

**nonuse values**   values people obtain without actually using a resource; nonuse values include existence and bequest values. (6)

**nutrient recycling**   the ability of ecological systems to transform nutrients such as carbon, nitrogen, and phosphorus into different chemical forms. (11)

**nutritional deficit**   failure to meet human demands for basic levels of nutrition. (11)

**open system**   a system that exchanges energy or natural resources with another system; the economic system is considered an open system because it receives energy and natural resources from the ecosystem and deposits wastes into the ecosystem. (7)

**open-access equilibrium**   the level of use of an open-access resource that results from a market with free entry; this use level may lead to resource depletion. (4, 14)

**open-access resource(s)**   a resource that offers unrestricted access such as an ocean fishery or the atmosphere. (2, 4, 14)

**opportunity cost of capital**   the rate of return available for alternative investment projects. (6)

**optimal depletion rate**   the depletion rate for a natural resource that maximizes the resource's net present value. (5)

**optimal pollution (level)**   the pollution level that maximizes net social benefits. (3, 16)

**optimum rotation period**   the rotation period for a renewable resource that maximizes the financial gain from harvest; determined by maximizing the discounted difference between total revenues and total costs. (15)

**option value**   the value people place on maintaining future resource use options. (6)

**organic techniques**   agricultural production systems that maintain soil fertility using organic materials and use natural methods of pest control. (17)

**overfishing**   a level of fishing effort that depletes fishery stock over time. (4, 14)

**over-harvesting of renewable resources**   rates of harvest that decrease resource stock or population over time. (2)

**pay-by-the-bag systems**   waste disposal systems in which customers pay a fee for each unit of waste discarded. (12)

**per capita GNP growth rate**   the annual change in per capita GNP, expressed as a percentage. (2)

**per capita output**   the total product of a society divided by population. (10)

**perfectly elastic supply**   a supply curve that is horizontal, meaning that the quantity supplied can be increased at the same price per unit. (4)

**physical accounting**   a supplement to national income accounting that estimates natural resource stock or services in physical, rather than economic, terms. (7)

**physical supply (of a resource)**   available reserves measured in physical terms, without regard to the economic feasibility of recovery. (12, 13)

**Pigovian tax**   a per-unit tax set equal to the external damage caused by an activity, such as a tax per ton of pollution emitted equal to the external damage of a ton of pollution. (3)

**point source pollution**   pollution emitted from an identifiable source such as a smokestack or waste pipe. (16)

**polluter pays principle**   the view that those responsible for pollution should pay for associated external costs such as health costs and damage to wildlife habitats. (3)

**pollution**   contamination of soil, water, or atmosphere by discharge of harmful substances. (1, 16)

**pollution haven**   a country or region that attracts high-polluting industries due to low levels of environmental regulation. (19)

**pollution tax(es)**   a per-unit tax based on the level of pollution. (3, 16, 18)

**population age profile**   estimated numbers of people classified by age groups in a given place and time. (10)

**population biology**   the study of how a species population changes as a result of environmental conditions. (14)

**population cohort**   the group of people born within a specific time period in a country. (10)

**population growth rate**   the annual change in the population of a given area, expressed as a percentage of the total population. (2, 10)

**population momentum**  the tendency for a population to continue to grow, even if the fertility rate falls to the replacement level, as long as a high proportion of the population is young. (2, 10).

**Porter hypothesis**  a theory asserting that shifting to more environmentally sound methods of production improves firms' long-run competitiveness. (17)

**positional analysis**  a policy analysis tool that combines economic valuation with considerations such as equity, individual rights, and social priorities; it does not aim to reduce all effects to monetary terms. (6)

**positive net present value criterion**  a decision rule stating that projects should be undertaken if they provide positive discounted net benefits (present value of benefits minus present value of costs). (6)

**precautionary principle**  the view that policies should account for uncertainty by taking steps to avoid outcomes damaging to health or the environment, especially when such outcomes are irreversible. (6, 7, 14, 19)

**present value**  the current value of a stream of future costs and/or benefits, calculated through the use of a discount rate. (5, 6, 11)

**preventive and adaptive strategies**  the contrasting perspectives of trying to prevent environmental damage versus trying to adapt to damage once it occurs. (18)

**price elasticity of demand**  the sensitivity of quantity demanded to prices; an elastic demand means that a proportional increase in price results in a larger proportional change in quantity demanded; an inelastic demand means that a proportional increase in price results in a smaller proportional change in quantity demanded. (3, 18)

**price elasticity of supply**  the sensitivity of quantity supplied to prices; an elastic supply means that a proportional increase in price results in a larger proportional change in quantity supplied; an inelastic supply means that a proportional increase in price results in a smaller proportional change in quantity supplied. (3, 11)

**price path**  the price of a resource, typically a nonrenewable resource, over time. (12)

**price taker**  a seller in a competitive market who has no control over the product price. (12)

**primary resource**  resource in a natural state, as opposed to a produced or recycled resource. (12)

**private choice**  individual preferences usually expressed through market behavior. (3)

**private optimum**  the optimal allocation or production of a resource based on market behavior. (3)

**private ownership**  the provision of certain exclusive rights to a particular resource, such as the right of a landowner to restrict trespassing. (14)

**process and production methods (PPM)  rules** international trade rules stating that an importing country cannot use trade barriers or penalties against another country for failure to meet environmental or social standards related to the process of production. (19)

**producer surplus**  the net benefit accruing to producers of a good, measured by the difference between the price received and costs of production. (3)

**product approach to GDP**  an approach for measuring GDP that adds up the dollar value of all new final goods and services produced in an economy. (8)

**production externalities**  externalities associated with production of a good, such as factory emissions of pollution. (19)

**production function method**  an approach to economic valuation that determines the monetary costs of duplicating or replacing environmental services. (6)

**productivity loss estimates**  an estimate of the reduction in the productive capacity of renewable natural resources, such as soil; used to supplement national income accounting. (8)

**property rights**  the set of rights that belong to the resource owner, such as a landowner's right to prohibit trespassing. (1, 3, 15)

**proxy variable**  a variable used to represent a broader concept, such as the use of fertilizer application rates to represent the input-intensity of agricultural production. (11)

**psychic benefit**  a benefit derived without the actual use of a resource, such as the existence benefits of species preservation. (4)

**public choice**  social preferences for policies; these preferences may not be expressed in market behavior. (3)

**public good(s)** goods available to all (nonexclusive), whose use by one person does not reduce their availability to others (nonrival). (1, 4, 15)

**purchasing power parity (PPP)** an adjustment made to national accounting measures that corrects for differences in the domestic purchasing power of different national currencies. (8)

**quota (system)** a system of limiting resource access through user limits on the permissible resource harvest. (4, 14)

**race to the bottom** the tendency for nations to weaken national environmental standards to attract foreign businesses or to keep existing businesses from moving to other nations. (19)

**real GDP** the GDP of a country adjusted for inflation. (8)

**real GNP** gross national product corrected for inflation using a price index. (2)

**recharge of aquifers** the refilling of groundwater reservoirs through seepage of surface and subsurface water through the earth's strata. (15)

**recycling** the process of using waste materials as inputs into a production process. (12, 17, 20)

**remanufacturing** replacing only the worn parts of a discarded product while retaining structural components in order to make the product reusable. (17)

**renewable energy sources** energy sources supplied on a continual basis such as wind, water, biomass, and direct solar energy. (2, 18, 20)

**renewable resource(s)** resources supplied on a continuing basis by ecosystems; renewable resources such as forests and fisheries can be depleted through exploitation. (1, 2, 5, 11, 14)

**rent dissipation** the loss of potential social and economic benefits in a market because of market failure. (14)

**replacement cost** an approach to measuring environmental damages that estimates the costs necessary to restore or replace the resource, such as applying fertilizer to restore soil fertility. (6, 8)

**replacement fertility level** the fertility level that would result in a stable population. (10)

**research and development (R&D)** efforts to increase technical knowledge for the production of new products or improvement of existing products. (13, 18)

**reserve base index** an estimate of available resource reserves divided by the annual consumption rate; uses a broad estimate of available reserves. (12)

**resilience** ecosystem capacity to recover from adverse impact. (14, 15)

**resistant pest species** pest species that evolve resistance to pesticides, requiring either higher pesticide application rates or new pesticides to control the species. (11)

**resource depletion** a decline in resource stocks through human exploitation. (1)

**resource depletion tax** a tax imposed on the extraction or sale of a natural resource. (5)

**resource lifetime** the number of years the economic reserves of a resource are projected to last under expected consumption rates. (12)

**resource recovery** mining or extraction of resources for economic use. (2)

**resource rents** income derived from ownership of a scarce resource. (12)

**resource substitution** the use of one resource in a production process as a substitute for another resource, such as the use of aluminum instead of copper in electrical wiring. (12)

**resource use profile** the consumption rates for a resource over time, typically applied to nonrenewable resources. (12)

**revenue recycling** using revenues from tax increases on certain products or activities to reduce other taxes. (18)

**revenue-neutral tax shift** policies designed to balance tax increases on certain products or activities with reductions in other taxes, such as a reduction in income taxes that offsets a carbon-based tax. (18, 20)

**right to pollute** a system that gives an entity a right to emit a certain quantity of a pollutant, such as a tradable emissions permit. (3)

**risk aversion** the tendency to prefer certainty instead of risky outcomes, particularly in cases where actions may cause significant negative consequences. (6)

**safe minimum standard** the principle that environmental policies on issues involving uncertainty should be set to avoid possible catastrophic consequences. (6)

**salinization and alkalinization of soils**   the buildup of salt or alkali concentrations in soil with the effect of reducing soil productivity. (11)

**satellite accounts**   accounts that estimate the supply of natural capital in physical rather than monetary terms; used to supplement traditional national income accounting. (7, 8)

**scale, composition, and technique effects**   the impacts of trade on economic growth, industrial patterns, and technological progress. (19)

**second law of thermodynamics**   the physical law stating that all physical processes lead to a decrease in available energy, that is, an increase in entropy. (13)

**second-best solution**   a policy solution to a problem that fails to maximize potential net social benefits but may be appropriate if the optimal solution cannot be achieved. (19)

**sensitivity analysis**   an analytical tool that studies how the outputs of a model change as the assumptions of the model change. (6)

**shortage**   a situation in which the quantity of a good or service that consumers wish to buy at a given price is greater than the quantity sellers are willing to sell at that price. (3)

**sink function**   the environment's ability to absorb and render harmless the by-products of human activity. (1, 14, 16, 20)

**social benefit**   the market and nonmarket benefits associated with a good or service. (3, 4)

**social cost**   the market and nonmarket costs associated with a good or service. (3, 5)

**social demand**   the vertical addition of individual demand schedules to obtain total willingness to pay for a given level of a resource. (4)

**social discount rate**   a discount rate that reflects social rather than market valuation of future costs and benefits. (6)

**social optimum**   an allocation of resources that maximizes net social benefits (equal to social benefits minus social costs). (3, 18)

**social rate of time preference (SRTP)**   a discount rate that attempts to reflect the appropriate social valuation of the future; the SRTP tends to be less than market or individual discount rates. (6)

**social sustainability**   the maintenance of social structure and traditions, for example among indigenous peoples. (15, 20)

**solar energy**   the energy supplied continually by the sun, including direct solar energy as well as indirect forms such as wind energy and flowing water. (1, 2, 13)

**solar flux**   the continual flow of solar energy to the earth. (9, 10, 13)

**solar hydrogen**   a virtually emissions-free system of energy relying on solar energy to release hydrogen gas from water, burning hydrogen to obtain useful energy, and obtaining water as a byproduct. (13, 17)

**source function**   the environment's ability to make services and raw materials available for human use. (1, 14)

**specificity rule**   the view that policy solutions should be targeted directly at the source of a problem. (19)

**spending approach to GDP**   an approach for measuring GDP that adds up the consumption and investment expenditures made by consumers, businesses, governments, and institutions on all new final goods and services within an economy. (8)

**stable equilibrium**   an equilibrium of, for example, a renewable resource stock level, to which the system will tend to return after short-term changes in conditions. (14)

**stable water supply**   the quantity of water available to a region for human use on a continual basis. (15)

**static equilibrium**   a market equilibrium that results when only present costs and benefits are considered. (5)

**static reserve index**   an index that divides the economic reserves of a resource by the current rate of use for the resource. (12)

**steady state economy**   an economy that maintains a constant level of natural capital by limiting the throughput of material and energy resources. (20)

**stock**   the quantity of a variable at a given point in time, such as the amount of timber in a forest at a given time. (13, 15)

**stock pollutant**   a pollutant that accumulates in the environment, such as carbon dioxide and chlorofluorocarbons (CFCs). (16, 18)

**strategic bias**   the tendency for people to state their preferences or values inaccurately in order to influence policy decisions. (6)

**strong sustainability** the view that natural and humanmade capital are generally not substitutable and, therefore, natural capital levels should be maintained. (7, 8, 20)

**structural adjustment** policies to promote market-oriented economic reform in developing countries by making loans conditional on reforms such as controlling inflation, reducing trade barriers, and privatization of businesses. (20)

**subeconomic resources** a resource quantity that cannot be economically extracted at current price and technology levels. (12)

**subsidies** government assistance to an industry or economic activity; subsidies can be direct, through financial assistance, or indirect, through protective policies. (3, 14, 15, 18)

**substitutability (of natural and manufactured capital)** the ability of humanmade capital to compensate for the depletion of some types of natural capital, such as the ability of fertilizer to compensate for the loss of soil fertility. (7, 8)

**sufficiency** the goal of limiting consumption to an amount necessary to live a comfortable but not extravagant lifestyle. (17)

**supply constraint** an upper limit on supply of, for example, a nonrenewable resource. (5)

**surplus** a situation in which the quantity of a good or service suppliers are willing to sell at a given price is greater than the quantity consumers wish to buy at that price. (3)

**sustainable agriculture** systems of agricultural production that do not deplete the productivity of the land or environmental quality, including such techniques as integrated pest management, organic techniques, and multiple cropping. (2, 11)

**sustainable development** development that meets the needs of the present without compromising the ability of future generations to meet their own needs. (1, 2, 20)

**sustainable (natural resource) management** management of natural resources such that natural capital remains constant over time, including maintenance of both stocks and flows. (2, 14)

**sustainable yield** a yield or harvest level that can be maintained without diminishing the resource stock or population. (7)

**sustainability transition** a transformation of patterns of population growth, industrial production, and agriculture to provide for human needs and preserve environmental systems. (20)

**system boundary** a boundary defining an area for study, such as a wetland or urban area; used in economic/ecological modeling. (9)

**technological innovation** increases in knowledge used to develop new products or improve existing products. (2, 10, 17)

**technological lock-in** the tendency of an industry to continue to use a given technology despite the availability of more efficient or cheaper technologies. (12, 20)

**technological thresholds** important industrial, agricultural, and energy technological innovations that make possible new production methods and may dramatically reduce environmental impact. (17)

**technology transfer** the process of sharing technological information or equipment, particularly among nations. (18)

**theoretical paradigm** the basic conceptual approach used to study a particular issue. (2)

**thermodynamic efficiency** minimizing the energy used to produce a given output or achieve a given task. (13)

**third-party effects** effects of market transactions that affect people other than those involved in the transaction, such as industrial pollution that affects a local community. (1)

**throughput** the total use of energy and materials as both inputs and outputs of a process. (1, 7, 12, 13, 17)

**total cost of pollution** a monetary measure of pollution damage, including both financial and social costs. (3)

**total net benefit** total benefit minus total cost. (5)

**total product** the total quantity of a good or service produced with a given quantity of inputs. (4, 14)

**total revenue** the total revenue obtained by selling a particular quantity of a good or service; equal to price multiplied by quantity sold. (4)

**tragedy of the commons** the tendency for common property resources to be overexploited because no one has an incentive to conserve the resource, while individual financial incentives promote expanded exploitation. (4, 14, 15)

**transactions costs**   costs associated with a market transaction or negotiation, such as legal and administrative costs to transfer property or to bring disputing parties together. (3)

**transboundary pollution**   pollution carried beyond the borders of a specific region or country and affecting those outside the region. (8, 19)

**transferable pollution permits**   tradable permits that allow a firm to emit a certain quantity of a pollutant. (16, 17, 18)

**travel cost method**   the use of statistical analysis to determine people's willingness to pay to visit a natural resource such as a national park or river; a demand curve for the resource is obtained by analyzing the relationship between visitation choices and travel costs. (6)

**true income**   an adjusted measure of income obtained by subtracting that portion of total income that would have to be invested at long-term rates to guarantee an indefinitely continued flow of income at the same level. (8)

**under-pricing**   prices of goods or services below the price that would result from taking full social costs into account. (15)

**undersupply of public goods**   the tendency for public goods to be supplied at levels below the social optimum because of a low effective demand. (4)

**uniformly mixed pollutants**   any pollutant emitted by many sources in a region resulting in relatively uniform concentration levels across the region. (16)

**unstable equilibrium**   a temporary equilibrium of, for example, a renewable resource stock level, that can be altered by minor changes in conditions, resulting in a large change in stock levels. (14)

**use value**   the value that people place on the use of a good or service. (6, 15)

**user cost(s)**   opportunity costs associated with the loss of future potential uses of a resource, resulting from consumption of the resource in the present. (5, 8, 11, 12)

**utility**   the level of satisfaction obtained from an activity. (3)

**value added method**   a methodology used in national income accounting that estimates the increase in dollar value at each stage in the production process of a good or service, equal to the value of output minus the value of purchased inputs. (8)

**virgin resource**   see *primary resource*. (12)

**waste mining**   obtaining resources used in a production process from waste products instead of using virgin resources. (17)

**water-abundant and water-scarce areas**   areas of the world where stable water supplies are either ample or limited; water scarcity has been defined as less than 1,000 cubic meters per capita of renewable supply. (15)

**water cycle**   the cycle of evaporation and precipitation that continually supplies fresh water. (15)

**watershed management**   the management of a watershed to preserve its ecological integrity; includes the management of agriculture, residential development, industry, and other human activities. (16)

**weak sustainability**   the view that natural capital depletion is justified as long as it is compensated for with increases in humanmade capital; assumes that humanmade capital can substitute for most types of natural capital. (7, 8, 20)

**welfare analysis**   an economic tool that analyzes the total costs and benefits of alternative policies to different groups, such as producers and consumers. (3)

**willingness to accept (WTA)**   the minimum amount of money people would accept as compensation for an action that reduces their utility. (6)

**willingness to pay (WTP)**   the maximum amount of money people are willing to pay for a good or service that increases utility. (6)

**World Environmental Organization (WEO)**   a proposed international organization that would have oversight on global environmental issues. (19)

**World Trade Organization (WTO)**   an international organization dedicated to the expansion of trade through lowering or eliminating tariffs and nontariff barriers to trade. (19)

# Index

*Note:* The letter n following a page number refers to a footnote.